SOCIALIST FUN

Youth, Consumption, and State-Sponsored Popular Culture

in the Cold War Soviet Union, 1945–1970

D1556992

Gleb Tsipursky

University of Pittsburgh Press

Published by the University of Pittsburgh Press, Pittsburgh, Pa., 15260
Copyright © 2016, University of Pittsburgh Press
All rights reserved
Manufactured in the United States of America
Printed on acid-free paper
10 9 8 7 6 5 4 3 2 1

Library of Congress Cataloging-in-Publication Data

Names: Tsipursky, Gleb.
Title: Socialist Fun: Youth, Consumption, and State-Sponsored Popular Culture in the Soviet Union, 1945–1970 / Gleb Tsipursky.
Description: Pittsburgh, Pa. : University of Pittsburgh Press, 2016. | Series: Pitt Series in Russian and East European Studies | Includes bibliographical references and index.
Identifiers: LCCN 2016007242 | ISBN 9780822963967 (paperback: acid-free paper)
Subjects: LCSH: Youth—Soviet Union—Social life and customs. | Youth—Government policy—Soviet Union—History. | Youth—Soviet Union—Societies and clubs—History. | Soviet Union—Social life and customs—1917–1970. | Cold War—Social aspects—Soviet Union. | Popular culture—Soviet Union—History. | Consumption (Economics)—Soviet Union—History. | Socialism—Social aspects—Soviet Union—History. | Western countries—Relations—Soviet Union. | Soviet Union—Relations—Western countries. | BISAC: HISTORY / Europe / Russia & the Former Soviet Union.
Classification: LCC HQ799.S69 T76 2016 | DDC 305.235094708/0904—dc23
LC record available at http://lccn.loc.gov/2016007242

SOCIALIST FUN

Pitt Series in Russian and East European Studies
Jonathan Harris, Editor

To Agnes Vishnevkin, my partner in life. Thank you so much for your support, patience, empathy, and understanding during the long years it took to complete this project.

CONTENTS

ACKNOWLEDGMENTS

I would like first of all to acknowledge Don Raleigh, a phenomenal scholar, teacher, and mentor. His support, advice, and guidance from my early days in the professional study of Soviet history were undoubtedly the most important factor in shaping my scholarly career and this manuscript. With his life wisdom, he taught me to be not only a scholar but also a much better human being.

I would also like to express my particular appreciation to Denise Young-blood, for her guidance and mentorship in my career and also for providing me with her wise life advice during times of trouble. Louise McReynolds's expertise in popular culture and Russian history and her no-nonsense approach to the academic profession have proved valuable to me. I have learned much from Christopher Browning, Anna Krylova, and Chad Bryant at the University of North Carolina at Chapel Hill. Emily Baran and Michael Paulauskas, with whom I spent a year abroad in Russia, deserve much gratitude both for their feedback on the manuscript and for helping me remember to have fun and relax as well as work. I am grateful for the guidance on my manuscript and my academic career from David Hoffman, my colleague and mentor at The Ohio State University. Sergei Zhuk and William Risch have given me much feedback on various stages of the project during our numerous professional collaborations.

For their suggestions on improving my manuscript, I wish to express my gratitude to Rachel Applebaum, Steve Barnes, Stephen Bittner, Eliot Borenstein, Jonathyne Briggs, Kate Brown, Karl Brown, Nick Breyfogle, John Bushnell, Bill Chase, Choi Chatterjee, Edward Cohn, Nancy Condee, Susan Costanzo, Michael David-Fox, Julie deGraffenried, Rossen Djagalov, Miriam Dobson, Theodora Dragostinova, Marko Dumancic, Robert Edelman, Christine Evans, Juliane Fuerst, Mischa Gabowitsch, Eleonory Gilburd, Anne Gorsuch, Helena Goscilo, Bruce Grant, Paul Hagenloh, Jeff Hardy, Steve Harris, Deborah Field, Anna Fishzon, Dan Healy, Jochen Hellbeck, Betsy Hemenway, Meri Herrala, Julie Hessler, Faith Hillis, Peter Holquist, Cynthia Hooper, Jeffrey Jones, Polly Jones, Catriona Kelly, Neringa Klumbyte, Diane Koenker, Pia Koivunen, Stephen Kotkin, Sharon Kowalsky, Denis Kozlov, Brian LaPierre, Christopher Lee, Scott Levi, Thomas Lindenberger, Mitch Lerner, Ann Livschiz, Eric Lohr, Stephen

Lovell, Elaine MacKinnon, Rosa Magnusdottir, Lynn Mally, Terry Martin, Polly McMichael, Paula Michaels, Sabina Mihelj, Ben Nathans, Amy Nelson, Joan Neuberger, Stephen Norris, Bella Ostromoukhova, Jennifer Parks, Margaret Peacock, Karen Petrone, Hilary Pilkington, Ethan Pollock, Karl Qualls, Sabrina Ramet, Patton Raymond, Susan Reid, Kristin Roth-Ey, Peter Schmelz, Jenny Siegel, Lewis Siegelbaum, Kelly Smith, Victoria Smolkin, Peter Stearns, Mark Steinberg, Tony Swift, Roshanna Sylvester, Richard Taruskin, Kiril Tomoff, David Tompkins, Kate Transchel, Ben Tromly, Christine Varga-Harris, Alexei Yurchak, Manfred Zeller, Vlad Zubok, Patrick Zuk, and many others. I wish to thank the manuscript reviewers from the University of Pittsburgh Press (UPP), whose constructive criticism enabled a substantially stronger final monograph. I am grateful to my editor and director of UPP, Peter Kracht, for seeing the promise in the manuscript and husbanding it along the long journey to publication. Alex Wolfe, the editorial and production manager at UPP, was a pleasure to work with and proved very understanding during delays due to health concerns. I likewise wish to express my gratitude to the scores of people with whom I conducted oral history interviews: thank you for trusting me to bring your story to light. A Mellon/ACLS fellowship, a Fulbright-Hays research abroad fellowship, and a University of North Carolina at Chapel Hill travel grant supported the necessary primary source research in Russia, where the staff at the Komsomol archive in Moscow, in particular G. M. Tokareva, proved very helpful. I have also benefited from grants by the Mershon Center, the Woodrow Wilson Center's Kennan Institute, and from The Ohio State University, all of which have enabled me to conduct additional research in archives in both the United States and the United Kingdom. Thank you all, and I take full responsibility for any mistakes remaining in the manuscript. I almost hope there are some mistakes, as I would love for future scholarship on this topic to uncover new areas that are as yet unexplored and might disprove some of my conclusions. The beauty of the scholarly endeavor is that we always improve on previous work, and I hope there is an abundance of future research on socialist fun!

SOCIALIST FUN

INTRODUCTION

The movie *Karnaval'naia noch'* (Carnival night), directed by El'dar Riazanov and released in 1955, depicts a New Year's Eve celebration in a *klub* (club), one of many institutions that hosted mass cultural activities.[1] Clubs hosted amateur music, dancing, and theater that attracted broad participation, termed *khudozhestvennaia samodeiatel'nost'* (amateur artistic creativity), along with festive events such as youth parties and New Year celebrations. In *Karnaval'naia noch'*, Comrade Ogurtsov has taken charge of the club just before New Year's Eve. Displeased with the plan for the festive evening, he demands that the program "be typical" and "most importantly, serious!" Ogurtsov thus forces a ballerina to put on less revealing attire and drains all the humor from the clown show. He bans the performance of the club's amateur ensemble, whose large complement of saxophones suggested controversial jazz overtones and therefore foreign cultural influence. Instead, Ogurtsov wants to invite a traditional, orthodox ensemble from the pensioners' association. He proposes starting the celebration with a speech on the club's achievements, followed by a propaganda lecture.

However, the young club workers and volunteer amateur performers refuse to accept Ogurtsov's plan for such a boring and politicized event and instead take matters into their own hands. They get the propaganda lecturer drunk, dress up as pensioners, and, after beginning their performance with staid classical music, launch into a jazz-style piece heavy on saxophone and brass. The viewer is witness to Ogurtsov's growing surprise and anger as the faux pensioners play and somersault about the stage. By the end of the movie, the club's young employees and amateur performers have managed to ensure a festive and fun evening for everyone except Ogurtsov.

The movie proved controversial from the first. Prominent officials disparaged the script for its focus on entertainment and fun rather than politics and for encouraging undue initiative from the lower ranks. Such attacks came from individuals who held what may be defined as a hard-line, conservative position, which included some combination of militant, narrowly defined Marxism-Leninism, the official Soviet ideology; demand for close control from above; support for a xenophobic version of Soviet nationalism; and espousal of traditional rural social and cultural values. Each cadre holding a hard-line view shared some or all of these elements, thus explaining the antagonism toward this film. Only the sustained advocacy of those bureaucrats expressing more liberal, moderate sentiments—advocating a combination of pluralism and tolerance in interpreting Marxism-Leninism, a more cosmopolitan and internationalist outlook, and greater engagement from and autonomy for the grassroots—enabled the filmmaker to complete the movie. Regardless of hard-line censure, *Karnaval'naia noch'* drew a huge audience, becoming one of the most popular Soviet films of all time.

The film's portrayal of the tensions in clubs between political propaganda and popular entertainment, between orthodox music and foreign jazz, and between popular initiative and bureaucratic directives reflects the broader strains within the state's cultural recreation offerings. This book examines these official cultural activities during the first quarter century of the Cold War, often called the First Cold War. It tells the story of how Soviet authorities attempted to construct an appealing version of socialist popular culture as an alternative to the predominant "western" model that had such enormous worldwide allure.[2] Soviet cultural functionaries strove to define the public norms for cultural fun. I use the term "fun" to refer to those cultural activities in which people found meaning, pleasure, and joy and into which they invested time, energy, and resources primarily out of their own volition and initiative. Many youngsters responded enthusiastically to the Kremlin's cultural policies and had fun within government-managed cultural spaces. However, popular desires did not overlap fully with top-level guidelines, resulting in hidden tensions and open conflicts.

This monograph brings to light a little-studied sphere that I call "state-sponsored popular culture"—cultural activities of the masses within government institutions. Looking at state-sponsored popular culture helps shift the traditional focus on the intelligentsia or intellectual elites as cultural creators in a different direction, spotlighting ordinary citizens. State-sponsored popular culture elides the traditional distinctions between "high" culture, or sophisticated artistic forms aimed at elite tastes, and "low" culture, or entertaining cultural activities intended to appeal to the masses, both of which were typically performed by professional artists. State-sponsored popular culture contained a broad spectrum of genres for a variety of tastes, all produced by nonprofessional volunteer artists in officially managed cultural settings.[3]

That 4.8 million Soviet citizens had performed as amateurs by 1953 (a number that rose to 9 million in 1962) underscores the broad appeal of organized cultural recreation.[4] The Communist Party managed this sphere through government institutions and party-controlled social organizations such as trade unions and the Komsomol, together known as the party-state complex. The Komsomol, the mass Soviet youth organization, accepted those ranging in age from approximately fourteen to twenty-eight, and this study defines "youth" as those eligible to join the Komsomol. This social demographic had significant divisions based on factors such as age, occupation, social class, gender, and geographical location. Nonetheless, since the party-state's cultural recreation policy treated this cohort in a largely unified fashion, which powerfully shaped the opportunities, experiences, and societal perceptions of the young, it makes analytical sense to consider young people as a cohesive category for this study.

Examining the artistic creativity of millions of amateurs belies typical classifications of Soviet cultural activities within the official/unofficial binary. The label "official" typically refers to thoroughly vetted cultural production by state-employed artists in government cultural venues; "unofficial" encompasses cultural activities that did not pass through cultural censorship and that occurred in nonstate settings. Amateur artists performed in party-state cultural institutions with some degree of oversight, making these activities official. However, amateurs had much greater room to maneuver due to their nonprofessional status, presumed lack of cultural knowledge, and performance for small audiences. Moreover, as most amateurs did not intend to build careers around artistic activities, they had much less to fear from pushing the boundaries. Likewise, the mass nature of amateur arts, with millions of participants, made it a challenge to impose thorough top-down controls. These factors resulted in substantially weaker censorship over state-sponsored popular culture as compared to professional cultural production.

The Soviet Union's vast network of club buildings, numbering more than 123,000 in 1953, functioned as the chief venue for cultural recreation.[5] A typical mid-size club had two halls for concerts, dances, theatrical performances, movie showings, lectures, political meetings, and other events; several smaller rooms for amateur groups to practice their artistic activities; a recreation area with various games, books, newspapers, and sports equipment; and a cafeteria. The club administration had the mission of providing financial and logistical support for amateur arts and cultural events, while ensuring that these activities followed the cultural policy dictated from above. The party-state leaders considered clubs an important site of socialist construction, where youth subjectivity—a sense of self and one's place within society—undergoes modification into that of a model Soviet subject ready to help the country transition to communism. Owing to the widespread popularity of state-sponsored cultural entertainment, clubs constituted central public spaces for youth entertainment, socializing, leisure, and romance. While this centrality made clubs a crucial location for the construction of a personal worldview and self-identity for young club-goers, such individual subjectivities did not always match top-level intentions.[6]

These disparities resulted from divergent visions of appropriately "socialist" fun. A key point of tension was the large proportion of young people enjoying western popular culture, such as jazz in the style of Louis Armstrong and John Coltrane, rock and roll by the Beatles and Elvis Presley, and dances such as the fox-trot and boogie-woogie, while not perceiving their behavior as anti-Soviet. By contrast, many militant ideologues considered western cultural influence to be subversive, especially in the Cold War context. These hard-liners proclaimed that young people should have fun by partaking in heavily politicized cultural activities or, at the very least, highly orthodox and traditional ones such as ballet, widely perceived as instilling appropriate cultural values. In some years, such militant perspectives prevailed in defining central policy. Yet, even then, certain club managers continued to host the controversial but popular western-inflected cultural forms, using deceptive practices to do so. A key motivation sprang from their need to fulfill the annual plan, which required enticing audiences to visit the club and encouraging amateurs to perform there voluntarily. Club administrators functioned at the uncomfortable intersection of carrying out top-level cultural mandates while organizing artistic activities that had wide popularity among the citizenry. Their experience shows that organized cultural recreation did not simply reflect the Kremlin's guidelines at any given point. State-sponsored popular culture was defined by the always evolving and frequently strained relationship among the leadership's directives, the varied incentives facing the cultural apparatus, and the desires and activism of ordinary citizens.

SOCIALIST FUN AND THE SOVIET PROJECT

Socialist fun was central to the overarching goal at the heart of the Soviet project: developing a socialist version of modernity. "Socialist modernity" refers to a society, culture, and a way of life widely perceived as progressive and advanced, informed by Marxism-Leninism, and actively constructed by human efforts. Scholars such as Anthony Giddens consider "modernity" a new stage in history defined by a break with notions of a static, tradition-based society. Replacing these assumptions with the conception that humans themselves construct and order social structures, modernity implicitly promised that people could build a perfect world on the basis of reason. From the beginning, the Soviet project endeavored to construct an alternative to the dominant western paradigm of a capitalist modernity; Zygmunt Bauman thus terms socialism the "counter-culture of modernity." Indeed, perceiving western modernity as characterized by class divisions, social conflict, consumerism, and individualism, the Communist Party sought a different path to the future—a socialist modernity, one placing greater value on egalitarianism, community-mindedness, altruism, and collectivism. However, the emphasis on these values, the vision of the specific form that such modernity would take, and the methods of attaining it changed over time.[7]

The early Soviet years involved a series of radical transformations aimed at building a utopian future. By the mid-1930s, the Stalinist leadership had proclaimed that the country had built the foundations of socialism, and thus it changed the focus to guarding those accomplishments. During the Thaw—the decade and a half following Joseph Stalin's death in 1953—the new leadership under N. S. Khrushchev revived the drive to move from socialism to communism. The term "Thaw" should not be read as equating the post-Stalin period with unvarnished liberalism but as conveying the series of thaws and chills in this ambiguous and multivalent but generally more pluralistic, tolerant, and grassroots-oriented era. The complexities, zigzags, and contradictions in Thaw-era policy resulted, to a large extent, from a combination of the Soviet Union engaging in the Cold War while trying to transition to communism.[8]

The post-Stalin authorities transformed the isolationist and top-down late Stalinist vision of socialist modernity into a novel Thaw-era model that aimed for grassroots engagement and for broad popularity at home and abroad. The new leadership rejected the previous tendency to simply dictate cultural norms from above and gave some weight to actual youth desires and preferences; moved away from demanding disciplined compliance to the officialdom and instead encouraged the young to express some autonomous initiative; and, finally, decreased the politicization of club activities and placed a much greater emphasis on entertainment and fun, including giving official sanction for a modicum of western-style cultural forms. Likewise, the post-Stalin administration increasingly pulled aside the Iron Curtain to showcase the Soviet Union, including its organized cultural recreation, as an attractive socialist alternative to western modernity. Indeed, the socialist alternative had wide global acclaim, especially in the 1950s and 1960s, when the Soviet project seemed most vibrant due to its apparent creation of social harmony, rapid economic growth, technological achievements, military might, and anticolonial internationalist orientation. Billions of people in East and South Asia, the Middle East, Africa, Latin America, and eastern Europe oriented themselves toward the socialist version of modernity rather than the western one. So did a significant minority of westerners.[9]

Yet, to secure legitimacy for a socialist modernity, the post-Stalin Kremlin needed to present an alluring version of socialist fun. This goal proved especially important and difficult to achieve in popular culture, the area in which western modernity had a vast global influence. The Soviet leadership wanted to forge a socialist popular culture, of equal or greater appeal than the western one, which would convey socialist values, as defined by whatever the current party line prescribed. In doing so, policy makers also aimed to ensure their cultural hegemony, meaning sure support among the masses for the cultural standards propounded by the ruling elites, which was necessary for maintaining political power and ensuring social stability.[10]

My analysis builds upon the work of Stephen Kotkin and David Hoffmann, who have demonstrated the Soviet project's ideologically driven rejection of capitalism as part of the drive to build a modern alternative to the western model in the pre–World War II Soviet Union. While extending their insights about the importance of Soviet ideology to the postwar years, my research indicates that World War II and especially the Cold War acquired a great deal of weight after 1945. The Cold War served as an existential threat to the Soviet Union and its achievements in building the foundations of socialism. On the other hand, it revived the possibility of socialism triumphing around the globe rather than in only one country, thus reinvigorating the dream of reaching communism in the foreseeable future.[11]

This book challenges the views of those scholars, such as Martin Malia, who treat the Soviet Union as unique. It also departs from the views of György Péteri and others who underscore the similarities between different socialist states in trying to build a socialist exception to the western version of modernity, without placing these modernizing projects in a global setting. The Soviet version of socialist modernity was one of many socialist modernities, though it functioned as the archetypal and most influential socialist modernity. Furthermore, I argue that the Soviet Union constituted one among many "multiple modernities," or countries that seek to forge a modern society different from the western model. Situating the Soviet Union among a field of multiple modernities allows us to move beyond the Eurocentric emphasis of traditional modernization theory, which assumes an inevitable, eventual convergence of all systems on a western modernity.[12]

A multiple modernities perspective highlights the contributions that the Soviet Union as a case study brings to other fields. Thus, this book develops the theory of multiple modernities by noting that, during the Cold War, the Soviet Union aimed to construct the most prominent alternative modernity and also presented itself as a model to emulate for all other countries striving to forge a modern society distinct from the western one. Likewise, I highlight the tensions inherent in the Soviet version of modernity. Differing ideas of what constituted a truly socialist modernity sparked conflicts within the Soviet Union. Comparing these to debates over modernization projects in other contexts produces illuminating insights.[13]

Scrutinizing clashes over state-sponsored popular culture from 1945 to 1970, my study also looks back to their origins. Adopting this wide-lens approach exposes the roots of these clashes in early Soviet and even pre-revolutionary disputes over "spontaneity" versus "consciousness," namely, whether a socialist cultural industry should privilege grassroots spontaneity or top-down ideologically conscious guidance, as well as the extent to which it should focus on ideological propaganda, on cultural enlightenment, or on pleasurable entertainment. The answers to these questions evolved throughout Soviet history, defining the nature of state-sponsored popular culture at any given time.[14]

Likewise, this monograph looks forward to the consequences of these struggles during the 1970s and 1980s, underscoring the key role that contingency played in the failure of socialist modernity. After the 1964 coup against Khrushchev, Leonid Brezhnev and his allies gradually turned away from soliciting initiative from below. This militant turn had an especially powerful impact on youth, as it went against the early, Thaw-inspired expectation that the party-state would grant them ever-increasing cultural autonomy. The Brezhnev administration's choice severely undermined youth commitment to the Soviet project, a conclusion complicating accounts that posit the inevitable triumph of western over socialist culture.[15]

Addressing the lived experience of socialist youth culture provides insights into the Soviet system's endeavor to build a modern socialist youth—the New Soviet (Young) Person. The Marxist-Leninist canon assigned the young a central role as those not only constructing but also slated to live in communist utopia; in turn, youth represented a major social demographic. Consequently, the Kremlin invested considerable resources into managing the young. Recent archive-based histories have revealed much about young post-1945 intelligentsia. Scholars have also investigated extensively the small numbers of countercultural youth. Such studies have shed much-needed light on the inadequacies in the party-state's cultural policies. Nonetheless, the cultural practices of the large majority of ordinary youth who did not openly deviate from official cultural norms remain largely in the shadows. This problematic dynamic implicitly reproduces the imbalance found in writings on western youth, which excessively privilege nonconformists. Consequently, the overarching image emerging from scholarship on Soviet and non-Soviet youth alike does not convey a representative picture of reality.[16]

An investigation of mass-oriented cultural entertainment casts doubt on the widespread notion, expressed by David Caute, Sergei Zhuk, and Reinhold Wagnleitner, among others, that Soviet youth generally longed for western culture and did not find pleasure and fun within official culture. Building on Alexei Yurchak's and Kristin Roth-Ey's work on other cultural spheres, my analysis of club activities indicates that many Soviet youngsters saw no contradiction between a full commitment to building communism and an appreciation for certain elements of western culture. In other words, loyal Soviet youth could like both communism and jazz, and Khrushchev as well as Coltrane.[17]

Moreover, Soviet organizations not only permitted but in some cases even encouraged a surprising amount of room for agency. Agency refers to behavior primarily motivated by an individual's personal interests and wants, as opposed to conduct imposed forcefully by external forces. Exploring Soviet organized cultural recreation underscores that grassroots agency did not necessarily translate to resistance or subversion, thus countering narratives that juxtapose state and society and postulate an inherent rift between a genuine, everyday culture and an official, state-managed one. Significant numbers among the young readily devoted themselves to cultural activities that bore a substantial ideological load, such as singing songs elegizing Stalin. Their conduct demonstrates what I term "conformist agency," or the conscious and willing decision, stemming primarily from one's internal motivations and desires, to act in ways that closely follow top-level guidelines.[18] Plenty, however, expressed their individual agency by abstaining from amateur arts with thoroughly politicized repertoires. Instead, they enjoyed singing folk songs and acting in Russian prerevolutionary plays, and a large number engaged in western-themed cultural activities in clubs. The most avid fans took deceptive measures to avoid censorship during periods of top-level militancy and antiwestern jingoism.

Early in the Thaw period, the authorities allowed young people to shape state-sponsored popular culture through a major campaign to promote initiative from below, greatly expanding the space for autonomous youth agency and self-determination within official settings. This drive helped lead to transformations in the behavior, worldview, and cultural tastes of those growing up in the period between the end of the war and Stalin's death, a group whom Juliane Fürst called the "last Stalin generation," and those coming of age in the turbulent mid- and late 1950s. I term this latter age cohort the "post-Stalin generation." Generations share many characteristics, but a shared sense of belonging to the same social group is a crucial component of a powerful generation. In this way, a generation parallels what Benedict Anderson has called an imagined community—a group, such as a nation, whose members share a common sense of identity and community, though their relations are distant and "imagined," rather than direct and personal. The post-Stalin generation, I find, possessed a much greater sense of belonging to the same age cohort, and consequently its generational cohesion was stronger than in the last Stalin generation, which helped the post-Stalin generation push for major cultural reforms and stand up to older authority figures. The post-Stalin generation met with some notable successes in changing top-level cultural policy and its grassroots implementation. The minute actions of millions of young people uniting with others of their age group to advocate for their personal and mutual wants not only shaped their everyday environment but also powerfully influenced the wider Soviet cultural field. Youth agency thus helped determine broad historical processes, a parallel to what Lawrence Grossberg has found about the social impact of young people in western contexts.[19]

State-sponsored popular culture helped define a socialist mode of cultural consumption. The burgeoning historiography on socialist consumption, which largely focuses on material consumer goods, has underscored the obstacles Soviet rulers faced in finding an appropriately socialist approach to consumption. This book proposes that mass-oriented collective cultural activities in clubs served as a lynchpin in the Kremlin's efforts to define and enact a socialist form of consumption and build a socialist version of a consumer society. However, deep tensions existed between ideological imperatives and marketlike financial consumerist forces in state-sponsored popular culture. Different party-state bodies gave more weight to one or the other, according to their varying missions and the political positions of the bureaucrats in each organ. These agencies frequently acted at cross purposes, undermining the imposition of a cohesive mode of socialist cultural consumption. This divide underscores the inefficiencies and contradictions within the Soviet top-down bureaucratic system. Such problems helped ordinary citizens and lower-level administrators alike maneuver within official institutions and challenge the center's cultural policy, ensuring that both groups possessed real agency. Furthermore, youth used their agency to refashion the nature and meanings of club cultural offerings to fit their own individual interests. These data expand our understanding of how individuals remake mainstream products to suit their own needs.[20]

Setting my case within an international framework highlights intriguing parallels and distinctions between how twentieth-century European authoritarian states, such as the Soviet Union, socialist eastern Europe, fascist Italy, and Nazi Germany, used cultural production for the masses as a tool for governance. The Soviet Union, in this regard, constituted what Bauman terms a "gardening state," referring to how modern authoritarian governments strive to transform—to garden—their populations, thus growing an ordered society that fits the leadership's needs and ideals. Drawing attention to commonalities and differences around the globe in the struggle against the postwar expansion of American popular culture, my work contributes to our understanding of how both socialist and nonsocialist societies resisted US cultural globalization. By emphasizing that governments could play a substantial role in shaping popular culture, consumerism, aesthetic tastes, and leisure, my project expands the western-centric academic models that used only North American and western European capitalist democratic contexts as the basis for their evidence and gave minimal attention to state structures.[21]

Investigating the grassroots impact of top-level cultural guidelines gets at the notoriously difficult issue of the reception of popular culture. At one end of the spectrum in my narrative stand young cultural activists and performers who embraced officially prescribed, orthodox cultural offerings. Many youths, however, found themselves closer to the middle, participating in mainstream club activities while occasionally testing the boundaries. On the far end of the range lie avid fans of western popular culture who pushed state-managed cultural institutions to host their favored musical genres. A crucial subgroup among the latter consisted of "jazz enthusiasts," my translation of the term *dzhazovye liudi* used by one of the most famous Soviet and post-Soviet jazz musicians, the late Georgii Garanian, to describe himself and his friends in his interview with me. "We were so into jazz that we had no other interests; it was jazz and nothing else," he stated. These jazz enthusiasts formed a fan community, getting together with other aficionados to listen to jazz, especially the newest and most fashionable styles; learn everything about this music and spread their knowledge to anyone interested; collect and trade jazz records; and, in many cases, to perform this music. While acknowledging their countercultural status in the late Stalin years, my study shows that many young jazz enthusiasts eagerly participated in state-sponsored popular culture once the post-Stalin leadership adopted a more pluralistic cultural stance. This finding challenges scholarship that treats jazz behind the Iron Curtain as embodying oppositional attitudes, a longing for freedom, and a desire for an American way of life.[22]

Speaking of "socialist fun" engages with literature that treats emotions not as simple biological givens but as largely cultural constructs of a specific society that reflect underlying social values. For instance, the psychologists Elaine Hatfield, John T. Cacioppo, and Richard L. Rapson have demonstrated how people's emotional experience results, to a significant extent, from the feelings expressed by those around them, as well as from what individuals consider to be the emotional norms in their society. Building on such research, historians have recently drawn attention to the historical significance of the evolution of emotions. William Reddy has used the term "emotional regime" to describe the normative sentiments prescribed by the political, social, and cultural authorities at any given time, along with the mechanisms enforcing these feelings. The term "emotional community," coined by Barbara Rosenwein, refers to a group whose members follow shared norms of emotional expression and possess the same outlook on appropriate affect. Any society has an overarching emotional community and subordinate emotional communities, which engage with but elaborate upon and occasionally oppose the affective values of the primary emotional community. Looking at organized cultural recreation helps illuminate the evolution of Soviet emotional regimes and emotional communities in the first decades of the Cold War. Soviet cultural policy strove constantly to ensure that young people expressed and experienced officially prescribed sentiments within state-sponsored popular culture. Yet, the nature of the emotional regime changed a great deal between 1945 and 1970. For example, a substantial shift occurred, from a restrictive and militant emotional regime in the late Stalin years to a more pluralistic one in the early Thaw period. This transformation represented a conscious step by the Khrushchev Kremlin to bring officially prescribed emotions closer to the reality of youth emotional communities as policy makers sought to mobilize feelings of enthusiasm and excitement among the young and channel them into renewing the drive toward communism. Still, top-level guidelines never entirely overlapped with the actual tastes and sentiments of young club-goers, resulting in gaps between youth emotional communities and the party-state's emotional regime. These fissures grew wider during periods of cultural conservatism, whether in the postwar Stalin era, at brief periods during the Khrushchev era, or in the late 1960s under Brezhnev, with many youths garnering pleasure and having fun by thumbing their noses at uptight prescriptions issued by the party-state.[23]

Exploring how youth cliques readily engaged in and invested deep personal meaning into state-sponsored cultural activities contributes to recent scholarship questioning the traditional distinctions drawn between the Soviet public sphere—everything associated with the party-state, such as official cultural production—and the private sphere—individual emotions, personal life, friends, sociability, family, and home. Organized cultural recreation embodied a liminal space that contained elements of what earlier scholarship labeled as public and private. These elements intertwined in a complex fashion to enmesh ordinary citizens within party-state structures and ideology. Simultaneously, the population's attitudes, preferences, and behaviors powerfully shaped the conditions local cadres and policy makers faced, as well as their perceptions of those conditions.[24]

The post-Stalin Kremlin's drive to build a modern and socialist popular culture that offered an alluring yet ideologically appropriate alternative to western popular culture placed the Soviet club network at the heart of the Cold War domestic cultural front. As recent publications have shown, the cultural struggle played a vital role in the Cold War's eventual outcome. In the contest for the hearts and minds of domestic and foreign audiences, both sides deployed culture as a weapon of soft power, that is, the ability to achieve international geopolitical goals through attraction rather than coercion. Scholars have furthered our understanding of western cultural diplomacy, or the government effort to promote its domestic culture abroad and thereby win over world publics. Yet, the more complex, and ultimately more revealing, question of the actual fruits of this soft power offensive on Soviet daily cultural life remains poorly explored. By illuminating the grassroots effect, and effectiveness, of western cultural diplomacy—an issue just now starting to receive serious attention from pioneering scholars—my work complements and enriches our comprehension of the Cold War.[25]

Exploring Soviet state-sponsored popular culture enriches our understanding of Soviet cultural diplomacy. There is surprisingly little scholarship on how authorities within socialist and nonsocialist contexts alike deliberately utilized internal cultural structures to sway the opinions of foreign visitors. I term this practice "domestic cultural diplomacy" to distinguish it from the traditional understanding of cultural diplomacy, which I suggest deserves the name "foreign cultural diplomacy." Existing scholarship has not drawn such distinctions and as a result has overlooked cultural diplomacy oriented toward foreign visitors. The party-state's leadership aspired to use its domestic mass cultural network to persuade outsiders that the Soviet Union had an attractive and socialist popular culture. State-sponsored popular culture also proved useful for foreign cultural diplomacy, as the Soviet authorities sent amateur artists to international cultural events, such as jazz festivals. Tracing the impact of these activities on both Soviet visitors and the foreigners with whom they interacted enriches the growing scholarship on the significance of Cold War cross-border interactions among nonstate actors. Moreover, examining both domestic and foreign Soviet cultural diplomacy helps place the Soviet Union within the context of twentieth-century transnational history.[26]

Grassroots events and exchanges in the mass cultural network constituted a critical daily experience of the Cold War for the population, while also representing a central component and microcosm of the superpower conflict as a whole, demonstrating the necessity of using micro-level case studies to grasp key elements of the Cold War. Such evidence suggests the validity of treating the Soviet Union as one among many "Cold War cultures," or countries that experienced the struggle between the blocs on an everyday cultural level. I wish to avoid Cold War determinism—the idea that every development from 1945 to 1991 stems from the superpower conflict—and acknowledge fully that the Cold War did not touch everything and that other international processes had important transnational impacts during this period. Likewise, each individual polity had particular historical trends that drove domestic developments prior to and after 1945. Nevertheless, the Cold War played a very significant role, including in Soviet cultural practices. My narrative shows that the superpower struggle influenced day-to-day lived experiences and that the cultural Cold War at the grassroots had real significance for Soviet rulers. Growing concerns about what many political elites saw as the subversive impact of western culture, along with top-level desires to influence foreign attitudes through domestic cultural diplomacy, influenced their actions in the domestic and foreign policy arenas.[27]

SOURCES AND STRUCTURE

A diverse complement of sources illuminates four interlinked elements of state-sponsored popular culture. First, my book examines the nature of and debates over policy formation within central institutions using central archives, including the files of the Komsomol, the trade unions, the Ministry of Culture, and the party. Second, recognizing that local practice frequently diverged from federal intentions, I have used for this project regional archives to compare top-level policy implementation in Moscow and Saratov. A regional center on the Volga, Saratov was the most provincial of Soviet cities and was closed to nonsocialist foreigners. It thereby offers a representative example of youth experience in the Russian heartland outside of the atypical, and exhaustively researched, settings of Moscow or Leningrad. This study closely surveys two working-class neighborhoods: Moscow's Krasnopresnenskii District and Saratov's Kirovskii District. The documents of several large enterprises and universities reveal ground-level policy enactment. These include Moskovskii gosudarstvennyi universitet

(MGU, Moscow state university), the Soviet Union's flagship educational institution, and Saratovskii gosudarstvennyi universitet (SGU, Saratov's state university), one of the strongest Soviet regional universities. The experience of working-class youth emerges from Saratov's Tret'ia gosudarstvennaia podshipnikovyi zavod (Third state ball-bearing factory) and Moscow's Krasnyi Bogatyr' (Red knight) and Trekhgornaia Manufaktura (Three mountain manufactory) factories. My work thereby brings to light both the daily life of and federal policies toward young urbanites—both middle class and working class, women and men, in the capital and in the Soviet Russian provinces—who attended official cultural events. While the center's directives applied to organized cultural recreation offerings for peasants and those in non-Russian regions, my study does not deal with their day-to-day cultural experience.[28]

This study also explores the depictions of organized cultural recreation in official discourse. Tracing the evolution in this rhetoric furthers our comprehension of the shifts in the official ways of thinking, talking about, depicting, and understanding Soviet reality, which also played a powerful role in constituting the worldview and cultural practices of young people. My sources here include national, regional, and local newspapers, instruction booklets for cultural officials, literary works, movies, and musical repertoires.

Finally, to comprehend how young people perceived and experienced state-sponsored popular culture on the day-to-day level, this work relies on firsthand accounts, including memoirs, diaries, and, most important, a series of open-ended interviews I conducted with scores of individuals. My interviewees include lower-level, mid-ranking, and top officials who participated in formulating and enacting organized cultural recreation. They include Liubov Baliasnaia, a high-level official in the Komsomol central hierarchy, and Anatolii Avrus, the leader of the Komsomol cell at SGU. I spoke with youth cultural activists who engaged extensively in state-sponsored popular culture; these activists included Iurii Gaponov, the leader of an innovative amateur artistic collective at MGU, and Iurii Sokolov, who participated in a variety of mass cultural activities. Jazz enthusiasts constitute the third category of interview subjects, whether Muscovites famous across the Soviet Union and in post-Soviet Russia, such as Georgii Garanian or Aleksei Kuznetsov, or Saratovites well known in that city, including Feliks Arons and Iurii Zhimskii.

Treating these oral sources as autobiographical texts, my methodology follows Donald Raleigh and other scholars in considering interview accounts to be a reflection of people's interpretation of the narratives of their lives rather than an entirely accurate portrayal of the past. Taking into account that the stories individuals tell about themselves change throughout the course of their own history caused me both to look for patterns across my interview subjects rather than trusting the memory of any one person and to remain aware of how new experiences shape recollections. My approach involves paying the greatest attention to those narrators who consciously differentiated between the values and emotions of their youth and their current sense of self. In analyzing the self-reported meanings that adults drew from their youthful lives and the feelings they experienced in state-sponsored popular culture, I most valued accounts that illustrated how behavioral changes arose from such emotions and meanings. In producing this work, I used archival and published sources to complement and test oral evidence, holding in highest regard those interviews that best correlated with written documents. The interviews served as invaluable tools for uncovering what happened behind the scenes of cultural events and within the interstices of youth cultural practices, spaces generally not reflected within archival documents and official publications. Furthermore, the interviews offer the best available instruments for getting insights on the meanings, emotions, and evaluations that young people associated with mass-oriented cultural activities. Informed by the work of Irina Paperno, I follow a similar approach in analyzing memoirs and diaries.[29]

The eight numbered chapters combine a chronological and thematic structure. Chapter 1 overviews Soviet organized cultural recreation from its origins to the end of World War II and then examines more thoroughly the immediate postwar period, 1945 and 1946. The next chapter investigates the extreme ideologization of the official prescriptions for club activities in the late 1940s and early 1950s. Chapter 3 takes an in-depth look at the attacks on western-style music and dancing during the same period. In chapter 4, the text explores how the pluralistic cultural turn during the early Thaw period, 1953–56, affected organized cultural activities. The fifth chapter presents a case study of Thaw-era transformations, particularly the explosion of youth enthusiasm, by focusing on novel institutions such as youth initiative clubs. Chapter 6 provides insights on the Kremlin's campaign to instill normative cultural tastes among youth in a brief hardline turn during the late 1950s. The seventh chapter deals with the revival of a more pluralistic approach to cultural policy from the end of the 1950s and into the early 1960s. Finally, chapter 8 teases out the ambiguities of the early post-Khrushchev years and the turn toward militancy by the end of the 1960s, concluding with the Sixteenth Komsomol Congress, in May 1970, which defined the shape of the overarching Brezhnev-era policy toward cultural recreation.

The book illustrates the evolution in the party-state's use of state-sponsored socialist fun in the Cold War context to help elucidate the primary alternative to the western paradigm of modernity. My research highlights the challenges faced by the authorities in achieving their goals, whether owing to disagreements among officials, incongruities within the Soviet institutional structure, or noncompliance by young people. At the same time, it demonstrates that the state's cultural policy, riven by tensions between hard-line and soft-line approaches, opened up significant room for youth agency and grassroots activism, with young people themselves playing a crucial role in defining state-sponsored popular culture.

CHAPTER 1

IDEOLOGY, ENLIGHTENMENT, AND ENTERTAINMENT

State-Sponsored Popular Culture, 1917–1946

The postwar Stalin years, from 1945 to 1953, are widely depicted as a time of cultural militancy, when official policy denied the population's desires for truly enjoyable cultural fun. Yet, a late 1945 Komsomol report commended Moscow clubs that "regularly show movies" and "hold evenings of youth leisure," meaning youth-oriented events with dancing.[1] In 1945 and early 1946, Komsomol official reports meant for internal policy guidance and Komsomol newspaper articles intended for public consumption frequently praised mass-oriented cultural institutions for staging entertaining and widely popular events with little or no ideological content, such as youth dances and foreign movies.[2]

To explain this unexpected cultural pluralism, the first part of this chapter examines the broader historical context of Soviet cultural production and provides the framework for the rest of the book by tracing the history of state-sponsored popular culture from its prerevolutionary origins through the end of World War II. It describes the basic institutions of organized cultural recreation and the primary tensions within them. The second part of the chapter focuses on the first postwar months, highlighting the tolerant policy toward state-sponsored popular culture. This postwar permissiveness resulted from the momentum of wartime cultural lenience, the immediate needs of physical reconstruction, and the Komsomol's lack of capacity to enforce a hard-line cultural position. Organized cultural recreation demonstrates that the late Stalinist authorities, for a few short months, actually sought to appeal to the population and satisfy popular desires for a more pluralistic society. Official discourse in this period presented a commitment to building a form of communism that was not irreconcilable with a desire for western popular culture, allowing young people a surprising degree of cultural space for maneuver and marking a break with prewar Stalinist policies.

THE ANTECEDENTS OF THE SOVIET MASS CULTURAL NETWORK

The antecedents of Soviet state-sponsored popular culture date back to the late nineteenth century. Some Russian industrialists, progressive officials, philanthropists, and members of the intelligentsia began to sponsor for the lower-class urban population forms of popular culture, such as popular theaters and *narodnye doma* (people's houses), intended to promote what they saw as healthy, appropriate, modern, and cultured leisure activities over supposedly wasteful or harmful ones, such as drinking.[3] Liberal pedagogues also established organizations that provided cultural education activities for lower-class youth.[4] Such initiatives responded to the social, economic, and cultural changes of industrialization and urbanization in imperial Russia. After the 1905 Revolution, there emerged autonomous workers' clubs in which workers gathered for cultural self-education, aided by intellectuals eager to assist them. These clubs occasionally served as cover for underground political groups, including the Bolsheviks, exacerbating some tsarist officials' antipathy toward organized cultural recreation.[5]

Organized cultural activities in Russia drew inspiration from institutions and developments in western Europe and North America.[6] During the eighteenth century, British authorities suppressed working-class popular culture without offering enjoyable cultural recreation in exchange.[7] By the nineteenth century, some middle-class social reformers began to sponsor what they perceived as fun, healthy, and "rational" leisure to British workers. The so-called working men's clubs, based on middle-class culture, were meant to wean workers from the traditional sociability of bars and dance halls.[8] In the United States, fin-de-siècle cultural elites disparaged the explosive growth of what they considered "low" cultural forms, such as blues and jazz, and instead promoted appreciation of "white" European "high" culture.[9] Social activists promoted the need for organized leisure activities for young people, founding organizations such as the Boy Scouts and Girl Scouts.[10] These initiatives represented part of a broader sweep of social interventionist measures within industrializing countries aimed at improving the discipline, cultural level, productive capacity, and social welfare of the population.[11]

The parallels between the efforts of Russian and western social reformers hint at broader congruencies between their visions of an ideal future. Both wanted all of society to share their middle-class cultural values and engage in "rational" and "modern," not "traditional" or commercial, leisure. Yet, these initiatives, without popular support or substantive government backing, had limited success in western countries and still less in imperial Russia.[12]

STATE-SPONSORED POPULAR CULTURE IN THE SOVIET UNION, 1917–1944

After the October Revolution, the Bolsheviks made state-sponsored popular culture a major sphere of activity for the Soviet party-state. The Bolsheviks took up many of the projects first elaborated by progressive professionals in late imperial Russia in the sphere of organized cultural recreation, just as they did in the realm of social reform more broadly.[13] Moreover, at least some imperial-era mass cultural establishments carried much of their staff and spirit across the revolutionary divide.[14]

During the civil war of 1917–22, the party leadership emphasized the role of mass-oriented cultural activities in promoting loyalty to the new regime.[15] The central government's focus on the war, however, left ample space for grassroots initiatives. Individual factory committees, village councils, and Komsomol cells created a network of semiautonomous trade union, village, and youth clubs at the local level.[16] These establishments often collaborated with the Proletkult, a semiautonomous cultural organization that strove to forge a "proletarian" culture via grassroots amateur cultural activities.[17]

Following the civil war and the transition to the New Economic Policy (NEP, 1922–28), these disparate activities coalesced into a centralized mass cultural network. This process involved a series of controversies about the most fitting cultural activities for the masses, which were part of larger debates about the best path to communism. Hard-line officials associated with the militant Left favored a rapid and coercive transition to communism led by an authoritarian elite committed to enacting Marxist-Leninist ideology with minimal consideration for public opinion. In contrast, soft-line cadres affiliated with the pluralistic Right supported a gradual path, one that relied more on persuasion over coercion, called for an alliance with nonparty technocratic specialists, and sought to both appeal to popular desires and elicit initiative from below as a means of achieving communism with grassroots support.[18] These conflicts date back to disagreements within the prerevolutionary Bolshevik Party over whether to depend on a small and ideologically conscious revolutionary vanguard or trust in broad-based worker spontaneity to forge communism.[19] While some officials consistently favored either soft- or hard-line viewpoints, most stood closer to the center of the political spectrum. They shifted their approaches and sometimes mixed elements from both, depending on the political, social, and economic situation, as well as on intraparty political struggles over leadership after Lenin's demise. The Right and Left thus constituted fluid coalitions rather than well-defined blocs within the party.

The difference between the militant and pluralistic approaches found its reflection in state-sponsored popular culture. One conflict centered on the main priorities of this cultural sphere. Three possible areas of focus existed: first, promoting communist ideology, party loyalty, Soviet patriotism, and production needs; second, transforming traditional culture into an appropriately socialist one by instilling socialist norms of cultural enlightenment; and, finally, satisfying the population's cultural consumption desires for entertainment and fun. More conservative officials held that state-sponsored popular culture needed to serve primarily as a "transmission belt" for Marxist-Leninist ideology, commitment to the party and the Soviet Union, and concern with production, with cultural enlightenment as a secondary goal. Soft-line cadres stressed satisfying the population's desires for engaging and entertaining cultural activities, thus making cultural enlightenment secondary and political-ideological education last in importance.[20] In another area of disagreement, pluralistic administrators expressed tolerance for western popular culture such as jazz music and foxtrot dancing, while those of a more militant persuasion condemned such cultural forms as ideologically subversive incursions of "foreign bourgeois" culture.[21] Finally, those holding a conservative position demanded close control from above over cultural activities at the grassroots, while those toward the opposite end of the spectrum were more welcoming of popular initiative and grassroots autonomy.[22] The latter point of tension proved especially significant for the fate of Komsomol-managed clubs that sprang up during the civil war and the early NEP period, with hard-liners expressing wariness of and striving to limit youth autonomy in state-sponsored cultural activities and those favoring a soft-line approach endorsing grassroots youth initiative.[23]

These divisions embodied two extremes of the political spectrum, with most cultural officials standing somewhere between these poles and holding a mixture of views. Further, their perspectives evolved over time due to changing domestic and external situations. Moreover, even those with the most extreme views largely agreed on the need for some cultural enlightenment and, more important, shared the common goal of trying to build a communist utopia. Still, the different stances generally correlated to fundamental tensions between conservative and liberal outlooks on the Soviet cultural field in the NEP years and afterward, continuing to inspire debates and reform drives throughout the history of the Soviet Union.

As the party-state recovered from the civil war and assumed more and more authority, those with more radical views increasingly dominated.[24] This hardening process accelerated in 1928, as Stalin took the reins of power and put an end to the cultural pluralism of the NEP. The government centralized organized cultural offerings for the masses. It directed cultural institutions to carry a much heavier ideological load, censured light entertainment as unacceptable "cultural excess" (*kul'turnichestvo*), and harshly condemned western-style popular culture.[25]

By the mid-1930s, the party-state had begun to step back from most of its militant policies, declaring that it had achieved victory in constructing the foundations of socialism. The state began to invest more resources into improving living conditions.[26] The number of clubs grew rapidly: between 1927 and 1932, the Soviet Union established 912 urban clubs, but, from 1932 to 1937, it established 2,951.[27] Clubs began to include more light entertainment.[28] The mid-1930s even witnessed a brief period of tolerance for western popular culture. Millions of people openly listened to and danced the fox-trot, tango, Charleston, Lindy hop, and rumba to jazz music played both by amateur ensembles and by professional jazz stars such as Alexander Tsfasman and Leonid Utesov.[29] Still, top-down directives and oversight rather than grassroots initiative pervaded the mass cultural network. Furthermore, young amateur artists had to conform to the cultural standards imposed by cultural professionals.[30]

In the late 1930s, official policy turned toward isolationism and publicly expressed fear of foreign ideological contagion, along with declarations of Soviet superiority in all spheres of life.[31] This development brought a renewed clampdown on jazz and western dancing, with jazz bands (*dzhazy*) either dispersed or forced to play variety (*estrada*) music. The repertoire for variety bands included an admixture of Russian classics, ballroom music, folk tunes, and mass-oriented patriotic and ideological Soviet songs. They also played a sovietized version of jazz cleansed of allegedly "decadent" elements. Official discourse expressed this division by speaking of acceptable sovietized jazz and contrasting it to harmful American-style jazz (*amerikanskii dzhaz*). Sovietizing jazz meant minimizing improvisation, syncopation, blue notes, and fast swinging feeling and instead playing in a smooth and slow style, with traditional jazz brass instruments, such as trumpets and saxophones, diluted by the addition of string and Soviet folk instruments. Fully choreographed and approved in advance by censorship organs, this sovietized jazz hardly measured up to the spontaneity and improvisation so essential to jazz as a musical genre; sovietized jazz most resembled big-band swing music, flavored with Soviet and especially Russian national themes.[32]

World War II caused tremendous disruption to youth lives across the Soviet Union and the European continent, including within the realm of

Soviet state-sponsored popular culture.[33] The state directed resources away from cultural activities, while most ordinary citizens had little leisure time or energy for culture. Despite these obstacles, some opportunities existed for mass music making and other forms of entertainment. Frequently, such entertainment occurred as a result of local initiatives by committed cultural enthusiasts. Moreover, concerts aimed at military personnel meant that cultural workers were engaged in efforts specifically for wartime needs. In fact, the government loosened the limitations on western popular culture imposed during the Great Purges. The party-state now welcomed American-style jazz tunes as a way of lifting the morale of the troops and populace and demonstrating a close relationship with wartime allies.[34]

THE MASS CULTURAL NETWORK

Regardless of the war, the framework of state-sponsored popular culture that emerged during the early 1930s survived largely unchanged throughout the Stalin period, and much of it carried over into the post-Stalin years as well.[35] Trade unions controlled most urban and some rural clubs. Like the party, trade unions had a hierarchical structure, with local enterprise committees overseen by district (*raion*, also translated as neighborhood), city, province (*oblast'* or *krai*, also translated as region), and republic-level committees. The Vsesoiuznyi Tsentral'nyi Sovet Professional'nykh Soiuzov (All-Union Central Trade Union Council) oversaw all trade unions. Government organs in each province, in collaboration with the Ministry of Culture, also established a number of large mass-oriented cultural institutions in most district capitals. This type of institution was known as a Dom narodnogo tvorchestva (House of folk creativity) or Dom khudozhestvennoi samodeiatel'nosti (House of amateur arts). These provided cultural guidance, assistance, and some limited oversight of organized cultural recreation. Village councils and large collective farms operated most of the smaller rural clubs. Parks of culture and leisure (*parki kul'tury i otdykha*), run by city-level cultural organizations, played a significant secondary role in the cultural life of young people in the larger cities from late spring to early fall, providing stages for concerts by professional and amateur artists, dance floors, and spaces for large celebrations. Libraries often had dedicated spaces and logistical support for amateur artistic collectives.

Urban clubs ranged from large, well-funded establishments, frequently called palaces of culture or houses of culture, to smaller, typically one-story buildings of a few rooms with a concert/movie hall referred to simply as clubs, down to one-room "red corners" (*krasnye ugolki*), typically featured in dormitories, factory shops, and large apartment buildings. Villages had smaller, poorly supplied clubs or tiny reading huts (*izba-chi-*

tal'nia). A manager directed clubs, hiring staff, planning and managing events, and balancing the budget; volunteer activists or housing supervisors managed red corners. In clubs, a volunteer club council (*pravlenie kluba*) helped run the institution. Clubs devoted most of their energy to cultural activities and political propaganda, but they also hosted such recreational pursuits as games and athletic activities and provided space for various community and political events.

The Gor'kii dom kul'tury (Gor'kii house of culture) in Moscow, owned by the bread-making trade union, exemplifies the largest club type. In 1947, it had a two-story building with a large hall that could seat one thousand, a smaller one that could hold three hundred, three rooms for amateur collectives, plus a leisure room, a library, a sports hall, a snack bar, and several additional rooms. Its inventory included a variety of musical, theatrical, movie, radio, and other cultural equipment. The club had a sizable budget of 2.9 million rubles and employed fifty-six people.[36]

The club manager's primary concern consisted of fulfilling the yearly plan, which outlined proper income and expenditures and the scope and number of cultural activities. Of these matters, financial management was usually more important than planning cultural activities, especially for trade union and village clubs and for parks of culture and leisure. Fulfilling and overfulfilling the plan, particularly the financial aspect, meant significant bonuses for club managers and workers, thus constituting a powerful incentive; failing to fulfill the plan could result in serious repercussions, including job loss.[37] By contrast, the Ministry of Culture expressed more concern with the ideological purity and quality of events than with financial revenue, thus generating friction with entities that had different priorities. Clubs served as the main hosts for amateur artistic circles, in which participants, mostly youth, gathered voluntarily on a regular basis to learn, practice, and perform music, acting, dancing, and other artistic activities. Each circle had a leader with some expertise in the relevant art form. The cultural organization hosting the amateur collective usually solicited volunteers to serve as circle leaders; however, well-financed clubs sometimes paid for professional artists and pedagogues to lead the circles.

Amateur collectives represented an obligatory function for clubs. The majority of circles lost money; they generally did not charge fees for amateurs to participate or, in most cases, for audiences to come to amateur concerts, in order to ensure sufficient numbers of both to fulfill the plan. However, some amateur collectives, frequently those playing popular music, helped to fill club coffers by drawing large enough audiences to hold paid events; they even performed in other venues besides their home institution on a contract basis. In other cases, some high-quality circles, even when their artistic genre lacked broad popularity, increased the club's prestige by winning amateur artistic competitions.

Amateur musical bands frequently performed at cultural events called "evenings" (*vechera*), a broad term encompassing events held for all sorts of purposes. Some had free entry, others required an official invitation or ticket purchase, depending on the event. Evenings frequently had two parts. The first generally focused on politics and ideology, such as a lecture or ceremony, and the second on entertainment, often with a concert or theatrical performance followed by dancing late into the night. Some evenings specifically targeted young people, with local Komsomol cells frequently assisting club administrators in the planning, organizing, and publicizing of the event and the distributing of tickets.

THE KOMSOMOL

Dedicated to socializing young Soviet citizens, the Komsomol (Vsesoiuznyi Leninskii Kommunisticheskii Soiuz Molodezhi, or All-Union Leninist Communist Youth League) had direct responsibility for carrying out the party's youth policies. The Komsomol's pyramid-like internal hierarchy paralleled that of the party and the trade unions. Its base consisted of primary cells located in most establishments with a youth presence, with larger establishments having several internal levels of cells. Primary cells were overseen by organizations at the level of the district and, above that, the city, the province, and the republic. At the top, the Komsomol Central Committee directed Komsomol policy and had a large central apparatus to further its goals. A bureau composed of top officials called secretaries headed the Komsomol Central Committee, with a first secretary in charge. Nikolai Mikhailov held that post from 1938 to 1952.[38]

The Komsomol enrolled only 10 percent of all Soviet youth in the mid-1930s, thus serving as a vanguard organization. However, the post–World War II years witnessed a major growth in membership, as the party leadership wanted the Komsomol to grow into a truly mass organization. In 1949, the Komsomol embraced 20 percent of those eligible, and, by 1958, its membership included about half of the Soviet Union's 55 million Komsomol-age youth.[39] Those who joined the Komsomol generally had social ambitions, such as attending college, becoming a party member or government official, or rising in rank at their workplace. Belonging to the Komsomol required expressing public dedication to Marxist-Leninist ideology, paying dues, engaging in volunteer work, and attending obligatory events, especially Komsomol meetings at primary cells, which featured discussions of and resolutions on various organizational activities and policies. Far from all members dutifully fulfilled these requirements, creating a significant point of tension within the Komsomol.

In a process loosely supervised by higher officials, Komsomol organizations elected their leaders at a special conference, usually held each year. These conferences also served as a forum to report on the activities of the Komsomol branch and to discuss plans for the upcoming year. Those chosen formed the Komsomol committee of the primary organization, which had responsibility for the daily management of the cell's affairs. A first secretary led each committee, with the other committee members responsible for distinct spheres of Komsomol work, such as propaganda, production, education, cultural events, athletics, and so forth. Often, these local-level officials had extra compensation or time off for their Komsomol organizational activities, depending on the size of the cell. Generally, the larger the primary cell, the more oversight higher-ups imposed on the election process. Above the primary cell level, higher-ups effectively selected officials to manage Komsomol organization, with yearly election conferences serving mainly as a venue in which to discuss the state of affairs in the Komsomol branch. District, city, and republic Komsomol mid-level officials formed part of the Komsomol bureaucracy, usually working full time for the Komsomol; the most well funded of these organizations, usually at the city and especially republic levels, also had hired staff, such as cultural inspectors, who helped manage and direct youth cultural activities.

The Komsomol organized occasional congresses that determined the organization's broad agenda; only one was held in the postwar Stalin years. Between the congresses, the most important rulings originated from Komsomol Central Committee plenums and the Komsomol Central Committee bureau. Each level of the regional Komsomol hierarchy had to adopt the directives enacted above and also passed separate resolutions relevant to its own needs. As a result, lower-level Komsomol committees faced a torrent of decrees, meaning that they had to mostly ignore some in order to work on others. New top-level initiatives generally pushed previous ones into the background, unless higher-level Komsomol committees repeated decrees or checked on implementation among lower-level cells.[40]

RECONSTITUTING STATE-SPONSORED POPULAR CULTURE AFTER THE WAR

With the transition to peace, the Soviet population widely expected a postwar relaxation of wartime pressures and a variety of improvements in living and working conditions.[41] The Kremlin dashed these hopes. Stressing self-sacrifice and discipline, the rulers aimed to mobilize the citizenry for an extensive, rapid, and exhausting reconstruction. Despite overcrowding, a lack of consumer goods, and famine in parts of the Soviet Union, the new Five-Year Plan (1946–50) focused on heavy industry, basic infrastructure, and military might. The Kremlin justified this course by stressing both the demands of reconstruction and the need to prepare for conflict with the United States and western Europe.[42]

The Komsomol tried to mobilize young people to pursue the Kremlin's goals, but World War II had ravaged the Komsomol. Thousands of primary cells disappeared, along with cash from dues, the Komsomol's main funding source. After the war the Komsomol Central Committee (CC) launched a membership drive to reestablish its structure, finances, and ability to influence Soviet young people.[43] Simultaneously, the Komsomol strove to enact the party's broader agenda, calling on young people to devote most of their scarce free time to the goals of rebuilding the country and preparing for a potential war.[44] Consequently, the Komsomol CC invested little energy in organized cultural recreation.

In addition, state-sponsored popular culture had suffered from extensive damage brought about by the war. Official statistics list 94,371 clubs in 1946, down from 118,032 in 1941.[45] However, even before the end of the war, the bureaucracies in charge of mass-oriented cultural institutions—trade unions and the Ministry of Culture—sought to reconstruct their cultural networks but paid little heed to the particular needs of young people or to the Komsomol itself.[46]

The central Komsomol organization did undertake limited efforts to increase organized cultural recreation for young people. By 1944, the Komsomol propaganda department had developed a comprehensive proposal to improve cultural recreation. It suggested having *Komsomol'skaia pravda*, the Komsomol's national newspaper, publish more articles on that topic, training Komsomol members to run amateur collectives, and having a secretary responsible for state-sponsored popular culture in each Komsomol committee. Most radically, it spoke of having local Komsomol branches establish youth clubs and amateur collectives.[47] Recalling NEP-era cultural establishments, these proposals paralleled top-level discussions at the time about the possibility of mobilizing the population through grassroots initiatives.[48] However, higher-ups rejected the idea of Komsomol-managed clubs, likely perceiving these as permitting youth too much autonomy, which was unacceptable to the party leadership at the time; proposals for activism from below in other spheres eventually suffered similar fates. Still, the Komsomol enacted many of the other elements proposed by the Komsomol propaganda department and sought to strengthen club services for young people.[49]

Komsomol newspaper rhetoric also promoted organized cultural recreation. A *Komsomol'skaia pravda* editorial about factory clubs claimed in January 1945 that young people wanted clubs to sponsor more youth-oriented events, including lectures, literary evenings, and amateur performances. The editorial specifically praised Moscow's Zuev club for lectures allegedly "based on the requests of youth," such as "The Dynamo and How to Care for It," "Electricity and Magnetism," and "Energy of the Future."[50] Representative of youth newspaper articles on involvement published at this time, this editorial presented a narrative of what idealized young New Soviet Men and Women should desire, including lectures on the domestic and international political situation, Russian history, science and technology, and literature.[51] Amateur arts concerts lay last on the inventory of model young people's priorities; dances and movies were not mentioned at all.

The editorial's pronouncements certainly diverged from the actual priorities of the young and instead depicted an idealized, hoped-for future. Thus, the journalist's writing embodied socialist realism, the Stalinist canonical style in rhetoric and cultural production that presented the officially prescribed model as the true reality, with the goal of transforming the imagined ideal into the real by remaking popular consciousness.[52] Simultaneously, this editorial served as a signal to the Komsomol's top-level cultural officials. Internal Komsomol messages repeatedly emphasized that political propaganda and production-oriented concerns had the most importance, cultural enlightenment was a distant second, and fun entertainment a low priority.[53]

These efforts from above faced serious problems. Regional Komsomol committees in Saratov and elsewhere made statements acknowledging the importance of state-sponsored popular culture.[54] However, such rhetoric frequently resulted in little follow-through, as cultural recreation remained a low priority. *Komsomol'skaia pravda* related that, although the Kirov Province Komsomol committee passed a decree promoting amateur arts, "there was a problem: a resolution existed, but no one worked on actually enacting it."[55] This situation was quite typical, as seen, for example, in Moscow.[56]

Factors relating to postwar conditions played a role as well. Clubs suffered from a deficiency in basic supplies such as fuel and furniture, which severely hampered their function.[57] The cultural network also lacked well-prepared club managers and amateur arts leaders.[58] Postwar lawlessness and hooliganism in club activities presented a further obstacle to the Komsomol's intentions.[59] German Krichevskii said in an interview that he and his friends targeted the members of an amateur art ensemble in his neighborhood, since, in his words, "street kids" like himself "despised the ensemble" for its association with officialdom.[60]

In many cases, the high cost of popular mass-oriented cultural events mandated by managers eager to fulfill the yearly financial plan prevented young people from enjoying organized cultural recreation. In the fall of 1945, the Komsomol propaganda department claimed that trade union clubs charged "unacceptably high" entrance fees, with tickets for concerts costing twenty to thirty rubles and admission for dances running at ten to twenty-five rubles.[61] Regional Komsomol branches related that young workers expressed "much displeasure" over high prices for tickets to club dances and concerts.[62] These complaints offer revealing insights into the actual popularity of club events, since dances and concerts drew youth into clubs. Lectures were notably missing from this list of points of complaint, a dynamic similar to that of the 1930s.[63] The Komsomol CC took some measures to deal with the costs, asking the Soviet leadership and the Tsentral'nyi Sovet Professional'nykh Soiuzov to lower the price of tickets.[64] The Komsomol press printed exposés of high ticket prices, using social censure to pressure cultural institutions.[65]

The Komsomol's promotion of youth access to such cultural activities reveals some of the ambiguities inherent within the Komsomol's cultural policy in the immediate postwar months. The most popular cultural forms deviated from the desired emphasis of the policy makers, who ranked political propaganda as primary, yet the actions outlined above promoted entertaining and nonideological events such as dances. Some statements in the internal and external Komsomol discourse even offered guarded blessings for such activities. In late 1945, the Moscow Komsomol praised clubs in the capital for regularly showing movies and holding youth dances.[66] A *Komsomol'skaia pravda* article lauded young workers from the Serp i Molot (Hammer and sickle) factory who organized dances.[67]

In contrast, certain Komsomol cadres censured what they perceived as excessive orientation toward fun entertainment. Some officials in the Komsomol propaganda department expressed concerns in a 1944 internal report over western-style dancing. The document proposed teaching "folk and ballroom dances to youth" as a means of "agitation against youth fascination with western dances."[68] The traditional preference of the intelligentsia for ballroom dances, perceived as calm, controlled, and rational, over western dances, considered wild, uncontrolled, and irrational, also likely played a role in this criticism.[69]

A BRIEF PERIOD OF POSTWAR PLURALISM, 1945–1946

Such criticism, nonetheless, proved exceptional and rarely entered public Komsomol discourse in the concluding stages of the war and the immediate postwar period. Foreign movies entered the Soviet Union largely as spoils of war and thus were known as "trophy" films. For instance, the 1944 German musical *Die Frau meiner Träume* (Dream woman) drew many more spectators than any of the staid and bombastic socialist realist movies. *Tarzan's New York Adventure* (1942) inspired young Moscow college students to imitate Tarzan's apelike howling in their dorms. The popular 1941 film *Sun Valley Serenade*, featuring the Glenn Miller jazz orchestra, helped advance the popularity of western music among Soviet youth.[70]

Foreign movies enabled club managers to fill depleted club coffers. The Gor'kii dom kul'tury declared in its 1946 yearly report that the club had taken in 1,164,100 rubles from movies, a whopping 69 percent of its total revenue, thus generating a tidy profit of 164,500 rubles. For comparison, the club made 268,700 rubles from theater performances, 221,200 from concerts, 22,800 from varied evening events, and a paltry 4,500 from lectures. Moreover, the club spent only 999,600 on the movies, hence its profit. While concerts also made money (12,700 rubles), the rest of the events cost more money than they brought in. Theater performances lost 34,500, evening events 32,200, and lectures 34,900 rubles, with the last category by far the most disproportionate in terms of cost of event versus revenue.[71]

The income from each event reflected the size and interests of the ticket-buying audience. The 1946 plan for the club called for lectures to bring in 109,800 rubles, instead of the measly 4,500 rubles they actually managed to get, which met only 4 percent of the planned goal. This sum underscores the abysmally low attendance at lectures. The club's 1946 plan also highlights another crucial point about lectures. According to the plan, the club expected movies, concerts, theater performances, and evening events to take in more money than they cost; the plan was overly optimistic about the latter two. Lectures, however, were written into the plan as a money-losing activity from the start, since the plan included anticipated revenue of 109,800 rubles versus expenditures of 141,600.[72] With the top-level demand for financial profit from cultural recreation institutions, the fact that financially unsustainable lectures figured prominently in the club's plan indicates the political pressure placed on clubs to have lectures and support them materially with profit from money-making events such as movies and concerts.

Western films went hand-in-hand with western dancing and music. Growing steadily even before the conclusion of the war, the number of youth from all social backgrounds dancing the fox-trot, tango, rumba, and Charleston exploded across the Soviet Union in the immediate postwar period. At dances, musical ensembles played everything from Soviet variety music to American-style jazz, with extensive improvisation, fast rhythms, and everything in between; many bands and musicians performed only or mostly American-style jazz. Utesov, Tsfasman, Eddie Rosner, and other popular jazz musicians brought their bands to Moscow and Leningrad, while plenty of talented amateur musicians joined professional groups.[73]

Western music and dances had clear financial benefits. A number of jazz ensembles performed in the Tsentral'nyi park kul'tury i otdykha imeni Gorkogo (Gor'kii central park of culture and leisure) in Moscow during 1946, including Rosner's band. That year, not coincidentally, the park dance hall greatly overfulfilled its plan, with an average of 487 people in attendance per dance instead of the 350 as anticipated, resulting in 759,000 actually coming to the dance hall that year instead of the planned 450,000.[74] Komsomol internal reporting similarly confirms the profits accruing to mass-oriented cultural institutions from western dances.[75] Youth interest in dancing served the Gor'kii park and other cultural recreation institutions well, helping cover the losses incurred by the much less popular lectures.

Soviet state-sponsored popular culture had roots in initiatives by social reformers in imperial Russia and took its subsequent shape in the dynamic and turbulent NEP years. During this period, several points of conflict emerged over organized cultural recreation, and they reflected broader struggles between hard-line and moderate visions of communist construction. In contrast to the militant perspective, the pluralistic one encouraged more space for youth agency and fewer restrictions on initiative from below; supported entertainment, cultural enlightenment, and political propaganda, in that order; and permitted a degree of western cultural influence. The conservative position had won out by the end of the NEP as Stalin took power. Wartime needs pushed the regime to adopt a more pluralistic approach, but the war itself severely damaged the system of mass-oriented cultural recreation. This fact, combined with general lack of attention to culture by the party-state in the immediate postwar months, limited youth access to state-sponsored popular culture.

However, such neglect helped satisfy youth wants. Policy makers expressed a predilection for heavily politicized club events, with a substantially smaller dose of cultural enlightenment activities, leaving little room for fun and pleasure. In spite of this focus, the vast majority of the Komsomol's statements on cultural activities from 1945 to mid-1946 lacked criticism of hedonistic behavior and western cultural influence.

A confluence of factors explains this dynamic. First, western-themed culture had genuine popularity among the young and provided an easy and cheap means of satisfying desires for a postwar return to a more relaxed peacetime setting. Likewise, movies, dancing, and jazz helped relieve the enormous strain of rebuilding the country. As they tried to reconstitute the Komsomol by recruiting new members and getting them to pay dues and serve as lower-level cadres, Komsomol higher-ups likely questioned the wisdom of fighting against such a popular form of entertainment. Conversely, the frailty of the Komsomol and its focus on assisting the party-state's infrastructural rebuilding drive in this period meant that the Komsomol had few resources left to change youth behavior. Furthermore, considering the top-down imperative for cultural institutions to fulfill the financial plan, the willingness of young cultural consumers to pay for light entertainment made the cultural network unlikely to change its offerings without strong pressure from policy makers. At the same time, the Komsomol would have been extremely unlikely to adopt a policy condemning western popular culture independently of the party, since the Soviet leadership would have seen doing so as a dangerously independent act. As a result, in state-sponsored popular culture the party-state actually did meet postwar expectations for relaxation of prewar constraints, at least briefly.[76]

In this fleeting period, then, young people could successfully reconcile a self-image of a good Soviet citizen and New Soviet Person with a real interest in western popular culture. This ability represented a significant shift from the way that official discourse depicted the model young New Soviet Woman and Man in the immediate prewar period as necessarily rejecting western popular culture. The findings here support the arguments that World War II represented a major break in Soviet life, as opposed to the view of those who see the Stalin period as cohesive and holistic.[77]

Youth hedonism did gain prominence outside the Soviet Union. In East and West Germany, the postwar period witnessed plenty indulging in jazz and dancing.[78] Such youth conduct spread widely throughout the Soviet bloc.[79] These years saw similar pleasure-seeking behavior across central and western Europe.[80] Within the United States, the end of the war brought a rapid increase in the number of youth dancing to jazz and watching movies at drive-in theaters.[81] These parallels among the countries participating in World War II indicate a postwar trend common to both capitalist and socialist states, with a large portion of young people reacting to the strains of the war by plunging into entertaining fun as the conflict ended.

CHAPTER 2

IDEOLOGICAL RECONSTRUCTION IN THE CULTURAL RECREATION NETWORK, 1947-1953

In stark contrast to its approach during the immediate postwar period, the Komsomol from the late 1940s and into the early 1950s vigorously censured events that devoted "excessive" effort to entertainment and lacked "sufficient" ideological content. Newspapers carried stories condemning clubs for focusing on dances and movies, instead demanding more politicized activities.[1] Komsomol leaders, such as Komsomol first secretary N. A. Mikhailov, called for "vigilantly defending youth from pernicious foreign influences."[2]

This chapter explains the transition in central policy from a more moderate to a militant stance. It considers the impact of this shift on cultural activities considered fully appropriate, leaving more controversial club events to the next chapter. Noncontroversial cultural forms, such as choruses and drama collectives, came to bear a hefty political load; they devoted much more effort to propagandizing Marxism-Leninism, loyalty to the party, and especially Stalin, Soviet patriotism, and Russian nationalism and to escalating economic production, while praising discipline, militancy, and a rejection of anything western. Nevertheless, many Soviet citizens enjoyed participating in such profoundly ideologized club activities. By illustrating the nature of conformist agency and emotions, this chapter brings to light the cultural life of the large numbers who toed the line on the newly militant official norms, a topic understudied in scholarship on the Soviet Union and youth culture more broadly. Still, some problems, such as the lack of commitment by lower-level cadres to organizing cultural events, undermined the effectiveness of central policy; likewise, officialdom's forcible imposition of the ideologically restrictive cultural standards in the late 1940s turned off many of those who otherwise enjoyed orthodox genres in state-sponsored popular culture.

SOVIET CULTURAL POLICY, 1946-1953

In the late 1940s, living conditions in the Soviet Union began to improve markedly. As the widespread postwar famine of 1946–47 drew to a close, the government ended systematic rationing. The initial wave of sovietization swept through western Ukraine, Moldavia, and the Baltic states, suppressing resistance by armed nationalists as the Soviet party-state imposed its authority. Currency reform, while disruptive at the time, led to more financial stability. The high levels of postwar crime also dropped. Housing stock and social services grew slowly, while price reductions made consumer goods slightly more affordable.[3]

Yet, many Soviet citizens considered these very gradual gains insufficient. The population looked forward to a better life and much faster improvements in living conditions. People proved more and more willing to speak and act against state demands in the late 1940s. The Stalin leadership, however, refused to accede to the population's desires. Considering its victory over the Germans to have fully validated its power and authority, the Kremlin strove to maintain its wartime insistence on Soviet people expressing absolute obedience and self-sacrifice for the good of the state, best embodied in Stalin's famous postwar toast praising Soviet citizens as "small cogs" holding together the "state machine."[4]

Moreover, Soviet authorities could mobilize the citizenry against a clear target as the Cold War escalated in the late 1940s. The Kremlin used the fear of another world war to justify maintaining a wartime footing, which enabled it to demand disciplined behavior from Soviet citizens, continued intense economic reconstruction, and a focus on heavy industry and basic infrastructure.[5] In this sense, the Cold War had just as much importance for domestic as for foreign politics in the Soviet Union, thus paralleling the impact of the Cold War on politics in western states.[6]

The authorities did make some improvements in consumer offerings, including clubs. Soviet cities reportedly had 6,450 functioning clubs in 1946, 7,970 in 1948, 9,170 in 1950, and 10,050 in 1953.[7] Trade unions controlled more than 8,000 mostly urban club institutions in 1951, with 600 having been built from 1946 to 1950 and many of the rest renovated after suffering wartime damage and neglect.[8] Amateur performers in club activities also gained more cultural materials; for example, the Komsomol's complaints over the lack of published repertoires for amateurs in 1950 were replaced with expressions of satisfaction over the quantity of such literature in February 1953.[9]

To a significant degree, such investment resulted from the potential for the cultural recreation network to convey political propaganda, a function that came to the fore in the late 1940s as part of a broader ideological reconstruction campaign. The political and ideological loosening in Soviet culture during the wartime and the immediate postwar period worried top-level authorities. The Kremlin also aimed to recast cultural production for its Cold War needs on the cultural front.[10] Consequently, once past the initial wave of postwar consolidation of power in 1945 and early 1946, the leadership placed increasing emphasis on ideological reconstitution. Soviet rulers ramped up Stalin's cult of personality in the late 1940s, stridently demanding that the population show extreme gratefulness to the party and its leader for victory over the Nazis and for any improvement in living conditions, as opposed to attributing developments to their own individual initiatives.[11] The Kremlin also intensified ideological and political propaganda and education in all spheres of life, emphasizing Soviet and especially Russian nationalism and hard-line interpretations of Marxism-Leninism.[12] The public discourse's focus on the cult of Stalin and increasingly xenophobic patriotism formed the core of Soviet ideological statements in these years, crowding out claims of advancing to communism, which made only rare and pro forma appearances.

Furthermore, the Kremlin launched the campaign against "cosmopolitanism," a label used to condemn anything perceived as foreign to the Soviet way of life. Beginning in late 1946, reaching its apogee in 1948, and continuing largely unabated throughout the rest of the postwar Stalin years, this campaign aimed to purge "anti-Soviet" elements, overtly targeting foreign influence of all sorts.[13] Anti-American propaganda proved especially prominent.[14] Less openly, this initiative also targeted Jews.[15]

In arts and culture, the first waves of this campaign began late in the summer of 1946. Instigated by Politburo member Andrei Zhdanov, a series of high-level Central Committee decrees on literature, theaters, and movies appeared in August and September 1946.[16] For instance, an August 1946 resolution censured drama theaters for putting on too few plays dealing with Soviet reality and too many by foreign playwrights.[17]

Although sporadic censure of western influence on music began in late 1946, such criticism took off only in late 1947, when a revived series of attacks on jazz appeared in the press. These attacks presaged the expansion of the anticosmopolitan campaign into the sphere of music with the infamous Central Committee resolution of February 10, 1948, condemning Vano Muradeli's opera *Bol'shaia druzhba* (Great friendship). The decree stated that Muradeli and other prominent Soviet composers had wrongly taken a "formalist path," with a style that "transformed music into cacophony," which "strongly recalls modern bourgeois culture."[18] The Central Committee forbade clubs, concert halls, and restaurants to play jazz and host western dances, directing these institutions and erstwhile jazz musicians to perform bland variety music, folk songs, and classical pieces, especially Soviet ideological and patriotic tunes. The political authorities removed jazz stars from their previously high positions in the cultural industry; some jazz players even ended up in the Gulag.

This campaign went substantially further than the attacks on jazz in the late 1930s. For example, the anticosmopolitan campaign's official discourse derided as completely incompatible with true Soviet music such jazz-style musical elements as syncopation, fast rhythms, and especially improvisation, elements that were partly tolerated in the late 1930s. The state banned saxophones, the instrument most representative of jazz, and suppressed valved trumpets and trumpet mutes. The word *jazz* acquired a highly negative connotation in official discourse. The previous binary between sovietized jazz and American jazz disappeared, with all jazz music now considered intolerable.[19] In another step that proved more extreme than any from the immediate prewar years, both public and internal official discourse frequently reproached clubs that preferred to stage entertaining musical events and other cultural performances rather than politicized activities.[20]

Following top-level signals, the central Komsomol authority's attention to mass cultural activities in these years focused primarily on censorship and control. The Komsomol propaganda department took the leading role in enacting the party Central Committee's 1948 decree. Less than a month after the censure of *Bol'shaia druzhba*, an internal policy document from the department called on all Komsomol organizations to implement fully the party Central Committee resolution.[21] Branch Komsomol committees quickly responded with detailed reports of how they strove to enact the decree.[22] Similar themes characterized the Komsomol's official discourse on cultural activities throughout the rest of Stalin's rule. In 1950, the Komsomol propaganda department underscored that the party and the population demanded "Bolshevik idealism" (*bol'shevitskaia ideinost'*) from the arts, which, according to the department, meant propagandizing the party's political line and helping the party nurture youth in the spirit of unconditional commitment to the Soviet system.[23] In this regard, Komsomol cultural policy in the late 1940s and early 1950s fit the pattern identified by recent scholarship, which argues that, in this period, ideological purity came to the forefront of the regime's goals for youth, as Stalin wanted to secure his legacy by ensuring that youth developed absolute loyalty to his vision of the future.[24] Hence, state-sponsored popular culture further illustrates how the later Stalin leadership sought to utilize everyday life to reinforce official ideological prescriptions.[25]

ORTHODOX AMATEUR ARTS AND THE ANTI-COSMOPOLITAN CAMPAIGN

The anticosmopolitan campaign powerfully influenced official prescriptions for state-sponsored popular culture. This section examines the new guidelines by focusing largely on instruction booklets and newspaper articles depicting model clubs and amateur collectives. These exemplary institutions best reveal the intentions of Soviet cultural authorities, as well as the day-to-day cultural life of some, but not all, young people.

Strict limitations affected what sort of music clubs could feature. Repertoire booklets and Komsomol conferences stressed performing pieces glorifying the party and Stalin, praising high production achievements, and instilling Soviet patriotism.[26] Club managers, amateur circle directors, and local Komsomol cadres clearly grasped what the hierarchy expected of them. Young amateur musicians performed many songs devoted to the Motherland, the party, Komsomol, Stalin, and heroic labor.[27] In a typical example, the first piece in an amateur concert at Odessa's Pervomaiskii dom kul'tury (First of May house of culture) was "Song about Stalin."[28] An instruction booklet from 1952 described how young women in an amateur sewing factory chorus wrote a song about their work, which ended with the following lines:

> We are forging our own happiness
> With our free labor.
> Our work will not fall behind
> Materikova herself.
> The sun is shining down
> There is nothing more beautiful than the Motherland.
> We send greetings,
> To our teacher and friend, Stalin.[29]

In these years, the authorities heavily promoted choruses above all other forms of amateur music collectives. In 1950, the Komsomol Central Committee highlighted the need to organize amateur choruses in industrial enterprises, collective farms, schools, and colleges.[30] V. K. Stepanchuk, a former secretary of a Komsomol district organization, also recalled the significance attributed to choruses at this time.[31] Choruses embodied the late Stalinist ideal. They constituted a mass, collective, and disciplined endeavor whose success depended on its members functioning together as "small cogs" holding together the "machine" of the chorus, evocative of Stalin's famous toast. Choruses also met the regime's emphasis on Russian nationalism, since they had a clear link to traditional Russian music. Lastly, with minimal equipment, amateur chorus circles were cheap.

The repertoire of drama collectives, which put on plays and held dramatic readings of poetry and prose, paralleled that of music circles. Frequently, they began their performances with praise to Stalin. One performance by students of technical colleges began with a dramatic reading of "A Word to the Great Stalin" and another with "Stalin—Equals Peace."[32] Amateur drama circles often performed Soviet plays. At Saratovskii gosudarstvennyi universitet (SGU), the Saratov state university, an amateur collective produced a play entitled *Pervyie radosti* (First joys) in 1952, based on a novel about Saratov in World War I written by the Saratovite Konstantin Fedin, who had received a Stalin Prize.[33] While official rhetoric did not ban classical Russian plays, the emphasis lay on Soviet productions.[34]

Amateur dance circles also carried an ideological load, though in a less direct fashion than music and drama collectives. Dance groups typically performed various forms of "mass dances," often staged for official celebrations.[35] Folk dances, especially Russian ones, represented the most common form of recommended dances, embodying the anticosmopolitan emphasis on Russian nationalism.[36] Likewise, cultural officials promoted novel "modern" and "socialist" ballroom dances with names such as "Vstrecha druzei" (Meeting of friends).[37] The party-state intended such new dances both to convey ideological messages and to replace western dances.

During the anticosmopolitan period, the vast majority of youth-oriented evening events centered on ideological themes. For instance, in 1949–50, the main topics of Leningrad's youth evenings included the struggle for peace and democracy, the great communist construction projects, and the image of Lenin and Stalin in the arts.[38] The Gor'kii dom kul'tury, for instance, in an attempt to woo youth to vote in elections, hosted an event that included games, songs, and dances before a lecture, entitled "The Stalin Constitution and Soviet Youth," and a play.[39] Another event, devoted to friendship between Moscow and Kiev college students, began with a speech praising the "great teacher and leader," Comrade Stalin, followed by an amateur concert, and, finally, dancing the waltz.[40]

While encouraging local Komsomol committees to help organize youth evenings, official Komsomol discourse emphasized the need for young cultural activists to exhibit disciplined obedience to adult authority figures and downplayed any hints of youth autonomy, spontaneity, or initiative. An instructional booklet produced in 1952 by the official Komsomol press, *Molodaia gvardiia*, on behalf of a Minsk factory trade union club represents an authoritative model of prescribed cultural organization for Komsomol committees. According to the text in this booklet, the club's council formulates the monthly plan in agreement with the factory party and Komsomol committees. The party committee "pays a great deal of attention to the upbringing of youth, and gives the club leadership much valuable advice and directives." Komsomol members helped organize youth evenings, consulting with the party committee on the topic of the lecture, finding a lecturer, and, together with the club management, organizing a concert. These evenings, always tied to the production goals of the factory, also endeavored to instill Soviet patriotism in young workers and expand their cultural horizons.[41] Another booklet from 1952, while stating that Komsomol cells "should be the initiators" of activities in cultural institutions, highlighted the need for all cultural work to serve the goal of bringing up youth in the spirit of Bolshevik ideology and Soviet patriotism.[42] Similarly, a former Moscow Komsomol neighborhood committee secretary, Valentina Miagkova, stressed the important role of local party committees, as well as trade union committees and Ministry of Culture organizations, in controlling clubs' repertoires of youth activities during the anticosmopolitan period. She noted that, by comparison, Komsomol cells had only a minor voice.[43]

In fact, the trope of discipline pervaded rhetoric on cultural recreation in these years. Thus, the railroad trade union instructed its cultural institutions to help "raise the discipline of each worker."[44] Komsomol rhetoric not dealing with state-sponsored popular culture likewise emphasized discipline.[45] Allusions to youth initiative figured only rarely in postwar Stalinist discourse on young people. When they did, such references frequently appeared in the context of discipline and management from above. For instance, the Komsomol's national organ published in December 1951 an article about the city of Melekess entitled "Develop Youth Initiative," which praised a local party committee for activating a dormant Komsomol cell.[46] The Saratov city Komsomol conference of 1952 censured the city Komsomol committee for not providing enough direction to local Komsomol cells.[47] This move mirrored the dynamic of the campaign for criticism and self-criticism of the late postwar Stalin years, when very narrowly prescribed rules permitted minimal scope for autonomous activism from below.[48] The stress on youth discipline dovetailed with the glorifying of Stalin as the source of all authority, which inevitably functioned to deprive youth of legitimate space for autonomy and grassroots initiative.[49] It also fit within the broader Stalinist efforts to continue wartime obedience among the young.[50]

Taken together, these messages clarify the anticosmopolitan campaign's image of the ideal New Soviet Youth. This model young person expressed loyalty to Stalin and the party, held a hard-line interpretation of Marxism-Leninism, and articulated xenophobic nationalism. Immediately obeying all orders from authority figures, such youth expressed enthusiastic activism within the narrow bounds of top-level directives and avoided any autonomous initiative.[51] Within the sphere of culture, the anticosmopolitan New Soviet Young Women and Men rejected any western influence and minimized light entertainment, preferring to spend their leisure time participating in heavily politicized club activities, especially propaganda lectures but also amateur collectives whose repertoires bore a heavy ideological load.

By trying to forge the anticosmopolitan model of the New Soviet Individual through a mass cultural network, the Stalinist Kremlin in the late 1940s and early 1950s paralleled the cultural policy of other European authoritarian states in the twentieth century. Victoria de Grazia has found that the Mussolini leadership in fascist Italy invested substantial resources in creating a large-scale centralized system of government-organized cultural recreation for adults and youth in order to forge what she termed the "new Italian." Such an individual would exhibit discipline and obedience, as well as loyalty to the nation and to the National Fascist Party.[52] Nazi Germany made similar efforts, if on a smaller scale and targeted mostly toward youth. Furthermore, the Nazi government launched strident attacks against jazz and western dancing, considering these cultural genres to be ideologically subversive agents of capitalist democratic influence—another clear parallel to the Soviet Union.[53]

Previous scholarship has shown that modern bureaucratic authoritarian countries constituted "gardening" states endeavoring to remake their citizenry to suit the needs of policy makers. A study of organized cultural recreation shows, however, that human gardening in the Soviet Union went beyond state violence.[54] Analyzing the large-scale programs to manage organized cultural recreation for youth expands our use of gardening as an analytical tool, helping us appreciate that these varied regimes recognized the importance of shaping mass cultural consumption desires and preferences as a means of building the model young socialist, fascist, or Nazi individual. The similar cultural policies exercised under these regimes indicate that the one-party structure and official ideology prevalent in all major modern authoritarian bureaucracies provided some common instruments for gardening the populace. However, each state adopted different methods and tools of gardening, and in all cases policy evolved over time. Thus, Soviet anticosmopolitanism relied on sharp shears to prune popular culture. In the late Stalin era, the party-state employed forceful coercion to create a formal garden in which a disciplined citizenry obediently followed top-level demands.

AMATEUR ARTS AND CONTROL ORGANS

Responding to pressure from above to improve controls over state-sponsored popular culture, cultural officials sought to monitor and guide amateur arts. Doma narodnogo tvorchestva (houses of folk creativity or folk arts) played a central role in exerting cultural control over amateur arts, as underscored by a top Komsomol official, V. E. Semichastnyi.[55] The most prominent folk arts house, located in Moscow, had oversight over the amateur arts in the capital and attendant influence over the rest of the Soviet Union.[56] Its functions included examining and approving all amateur circle repertoires and giving the collectives guidance, training, and support, with the goal of managing their artistic content.[57] Clubs established or strengthened art councils, which were committees composed of various officials and professional artists who reviewed the repertoire for amateur arts at individual clubs.[58]

Amateur cultural competitions served as another instrument both for encouraging and for controlling organized cultural recreation. These contests began at the local level, for example, pitting amateur circles against each other within a local establishment, such as a factory or university.[59] Collectives that won at the local level met in district and then city-wide competitions.[60] Groups awarded top honors in these contests sometimes went on to province-wide and then national competitions, with official financial support for their travel.[61] Victories by circles garnered prestige for their host institutions, helping explain why they granted members of the better-quality collectives time off and extra funding.

These contests likewise offered an opportunity for the hierarchy to evaluate and pass judgment on grassroots amateur arts, mirroring how Soviet industrial competitions intensified production.[62] In contrast to industrial contests, however, amateur art competitions also served as a way to monitor repertoires and send signals about appropriate programs for amateur art. For instance, the Komsomol propaganda department's report on the 1947 competition for Moscow's technical college students stressed that "in the repertoire of circles, there now appear works reflecting the might and steadfastness of the Soviet system, instilling love in the Motherland."[63] Such statements are strongly indicative of the differences between officially recommended amateur art competitions in the anticosmopolitan years and those held earlier, which featured more entertainment-oriented and less ideological pieces.[64] Amateur competitions likewise served to reveal problems in the repertoire. Semichastnyi criticized amateur cultural competitions in 1950 for "apolitical, low-quality works lacking in ideological content."[65]

POLITICAL PROPAGANDA AND SOCIALIST MODERNITY

The fact that high officials had to use strong pressure to promote strongly ideological cultural activities illustrates the gaps between official prescriptions and the actual desires of many Soviet youth. After all, clubs had a powerful incentive to offer the kinds of activities that appealed most to youth because their entry fees would make it possible to fulfill financial plans. Club officials at the grassroots were best positioned to know what kinds of cultural products sold well and which ones did not. Despite the apparent wishes of the Soviet authorities, simply decreeing that all young people should enjoy listening to political and production-oriented propaganda did not make it so. Far from all young Soviet citizens matched the anticosmopolitan model of the disciplined, obedient, and politicized New Soviet Person.

In fact, as had been the case in the immediate postwar period, there continued to be a great many youth who found political propaganda unappealing. Lectures continued to draw only small audiences. The most revealing evidence comes from a keynote speech at a conference of Krasnopresnenskii District Komsomol cadres, a semi-closed forum that permitted more honesty. The secretary of the Krasnopresnenskii neighborhood Komsomol disparaged the club of the silicate factory for holding too few lectures on youth themes. The secretary of the silicate factory Komsomol cell received censure for not doing anything about the lack of lectures. Additionally, the speaker criticized the club of the Stromynka dormitory at Moskovskii gosudarstvennyi universitet (MGU, or Moscow State University) for its poorly attended lectures. The club's plan, according to the speech, failed to respond to the demands of the students, for example, by not propagandizing Soviet patriotism sufficiently.[66] Yet, as shown by the lack of audiences for lectures, such socialist realist claims did not correspond to reality. In fact, lecture-style political propaganda in club spaces proved unpopular among youth in other Soviet bloc states as well, for example, in Stalinist Poland.[67]

The restrictive vision of state-sponsored popular culture put forward during the anticosmopolitan campaign indicates that the postwar Stalinist leadership did not strive to forge a domestically and globally appealing vision of a socialist modernity as an alternative to the western one. The Kremlin did not prioritize meeting the actual desires of its young citizens in the cultural sphere. Instead, it used propagandistic rhetoric and the coercive imposition of discipline to try to achieve its goals of maintaining social stability and enforcing social control. Using these strategies of rule hardly contributed to building an appealing alternative modernity, since this model had to be attractive in order to persuade people at home and abroad to adopt it as their guiding model for thought and behavior. Wary of giving up its oft-stated claims to total authority and absolute control, the Stalinist leadership from the late 1940s explicitly refused to provide any room for youth autonomy and agency in the cultural sphere, which might have elicited popular enthusiasm and initiative, despite some internal discussions about this possibility in the mid-1940s.

Moreover, the late Stalinist Kremlin drastically limited interactions with the outside world, with the anticosmopolitan campaign representing the apogee of a defensive and isolationist position. Even the Soviet party-state's highly successful efforts to mobilize its citizens to participate enthusiastically in the Soviet-led international peace campaign focused on signature gathering and donations, not direct citizen diplomacy toward outsiders.[68] The postwar Stalinist government, in other words, tried to sell Soviet foreign policy and its geopolitical role as beneficial to outsiders but made minimal efforts to demonstrate the Soviet Union's domestic system as an appealing model of socialist modernity to the world outside the socialist bloc. In turn, within socialist eastern Europe, the Stalin Kremlin relied much more on coercion than persuasion when instilling the Soviet socialist model. With its coercive methods, along with its defensive and enclosing orientation, the anticosmopolitan campaign represented the Kremlin's effort to consolidate and maintain power and rebuild what Stalin earlier termed "socialism in one country," which was no recipe for a globally attractive modernity. This approach was at some variance with Soviet policies in the 1920s and early 1930s to showcase the Soviet Union to nonsocialist visitors, especially westerners, as a means of promoting the socialist model as an appealing alternative. However, it fit well with the shift toward isolationism in the late 1930s, suggesting continuities between the immediate prewar period and the postwar Stalin years. Of course, the Soviet victory in World War II and the regime's international position as a superpower, along with the escalating Cold War and its impact on the Soviet Union, made it impossible to rebuild the prewar system as it had existed previously.

Regarding ideology, the later Stalin leadership did not seek to move toward communism. It sought to prioritize maintaining power and stability, rather than further transforming Soviet society along Marxist-Leninist lines by introducing societal reforms that would destabilize the system. Thus, public discourse made only minimal claims about moving toward communism, instead emphasizing the cult of Stalin and xenophobic nationalism as the central ideological bases for the postwar Soviet system. By doing so, the Stalinist leadership exhibited a yearning to return to the immediate prewar period, a time that it considered, at least during the late 1930s, the ideal, pragmatic embodiment of socialism.[69] Yet, evidence indicates that the Stalin leadership's militancy and conservatism in cultural policy from the late 1940s onward went beyond those of the immediate prewar years. Here, a range of factors played a role, including the mounting cultural struggle with capitalist states, the perceived needs of postwar ideological reconstruction, the Stalinist Kremlin's desire to maintain strict wartime-style controls, and the increased sense of legitimacy and power it gained through the victory against Germany. In this sense, the late 1930s and the postwar Stalin years were distinctly different.

As the Kremlin took over eastern European states, it pushed its satellites to adopt similar cultural policies. East Germany, Bulgaria, Hungary, and others enacted a top-down, isolationist approach to building a modern socialist popular culture.[70] The Soviet Union spread the late Stalinist version of socialist popular culture, and socialist modernity, throughout its sphere of control, although substantial regional variation existed throughout the Soviet bloc.[71]

EMOTIONAL LIFE AND CONFORMIST AGENCY IN OFFICIALLY PRESCRIBED CLUB EVENTS

The recollections of former cultural activists whom I interviewed demonstrate that young people generally joined amateur art circles based on personal enthusiasm for such cultural activities. Participation in an amateur collective did count as a low-level form of social service in one's official file, which was of particular importance to those amateurs who also belonged to the Komsomol. However, amateur arts did not have nearly the same political value on the official scale as giving lectures or exhorting voters to come to the polls, even though they generally required much more time and energy; thus, amateurism drew young people interested in cultural activities rather than simply politically ambitious ones, whether Komsomol members or not.

The most lucid description of this topic comes from Dmitrii Gal'tsov, who participated extensively in amateur arts at MGU and had intimate familiarity with both the creative and the organizational aspects of state-sponsored popular culture. He stated that "the [college] administration considered participation in amateur arts as social work, and every [student] had to have some sort of social work," which "was included in one's official file." Otherwise, the student might get criticized as an "antisocial element" and encounter potential obstacles in her or his life path. Yet, amateur cultural activities, in his words, counted as least important in the hierarchy of prescribed social work. He underscored that he would have undoubtedly participated in amateur arts without getting official credit for it, since "people engaged in amateur arts out of their own personal wish."[72] Likewise, O. V. Cherniaev, who both participated in and organized amateur music events, said that amateur arts activity "was not something that you were forced to do, but did by choice out of your own personal desire." Yet, it had the added benefit that "your official file stated: active participation in social work through amateur arts."[73] Interviews with other young amateur artists reveal similar motivation.[74] The future Soviet leader M. S. Gorbachev, who was fourteen in 1945, related in his memoirs that in the late Stalinist years when he went to school, "everybody was keen to participate" in officially organized recreation. At his school, amateur theater "became such a craze that the drama group could not admit all the enthusiasts" and "new members had to be carefully selected."[75] These youth joined amateur circles of their own volition, finding pleasure, joy, and other desirable emotions in state-sponsored popular culture.[76]

The heavily ideologized repertoires in the late 1940s and early 1950s did not prevent many young people from finding deep emotional meaning in these activities. Nina Petrova, a participant in a dramatic collective in the postwar Stalin years and currently a historian, spoke with me among the files in Moscow's Komsomol archive. She told me how she had performed a dramatic reading of a selection from a Stalin Prize–winning novel, A. A. Fadeev's *Molodaia gvardiia* (Young guard), at a province-level amateur art competition in Ukraine. She experienced such intense emotions that she burst into tears, and audience members cried as well.[77] Valentina Iarskaia, currently a sociologist in Saratov, performed in amateur plays in a drama collective while growing up in the postwar Stalin years. Even more than fifty years later, she lucidly recollected the details of a scene in which she played the role of a spy interrogated by the Soviet political police, and she pointedly recalled her enthusiasm in playing this and other roles.[78] Petrova's and Iarskaia's clear and poignant memories underscore the powerful emotional impact of youth participation in heavily politicized club programs.

Other forms of amateur arts evoked emotional resonance as well. A historian of imperial Russia who attended SGU in the late Stalin years, Nikolai Troitskii performed in an amateur university chorus. He told me that patriotic songs formed a compulsory part of a concert program but insisted that he and other youth sang such songs with sincere feeling, despite the obligatory nature of the selections. He remembered "believing, with pleasure" in the content of songs about the civil war, World War II, and the Soviet Motherland.[79] The Saratovite Francheska Kurilova, who served as a lower-level Komsomol official while in school and in college, shared her memories with me over tea and refreshments. She had sung and read poetry in amateur arts during her youth, and she recalled her feelings of excitement over going through all levels of an amateur art competition, up to the final performance at the province level.[80] Svetlana Shchegol'kova gained pleasure from the state-sponsored opportunities to learn ballroom dances, such as the waltz and the mazurka.[81] All of these feelings conformed to the intentions of the party-state leadership, who hoped that young people would emulate the anticosmopolitan model of the New Soviet Individual by finding deep emotional meaning, joy, and fun in officially prescribed amateur cultural activities.[82]

Many of the millions of young people who chose to sign up for amateur arts in the postwar Stalin years shared similar emotions. In 1945, amateur circles had slightly more than 2 million performers. This number had risen to 3.5 million by the end of 1947, and in 1950 it topped 4 million. By February 1953, 4.8 million people were engaged in amateur arts in 324,000 circles across the Soviet Union. Drama collectives, despite their explicitly ideological repertoires, garnered the highest popularity, with about 2 million participants.[83] Scholarship on Soviet mass songs also shows that the population appreciated and sang tunes that had explicit ideological messages.[84]

That millions of people opted to voluntarily devote their time and energy to orthodox cultural activities during the heyday of the anticosmopolitan campaign, regardless of the heavily ideological repertoires, illustrates what my approach calls conformist agency. Such agency, along with its complexities and nuances, deserves respect, acknowledgment, and attention from historians on par with the spectacular public nonconformism expressed by the small minority of countercultural youth studied by the large majority of scholars on postwar Soviet youth cultural practices. This does not mean that all those who participated in officially recommended amateur arts in the culturally conservative late 1940s and early 1950s fully supported a hard-line vision of Marxism-Leninism, intense devotion to Stalin and the party, and xenophobic Soviet and Russian nationalism, just as far from all countercultural Soviet youth necessarily opposed the Soviet system or preferred a western lifestyle.

The concept of conformist agency is best thought of as a heuristic tool of analysis representing an ideal type at one end of the spectrum, with full-scale nonconformism at the other end, and all shades of behavior characterizing the reality of youth cultural practices occupying the space in between. In fact, young people sometimes engaged in a multiplicity of cultural practices: fully conformist ones, such as chorus or drama collectives with profoundly ideological programs; less conformist cultural activities that did not receive unqualified support from above, such as listening to variety music performances; and, finally, nonconformist ones such as western dancing. Regardless, we should not treat less conformist or nonconformist cultural activities as somehow necessarily more authentic than conformist ones. After all, young people generally participated in amateur arts on a voluntary basis out of a personal enthusiasm and interest and frequently had a deep emotional connection to their artistic activities.[85]

PROBLEMS IN CONFORMIST CULTURAL ACTIVITIES

Some among the young participated in conformist cultural activities in ways that departed from the intentions of the leadership; they failed to experience and express prescribed feelings. One challenge to the goals of the Soviet rulers involved the glacial rate of expansion in conformist activities during the late 1940s and early 1950s, illustrating how real life departed from the model clubs and collectives described earlier. Club institutions and Komsomol organizations came under criticism for devoting much more energy to amateur arts shortly before and during amateur artistic competitions, which higher-ups evaluated closely. In 1947, for example, the Krasnopresnenskii neighborhood Komsomol lambasted the fact that amateur circles functioned primarily during competitions.[86] Similarly, three years later the Komsomol propaganda department disparaged such behavior, testifying to the scale and continuity of this problem.[87]

Cultural offerings for young people were scarce in large part because local-level Komsomol cadres were reluctant to invest much effort in cultural recreation activities. Thus, the director of a park of culture and leisure in the city of Gor'kii complained in 1949 that neighborhood Komsomol committees expressed no interest in the park's work.[88] The Komsomol branch in the Avtostal' factory in Stalin province came under criticism from the Komsomol propaganda department in 1952 for its failure to organize adequate cultural activities for young people; out of six thousand young workers, only eighty-eight participated in amateur arts circles.[89] Considering the fact that the Komsomol leadership paid minimal attention to improving state-sponsored popular culture, such statistics are not surprising, as the already overloaded Komsomol administrators had little incentive to put more than token efforts into club events.

Liubov Baliasnaia confirmed that few Komsomol officials who organized substantive cultural work during the postwar Stalin years generally acted out of their personal enthusiasm and commitment, as opposed to responding to directives and incentives from above. Baliasnaia provides an especially valuable source, as throughout her extensive career she focused a great deal of her attention on organized recreation for young people.

Baliasnaia served as a mid-level Komsomol official in Ukraine during the postwar Stalin years. She had moved up to a high-level position within the Ukrainian Komsomol by the mid-1950s. In 1958, Baliasnaia came to Moscow and became a secretary in the Komsomol Central Committee bureau, thus becoming one of the top officials within the Komsomol. In the mid-1960s, she transitioned to assistant minister of enlightenment of the Russian Soviet Federated Socialist Republic (RSFSR).[90]

The general demographic profile of Komsomol bureaucrats contributed to their lack of concern over state-sponsored popular culture. War veterans occupied a high percentage of Komsomol administrative positions at all levels, especially at the bottom. As a result, a significant age and experience gap existed between them and their cell members, an increasing number of whom had not fought in the war. The former soldiers who served as Komsomol cadres focused their energy on education, job training, and political activism and had little time left for Komsomol work, such as club activities, which they quite accurately perceived as not advancing their careers.[91] The historian and SGU professor Anatolii Avrus, who matriculated at the university in 1948, described another aspect of this generation gap to me in an interview in his office at the university. He recalled that veterans preferred to spend their free time on paramilitary training and sports and considered cultural recreation intrinsically less important.

This dismissive attitude toward organized cultural recreation led to some tensions with nonveteran Komsomol members. Avrus related that nonveteran students not only sought to acquire an education for a career but also to find a path into adult society and an identity, and some even wanted to "spend five years having fun." Consequently, nonveteran college students tended to spend much more time in club activities, especially since many developed their artistic talent by participating in amateur circles in schools and after-school programs. Overall, Avrus recalled that "during this time there was a comparatively strong desire among students to engage in amateur arts," owing to the end of the war and the accompanying "longing for a peaceful life," with participation in amateur arts showing that peace had arrived. Further, according to Avrus, students lacked other forms of entertainment in those years, with the exception of movies, making "amateur arts or participation in sports the only way of relaxing."[92] Others, such as Troitskii, who studied at the university together with Avrus, similarly recalled student enthusiasm for amateur arts in the postwar years.[93] This evidence furthers our understanding of the tensions resulting from the gap in age and veteran status between lower-level Komsomol officials and Komsomol members.[94] Moreover, it illustrates the party-state's inability to deliver sufficient conformist cultural consumption options to satisfy the desires of at least some young people who wanted such orthodox cultural recreation, frustrating these youths and hampering the Kremlin's effort to forge an anticosmopolitan version of New Soviet Individuals.

In a further challenge to the designs of Soviet rulers, a subset of those youth who enjoyed participating in officially approved forms of state-sponsored popular culture disliked certain aspects of the official repertoire. Troitskii wrote in his memoirs that, during his youth, he and the other young people he knew did not express dissenting thoughts even in private conversations and "truly believed in Soviet power."[95] However, my interview with him revealed a more complex story. While he and the other young amateur singers performed patriotic songs with true feeling, other elements of the repertoire provoked mixed emotions. Most notably, he told me that concerts had to open with a song about Stalin. Yet, at least among his clique, this feature "was perceived as a formality" that did not reflect the actual sentiment and values of young people.[96] Thus, while Troitskii and his friends were faithful to the Soviet system and emotionally invested in highly ideological and patriotic songs, they did not experience the officially prescribed emotions of intense love for and gratitude to Stalin.

Iarskaia, while finding pleasure in her drama circle, rejected other aspects of the cultural policy in the anticosmopolitan period, namely the xenophobic nationalism that sought to sovietize all forms of cultural expression. A case in point comes from a field trip by a group of students from her class at school to see an opera, *Iz vsego serdtsa* (From the whole heart), by a Soviet composer. While hesitant over the prospect of attending an opera in the Soviet genre of socialist realism, she decided to give it a try. She described how, sitting in the nosebleed section, she and other members of the class "listened with horror" as the tenor launched into song: "and so, we begin the party commit-tee mee-ting." Despite the quality of the singing, which she praised, the content of the song inspired the whole gallery to laugh, and she and her classmates decided to walk out before the end of the performance.[97] Mocking laughter among youth who exhibited conformist agency in other settings does not fit the emotional expression that the cultural authorities had hoped to elicit.

Likewise, archival documents reveal some of the tensions inherent in officially approved forms of amateur activities. For instance, some drama circles received censure for not putting on ideological plays. The Moscow city Komsomol criticized certain amateur theater groups in February 1953 for performing "vulgar" plays, such as *Babushkiny skazki* (Old wives' tales).[98] In another example, the author of an instruction booklet described how the amateur collective of the Labinsk dom kul'tury had great success among audiences with its first few performances. However, the district party committee rebuked the group for putting on excessively light and entertaining plays, warning the house of culture management that such pieces "might lead to rolling down a slippery path to apolitical cultural entertainment." Instead, the party organization recommended that the theater circle put on a play critical of foreign warmongers and another praising collective farm production. The circle dutifully followed these directives.[99] Political authorities had to use coercion to impose ideological repertoires on some amateur cultural collectives. Such tactics hardly lead to the kinds of emotions that the authorities sought to inspire among the young amateurs.

Not all club events devoted to ideologically approved themes fit the confines of officially recommended practices, as exemplified by an unusual SGU amateur concert held on May 9, 1950, to mark the fifth anniversary of the end of the war. While Stalin canceled the nationwide celebration of Victory Day soon after the war, many veterans celebrated it on the local level.[100] Student veterans decided to mark the occasion with a concert, finding support from the university Komsomol. The performance featured a student veteran who sang what Avrus labeled "folklore from the front," including pieces that Avrus had never heard before or since and that had not been cleared by the censorship apparatus. During the concert, the two hundred audience members apparently "did not make one sound" because of "how interesting the songs were."[101] Such events, repeated across the Soviet Union during these years, conveyed the individual soldier's perspective, rather than the vision prescribed by authorities. Although promoting patriotism, these songs undermined some aspects of the official narrative of the war, for example, the attribution of the victory to Stalin's genius. "Folklore from the front," then, evoked a complex range of emotions and values, not all of which matched the Kremlin's aims.

During the late 1940s and early 1950s, the Stalinist leadership aimed to ensure social stability, maintain iron discipline, quickly rebuild the country, and prepare for another world war. In the cultural sphere, the Soviet rulers pursued these goals through the anticosmopolitan campaign, which stressed a hard-line vision of Marxism-Leninism, unquestioning faith in the party and especially Stalin, and xenophobic Soviet and Russian nationalism in the context of the escalating Cold War. The Kremlin sought to garden Soviet youth, cultivating an anticosmopolitan version of New Soviet People: highly ideological and politicized, disciplined and obedient rather than initiative-oriented, well prepared to serve as Cold Warriors through rejection of all traces of western cultural influence, and exhibiting conformist agency and emotions. The tenets of the anticosmopolitan campaign insisted on a broad escalation of the ideological elements of club activities, along with an extensive centralization of content management. Central policy demanded that youth perform the newly politicized repertoire passively, instead of having youth express their voices as creators who shape the repertoire actively. These initiatives achieved significant successes in imposing top-down controls over noncontroversial, orthodox forms of club activities. While the infrastructure of the cultural recreation network improved, its range grew much more limited.

This dynamic corresponds to what occurred in state-sponsored popular culture during the late 1930s, which also witnessed a crackdown on foreign influence, a turn toward Soviet and Russian nationalism, and a stress on loyalty to the party and Stalin in Soviet cultural institutions. The late Stalinist Kremlin envisioned a modern socialist society achieved by establishing a centralized and top-down structure determined entirely by the party elite's mandates, enforced by coercion, and closed off from outside interactions—another parallel to the late 1930s. In both cases, this model was unlikely to offer a broadly popular and appealing socialist alternative that attracted domestic and global mass audiences. The similarities between the cultural policy of the late 1930s and late 1940s indicate that the Stalinist leadership may have tried to reach back and reconstitute certain elements of the cultural sphere that it considered most worthwhile.

In spite of its high ideological load during the anticosmopolitan campaign, the amateur arts had 4.8 million participants on the eve of Stalin's death. A large number did not express any hesitation about their participation, sincerely believing in the ideals and values propagandized in the plays and songs. Oral evidence illustrating this loyalty has particular credibility, as the vast majority of those interviewed turned against Stalin only after his death in 1953. The willing and enthusiastic performance of pieces celebrating the party line likely strengthened acceptance of the official rhetoric among the young performers, and perhaps their audiences as well. The party-state encouraged autobiographical writing to forge people into model Soviet citizens.[102] My findings highlight another mechanism of constructing Soviet subjectivity, one deployed on a mass scale and in a collective, communal setting. Besides writing themselves into New Soviet People, individuals could sing, act, or dance themselves into this subject position. For many youths, individual agency proved fully compatible with participation in orthodox state-sponsored cultural activities. In other words, structure, as represented by the party-state, and agency, self-willed and individually motivated behavior, did not necessarily oppose each other, as shown by conformist agency. Similar developments took place in organized recreation within other socialist states, such as East Germany.[103]

The image of appropriately socialist fun changed during the anticosmopolitan campaign. During the war and the immediate postwar months, public discourse and policy did not stringently dictate the sentiments that young people were to feel and articulate in club activities. But official rhetoric of the late Stalinist period obliged young club-goers to express and experience love for the party and especially Stalin, absolute faith in a narrowly interpreted Marxism-Leninism, disciplined submission and obedience to the hierarchy, and eagerness to increase production—the obligatory affective standards of the anticosmopolitan campaign years.[104] In other words, the propaganda apparatus directed youth to find pleasure, meaning, and emotional satisfaction in highly politicized and strictly conformist club activities.

Thus, the anticosmopolitan initiative spurred a makeover of the Soviet emotional regime. The affective norms of expression and experience propounded by the authorities at any given time shifted from a loose to a strict emotional regime. William Reddy has used the term "strict" to define regimes with tightly delimited and closely managed affective norms, whose violation, if uncovered, drew harsh disciplinary measures. The fact that many young amateurs found deep emotional meaning in the narrowly limited orthodox cultural activities of the anticosmopolitan drive accords with Reddy's framework. He shows that strict emotional regimes had success in creating a core of conformist subjects who adopted the prescribed emotional norms for themselves.[105] The multitude of young amateur artists articulating and, to varying degrees, feeling officially sanctioned emotions underscores how the anticosmopolitan campaign shaped youth emotional communities—groups whose participants share a similar set of emotional values—on the grassroots level. These findings fit well with recent scholarship, which has shown that many Soviet citizens were in emotional accord with the late Stalinist leadership's international campaign for peace after World War II.

That young people experienced positive emotions in heavily ideologized cultural activities challenges previous conceptions of the public and private in the Soviet Union. Scholars such as Vladimir Shlapentokh and Oleg Kharkhordin have traditionally drawn sharp lines between the public, official sphere (meaning everything associated with the Soviet party-state) and the private, unofficial sphere (referring to personal emotions and interests, pleasure, sociability, friends, romance, family, and home).[106] More recently, Lewis Siegelbaum and others have offered an alternative viewpoint, arguing for the notion of multiple and layered public and private spheres in the Soviet contexts, with porous, shifting, and unstable boundaries between the official and the unofficial.[107] In the cultural sphere, the latter perspective is closer to the mark. As we have seen, young people found fun, excitement, and emotional meaning in orthodox cultural activities. Their experiences clearly do not fit within the traditional official-unofficial binary and instead suggest the need for a more complex understanding of Soviet culture.

The party-state, however, faced a series of obstacles in using officially approved forms of cultural recreation to forge young New Soviet People. The Soviet leadership placed little emphasis on increasing organized cultural activities, while the many war veteran Komsomol cadres expressed little self-motivated concern for this sphere. Consequently, the cultural consumption demands of many rank-and-file Komsomol members and non-Komsomol youths, even for prescribed cultural forms, remained unmet. The resulting tensions between conformist youth and the Komsomol hierarchy weakened the project of building an anticosmopolitan version of New Soviet People. The leadership's own policies contributed to undermining its intentions.

Another challenge to the party-state's goals emerged from a number of amateurs who enjoyed orthodox cultural genres but actively disliked the politicized anticosmopolitan restrictions. Participating in only prescribed forms of amateur arts for lack of other options, these youths distanced their personal sentiments from some facets of the ideologized repertoires, especially relating to the Stalin cult. They did not easily fit into the late Stalinist emotional regime in regard to amateur arts, often feeling disillusioned with the requirement to "sing Bolshevik." Stephen Kotkin uses the term "speaking Bolshevik" to refer to the Stalin-era practice of using "obligatory language for self-identification" and as a "barometer of one's political allegiance to the cause," especially when interacting with official figures.[108] My findings show that our notion of "speaking Bolshevik" must also account for Soviet citizens' emotional experience of using regime-sanctioned language, particularly when discursive tropes failed to match the speakers' own sentiments and beliefs.[109]

Indeed, performing normative pieces did not lead such young people to adopt officially approved values and feelings, a conclusion that reflects research on other times and places.[110] A substantial cohort reinterpreted the meanings, symbols, and emotions associated with outwardly conformist cultural activities beyond all recognition. This reworking underscores the fact that young amateurs who performed conformist pieces had substantial power to interpret these cultural texts for themselves, instead of simply following the intentions and guidelines of the professional cultural intelligentsia authors who wrote the conformist scripts or the political authorities whose censorship apparatus oversaw the repertoire.[111] These youths took the cultural recreation options offered to them by the cultural apparatus and, to a greater or lesser extent, adapted these activities to their own individual cultural consumption desires. In doing so, they engaged in the equivalent of what Michel de Certeau has termed "secondary production" in his analysis of consumption in capitalist systems.[112] This finding underscores parallels between everyday consumption practices in socialist and capitalist systems. Moreover, the Soviet youngsters developed a strategic approach to interactions with the system, maneuvering within the clubs to acquire access to the artistic activities they desired, a skill that would serve them well in their adult lives.

CHAPTER 3

IDEOLOGY AND CONSUMPTION

Jazz and Western Dancing in the Cultural Network, 1948–1953

"Beautiful Russian musical ball dances have almost completely forced out vulgar western fox-trots and tangos" from state-sponsored popular culture, boasted the introduction of a Komsomol propaganda department report on Moscow youth dancing in 1952. However, much of the document described "serious problems," most notably that several cultural institutions continued to host western dances to jazz-style music.[1] If the party Central Committee banned these cultural genres, why did they appear within official establishments?

Solving this puzzle requires an examination of the anticosmopolitan campaign's attack on jazz and western dancing. The party-state leaders attempted to accomplish their ideologically militant goals through central directives aimed at purging these western-style cultural genres from the cultural recreation network. Getting rid of western-inflected cultural forms proved extremely difficult, as they remained very popular among the young. Hosting these activities helped club managers achieve the financial demands of the annual plan, which pitted ideology against consumption-oriented market forces. Likewise, the anticosmopolitan drive bred deviance by creating a new counterculture of jazz enthusiasts, who were forced to engage in shady dealings and even crime in order to access their favorite music. While jazz enthusiasts represented a small minority, many more youth continued to enjoy western dancing, evading top-level directives. Such evidence indicates both the high level of confidence among the young and the difficulties experienced by the Stalin administration in forging an anticosmopolitan version of New Soviet Youth.

THE STRUGGLE TO PURGE WESTERN CULTURAL INFLUENCE FROM THE MASS CULTURAL NETWORK

As part of the anticosmopolitan campaign, Soviet rulers clearly prohibited western-style culture in club activities. These cultural policies, along with those described in the previous chapter, significantly affected the everyday experiences of millions of young amateur artists and those who attended dances and listened to concerts in the mass cultural network. My account thus questions the notion that the anticosmopolitan campaign had little meaning for or influence on the day-to-day life of the young.[2]

For popular music, the new drive vetoed all American-style jazz and even sovietized jazz that interspersed balalaikas among the saxophones. The ban also targeted comparatively recent dances associated with jazz music, such as the Lindy hop and Charleston. However, the prohibition extended, in a softer form, to the fox-trot, tango, and rumba. In doing so, the postwar Stalinist authorities went significantly further than they had in the immediate prewar years, a time of more permissive attitudes toward sovietized jazz and the fox-trot, tango, and rumba. From among dances that originated in western settings, only courtly ball dances such as the waltz and polonaise that appeared in Russia before the twentieth century and were considered to represent the classical European heritage, as opposed to the decadent "bourgeois" influence, remained acceptable. Consequently, the rhetoric of the ideologically militant anticosmopolitan initiative greatly expanded the range of cultural activities labeled as "western" and intensified the stigma associated with this label. Such evidence underscores the flexibility of the term "western" and the meanings associated with it in public rhetoric, which changed over time in accord with the needs of those in charge.

Following the tenets of the anticosmopolitan campaign, the Komsomol took a series of steps against western popular culture. Komsomol-owned newspapers played a central role in this top-down initiative. *Komsomol'skaia pravda* in 1951 published a letter to the editor that condemned a club for playing "melancholy tangos and vulgar fox-trots."[3] *Moskovskii komsomolets* critiqued the administration of the Bauman factory club for thinking that "the only entertainment for youth should be dancing the fox-trot to the sound of jazz."[4] Komsomol cells sent brigades to cultural institutions and restaurants with the goal of uncovering and denouncing forbidden tunes.[5] The Komsomol leadership pressured other party-state bodies to comply fully with the anticosmopolitan campaign. For instance, in a note to Deputy Prime Minister G. M. Malenkov, Nikolai Mikhailov criticized the content of gramophone records that included "dance music in jazz style," and he condemned Soviet radio broadcasts of "American" dance music.[6]

Cultural control organs likewise endeavored to enact the party's policy shift, as illustrated by the Moscow Dom narodnogo tvorchestva, which served as a guide to other cities' houses of folk creativity. In 1949, the Moscow house censured certain local amateur variety orchestras that played "western European and American music."[7] By 1951, this institution had found the activity of amateur variety orchestras to have "noticeably decreased over the last years," and it expressed no complaints about their repertoires.[8] This finding suggests that the anticosmopolitan campaign generally succeeded in expunging jazz-style music from Moscow amateur circles. The drop in the number of amateur collectives devoted to variety music likely resulted from the ban on western music in their repertoires and resultant lack of youth interest in such groups. The Gor'kii dom kul'tury (house of culture) reported that, after the party's shift on the ideological front, the club got rid of its own in-club jazz ensemble.[9]

This policy shift helps explain the substantial slowdown in the previous growth in amateur artist numbers in the late 1940s and early 1950s. From 1945 to late 1947, the beginning of the anticosmopolitan campaign, the number of participants grew by 1.5 million. From that date to early 1953, however, membership increased by only 1.3 million.[10] The 1945–47 period undoubtedly witnessed a postwar upswing in amateur arts participation, but this change does not adequately explain the rapid decrease in the growth rate of the amateur arts, especially because club infrastructure improved, giving cultural recreation organizations more space, equipment, and repertoires. Part of the reason for the decline stems from the ban on western music in early 1948, which led to the dissolution of many variety amateur collectives and the repertoire of others shifting to a focus on ideologically prescribed themes, which likely discouraged many Soviet youth from engaging in amateur arts. Moreover, amateur artistic circle membership grew more rapidly after the anticosmopolitan campaign ended with Stalin's death, a process detailed in the next chapter.

The records of the Moscow Dom narodnogo tvorchestva also provide insights into the struggle against western dancing. Responding to what it termed "foreign influences" in dancing, the house sent its representatives on 236 inspections of mass dances in Moscow's cultural institutions in 1951 and continually promoted new ballroom dances. It even created an attestation commission, intended by the house to evaluate all candidates for positions as dance managers in Moscow's cultural institutions.[11]

Still, western dancing in state-sponsored popular culture continued. In 1952, a Komsomol propaganda department report on Moscow criticized club officials whom it termed "dance poachers, who distort the tastes of Soviet youth" by "propagandizing degenerate western fox-trots, languid tangos, and vulgar rumbas." It claimed that youth complained about western dances, quoting a letter to *Komsomol'skaia pravda* by three young people who blew the whistle on a dance floor where "a jazz ensemble" performed "cosmopolitan 'fox-trots' and 'crying' tangos." The attestation commission seems not to have functioned as intended, since the report blamed many of the problems on the lack of a centralized system of management over dancing directors, which apparently allowed club managers to hire whomever they wanted.[12]

JAZZ ENTHUSIASTS AND STATE-SPONSORED POPULAR CULTURE

Some club and park directors continued to offer western popular culture because, as the Komsomol propaganda department admitted in 1952, there was a substantial "group of fans of western dances" among the young.[13] Distressingly for the department, "a significant portion of youth" tried to "make themselves look like 'foreigners' and recreate the most repulsive western European and American fox-trots." It stated, "Among these emulators of foreigners, new dances appeared, such as 'Get Your Hands Off Korea' and 'The Wall-Street Smile,' as well as terms such as the 'Truman style.'"[14]

Such evidence hints at the rise of *stiliagi*, a youth counterculture that appeared in the Soviet Union at the end of World War II. Popularized by an infamous article published in the satirical journal *Krokodil* in 1949, the term "stiliagi," loosely translatable as "the style-obsessed," was used by official discourse to homogenize and stigmatize young people enamored with cultural practices associated with western Europe and America.[15] These young people, mostly males, emerged from among the children of Soviet elites in the mid-1940s. By the early 1950s, some middle- and even working-class youth had begun to join the ranks of the stiliagi as the living conditions, purchasing power, and cultural knowledge of Soviet citizens improved.

Stiliagi made adopting a style they considered western central to their lives and self-definition. Indeed, the *Krokodil* article tellingly condemns the protagonist, a young male, for "complex and absurd dance moves" in the dance hall, a reference to American-style dancing, and for wearing a jacket with an orange back and green sleeves, yellowish-green pants, and socks in colors suggestive of the American flag. More generally, it censured stiliagi for "developing their own style in clothing, conversations, and manners," in which "the main thing is to not be like normal people."[16] This official condemnation references important signifiers in stiliagi cultural practices, including music and dancing, fashion, an argot, and mannerisms in which these youth affected a western style.[17]

Perhaps somewhat surprisingly in light of the anticosmopolitan campaign, the postwar Stalin leadership expressed little concern with such youth. Stiliagi suffered minimal public denunciations from the central Komsomol bureaucracy, although some militant local Komsomol secretaries made efforts to censure stiliagi. Recent archival-based scholarship has substantially advanced our understanding of the history of this alternative youth culture in the postwar Stalin years.[18] However, other Soviet youth who did not belong to the stiliagi alternative culture also expressed a genuine interest and even fascination with certain aspects of western popular culture, a topic poorly illuminated in the current historiography.

A study of young jazz enthusiasts in the late Stalin years shows that they constituted an alternative youth culture distinct from, although with similarities and links to, stiliagi. Many jazz enthusiasts were intense fans of this music and eventually became the most famous jazz musicians, promoters, organizers, and critics in the Soviet Union and post-Soviet Russia. With rare exceptions, jazz enthusiasts did not self-identify as stiliagi, as the former considered the aesthetics of jazz music, its sound and feel, much more significant than its origins in the United States.[19] For example, during my interview with A. A. Kuznetsov, a prominent Moscow jazz musician, he emphasized that he "was not among the stiliagi."[20] Valentina Iarskaia, the Saratovite who performed in the amateur play about the Soviet political police described in chapter 2, sang jazz pieces during the mid- and late 1950s. One of the rare women performing jazz music, Iarskaia considered stiliagi fashion amusing and expressed apathy toward stiliagi in general.[21] Speaking to me at a Moscow restaurant, Georgii Garanian suggested a clear difference between stiliagi and jazz enthusiasts. Stiliagi, in his words, had their own way of dressing, slang, everything, "all with an air of superiority." Garanian stated that he did not really have any contacts with stiliagi cliques.[22] Others expressed similar sentiments.[23] Autobiographical accounts reveal widespread dislike for stiliagi among the population.[24]

Generally well educated, jazz enthusiasts tended to come from middle-class social backgrounds. The cultural and financial resources provided by middle-class backgrounds, especially access to postsecondary education, proved conducive to acquiring the taste for and access to jazz music and information on jazz. The children of the Soviet elites rarely joined the ranks of jazz enthusiasts, whose cultural practices left less space for the sort of spectacular nonconformism embodied in the stiliagi. With rare exceptions, jazz enthusiasts were male, as were stiliagi and jazz musicians in non-Soviet contexts.[25] The jazz fans' interactions with each other thus created a homosocial male space that provided an alternative vision of Soviet youth masculinity.[26]

Interviews with jazz enthusiasts reveal the powerful impact of the anticosmopolitan campaign on their everyday existence. Garanian described the party Central Committee's 1948 resolution as a crucial juncture after which the authorities did not allow jazz.[27] Iurii Zhimskii, a prominent Saratov jazz musician during the post-Stalin years, told me that the resolution resulted in the "harassment" of jazz ensembles, with "saxophones replaced by clarinets."[28] Another Saratov jazz musician, Lev Figlin, stated that a broad consensus emerged that "jazz is not our music."[29]

Even so, young people fascinated with jazz had a number of options, some of them legal. Iarskaia recalled, for example, how she repeatedly watched *Veselye rebiata* (Happy-go-lucky guys), a Soviet jazz comedy from 1930s, when the authorities permitted jazz.[30] A Muscovite jazz musician and promoter, Vitalii Kleinot, described the high esteem in which jazz enthusiasts held trophy films, as these often featured jazz music.[31] According to Zhimskii, plenty of old prewar Soviet records survived the ban on jazz music, thus allowing middle-class young people with gramophones to listen and dance to these tunes at home. This music was preserved because many well-educated adults ignored the ban on jazz music, the music they grew up with in the 1930s, and even danced the fox-trot and tango to jazz-style music themselves.[32] Furthermore, veterans brought home foreign jazz records as trophies.[33]

Those who were really enthusiastic about jazz also adopted illicit methods to access the newest foreign jazz pieces and information on jazz—virtually requisite for those who considered themselves part of a jazz fan community. They used the black market to acquire illegal records, such as those made by Soviet underground music production studios. Such establishments, which appeared soon after the war, demonstrate how entrepreneurially minded citizens found ways to satisfy grassroots cultural consumption demands in ways that went around the party-state's system of cultural provision and control.

The Zolotaia sobaka (Golden dog) represents a paradigmatic case of one such underground enterprise. In late 1946, several young people, including Boris Taigin, opened the Zvukozapis' (Sound recording) music studio as part of an officially sanctioned cooperative, using recording equipment brought from Germany. Overtly, this studio's business model consisted of making recordings for people who wanted to record themselves giving short speeches or singing songs. As Taigin reveals, "This served as an official cover, since the primary purpose of this studio lay in illegally producing 'profitable goods' for sale." The actual work of this studio began after the end of the formal business day, when it recorded popular music, including foreign pieces, on used x-ray films, which received the name of "music on bones," also known as "music on ribs." This studio, one among many underground production studios in Leningrad, distributed its black market recordings through a network of dealers for several years. However, in November 1950, the police made mass arrests of approximately sixty people involved in making and distributing "music on bones" in Leningrad, with Taigin receiving a five-year sentence.[34]

The official network of state-owned retailers also made efforts to cash in on the passion of youth for western music, with the Komsomol propaganda department complaining that, in music stores, "there are cases when records with American fox-trots have the labels of Russian ballroom dances."[35] Young people in Moscow and Leningrad undoubtedly had much better access to illegal jazz records than those in other regions, yet interviews with jazz enthusiasts in Saratov illustrate that such black market practices occurred there as well. Thus, Figlin recollected that youth in Saratov got access to jazz via black marketers making records on x-rays in the postwar Stalin period.[36] The illegal purchases of western-style goods even received its own term, *fartsa*, part of the broader gray economy that permeated the Soviet Union.[37]

Another option for young Soviet jazz enthusiasts involved listening to western jazz on foreign radio stations. In the context of the Cold War, such behavior was more overtly politicized than listening to jazz on 1930s Soviet records and movies, with much greater potential for punishment. Soon after World War II, radio stations financed and managed by the US and British governments started broadcasting into the Soviet Union. These included the United States Information Agency (USIA)'s Voice of America, the Central Intelligence Agency's Radio Free Europe, and the Russian Service of the British Broadcasting Corporation. Despite Soviet state efforts to jam foreign radio stations during this period, some signals got through.[38] Voice of America proved the most prominent radio station for jazz in the postwar Stalin years, notably hosting Leonard Feather's *Jazz Club USA* program.[39] Iarskaia described how, in the early 1950s, she listened to "American music" on Voice of America.[40] Konstantin Marvin, a Saratovite who became a jazz musician, recalled trying to listen to Benny Goodman and Louis Armstrong during the postwar Stalin period.[41] Another Saratovite jazz musician, Feliks Arons, related how he managed to catch jazz on Voice of America and that he "understood already back then that this is a very interesting music, literally jumping up in the air" with excitement.[42] These broadcasts allowed many young people who had a passion for jazz to both listen to and acquire information on this musical genre, such as the names of prominent musicians, the varied jazz styles, the playing techniques, and so on—all necessary to the creation and maintenance of a jazz fan community, in socialist and capitalist contexts alike.[43] In the Soviet Union, however, this fan community cohered into a youth counterculture due to the politicization and criminalization of jazz.

American government broadcasting constituted a direct challenge to the Soviet Union on the Cold War's cultural front. USIA-sponsored radio, as well as British and other broadcasters, promoted two goals perceived as inherently intertwined by western officials, with the first believed to inevitably follow the second. The primary aim consisted of instilling a western-oriented and anti-Soviet political perspective; the secondary and subordinate goal involved spreading interest in and admiration for American culture.[44] The USIA used a variety of means to track its radio broadcasting's impact. For instance, an analysis based on interviews with 210 western Europeans who spent substantial amounts of time in the Soviet Union found a significant Soviet audience for Voice of America.[45] A report based on the opinions of western visitors found that American jazz music constituted the most popular programming on Voice of America but also found "considerable interest in programs which describe how Americans live." In contrast, "many Soviet citizens openly resented 'political' fare on the Voice."[46] Another USIA analysis based on similar sources reached largely parallel conclusions.[47]

These American sources correlate with my interviews, and together they indicate that the United States had some success in reaching its cultural goals among jazz enthusiasts. Finding out information about American jazz from the radio, many young jazz enthusiasts developed an interest in the western way of life and culture. For instance, Garanian, Kuznetsov, Zhimskii, Figlin, and Kleinot remembered that they grew to like certain elements of US culture and had a positive view of the United States in general as the most advanced country in terms of their favored cultural genre. They often wore what they considered somewhat American-like clothing when going to concerts and dances.[48]

Still, the interest of jazz enthusiasts in US culture writ large was decisively secondary to their passion for jazz; their appreciation for American jazz did not necessarily translate to admiration for American culture more broadly, contradicting the operating presumptions of US government officials. Thus, in contrast to most stiliagi, jazz enthusiasts generally did not self-identify with the United States or western Europe. Neither did they seek to adopt what they imagined to constitute a western style in their everyday behavior and fashion outside of youth hangouts and parties, as did stiliagi. Even the special occasion outfits of jazz enthusiasts proved distinctly less spectacular, provocative, and expensive than those of stiliagi, and they did not always seek to emulate foreign accoutrements.[49] Figlin, for instance, differentiated the United States' jazz culture, which he greatly admired, from its broader culture, which he did not consider better than Russian culture. He also had no interest in adopting American ideology and ways of thinking while young, which he attributed in my interview with him to the effectiveness of Soviet classes in political economics.[50] Two hard-core jazz enthusiasts, Oleg Cherniaev from Voronezh and Viktor Dubiler from Donetsk, expressed a strong passion for jazz but little interest in adopting other aspects of American culture, even fashion.[51] Consequently, for the large majority of young jazz fans, listening to American jazz on foreign radio did not spark a general attraction to American culture and lifestyles. Such broadcasts provided cultural information and entertainment that contributed crucially to the formation and maintenance of the jazz enthusiast alternative youth culture, instead of leading to radical cultural nonconformism or political opposition.

American cultural programming did explicitly influence the politics of a small minority. Aleksei Kozlov, a rare exception to the general pattern for jazz enthusiasts, adopted many American-style cultural practices in his daily life, terming himself a stiliaga. Furthermore, departing from many stiliagi and jazz enthusiasts alike, Kozlov voiced an explicitly pro-western and anti-Soviet political perspective.[52] The future political dissident B. P. Pustyntsev, not an avid jazz enthusiast, still enjoyed listening to jazz on foreign radio stations in the postwar Stalin years, which helped inspire his hostility to the Soviet state.[53] Hence, American cultural propaganda succeeded in rousing some limited political opposition to the Soviet system.[54]

In another contrast to stiliagi, many jazz enthusiasts made serious efforts to perform their favored music and frequently joined amateur music circles for this purpose. The vast majority received no formal education in music—many could not read musical notation—and taught themselves to play jazz by ear.[55] Garanian recalled that his participation in amateur arts at his Moscow institute enabled him to access the piano after hours, which he used to figure out the notes of the jazz pieces he had memorized from the radio. This practice involved some risk since, according to him, if the college administration found out that a student musician played jazz, then "the student might have been kicked out."[56] Such punishment, likely in association with expulsion from the Komsomol, though relatively mild in the context of the harsh late Stalin era, posed a serious threat to young people who wanted to achieve a white-collar career and middle-class lifestyle in the Soviet Union.[57] Amateur jazz musicians occasionally joined professional variety ensembles that played light music, with some minimal elements of jazz, in restaurants and movie theaters, which were explicitly entertainment-oriented venues funded by the private payments of patrons.[58]

Despite the risk of punishment, certain amateur collectives in the Soviet regions used subterfuge to introduce jazz elements into club activities. Zhimskii described how he belonged to one Saratov amateur group in high school that played pieces such as "Chattanooga Choo-Choo," calling them different names for the official records. Occasionally, teachers made them stop playing jazz-style music, but the collective never got into serious trouble over this unofficial repertoire.[59] Figlin got his start in a twenty-member variety ensemble at the Saratov Medical Institute in the early 1950s, which played what he called "elements of jazz." The ensemble managed to play jazz-style compositions by deceptively listing a different name and author to get through censorship and learning to avoid various control organs. According to Figlin, such maneuvering to play jazz music taught him some of the strategies he later used to maneuver within the broader Soviet system as a whole.[60] None of the Muscovite jazz enthusiasts, however, reported publicly performing jazz-style pieces in amateur ensembles during the postwar Stalin years, though they frequently participated in amateur arts and used musical instruments to learn jazz after hours. Although a further investigation may reveal that some jazz enthusiasts in Moscow or Leningrad may have attempted to introduce a jazz note or two into club concerts, evidence shows that Saratov provided a much more permissive environment for jazz amateur musicians.

Thus, in some Soviet regions, jazz-inspired music survived the anticosmopolitan campaign's ban on western influence in state-sponsored popular culture. The capital, in contrast, contained many more dangers for amateur musicians who wanted to play jazz. Discovery was much more likely due to the presence of so many hard-line cultural officials and the diligent efforts by the militants in the Moscow folk arts house to suppress this music. As Figlin told me, in Saratov he could imagine easily getting away with claiming to have himself written the popular jazz standard "Take the 'A' Train," due to the low level of knowledge by local music controllers. In Moscow, this step would have carried much more risk.[61] Such evidence suggests the danger of relying on sources only from the capital and illustrates the necessity of local studies to fully comprehend the Soviet experience. Other scholarship shows that some regions provided safe havens for professional jazz musicians as well, especially the Baltics.[62] Still, even in the periphery, slipping a modicum of jazz into club activities depended on the presence of either more tolerant local cultural officials or incompetent ones incapable of identifying such music, while state policy continued to tilt heavily against this music on the eve of Stalin's death.

The anticosmopolitan campaign labeled the activities both of jazz enthusiasts and of stiliagi as "deviant," despite the distinctions between these alternative youth cultures. In contrast to stiliagi, the jazz enthusiast counterculture was not driven by deliberate attempts to juxtapose themselves with the cultural mainstream.[63] The Kremlin's censure of jazz transformed this cultural form into forbidden fruit that drew some of those inclined toward nonconformist youth behavior; however, young rebels were much more likely to join the stiliagi counterculture, which emphasized spectacular opposition to Soviet cultural norms as opposed to single-minded dedication to jazz. In this regard, jazz enthusiasts also differed from western alternative youth cultures during the postwar decades, such as British Teddy Boys, American beatniks, and German and Austrian Halbstarken, as well as the prewar zoot suiters in the United States and swing youth in Nazi Germany, all of whom deliberately and provocatively deviated from their society's vision of acceptable cultural practices.[64]

The postwar Stalin leadership chose to politicize and denigrate the jazz enthusiasts' cultural consumption desires, marginalizing jazz enthusiasts not because of something they actively did but because of a change in state policy. The party Central Committee's 1948 decree functioned to create "deviance" where none existed beforehand by relabeling behavior previously considered quite acceptable as subversive and intolerable.[65] This move formed part of a broader pattern of the Kremlin's increasingly exclusionary approach to governing at this time.[66]

By denouncing people who found pleasure in listening to jazz, the party hierarchy excluded jazz enthusiasts from the overarching Soviet emotional community. The Kremlin's abrupt transformation, which rapidly established a strict emotional regime, inevitably caused alienation among jazz enthusiasts. Jazz fans instead were forced to become a nonconformist emotional community, one whose shared emotional norms departed from the official emotional regime and the mainstream emotional community. This alternative emotional community enabled fans of jazz music to find emotional meaning and self-fulfillment together with their fellow enthusiasts.

The "deviant" conduct and emotional alienation of jazz enthusiasts from the party-state leadership, however, cannot be called resistance in the sense of political opposition.[67] The reason is that, especially at this time, other Soviet youth formed underground groups dedicated to political reform and suffered harsh punishments for doing so.[68] Moreover, according to Garanian, jazz enthusiasts, while seeing many flaws within the Soviet system, accepted the Soviet way of life in general and did not actively attempt to resist the authorities. Garanian told me that he supported "Soviet power" overall, if "with some major qualifiers" (*s bol'shimi ogovorkami*).[69] Kuznetsov stressed that the marginal position of jazz and its association with US culture did not serve as a draw for him, as his interest in this music stemmed from the aesthetic qualities of jazz itself, not from the fact that the regime frowned upon this music.[70] N. Sh. Leites, who organized jazz activities during the Thaw, likewise emphasized that the "music itself attracted him," as opposed to any aura associated with the music. He went on to describe himself as having "believed in socialism."[71]

These interviews with prominent jazz enthusiasts complicate the dominant perspective on Cold War–era jazz in the post-Soviet space. After 1991, most commentators generally celebrated jazz in the Soviet bloc, especially in the early Cold War, as expressing freedom and authenticity through cultural opposition to the party-state and articulating an implicit preference for a western way of life. Even many scholarly works offered this perspective, for instance, in an edited volume that published the results of a conference on jazz in the Soviet bloc whose organizers focused on how jazz "acquired its role as a platform for oppositional thinking and behavior."[72] One contributor to this volume states that jazz was "seen as a code for the *American way of life*."[73] Some other scholarship on Soviet bloc consumption posits that people consumed western products to express "contempt for their government."[74]

The oral history interviews cited above show that playing and promoting jazz in the Soviet Union did not necessarily mean resisting the Soviet authorities or preferring the western way of life. Furthermore, the fact that the interviewees cited above did not parrot the tropes of the dominant paradigm helps illustrate their awareness of their past historical selves and their ability to differentiate between their current beliefs, values, emotions, and set of meanings and those they held when young. This makes their contributions particularly credible and valuable for evaluating the lived reality of the late Stalin years.

WESTERN DANCING IN SOVIET CLUBS

Dancing the tango, fox-trot, and rumba—pastimes enjoyed by many more Soviet youth in comparison to the numbers enamored of the more heavily censured jazz—received less intense denunciation in the official discourse and occupied a more ambiguous position in organized cultural recreation. Due to the relatively prominent presence of western dancing in state-sponsored popular culture, fans of this cultural form had no need to establish an alternative youth culture or emotional community. Many of those interviewed recalled young people frequently engaging in these dances during the years of the anticosmopolitan campaign. Anatolii Avrus, a Saratovskii gosudarstvennyi universitet (SGU, Saratov's state university) student and Komsomol activist, described how students often danced the fox-trot at university dances because, unlike jazz, it was permitted.[75] Nina Petrova remembered many people doing the fox-trot and tango at dance halls in Briansk, Ukraine.[76] The future Komsomol Central Committee (CC) secretary Liubov Baliasnaia recalled the fox-trot and tango as widespread in dance halls in Ukraine.[77] Such testimony evinces the late Stalin leadership's failure to impose "Bolshevik dancing" on the young.

In the context of the resource-scarce postwar Stalin years, the willingness of many young people to part with the rubles necessary to gain admittance to a dance floor indicates their enthusiasm for these dances and the substantial role played by western popular culture in their everyday lives.[78] Still, not all of those who danced the fox-trot, rumba, or tango had a passion for western dances. Many youth attended the dances because the fox-trot, tango, and rumba lay at the core of youth sociability, especially in regard to romantic relationships. For young men, as Zhimskii described, these dances provided an opportunity for "meeting girls, this is what we dreamed of: these [dances] offered us our first romantic adventures, our first loves."[79] Nelli Popkova, who attended SGU, emphasized the importance of dancing for meeting young men, as these dances enabled the young to engage in "intimate socializing."[80] The official censure of the fox-trot, tango, and rumba, which imbued these dances with a rebellious character, likely contributed to their romantic appeal for some youths.

In many cases, those to whom the party-state assigned the task of ideological control did not fulfill this mission to the expected degree. During the beginning of the 1950s, the Saratovite Francheska Kurilova served as a Komsomol secretary in her all-female school, where school-sponsored youth evenings run by the Komsomol, which invited visitors from all-male schools, provided one of the few opportunities for public interaction between boys and girls.[81] She related to me that before such events, the school's principal would inform her that, "according to official guidelines, the fox-trot and tango should not be danced." Nonetheless, using her prerogative as the Komsomol secretary, Kurilova allowed one or two tangos or fox-trots danced in a calm and unprovocative manner each evening. Still, she "immediately chased away the boys" visiting her all-female school if "fox-trot dancing began to get out of control" (*nachinalos' buistvo v foxtrote*). Once some boys even tried to take revenge on Kurilova for kicking them out by jumping her and her friends after school during the winter. She managed to get away, but her friends were not so lucky, and the boys rubbed them down with snow. Kurilova, however, danced the tango and fox-trot at private, nonofficial parties without any guilt.[82]

If the Komsomol enforced controls at Kurilova's school, teachers took on this role at Zhimskii's school. There, despite knowing about the ban on the fox-trot and tango, the students, who "had control over the gramophone," put on the fox-trot and tango music, resulting in conflicts with teachers who "disapproved of this" and told them to stop.[83] Figlin suggested that one way that the fox-trot and tango avoided censorship involved deceptive renaming: "the fox-trot and tango became slow and fast dance," respectively.[84]

This creative labeling, similar to the techniques used by jazz enthusiasts, indicates the need to revise previous scholarship. Alexei Yurchak has argued that Stalin's death and the consequent collapse of legitimating authority resulted in official discourse increasingly seeking validation from past canons and growing divorced from everyday life. At the grassroots, this resulted in what Yurchak calls a performative shift, namely, a growing disconnect between the discourse's constative aspects, referring to the formal meaning of various phrases, and the performative aspects, the goals that this rhetoric aimed to achieve. As a consequence of this shift, local-level cadres fully heeded the tenets of official discourse in their interactions with higher-ups, while actually doing quite another thing at the local level. He specifically used the example of Komsomol officials condemning rock and roll publicly and then organizing rock music events.[85] The evidence adduced here demonstrates that such practices, in regard to jazz and western dancing, were already occurring in the anticosmopolitan years. Illustrating that Stalin's discursive authority was hardly absolute, such evidence challenges Yurchak's notion of what transformations took place in official discourse after Stalin's death.

CULTURAL HEGEMONY, CULTURAL CONSUMPTION, AND THE ANTICOSMOPOLITAN CAMPAIGN

In trying to ensure its cultural hegemony and garden the population by forcefully imposing cultural standards that went against the actual desires of young people, the party hierarchy encountered substantial obstacles. The managers of cultural institutions faced strong pressure from above to run economically healthy establishments despite the postwar Stalinist scarcity.[86] Western dances helped these officials achieve their institutional aims, as the Komsomol propaganda department report of 1952 acknowledged: "certain club and park directors, seeking to attract more visitors to the dance halls to fulfill the financial plan, allow western dances."[87]

In addition, cultural institutions frequently held dances after lectures as part of a larger evening event, drawing in young people who came to the first, politicized part of the evening in order to access the second, entertaining portion. This strategy raised the audience numbers for lectures, which helped fulfill the attendance component of the annual plan. Permitting amateur groups to perform music with jazz elements occurred more rarely, as doing so was a less profitable and more perilous undertaking. Still, allowing jazz elements in an amateur music circle attracted more young people to participate in amateur arts, permitting club managers to claim greater successes on their annual reports. At the same time, these amateur collectives played jazz-style music at the dances hosted by the club, attracting ticket-buying audiences.

The leaders of local Komsomol cells also had many reasons for allowing their constituents to consume western popular culture. Tolerating jazz music and western dancing led to better statistics for youth participation in organized social activities in reports to higher-ups. A permissive stance contributed to increasing membership in the Komsomol and more fees paid, a central priority of the Komsomol hierarchy at this time. Additionally, the success of lower-level Komsomol officials in collecting dues, organizing cell members to complete volunteer projects, and even achieving production goals rested on the attendant goodwill of their constituents, with a militant position on western popular culture having the potential to undermine these crucial social bonds. This last scenario was a particular problem, since the leaders of local cells not only managed their members but also socialized and often lived with them, for instance in factory or university dorms. For those lower-level Komsomol officials disinclined to pursue the Komsomol career track, the likelihood of undercutting their long-term relationships with their friends and coworkers made them even less interested in vigorously implementing the anticosmopolitan campaign. It is no wonder, then, that official statements condemning young people's interest in western culture appeared only rarely at branch Komsomol conferences during these years.[88] The Komsomol propaganda department's investigations into how regional Komsomol cells followed central Komsomol policy also revealed serious problems; in one instance it condemned the Orlov Province Komsomol for the fact that youth evening events "have nothing but western dances," frequently with alcohol consumption and fights.[89]

Such evidence underscores the notion that club and Komsomol officials in the anticosmopolitan years had to negotiate the powerful tensions resulting from the conflicts between top-level ideological militancy and the massed power of grassroots popular desires from below. These cadres maneuvered between the Charybdis of ideological militancy and the Scylla of "excessive" entertainment, with some choosing to sail their ships closer to the latter. The strong pressure that youth consumption desires exerted on clubs and Komsomol organizations spotlights the powerful role of market forces in the Soviet system of organized cultural recreation. This finding suggests that Stephen Lovell's point that market forces had little impact on official Soviet cultural production until the late 1980s needs to be read more narrowly as applicable to literary production but not necessarily other official cultural production, such as music and dancing.[90] It also illustrates that the conflicts within official culture between audience demands and top-level directives that other scholars have found for the post-Stalin decades already existed in the late Stalin years and undoubtedly earlier as well.[91] Likewise, such tensions illustrate parallels to struggles in western settings over complex art forms such as classical music, with some seeking to make such music more appealing to mass audiences while others advocate for esoteric pieces.[92]

Exacerbating these systemic incentives, some central agencies were financially oriented, while others centered on ideology and control.[93] Trade union club managers reported both to the directors of their enterprises and to higher-ups in the trade union hierarchy, for whom financial matters generally held sway. Houses of folk creativity answered to regional governing organs and the Ministry of Culture, which focused their attention primarily on ideological purity. Thus, houses of folk creativity placed much less priority on financial profit. In the case of the Komsomol, the ideologically oriented propaganda department did not have to contend with the need to raise membership and dues, in contrast to the cadres leading local Komsomol cells.

Thus, the Stalinist Kremlin's own policies and system of governance subverted the implementation of the anticosmopolitan campaign at the grassroots level. Soviet rulers undoubtedly wanted to purge every trace of western popular culture. However, policy makers continued to stress that clubs and parks must meet plan targets for fiscal revenue and that Komsomol cells had to increase membership and dues payments. These two sets of priorities contradicted each other, and the late Stalinist leadership proved unwilling to invest the resources necessary to eliminate all elements deemed unacceptably western from the government's cultural recreation network.

Faced with competing objectives, club managers and lower-level Komsomol officials made a wide variety of choices regarding western popular culture. Among the many variables affecting their decisions was their locale. For example, the vigilance of the control organs in the capital increased the difficulty of sponsoring western popular culture in Moscow, whereas the provinces provided more opportunities for doing so. In turn, a large number of young people interested in the fox-trot, tango, rumba, and jazz in a given Komsomol cell, usually within an institution of higher education, offered more incentives for hosting western dancing and jazz.

The personal ideological predilections of local cultural officials also played a role. This situation best explains why cultural establishments facing similar systemic incentives and political conditions, such as neighboring clubs with largely overlapping populations of young people and nearly identical control structures, adopted different offerings. The cadres in charge of organized cultural recreation during the anticosmopolitan campaign invariably knew the ideological implications of their activities. This suggests that the local officials who allowed elements of western popular culture tended to have a more pluralistic vision than the hard-line official Soviet policy at the time. The fact that many grew up in the 1920s and 1930s listening to jazz and dancing the fox-trot, tango, rumba, and even the Charleston and Lindy hop likely contributed to their tolerant perspective on western popular culture. The diversity of ideological perspectives, while largely submerged during the postwar Stalin years, would bloom during the post-Stalin period.

Official rhetoric in the late Stalin years further vilified cosmopolitanism and greatly expanded the scope of cultural activities deemed unacceptably western. American-style jazz and the Charleston, and even, to a lesser extent, sovietized jazz and the fox-trot, tango, and rumba, were tarred by association with western popular culture. The anticosmopolitan campaign denied any legitimate ideological, cultural, or emotional space to music and dancing labeled as western and called on New Soviet Women and Men to denounce any "bourgeois" cultural influence.

The anticosmopolitan drive instigated the formation of an alternative youth culture and emotional community of jazz enthusiasts. These avid fans found deep aesthetic pleasure and emotional meaning in jazz music, but the overwhelming majority did not strive to oppose the authorities. The anticosmopolitan campaign created deviance by labeling jazz enthusiasts as "other," disparaging jazz, and criminalizing some behaviors associated with jazz fandom. The jazz enthusiast alternative culture offered its members a safe community in which to socialize with other jazz devotees. It offered mutual emotional support, as well as an opportunity to listen to, discuss, and play most contemporary jazz pieces, even within official cultural establishments. Owing to party-state pressure, the jazz enthusiast youth culture consisted of small cliques, often centered around a pluralistic cultural institution, which had little contact with each other even within the same city. Moreover, their range of activities differed geographically in surprising ways. By comparison to Muscovites, provincial urban youths in many cases could more safely perform jazz, owing to weaker cultural controls in the regions. This situation complicates the prevalent assumption that the residents of the capital inevitably had better access to western popular culture than those in the Soviet heartland.

The much greater number of fans of the tango, fox-trot, and rumba had a far easier time. Club directors, responding to a mix of systemic incentives and personal ideology, chose to host western-style dances. This finding underscores conflicts over hard-line versus soft-line interpretations of Marxism-Leninism and between top-level directives versus the massed power of popular desires and consumerist market forces. The late Stalin years, then, often regarded as the ones most closely approaching the totalitarian model of a monolithic authoritarian state fully dominating a passive citizenry, actually prove to have been much less than totalitarian on close examination. The party-state did respond to grassroots desires and offered both local officials and ordinary youth some room to maneuver, if much less than in the post-Stalin period and owing to systemic inefficiencies rather than leadership intentions.[94]

By emphasizing the implicit negotiations between young people and local cadres, my account departs from the Frankfurt school view of popular culture as simply a tool for social control over the masses.[95] The conduct of Soviet young people illustrates how many shaped their day-to-day environment to fit their personal interest in consuming western culture, thus expressing their agency while influencing broader historical processes. Such evidence points to parallels between the socialist and capitalist systems regarding the power exerted by popular demands, as scholarship on western Europe and the United States demonstrates that individuals used their agency as consumers to influence the mainstream offerings in the capitalist marketplace.[96]

Many young Soviet citizens satisfied their private and officially proscribed desires for western dancing and music in government-managed clubs—spaces unmistakably part of the public realm yet which occasionally acted against the Kremlin's hard-line ideological directives. The mass cultural network thus represented a distinct layer within the Soviet public sphere, one that illuminates the interpenetration between the public and private and the diffuse boundaries between them. Each cultural institution constituted a distinct node in the Soviet public sphere, with its approach to western popular culture dependent on the individual choices of those local cadres in charge. Overall, the jazz enthusiast counterculture and the mass presence of fox-trots, tangos, and rumbas in clubs indicates that the anticosmopolitan campaign resulted in an estrangement by large segments of young people from the top layers of the public sphere: the center and its official discourse.

An important goal of the anticosmopolitan campaign was creating ideologically fit young Cold Warriors. That many young people enthusiastically participated in organized cultural recreation directly targeting foreign influence, as the previous chapter has related, indicates some of the successes of this drive. So does fresh research pointing to the growing anti-

American feeling among the population owing to the anticosmopolitan initiative.[97] The anticosmopolitan drive reveals how the escalating Cold War had a deep impact on domestic policies and local experiences in the Soviet Union, just as it did around the globe. In another parallel, many western countries cracked down on postwar youth countercultures, citing the need to remake their youth into young Cold Warriors.[98]

Moreover, the anticosmopolitan campaign opened substantial room for western soft power in the Soviet Union. Cultural diplomacy, in the form of cultural propaganda via radio broadcasts, influenced the attitudes, emotions, and identities of certain segments of Soviet youth. Still, listening to jazz on western radio broadcasts did not necessarily lead jazz enthusiasts to adopt American styles in the rest of their cultural practices or western political perspectives, contrary to the presumptions of American officials at the time and many scholars today.

Official club activities offer insights into the cohort of young people growing up in the postwar Stalin years, whom Juliane Fürst termed "Stalin's last generation." She correctly notes that these youth, despite all growing up in similar circumstances, did not develop a generational consciousness, meaning an age cohort's self-awareness as a distinct generation. Nonetheless, Fürst argues that this generation had shared experiences and developed signal common values and beliefs. Specifically, "consumption, not ideology, became the dominant identifier for young people," along with the sidestepping of prescribed norms, resulting in a growing distance between the party-state leadership and Stalin's last generation.[99] This study supports Fürst's argument of a growing gap. However, data on what youth consumed complicate the presumption that consumerism necessarily opposed ideology or indicated sidestepping of prescribed norms. While many youth engaged in western dancing in clubs, plenty expressed conformist agency by willingly performing in amateur art circles and other club activities with a heavy ideological load. By doing so, the latter found deep emotional meaning and pleasure, even if the reasons for such meaning and joy did not overlap fully with the intentions of the late Stalin authorities.[100] Since cultural consumption desires and aesthetic tastes represent a crucial component of individual subjectivity and group identities, voluntary mass participation in diverse cultural activities, prescribed and proscribed alike, sheds light on the vast differences among postwar youth. This diverse, widespread engagement suggests a lesser commonality of beliefs and ideals among Stalin's last generation than claimed by Fürst.

Soviet youth were aware of the borders of toleration within the Soviet system and were willing to stretch these limits, as their adroit maneuvering within the mass cultural network shows. Some, like Iarskaia, participated in cultural activities banned by the Kremlin, in some that were on the margins of acceptability, and in orthodox, sanctioned cultural forms.

Many youth who enjoyed western popular culture, especially educated, middle-class urbanites, thought of themselves as fully integrated into postwar Soviet society. Such youth generally did not perceive their conduct as anti-Soviet but as lying within the broad limits of the Soviet public sphere while departing from the leadership's current cultural policy. They used the space offered by state-sponsored popular culture to test and negotiate the boundaries of the permissible, in ways familiar to many young people around the globe.[101] Their successful socialization into the Soviet system expressed itself in ways diametrically opposed to the status of the diarists who sought to write themselves into the social and political order of the Soviet Union. This distinction speaks to the substantially greater sense of self-confidence and comfort with their society among those who grew up after the war.

Such youngsters, furthermore, hardly "spoke Bolshevik," as Stephen Kotkin has defined it, when interacting with club officials. They instead explicitly—and often successfully—demanded banned dances and music. This finding challenges our notion of "speaking Bolshevik" and indicates the need for further attention to grassroots interactions between local officials and Soviet citizens. However, such youngsters did not reject the broad outlines of the Soviet way of life or consciously resist the party-state. Instead, they articulated a personal vision of "Sovietness" that did not fit the narrow strictures of the anticosmopolitan model of the New Soviet Women and Men, highlighting the late Stalinist Kremlin's failure to garden all postwar youth into disciplined Cold Warriors.

CHAPTER 4
STATE-SPONSORED POPULAR CULTURE IN THE EARLY THAW, 1953-1956

In 1958, the newspaper of Saratovskii gosudarstvennyi universitet (SGU, Saratov's state university) published a cartoon that depicted Iurii Zhimskii, an amateur jazz musician, playing a saxophone and an accordion while wearing western-style clothing (fig. 4.1). During the anticosmopolitan campaign, this image would have illustrated proscribed cultural practices. Yet, rather than denouncing Zhimskii, the cartoon appeared in a series of "Friendly Drawings," and the caption praised Zhimskii's talents as a jazz musician.[1]

After Stalin's death in March 1953, the new Soviet leadership introduced a cultural policy that was more pluralistic and oriented toward appealing to the real desires of young people. This new policy involved decreasing the political elements in club events, endorsing more entertaining activities, and tolerating sovietized jazz and the less controversial forms of western dancing. By doing so, the new leaders extended a new social contract, while also bringing young people into government-managed social spaces. The post-Stalin administration also strove to create a socialist alternative to western modernity, one that appealed to domestic and foreign audiences alike. Such reforms met with widespread approval among Soviet youth, but these cultural reforms appalled militants, who fought diligently if unsuccessfully against their enactment between 1953 and mid-1956.

CENTRAL POLICY AND OFFICIAL DISCOURSE ON CULTURAL RECREATION FOR YOUTH

Following Stalin's death, power passed to a collective leadership. After a series of conflicts, Nikita Khrushchev emerged triumphant by late 1955, and he had fully consolidated his power by mid-1957.[2] The new top officials launched a reenergized drive to reach communism. This effort included transforming *byt'*, an idiomatic term referring to the population's everyday

FIG. 4.1. A cartoon depiction of Iurii Zhimskii, a prominent jazz musician in Saratov, in the *Leninskii put'*, the newspaper of Saratov's state university.

way of life, in a fashion perceived as befitting the idealized future.[3] The Kremlin ended the anticosmopolitan campaign, began to give amnesty to Gulag prisoners, and opened up space in public discourse to question the status quo and future course of the Soviet Union.[4] Khrushchev's denunciation of Stalin's crimes in 1956 in the so-called Secret Speech at the Twentieth Party Congress accelerated these processes.[5] Previously accepted versions of truth eroded, and the dominant model of socialist realism in cultural production faced intensifying challenges.[6] The Soviet Union began to open the Iron Curtain to the outside world and adopt a more peaceful foreign policy stance.[7]

The early Thaw period also saw young people rise to a position of greater prominence.[8] An essential component of building communism was gardening youth into well-prepared adults, ready to construct and, it was hoped, to live in the communist utopia; official discourse frequently associated the spirit of optimism and rejuvenation in the Thaw with youth itself.[9]

Within a few months of Stalin's death, the Kremlin initiated a massive expansion in the provision of consumer goods and services. The drive to build apartment complexes enabled growing numbers of families to move from communal housing into private apartments.[10] Soviet consumers acquired better food, more fashionable clothing, modern appliances, and more opportunities for travel.[11] While scholars have shed much light on material consumption, exploring the cultural consumption of organized cultural recreation provides important insights on the transformations in the mid-1950s.[12]

In contrast to the anticosmopolitan campaign, early Thaw policy on cultural recreation stressed the need for official institutions to provide fun entertainment for young people. In October 1953, the Komsomol called on club managers to deemphasize political agitation and focus on cultural recreation.[13] Komsomol first secretary Aleksander Shelepin's keynote speech in 1954 at the Twelfth Komsomol Congress devoted about five times as much space to discussing clubs, amateur music, and amateur theater as did the keynote of the 1949 congress.[14] According to Liubov Baliasnaia, a high-level Komsomol official, there was a general transition toward emphasizing cultural recreation, a shift also in evidence in Komsomol newspapers.[15]

The post-Stalin administration also expanded leisure time, giving young people more opportunity to participate in state-sponsored popular cultural events.[16] Moreover, the government also sought to assist women with the "double burden" of working and domestic chores by supporting collective social services, such as day-care centers and community kitchens.[17] Young people in particular received more hours per week free from work and study.[18] The Komsomol cast this measure as an example of the state's concern and care for youth.[19] The party-state's emphasis on increasing leisure time shows that, contrary to Stephen Hanson's view, the Kremlin did not continue to demand time-transcending heroic labor from the population after Stalin's death.[20]

Anticosmopolitan rhetoric, which claimed that most young people truly wanted to listen to lectures on politics, ideology, science, and economic production, bore little resemblance to reality. By contrast, post-Stalin policy makers advocated cultural activities that appealed to ordinary youth. As the Komsomol propaganda department noted in November 1953, "Young people want[ed] to sing, dance, have fun, read a good book or simply get together at a club."[21] In fact, the Komsomol Central Committee (CC) made an explicit connection between cultural reform and de-Stalinization. In a 1956 report, the CC blamed a lack of cultural recreation options for young people on "[Stalin's] cult of personality," which had demanded "rote memorization of what Stalin said or wrote" rather than appealing cultural offerings.[22]

Official regard for juvenile delinquency also changed. In the late Stalin years, the party-state generally ascribed even the most violent crimes to insufficient political enlightenment and education, relying on political propaganda and police repression to deal with youth misbehavior.[23] However, during the Thaw, official pronouncements, such as the resolutions of the Komsomol congress in 1954, began to ascribe youth misbehavior to a lack of organized cultural activities.[24] Shelepin's speech at a Moscow city Komsomol conference in 1957 highlighted the change from earlier methods of dealing with juvenile delinquency, arguing that Stalin-era "administrative measures"—police actions—had proven insufficient to stem juvenile delinquency. To do so, he maintained, the Komsomol needed to organize youth leisure with "real Komsomol energy."[25] Baliasnaia confirmed that, before the mid-1950s, the Komsomol had no systematic policy of using organized recreation to combat youth hooliganism.[26] Similarly, M. S. Gorbachev, who led the Stavropol city Komsomol organization in the mid-1950s, recalled that he sought to provide organized cultural recreation for youth as a means of dealing with youth hooliganism.[27]

Such evidence indicates that historians must revise their understanding of Thaw-era cultural innovations. These changes emerged from a new course consciously set by the post-Stalin Kremlin, rather than as a result of structurally determined policies associated with postwar reconstruction, as some scholars have argued.[28] My investigation of organized cultural recreation shows that, though there was some continuity across 1953, Stalin's death and the coming to power of new leadership was a substantial break. Undoubtedly, state-sponsored cultural policy for youth in the mid-1950s built upon the gradual postwar reconstruction of the cultural network, and the swift changes in the years after 1953 suggest that many administrators already disagreed with existing polices in the late Stalin years. Indeed, bureaucrats in a variety of fields had already discussed some of the liberalizing reforms implemented in the early Thaw before March 1953, but only the ascension of new, pluralistically oriented leadership enabled these discussions to bear fruit.[29] Such evidence illustrates that the transformation in Soviet official cultural offerings away from ideology and enlightenment and toward cultural entertainment that Kristin Roth-Ey associates with the growing predominance of television in the 1960s had originated in the early Thaw.[30]

The post-Stalin Soviet rulers extended a new and populist social contract, aimed to appeal to young people's consumption wishes and cultural tastes and to thereby solidify their political legitimacy, a major concern in the context of the uncertainty following Stalin's death. The new administration extended the consumerist benefits given by the late Stalinist Kremlin to managers and high officials—what Vera Dunham has termed the Big Deal—to include youth, at least in regard to state-sponsored popular culture.[31] In this sense, the social contract represented a form of welfare granted to the young.[32] It provided a way to meet the population's long-delayed hopes for a good life after the war, dashed by the harsh late Stalinist policies.[33] Notably, the new social contract encompassed the provision not only of state-sponsored popular culture but also consumer goods and services as part of a more holistic turn toward improving living conditions and appealing to mass desires.[34]

Rather than having the social contract serve only as a social palliative, the post-Stalin rulers also intended this offer to advance ideological revivalism. The Kremlin aimed to draw youth to participate in forging communism by illustrating the promise of a communist utopia on a day-to-day level. By contributing actively to building communism, young people would achieve the satisfaction of their personal desires and interests.

In offering state-sponsored cultural recreation to youth, the post-Stalin authorities wanted to expand the reach of what I call "socialist time"—the period that people spent in collective settings. There, official bodies could surveil and influence the conduct and self-expression of Soviet citizens, encouraging them to behave and express themselves in a fashion concordant with the standards for New Soviet People. The early Thaw witnessed an effort to expand socialist time from workplaces, which were already well surveilled, to leisure periods as well.[35] By getting young people to spend more of their free time in state-monitored settings, the new leadership hoped to make youth leisure more visible, organized, and productive—more "rational" (*razumnyi*), in the official rhetoric—thus echoing the efforts of prerevolutionary reformers, described in chapter 1.[36] The concept of socialist time offers a useful heuristic tool for understanding how the party-state used surveillance of leisure to intensify social controls and forge youth into model communists during their free time.[37]

The post-Stalin leadership's attempt to increase socialist time, together with its acceptance of young people's actual desires and tastes, contributed to a new, populist ruling style. The Stalinist rulers had relied heavily on what Michael Mann has termed "despotic power," meaning forceful authoritarian actions that do not consider the true interests and wants of ordinary citizens. However, the official recognition of and attempts to appease popular wants during the early Thaw speak to the movement away from the large-scale reliance on the harshest aspects of coercive power and the incorporation of "infrastructural power" elements. The latter constitutes the state's capacity to bring about changes in everyday life by its interpenetration, integration, and negotiation with society, as opposed to the use of brute authoritarian force. This change denoted a major revision in the party-state's methods of gardening the population. The late Stalinist approach involved using forceful coercion in an effort to create a well-disciplined citizenry closely obeying top-level guidelines on appropriate desires, wants, and emotions—what I earlier termed a formal garden. In the early Thaw, the gardening style of the Soviet leadership shifted to coaxing the plants into a naturalistic-style garden, negotiating with the populace, and accommodating actual grassroots cultural consumption desires.[38] The Soviet example consequently helps illustrate that the gardening state did not represent a cohesive or stagnant entity. Instead, it evolved dynamically over time, and divergent voices in the government advocated varying approaches to gardening the citizenry. Nonetheless, both hard-line and soft-line functionaries strove to manage the culture of the population in a fashion they saw as conducive to building communism and winning the Cold War.

The Cold War context was essential because, by appeasing young people's cultural preferences, official discourse presented the Soviet Union as an attractive model for domestic and global audiences. The Khrushchev leadership from 1957 onward began comparing the Soviet Union's achievements to western and especially American ones—as opposed to those of imperial Russia or the prewar Soviet Union—and promising to overtake its adversaries.[39] At the same time, the post-Stalin Kremlin rekindled cultural diplomacy efforts to appeal to nonsocialist outsiders, presenting the Soviet domestic system as an attractive model for emulation, a tactic largely abandoned in the late Stalin years. Soviet musicians, writers, scientists, cosmonauts, and other notable figures began to travel around the globe, seeking to convey positive impressions of the Soviet Union's domestic system and foreign policy alike and to counter American public diplomacy censuring the Soviet Union.[40]

As for domestic cultural diplomacy, the state revamped youth-oriented popular culture to target foreign visitors, elites and ordinary people alike. Shelepin's speech in 1956 at the Twentieth Party Congress demonstrates how the Thaw-era Soviet Union broke with the isolationist tendencies of late Stalinism and began to showcase itself to foreign youth. Moreover, Shelepin's words revealed a strong desire to shatter the image of an isolated, hostile entity ascribed to the Soviet Union by western rhetoric. Thus, Shelepin castigated the "reactionaries" in the United States and other capitalist countries who claimed that "the Soviet Union supposedly walled itself off with an 'iron curtain' from other peoples." Calling this statement a "dirty lie," Shelepin cited the fact that in the previous couple of years, more than four hundred foreign youth delegations with more than thirteen thousand participants had visited the Soviet Union. Moreover, Shelepin pointed to the upcoming Shestoi Mezhdunarodnyi molodezhnyi festival' (Sixth international youth festival), to be held in Moscow in July 1957, to which more than thirty thousand young people from a variety of countries and political and religious beliefs had been invited.[41] Komsomol newspapers directed youths to prepare clubs for the festival, and the Komsomol CC launched union-wide amateur artistic competitions.[42] One high-level official told amateur artists that their successful performance at the festival would "demonstrate to the youth of all countries the flowering of the arts and culture of the Soviet Union," as the better they prepared for the festival, the "higher the reputation of our country will grow."[43]

To better reach Americans with its public diplomacy, Soviet authorities established a bilateral agreement with the United States in 1956 to permit each superpower to publish a monthly magazine on the other's territory. Initially called *USSR*, and later *Soviet Life*, the journal published by the Soviet embassy in Washington embodied the kind of messages that the Soviet Union's propaganda intended to convey. One of its early articles described Soviet college student life, praising the "wide and varied" extracurricular activities available, including "amateur theatrical groups, student orchestras and choruses, dances," and others. The journal published a photograph that purportedly depicted the typical cultural student leisure, with well-dressed youth enjoying themselves listening to a student play the piano (fig. 4.2).[44]

A 1956 journal piece on the upcoming international festival in Moscow promoted the event by describing how it would begin with "mass performances on the theme of peace and friendship." The festival itself had 350 to 400 planned activities per day, many held in clubs, concert halls, and at specially built open-air concert stages.[45] The journal also celebrated the five Kravchenko brothers who worked in an Odessa machine manufacturing plant and formed an amateur string quintet. The Kravchenko quintet proved "very popular," and the brothers were described as "excellent musicians" who played Tchaikovskii, Moussorgsky, Chopin, Strauss, and folk music (fig. 4.3).[46]

Such rhetoric exemplifies the Soviets' use of domestic club activities for foreign propaganda purposes. Post-Stalin authorities aimed to showcase the Soviet Union and its state-sponsored popular culture for foreign

FIG. 4.2. Appearing in a journal published by the Soviet embassy in Washington, this photograph provides an image the Soviet Union presented as typical student cultural leisure.

FIG. 4.3. The Kravchenko brothers' string quartet, featured in the journal the Soviet Union published in Washington for American readers.

audiences, presenting Soviet culture as an appealing alternative to western culture. With the Thaw-era opening up of the country to the outside world, the party-state wanted to broadcast the Soviet model as a fun, attractive, and progressive way of life—a crucial message in the Cold War competition between socialism and capitalism. The leadership sought to mobilize young amateur artists to serve as Cold War cultural warriors, with these youths displaying their artistic talents in grassroots cultural diplomacy targeted directly at foreigners who visited the country or indirectly at global audiences through publications such as *USSR*.

These early Thaw reforms had some effect among foreign youth. Post-Stalin public diplomacy included encouraging western youth associations to send delegations to the Soviet Union. For instance, fifteen young people from the Scottish Union of Students traveled to Moscow, Leningrad, and Kiev in December 1953. They later reported to the British Foreign Office that they had found a "surprisingly high standard" in many amateur folk dancing performances at university concerts.[47] Five Cambridge University students who went to Moskovskii gosudarstvennyi universitet (MGU, Moscow State University) in September–October 1956 wrote that Soviet students "tended to rely very largely on the official apparatus of entertainment," which offered a wide variety of activities, including "musical circles, choirs and a dance band, dancing (ballet, folk and ballroom), photographic, linguistic and scientific societies, and the publishing of a university newspaper." The visiting students praised the university club as "modern," with "amenities [that] are very impressive."[48] Such accounts show that the post-Stalin Soviet system successes fully enrolled domestic organized cultural recreation in public diplomacy efforts directed toward nonsocialist outsiders, just as Soviet successes had appealed to foreign intellectuals in the 1920s and early 1930s.[49] In a notable difference from early Soviet policy, Thaw-era domestic cultural diplomacy did not focus primarily on notables but also appealed to ordinary foreigners; the post-Stalin leadership recognized that winning the hearts and minds of the global populations, elites and non-elites alike, was essential to the Cold War struggle.

The party-state's improved provision of official cultural activities in the mid-1950s likely had a particularly strong impact on foreign audiences because it came at a time when analogous programs in the west were losing government support. In Britain, the newly elected conservatives moved away from the Labour Party's program of subsidizing mass-oriented leisure-time activities.[50] By comparison to the 1930s, American government organs invested substantially fewer resources in recreational activities.[51]

The changes in official policy and rhetoric demonstrate a post-Stalin transformation in the party-state's efforts to achieve a socialist version of modernity. In the late Stalin years, the authorities had endeavored to build a top-down, centralized, coercive, vanguard-led, and isolated modern socialist society. The new Thaw-era officials in the Kremlin instead strove to construct a populist, appealing, mass-oriented, and increasingly open version of a socialist modernity. The novel social contract, revamped ideological revivalism, and the Cold War's cultural front represented intertwining and mutually reinforcing motivators for reforming state-sponsored popular culture, part of a Thaw-era re-visioning of what constituted a modern socialist society. Such findings also suggest that the newly opened window to the outside world and search for a more peaceful relationship with foreign countries resulted primarily from domestic needs and ideological priorities, as opposed to external geopolitical motivations. This conclusion also fits within the framework of scholarship that illustrates the large extent to which Soviet post-Stalin foreign policy depended on domestic concerns and modes of thinking regnant within the Soviet Union at the time.[52]

ENACTING THE EARLY THAW REFORMS IN THE MASS CULTURAL NETWORK

The post-Stalin administration invested substantially more resources in providing club activities for the masses. Trade unions had more than 8,000 clubs and larger cultural recreation institutions in 1951, with only 600 built from 1946 to 1951, plus 80,000 red corners.[53] By 1956, the trade unions had more than 10,500 clubs and 112,000 red corners.[54] The number of workers in urban clubs belonging to the Ministry of Culture more than doubled during this period, from 846 in 1951 to 2,200 in 1956, while those in trade unions increased by nearly half, from 19,400 in 1951 to 28,854 in 1956.[55]

The Komsomol greatly increased its efforts to provide more organized cultural activities for young people. Although it lacked the financial capacity of the trade unions, the Komsomol leadership had access to the volunteer labor of Komsomol members, and in contrast to the Stalin years, it emphasized the importance of having Komsomol youth help build clubs. Komsomol newspapers and regional committees also promoted volunteer club construction by young people. Top Komsomol officials also requested permission from party leaders to have clubs devote less time to movies and more to youth-oriented events and to have youth pay smaller club fees. The Komsomol directed its members to work and serve in the mass cultural network, including on club councils as volunteers.[56] As a result of these efforts, Komsomol organizations frequently acquired more influence on club activities. For instance, in Pugachevsk, Saratov Province, after a wood production enterprise's Komsomol members fixed up this establishment's club, the Komsomol cell received a significant voice in shaping club activities.[57]

The result was an increasing number of state-sponsored popular cultural activities, such as youth evenings, after March 1953. For example, the Moscow Gor'kii dom kul'tury (house of culture) had ten youth evenings in 1950, one-third of the total evening events that year.[58] Yet, between October 1955 and October 1956, it held sixty-three youth-oriented evenings, more than two-thirds of the total ninety-one evening events during that time and more than six times the number of youth-oriented evenings in 1950.[59] In 1956, the cultural-enlightenment department of Moscow's Krasnopresnenskii District for the first time reported on club engagement with youth, suggesting that the hierarchy put greater stock in youth cultural entertainment.[60]

The increase in club activities for youth comes through even clearer in amateur arts. In 1950, the Soviet Union had more than 200,000 amateur art collectives with 4 million participants, mostly youths.[61] By 1954, around 5 million individuals performed in 350,000 circles.[62] However, the number of those involved in amateur arts reached 9 million participants in 600,000 collectives by 1962. Amateur arts participation grew by only 250,000 persons per year from 1950 to 1954, but the rate of growth doubled to 500,000 annually from 1954 to 1962.[63]

The growth in the number of amateur arts participants reflected the efforts of Komsomol cells in the mid-1950s to promote youth involvement. In a conference held in December 1953, for instance, the Komsomol organization of Saratov's Tret'ia gosudarstvennaia podshipnikovyi zavod (Third state ball-bearing factory), used much stronger rhetoric to promote amateur arts than it had during the previous year.[64] A similar impression comes from comparing the statements on amateur arts made in the 1956 Moscow city Komsomol conference to those from the 1951 conference.[65]

The ideological load of club activities decreased substantially. Anatolii Avrus, a Komsomol official at SGU from the late 1940s to the late 1950s, told me that cultural recreation "took on a more entertaining character" and "less attention was paid, much less than in the [postwar Stalin years], to ideological purity."[66] A perusal of instructional booklets on state-sponsored popular culture confirms his statements. Propaganda lectures grew less prominent, while their themes increasingly shifted away from a focus on domestic and foreign politics, production concerns, and Marxist-Leninist dogma and instead dealt more with issues of greater interest to youth, with lectures bearing titles such as "About Love, Comradeship, and Friendship."[67]

More militant Soviet leaders opposed the pluralistic early Thaw reforms, underscoring the tensions associated with de-Stalinization. Some conservative officials disparaged the turn toward entertainment and pleasure. "Comrades have said that our Komsomol cells are losing their political face and are becoming sport and cultural clubs," railed one speaker at MGU's Komsomol conference in 1956.[68] The party propaganda department criticized *Moskovskii komsomolets* for its proposal to replace existing forms of political education with dancing, watching movies, listening to records, and studying new songs.[69]

WESTERN CULTURAL INFLUENCE IN EARLY THAW CLUB ACTIVITIES

The willingness of post-Stalin officials to overcome their anxieties about jazz and western dancing represented the truest test of the new leadership's commitment to satisfying youth cultural consumption desires and presenting socialism as fun to both domestic and global audiences. The authorities slowly brought jazz and western dancing from the margins of the Soviet cultural arena after 1953. An unofficial Soviet poet, V. K. Khromov, recalled his shock over hearing music for the fox-trot and tango broadcast over Soviet radio soon after Stalin's death.[70] Variety ensembles in restaurants started to include more syncopated rhythms in their repertoire, and formerly prominent jazz musicians returned to Moscow and Leningrad from either voluntary exile or prison. Sovietized jazz became increasingly acceptable.[71] The movie *Karnaval'naia noch'* (Carnival night), described at the beginning of this book, similarly illuminates how tolerance for jazz was growing.

Party-state organizations dropped anticosmopolitan language from their cultural policy statements. The 1956 Central Council of Trade Unions plenum decree on cultural recreation, in contrast to the 1951 plenum decree, did not censure "antisocial" amateur art pieces, and Shelepin's keynote speech in 1954 conspicuously failed to mention western music as a problem.[72]

Moscow's Dom narodnogo tvorchestva (House of folk creativity or folk arts house) provides a case study of how new cultural policies were manifest at lower levels. This institution's conservative administration contested the soft-line changes in the early Thaw. A letter sent by the director of this institution, N. A. Astriev, to the Ministry of Culture on December 27, 1953, acknowledged that Soviet radio broadcast western dance music, but Astriev insisted that the folk arts house in Moscow would continue to "*stop any attempt* to dance fox-trots and tangos in the clubs and parks of the capital," given the lack of specific directives to the contrary.[73] The next year, the Moscow folk arts house complained about the pervasiveness of people doing the fox-trot and tango on dance floors.[74]

However, a different attitude toward dance gained ground among the cultural authorities. In a letter to the Ministry of Culture in 1956, A. K. Azarov, a Moscow dance teacher, disparaged his city's Dom narodnogo tvorchestva for prohibiting the teaching of the fox-trot and similar dances even after the end of the anticosmopolitan campaign, which resulted in youth learning western dancing from the "back door," giving birth to *stiliagi*-style dancing, "with jaunty bodily movements and indiscreet poses."[75] His letter embodies a new approach, namely, taming aspects of western dances perceived as wild, uncontrolled, and sexualized, and turning them into rational cultural leisure, a mode of dancing traditionally preferred by the cultural intelligentsia.[76] Likely due to its reluctance to engage in this novel course, the attestation commission for dance teachers in Moscow's Dom narodnogo tvorchestva was closed by higher organs in 1956.[77]

Other sources confirm the increasing acceptability of some forms of western dancing. An instruction booklet from 1957 for trade union club officials, a type of publication that certainly did not press the boundaries of acceptability, approvingly mentioned the dancing of a tango in a club.[78] A jazz musician told me that SGU students danced the fox-trot, tango, and boogie-woogie in the late 1950s.[79] The former Komsomol secretary of the university, Avrus, remembered that, at university-sponsored evening danc-es in the mid-1950s, youths danced the fox-trot and tango freely. However, boogie-woogie remained "officially forbidden," with the Komsomol trying to prevent young people from dancing it.[80]

Thus, while the mid-1950s witnessed controversies over boogie-woogie, the fox-trot and tango became commonplace, despite disapprov-al from some militant officials. In Saratov, the Komsomol city newspaper adopted a conservative position on western dancing. An editorial cartoon from 1955 disparaged young people who supposedly emulated foreigners and "inspired nausea" with their western-style dancing, including the fox-trot (fig. 4.4).[81]

Baliasnaia related that when she visited a school in Khar'kov in the mid-1950s, she found that the principal refused to hold a school evening dance because he disapproved of the students' preference for boogie-woogie over waltzes. When he told Baliasnaia that he would "quit his job before allowing the boogie-woogie, she responded that he might as well resign, because she would not leave Khar'kov until the school hosted "a dance with boogie-woogie." According to Baliasnaia, this episode reflected a broader tension between the more progressive Komsomol and less pluralistic institutions such as schools. The former "forcefully promoted" youth evenings with western dancing in order to, as she stated, "satisfy youth interests" and ensure that young people attended official cultural events in large numbers. She emphasized that the Komsomol leadership, and she herself, adopted this approach because they considered it most conducive to building communism, despite her own personal feelings that the boogie-woogie "was a truly alien dance for us."[82] Such incidents underscore both the conflicts over western dancing and the commitment of soft-line Komsomol officials to appeal to young people and get them involved in the Soviet project.

The attitude toward jazz music in state-sponsored cultural events also changed in the early Thaw. The annual report for 1954 prepared by Moscow's Dom narodnogo tvorchestva noted the rapid growth of variety ensembles. Complaining that, "both in their repertoire and their manner and style of performance," these variety ensembles sought to emulate western jazz artists, the document underscored the "intensive struggle to rid these ensembles of everything superficial and alien to the Soviet listener."[83] The Moscow folk arts house did not fare well in this battle, reporting in 1955 that the number of variety collectives that "emulate bad jazz ensembles" had continued to increase, especially in universities.[84]

Likewise, this new course fit in well with existing incentives for grassroots cadres. For mass cultural institutions, ideologically oriented events such as political lectures continued to draw tiny audiences.[85] The post-Stalin leadership's soft-line policy on hosting western dances and jazz ensembles lowered the barriers for clubs trying to fulfill plans for financial revenue and participation in amateur arts. For local Komsomol officials, the new approach helped ensure the growth of their cells, the timely payment of dues, and the willingness of members to undertake social obligations.

Interviews and memoirs confirm that clubs increasingly opened their doors to jazz in the early 1950s. In Moscow, Georgii Garanian's underground jazz group, the Zolotoi vosem' (Golden eight), participated in open club performances by joining one of the most prestigious youth orchestras at the time in the Tsentral'nyi dom khudozhnika (Central house of artists) under B. S. Figotin and, later, Iu. V. Saul'skii.[86] Aleksei Kozlov recalled that the Komsomol committee at MGU helped him purchase a saxophone for university-sponsored amateur arts.[87] In Saratov, Valentina Iarskaia remembered her amateur student ensemble playing jazz-style songs from the film *Karnaval'naia noch'*.[88] According to Zhimskii, many new jazz-oriented collectives were formed during the 1950s. He supplied me with a photograph of his jazz group performing at the Saratov pedagogicheskii

Fig. 4.4. An editorial cartoon from the Komsomol newspaper *Molodoi stalinets* illustrates "improper" dancing, 1955.

institut (Saratov pedagogical institute), visually illustrating the growing acceptability of jazz (fig. 4.5). Formally dressed and well groomed, the band members looked nothing like stiliagi and thus helped legitimate jazz-style music.[89]

Further proof of the growing acceptability of jazz, as well as the pattern of increasing conflict between liberal and conservative figures, comes from a debate by the jury of an amateur art competition for variety ensembles, a contest held in preparation for the Mezhdunarodnyi molodezhnyi festival' (International youth festival). The discussion centered on Saul'skii's ensemble, in which Garanian played. One jury member censured the ensemble for "playing in the modern style, the style of an American jazz ensemble," warning that presenting any award to this ensemble would indicate to others that such music was permitted. Leonid Utesov, a professional jazz musician popular since the 1930s who also sat on the jury, took a more tolerant view: "we should not think of this collective as flawed," owing to the "several sharp techniques used from the arsenal of American jazz ensembles." A Komsomol representative also defended the group.[90] Saul'skii's ensemble ended up getting a bronze medal and permission to perform at the upcoming festival. This exchange undoubtedly demonstrated the growing acceptability of jazz elements deemed "American," such as improvisation, syncopation, and blue notes, to young musicians, just as the more orthodox jury member feared. Other fields of cultural production, including films, art music, and literature, also witnessed extensive struggles between those who wanted to maintain a hard-line, Stalin-era approach and those who pushed for liberalizing reforms.[91]

Such conflicts underscore how tensions between those holding opposing views of the post-Stalin cultural reforms had a larger impact on the daily life of the population than has been suggested by some recent scholarship.[92] My approach does not propose the existence of an unchanging camp of hard-liners who opposed de-Stalinization during the early Thaw or that such a conflict explains the main developments during this period. Nonetheless, because the late Stalinist leadership pursued a radically militant position on mass cultural offerings, advocating a hard-line approach during the Kremlin's pluralistic shifts in the early Thaw marked one as an opponent of cultural de-Stalinization. In turn, strong supporters of reforms generally held a more liberal position toward state-sponsored popular culture than the party line in the mid-1950s, endorsing American-style jazz music and the boogie-woogie and pushing the Soviet leadership to allow further cultural pluralism. These positions marked the two ends of a broad and variegated political-ideological spectrum. The majority of Soviet officials and ordinary citizens, including the majority of those at the

Fɪɢ. 4.5. Iurii Zhimskii's ensemble performing at the Saratov pedagog-icheskii institut (Saratov pedagogical institute). Courtesy of the private archive of Iurii Zhimskii.

highest levels of power, stood somewhere in the middle ranges. They expressed some limited and hesitant endorsement of the post-Stalin changes, along with concerns about the potential outcomes of these reforms. Furthermore, neither officials nor ordinary people necessarily held a consistent position on de-Stalinization. A combination of the struggles between those at the ends of the spectrum, historical developments, top-level policies, and systemic incentives influenced the views of the many closer to the middle.

Uncertainties and hesitations among cadres resulted from conflicting values within the Soviet cultural sphere. Baliasnaia, for instance, personally recognized and promoted the need to satisfy youth interests in order to involve youth in cultural activities and, ultimately, in the building of communism. As noted above, she even directly opposed conservative officials, such as the Khar'kov school principal, but expressed reservations about using "alien dances" to appeal to youth desires. Expressing a belief held by many other Soviet officials, Baliasnaia insisted that "together with [alien] music and words comes foreign ideology."[93] The doubts and ambiguities accompanying such conflicting imperatives defined the future course of and shifts in Soviet policy toward youth-organized cultural recreation in the Thaw and reflected the dilemmas and ambiguities of de-Stalinization as a whole.[94]

Public conflicts between hard-line and soft-line approaches to organized cultural recreation in the Thaw recall similar disputes during the 1920s. Despite the major differences between the mass cultural networks in these periods, the post-Stalin leadership's reforms, with their greater focus on entertainment or tolerance for western popular culture, resembled the doctrines of the Right during the New Economic Policy era. This pattern fits the broader trend in which the Kremlin during the early Thaw tried to revive what official discourse termed the "Leninist principles" of the 1920s, as a means of finding a road to communism untainted by Stalin's "cult of personality."[95] In a marked difference from NEP-era discussions, the mid-1950s discourse linked youth initiative to two uniquely Thaw-era developments: de-Stalinization and building communism in the context of the Cold War. Nonetheless, the similarities indicate that the foundational struggles that determined the shape of the Soviet system, although seemingly settled in the 1920s, emerged anew in the early Thaw and powerfully affected government policy and everyday life.

THE EMERGENCE OF THE SOVIET JAZZ SCENE

The post-Stalin transition paved the way for the establishment of a Soviet jazz scene. Jazz enthusiasts increasingly felt free to meet each other openly, discuss and listen to jazz, share information, and exchange records, resulting in the establishment of city-level jazz networks. In Moscow, this new sense of cultural freedom led to the emergence of what Aleksei Kuznetsov and other jazz musicians termed the *birzha* (exchange). This term referred to an open-air music labor market in Moscow, at the intersection of Neglinnaioa and Pushechnaia streets. There, jazz musicians gathered to talk about new jazz-related developments, evaluate other jazz musicians, and organize various jazz activities. Kuznetsov especially appreciated birzha's "creative jazz-like atmosphere and discussions."[96]

One of the most important functions of the Moscow birzha involved facilitating official but closed jazz dance evenings, which experienced explosive growth during the mid-1950s. Limited to the members of the institution hosting the evening and thus less accessible for external monitoring by control organs, such events enabled young amateur jazz musicians to play more daring jazz and western dance music. In fact, Garanian formed his underground jazz group, Zolotoi vosem', primarily to play at these closed dances, called *khaltury* (moonlighters) in jazz lingo. These events, especially those held in higher educational institutions, "were the height of modernism": the audiences usually wanted to hear "forbidden American" pieces and, more rarely, popular Soviet songs or other tunes. Jazz musicians moonlighting at these dances, as Garanian stated, had the opportunity to increase their musical talent and also connect with other jazz musicians.[97] Indeed, plenty of other jazz musicians, such as A. A. Kuznetsov, Vitalii Kleinot, and M. I. Kull', played at similar khaltury.[98]

Jazz musicians competed avidly with each other at these closed jazz dances. Garanian recalled that "we always wanted to be the most hip."[99] Overall, as Zhimskii told me, "dancing to jazz was considered very fashionable" in that period.[100]

Musicians received cash on the side for such performances, generally from trade union club officials. Lev Figlin described how, at an institute in Saratov, the organizers of one closed event invited him and other jazz musicians, paid them some cash and gave them free food, and allowed them to play whatever they wanted.[101] Garanian recalled getting six rubles for one performance, enough to take his girlfriend out for a night on the town with a fancy dinner and drinks.[102] These closed jazz-style dance evenings, with semi-legal cash payments to musicians by club officials, further blurred the supposedly rigid boundaries between the private and public.

Young people also organized a new wave of jazz-themed nonofficial events in the mid-1950s. Feliks Arons described private parties in Saratov during which, if someone "played [jazz], then it was simply a dream, as it was very unusual to get into a clique where someone played jazz."[103] Figlin told me about private youth jazz parties in Saratov organized by jazz enthusiasts in individual apartments. In one case, a well-off friend of Figlin hosted a jam session in his large apartment, which already had a piano. Supplied with a saxophone, drums, and other instruments brought by amateur jazz musicians, along with vodka, beer, and meat dumplings, the musicians jammed late into the night. Such parties acquired notoriety among Saratov student youth. Among the twenty to twenty-five attendees at each event, there were plenty of young women. Jazz musicians had many opportunities to get together with women whom Figlin termed "liberated." His experience apparently belies the famous quote that there was no sex in the Soviet Union, and this situation evinces an evolution in the homosocial sphere of jazz enthusiasts.[104] With the growing tolerance of jazz by the authorities, young women increasingly participated in jazz activities as fans and groupies. Still, the vast majority of jazz musicians remained male, retaining the homosocial space. Women occasionally sang jazz vocals, as did Iarskaia, for instance, but Soviet jazz bands rarely performed songs, leaving little space for gender diversity on the stage.[105]

The exponential growth in the popularity of these activities suggests that jazz music and those who played it achieved a high social status among Soviet youth. Sarah Thornton has insightfully critiqued Pierre Bourdieu's depiction of cultural tastes as dependent upon social class and as functioning to legitimate the higher status of the middle class. Thornton instead proposes that youth in particular formed complex and inherently unstable social status hierarchies based on rapidly shifting tastes in popular culture, a view borne out by my findings on Soviet youth and their quick changes in cultural preferences.[106] However, in contrast to the western settings studied by Thornton and Bourdieu, the Soviet case evinces the powerful role of governing structures in influencing these hierarchies, as the pluralistic early Thaw policy enabled growing access to jazz and thus an explosion in the popularity of this music. The Kremlin undoubtedly did not intend to put jazz and its practitioners so high on taste-based social status hierarchies, as top officials preferred and advocated for orthodox musical genres and wanted youth to favor these as well. Nonetheless, the combination of increasing official tolerance alongside restrictions and hand-wringing made jazz irresistible to many among the young. This development underscores the potential for the unintended consequences of government policies even within authoritarian settings.

However, certain youth refused to conform to even the more pluralistic culture of the mid-1950s. Kozlov described what seems like a standard maneuver for him and his *stiliaga* friends at a school evening: "one of us would get into the playing booth, lock the door, and put on American music," by which he meant jazz. Then, "in the dance hall, several pairs would begin to dance, while the rest, the 'proper' students, looked on with wonder and jealousy."[107] In a letter to the editor published in *Komsomol'skaia pravda* in 1955, a group of young factory women condemned their coworker, Valia. According to the letter, Valia was forced to leave an evening event for youth because she danced "differently" than everyone else. Valia also apparently wore immoderately revealing clothing and excessive makeup.[108] The growth in the number of stiliagi during the mid-1950s, and the further expansion of this counterculture to middle-class and even working-class youth such as Valia, made such confrontations increasingly common.[109] Simultaneously, stiliagi experienced much greater persecution under the new Thaw-era initiative against juvenile "delinquency" than they had under Stalin.[110] This post-Stalin policy marked a break between the official treatment of stiliagi and jazz enthusiasts and their resulting everyday experience.

Unquestionably, the early Thaw version of sovietized jazz did not satisfy the consumption desires and cultural tastes of avid jazz enthusiasts fully, leading them to continue some nonconformist behaviors. They still listened to the newest jazz pieces on foreign radio broadcasts, especially as western cultural propaganda grew less blatant. The launch of Willis Conover's *Music USA* program on the Voice of America in 1955 proved a key development.[111] The Saratov jazz musician Figlin told me that he and other jazz fans in his clique listened to *Music USA* on a regular basis.[112] Viktor

Dubiler, a jazz organizer who lived in Donetsk, Ukraine, in his youth-hood, called Voice of America the "voice of God."[113] Progressive cultural elites, including Joseph Brodsky and other young Leningrad poets, also listened to jazz on Voice of America, even incorporating jazz themes into their poetry.[114] Many jazz enthusiasts not only listened to *Music USA* but recorded its pieces. Turning up the radio volume to full blast and covering the radio speaker with a pillow, Figlin recorded jazz pieces directly from this program to a Dnepr-3 recorder.[115] The Muscovite jazz musician and promoter Kleinot also recalled frequent recording from Voice of America.[116] While both knew that these recordings went against official strictures, neither jazz enthusiast considered his actions as dissent against the system in a broader sense. This finding challenges the recent efforts to extend the concept of dissidence to unofficial musical production.[117]

Such recordings served as one crucial source for the large number of records collected by fans. At the time of our interview, much of Dubiler's Soviet-era collection remained intact.[118] Another source for jazz records was those who traveled abroad; their numbers rose rapidly after 1953.[119] Underground music studios ramped up their efforts, using better equipment to produce higher-quality products.[120]

Moscow and Leningrad were key jazz distribution centers for the Soviet provinces. According to Figlin, Saratovite jazz enthusiasts traveled to Moscow and brought back high-quality jazz records for the Saratov jazz scene.[121] Dubiler recollected how jazz enthusiasts from Donetsk traveled to Leningrad, as this city had a major port with extensive ties to the outside world, which facilitated the smuggling of jazz records.[122]

Jazz enthusiasts continued to use subterfuge to overcome censorship and to bring more controversial jazz elements into amateur repertoires, adopting more daring tactics alongside those employed previously. The Muscovite Garanian spoke of playing jazz music in satirical skits making fun of the United States, an approach that had roots in the 1920s.[123] For example, when the performer representing the United States danced in a scene about the conflict between the superpowers, Garanian's group played jazz music. This move, he recalled, "was one of the naïve strategies to play a couple of jazz notes," with "the audience listening to jazz gladly."[124] Jazz-accompanied satirical sketches appeared in Saratov during the mid-1950s according to Figlin, who stated explicitly that such activities did not take place before Stalin's death.[125]

Nonetheless, jazz enthusiasts relied less and less on shady practices in the mid-1950s as cultural policy swung their way. The growing tolerance for the music that stood at the center of their social and cultural life provided jazz enthusiasts with the opportunity to move toward the mainstream of state-sponsored popular culture. The vast majority among jazz enthusiasts did so gladly, further differentiating them from stiliagi. Jazz enthusiasts did not primarily use jazz as a subversive signifier of oppositional cultural politics. True jazz fans focused on the aesthetics of jazz itself, not on showcasing their defiance of the mainstream by adopting spectacular nonconformist styles, unlike stiliagi or western youth countercultures. Moreover, the public campaign against stiliagi drew hyperbolic portrayals of western-influenced youth (fig. 4.6).[126]

These extremist caricatures aimed to mobilize public support against stiliagi, and they achieved some success.[127] Still, such exaggerated depictions fit only a small minority of full-fledged stiliagi. Young people who adopted only a limited degree of western culture, such as jazz enthusiasts, could avoid perceiving themselves, and having others see them, as beyond the bounds of Soviet legitimacy.[128] This helps explain why the large majority of jazz enthusiasts, such as Garanian, Kuznetsov, Iarskaia, and Kleinot, chose not to identify as stiliagi, despite the parallels between jazz enthusiasts and stiliagi and the fact that those who were more militant occasionally equated jazz enthusiasts with stiliagi.[129] Kozlov, an exception to this tendency, even received criticism from other jazz musicians for being a stiliaga; Vadif Sadykhov castigated Kozlov as lacking true talent for jazz, linking this supposed deficiency to Kozlov's stiliaga-like behavior.[130]

The growing tolerance of western music and dancing indicates that the new Soviet leaders, striving to co-opt young people into helping build an enticing socialist modernity, reconceptualized the standards for New Soviet Youth. During the anticosmopolitan campaign, the Kremlin had prohibited model young Soviet citizens from bearing any trace of western influence. After 1953, the party-state compromised with the mass of Soviet youth tempted by some aspects of western popular culture. Official discourse now permitted young people to appreciate and adopt some elements of western style and still perceive themselves as loyal citizens who participated fully in communist construction and supported the socialist way of life. It is no wonder that the prominent jazz musician and promoter Kleinot recalled his faith in communism throughout the Thaw, praising the freedom made possible by the Khrushchev years and calling himself and his generation of jazz musicians "children of the Thaw."[131] Other jazz musicians, such as Sadykhov, similarly told me of how the Thaw brought faith in a bright future.[132] Such evidence further challenges scholarship that equates jazz behind the Iron Curtain with opposition to the authorities and a preference for a western way of life.

Through these transformations within its mass cultural network, the Soviet Union provided a model eventually emulated by the cultural ap-

FIG. 4.6. This editorial cartoon in the Komsomol newspaper *Zaria molodezhi* visually illustrates and defines *stiliagi*.

paratus in eastern Europe. In 1956, official policy in East Germany and Hungary expressed some tolerance of jazz, as did Bulgaria by the end of the 1950s.[133] In later years, certain Soviet bloc countries would surpass the Soviet Union proper in liberalizing cultural policy, serving as both models and challenges to the Soviet cultural sphere.[134]

Early Thaw official discourse discarded the emphasis on didactic lectures typical of the late Stalin years, underscoring instead the need to satisfy youth desires by promoting more entertaining cultural activities. The party-state invested greater resources into clubs, both increasing the number of events and orienting the cultural network toward young people. Authorities expressed growing tolerance for cultural forms previously depicted as unacceptably western, including sovietized jazz and the fox-trot, tango, and rumba; even American-style jazz and boogie-woogie had begun to compete for legitimacy by the mid-1950s. The label "western" lost some of its stigma, demonstrating the ambiguity and fungibility of the term, which could serve the political needs of varying constituencies at different times. Greater openness to western popular culture served many young people well, especially jazz enthusiasts, who quickly rose in youth social status hierarchies.

All of these changes suggest that the new cultural policies of the early Thaw reflected deliberate choices by the post-Stalin rulers, rather than primarily an evolution occurring organically as part of postwar reconstruction processes. Liberally oriented cadres at the center and the regions were already seeking to implement some elements of reform prior to March 1953, but the Stalin leadership blocked most of these suggestions. Only the change in leadership made possible the new course in culture, as well as in other spheres. Almost immediately after ascending to power, the post-Stalin leadership offered a novel consumerist social contract, both to ensure political legitimacy for itself and to attract youth alienated from the state during the anticosmopolitan years. By 1955, as Khrushchev assumed more and more power, ideological revivalism had increased in significance, hinting at his personal preferences. Striving to attract young people into building communism by persuading them that doing so would satisfy their personal interests and desires, the Khrushchev leadership's cultural course redefined socialism to offer a richer and more fulfilling cultural life and day-to-day experience. At the same time, the post-Stalin Kremlin hoped that engaging club activities would get young people to spend their leisure time in official collective settings, thus increasing what was termed socialist time. All these innovations speak to how the new rulers shifted toward a softer, populist ruling style that relied more on infrastructural power in and negotiation and compromise with mass desires for gardening the population. Public discourse broadened the previously strictly limited cultural standards for New Soviet Individuals, permitting many more young people to consider themselves loyal citizens while still admiring western popular culture.

The gradual opening of Soviet space to the outside world moved the cultural front of the Cold War closer to the center of state-sponsored popular culture. Breaking with anticosmopolitan policies, the early Thaw Soviet authorities strove to convince internal and external audiences that socialist culture provided genuine fun, offering a valid alternative to the western model of modernity. Particularly noteworthy here, the party-state endeavored to use its internal club activities in domestic cultural diplomacy efforts aimed at foreigners who visited and read about the country to convey the image of an appealing socialist modernity and an interesting and engaging popular culture. Soviet-dominated eastern European states followed the Soviet Union in adopting a similar policy of revising their organized recreation offerings to appeal more effectively to internal and external audiences, in regard to both popular culture and other areas, such as sports.[135]

While the party-state constituted the key active agent in changing the framework for club activities in the early Thaw, the Kremlin responded to the power of grassroots youth demands in its move to liberalize official cultural norms. The late Stalinist rulers had failed to change the cultural consumption desires, preferences, and emotions of large numbers of the populace, with many persons continuing to prefer western-style popular culture and others disliking the anticosmopolitan drive's high politicization of noncontroversial amateur arts. In consequence, as the post-Stalin top officials sought to gain legitimacy and co-opt young people into forging communism and fighting the Cold War, policy makers increasingly swung to meet actual youth wishes. The public opinions of young people, to a significant extent, drove the Soviet state's policy shift, underscoring how the individual desires and grassroots agency of millions of young people combined to influence the cultural field and thus broad historical processes.

These transformations did not occur without a struggle; ideologically militant officials wanted to preserve the status quo of the late Stalin years. Those pushing for reforms believed that, to win the Cold War and build communism on a global scale, the Soviet Union had to offer a widely attractive, socialist version of fun. The revisionist viewpoint won out in the mid-1950s, permitting the wide expansion of western popular culture in the cultural network. Moreover, the public discussions over appropriate cultural norms left much room for individual youths to formulate their own viewpoint, thus developing individual agency.

Conflicts over Soviet state-sponsored popular culture bear some parallels to the struggles over cultural hegemony in the popular cultures of capitalist states. In the latter, however, contests for hegemony have revolved primarily around issues associated with social class.[136] In contrast, ideological conflicts between liberal and conservative figures over the correct path to communism played a crucial part in the public contests over Soviet popular culture in the early Thaw period.

Making cultural standards the topic of widespread public debate at all levels undermined the party-state's cultural hegemony. The ruling group consciously introduced confusion and instability into the previously established cultural framework, which was a strategy seemingly at odds with the goal of maintaining cultural stability and, consequently, power. However, the new leadership, in reforming late Stalinist practice, aimed to bring official cultural standards closer to the actual cultural consumption desires and preferences of the young. The Kremlin saw this strategy as requisite for building an appealing socialist modernity, which would reinforce the long-term success of the ruling group. The Soviet case study illustrates that simply maintaining cultural hegemony and fighting off challenges might not be enough to ensure power; sometimes, opening up cultural standards to challenge may eventually strengthen those in charge.

Indeed, many young people found the new club activities genuinely appealing. They participated eagerly in the more entertaining official cultural events, especially in jazz and western dancing. Notably, jazz enthusiasts streamed willingly into state-sponsored popular culture, demonstrating a marked difference with the spectacular nonconformism at the heart of stiliagi and western youth countercultures. Interviews indicate strong support for the early Thaw course in navigating organized cultural recreation, and they suggest appreciation for the post-Stalin Kremlin due to its new policies. With the shrinking of the gap between the authorities and the young, the latter arguably grew more committed to building communism, participating in the public sphere, spending more of their leisure in socialist time, and supporting the Soviet way of life during the Cold War. They thus engaged actively in the project of forging a post-Stalinist, widely appealing model of socialist modernity.

Such data suggest a transformation within the officially sanctioned emotional regime.[137] The strict anticosmopolitan emotional regime, while satisfying for many true believers, bred feelings of cynicism and disillusionment among others who did not believe wholeheartedly in all aspects of rigid cultural norms during the late Stalinist period. Early Thaw public discourse broke from late Stalinist claims that model young citizens garnered pleasure from ideologically charged cultural activities and rejected any hint of foreign influence. Instead, the leadership began to use emotional prescriptions to encourage young people to enjoy entertaining cultural activities that had few or even no political overtones and to openly admire fun and exciting club events, including those with western elements, which satisfied the desires of the public. The post-Stalin rulers thus adopted a looser emotional regime and broadened the emotional norms of the overarching Soviet emotional community, making it more inclusive. This approach proved quite effective in bringing official policies closer to young people's actual emotions. In the mass cultural network of the mid-1950s, cynicism and disillusionment decreased while pleasure and joy grew substantially, improving youth lives overall.[138] Still, some of those who felt fully comfortable with the narrow Stalinist emotional guidelines inevitably lost their bearings and felt unmoored with the new ambiguities introduced into the broadened emotional community of the early Thaw.

Those bureaucrats wary of the reforms had some valid concerns. Acknowledging that young people had legitimate cultural consumption desires that the party-state needed to assuage, the post-Stalin authorities unwittingly initiated a permutation in the grassroots perception of state-sponsored popular culture. Recent research has shown that the consequences of the post-Stalin leadership's stress on satisfying popular material consumption desires eventually transformed goods previously seen as luxuries into items considered both necessary and rightfully theirs to possess.[139] A parallel development took place in cultural consumption within state-sponsored popular culture. The official emphasis on satisfying popular cultural consumption desires spurred Soviet youth to increasingly perceive the mass cultural network as obliged to provide them with joy, pleasure, and happiness—true fun, not the socialist realist version. This tendency reflected and helped constitute a wider mid-1950s pattern, with the Kremlin implicitly promising increasing happiness for the population.[140] The rising sense of entitlement to happiness paralleled earlier developments in the western paradigm of modernity.[141] The Soviet Union differed in that the expectation of happiness intrinsically challenged the Khrushchev Kremlin's efforts to ensure that state-sponsored popular culture not only entertained the population but also helped forge New Soviet People by reshaping youth. Furthermore, the stress on satisfying popular desires made the Soviet Union more vulnerable to western Cold War propaganda stressing consumerism.[142] Building a socialist version of modernity that functioned as an appealing alternative to the western model at home and abroad proved no easy task.

CHAPTER 5

YOUTH INITIATIVE AND THE 1956 YOUTH CLUB MOVEMENT

Iurii Sokolov, a young factory worker in Kaluga during the mid- and late 1950s, enthused over the Kaluga Fakel (Kaluga torch), a novel, initiative-based youth cultural collective. He termed it a "child of the Thaw," explaining that, in contrast to Stalin-era practices in which "everything came from above," this new establishment "originated from below, because of the Thaw." Sokolov told me that a group of young enthusiasts came together to create Fakel, later receiving sponsorship from the Kaluga city Komsomol.[1] My archival research revealed a more complex story. Rather than a spur-of-the-moment creation from below, the Kaluga Fakel drew its inspiration from an article published in the Kaluga Komsomol newspaper, *Molodoi leninets*, promoting the establishment of youth initiative clubs (*molodezhnye initsiativnye kluby*).[2] The article in question, printed in 1956, came about as the result of a campaign by Komsomol higher-ups calling for new cultural forms based on youth communal involvement. Even so, we should not underestimate the emotional power of the enthusiasm expressed by Sokolov. Shared by many, these feelings and perceptions, and the behavior that followed, constituted a signal component of young people's cultural life during the early Thaw.

This chapter first examines the new top-level guidelines promoting grassroots activism. The Khrushchev leadership considered the strategy of soliciting initiative from below to be central to forging a post-Stalin version of model young communist citizens. Likewise, the Kremlin perceived its endorsement of grassroots leadership as fundamental to the construction of a broadly appealing socialist modernity. The chapter then turns to the enactment of this new departure in cultural policy, showing that these novel, initiative-based cultural forms ensured that the actually existing wants, sentiments, and tastes of the young generation powerfully influenced state-sponsored popular culture. At the same time, since many young people willingly invested a great deal of time, energy, resources, and emotions in the new grassroots-based cultural forms, such official cultural collectives helped the party-state hierarchy mobilize popular enthusiasm for engaging with the Soviet project.

YOUTH INITIATIVE IN TOP-LEVEL POLICY AND OFFICIAL DISCOURSE

The post-Stalin Kremlin's emphasis on grassroots community activism dates back to discussions within the prerevolutionary Marxist movement over whether to rely on mass initiative from below or a small revolutionary vanguard that imposed centralized control over popular activism. This tension, known as the spontaneity-consciousness paradigm, defined many issues of debate once the Bolsheviks seized power. The hard-line perspective, which minimized the space for any youth autonomy and instead demanded that young people exhibit full obedience to party-state officials, won out under Stalin. The anticosmopolitan campaign witnessed a particularly strong emphasis on youth discipline, with the use of the term "initiative" being rare and generally referring to heavily circumscribed behavior directly responding to directives from adult officials. This strategy left little legitimate space for young people to exhibit activism that had any degree of autonomy beyond the close oversight of the hierarchy.

Soon after March 1953, the party-state's policies changed. Official discourse not only placed much more emphasis on initiative from below but also revised the semiotics associated with this term to refer to young people expressing a genuine voice in shaping community affairs. The final resolution of the Twelfth Komsomol Congress, in 1954, underscored the importance of "strengthening the control of Komsomol members over Komsomol organs."[3] A major internal report issued in January 1956 by the Komsomol Central Committee (CC) on the state of the Komsomol lambasted what it identified as the main problems of Komsomol work: an insufficient number of interesting activities for youth due to excessive bureaucracy, authoritarian methods that violated Komsomol democracy, and a lack of concern with the actual interests of young people.[4] At the Twentieth Communist Party Congress, held in 1956, Aleksander Shelepin called for "developing initiative and grassroots activism" to deal with these issues.[5] The Komsomol CC passed a series of decrees and changed the Komsomol's bylaws to underscore the importance of youth initiative.[6] Komsomol press discourse, advice literature, and regional committees expressed strong support for grassroots activism.[7]

Official rhetoric linked youth initiative to the renewed drive to achieve communism and to implement de-Stalinization. Inspiring grassroots activism had ideological significance since the post-Stalin leadership revived the idea, virtually abandoned under Stalin, of the state eventually

withering away in the *eschaton* of communism, necessitating the preparation of young people for self-governance.[8] In 1958, Khrushchev gave a major speech at the Fourteenth Komsomol Congress in which he stated that
"the Komsomol is increasingly becoming an organization that is instilling
in youth an ability to live in a communist society and manage its activities.
What is needed for this? A wider development of grassroots activism."[9]
Shelepin's speech at that congress underscored similar themes and also
praised the Komsomol's work in dealing with the problems caused by Stalin's "cult of personality."[10] Decreasing administrative expenses by relying
on youth to manage themselves rather than using state-paid administrators served as an additional motivation, but it was a motive that was clearly
secondary and rarely mentioned publicly or internally.[11] Notably, Yugoslavia began to promote initiative from below after Josip Broz Tito broke
with Stalin in 1948, which further supports the connections between official endorsement of grassroots activism and de-Stalinization. This Yugoslav development also illustrates that the tension between the values of
discipline and initiative, consciousness and spontaneity, had widespread
relevance across the broader socialist sphere.[12] After Stalin's death, other
socialist states, such as East Germany, began to promote grassroots activism in organized cultural recreation and other spheres.[13]

The Thaw-era leadership's elevation of youth community activism
served as a central component of the post-Stalinist effort to build an attractive socialist alternative to western modernity. The early Thaw drive
sought to distinguish the Soviet way of life from what official rhetoric
presented as typical western youth practices. Instead of exhibiting westernlike individualistic egoism and apathy toward public life, public discourse depicted Thaw-era versions of New Soviet Women and Men as
collective-oriented and community-minded enthusiasts. While retaining
their individual identities and personal preferences, these model youths
engaged in and shaped public life within their communities, expressing
their interests, passions, and opinions within state-sponsored, as opposed
to private, settings. This new line aimed to present audiences at home and
abroad with a more appealing image of the idealized young builder of
communism and thereby gain wider support for the socialist model and
way of life, an essential goal in the Cold War competition for hearts and
minds. In doing so, the Soviet Union participated in a broader tendency in
recent history to deploy children and youth for symbolic political goals.[14]

By moving grassroots activism to the heart of prescribed youth
behavior in the mid-1950s, the authorities strove to make the feeling of
enthusiasm a central component in the new emotional regime and the
overarching Soviet emotional community of the early Thaw.[15] This ap-

proach also aimed to institute its novel populist ruling style, character-ized by a greater reliance on infrastructural power and softer gardening methods. Young people engaging in public activism and community self-management helped the Kremlin both penetrate into and negotiate with society to reach goals that, to a large extent, served the interests of a sig-nificant portion of youth and the political elites alike.

YOUTH INITIATIVE AND STATE-SPONSORED POPULAR CULTURE

The post-Stalin Komsomol encouraged youth initiative through a number of novel institutions. Komsomol members policed their communities in volunteer patrols.[16] Grassroots Komsomol construction brigades traveled to "heroic" construction sites at hydroelectric power stations and in the so-called Tselina (Virgin lands).[17] The latter constituted part of a campaign by the Khrushchev authorities to mobilize youth enthusiasts to cultivate steppe lands.[18] The Komsomol also took on much broader responsibili-ties in managing tourism and sports activities.[19] Youth-themed television shows presented role models of initiative-oriented youth.[20] The Komsomol took on a much bigger role in organizing cultural agitation brigades, which grew rapidly and acquired a mass character during this period.[21] Young writers benefited from a spate of new grassroots organizations that provid-ed a venue for youth literary enthusiasm.[22]

The Komsomol's fresh policies strongly affected state-sponsored popular culture.[23] Youth newspapers promoted Komsomol members who enthusiastically took on leadership roles in creating spaces for organized cultural recreation.[24] Regional Komsomol committees highlighted their success in doing so.[25] Official rhetoric directed trade union club officials to stimulate youth activism and initiative. As an example, one instruction booklet offered a model story of how a club director inspired a youth to organize an amateur movie-making group.[26]

Still, the Komsomol CC drew attention to ongoing problems with organizing youth cultural activities through trade union clubs.[27] It com-plained that, since trade union committees frequently evaluated the work of clubs based on their fulfillment of financial plans, these clubs showed too many movies. Komsomol organizations lacked the opportunity to use trade union club spaces for youth-oriented events.[28] To address this issue, the Komsomol CC proposed creating innovative cultural collectives man-aged by young people themselves, most notably youth clubs.[29]

In contrast to the late Stalin years, in the mid-1950s the Komso-mol's youth-managed cultural collectives met with success. The new youth clubs gained an independent official status and budget, though they had to rely on other organizations to provide them with space to host activities. Youth clubs, while breaking with Stalin-era practices, harked back to the Komsomol-managed clubs of the New Economic Policy (NEP), making the youth club movement part of a broader Thaw-era search for a path to communism based on "Leninist principles." Likewise, with authority placed in the hands of ordinary youth, the youth clubs represented a turn against the professionalized management of club activities and grassroots amateurism that had been prevalent since the mid-1930s.[30]

THE EMERGENCE OF INTEREST-BASED CLUBS

Interest-based clubs (*kluby po interesu*) constituted one type of youth club. In these collectives, young people got together to enjoy a common hobby; in another variant, such clubs united a specific social demographic presumed to share similar interests. With encouragement and support from the Komsomol CC, such clubs spread throughout the Soviet Union in the mid- and late 1950s.[31] My findings revise previous assessments of Soviet youth clubs as a phenomenon of the 1960s.[32]

Exemplary of clubs united around a specific hobby was a plan to construct a *dvorets iunosheskogo* (youth palace) in Moscow to include rooms for youth clubs dedicated to everything from aeronautics to stamp collecting, as well as rooms serving particular demographic groups, such as young women and college students.[33] Similarly, in Saratov, clubs for senior school students sprang up. Saratov newspapers praised such clubs, which were organized primarily by the students themselves (fig. 5.1).[34] In Kemerovo, chess, tourism, and photography clubs appeared. Photography clubs created photo displays, helped produce satirical newspapers, and prepared albums with views of the city and the countryside.[35] The Rostov Province Komsomol established a club for young writers.[36] Nature protection clubs began to appear.[37] International clubs emerged, with their young members learning about and exchanging letters with foreigners.[38] Besides providing an outlet for youth interested in these activities, such clubs supported other Komsomol functions and reduced expenditures, since they relied mainly on youth initiative.

The stress on youth activism and initiative points to a crucial difference between interest-based clubs and the previously existing hobby circles, in which adult leaders organized and directed activities. Circles were also didactic, often featuring a program of instruction. In contrast, young club members themselves took charge of an interest-based club's organization and governance, though within the limits defined by the club's mission and oversight institutions; likewise, clubs placed more emphasis on uniting rather than teaching participants.

FIG. 5.1. This photograph accompanied an article in the Komsomol news-paper *Zaria molodezhi* that described the collective nature of clubs for older school students.

An interview with Boris Pshenichner, a club official in Moscow's Dvorets pionerskaia (Pioneer palace) who worked with circles and interest-based clubs dedicated to aeronautics and astronomy during and after the Thaw, further illuminates these differences. When asked to compare circles and clubs, he stated that clubs had an element of self-management, more autonomy, and less bureaucracy. He also highlighted the popularity of the interest-based clubs, giving an example of how the club he oversaw filled up very quickly in 1962, with many young people eager but unable to get in.[39]

For the authorities, satisfying youth interests and increasing the amount of socialist time—by ensuring that youth spent their leisure time in official collectives—were the primary goals of these clubs. Interest-based clubs arose not only for those activities perceived as fun by young people but also for those considered useful for the party-state. For instance, the authorities intended aeronautics clubs to promote youth knowledge about and interest in aviation, a profession for which there was high demand. Hunting and fishing clubs served to advance military preparation, and music-oriented clubs spread normative cultural standards. Still, the new clubs were more focused on entertainment and grassroots initiative than Stalin-era circles, and they catered to a much wider variety of interests. Clubs devoted to social demographics, which brought youth together to enjoy the company of like-minded peers, had no direct Stalinist equivalents.

Both kinds of interest-based clubs legitimated young people's active pursuit of their own individual passions, while acknowledging differences between social groups based on age, gender, education, and other categories. Easing the standards of behavior and scope of acceptable interests for New Soviet People, they denoted a departure from the postwar Stalinist pattern of condemning any expression of individualism or peculiarity.[40] These clubs fit a broader trend in the Thaw of recognizing diversity within society, as did the rebirth of sociology.[41] Similarly, a spate of Thaw-era films recognized and offered tolerance for a variety of identities.[42] Such findings suggest the need to refine Stephen Lovell's argument that official culture for the masses promoted a cohesive and unified vision of a Soviet cultural consumer that hid the cultural and social differences among the populace.[43] While his conclusions may fit the publishing industry, club activities indicate that they apply less well to the broader Soviet cultural sphere. The post-Stalin Kremlin, in its approach to state-sponsored popular culture, publicly admitted the existence of cultural diversity in Soviet society and oriented its cultural policy toward this social reality, thereby discarding the late Stalinist image of a homogeneous Soviet community, composed of undifferentiated individuals who fully shared all interests and preferences.

YOUTH INITIATIVE CLUBS
STRUCTURE AND GOALS

The Komsomol also promoted another type of novel youth collective: youth initiative clubs. If interest-based clubs catered to specific interests and demographics, youth initiative clubs offered young people of all social groups the opportunity to come together to pursue a diversity of interests in a single collective.

The origins of these institutions sprang from local and global influences alike. Youth initiative clubs bore similarities to the Komsomol-managed clubs of the 1920s. Another source of inspiration came from abroad. During a trip to Norway in 1955—the visit itself a result of de-Stalinization—Liubov Baliasnaia recalled being impressed with a college club designed to encourage independent student self-management. She successfully promoted the establishment of analogous institutions once she returned to Ukraine.[44] Similar clubs existed in eastern Europe, possibly serving as another model.[45]

The first Soviet youth initiative clubs emerged at the local level in 1954 and 1955, due to the individual efforts of Komsomol officials such as Baliasnaia. However, the clubs received widespread notice only after the Komsomol CC promoted their establishment in early 1956. Komsomol committees quickly responded to this directive, for instance, in the Komsomol conferences for the city of Moscow in 1956, at Moskovskii gosudarstvennyi universitet (MGU) in 1956, and at Saratovskii gosudarstvennyi universitet (SGU) in 1957.[46] Youth newspapers published articles praising the establishment of youth initiative clubs and providing instructions for doing so.[47]

Such sponsorship from the Komsomol hierarchy and press organs made possible and encouraged the wide development of grassroots youth activism in creating these clubs. According to *Komsomol'skaia pravda*, for instance, a Leningrad club known as Petrogradskaia storona (Petrograd side) had given local youths an avenue for initiative and creativity. Whereas youths had been reluctant to attend organized cultural events, local Komsomol cultural cadres, realizing that the problem lay with the fact that youth "felt themselves not owners, but guests" at such occasions, decided to establish a youth initiative club, where "the creative energy and imagination of youth set the tone," since young people themselves organized evening parties, balls, lectures, debates, and exhibitions.[48]

The Moscow club Fakel proved even more influential for the youth initiative club movement. Located in the Kuibyshev neighborhood, this club had 200 members in 1957. The Komsomol propaganda department described it as a "friendly collective that came together during youth evenings, meetings, debates, tourist trips."[49] Many local Komsomol newspapers reprinted an ad about Moscow's Fakel, most likely because of a top-level directive to popularize the creation of such clubs.[50] One such article in a Kaluga newspaper helped inspire the Fakel club described by Iurii Sokolov. Kaluga's Fakel even borrowed many of its organizational forms, such as its bylaws, from the Moscow Fakel club. The Kaluga Fakel had a largely working-class character, with 112 of its 172 members employed as workers (in November 1957).[51]

The Komsomol CC helped develop the work of youth initiative clubs by asking the party Central Committee to make district houses of culture available for youth-centered activities at least four times a month. It also acquired the right to raise money for youth cultural recreation from volunteer Komsomol-organized events by selling tickets to youth amateur concerts and collecting scrap metal and paper without having to pay taxes on the proceeds.[52] Youth initiative clubs also received assistance from institutions ranging from local enterprises to artistic and hobby associations and educational establishments. This support defrayed most or all of the expenses for their activities.[53] Consequently, the creation and financing of youth initiative clubs depended heavily on advocacy by the Komsomol CC, on the organizational impetus of local Komsomol committees and youth newspapers, on the support of local enterprises, and especially on the enthusiasm of Komsomol members themselves.

The 1956 youth initiative club campaign took off quickly, as a Komsomol propaganda department report from 1957 indicates. Calling for creating youth initiative clubs as part of every cultural establishment, the report's authors praised these new institutions for their embrace of grassroots enthusiasm, volunteerism, and youth autonomy. Participating in such clubs, the document noted, involved youth in what the department called rational leisure, created a core of activists around Komsomol committees, and developed a collective spirit among youth. It also encouraged friendship among young people and between ordinary youths, Komsomol committees, and youth newspapers.[54] This report illustrates the Komsomol's goal of using youth initiative clubs to strengthen grassroots activism and enthusiasm, while directing young people's interests and cultural consumption desires into appropriate channels in order to garden the young into model builders of communism.

Similarly, the authorities wanted youth clubs to extend the Komsomol's institutional reach into young people's everyday lives, an example of the transition to the infrastructural power–based rule. Thus, in a major speech in 1963, Sergei Pavlov, first secretary of the Komsomol from March 1959 to June 1968, called for Komsomol committees to nurture enthusiasts who actively organized youth collectives "and through them [to] ensure the influence of the Komsomol" among the young.[55] In this way, clubs served to increase socialist time.

Sokolov, who eventually became a Komsomol cultural official and organizer, highlighted another motive, one explicitly associated with the Cold War. Many western youth organizations did not want to have any official dealings with the Komsomol, which they regarded as a tool of social control. Although Komsomol cultural activists managed youth clubs and other novel institutions, collaborating with these establishments enabled western organizations to have relationships with Soviet youth organizations while avoiding direct involvement with the Komsomol.[56] Thus, youth exchanges between British and Soviet governments occurred through a Soviet entity called the Komitet molodezhnykh organizatsii SSSR (Committee of youth organizations of the USSR).[57] Although the Komsomol oversaw this body, its apparent autonomy meant that westerners could avoid both the stigma of working with the Komsomol explicitly and the potential political backlash from the domestic Right.

As youth clubs had neither paid staff nor ownership of a dedicated building, the archival records leave much to be desired, especially regarding statistics. Nonetheless, a close perusal of the sources indicates the rapid growth of these institutions. In 1957, more than twenty youth initiative clubs existed in Odessa alone, a sizable number given that Shelepin had called for such clubs only in 1956.[58] In 1962, Moscow had 214 youth clubs, and, by 1967, there were 12,000 such institutions across the Soviet Union.[59] Reports from individual youth initiative and interest-based clubs indicates that they had between several dozen to several hundred members; thus, total membership in 1967 likely ranged from half a million to a million youths. Given that the clubs existed until 1991, many millions of young people participated in such cultural collectives.

RANGE OF ACTIVITIES

Youth initiative clubs aimed to engage youth and appeal to their interests and desires by offering activities with much less explicitly political content than clubs affiliated with trade unions or the Ministry of Culture.[60] For instance, an Odessa youth group known as the Klub interesnykh vstrech (Club of interesting meetings) hosted gatherings for newlyweds at which young people discussed love, friendship, loyalty, and jealousy in a warm and informal atmosphere. Organizers of these gatherings collected questions from young people on the topic of the evening in advance. Among these were "How can one learn how to love for real?" and "Can one love a second and third time?" and "Is it good to be jealous?" A young philosophy teacher addressed these issues in a presentation, followed by a question-and-answer session with the audience. Youth also posed questions to long-wed couples, something that may have had particular relevance due to the low level of knowledge about sex among the population in the Khrushchev era.[61] Another meeting, promoted as "Girls! Let's Talk about Taste," featured advice on "proper" haircuts and clothing.[62] These events embodied the attempts to guide youth cultural consumption desires to fit "appropriately" socialist norms.

In contrast to such Stalinist-era offerings as dull and ponderous propaganda lectures for young people, youth initiative clubs began to organize debates, which, although politically themed, were comparatively open and dynamic.[63] Petrogradskaia storona sought to engage youth in issues that had fundamental relevance to their lives, holding events with themes such as "On Love and Loyalty," "The Question of Happiness Is on the Agenda," and "How Should One Lead a Communist Life?" The debates apparently drew large crowds, with the hall proving too small to accommodate all those who wished to attend.[64]

The Komsomol hierarchy encouraged such events. The Komsomol propaganda department called for "heated debates" to take place in youth initiative clubs so that "youth find answers to all questions that concern them there."[65] The Komsomol CC emphasized the need for more such debates, to deal with "the most important questions of modern life—moral themes, books, movies, plays, friendship, love, comradeship."[66] The committee believed that debates expunged negative tendencies from youth collectives and confirmed the best and newest in youth lives. It even sent an instructional letter to all Komsomol cells on conducting these events.[67] Thus, Komsomol policy makers viewed debates as encouraging youth to interrogate the tenets of official ideology, morals, and ethics within the contexts of Komsomol-managed events, with the intention of shaping the outcomes of debates and strengthening young people's faith in the system.

The Komsomol's internal discourse reveals a further purpose to debates, namely, the need to have youth discuss issues of importance within Komsomol-run collectives. In 1956, the Komsomol CC criticized the fact that, although young people enjoyed talking and arguing, "debates among youth generally take place outside of Komsomol organizations."[68] Nelli Popkova, an SGU student and cultural activist during the Thaw, told me of a typical informal debate that took place in her dorm in 1956. Fellow students threw pillows at her when she expressed an unpopular position.[69]

A number of underground youth groups devoted to discussing issues of concern to young people had sprung up in the postwar Stalin years and suffered repression from the Stalinist secret police.[70] The reformist spirit of the early post-Stalin period spurred a new wave of such groups, which felt freer to express themselves publicly.[71] The keynote of the 1957 SGU university-wide Komsomol conference, delivered by the cell leader, Anatolii Avrus, related how several students, without consulting any official organs, had decided to create a discussion club and even publish their own newspaper. Its articles expressed what Avrus termed an "improper interpretation of modern bourgeois art." Avrus maintained that the Komsomol needed to prevent such "ugly forms of initiative" from below by creating Komsomol-managed discussion clubs.[72] In other words, state-sanctioned debates aimed to bring unofficial discussions into spaces with government oversight and management.

Such officially sanctioned debates show that youth initiative clubs served as incubators of public opinion and promoted a civic spirit of public engagement, enabling youth to reflect on pressing issues relevant to their day-to-day lives.[73] Moreover, youth initiative clubs prompted youth to take action to confront some of the problems they saw in Soviet cultural life. Namely, youth had the opportunity to organize innovative and semiautonomous events that satisfied desires and wants not met by other components of the party-state cultural apparatus. Consequently, youth initiative clubs contributed to the growth of civic spirit among the young.

Other club activities served both entertainment and didactic functions. For instance, *Molodoi leninets* described a skiing trip organized by the Kaluga Fakel club during which one youth, Valentin Kriukhin, underwent a transformation, from an individualist into a willing part of the community. Initially, Kriukhin had tried to set himself apart, but when he met with difficulties, everyone helped him, and "soon his arrogance was gone, as the young man felt the strength of the collective."[74] In this way, clubs simultaneously promoted Soviet collectivism, in contrast to "arrogant," westernlike individualism, and imposed social control on individuals who deviated from accepted norms. Similar reprimands of misbehaving club members took place at other events.[75]

Clubs also engaged in more explicit and violent forms of social control, such as patrolling the streets and fighting hooligans and *stiliagi*. The Kaluga Fakel provides a particularly interesting case in point, because the well-known Soviet bard Bulat Okudzhava participated actively in its patrolling activities prior to his move to Moscow in 1956. The club formed a "flying brigade" that rode around on motorcycles to deal with public disturbances. The brigade targeted stiliagi, catching them and cutting up their western-style clothing. They also raided dormitories to stop sexual contact between young men and women. Okudzhava later expressed his regrets over his participation in these two areas of brigade work.[76]

The role of youth initiative clubs both as social control institutions and as spaces for the development of civic spirit emerges particularly clearly from the Komsomol's interactions with *kompanii*, or bohemian youth cliques, many of which formed during the Thaw. While only a minuscule proportion of all young people belonged to kompanii, these groupings included many young cultural elites.[77] The most evocative case of relations between the Komsomol hierarchy and kompanii of relevance to state-sponsored popular culture comes from the attempt to create a club for the unofficial poets of Moscow's Maiakovskii Ploshchad' (Maiakovskii Square). Since 1958, Maiakovskii Ploshchad' had served as a gathering place for young amateur poets who read their poetry without it first passing through official censorship. These poetry readings drew huge crowds, and, although the gatherings were initially tolerated, by 1960 the poems were increasingly critiquing the government, leading to state harassment.[78] At one point, however, a group of Komsomol officials and activists, along with some poets and their supporters, pursued a compromise. Lower-level cadres persuaded mid-level officials in the neighborhood Komsomol committee to offer the young poets an autonomous youth club in a local cultural establishment.[79] For Komsomol officials, providing such a club aimed to solve the immediate problem of public censure by redirecting it into a less open context.

Juliane Fürst has insightfully argued that kompanii tried to privatize public spaces and escape official collective structures. However, the example cited above shows that, in some cases, Komsomol authorities negotiated with kompanii over the boundaries between public and private, illustrating the diffuse and uncertain borders between these spheres. This negotiation also demonstrates that kompanii did not always seek to reject official spaces and collectives; a more nuanced reading of these groupings thus becomes necessary.[80] Our understanding of kompanii would benefit from comparing them to those cliques that formed in youth initiative and interest-based clubs. In such clubs and in kompanii alike, young people came together voluntarily to pursue mutual interests and enjoy their leisure time together. Kompanii differed because of their unofficial status and their connections to the cultural intelligentsia. Owing to the high social status of intelligentsia, members of kompanii generally had much greater access to cultural capital and economic resources, making intelligentsia members less interested in state-sponsored cultural activities. At the same time, those youth who most disagreed with party-state cultural norms were much more likely to gravitate to kompanii than to official youth clubs.

Shelepin's call in 1956 for new cultural forms led to innovative amalgams such as the Arkhimed (Archimedes) studio, which combined elements of a youth initiative club, an amateur art collective, and a festival planning committee, all centered on the performance of the opera *Arkhimed*. This studio emerged from the MGU physics department, perhaps the most prestigious department in the university.[81] Physics students there had a tradition of writing and performing operas that had begun in 1955 with *Dubinushka* (Dummy) and then *Seryi kamen'* (Gray rock) in 1958. Students put on these two operas or scenes from them at graduation celebrations, amateur arts competitions, and student evenings.[82]

Some of these productions were massive in scale. *Arkhimed* was one such production. Its origin was a 1959 physics department Komsomol conference, the participants of which had resolved to prepare a fun springtime celebration for 1960 and to create a festive new holiday, Den' fizikov (Physicists' day), celebrated on the supposed birthday of Archimedes (May 7). The fact that young college students had the audacity and confidence to establish a new holiday without explicit approval from above speaks volumes about the rapid expansion of autonomous youth community activism in the Thaw.

Over the following months, physics students invested a great deal of time and energy into preparing the festivities. The 1960 celebration, attended by a huge crowd, began with performances of amateur arts, followed by a carnival-like parade, led by floats with students dressed up as famous physicists. The world-famous physicist L. D. Landau, the faculty patron of the celebration, joined the fun on one of the floats (fig. 5.2).

Fɪɢ. 5.2. The first Den' fizikov (Physicists' day) parade. Professor Landau is in the center, wearing a black suit. Courtesy of the private archive of Marina Lebedeva.

After circling the university, the procession ended at the university's club building, where the students put on the opera *Arkhimed* for the first time. The opera depicted the heroic Archimedes, a dean at the University of Syracuse in Sicily, fighting for the future of physics against the Greek gods, who feared the progress of science (fig. 5.3).

The gods encouraged university staff to engage in corrupt behavior and tempted students to drink and dance the twist, officially forbidden at the time. A key moment in the show came when, as the opera's libretto states, "the students, tempted by the gods, for a minute lose their humanity, and a general dancing of the twist [*tvistopliaska*] begins." The opera's first performance was so popular that students barely fit into the

FIG. 5.3. The scene from the opera *Arkhimed* in which the hero challenges the Greek gods. Courtesy of the private archive of Marina Lebedeva.

overcrowded hall (fig. 5.4). This production combined three elements of Thaw-era official discourse: promotion of science and technology, criticism of bureaucratism and corruption, and disparagement of "negative" student behavior such as stiliagi-style dancing. The formal attire of most audience members (see figs. 5.2 and 5.4) differentiated such cultural activities from those of the stiliagi.[83]

Through the initiative-based cultural forms of the mid-1950s, the post-Stalin Komsomol leadership aimed to present an appealing vision of socialist fun. These activities also met the demands of lower- and mid-level Komsomol bureaucrats, who sought to encourage rank-and-file Komsomol members to engage in Komsomol activities within official collectives,

Fɪɢ. 5.4. The audience at the first performance of the opera *Arkhimed*. Many audience members had to stand in order to fit into the hall during the show, and some sat on the banisters. Courtesy of the private archive of Marina Lebedeva.

making them more likely to attend Komsomol meetings, perform volunteer labor duties, and pay dues.

For the managers of trade unions, for the Ministry of Culture, and for village cultural institutions, the initiative-based youth cultural collectives proved more of a challenge. Hosting youth clubs took time away from profitable movie and dance nights. However, these new activities meant that the total number of events held increased, along with the number of persons involved in club activities. Moreover, the clubs permitted cultural institutions to claim success in specifically youth-oriented work, a factor that acquired growing prominence in the post-Stalin years.

NEW CULTURAL FORMS AND YOUTH LIVES

As we have seen, new initiative-based cultural forms spread widely. Sources describe overcrowded halls along with great youth interest and participation in novel cultural forms. Such evidence helps emphasize that many among the young expressed a genuine and powerful enthusiasm for these innovative cultural collectives.

Interviews with participants ground these broad developments and offer an in-depth look at their impact on the lives, emotions, worldviews, and perceptions of self among the young. My interviews with former

FIG. 5.5. This banquet was held after a performance of *Arkhimed*. Courtesy of the private archive of Marina Lebedeva.

Arkhimed performers invariably revealed their eagerness for engaging in this Komsomol-organized cultural activity. Tatiana Tkacheva enjoyed an "enormous emotional lift" from performing in the opera.[84] For Dmitrii Gal'tsov, it "was just fun."[85]

Arkhimed played a deep social role as well. The opera experience involved not only singing and acting but also the customary post-performance banquet for its members, remembered with pleasure by Sergei Semenov (fig. 5.5).[86]

According to Ol'ga Lebedikhina, a professional vocal instructor who served as the chorus master of Arkhimed, this collective represented "real life" for its members and was the center of their social world.[87] Svetlana Shchegol'kova confirmed the key role of the clique that formed around the opera, describing the clique's members as "friends with whom we are close and hang out with pleasure" in the present as well.[88] The dance leader and later historian of the Arkhimed collective, Svetlana Kovaleva, similarly stressed the importance of the friendships forged through *Arkhimed* and said that the opera had inspired her to consider that "we can achieve whatever we want."[89] The coauthor of the opera, Valerii Miliaev, likewise underscored its crucial role in personal growth and developing social skills. For Semenov, the opera helped him gain confidence in public speaking.[90]

As related by the Arkhimed studio director Iurii Gaponov during a five-hour interview conducted while strolling in a Moscow park, for him, "creating a collective" from among the opera participants was the key goal of the Arkhimed project. Notably, Gaponov and other Arkhimed members considered service in the physics department's Komsomol cell and their involvement with the Den' fizikov celebration as part of the broader complex of Komsomol work.[91]

Interviewees may have been romanticizing their youth, and the passage of time inevitably reshapes the stories people tell about their personal experience. Still, the recollections of Arkhimed members about their enormous investment of emotion, time, and energy into this official cultural activity and its impact on their social lives and worldview, along with the fact that many participants have remained lifelong friends who continue to treasure their memories, underscore the outsized role that the Arkhimed collective played for many of those who performed in it. Furthermore, Arkhimed problematizes scholarly claims that strong friendship relations and emotional bonds lead to individualization.[92] Instead, Arkhimed and similar state-sponsored cultural groups emphasize how such friendships could and did lead to more intense and enthusiastic collectivism, along with deeper involvement with the official party-state structure. In this way, the Soviet authorities provided opportunities for young people to build deep social bonds, of the type that recent neuroscience research indicates contributes much to mental well-being and physical health.[93]

Indeed, Arkhimed was hardly a unique phenomenon and had many parallels to other youth-oriented institutions, such as the Kaluga Fakel group.[94] Even some ordinary Komsomol cells functioned in a similar fashion during the Thaw. Irina Sokol'skaia, who served as the Komsomol organizer for her college Komsomol class, adopted the sentiment that "the best Komsomol work" involved "doing something positive for her group" and ensuring lasting friendships through entertaining organized cultural recreation, which also fit into the Komsomol's broad agenda for normative leisure. Much like Gaponov, she said that it was important for her "to create a good life for the students out of the directives coming from above."[95]

Interest-based clubs provided many of the same benefits, according to officials in Moscow's Dvorets pionerskaia. During my visit to the palace in April 2009 I spoke with Pshenichner and Nona Kozlova, both employed there since the 1960s to work with groups dedicated to aeronautics and astronomy. Kozlova described palace activities aimed to harness young people's enthusiasm for astronomy in the interest both of education and *vospitanie* (moral upbringing). Both Kozlova and Pshenichner told me that young members also benefited from professional preparation and from becoming part of collectives that have continued to connect individuals to each other. Apparently, former affiliates still meet to partake in astronomy-oriented activities or to socialize together at reunions.[96] According to Valentina Miagkova, similar goals and outcomes characterized a broad range of interest-based clubs at the Dvorets pionerskaia, which served as "a ticket to life for very many."[97]

Youth who performed in such initiative-based cultural groups generally supported most of the de-Stalinizing changes and the revived drive to build communism under Khrushchev. Frequently, they portrayed themselves as having believed in a romantic vision of communism "with a human face" during their youth. Tkacheva recalled her faith and that of her friends in constructing communism.[98] Miliaev attributed the popularity of Arkhimed to the notion that the opera of the same name fit "the liberal spirit of the time, a spirit of freedom of expression."[99] Nina Deviataikina described herself as "growing up in the freedom of the Khrushchev era," which permitted her and her friends to "breathe in a new" and "relatively free fashion."[100] Such statements correlate with recent findings that young people in the post-Stalin years were optimistic about communism and the Soviet system, whether in the center, in the Russian provinces, or in the Soviet republics.[101]

Such feelings accorded well with the goals of the Khrushchev leadership. In the view of Lebedikhina, the success of amateur arts depended on the support of both the "authorities and . . . ordinary people themselves." Enthusiastic grassroots participation in state-sponsored popular culture allowed political elites to present "Soviet life as a happy life," while simultaneously enabling the amateur artists to "find and express themselves."[102] Cultural innovations forged real emotional attachments between young people and the new institutions, pushing them into closer alignment with the Kremlin's Thaw-era prescriptions for appropriate emotions. The existence of such emotional bonds belies the image of mask-wearing, inauthentic Soviet selves who expressed their authentic, true feelings only in private settings.

Furthermore, initiative-based cultural groups provided young people with an opportunity to find and cultivate a personal sense of meaning and purpose in life. Recent psychological research on meaning and purpose reveals that a personal sense of meaning and purpose stems from three crucial elements: (1) reflection on one's sense of meaning and purpose in the context of broader life events; (2) activities that enable one to cultivate social and community bonds; and (3) social service to others. In youth initiative clubs and similar settings, young people had an opportunity to reflect on the meaning of events in their lives through debates, discussions, and study groups. These institutions enabled youth to cultivate bonds with each other through cultural and social activities. Finally, through volunteering together and playing for audiences, young people gained the opportunity to serve others.[103]

While bringing people together in deep and meaningful ways, initiative-based cultural forms also functioned to ensure that a sizable number of youth became socialized in state-sponsored settings, thus spending their leisure in socialist time. The trope of youth clubs and brigades forging true collectives, which resounds throughout the interviews and official sources alike, fit ideally with the Khrushchev leadership's goals. Youth clubs were not hollow façades; they helped form close-knit, long-lasting community ties and social bonds, and many club members explicitly supported Khrushchev-era populist reforms. Such evidence illustrates some of the successes of the Kremlin's populist turn in cultural policy, as the new leadership moved away from Stalinist authoritarianism toward reliance on a new social contract, infrastructural power, softer methods of gardening, and grassroots activism that involved a significant number of young people in the Thaw-era vision of building an appealing socialist modernity. These were not "short flames of new enthusiasm" that masked a general "shirking [of] the system" but rather an expression of genuine enthusiasm.[104]

POINTS OF TENSION OVER YOUTH INITIATIVE

Nevertheless, conflicts arose as a result of differences between soft- and hard-line visions of appropriate cultural activities. The first speaker at a Komsomol-sponsored conference on youth clubs in 1962 described how, at the dawn of the youth club movement, many officials "expressed suspicion and lack of faith" in these novel collectives.[105] Liubov Baliasnaia attested to the gap between Thaw-era officials who supported grassroots initiatives and those functionaries (whom she labeled "not very wise") who could not shed their attachment to top-down discipline, which she believed alienated youth.[106]

Youth initiative clubs drew much more flak from hard-liners than did interest-based clubs, as the former had a broader membership base, greater autonomy, and relied more on initiative from below. Moscow's Fakel, the youth initiative club that served as a model for many others, was nearly shut down because of opposition from conservative authorities in the Moscow city Komsomol committee and the local house of culture, which distrusted the club and denied them space for events, forcing the Komsomol propaganda department to intervene.[107] In this case, pluralistically oriented lower-level Komsomol officials and activists in youth initiative clubs clashed with more orthodox mid-level officials and trade union club managers who were reluctant to permit innovations and support community activism. The soft-line stance of the Komsomol propaganda department proved crucial, as its representatives reprimanded intransigent mid-level officials and defended grassroots engagement in Moscow's Fakel and similar institutions.

Kaluga's Fakel club encountered similar problems. On November 20, 1956, the Kaluga city party committee condemned the "intolerable autonomy" exhibited in the establishment of Fakel, decreeing the closing of the club and imposing punishments on Fakel activists, including *Molodoi leninets* editors. The latter, in a complaint to the party Central Committee, maintained that such misguided "vigilance" could come only from "people poisoned by bureaucracy," who, guided by the "spirit of the cult of personality," sought to regulate everything, including the "enthusiastic creativity of the masses."[108] The editors thus condemned the Kaluga city party for practices explicitly associated with the Stalinist "cult of personality" and instead upheld the initiative, creativity, and autonomy associated with de-Stalinizing reforms.

Fakel supporters appealed to a series of organs in Moscow. Ultimately, the party Central Committee apparatus launched an investigation, which came down primarily on the side of Fakel and against the Kaluga party committee. This outcome ensured the continued existence of the club and the revocation of party reprimands of the club's activists.[109] During our interview, Sokolov recalled an article in *Komsomol'skaia pravda* defending Fakel, thus indicating the resonance of this conflict with the public and the significance of the club in the lives of at least some Kaluga youth.[110] Intervention by the central authorities expressed strong support for youth grassroots activism and served as a warning for obstructionist officials.

Youth initiative clubs even caused tensions with well-established cultural recreation institutions, as revealed in December 1956 in a note by a high administrator in the Ministry of Culture. The official suggested that the best cultural activists and artists might quit trade union clubs and "form some sort of elite caste" within youth initiative clubs. He bristled at clubs' autonomy, accusing them of creating a "Komsomol within the Komsomol." Specifically citing the Kaluga Fakel as a prime example of such problems, the official censured *Komsomol'skaia pravda* for defending it.[111] The reference to the Kaluga Fakel hints at how this local struggle achieved the status of a notable point of conflict within the central party-state apparatus.

This note from 1956 demonstrates that there was implicit support for a militant vision of the path to communism that did not rely on grassroots spontaneity. The warning of a "Komsomol within the Komsomol" evoked the traditional bugaboo of party-state factionalism that hard-liners had used to bash youth cultural self-management since the 1920s. Warning against the weakening of trade union clubs, the memo evinced concern with defending bureaucratic turf against an unwelcome incursion from the Komsomol. In other words, systemic incentives intertwined with a conservative outlook to prompt the official's actions.

THE EVOLUTION OF YOUTH INITIATIVE CLUBS IN THE EARLY 1960S

Despite such opposition, the promotion of cultural collectives by soft-line bureaucrats, and the popularity of these institutions among youth, ensured their expansion. By 1959, the Ministry of Culture seems to have accepted their existence; a textbook for club employees mentioned youth initiative clubs as a new form of club work.[112] In 1962, their main concerns shifted from defending their very existence to searching for space and financial support.[113]

In the early 1960s, *kluby na obshchestvennykh nachalakh* (volunteer clubs) began to spring up. Unlike youth initiative clubs, volunteer clubs had individual spaces assigned to them by the party-state. The volunteer clubs, consequently, had greater power, authority, and permanence. The first such club in Moscow, Aktivist, in the Krasnopresnenskii neighborhood, provides an example of these new organizations. Created in October 1959, Aktivist managed its own space, which included a hall that could hold two hundred people, seven rooms for various cultural activities, a library with six thousand titles, and a photography lab. The club's volunteer activists chose a motto: "we have one paid staff member—enthusiasm."[114]

The director of Moscow's Entuziast (Enthusiast) volunteer club stressed that youth initiative formed the basis for the success of the club, which boasted a well-maintained hall for 120 people and fourteen small rooms. The director ascribed Entuziast's fine appearance to its members, who voluntarily spent their free time renovating the run-down basement. Attesting to this volunteer club's appeal, he related how a group of amateur musicians felt uncomfortable in trade union clubs, where the management ordered them to write and perform specific songs. Further, the trade union clubs refused to dedicate a room where youth could just hang out. Entuziast, however, did not place demands on young people to write certain songs, offering them broad leeway to indulge their creative talents. It also provided them with spaces in which to spend time talking and relaxing with one another, engaging in sociability instead of directed cultural activities. As a result, these talented amateurs relocated to Entuziast and wrote a series of songs that grew popular among Moscow youth.[115]

These amateur singer-composers represented part of the bard movement—performers who composed and sang poetic songs accompanied by guitar music. Originating from prerevolutionary traditions of popular romances, folk music, and gypsy and criminal-style songs, this guitar poetry struck a powerful chord with Soviet audiences from the late 1950s onward, at first with cultural elites and college students and later more broadly among the middle and working classes. Newly available tape recorders made possible the rapid spread of bard music without going through official organs, thus allowing individual singer poets to achieve national fame. Some of the most prominent bards, such as Aleksandr Galich, Bulat Okudzhava, and Vladimir Vysotskii, wrote edgy songs that challenged the limits of the party-state's tolerance and grew highly popular as a result.[116] Eastern Europe also had bards, such as Wolf Bierman in East Germany.[117] While much of the historiography has focused on bards in socialist states, recent literature indicates that bard poetry was popular elsewhere among left-leaning musicians, including Americans Pete Seeger and Bob Dylan, as well as Georges Brassens of France.[118]

While most scholars have focused on a few of the most controversial bard celebrities, an examination of Thaw-era youth culture shows that the bard phenomenon had broad social resonance.[119] In 1959, the Moscow Dom narodnogo tvorchestva noted that guitars had already gained wide popularity among Moscow youth and that many clubs had recently created guitar circles.[120] Valerii Miliaev, who was also a well-known bard, recalled hearing original guitar poems at official university concerts under the rubric of *studencheskaia pesnia* (student song) or *samodeiatel'naia pesnia* (self-written song). The authorities even sponsored festivals of bard songs.[121]

Furthermore, in contrast to studies that have emphasized the opposition between bard superstars and official cultural production, my data indicate that plenty of young people composed guitar poetry that did not provoke the government's ire.[122] Even the conservative Dom narodnogo tvorchestva in Moscow supported and praised controversial guitar poetry. Sergei Krylov, a prominent bard and festival organizer, described how his and other bards' music did not criticize the state but instead aimed to bring entertainment and joy. As a festival organizer, he had to defend bard songs against skeptical party functionaries in Magadan Province who associated guitar poetry with oppositionist bard celebrities. Krylov succeeded by arguing that, when youths sang bard songs, they were not indulging in western music. He also emphasized that many bard songs focused on Soviet patriotism and love for nature—themes supported by official discourse.[123] Different club managers competed to attract amateurs from Entuziast, indicating the prestige and lack of controversy associated with hosting young bards.

With the support of youth enthusiasm from below and top-level advocacy from above, volunteer-based cultural forms grew rapidly in the early 1960s. By the end of 1962, twenty-six volunteer clubs were serving Moscow residents, with sixteen of them opening up that year.[124] SGU established one such club in the early 1960s through the cooperative efforts of the university's Komsomol, trade union, and administration. Named Klub kul'tury (Club of culture), this institution's leadership came from young Komsomol activists such as Mark Pinkhasik. Soon, the volunteer Klub kul'tury became the official club of the university, with Pinkhasik hired as the director.[125]

Because of their growing integration into the state-sponsored popular culture system by the early 1960s, youth cultural collectives proved increasingly capable of defending their own interests against militant local officials who disliked youth initiative. The organizers of Arkhimed, for instance, had to deal with hard-liners in the physics department administration and its party committee from the start, in 1960. According to Svetlana Kovaleva, opponents of the club tried to "limit youth activism," demanding a preview of the opera and attacking Arkhimed supporters.[126] The hard-liners managed to have some parts of the opera censored, including a depiction of volunteer construction labor on the Egyptian pyramids, which they believed hinted at slave labor in the Tselina and on other construction projects. The most militant officials also complained about other aspects of Arkhimed, such as its satire of corruption and drunkenness among university staff and the implication that dancing the twist and intoxication were widespread among physics students.[127]

In 1961, militant members of the physics department party committee almost succeeded in shutting down the Den' fizikov celebration. Yet, the Arkhimed collective, with the assistance of Professor Landau, saved the Den' fizikov event from cancellation by inviting Niels Bohr to the festivities (fig. 5.6).

The students understandably expressed great enthusiasm over Bohr's presence. Bohr, in turn, loved the festival and opera, writing in the MGU guest book that "the artistic talent and sense of humor expressed at the yearly celebration in honor of Archimedes and his service to humanity, left a truly indelible impression on my wife and myself." Moreover, after watching the opera, Bohr apparently said that "if these students are capable of the same creativity and wit in physics, then I am not worried about the future [of physics]."[128]

Fig. 5.6. Niels Bohr is shown giving a speech after a performance of *Arkhimed*. Professor Landau is to his right. Courtesy of the private archive of Svetlana Shchegol'kova.

Bohr's visit illustrates the intersection of domestic cultural diplomacy and initiative-based cultural activities. He expressed much admiration for Soviet organized cultural recreation, a goal that Soviet cultural authorities pursued for domestic cultural diplomacy. Moreover, Bohr's presence not only energized and excited students but also shaped Soviet organized cultural recreation at MGU by ensuring that the festival and opera performance took place.

Despite continuing opposition, Den' fizikov and the opera *Arkhimed* received praise at the university-wide Komsomol conference in 1963. A visit by the cosmonaut German Titov to the Den' fizikov celebration in 1963 nearly causing a stampede of star-struck students. The journal *Iunost'* (Youth) called for extending such festivals to other departments that year, and indeed physics departments in other higher educational institutions held celebrations based on MGU's model. In 1964, television and radio broadcasts covered MGU's Den' fizikov, and a Soviet film, *Gvozdiki nuzhny vliublennym* (Lovers need carnations), even included a depiction of it.[129]

Still, some of the more orthodox bureaucrats in the administration continued to pressure Arkhimed and complain about Den' fizikov. Moreover, they punished some of the outspoken defenders of these daring cultural activities, including Gaponov, through measures that impeded their careers, such as blackening their official files.[130] The tensions over Den' fizikov represented just one of several key points of conflict between what Miliaev identified as the "physics department's conservative administration" and the department's Komsomol committee, which he termed "liberal." Specifically, he praised the latter for giving young people such as him a chance to "express their opinion, to argue," and to make a difference by individually engaging in and shaping official activities.[131]

Tensions over the youth initiative movement help confirm the key role played by conflicts between liberal-leaning and more conservative individuals in shaping Thaw-era mass cultural activities, and thus everyday youth cultural practices, which paralleled high-level policy debates during these years.[132] This book does not argue that struggles between two static and fixed camps dominated and defined the Thaw; instead, it posits that the pluralistic and militant outlooks represented the two ends of the political spectrum as it related to state-sponsored popular culture. Moreover, bureaucrats' attitudes toward youth initiative evolved over time. If, in the mid-1950s, many officials were hesitant about and wary of youth clubs, by the early 1960s only a minority of militant bureaucrats were expressing public skepticism over the principle of youth initiative. Nonetheless, the extent of grassroots activism remained a central point of conflict over club activities throughout the Thaw and exerted a powerful influence on youth day-to-day experience. On the question of youth initiative, party-state cadres stood at various intermediate points between the two ideological extremes. Officials who held soft-line positions expressed varying levels of tolerance for youth cultural collectives and different perceptions of permissible behavior.

Nonetheless, the borders of permissibility proved difficult to define and enforce at the grassroots level, thus permitting the more daring initiative-based youth cultural collectives a significant, if not unlimited, degree of leeway to push boundaries. A major point of conflict over the opera *Arkhimed*, for instance, emerged over the Greek god Apollo's back-up dancers. In a scene about seducing the students of Archimedes to turn away from physics, the dancers performed a cabaret in daring costumes (fig. 5.7).

Shchegol'kova, one of the dancers in the photograph, related that the students had made the attire by shortening their gymnastics costumes. They even wanted to dance the Charleston or twirl a baton but decided against it. In her words, when university officials saw their costumes, "of course, their jaws dropped." Many bureaucrats found the costumes excessive and frivolous and tried to get the dancers to at least take off their

Fig. 5.7. This photograph of the opera *Arkhimed* features the scene with Apollo's backup dancers. Courtesy of the private archive of Marina Lebedeva.

gloves for a more "sportlike look." Yet, with the support of more pluralistic members of the party committee, the students managed to talk their way into leaving the costumes unchanged, insisting that they sought to depict the spirit of the young Greek women dancing for Apollo. According to Shchegol'kova, the chance to publicly dance a western cabaret in appropriate garb constituted another, unvoiced motive for the costumes and the number itself.[133]

Kovaleva, who also appears in the photograph, recalled that the western-style dancing itself spurred the indignation of hard-line individuals on the party committee, though the student audience "liked [the dance] very much."[134] Thus, the dancers' risqué costumes pushed the limits of appropriate garb for women in official student performances, continuing a tradition of Russian students' questioning of official gender norms.[135]

The cabaret-style dancing also undermined the state-prescribed mission of expunging stiliagi-like, excessively western behavior, as did the opera's ostensibly negative depiction of the twist. The coauthor of *Arkhimed*, Miliaev, told me that he disliked stiliagi and meant no irony or subversion in the scene in which the students danced the twist.[136] Regardless of Miliaev's intention, the opera director, Gaponov, emphasized that such scenes were deliberately included, both in *Arkhimed* and in other performances, as a means of exhibiting officially censured dances in state-sponsored venues.[137] Indeed, plenty of students, as *Arkhimed* participant Dmitrii Gal'tsov commented to me, welcomed a chance to perform proscribed dances on officially sanctioned stages.[138] Sergei Semenov liked that scene most of all, both for its "beautiful young women, dancing well," and for its realistic depiction of everyday life in the physics dormitory.[139] The tactic of featuring a proscribed dance in *Arkhimed* parallels the one jazz enthusiasts deployed when they played American-style jazz in skits that publicly disparaged the United States. This parallel illustrates how the context of Soviet cultural censorship and the Cold War conflict opened up the potential for multiple meanings, including nonconformist ones, within seemingly straightforward cultural events, even when the author might not have intended or even explicitly and genuinely rejected the alternate interpretation. This conclusion enriches the findings of previous studies about the room available for unorthodox readings of Soviet music, further underscoring the challenges experienced by the authorities in having audiences receive officially prescribed messages through various cultural forms.[140]

Some initiative-based youth cultural collectives pushed the boundaries by providing cover for marginalized or even illegal activities. Moscow's Fakel offered a platform for a literature circle in which unofficial poets, such as G. V. Sapgir, A. V. Laiko, and other members of the Lianozovo poetry group, had a chance to perform their poetry and make connections.[141] In the interest-based clubs devoted to stamps, avid collectors illegally purchased stamps from each other.[142] Youth clubs provided space for everything from unsanctioned Ukrainian nationalist activities to the study of Asian alternative medicine.[143]

In one case, a youth initiative club in Kuibyshev even rivaled the Komsomol in the realm of youth loyalty. In 1964, the leadership council of the Kuibyshev Gorod molodezhnyi klub informed the Komsomol leader Sergei Pavlov that, although the club was very popular among youth, with four hundred "fanatic-enthusiasts" and club events drawing up to thirty-five thousand people, it lacked a space of its own. The province-level Komsomol and party organizations had promised the club a venue for its activities, but they had failed to deliver. This lack of space, the club leadership's letter alleged, put the club at risk of collapse and could result in the young club-goers losing "faith in the Komsomol organization of the province and in all guarantees and promises of Party organs."[144] That initiative-based cultural forms could be more meaningful than the Komsomol directly contradicted Pavlov's call for the Komsomol committees to use such cultural institutions to extend their influence among youth. The case of the Kuibyshev Gorod molodezhnyi klub illustrates some of the limitations of this endeavor and also points to the potential problem of grassroots disillusionment when initiative from below did not receive sufficient support from above.

In most cases, conflicts over the extent of youth initiative led to negotiated solutions between the authorities and young people. On some occasions, however, the party-state shut down cultural collectives that refused to compromise and blatantly went beyond the limits. The Maiakovskii Ploshchad' poets, for instance, had been granted a club by the Komsomol authorities, along with a promise of autonomy. The poets organized a literature section, but, when they tried to stage an exhibit of abstract art, the director of the cultural establishment that had provided the club's meeting space refused permission. The Komsomol district and city committees chose not to force the issue. In response, the poets returned to the square. Soon afterward, local officials used force to disperse the poets.[145] By openly going far beyond the boundaries, the poets placed themselves in clear political opposition to the party-state, resulting in their repression.

Youth debates also had the potential to generate friction with political authorities. SGU held a debate about V. D. Dudintsev's *Ne khlebom edinym* (Not by bread alone), a powerful, controversial, and popular 1956 book that dealt with bureaucratic corruption.[146] This book received positive coverage in the pluralistic environment following Khrushchev's Secret Speech in February 1956. However, with the fallout from the speech leading to popular disturbances inside and outside the Soviet Union, culminating with the invasion of Hungary, the atmosphere turned more conservative in late 1956, resulting in a new official line calling for condemnation of Dudintsev's work.[147] However, according to the Saratov Komsomol activists Liudmila Gerasimova and Anatolii Avrus, the vast majority of the audience in the late 1956 debate at SGU supported Dudintsev. Arguing against the new official line, some students and faculty members claimed that Dudintsev's account ran true to life.[148] Unsurprisingly, SGU's party and Komsomol organizations and the university newspaper condemned this debate and its outcome. In his 1957 speech at the university-wide Komsomol conference, Avrus, as the leader of the university-wide Komsomol organization, explicitly censured the viewpoints that had been expressed by debate participants. He even stated that the incident "illustrates the weak political education [*politicheskii zakal*] of our students."[149]

Another example of a problematic debate, described at an MGU Komsomol conference in 1963, was one dealing with abstract art. Apparently, certain students "showed political immaturity, failing to understand the Party's positions on art."[150] This episode constituted part of a broader crackdown on abstract art by the Khrushchev administration after late 1962.[151] Such instances underscore some of the limitations in top-level promotion of youth grassroots initiative, which were especially apparent when the leadership changed course toward a more conservative official line. Nonetheless, the Komsomol CC continued to promote youth debates, believing that their benefits outweighed the risks.[152]

The Khrushchev administration departed from the late Stalinist period stress on discipline, encouraging initiative from below to get the young engaged in the Soviet project and prepare them to manage society as the state withered away with the approach of communism. By sponsoring grassroots activism, the new rulers also aimed to achieve a victory in the Cold War contest for hearts and minds at home and abroad. They did so by depicting the Thaw-era socialist alternative, with its supposedly publicly engaged and enthusiastic youth, as preferable to the western modernity, purportedly characterized by individualistic consumerism, egoism, and apathy. Post-Stalin policy makers rejected the late Stalinist vision of a homogeneous collective and instead began to openly acknowledge cultural and social differences.

The party-state's engagement with young people speaks to the powerful new role of youth in the early Thaw period. The wants, tastes, and emotions of this social group increasingly assumed a significant role in defining state-sponsored popular culture. To a large extent, youth voluntary enthusiasm determined the success of the new initiative-based cultural forms. Allowing and even encouraging young people to shape these novel youth-managed official collectives resulted in greatly increased room for agency within the official cultural sphere. Combined with debates and other innovations, such post-Stalin developments in the mass cultural network encouraged young people to engage in public activism to achieve their goals and desires, helping develop a civic spirit among the young.

In extending more agency to young people, the Thaw-era Soviet cultural system arguably compared favorably not only to the Stalinist one but also to those in other societies. In his analysis of western modernity, Arjun Appadurai famously proclaims that "where there is consumption, there is pleasure, and where there is pleasure there is agency." People voluntarily choose which mass consumer products to consume and enjoy. However, as

Appadurai has noted, "freedom . . . is a rather more elusive commodity": individual consumers had little say regarding what offerings the market system provided, thus limiting the extent of popular agency.[153] In contrast, early Thaw state-sponsored popular culture both offered pleasure and gave young people a surprising degree of autonomy to define the nature of what they consumed. In Appadurian terms, the Soviet case offered a greater degree of agency than the western cultural industry.

The post-Stalin initiative-based cultural forms marked a stark break with not only Stalinism but also the Nazi German and fascist Italian systems of organized cultural recreation. Neither the Nazi nor the fascist Italian structures intended to inspire grassroots self-management at any point in their existence.[154] However, many eastern European countries did undergo an evolution similar to the Soviet one during the mid- and late 1950s. This transformation suggests a confluence of efforts among Soviet bloc states in relying on initiative from below to present socialist modernity as a comprehensive and engaging alternative to the western version.

The new Soviet leadership expanded considerably the previously narrow boundaries of acceptable emotional norms, self-identities, and worldviews for Soviet youth. It regarded young people's pursuit of a wide variety of interests as legitimate and as part of a greatly broadened path toward communism. This shift sparked widespread enthusiasm and excitement, helping bring many young people into the fold. Enthusiasm became a hallmark emotion of the early Thaw. The authorities succeeded in appealing to the feelings of a substantial portion of the Soviet youth and getting them engaged in grassroots community-level cultural management. This finding parallels recent scholarship on other locations, pointing to the powerful role of emotions as a mobilizing mechanism for public participation.[155]

Young cultural activists invested a great deal of their time, effort, energy, and emotion into the new cultural forms. Youth club enthusiasts participated in exciting and innovative official cultural activities and, consequently, in the civic life of Soviet society. Moreover, the new top-level policies enabled young people to create new forms of socialist fun, which legitimated and uplifted the socialist version of modernity. Young people's participation in the new cultural forms also yielded personal benefits, including friendships, a sense of community, skills and abilities, excitement, joy, and a sense of personal meaning and purpose.

As a result, young people spent more of their leisure in socialist time rather than in the growing number of private apartments. Some of these new cultural institutions permitted a greater degree of western-style cultural expression than the party line allowed. Yet, they also encouraged more young people to engage with the official Soviet cultural sphere, even as youth felt somewhat distanced from the traditional forms of state-sponsored popular culture. By accommodating such behavior within organized cultural recreation, the party-state opened room for mild forms of youth rebellion and nonconformism to take place within government-managed settings. This accommodation helped encourage potentially deviant young people to stay within the party-state's cultural sphere and contributed to minimizing spectacular public youth divergence from official norms of the type that occurred widely in western settings at this time.[156]

This escalation in time spent in official collectives does not bear out Oleg Kharkhordin's broad claims that Soviet collectives grew more powerful and repressive during the Khrushchev years or that cynical strife dominated the internal dynamics of such groups.[157] Kharkhordin also claims that interest-based clubs were defined by an internal core group that opposed official club activists, which illustrated the fundamental antagonism between the official and unofficial in the Soviet Union.[158] My study of youth clubs shows that such was often not the case. Kharkhordin's notions fail to account for the historical reality that officially registered leaders such as Gaponov in fact constituted the genuine, fully acknowledged leaders of many youth cultural collectives. More generally, within Thaw-era state-sponsored popular culture, official collectives such as initiative and interest-based clubs blurred the boundaries between public and private according to the traditional scholarly understanding of them. Many young people found pleasure and fun, cultural self-fulfillment, deep emotional meaning, a close-knit community, and lifelong friendships in official cultural collectives, which helped define youth worldviews, cultural practices, and self-identities. Such evidence helps illustrate that Komsomol-managed organizations functioned less like a social control mechanism than envisioned by some scholars.[159]

Militants within the bureaucracy expressed "conservatism and mistrust" toward initiative-based cultural collectives, resulting in conflicts with those holding soft-line positions. Such conflicts had powerful implications for the everyday cultural practices of the many millions of young people who participated in youth clubs. Dating back to prerevolutionary debates between reliance on grassroots spontaneity versus top-level directives, such struggles indicate that tensions over these contradictory values continued to stand close to the heart of ideology, discourse, and policy throughout the Soviet Union's later history. The question of youth initiative within official cultural settings meant a great deal to young cultural activists of the Thaw era who passionately and publicly defended these official collectives against conservative bureaucrats. There is thus a need to complicate Alexei Yurchak's argument for the increasing irrelevancy of official discourse for everyday youth experience from 1953 onward, a point that may apply better to the 1970s and 1980s than to the Thaw.[160] Furthermore, the willingness among these young people to voice opinions contrary to those of authority figures and to insist on the importance of individual desires further challenges Stephen Kotkin's notion of Soviet citizens as generally "speaking Bolshevik" to officials, at least during the post-1953 period.

The stress on satisfying youth desires and developing youth initiative resulted in young people acquiring an increasingly cohesive sense of themselves as a distinct social group. More and more, the young perceived themselves and their peers as a unique demographic. Young people increasingly came to consider their own opinions and interests as deserving attention and respect, giving rise to the formation of a recognizable generational consciousness among the young, meaning an age cohort's self-awareness as a unique generation at variance with other age groups. I term this cohort the "post-Stalin generation," a reference to them growing up in the whirlwind of changes during the mid- and late 1950s following the dictator's death.[161] In contrast to Stalin's last generation, the post-Stalin generation constituted what June Edmunds and Bryan Turner would have termed an "active" generation, meaning one whose members identified with other members of their age group, uniting around their common youthhood to struggle for mutually desirable social change.[162] Those belonging to the post-Stalin generation joined with each other in initiative-based cultural collectives, engaging in grassroots activism to pursue their goals and developing their civic spirit and generational consciousness.

Notably, promoting youth initiative and appealing to popular interests occasionally challenged the goals of the early Thaw leadership. The official discourse's novel stress on youth desires and grassroots activism legitimated young people paying more conscious attention to their personal needs and wants. Policy makers hoped this approach would lead to a socialist version of modernity characterized by a balance between advancing individual desires and engaging in communist construction via official collectives, in the context of competing with the Cold War image of western individualism and consumerism. However, the leadership found that its viewpoint on appropriate initiative from below did not always match the vision of young people. From the perspective of those in charge, in some cases youth went too far in expressing their agency and initiative, whether through critical comments, unruly activities, provocative conduct, or excessive adoption of western cultural elements.

CHAPTER 6

THE 1957 INTERNATIONAL YOUTH FESTIVAL AND THE BACKLASH

At the Seventh Komsomol Central Committee Plenum, held in February 1957, Alexander Shelepin called for decisive actions to develop youth "aesthetic tastes" (*esteticheskie vkusy*), both to help achieve communism and to respond to the "propagandists of western culture who constantly strive to impose foreign views and tastes on Soviet youth."[1] These words reflect the essence of a campaign for "aesthetic upbringing" (*esteticheskoe vospitanie*) that the Komsomol undertook in 1957. A far-reaching endeavor to garden young people's conception of what constituted tasteful and beautiful cultural expression, aesthetic upbringing denoted a hard-line shift away from the early Thaw emphasis on appealing to existing cultural consumption desires and proclivities.

This new initiative responded to a perceived excess of western cultural influence and unruly youth activism resulting from early Thaw cultural liberalism, the sixth Mezhdunarodnyi molodezhnyi festival' (International youth festival), and western Cold War propaganda. Officials clamped down on western popular culture and even somewhat limited youth initiative. Still, rather than focusing on suppression, the Komsomol emphasized providing an abundance of orthodox cultural recreation options, including *universitety kul'tury* (universities of culture), which were didactic cultural institutions meant to turn youth aesthetic tastes toward prescribed cultural norms. Many young people readily engaged in the normative cultural forms of the aesthetic upbringing campaign, exhibiting conformist agency and indicating some party-state gains in molding cultural preferences. However, the institutional problems in enacting the new top-level undertaking, along with the challenges of reaching those young people who enjoyed western popular culture, weakened its impact.

THE HARD-LINE SHIFT AND YOUTH CULTURAL POLICY

The Khrushchev leadership found itself in a bind in late 1956, as a result of the unanticipated ripple effects of his Secret Speech the preceding February. Khrushchev placed the blame for Stalin-era terror squarely on the shoulders of Stalin and certain secret police bureaucrats, thus absolving the party-state system as a whole of any guilt. Nonetheless, some of the most liberal individuals among the Soviet youth and intelligentsia went further, pointing to systemic failures and calling for fundamental reforms. Conversely, some militant officials and citizens openly rejected Khrushchev's criticism of Stalin; the republic of Georgia, Stalin's birthplace, experienced mass protests in defense of Stalin.[2] Khrushchev's revelations also sparked disturbances in eastern Europe, especially in Poland and Hungary, the latter suppressed by Soviet military force. Such reactions emboldened conservatives to attack post-Stalin reforms and helped persuade the many officials closer to the center of the political spectrum that de-Stalinization had gone too far and too fast. Furthermore, they gave pause to those inclined toward a moderately pluralistic approach, including Khrushchev. Indeed, an attempted coup in June 1957 almost removed the Soviet leader.[3]

As a result, by the end of 1956, central policy had begun to scale back the openness and decentralization of the early Thaw. In literature, B. L. Pasternak came under severe criticism for publishing *Doctor Zhivago* abroad, and the Soiuz Pisatelei (Writers' union) curtailed the freedoms granted to young writers in the immediate post-Stalin period.[4] At Moscow's Gnesinykh Muzyka Pedagogika-institut (Gnessin music-pedagogy institute), faculty restricted students' exposure to western classical music composers, such as George Gershwin.[5] Soviet ballet suffered from similar turmoil.[6]

For youth cultural policy, the plenum held in February 1957 represented the key shift. Shelepin condemned western propaganda as "fairy tales" and "bourgeois lies," calling on Komsomol cells "to struggle against blind kowtowing to everything western." He decried young people's excessive interest in western dances and jazz and their habit of buying records underground. He noted that preparations for the 1957 Mezhdunarodnyi molodezhnyi festival' in Moscow had led to the creation of too many jazz ensembles, "often with a poor program."[7]

To some extent, conservative central agencies had forced the Komsomol's hand. A report from the party's propaganda department criticized Komsomol newspapers for failing to conduct a "frontal assault against bourgeois ideology."[8] After a delegation of English students visited the Soviet Union, the Ministry of Foreign Affairs published an article entitled "Speculators and Hooligans" in an English newspaper, the *Observer*. It related how a minority of Soviet youth tried to emulate western ways and purchase western products from foreigners. The ministry suggested that youth organizations deal with the problems described to prevent any more negative press, especially due to the upcoming international festival, but western newspapers kept publishing stories about Soviet youth who longed for western material and cultural products.[9] In the context of Cold War cultural diplomacy, such pieces were especially problematic.

The question of including western elements in state-sponsored popular culture inspired much bureaucratic infighting. Shelepin sent a letter in early 1957 to the cultural department of the party Central Committee complaining that, in a speech, the first secretary of the Soiuz kompozitorov (Composers' union), Tikhon Khrennikov, had accused the Komsomol CC apparatus of over-promoting jazz collectives for the 1957 international festival. According to Shelepin, B. M. Iaroslavskii, a high-ranking cultural official, had inserted this phrase into Khrennikov's speech. Shelepin denied the charge, highlighting the fact that the Komsomol CC specifically condemned excessive preoccupation with creating jazz ensembles for the upcoming festival. In response, Iaroslavskii criticized the Komsomol CC for its support of an "Americanized form of western jazz," with its overuse of brass and percussion instruments and "cacophonic sound."[10] Attacks on the Komsomol by the Soiuz kompozitorov, the party propaganda department, and the foreign affairs ministry demonstrate that the Komsomol's soft-line position had left it vulnerable to censure from conservatives in other, generally more militant, central bureaucracies.

Such data spotlight the complex relationship between historical processes and Soviet central policy. Domestic and foreign disturbances and the growth of western cultural influence undoubtedly inspired anxieties among the political elites.[11] However, conflicting interpretations of these developments among hard- and soft-line officials were at least as important as their emotional reaction. Conservative bureaucrats successfully used the concerns that arose in officialdom to promote their position and cast doubt on early Thaw liberalization.

THE AESTHETIC UPBRINGING CAMPAIGN

Hard-liners' concerns about youth aesthetic tastes precipitated the aesthetic upbringing campaign. Komsomol leaders discussed raising cultural levels after the war but did not acknowledge problems with young people's cultural tastes until 1957, when the Komsomol CC bureau first mentioned youth aesthetic tastes.[12] However, branch Komsomol conferences, such as the one held in Moscow, began to pay serious attention to cultural tastes in 1956, suggesting that such concerns bubbled from lower- and mid-level conservative officials to influence the upper echelon.[13] The Komsomol leadership launched its aesthetic upbringing campaign at its plenum in February 1957, during which Shelepin advocated improving the "cultural level" and "aesthetic upbringing" of youth as part of the progress toward communism, a view that Khrushchev supported.[14] To this end, he argued that Komsomol cells needed to strengthen their struggle with western tastes by helping young people to "figure out what is truly artistic and beautiful," as many youth "emulated the bad tastes of the bourgeois West" because of foreign propaganda.[15] Liubov Baliasnaia attested to the powerful impact of the plenum on shaping youth cultural activities.[16] Discussions of tastes in music and dancing paralleled and intertwined with debates over appropriate fashion, in the Soviet Union as well as in other socialist countries.

The intensifying efforts to inculcate officially prescribed cultural tastes among youth amounted to a Thaw-era version of culturedness. This drive had some similarities to the Stalinist government's endeavor in the 1930s to instill culturedness, which encompassed cleanliness, sobriety, literacy, and disciplined labor for the whole of the population. However, Stalin-era policy imposed higher cultural standards on elites and the upwardly mobile, focusing on appropriate manners and dress, as well as normative aesthetic tastes and cultural knowledge, echoing the cultural values espoused by the prerevolutionary middle classes.[17] The Thaw-era campaign for aesthetic upbringing called for appropriate cultural tastes and knowledge among all youth, not just elites, making Thaw-era culturedness qualitatively different from its predecessor. At the same time, in reversing the loosening of cultural norms characteristic of the early Thaw, the drive in 1957 adopted gardening methods similar to those deployed during the anticosmopolitan period, if not nearly as harsh. Furthermore, Thaw-era culturedness built upon and advanced the post-Stalin administration's endeavor to use a variety of tools, including more thorough social controls, to transform daily life and help forge New Soviet Young Women and Men ready to build communism.

The Komsomol leadership's aesthetic upbringing campaign stemmed not only from the drive to construct communism but also from the need to fight the Cold War on the domestic cultural front. Shelepin's concern with western-influenced aesthetic tastes among youth shows that winning the cultural competition between the superpowers played a particularly important role in the attempt to shape youth aesthetic preferences. Furthermore, having western newspapers report on Soviet youth's proclivity for western culture hardly fit the Thaw-era goal of showcasing the Soviet project and its popular culture for international audiences. As in the 1930s, Soviet authorities paid close attention to what foreigners saw, thought, and reported.[18]

Top Komsomol officials did not denounce western cultural propaganda simply to achieve the aims of the newly conservative Kremlin;

they also responded to a transformation in American public diplomacy. In the late 1940s and early 1950s, the United States followed a brash and heavy-handed style in its foreign propaganda, while investing relatively few resources into the cultural elements of soft power. In 1954, however, President Dwight D. Eisenhower persuaded Congress to fund an expansion of cultural diplomacy measures. American propaganda acquired a much softer tone, emphasizing US cultural products that appealed to youth around the world, including those in the Soviet bloc.[19] The Komsomol's intensified condemnation of western efforts to subvert youth cultural tastes reflects the party-state's attempt to confront reforms in US cultural diplomacy, hinting that the changes in American cultural propaganda had proven effective.

The plenum in 1957 also revealed top-level anxieties over generational tensions. According to the plenum resolution, the youth cohort of the mid-1950s had grown up in a time when socialism triumphed and young people won many rights and privileges. The "current generation did not pass through the harsh school of revolutionary battle" as had their elders. Consequently, some among this young generation did not value the price paid "in blood and sweat" for its current situation, accepting their benefits and lifestyle as a given, "demanding much from the state and giving it little in return." The document criticized Komsomol organizations for failing to pay sufficient attention to this problem.[20]

This text makes clear the party's willingness to talk about generational tensions, thus challenging scholarship suggesting that the Soviet leadership avoided dealing with generational conflict as the Soviet Union matured in the postwar decades.[21] As shown by the plenum resolution, published in youth newspapers and discussed at Komsomol meetings, problems relating to generations certainly figured within the party-state's public rhetoric during some periods of the Thaw.[22] The Thirteenth Komsomol Congress, in 1958, also spotlighted generational tensions in Soviet society, using language similar to that employed in the plenum.[23]

By openly acknowledging the existence of a generation gap, the Komsomol CC stressed its determination to solve this problem. Thus, film directors highlighted generational tensions in Thaw-era movies, as in *Karnaval'naia noch'*, acting in some accord with top-level policies. Sometimes, they went beyond what the party line permitted, for instance, in Marlen Khutsiev's *Leninskoi gvardii* (Lenin's guard).[24] Showing intriguing similarities to the Soviets, the United States also had prominent public figures at this time openly worrying about its young generation growing "soft" and failing to appreciate personal sacrifice.[25] Such parallels indicate mutual concerns among the political elites in both superpowers over the quality of their young as Cold Warriors on the domestic front and speaks to conservative backlashes in the United States and Soviet Union over postwar cultural hedonism among the youth.

THE MOSCOW INTERNATIONAL YOUTH FESTIVAL

Soviet cultural diplomacy powerfully influenced the domestic front. Although Komsomol leaders launched the aesthetic upbringing campaign in February 1957, they delayed applying its most repressive elements until after the international youth festival in July and August. These international socialist youth festivals had begun in 1947 in Prague, followed by Budapest in 1949, East Berlin in 1951, Bucharest in 1953, and Warsaw in 1955. After Stalin's death, the new leadership made the bold choice of hosting one in Moscow, charging the Komsomol with organizing it.[26] The Kremlin wanted to use domestic cultural diplomacy to counter negative western propaganda that the Soviet Union was a repressive and isolated country. Instead, policy makers aspired to create a positive image among foreign audiences, both among the visitors themselves and in foreign press organs, through Soviet commitment to values such as internationalism, openness, youthhood, peace, and global unity.

Cognizant of Soviet intentions, the American and British governments countered by representing the event as nothing more than communist propaganda. To weaken the festival's legitimacy, US and UK officials strongly discouraged their citizens from attending, though they did not ban travel to it, lest such repressive measures undermine the idea that they defended the values of liberty and democracy. An inquiry from the US National Student Association about involvement in the festival led a US State Department official to reply that, while no formal ban existed, the department believed "that representation of respectable American student organizations could only contribute to the prestige of the Communist-dominated sponsors" and that such "participation therefore should be discouraged."[27] The president of this association, which was a supposedly independent institution that in reality received the large majority of its funding covertly from the American government as part of a state-private network of similarly financed organizations established in the early years of the Cold War, unsurprisingly agreed with this perspective.[28] Similarly, though the British embassy in Moscow generally favored organizing youth exchanges between the United Kingdom and Soviet Union, it insisted in an April 1957 letter that "international youth exchanges be kept outside politics." The author argued that the upcoming festival did not meet this criterion and recommended that British youth organizations not participate in the event.[29] Somewhat like their American counterparts, British youth organizations received support from government and private sources.[30] The British Foreign Office advised the Imperial Society of Ballroom Dancing to refuse a Soviet invitation to the festival, pointing out that the society, by participating, "would be lending themselves to a particularly blatant piece of Soviet propaganda aimed at influencing young people in favour of the communist way of life." Taking the hint, the society turned down the invitation, noting in its letter to the Soviet organizers that "a preference has been expressed by cultural authorities in this country that we should not take part."[31]

The same message awaited Barbara Perry, a Chicago ballerina, who requested State Department approval to participate in the festival. State Department officials responded that in the eyes of the government, the festival was "an instrument of communist propaganda," and they advised Perry that she should "not engage in any effort to encourage participation in the Moscow festival." Unusually, Perry pressed her case, arguing to a State Department staffer that American participation would "provide a wonderful chance for young Americans to show what our country and its people are really like," thus making "use of the Festival or even 'capture it' for our own purposes." The State Department bureaucrat rejected Perry's claims, yet Perry persevered, acquiring support from the *Chicago Daily News* and Rep. Barratt O'Hara and collaborating with the Chicago Council of Soviet-American Friendship.[32] Her efforts became a communist cause célèbre; *Komsomol'skaia pravda* interviewed her about this opposition from the State Department.[33] In spite of obstructionism from the British and American governments, a number of young people from these countries, including a delegation that Perry organized, managed to attend the youth festival.

To these and other festival visitors, the Soviet leadership strove to convey that the Soviet Union's version of popular culture represented a progressive and appealing alternative to the western model. The implementation of these plans illustrates Soviet Cold War cultural diplomacy on the domestic front. Komsomol newspapers called on young people throughout the country to prepare for the upcoming festival.[34] The Komsomol CC mobilized its branch organizations to assist.[35] In a marked change from late Stalinist insularity, clubs organized numerous events for young people to learn about foreign cultures, customs, histories, social structures, and languages.[36]

Local youth festivals helped the Komsomol prepare for the international festival. These festivals originated from late Stalin-era youth sports contests and amateur arts competitions. The genre of the *festival' molodezhi* (youth festival) represented a departure in state-sponsored popular culture, however. These events combined youth festivities, such as parades and evening parties, with amateur arts and sports competitions, with at least one held in January 1953.[37] The Komsomol's central apparatus began supporting these events in 1954.[38] The preparation for the 1957 international festival proved the key element for youth festivals attaining a mass character, as the central Komsomol apparatus called on local and regional Komsomol cells to organize a series of youth festivals to gear up for the big event.[39]

Amateur performances were considered vital to convincing visitors that the Soviet Union had an attractive popular culture. National, regional, and local press articles underscored the importance of demonstrating a high level of achievement in amateur performances for foreigners.[40] For example, a wall newspaper in the Moscow factory of Trekhgornaia Manufaktura called for worker youth to "learn new songs and dances" in the club to prepare for the festival.[41] Cultural institutions devoted considerable energy to getting their amateur arts ready for the festival.[42]

Furthermore, the Komsomol leaders decided to permit American elements in official jazz performances to a degree not seen since the war; the goal was to undermine western propaganda claims about Soviet cultural censorship and truly impress young foreigners with the young artists' talents in the most fashionable musical genre among youth around the globe.[43] Consequently, many jazz collectives appeared, assisted, as the exchange between Iaroslavskii and Shelepin hinted, by the Komsomol CC. Its decree in January 1956 on amateur music competitions for the festival included a contest for jazz and light music ensembles, which contributed to the widespread formation of such groups. Komsomol CC representatives built up the number of jazz collectives as well. For instance, one Komsomol official recommended that the Moskovskaia konservatoriia (Moscow conservatory) establish a jazz ensemble.[44] Other central agencies also helped promote jazz prior to the festival, including the Soviet Council of Ministers, which approved the festival's holding of jazz and light music amateur competitions.[45]

Responding to such signals, trade union clubs, educational institutions, and youth initiative clubs established jazz-style variety ensembles in droves.[46] It is thus no wonder that hard-liners in the Moscow Dom narodnogo tvorchestva (House of folk creativity or folk arts) complained that out of thirty-six ensembles that took part in a preliminary competition for the upcoming festival, thirty-three played "in the spirit and style of a western jazz ensemble." Since the ideological militants at the folk arts house controlled the jury for that particular contest, they permitted only those three groups that did not perform explicitly western music to advance.[47] However, plenty of competitions had more pluralistically oriented officials in the jury, encouraging the performance of the most daring, American-style jazz elements.[48] This situation resulted in a widespread perception that there was ever-growing room for jazz in the Soviet Union, as recalled by Lev Figlin, a Saratov jazz musician who played jazz-style music in one such preliminary festival contest.[49]

Jazz was prominent at the festival itself.[50] Aleksei Kozlov recalled jazz concerts as the most fashionable and difficult-to-access events.[51] Iu. V. Saul'skii's collective impressed both Soviet citizens and visitors from abroad, winning a silver medal.[52] Other Soviet ensembles with western musical elements also lit up the scene, prompting hard-line opposition. One jury member lambasted the Uralmash factory collective as "the most vulgar expression of western popular music," stating that, if he had had his way, the group would not have been allowed to perform. But other jurors, including a representative from the Komsomol, commended the Uralmash ensemble for its superb performance and proposed awarding it the second-place prize in its category. With the endorsement of soft-line jurors, the Uralmash collective received its prize.[53]

Thus, a tolerant perspective triumphed at the festival, which certainly had an impact on the jazz scene and western dancing in the Soviet Union. Foreign jazz-style bands brought expert knowledge of the newest jazz forms—bebop and cool jazz—and impressed Soviet jazz enthusiasts greatly. A Czechoslovak jazz group just beat out Saul'skii's ensemble to win the festival's gold medal in amateur light music performance. Interacting with foreign jazz collectives enabled Soviet jazz musicians to make transnational connections that paved the way for later exchanges.[54] This proved especially true for jazz musicians from socialist states. Contacts with those counterparts had already begun before the festival, as when the Polish Blue Jazz Band toured the Soviet Union in 1956.[55] Such cultural influence from eastern Europe shows that western Europe and the United States did not represent the only "Other" for the Soviet Union. Still, western and especially American groups left a particularly strong impression. Both Kozlov and Aleksei Kuznetsov recalled their admiration for the English jazz quintet led by Jeff Ellison.[56] The Muscovite Vitalii Kleinot described how he enjoyed dancing the boogie-woogie with foreign youth.[57]

The festival's cultural influence worked both ways. Soviet jazz activities had a positive impact, including at the level of person-to-person interactions. Kozlov's knowledge of and love for jazz left a very good impression on Ellison's quintet. Kozlov felt proud that he had helped "improve the image that foreigners had about the country," and in the process he "felt [himself] a patriot."[58] Postfestival discourse in American newspapers spoke of the popularity of jazz among Soviet youth during the festival, thus humanizing the Soviet Union's population for the wary American public.[59] The skills of Soviet jazz musicians dazzled foreigners, who began to invite the best Soviet jazz players to perform, including Georgii Garanian, although travel restrictions prevented Soviet jazz musicians from going abroad.[60]

The successes of Soviet cultural diplomacy went beyond jazz and dancing, however. For instance, the Soviet press published an article about Barbara Perry's festival experience in which she praised the warmth of the Soviet people and officials in greeting the American delegation. Convinced that "the Soviet people want peace and friendship" with the United States, she disagreed with her government's claim that the festival pursued Soviet propaganda aims.[61] Similarly, Charlotte Saxe, a young American festival-goer, wrote a letter to President Eisenhower stating that

> the ardent and intense desires of the Russian people for peace touched the hearts of all the American delegates at the Festival, even though many of the Americans who attended the Festival were conservative and in no way sympathetic towards communism. . . . The Russians are such a kind and friendly and hospitable people, Mr. President, that I am certain that if you had been in Moscow during the Festival your heart would have been touched too and you and the State Department would increase your efforts to find a solution whereby we could live in peace and harmony with such a wonderful people. And not only the people, but also the Soviet government wants peace above all else.[62]

To help achieve peace, Saxe asked the president to dissolve the North Atlantic Treaty Organization (NATO) and remove the air bases surrounding the Soviet Union. At another point in her letter, Saxe wrote, "I had believed what I read in our newspapers—that the Russian people had a low standard of living, that they were badly dressed, and that Moscow was a drab city. But I found that what I read in the newspapers wasn't true at all, because in Moscow I was impressed with how high the standard of living is. And the people are well-dressed and in my opinion Moscow is certainly not a drab city." Apparently, the president read this letter, discussed it with Secretary of State John F. Dulles, and had a State Department official answer Saxe at length, telling her that her letters faithfully reflected "the propaganda image of Soviet-American relations now promulgated by the Soviet government."

British youth also felt the impact of the festival. For instance, one young factory worker from London told UK officials that he had a "leftish leaning which deepened during my stay in Moscow." Another young Londoner spoke very favorably about the festival and his reception in the Soviet Union.[63] A UK government memorandum noted that, overall, the festival had inspired only modest sympathy for the Soviet Union among western youth but had had a substantial impact on Asian and African visitors, adding that "this was no doubt the field in which [Soviet authorities] had been most eager to score a success."[64] Considering Saxe's letter and the many positive depictions of the festival in the western press, the British may have underestimated the festival's impact on westerners.

Long-term UK and US Cold War interests would arguably have been better served by a more active and strategic cultural diplomacy effort regarding the festival, rather than simply denouncing the event and discouraging their citizens from attending. A more effective tactic might have included educating western attendees about the Soviet system, debriefing festival-goers about their experiences, and, perhaps most importantly, sending the best artists and athletes to perform in the festival competitions. As it was, foreign competitors often outdid their Soviet counterparts, prompting conservatives in the Moscow Dom narodnogo tvorchestva to complain about the poor organization of the festival's ballroom dancing contest, saying that it had turned into "an advertisement and propaganda only for western dances." The folk arts house lamented that the dancers representing foreign countries "were clearly not of festival age" but substantially older, "not ordinary youth but European champions with multiple titles."[65] This statement suggests that the British government had lost a valuable opportunity for scoring a victory in the Cold War's cultural front by discouraging the Imperial Society of Ballroom Dancing from sending a delegation, despite the society noting that its participation would "provide an admirable shop-window for British ballroom dancing—a field in which we could certainly beat all comers."[66]

Such missteps underscore some of the problems in US and UK foreign cultural diplomacy efforts toward socialist states. Scholars have shown that cultural exchanges in later years had a powerful impact on Soviet citizens; starting such programs earlier might have reaped considerable rewards for western states. Furthermore, even when the US and UK governments began to engage in substantial cultural exchanges at the end of the 1950s, they invested relatively few resources in such endeavors.[67] In short, western governments failed to take full advantage of the opportunity to present their models of modernity in the best light to the citizens of socialist and nonsocialist states alike, weakening western positions on the Cold War cultural front.

AESTHETIC UPBRINGING AND WESTERN POPULAR CULTURE AFTER THE FESTIVAL

The immediate postfestival future looked gloomy for youth interested in jazz. The Komsomol no longer needed to support this music for the sake of public diplomacy, which had been a key argument for pluralistically in-clined officials. Moreover, the impact of foreign jazz ensembles on the So-viet Union, as part of a broader inflow of western cultural influence during the festival, inspired a hard-line backlash. Liubov Baliasnaia recalled that Komsomol officials at the time perceived the increased access to the out-side world as something that "needed to be opposed."[68] Furthermore, the next major celebration, the fortieth anniversary of the 1917 October Rev-olution, proved conducive to more conservative musical styles, with pieces oriented toward political propaganda and military parades.[69]

As a result, a hard-line shift in cultural policy that occurred in late 1957 included assaults on jazz. Soon after the festival ended, the journal *Sovetskaia kul'tura* denounced Iurii Saul'skii's ensemble as "musical *stili-agi*" who played vulgar music. Despite winning the festival's silver med-al, Saul'skii's group had to disband. Garanian joined Oleg Lundstrom's variety band, which, Garanian complained, played only one or two jazz pieces out of every twenty-five numbers it performed.[70] At a Komsomol conference in Saratov's Kirov neighborhood in November 1957, the key-note censured the many amateur music circles "that perform pieces lacking in ideological content," such as numbers by the American swing-style jazz trumpeter Harry James.[71] Moscow's Komsomol also censured jazz bands.[72]

Many club managers disbanded their jazz collectives under pres-sure from militants. The amateur competitions that had preceded the 1957 international youth festival played an important role in enabling the hard-liners at the Moscow Dom narodnogo tvorchestva to identify and target groups that performed American-style jazz music.[73] With support from the central cultural bureaucracy, the Moscow folk arts house ac-quired the right to confirm all directors for Moscow's amateur collectives in 1958, giving them much more control over amateur circles.[74] While the hard-line turn strengthened control organs, militant lower-level Komso-mol cadres revived the anticosmopolitan-era groups known as *muzykal'nye patruli* (music patrols), which checked music ensembles' repertoires, de-nouncing those that played American-style jazz.[75]

Yet, the pendulum of top-level cultural policy did not swing back fully to the wholesale rejection of western popular culture characteristic of late Stalinism. Thus, Shelepin wrote a letter to the Council of Ministers in 1957 asking for an increase in the production of musical instruments, in-cluding saxophones, to raise youth participation in amateur circles.[76] A re-quest for the instrument symbolizing jazz would have been unimaginable during the anticosmopolitan years.

Instead of a ban on jazz, the fall of 1957 witnessed limitations on jazz, and the vast majority of existing jazz groups found ways to accommo-

FIG. 6.1. A jazz-style variety ensemble performance at the Saratov peda-gogicheskii institut (Saratov pedagogical institute). Courtesy of the private archive of Iurii Zhimskii.

date the party-state's new restrictions. Bands like that of Oleg Lundstrom played a mix of mostly light variety music with a few jazz pieces per evening performance. Konstantin Marvin related that his quartet combined jazz pieces with what he termed "patriotic songs."[77] The groups had less improvisation and other elements associated with an Americanized jazz style. Ensembles relied less on brass and percussion instruments, which Iaroslavskii had condemned, and included many more string and other instruments. The Saratov jazz musician Iurii Zhimskii's ensemble combined a saxophone, clarinet, piano, drums, accordion, maracas, and a guitar. The group had a female pianist, a rare exception to the general trend of all-male jazz musicians, but was otherwise representative (fig. 6.1).

The party-state's despotic tactics curbed the rapid growth of jazz ensembles and their inclusion of American-style elements in their repertoires, such as pieces in the bebop and cool jazz styles. Still, these revisions in music proved relatively mild. In 1957, the authorities launched a massive clampdown against dissent that resulted in the highest rate of arrests during the Khrushchev era.[78] Yet, unlike in the anticosmopolitan campaign, jazz musicians were under no threat of being jailed. They performed at *khaltury* (moonlighters or jazz evenings) with nary a trace of fear, with the preferences of their audiences serving as the only limitation on their music. Within more open settings, they continued to use deceptive tactics to get around restrictions. Some do not even recall 1957 as a particularly bad year, with their impressions of the jazz at the international youth festival crowding out the antijazz campaign.[79]

Besides the attacks against jazz, the government's hard-line turn in 1957 resulted in some hesitancy regarding youth self-management. In his speech at the Seventh Komsomol CC Plenum, held in 1957, Shelepin praised initiative from below by local Komsomol cells but also underscored the need to maintain unity of purpose in the Komsomol's work.[80] By doing so, Shelepin stepped back from the unvarnished support of youth grassroots activism that he had offered only a year prior to that, at the Twentieth Party Congress, in 1956.[81] In their reports on the implementation of the 1957 plenum, some Komsomol committees in the provinces went even further. The Kemerovo Komsomol, for instance, stated that "youth initiative requires a degree of direction and close management."[82] While many mid-level Komsomol cadres who came to power under Stalin may have thought so privately, making such claims in official internal documents constituted a radically hard-line position. Most reports on the enactment of the plenum instead spotlighted attempts to develop youth initiative, not manage it from the top.[83] The Komsomol hierarchy exerted more control over initiative-based cultural institutions, such as the youth initiative clubs that had opened in Minsk during 1956 and early 1957. After the militant shift, the Kemerovo Komsomol committee created the Tsentral'nyi Komsomol'skii klub (Central Komsomol club) to unify such collectives, which resulted in closer oversight from above.[84]

This pattern—cultural liberalization followed by a backlash against youth "excesses"—paralleled what occurred in other twentieth-century authoritarian states. In Italy, for example, the Mussolini government granted youth significant autonomy and support for their cultural expression to involve them in the project of forging a fascist modernity. However, this resulted in some young people using the arts to challenge the fascist social hierarchy and call for social justice, prompting the authorities to impose more stringent restrictions.[85] In China, the party-state encouraged a wide variety of pluralistic voices on policy issues through cultural expression and public criticism in the 1956–57 Hundred Flowers campaign. Meant to advance the cause of building communism, this initiative, in the eyes of the leadership, had gotten out of control by July 1957, resulting in a crackdown on grassroots youth autonomy and public criticism.[86]

These similarities reflect a recurrent tension within modern authoritarian efforts to create an ideologically informed vision of a nonwestern modernity. Perceiving a lack of popular engagement, policy makers attempted to inspire enthusiasm and activism among the masses, including through granting some independence. Often, doing so led to what many among the officialdom perceived as "excesses," prompting the hierarchy to rein in popular autonomy and reimpose centralized controls. Top-down management, in turn, led to a deficit of grassroots involvement and loss of faith, causing concern among officials, who then advocated for getting the population engaged, restarting the cycle once again.

THE MARCH FOR CULTURE

In the aesthetic upbringing initiative's efforts to garden the cultural tastes of young Soviet people, despotic power elements represented a relatively small component. The new campaign focused instead on infrastructural power strategies designed to increase youth access to orthodox state-sponsored popular culture and to teach young people about prescribed cultural tastes. At the Seventh Komsomol CC Plenum, in 1957, Shelepin proposed assisting young people in "appropriately evaluating literature, art, sculpture, and music," a sentiment echoed in Komsomol newspapers.[87] Similarly, in November 1957, the Ministry of Culture ordered all cultural institutions to make youth aesthetic upbringing an obligatory part of their plans.[88]

To do so, the Komsomol hierarchy launched the "pokhod komsomol'tsev za dal'neishii pod"em kul'turnogo urovnia molodezhi" (Komsomol march for further elevating the cultural level of young people), or what I shall term the "march for culture."[89] One detailed report described how the Bashkiriia Province Komsomol committee directed each of its members to participate, over the next two years, in an amateur arts circle, interest-based association, or sports group and to get at least one other youth involved as well. All Komsomol members would "learn how to dance" (that is, in a nonwestern manner), watch movies about once a week, visit the theater once or twice a month, go to a museum once a year, and read actively. Each member would volunteer four times a month for construction work of relevance to the march for culture. Finally, members with a higher education would be trained to direct an amateur circle or sports group.[90] This list demonstrates the cultural practices and personal duties that the Bashkiriia Komsomol saw as congruent with Thaw-era culturedness.

Bashkiriia Komsomol organizations also took on a set of institutional obligations. During 1957 and 1958, each local Komsomol cell had to organize amateur circles, youth clubs, and local movie festivals. The provincial Bashkiriia Komsomol branch promised to help build 150 new club buildings, renovate 300 existing ones, and purchase equipment such as musical instruments, radios, record players, televisions, and so on. In addition, it would direct one thousand Komsomol members to work in the cultural network and organize a series of events, including a large amateur competition and a youth festival.[91]

Plans from elsewhere, in Voronezh and Rostov provinces, for instance, set similar goals.[92] Among the events that Komsomol organs planned were Komsomol weddings, a novel ritual for youth that used cultural activities to inculcate not only officially prescribed cultural tastes but also gender norms, part of a broader post-Stalin drive to ascribe civic meaning to ceremonies and ritual.[93] First mentioned in 1954, these weddings began to appear across the Soviet Union with the enactment of the 1957 aesthetic upbringing initiative.[94] Official discourse, as expressed by *Komsomol'skaia pravda*, touted state-sponsored weddings in clubs as a way to undermine religious wedding traditions, in keeping with Khrushchev's antireligion campaign, and to minimize the drunkenness and untoward behavior prevalent at private wedding feasts.[95] The authorities also intended Komsomol weddings to ensure the stability of the family. As noted by Shelepin in 1957, private marriages often ended in divorce, but "when someone gets married openly, in front of the people, his friends and comrades—it is another matter altogether."[96] Such rituals aimed to place relationships between young men and women within the boundaries of government-monitored official collectives, in effect reframing the norms of courting and family life from private to more public settings and ensuring the performance of officially preferred gendered behavior.[97]

By 1958, all province- and republic-level Komsomol organizations had laid out two- and three-year plans for raising youth cultural levels. Altogether, they took on the obligation to use youth volunteer labor to help build more than 25,000 clubs and other buildings used for cultural activities, as well as to renovate and beautify 40,000 such structures and to train more than 30,000 cultural workers.[98] The Komsomol achieved some successes in its march for culture. In 1957, Saratov's provincial Komsomol committed youth volunteer labor to the construction of 350 clubs and libraries over the next two years. By 1958, the Komsomol had assisted in completing 204 such buildings.[99] The Bashkiriia Komsomol's efforts proved so exemplary that the Komsomol's publishing arm, Molodaia gvardiia, published an instruction booklet about Bashkiriia's march for culture.[100] According to the Eighth Komsomol CC Plenum, held in 1960, young volunteers participated in building more than 12,000 clubs and 16,000 movie theaters, renovating more than 40,000 cultural structures, and training 25,000 cultural workers, nearly fulfilling the 1957 plan.[101] However, as the Saratov Komsomol indicated in 1959, getting individual Komsomol youth engaged in prescribed cultural activities proved more difficult.[102]

Many aspects of the aesthetic upbringing drive continued into the end of the 1950s and early 1960s. At the Twenty-First Communist Party Congress, held in 1959, the Soviet leadership spoke of the need to promote aesthetic upbringing, a sentiment echoed at the Eighth Komsomol CC Plenum, in 1960, and the Fourteenth Komsomol Congress, in 1962.[103]

The Komsomol's institutional priorities were apparent in its emphasis on the infrastructural power the march for culture would have in enacting the aesthetic upbringing campaign, as opposed to using despotic tactics. An extensive crackdown on all things western would have alienated many youth from the Komsomol, thereby undermining the goals of increasing membership, soliciting youth volunteers, acquiring financial stability, and meeting the overarching Thaw-era goal of mobilizing young citizens to build a socialist modernity. Consequently, while Komsomol rhetoric both condemned western culture and called for increasing the supply of more noncontroversial club activities, the Komsomol apparatus focused its policy enactment on the latter, something that Soviet youth could embrace, or at least not oppose.

The Komsomol's march for culture also found widespread approval among party-state cultural agencies, whose officials considered participation in orthodox state-sponsored popular culture conducive to cultivating normative aesthetic tastes. Tikhon Khrennikov, in a letter to the party Central Committee, wrote that amateur music collectives "play a major role in the ideological and aesthetic upbringing of a member of the new communist society."[104] Cultural institutions benefited on a pragmatic level from the Komsomol's drive to have youth volunteers build clubs and to train Komsomol members to staff these establishments.

The rapid increase in orthodox cultural activities fit well with the party-state leadership's post-Stalinist shift toward satisfying desires to consume. Khrushchev, at the April 1958 Komsomol congress, censured ongoing state-sponsored popular culture as insufficient to meet the growing "spiritual needs of the population." He encouraged the Komsomol to pressure enterprises to build more clubs and to construct some using youth volunteer labor.[105] At that same congress, Shelepin directly tied aesthetic upbringing to the fight against "the propagandists of western culture who try to instill tastes and views foreign to us among our youth."[106] Khrushchev's speech, read in the context of Shelepin's words, suggests that policy makers intended the growth in the provision of more orthodox state-sponsored cultural activities to counterbalance the limitations set on western popular culture, continuing the legitimating impact of the post-Stalin social contract.

Likewise, cadres across the political spectrum could agree on certain aspects of the march for culture. For those more conservative, increasing the number of prescribed cultural activities helped inculcate the party line and fight western popular culture. For the liberally inclined, it appeased youth desires, and the construction efforts provided a framework for future pluralistic cultural initiatives.

UNIVERSITIES OF CULTURE
MISSION, STRUCTURE, AND GROWTH

Universities of culture, which offered free or very cheap courses on cultural topics, embodied the didactic elements of the aesthetic upbringing initiative. Largely established in clubs, these institutions received endorsement from both Komsomol and party central committees, the Ministry of Culture, trade unions, the Vsesoiuznoye obshchestvo po rasprostraneniiu politicheskikh i nauchnykh znanii (All-Union society for the dissemination of political and scientific knowledge, known better as the Obshchestvo znanii (Knowledge society), and other agencies.[107] The mission of these institutions was to promote cultural enlightenment and aesthetic upbringing. In a typical statement, the Arkhangel'sk party propaganda department reported that the universities provided the population with cultural knowledge and refined their "artistic tastes," helping create "fully developed and prepared members of communist society."[108]

Universities of culture consisted of courses covering topics considered requisite for cultured New Soviet Women and Men, including music, theater, art, cinema, and literature. The university at Saratov's Enterprise No. 447 had two-year courses from mid-September to mid-April, with four-hour weekly sessions.[109] In 1959, the Ministry of Culture presented a recommended educational program, which suggested 114 total educational hours for a music course. Course hours were divided between the study of Russian and foreign classical music, Soviet music, music theory, Marxist-Leninist aesthetics, and party resolutions regarding cultural policy. Some lessons explicitly targeted western popular culture. One class meeting bore the title "Modern Ballroom Dances and the Struggle with Foreign Influence in Dancing." Another was "Criticism of the Reactionary View of Bourgeois Art Theorists."[110] With some variations, the curriculums of other universities generally corresponded to this one.[111] The program of these universities, which included Soviet cultural products, Russian and foreign classical traditions, folk themes, Marxist-Leninist aesthetics, recent political statements on culture, and an antiwestern orientation, reflected the canon for Thaw-era culturedness.

Universities spent most of their time on less explicitly politicized topics, and they also combined lectures with more engaging and active events. Thus, the universities held seminars and organized conferences, debates, lecture-concerts, meetings with artists, and collective discussion of art exhibits, movies, and music, and these events reportedly drew in many attendees.[112] For instance, the first day of a university of culture in a club for young construction workers in Leningrad featured a lecture, concert, art exhibit, movie, and meetings with musicians and artists.[113] University of culture lecturers used group visits and subsequent discussions to ensure a normative interpretation of the cultural activity.

Universities of culture had antecedents in imperial Russia, where the progressive intelligentsia offered lecture cycles that provided cultural knowledge to the masses in establishments called Narodnyie Universitety (People's universities) and Narodnyie Teplitsy (People's conservatories).[114] Bolshevik cultural organs promoted similar institutions and events during the civil war and the 1920s, but they generally faded away under Stalin in favor of lectures on culture that lacked entertaining components. The 1920s saw some Soviet clubs provide lectures in series called *vecherniie universitety* (evening universities) or *voskresen'ie universitety* (Sunday universities), which focused on literacy and basic knowledge, including cultural elements.[115]

The Thaw-era universities of culture movement originated in lower-level Komsomol organizations during the early post-Stalin years. The Bashkiriia and Voronezh Komsomol organizations spoke of establishing universities of culture in response to the 1957 plenum.[116] This notion percolated up to the Komsomol leadership. In 1958, Shelepin spoke of universities of culture as a praiseworthy new form, and he singled out the Bashkiriia and Voronezh Komsomol cells as good models for organizing cultural activities.[117]

The center's adoption of initiatives pioneered at lower levels shows the potential for local initiatives to have a widespread impact during times of reform. The Komsomol cadres from the Bashkiriia and Voronezh Komsomol organizations received credit for an innovation that the Komsomol CC found worthy, an example of what might be called "socialist entrepreneurship." Baliasnaia also confirmed that the Komsomol leadership sought out worthy grassroots innovations and promoted them as recommended best practices.[118]

Such methods show similarities to how the leadership of other authoritarian states introduced novel developments into their own governance and policies. For an example unrelated to culture, Nazi German leaders took up innovative practices from local cadres for implementing the Holocaust and enacted them throughout the eastern front. This suggests intriguing parallels between the ways different modern autocratic government structures channeled and made use of the entrepreneurial energies of grassroots officials.

Other central agencies also promoted the universities of culture. The Ministry of Culture directed all local cultural institutions to assist the universities in implementing a decree issued in February 1959, and even the party Central Committee enacted, in October 1960, a resolution on improving the universities of culture.[119] Such top-level endorsement led to rapid growth. The total number of universities of culture in the Soviet Union grew from more than 2,200 in 1959 to 8,000 in 1961, serving well over 1.25 million participants.[120] Growth slowed thereafter, with the total reaching 10,000 universities of culture by 1963.[121] A small but growing number of universities began to specialize in nonartistic matters, such as health, agricultural knowledge, and science and technology.

ORGANIZATION, CHALLENGES, AND IMPACT

Club managers generally took on the organizational tasks related to setting up universities of culture. They received assistance from volunteer councils that planned and managed university activities. Officials from the Komsomol, party, trade unions, and elsewhere, as well as cultural professionals, performers, teachers, and other interested members of the intelligentsia, staffed the universities of culture. Members of the cultural intelligentsia helped create the educational plans and led the lessons, while party-state officials reviewed the plans and provided the material resources required. Official rhetoric frequently emphasized that the universities relied on the volunteer labor of party-state cadres and cultural professionals.[122]

To some extent, therefore, the universities of culture served as a collaborative effort between political elites and the intelligentsia. For the latter, serving the universities of culture contributed to the traditional intelligentsia goal of bringing culture to the masses.[123] Their participation also allowed cultural intelligentsia professionals to improve their official biographies through volunteer social activism, which was particularly important for party members. Community service in universities of culture enrolled the cultural intelligentsia as Cold War combatants on the domestic cultural front, particularly since official rhetoric tied aesthetic upbringing to the fight against western cultural propaganda. Furthermore, the cultural intelligentsia's volunteer activities at the universities added to the Khrushchev leadership's endeavor to mobilize the population into active societal self-management.

Local organizations helped the universities both practically and financially. Concert halls, music colleges, theaters, cinemas, museums, and other cultural establishments sometimes assisted the universities of culture as part of their public service. They offered free or cheap tickets, sent cultural professionals to give lectures and perform at concerts, and provided musical instruments, movie reels, and other forms of cultural equipment.[124] In many cases, enterprises, trade unions, party cells, and other organizations provided direct funding to clubs for the costs associated with hosting universities of culture.[125]

Volunteer labor by cultural intelligentsia and support from local organizations helped the universities offer free or heavily subsidized courses.[126] Aleksander Vygnanov, a mid-ranking Komsomol official at a Moscow technical institute from 1958 to 1963, boasted to me in an interview that students received inexpensive subscription cards to the university of culture hosted by the institute's club. Some even received the cards for free as rewards.[127]

Top officials wanted the universities to target workers and collective farmers in particular as part of the Khrushchev leadership's effort to uplift the lower social classes through education in a Soviet version of cultural affirmative action.[128] Such endeavors provide nuance to scholarly claims about the lack of state-sponsored entertainment offerings for the working classes.[129] In 1959, the Ministry of Culture, Komsomol leadership, and Obshchestvo znanii passed a joint circular suggesting that the universities of culture give preference for entry to those with less interest in the arts, implying that they needed cultural education the most.[130] Four years later, the Ministry of Culture disparaged inadequate efforts in getting workers and collective farmers to visit the universities.[131] Such statements indicate that, although the leaders wanted to enroll more members of the working class, those from middle-class backgrounds with a better education and higher interest in cultural activities took greater advantage of the universities. In part, this imbalance resulted from workers and peasants rejecting the kind of middle-class cultural values inherent within the aesthetic upbringing campaign.[132] This development paralleled similar issues faced by cultural intelligentsia in earlier periods when they sought to use cultural programs to uplift working-class cultural tastes.[133]

Attendance represented another point of concern. Some universities of culture received praise for their success in maintaining audience interest.[134] Conversely, a report in 1960 criticized universities in Stalinsk Province because less than 50 percent of those who signed up finished the courses. Apparently, "the low quality of lectures" led to audience dissatisfaction.[135] The Ministry of Culture complained in 1963 that most universities of culture failed to organize "active learning," including seminars, conferences, discussions, debates, and collective excursions.[136]

Additional problems stemmed from local institutions providing inadequate aid. The Komsomol CC in 1960 demanded that concert halls, cinemas, museums, and other cultural establishments provide the universities of culture with more art exhibitions, movie reels, concert brigades, and the like.[137] Officials at the university of culture affiliated with Saratov's Enterprise No. 447 requested that the provincial Ministry of Culture supply artists to perform for the university audience without requiring fees. They also asked that the philharmonic discount prices for the students.[138]

Such financial issues proved a particularly sore point for the universities of culture. The Komsomol propaganda department admitted in 1960 that some cultural workers saw giving lectures as "a means of financial support," with a number of lecturers in Leningrad apparently demanding very high sums.[139] In 1963, a Moscow metallurgical enterprise's university of culture accused the local branches of the Obshchestvo znanii and concert organizations of placing themselves in a ludicrous position by demanding money for propagandizing Soviet ideology, "a despicable practice that causes significant harm to ideological work." As a result, the university had to charge fees, which upset audience members who expected free classes, and a number dropped out.[140] Thus, consumption motives and market forces conflicted with and undermined the ideological goals of cultural officials, who had to use financial incentives to motivate many cultural professionals to respond to ideological exhortations.

It is thus no wonder that some club managers, behind closed doors, grumbled over universities of culture. At a conference of Moscow club workers in 1962, the assistant director of Zueb, a Moscow club, lamented the fact that "all clubs are obliged to establish these universities of culture." He claimed that this innovation fit less well in some clubs than others.[141] His words underscore the excesses that resulted from top-level efforts to spread innovations that worked well in one context but poorly others, an example being the Thaw-era corn campaign.[142] This finding suggests broad similarities among problematic aspects of post-Stalin governance.

Although these universities of culture embodied the aesthetic upbringing initiative associated with the militant turn in late 1956, they still constituted a place of conflict between hard-line and soft-line cadres. Some criticized these universities for placing undue emphasis on cultural activities and not enough on political propaganda. In 1959, a Komsomol, Ministry of Culture, and Obshchestvo znanii circular was already critiquing the fact that many university educational plans primarily stressed cultural themes. The three agencies instead stated that, together with cultural topics, the universities had to address science and technology, the Seven-Year Plan, and the general goals of communist construction.[143] An investigation into an agricultural institute's university of culture in Saratov resulted in its program being censured for the predominance of cultural and prerevolutionary topics and insufficient attention to the political position of the party and the achievements of Soviet technology.[144] In contrast, an internal Ministry of Culture report from 1961 criticized the view that the study of the arts in the universities of culture constituted "an expression of 'cultural excess' condemned by the Communist Party."[145] The more liberal position thus tilted more toward cultural activities, as opposed to political propaganda.

Archival party-state reports and publications suggest that the universities made substantial achievements in aesthetic upbringing for their students. The Arkhangel'sk Krasnyi Nakoval'nia (Red anvil) factory's university of culture reportedly helped its audience members develop an interest "in serious musical compositions and paintings."[146] A worker from the Uralmash factory credited his attendance at a university class with expanding his cultural horizons and enriching his knowledge of literature and the arts. Two workers at a clothing enterprise in Moscow mentioned that they had learned a great deal about art at a university class.[147]

Those who compiled official sources may well have exaggerated the positive influence of the aesthetic upbringing campaign. However, interviews with those who were the objects of the campaign help confirm that aesthetic upbringing programs combining cultural education and entertainment appealed to and influenced those who participated in them. Nelli Popkova, who emerged from a middle-class, well-educated background, described how she and her friends went to "unforgettable" free courses on art in Saratov's Radishchev Gosudarstvennyi khudozhestvennyi muzei (Radishchev state art museum) during her youth. She and her clique "went with great pleasure" and "learned a great deal about music" at lecture-concerts offered by the Saratovskii gosudarstvennyi filarmonicheskii (Saratov state philharmonic), which cost a nominal sum. In the mid-1970s, Popkova worked as a librarian at Saratovskii gosudarstvennyi universitet (SGU, Saratov's state university) and delivered lectures on literature at a university of culture.[148] Iurii Sokolov, a worker who came from Kaluga to attend the Moskovskii energeticheskii institut (Moscow energy institute), recalled feeling that he and others who came from outside Moscow felt culturally inferior, "with a big gap" in comparison to Muscovites. The institute's house of culture, however, provided many superb educational and cultural activities. According to Sokolov, the events there, free for students, greatly advanced his cultural growth.[149]

Interviews with officials who worked directly with youth attest to their perception of the importance and impact of aesthetic upbringing, both through universities of culture and amateur activities. Vygnanov, for example, believed his Moscow technical institute needed to produce engineers who had some knowledge of poetry, literature, and the arts. The university of culture at the institute's club, in his view, "gave [students] serious knowledge of the art of dance, cinema, theater, and so on." He expressed pride in the fact that the students who left Moscow for work in the regions carried this cultural knowledge with them wherever they went.[150] A former secretary of the university Komsomol committee at SGU, Liudmila Gerasimova, underscored the central role of aesthetic upbringing for the university club's enthusiasts. Viktor Sobolev led a dance collective for adolescents and thought that this group helped participants to acquire good cultural tastes.[151] The former director of a theater collective stated that, by performing in shows, youth broadened their interests and obtained an artistic upbringing.[152] Baliasnaia praised universities of culture for molding the culture of young people.[153]

The aesthetic upbringing initiative sought to instill orthodox cultural preferences among young people, as policy makers made a hard-line turn to reimpose cultural hegemony after loosening the reins of cultural control in the early Thaw wave of liberalization. The new campaign deserves acknowledgment as promoting a novel, Thaw-era version of culturedness, one that sought to garden the aesthetic tastes and cultural perceptions of all youth, not just elites (as in the 1930s). The campaign was also distinct because the Cold War cultural competition, and especially western cultural propaganda, functioned as a key motivating factor for the Thaw-era version of culturedness.

The Cold War's cultural front complicated the enactment of the aesthetic upbringing initiative. Militant officials pushed the Komsomol to launch the initiative in February 1957. Policy enactment lagged behind rhetoric, however, owing to a combination of pressure from liberal officials and the need to demonstrate an appealing socialist popular culture, including American-style jazz, to foreign visitors at the international youth festival in July and August 1957. The aesthetic upbringing initiative underscores that Soviet political decision making resulted from a confluence of emotional reactions to historical developments, internal political conflicts, and officialdom's sense of the overarching political needs. It also shows how domestic cultural diplomacy demands shaped Soviet cultural policy, illustrating the value of adopting a multipolar and multilevel model of analyzing foreign relations, one that acknowledges a major role for transnational interactions below the level of formal diplomacy.[154]

Both the Moscow international youth festival and the aesthetic upbringing initiative illustrate how Soviet cultural life was increasingly influenced by the clash between the superpowers. This finding points to the need for in-depth microstudies of the local experience and influence of the Cold War as a means of grasping key elements of this contest.[155] Likewise, such evidence highlights that we need to treat the Soviet Union's culture during that period as a truly "Cold War culture," in other words, the Soviet Union was a country, one of many, whose daily cultural life was powerfully affected by the struggles between the capitalist and socialist blocs.[156] The Soviet Union, of course, was distinct in this regard, owing to its greater level of state authority and centralized cultural policy, as well as its role as one of the two bloc leaders. Analysis of Cold War cultures needs to avoid a deterministic perspective that ascribes all historical developments to the Cold War, however. Indeed, the Soviet Union experienced major changes during the Thaw owing to preexisting social dynamics such as postwar recovery and growing urbanization, as well as to the Khrushchev administration's relaunching of ideological revivalism. Nonetheless, my findings suggest that the historical literature has underestimated the impact of the Cold War on Soviet society. This is especially true for scholarship by those arguing that World War II defined the key beliefs and values in the Soviet Union after 1945.[157]

The new aesthetic initiative bears significance for our understanding of the molding of popular tastes. Scholars have illuminated how professional musicologists constructed public notions of appropriate music tastes, described the role of artists and performers as creators of taste, and discussed how marketers and advertisers helped instill the prescribed cultural tastes among consumers.[158] Such works, however, rely on western capitalist contexts in their commentary on how tastes emerged, developed, and changed. This chapter's examination of a socialist setting underscores the need to expand our understanding of the social formation and function of aesthetic taste to include the role of a state apparatus and an official ideology. The Soviet party-state sought to socially engineer normative tastes in order to forge youth cultural practices, worldviews, subjectivities, and individual identities suited to the needs of the political leadership and its ideological and cultural prescriptions. To a lesser extent, other modern authoritarian regimes likewise consciously strove to change the preferences of their populations, suggesting that their state structures also considered such policies appropriate and effective methods of governing the country and gardening the population.[159]

While policy makers pressed for aesthetic upbringing, that campaign also demonstrates the clout of grassroots youth desires. The new initiative, after all, represented the reaction of the authorities to what they perceived as "excessive" fascination with western popular culture among the youth. Furthermore, the Komsomol's implementation of aesthetic upbringing emphasized the use of infrastructural as opposed to despotic power in the attempt to appeal to at least some facets of youth desires. In another indication of the influence of grassroots opinion, the new top-level drive did not go nearly as far as the anticosmopolitan campaign in condemning western popular culture.

Aesthetic upbringing elucidates the emerging outlines of the Thaw-era attempt by policy makers to define a socialist version of a consumer society, with the goal of having young people consume their way into communism through wanting and taking in only officially prescribed options. The Soviet leadership's approach here had some parallels to those in other socialist contexts. Paulina Bren has found that the post-1968 Czechoslovak government, in competing with western Europe with regard to living conditions, did not try to produce more consumer goods than the western capitalist system. Rather, the Czechoslovak party-state offered better working conditions, more leisure time, and a variety of social welfare benefits, claiming that they resulted in a lifestyle superior to the western one.[160] The campaign for aesthetic upbringing emphasizes that rhetoric concerning socialism's superiority over the western way of life was already playing a prominent role in some socialist contexts before 1968. Instead of trying to compete with western modernity by providing youth with more western popular culture, the Kremlin in 1957 chose to emphasize the prescribed cultural canon and normative cultural activities as uplifting, enlightening, and in all ways superior to western ones.

By gardening youth cultural consumption desires and aesthetic tastes more forcefully, the authorities restricted the scope of cultural activities from which New Soviet People could legitimately derive joy, thus narrowing the scope of socialist fun. In doing so, the political elites promulgated a stricter emotional regime than the one prevalent from 1953 to 1956, although it was not nearly as harshly authoritarian as the one that prevailed during the anticosmopolitan era. The newly restricted emotional regime well served those who, like Popkova, already derived pleasure from non-controversial cultural genres; likewise, it helped many who, like Sokolov, wanted clearer emotional guidelines and prescribed cultural knowledge. However, this shift caused substantial discontent among a multitude whose proclivities did not fit fully within these categories. The large numbers who enjoyed western dancing resented the new restraints, especially in the context of the growing popularity of the controversial boogie-woogie and rock-and-roll-style dances. Fewer in number, jazz enthusiasts experienced the most intense emotional strain, with renewed attacks on their beloved artistic genre and their own cultural practices.

Still, many other youths had a more positive emotional association with the aesthetic upbringing initiative, as this drive helped young social strivers acculturate to a higher status, thus paving their way into the middle class. The Soviet Union experienced fast-paced urbanization and quickly growing college enrollments in these years.[161] Many upwardly mobile youths wanted a higher degree of cultural awareness. The aesthetic upbringing initiative functioned to ensure that the cultural capital of such young citizens matched their economic and social status as urbanites and college graduates. In this endeavor, party-state officials allied themselves with members of the cultural intelligentsia who held to their traditional ideal of cultural education for the populace.

Exhibiting conformist agency, a large number of young persons engaged readily and enthusiastically in the orthodox cultural activities of the aesthetic upbringing initiative, indicating that the new policy achieved some success in shaping aesthetic tastes among a segment of the young. The case study of the universities of culture underscores that, despite their many problems, millions voluntarily spent their free time studying there and willingly took in the party-state's guidance on what constituted appropriate cultural knowledge and aesthetic tastes. Many of these youth perceived themselves as becoming cultured owing to their participation in normative cultural activities. In effect, they adopted many or all elements of Thaw-era culturedness into their individual daily cultural practices, aesthetic sensibility, emotional expression, and self-identity. Yet, those who went to universities of culture did not necessarily accept all the tenets of the official cultural canon, since individuals refashioned mainstream consumption products and messages to suit their personal needs.

In addition, the complex nature of the aesthetic upbringing initiative's didactic elements challenged top-level goals. The Khrushchev Kremlin envisioned the New Soviet People as the most culturally educated individuals in the world, an obligatory aspect of building an appealing socialist version of modernity. The administration considered such cultural knowledge necessary, both for preparing people ready to live in communism and for winning the Cold War's cultural struggle, and achievable by informing its population about what constituted appropriate cultural standards and by showcasing the high cultural level of Soviet citizens for the outside world.[162] This approach resulted in the official conception that Soviet citizens needed to appreciate the classical western canon, prerevolutionary Russian culture, and foreign socialist culture, to be aware of and reject western popular culture, and most of all to know and like Soviet culture. Consequently, the university of culture curriculum offered an extensive education in foreign arts and culture. The authorities set a very high standard for themselves to meet in this hierarchy of cultural knowledge and appreciation. A great deal could go wrong, as young citizens could potentially like the classical western canon, prerevolutionary Russian culture, foreign socialist culture, or, worst of all, western popular culture more than prescribed Thaw-era culturedness. The difficulty of drawing a sharp line between what belonged in the classical western canon and what represented vulgar and subversive "foreign bourgeois" cultural expression offered a particular challenge in a time of a rapidly shifting party stance on culture. It is no wonder that young people who explicitly deviated from the Soviet cultural canon frequently pointed to Soviet official cultural education as the impetus for their nonconformist cultural practices.[163]

Moreover, the universities of culture faced a number of problems on the institutional level. Individual lecturers and local cultural establishments frequently refused to extend volunteer aid to the universities, despite top-level exhortations, thus showing how systemic financial matters on the ground undermined ideologically motivated goals in the center. In the top-level blindness to grassroots institutional realities, the aesthetic upbringing drive faced problems similar to those of many other social engineering schemes of gardening states.[164]

Likewise, the authorities struggled to reach those youth who did not wish to participate in the aesthetic upbringing drive's cultural forms. Young members of the working class who did not enjoy such cultural activities or strive for upward mobility had little reason to attend educational cultural events, despite the center's affirmative action efforts to target them. Perhaps more problematic, a large proportion of youth who enjoyed western popular culture, working class and middle class alike, found the aesthetic upbringing drive contrary to their cultural consumption desires, aesthetic tastes, and emotions. Consequently, they generally did not attend the universities of culture and spent less of their overall leisure in organized cultural recreation during the aesthetic upbringing initiative, thus minimizing their exposure to socialist time.

The campaign for aesthetic upbringing exacerbated generational differences. By openly upbraiding the young generation at the highest level of policy rhetoric in 1957, top officials introduced generational difference as a category for commentary in Komsomol cell meetings and youth publications. The emphasis on generational differences drew the attention of many young people to this issue and likely contributed to their seeing themselves as part of a separate generation. The rise of global youth movements at this time, combined with the greater exposure of Soviet young people to the outside world, exacerbated this sense of generational tension.[165] The attacks on western popular culture in 1957 also played a role. All these contributed to the formation of a full-scale generational consciousness among the active post-Stalin generation.

CHAPTER 7

A REFORMIST REVIVAL

Grassroots Club Activities and Youth Cafés, 1958–1964

At a club workers conference in Leningrad in May 1962, Leonid Likhodeev, a journalist from the newspaper *Literaturnaia gazeta*, criticized traditional club events as excessively organized and controlled; he quoted club workers as claiming that the strict environment was necessary since they "found it hard to imagine that an individual can be trusted to control himself," to "not rip out a microphone, tip over chairs, kill a police officer, or gnaw through trolleybus cables." Disagreeing with this characterization, Likhodeev threw his support behind a new cultural form—*molodezhnye kafe* (youth cafés)—that he believed would promote "the natural human condition" by encouraging "sociability" (*obshchenie*), primarily by providing an intimate and relaxed atmosphere for socializing and for free-flowing discussions.[1] When a hard-line official had challenged Likhodeev's views at an earlier conference, held in Moscow in March 1962, he had responded that, although cafés originated in the west, "it does not matter where they came from." Moreover, Likhodeev opposed club workers who disparaged youth cafés as kowtowing to western influence, saying that "it may be kowtowing, but so what?"[2] At both meetings, many expressed vociferous support for Likhodeev's ideas, unimaginable in the period from late 1956 to early 1958, when hard-line views predominated.

This liberal shift resulted primarily from the hierarchy's realization that large numbers among the young abstained from the didactic club events of the aesthetic upbringing drive. To satisfy popular desires and to get as many as possible involved in state-sponsored popular culture, the leadership once again encouraged grassroots initiative and opened much more room for controversial western music and dancing in cultural institutions, while continuing to promote the normative cultural canon. Although hard-liners opposed the new approach, the combination of endorsement from the top and mass support from below enabled the new departure in cultural policy to achieve some notable victories, best embodied by the innovative youth cafés. Minimizing politicized content, these establishments provided spaces for jazz musicians to play American pieces while youth drank coffee and sometimes wine and talked quite freely with other young people, together embodying what this book calls "state-sponsored sociability." Their rapid growth in the early 1960s slowed down during a cultural tightening in 1963 and 1964, yet these two years did not mark nearly as much of a break as is often assumed.

CONTINUITIES IN TOP-LEVEL CULTURAL POLICY, 1958–1962

Some aspects of the Kremlin's approach to organized cultural recreation for youth continued from the hard-line period of late 1956 to early 1958. In 1960, the Kremlin announced a transition to a seven-hour workday, giving more leisure time to the population. The Programma Tret'ia partiia (Third party program), a central guiding document for the Communist Party adopted at the Twenty-Second Communist Party Congress, in 1961, also increased the population's free time.[3] State policies expanded the free time of the citizenry by perhaps as much as 25 percent from 1959 to 1963.[4]

The Komsomol trumpeted this achievement of increased leisure time. In the summer of 1960, *Komsomol'skaia pravda* compared the length of the Soviet work week favorably to those of the United States, United Kingdom, France, and West Germany, explicitly demonstrating the benefits of socialism over capitalism.[5] Such direct comparisons aimed to promote the superiority of socialist modernity over the western version in the Cold War context.

At the same time, the increase in free time emerged as a source of concern because, as one official put it at a Moscow city Komsomol conference in 1960, "there is more leisure time, but the time span of 'communist influence' should not decrease."[6] The impact of western culture constituted another reason for anxiety. In a frank internal memo, prepared in December 1960 for the Komsomol CC by Len Karpinskii, head of the Komsomol propaganda department, "contemporary bourgeois influence" was generally tied to "pleasure and culture" and expressed itself as "ideological subversion through satisfying leisure desires."[7] The director of the Dom narodnogo tvorchestva (House of folk creativity or folk arts house) in Moscow declared in 1962 that West Germany promoted "American songs" to turn East German youth toward a western way of life and drew an analogy to the situation in the Soviet Union.[8] These statements represented a new and unprecedented focus of the party-state on the corrosive influence of western cultural influence.

To deal with such worries, the Komsomol placed a new emphasis on providing orthodox organized cultural recreation activities. The Eighth Komsomol CC Plenum in 1960 insisted that Komsomol cells ensured that all youth knew how to spend their free time "correctly."[9] Youth newspapers and instruction booklets reinforced this message.[10] Sergei Pavlov, first secretary of the Komsomol, explicitly tied aesthetic upbringing to socialist modernity in 1962 at the Fourteenth Komsomol Congress. In his words, the only appropriate "modern style" in culture involved a rejection of traditional capitalist styles and the expression of the "spirituality and worldview of the new person."[11] This quote referred to the Programma Tret'ia partiia's "Moral Code of the Builder of Communism," the model for New Soviet People from 1961 onward.[12]

Such rhetoric soon found expression in Komsomol policy. The Komsomol CC plenum in 1960 instructed Komsomol cells to use volunteer youth labor to build fifteen thousand clubs and renovate fifty thousand cultural institutions.[13] The party-state continued to pour resources into universities of culture and created other cultural forms designed to inculcate aesthetic upbringing, such as music interest clubs and musical salons.[14]

Reaching out beyond traditional club spaces, the Komsomol also promoted cultural "work where one lives" (*rabota po mestu zhitel'stva*) beginning at the end of the 1950s as a means of managing youth leisure time on the local community level through official collective activities.[15] Such endeavors had particular resonance due to the Thaw-era apartment building campaign, which created more noncommunally controlled spaces.[16] In 1960, the Komsomol propaganda department and Komsomol press called for the wide development of this new concept of cultural work.[17] Komsomol cells took up the implementation of this initiative in, for instance, Saratov and Moscow.[18]

BREAKS IN TOP-LEVEL CULTURAL POLICY, 1958–1962

Soviet authorities realized, however, that such novel types of cultural activities failed to have an impact on the large numbers of young people who avoided orthodox cultural events. The 1960 plenum's decree on organizing youth leisure required Komsomol organizations to pay particular attention to those who shunned amateur circles and other collective activities.[19] This emphasis on noninvolved youth did not appear in policy statements associated with the militant turn of late 1956 to early 1958. Komsomol higher-ups chose to make an example of the Voronezh Province Komsomol organization, censuring it for ignoring youth who avoided official cultural activities, leaving them "to fend for themselves, often being subjected to bourgeois influence through foreign films, literature, anti-Soviet radio programs, and rumors."[20]

To draw youth into state-sponsored popular culture and thereby into socialist time, the Komsomol leadership took steps to make organized cultural activities more appealing, including offering young people more space for local autonomy. After expressing some hesitancy during the hard-line turn of late 1956 to early 1958, the Komsomol CC once again accentuated grassroots activism as a core value. At the Thirteenth Komsomol Congress, in 1958, Aleksander Shelepin strongly emphasized the development of community leadership.[21] Initiative from below received further support from the party congress in 1961. Youth initiative club activists referenced this congress by advocating for their institutions.[22]

Discussions of organized cultural recreation during the mid-Thaw years also stressed developing popular initiative to oppose western propaganda that portrayed the Soviet Union as less free and democratic than the United States. In his internal memo from 1960, Karpinskii wrote that foreign ideology influenced Soviet youth "by presenting the idea of freedom of behavior" as attractive. He asserted that the Komsomol's "reliance on prohibitions" could not compete successfully with the deceptive image of freedom and democracy offered by the west.[23] Other Komsomol leaders, such as Pavlov at the Fourteenth Komsomol Congress, in 1962, began to voice the idea that western propaganda attempted to subvert youth "by advertising false bourgeois freedoms and democracy."[24] Such evidence suggests that western public diplomacy was quite influential among Soviet youth, and it also shows that the Komsomol higher-ups were aware of the need to use this image to their advantage.

Another new motivation for soliciting youth activism was the authorities' attempt to deal with what they described as the excessively consumerist outlook of some youth, which official discourse also associated with western propaganda. Pavlov's Fourteenth Komsomol Congress speech blamed foreign propaganda for presenting "illusions of personal enrichment" to youth.[25] Such public pronouncements reflected internal worries over the failures of the Komsomol's socializing work, as illustrated by Karpinskii's internal memo for the Komsomol CC. He tied concerns over consumption to poorly organized cultural activities for young people, that is, events that lacked sufficient space for initiative from below.[26]

To get more young people involved in state-managed cultural institutions, the Soviet authorities allowed greater room for western popular culture. According to Liubov Baliasnaia, the Mezhdunarodnyi molodezhnyi festival' (International youth festival) held in Moscow in 1957 brought in so much western cultural influence that "stubbornly opposing all of it" on the leadership's part "was simply unreasonable." She regretted that youth wanted western dances and jazz but noted that Komsomol cadres, including her, "accommodated their wishes," because "if only the waltz was offered, no one would come to the evening dances."[27] Recognizing this dilemma, the Soviet leadership gradually abandoned the hard-line approach, most notably in the party Central Committee decree of May 1958 on correcting the mistakes in its resolution of February 1948 that censured the opera *Velikaia druzhba* (Great friendship).[28] Since the latter decree had formed the basis for the attacks on western popular culture and remained in force until the new statement, the 1958 resolution thus opened up much more room for jazz and western dancing in clubs.[29]

Komsomol newspapers began to publish articles voicing open-mindedness toward jazz. In one such article, the controversial young writer Vasilii Aksenov described a variety of different jazz styles, from Dixieland to the most fashionable cool jazz, presenting the latest American-style jazz as fully appropriate. Aksenov explicitly mocked the view that cultural forms created in the United States necessarily served western imperialist goals, and he defended jazz as a "true folk art."[30] Other newspapers also printed articles that suggested jazz was a mainstream cultural form.[31]

Aksenov, a longtime jazz lover, and other liberally minded authors began to portray jazz positively, legitimating jazz as part of Soviet cultural life.[32] Seventeen-year-old Dimka Denisov, the hero of Aksenov's most famous novel, *Zvezdnyi bilet* (Ticket to the stars), published in 1961, danced to jazz in the courtyard of his apartment complex, despite adult disapproval. In Aksenov's novel *Apelsiny iz Marokko* (Oranges from Morocco), published in 1963, the protagonist, a young engineer, enjoys spending time with his friends in a private apartment listening to western-style jazz.[33] Liudmila Gerasimova recalled that Aksenov had great popularity among Saratov university youth and developed or strengthened their interest in jazz.[34] Other prominent Soviet authors, such as the Strugatskii brothers, also defended listening to jazz; they did so in their science fiction book *Ponedel'nik nachinaetsia v subbotu* (Monday begins on Saturday), published in 1965.[35]

The authorities went even further, inviting western jazz musicians to tour the Soviet Union. The first tour by a western troupe officially invited to play jazz took place in the summer of 1962. A 1930s swing-style jazz big band led by the clarinetist Benny Goodman visited five Soviet cities. The performances met with great success among the audiences and authorities alike. Jazz enthusiasts jammed together with Goodman's sidemen in Moscow, Leningrad, and other cities, despite some police intimidation.[36]

The tour resulted from a 1957 agreement between the Soviet Union and the United States on mutual cultural exchanges, part of a series of pacts between the Soviet Union and nonsocialist states that built upon the post-Stalin opening to foreign visitors and resulted in appearances by foreign performers and exhibits of foreign goods.[37] These agreements enabled the Soviet Union to send numerous musicians, dancers, and other cultural figures abroad.[38] For instance, the famous Baletnaia truppa Bol'shogo teatra (Bolshoi ballet) and the Moiseyev tantsa (Moiseyev dance company), which performed stylized folk dances, toured the United States in 1959 and 1960, with both proving very popular.[39] The Moiseyev tantsa even prepared a twist-style number for their American tour, which they later exhibited back in the Soviet Union under the label "Parodiinyi tanets" (Dance parody).[40] The excellent quality of Soviet "high" cultural performances sent abroad appealed to audiences around the world and raised the Soviet Union's cultural prestige to unprecedented heights during the early 1960s.[41] The Soviet bloc further improved its international reputation by exporting other innovations across the Iron Curtain, such as the Lamaze childbirth method.[42] The Soviet authorities increasingly permitted ordinary citizens to travel to capitalist countries as tourists, hoping they would serve as grassroots "citizen" ambassadors.[43] All these activities illustrate the Soviet leadership's intention to harness the soft power of cultural diplomacy in order to showcase the Soviet Union as an appealing socialist alternative to western modernity.

The Kremlin also expanded the number of foreigners—including youth—permitted to visit the Soviet Union.[44] In 1958, the Komsomol established its own tourist agency, Sputnik, to host visiting young people.[45] As the number of foreign youths pursuing higher education in the Soviet Union grew, the Khrushchev authorities sought to spread the Soviet model through education.[46] The American government closely tracked the rise in foreigners studying in the Soviet Union, considering this a significant area of Cold War competition.[47]

To supplement foreign youth delegation trips to the Soviet Union sponsored by nongovernmental organizations (NGOs), Soviet youth organizations negotiated with nonsocialist governments to establish mutually sanctioned and funded bilateral youth exchanges. For instance, in 1958, the British Foreign Office invited forty Soviet youths to the United Kingdom for three weeks, following negotiations that had begun in 1956.[48]

Western authority figures mirrored the Soviets' efforts to influence youth through domestic cultural diplomacy. In a letter to the British Foreign Office, Sir Philip Norris, chair of the Committee of Vice Chancellors and Principals, stated that "amongst young people, especially students, in the Soviet Union, there may be a possibility that contacts with the West would make some valuable and deep impression."[49] An internal memo suggested targeting youth in Soviet Georgia for invitations, "on grounds of vulnerability and traditional English sympathies."[50] The British even developed specific guidelines for the most successful ways to influence young

Soviet visitors. They thought that the smaller the number of foreign visitors, the better, because Soviet youth group leaders maintained better control of larger groups. Ideally, the British wanted to make individual hosting arrangements, to expose each guest to maximum western influence.[51] The US government also invested in such domestic cultural diplomacy. For instance, during the Cold War, US officials collaborated extensively with NGOs and thousands of volunteers to plan a variety of activities and events for foreign participants in exchange programs, all designed to present the United States in the best possible light.[52] Such data spotlight the importance of domestic cultural diplomacy in western settings and highlight the need for further research on all aspects of this understudied field in socialist and nonsocialist contexts.

The Soviet authorities certainly knew about the intentions of western governments; after all, the party-state hierarchy sought to achieve similar goals with visiting foreign youngsters. The Soviet Union participated in these exchanges because the Soviet leadership was confident that their socialist alternative would be well received among domestic and foreign audiences. A desire to ameliorate hostilities with western states, as well as to acquire international legitimacy and respectability through bilateral agreements that treated the Soviet Union as an equal, also played a role.[53] More broadly, Soviet tourism speaks to the powerful impact of this sphere on contemporary societies, socialist and capitalist alike.[54]

The top-level liberal policy shift greatly expanded opportunities for grassroots initiative and for western popular culture to become part of the cultural practices of New Soviet People. This finding contradicts recent claims that, in the Khrushchev years, officials and civilians more than forty years of age could not imagine a jazz enthusiast being a good Soviet citizen.[55] Policy makers responded to youth behavior and desires, as well as sought to get young people into socialist time, to oppose western propaganda, and to reinvigorate the social contract of the early Thaw.

These issues gained particular urgency due to the building campaign and the provision of leisure, as youth had substantially greater opportunities to enjoy banned western popular culture in nonofficial settings, and to socialize there as well. As a result, the Soviet system grew increasingly irrelevant for the formation of identities, relationships, and community bonds that occurred during free time. Such findings underscore the unexpected consequences of party-state policies that at first glance seem unrelated to state-sponsored popular culture but in actuality intertwined in complex ways, threatening the Kremlin's long-term goals.

Statements by Karpinskii, Baliasnaia, and other Komsomol leaders offer further proof that top-level anxieties did not necessarily lead to conservative policy outcomes. Most political elites shared broad goals; they wanted to involve young people in officially sponsored collective activities and to cultivate faith in the party-state, all while avoiding excessive consumerism and a preference for the western way of life. Official unease arose when youth behavior seemed to counter such aims. Hard-line and soft-line cadres, who disagreed on the best way to deal with such problems, promoted their favored solutions in a battle for the allegiance of those closer to the middle. At the end of the 1950s and the beginning of the 1960s, the liberal perspective generally won out. Indeed, the pluralistic transformations in state-sponsored popular culture at the end of the 1950s paralleled liberalizing reforms in, for example, Soviet radio production and criminal rehabilitation.[56]

YOUTH INITIATIVE AND WESTERN CULTURAL INFLUENCE IN CLUBS, 1958-1962

Top-level support paved the way for an upswing in youth initiative. Amateur activities garnered more support and achieved a grander scale. The cultural bureaucracy approved the transformation of some elite amateur theaters into *narodnye teatry* (people's theaters).[57] Some of the best amateur classical music circles became volunteer philharmonics and symphony orchestras.[58] Besides gaining prestige, such collectives obtained more financial resources, including paid staff. Ever more frequently, reports from cultural institutions included sections devoted to grassroots activism, indicating the importance of this issue to higher-ups.[59]

Nonetheless, tensions over youth initiative manifested themselves in many settings, most notably at several 1962 club worker conferences. The Rusakov dom kul'tury (house of culture) director stated that the many "excessively organized" trade union club events led to "boredom" among youth, and the director thus advocated that clubs give young people more room to organize cultural activities on their own.[60] L. S. Zhuravleva, the organizer of one of these conferences, bemoaned the fact that "some of our club workers are still beholden to old traditions."[61] Hard-liners took a different view. The manager of the dom kul'tury for the Krasnyi proletarii izdatel'skaia (Red proletarian press), Slutskaia, disagreed with Zhuravleva, criticizing those cultural officials who "let youth take the lead" and did away with "old traditions." At Slutskaia's club, activities centered on ideology and propaganda, such as lectures and book discussions.[62] Slutskaia and other conservatives, however, generally occupied defensive positions at these conferences.

High-level tolerance allowed jazz to acquire more prominence in amateur collective repertoires. The Moscow folk arts house's ideologically militant administration complained in 1959 that amateur variety ensembles were "trying to copy western jazz bands."[63] In 1962, the director complained that "variety ensembles play many Negro and American songs."[64]

The authorities allowed interest-based clubs that played jazz. A group of enthusiasts in Leningrad created the first in 1958, the D-58, which played jazz music and held lectures on jazz.[65] Jazz fans established a club in Moscow in 1960, and other clubs soon opened their doors in major cities, often with Komsomol sponsorship.[66]

Attitudes toward western dances underwent a similar transition. By the late 1950s, the fox-trot and tango had given way to the boogie-woogie and Charleston, while the most daring youth began to do the twist, shake, and other rock-and-roll dances. Those engaging in rock-and-roll dances during the late 1950s occasionally suffered official censure, yet the expanded authority of primary-level Komsomol cells during the decentralizing initiatives of the early Thaw protected many youth. Abram Derzhavets, who served as a Komsomol secretary for his class at a Moscow technical college, told me that he simply ignored repeated suggestions from his department's Komsomol to criticize the western dancing of his cell members. Still, some other primary Komsomol cells in his college did reprimand such youth, while parents often berated children doing the twist and similar dances.[67]

By the early 1960s, official tolerance had increasingly extended to the Charleston, twist, boogie-woogie, and other dances as young people began to adopt them en masse. Many of my interviewees recalled youth eagerly doing these dances, in private settings and in state-sponsored events, during the early and mid-1960s.[68] Irina Sokol'skaia recalled that the Komsomol disparaged the twist when it first became popular, but such criticism had grown muted by the time she began learning it as a schoolgirl in the early and mid-1960s, though her father still expressed disapproval. Sokol'skaia herself initially disliked the twist, considering it ugly and vulgar, and overly individualistic, since each person danced it alone, separated from the collective. Sokol'skaia's testimony evinces the power of Soviet official discourse in shaping perceptions of aesthetic norms in dancing. She did eventually accept the twist after watching her friend, an amateur gymnast, perform the dance well, making what she called "an ideological leap" to get over her discomfort. At no time did she feel disloyal to the Soviet system in her dancing, emphasizing to me that she believed in official rhetoric during her youth.[69]

The shifting dynamics of youth cultural practices and tastes forced policy makers to adopt a more tolerant attitude. As small minorities of young people took up new dances like the twist, they made their way up the youth social hierarchies, paralleling similar processes in western youth cultures.[70] Early adopters, such as Sokol'skaia's gymnast friend, offered an appealing model to emulate for more mainstream and committed youth like Sokol'skaia. To keep up with the shifts in grassroots youth cultural preferences and behavior, leaders had to stretch the boundaries of the acceptable, at least if they wanted to build a socialist modernity perceived as appealing by the population, a project to which the Kremlin recommitted itself in mid-1958.

A major impetus for these western dances came from the influx of foreigners to the Soviet Union in the late 1950s. Through the international youth festival, Soviet youth learned western dancing from young people from across the globe. While at a Soviet summer youth camp, Francheska Kurilova learned to dance the boogie-woogie from a Czech visitor.[71] Svetlana Kovaleva remembered learning about both western dances and fashion from foreign students whom Moskovskii gosudarstvennyi universitet (MGU, Moscow's state university) hosted during the festival. Soviet youth visits abroad played a similar role. Kovaleva toured Czechoslovakia as part of an amateur student troupe, learned the jive, and brought it back to the Soviet Union.[72] Such evidence highlights the importance of the role of everyday relationships among varied international actors, including ordinary people at the grassroots, in defining the outcome of the Cold War. The day-to-day interactions between Soviet and non-Soviet youth played a vital role in young Soviet citizens learning about and adopting elements of western popular culture, thus shaping the Cold War's cultural front.

Western popular culture continued to inspire wide-ranging debates among club workers. The assistant manager of the Zuev club asked the audience to recall that, before 1953, the official line had precluded all western dances, and he then asked, "Why are we so scared that someone will dance rock and roll?" He observed that the intolerant stance of many club officials "drove young people away into private apartments," where they danced the twist anyway.[73] Others rejected the soft-line position. A speaker labeled such dances an example of "true bourgeois ideology, which enters our souls through the feet, through shaking."[74] A representative from the Leningrad city Komsomol committee associated such dances with youth vulgarity and improper relationships with women.[75]

Some youth opted to dance recent western dances in nonofficial contexts to avoid any monitoring at all. In 1960, a group of young people in Orsk began to gather in private apartments for what the Komsomol propaganda department termed "drunken orgies," where they played cards, drank alcohol, "danced rock and roll without any clothes on," and had promiscuous sex. News about the group spread to Sverdlovsk, Kuibyshev, and other nearby cities, and young people began to come to Orsk to participate in these activities. The police shut this group down in early 1962.[76] It would be an understatement to say that no club in the Soviet Union would have agreed to sponsor such activities, which bore some parallels to hippie communes in the United States and presaged the *sistema*, the hippie counterculture that developed in the Soviet Union from the late 1960s onward.[77]

YOUTH CAFÉS, 1958–1962
STRUCTURE, MOTIVATIONS, AND CULTURAL DIPLOMACY

During the early 1960s, young Soviet urbanites acquired a new place to spend their leisure: youth cafés. These volunteer-based cultural institutions, managed by local Komsomol cells, mostly operated out of restaurants and more rarely partnered with trade union clubs. A hall set up in a youth café style had tables and chairs placed sufficiently far from each other to enable young people to talk together comfortably, as opposed to the traditional cultural events settings with rows of chairs facing the stage. The youth café format thus shifted the center of gravity to the interactions among café visitors themselves, not between the stage and the audience. Youth cafés served light and inexpensive meals, coffee, and, at some cafés, wine, with patrons sitting at their tables for many hours, drinking, eating, and, most of all, talking. In many youth cafés, the entertainment largely consisted of ensembles playing American-style jazz (fig. 7.1). Frequently, they also held special events that resembled those at youth initiative clubs, such as debates, meetings with prominent musicians, artists, and writers, fashion shows, and other engaging activities, as opposed to propagandistic lectures. Most cafés had dance floors, and some had recreational rooms where youth hung out, socialized, and played chess, table tennis, and billiards.[78]

Youth cafés sought to convey a modern and progressive sensibility through a sleek and elegant, post-Stalinist, Thaw-era décor and design.[79] This is what the director of the Moscow youth café Molodezhnoe (Youth) meant when he called for such cafés to have "a modern [*sovremennyi*] hall."[80] Youth cafés needed to "have beautifully decorated and comfortable" spaces, with appropriate paintings, decorations, and furniture.[81] Coffee conveyed the spirit of novelty and progress, since this beverage was just beginning to become more popular and available in the Soviet Union. Furthermore, it had an aura of western influence, explicitly different from the tea-drinking Slavic tradition.[82]

The personnel working in youth cafés were similar to those in the youth initiative clubs in terms of their enthusiasm, and many elements

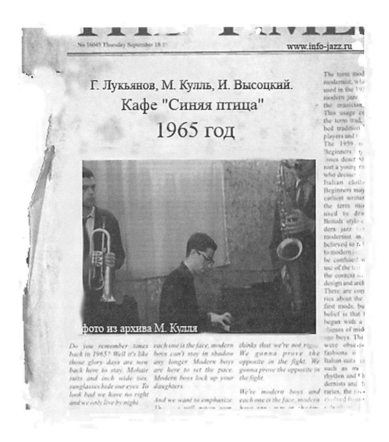

FIG. 7.1. This photograph from 1965 shows jazz musicians playing in a youth café. The photograph is from the personal archive of M. Kull', accessed November 1, 2013, http://info-jazz.ru/community/jazzmen/?action=show&id=264.

of the youth cafés originated in those clubs.[83] Youth cafés relied mostly on volunteer activists, particularly in the form of a café council whose members were generally lower-level Komsomol cadres, along with a few officials from other agencies, jazz enthusiasts, cultural figures, and white-collar professionals.[84] The large majority of those serving on café councils did so out of passion for the youth café movement, spending long hours with minimal reward from officialdom. The Vostochnoe (Eastern) youth café had a council described as an "initiative-based group of comrades who are avid supporters of the café."[85] Vadif Sadykhov, a jazz musician, described how one council, made up of Komsomol cadres, organized everything needed to hold jazz evenings. Many had good relationships with jazz musicians and hung out with them during performance breaks.[86]

Local Komsomol cadres carved a niche for these innovative cultural forms within the Soviet system. In Moscow in 1959, at one of the first serious discussions about youth cafés, Timiriazev neighborhood Komsomol officials convinced higher-ups to try out youth cafés as an experiment, and, by July 1960, the Komsomol CC itself had offered strong support for youth cafés.[87] Komsomol conferences and newspapers promoted cafés, and, with such support, youth cafés soon opened their doors in the early 1960s in Moscow and Leningrad.[88]

Molodezhnoe, one of the best-known Moscow cafés, offers a detailed view of youth café activities. In the words of Valerii Ponomarev, a Moscow jazz musician, during the 1960s Molodezhnoe "was considered the most fashionable and modern establishment in Moscow."[89] Like many of its counterparts, this café functioned in the mornings and afternoons as a regular restaurant run by the food bureaucracy. In the evening, the Komsomol took charge and transformed this space into a youth café. Each program began with contemporary jazz music and later proceeded to some special event.[90] Prominent artists performed in Molodezhnoe, including the actor-bard Vladimir Vysotskii. The café hosted discussions on controversial issues, including, for example, one on art, with "young artists from the most leftist to the most rightist, with passionate debate ensuing." Sometimes, audience members came on stage and read their own poetry, and artistically inclined college student amateurs, especially from MGU, offered their talents.[91]

Moscow's Vostochnoe offers an example of a more modest and typical café. Most evenings involved jazz music, and each Wednesday and Saturday Vostochnoe held special events, such as a cycle of lectures on the history of jazz, a fashion show, or amateur performances.[92]

Some cafés, especially those in Leningrad, focused less on jazz music, instead providing more targeted activities for particular audiences, such as avant-garde painters, poets, and other members of the progressive cultural intelligentsia. Leningrad's Kafe poetov (Poets' café) acquired widespread popularity among poets as a safe space for controversial poetry.[93] Patetich-eskoe (Pathos), a café in Moscow, had a similar function for writers and poets.[94] An abstract-style painter reportedly painted the tiles of the famous Saigon café in Leningrad.[95]

These new cultural institutions emerged from western models. An article from May 1961 depicted a well-run foreign college student youth café, suggesting that this form deserved emulation in the Soviet Union.[96] The western-style café culture of the Baltics provided another source of inspiration.[97] Both Baliasnaia and the Saratovite Konstantin Il'in regarded youth cafés as, in Il'in's words, a "breach made by the western way of life" into the Soviet Union.[98] Western-influenced, jazz-focused cafés spread in other nonwestern settings during the postwar decades as well, such as in Japan and in other socialist states.[99]

Despite the western origins of the cafés, the Komsomol leadership was willing to experiment with these new cultural institutions in order to appeal to youth desires. According to a Komsomol propaganda department internal report, these cafés interested young people by enabling them to listen to new music, dance, laugh, hang out with other youth, talk with famous people, and discuss and argue about important questions of everyday life. The department wanted youth cafés, with their "relaxed, unrestrained atmosphere," to imitate gatherings at individual apartments, with the implication that cafés should serve as a nonprivate setting for youth sociability and entertainment, one that allowed for Komsomol guidance.[100] Youth cafés aimed to increase socialist time, especially among young people who preferred relaxing in private apartments to orthodox organized cultural activities. The Komsomol leadership also viewed cafés as a means to advance the goal of aesthetic upbringing and to develop "the volunteer initiative of Komsomol member enthusiasts."[101]

The Komsomol hierarchy also endorsed these new institutions because of the crucial role that youth cafés and jazz had acquired in Cold War domestic cultural diplomacy. Aleksei Kozlov, the jazz musician who helped establish Moscow's Molodezhnoe café, related how Soviet jazz proved its usefulness as a tool of cultural diplomacy at the Mezhdunarodnyi forum molodezhi i studentov (International forum of youth and students) in Moscow in 1961. The Komsomol needed to create what Kozlov termed a "relaxed and modern atmosphere" for meetings between Soviet and foreign students in a club. Komsomol cadres invited Kozlov and other jazz musicians to play "modern American jazz."[102] The British ambassador to the Soviet Union described this event as having been well attended by many young Africans, Asians, Latin Americans, and eastern Europeans. The party-state gave delegates "lavish treatment," including cultural programs: "it is difficult to see how" such activities "can fail to have had an effect on many of the delegates, particularly from newly-emerging countries," claimed the ambassador.[103]

Moscow's youth cafés, especially Molodezhnoe, became favored destinations for the Soviet authorities to take foreign dignitaries and delegations.[104] Molodezhnoe began operating in October 1961, just before the Twenty-Second Communist Party Congress, with the café opening timed to correspond to the arrival of the foreign communist visitors, according to Kozlov. A Cuban delegation led by Raul Castro visited Molodezhnoe, and Kozlov's jazz band performed the "Marcha del 26 de julio" (July 26 hymn), a Cuban revolutionary piece, to great effect. On one occasion, a group of Americans, including businessmen, Ford Foundation representatives, and reporters from *Look* magazine, visited Molodezhnoe.[105] Ordinary foreign tourists frequently visited youth cafés as well. Ponomarev recalled that Molodezhnoe was "always full, mainly of European tourists." He believed the authorities intended Molodezhnoe to "amaze western guests with the freedoms available" in the Soviet Union.[106] Kleinot stated that Soviet advertising materials aimed at tourists explicitly promoted youth cafés to demonstrate "what constitute[d] Soviet modern culture."[107] Harding Ganz, an American tourist, remembered a Leningrad youth café he visited in 1966 as "a swinging place," with contemporary jazz music and free-flowing, lively conversations. Ganz expressed surprise to me at finding such an "open" establishment in the Soviet Union.[108]

These data support the argument that showcasing the Soviet Union for foreign observers had a great deal of importance to the party-state. Michael David-Fox, looking at the 1930s, has concluded that the authorities specifically built model sites of Soviet socialism, such as new cities, with foreign visitors in mind.[109] Similarly, impressing foreign guests served as a core function of youth cafés; this goal shaped their construction, design, and range of activities, especially for cafés in the capital cities frequented by foreigners.

EVERYDAY LIFE IMPACT

Youth cafés acquired immense popularity among the young. The challenge of gaining access to a youth café in the early 1960s testified to their appeal. An instruction booklet from 1962 portrayed the cafés as immensely popular, with "lines forming long before the café open[ed]," a phenomenon that Ganz remembered.[110] By promoting youth cafés to ensure grassroots support, the Komsomol ended up creating consumer demand that it had trouble satisfying in the short run. Frustrations over long lines undermined some of the legitimating function of these establishments, illustrating some of the challenges in building an appropriately socialist consumer society.

What drew young people to youth cafés? Certainly, the nontraditional, western aspects of the café setup—drinking coffee at a table, socializing with interesting people, and taking in exciting and often western-style cultural entertainment—appealed to many. The music in particular drew plenty of jazz fans. Others went to the cafés because they seemed exotic or because they offered the chance to meet foreigners.[111]

Most former café visitors recall the spirit of these cafés as the fundamental element in their appeal, namely their intimate and unconstrained environment, a pluralistic space of state-sponsored sociability. In Kozlov's words, "At that time, the unconstrained discussion of two strangers in a public setting where one's words might be recorded constituted a very new and exciting phenomenon."[112] Sadykhov characterized the social atmosphere of youth cafés as "wonderful."[113] The Saratovite Mikhail Ryskin found the "spirit of freedom" exciting.[114] Many others referenced sociability as crucial to youth cafés.[115]

Youth café organizers put unrestrained socializing front and center. The director of Moscow's Molodezhnoe proclaimed that young people "need[ed] a café-club where they can have debates, meet with interesting people in a relaxed atmosphere," and "talk with a friend."[116] Likhodeev depicted youth cafés as essential since, when young people go to cafés, "they engage in socializing and behave themselves like human beings should," a statement dovetailing with the emphasis on sociability in 1960s Soviet culture.[117]

Attracted by the atmosphere of cafés, many pluralistically inclined members of the cultural intelligentsia also frequented these institutions. Likhodeev, at the conference of club workers held in May 1962 in Leningrad, observed that traditionalist cultural figures, such as Vasilii Solov'ev-Sedoi, would not come to youth cafés. Likhodeev stated, however, that he and others like him, such as N. V. Bogoslavskii, a prominent cultural figure who liked "laughing and making witty comments," would indeed attend and perform.[118] The café Molodezhnoe had a variety of patrons from the realms of theater, cinema, and music.[119]

Jazz enthusiasts greatly enjoyed these institutions. Appreciating the relaxed and intimate atmosphere and the western-style forms, as well as the attentive audiences and the chance to socialize with other jazz musicians, musicians performed for free or minimal payments. Former jazz artists loved playing for audiences "who greatly desired to listen to jazz," in an atmosphere that was, in Sadykhov's words, "a celebration for the soul."[120]

Still, in the early days of youth cafés, musicians ran into difficulties playing the most contemporary jazz, bebop, and cool jazz. Characterized by intricate arrangements and extensive improvisation, these complex jazz styles had gained prominence among Soviet jazz enthusiasts by the end of the 1950s. Bebop and cool jazz were meant primarily for concert performances attended by audiences highly knowledgeable about jazz. Those listeners accustomed to hearing jazz only as an accompaniment to dancing found the novel styles difficult to appreciate. At some *khaltury* (moonlighters, or jazz evenings), modernist jazz musicians performing bebop and cool jazz faced pressure from audiences and club managers who wanted them to play Soviet popular songs or swing-style jazz suitable for dancing. Generally, jazz musicians ended up performing these numbers for additional payments from listeners, although on some occasions they received money to play modern-style jazz.[121] Although the vast majority of café visitors had a high regard for bebop and cool jazz, Kozlov described how some uninformed patrons tried to dance to this music. He decided from the first to "fight with these uncultivated [*obyvatel'skie*] habits of the masses," in order to raise what he termed the "cultural level" of the population. He called on Komsomol patrols to manage such audience members. Other jazz musicians confirm the role of Komsomol patrols in maintaining order in cafés.[122] This development represents a telling reversal of the role of such official groups in the aesthetic upbringing drive, when Komsomol patrols participated in surveilling and suppressing western music and dancing. Furthermore, Kozlov's actions paralleled the party-state's and cultural intelligentsia's goals of bringing "culture to the masses," as did those of other jazz performers, such as Oleg Cherniaev and Lev Figlin, who read lectures on jazz in youth cafés and jazz interest-based clubs.[123] Such data reinforce earlier findings on the growing integration of jazz enthusiasts into the Soviet cultural mainstream.

Most café activists and visitors saw this space of state-sponsored sociability as fully compatible with forging an appealing, Thaw-era version of a socialist modernity. Likhodeev, for instance, regarded conversations in an intimate atmosphere as the key to youth upbringing in the spirit of the Twenty-Second Party Congress, which he described as having at its heart the idea that "human beings are friends, comrades, and brothers to each other," a frequently used slogan.[124] Interviews with café patrons and activists also bear out this proposition, as many, such as Kleinot, revealed their belief in building communism during the early 1960s.[125] Sadykhov associated his faith in a Thaw-era vision of communism with youth cafés.[126] These institutions and their spirit, therefore, helped get café visitors engaged actively with the Thaw-era project of forging an appealing socialist modernity.

The relaxed atmosphere of cafés fit the intentions of the Komsomol hierarchy at this time. Karpinskii called for aiming "our best political forces at small audiences and intimate conversations."[127] The Komsomol propaganda department wanted youth cafés to provide the "opportunity for interesting conversations, discussions, and debates with other youth around the table."[128] For the Komsomol leadership, providing youth with an intimate atmosphere brought youth into official, collective, and state-managed spaces. In contrast, for youth café activists, such as Likhodeev, the sociability itself represented the primary goal. This divergence of emphasis did not pose a serious problem during the early 1960s, when the policy makers adopted a soft-line course.

Youth cafés show that western and especially American cultural and material products had a powerful impact on global cultural practices after 1945, but local residents and institutions did not adopt such culture wholesale, instead transforming it to fit their own individual needs, forging novel hybrid forms out of native and global influences.[129] Soviet youth cafés, which embody such hybridization, stretch the current scholarly models of how western popular culture gets refashioned to serve local desires. The vast majority of the literature explores how private individuals and the market mediated this process.[130] Youth cafés, by contrast, represent a state-managed official institution. The Soviet case enables us to further understand the role that governments played not only in opposing western popular culture, the traditional emphasis of much of the research on the globalization of western cultural influence, but also in adapting this popular culture to serve the goals of the state apparatus.

Combining western and Soviet influences contributed to the role of the youth café as a crucial site for the forging of the *shestidesiatniki* (people of the sixties). First appearing in the literary magazine *Iunost'* (Youth) in 1960, this term refers to a cohort of young intelligentsia sharing a broad set of values, including a commitment to cultural liberalism, truth and openness, and an international and peaceful orientation, as well as to forging an idealized vision of communism purged of what they considered Stalinist traits.[131] Unlike some scholarship, my narrative does not equate the shestidesiatniki with a new generation of young intelligentsia.[132] Instead, it suggests that the shestidesiatniki formed what Karl Mannheim has termed a "generational unit," a subgroup within a generation that interprets its experiences in similar ways, consequently acquiring shared values and beliefs. These may be dissimilar and even antagonistic to the worldview of other generational units within that generation.[133] The shestidesiatniki ethos did not characterize all young intelligentsia, as many espoused a deep commitment to ideological orthodoxy or, in growing numbers, to Russian and other ethnic nationalisms.[134] With their bohemian, liberal, modern, and western-influenced environment, youth cafés helped forge the values and beliefs of the shestidesiatniki. Likewise, youth cafés embodied the civic spirit of the shestidesiatniki, depending as they did on the enormous investments of time and energy on the part of young, liberal-minded activists and cultural intelligentsia willing to reform the Soviet system and to push the Soviet Union toward a more pluralistic socialist modernity.

Unsurprisingly, officials who were more militant spoke out against youth cafés, for instance at the club worker conference in 1962. A characteristic comment censured youth café activists' rejection of lectures.[135] A speaker criticized individualized socializing in cafés and called for cultural and aesthetic upbringing through cultural events with large audiences in traditional clubs.[136] A hard-liner challenged the director of Molodezhnoe on how the café propagandized the decisions of the Twenty-Second Party Congress. The director replied that the café did not propagandize them.[137]

In contrast, pluralistic cadres expressed support for cafés. The Moscow Komsomol defended the Molodezhnoe director, while the Zuev club's assistant manager argued that lectures failed to reach young people, thus driving them to attend youth cafés instead of clubs. He suggested organizing for the club events that would be similar to youth cafés themselves.[138] Similarly, the manager of a house of culture expressed a willingness to experiment with forms that resembled youth cafés.[139]

This debate, as well as the broader controversies surrounding the mid-1958 shift, highlights the continued significance of tensions between liberal and conservative perspectives on state-sponsored popular culture. To a degree, the vacillation of Thaw-era Soviet cultural policy resulted from systemic problems associated with pursuing either a hard-line or soft-line course. As mentioned above, a more conservative policy alienated young people from participating actively in the Soviet system, thus undermining a goal pursued ardently by the Khrushchev leadership. Conversely, a pluralistic approach toward culture led to what many officials perceived as excess youth initiative and subversive penetration by western cultural influence. These internal dynamics of cultural policy, together with the broader context of Soviet domestic and foreign developments, form one part of the explanation for the policy zigzags.

However, variation at the level of the individual also played a fundamental role in determining the shape of state-sponsored popular culture. Regardless of the party line at any specific time, liberally inclined officials expressed strong support for grassroots autonomy and open-mindedness with regard to western popular culture, reflecting the hard- versus soft-line alignments dating back to early Soviet history. Vigorous public conflicts continued throughout the post-Stalin years, testifying to their significance in the shaping of state-sponsored popular culture. Furthermore, the viewpoints of different local officials affected the day-to-day experiences of individual youth, defining the scope of their access to western popular culture and autonomous activities in organized cultural recreation.

Bureaucrats were not the only ones who mattered. The pluralistic perspective of the mass of young people who wanted western popular culture and grassroots initiative provided a powerful motivating force. Their desires served as a systemic factor driving the actions both of local officials striving to achieve plans and of the leadership seeking to appeal to youth desires. Besides voting with their rubles and feet, many committed young activists worked daily to advance popular initiative and western cultural forms. Their efforts included engaging in sustained debates with skeptical officials, thus casting further doubt on claims that official discourse lost relevance for everyday youth experience from 1953 onward.

Youth cafés experienced some growing pains. Organizers had difficulty attaining financial sustainability and finding the necessary resources, including coffee, wine, food, and stylish furniture.[140] With endorsement from the Komsomol hierarchy and press, the obstacles slowly became more manageable.[141] Gradually overcoming initial organizational problems and official recalcitrance, the cafés by mid-1962 stood on the verge of rapid growth, drawing on support from young people not only in major cities but also in smaller towns and even rural settings, in part encouraged by positive depictions of cafés on television.[142] Twenty youth cafés aimed to open their doors in Moscow from March to the end of 1962, and they slowly began to appear in the regions as well.[143]

Such growth in youth cafés showed that the Soviet Union offered significant space for youth cultural emancipation and agency during the early 1960s, as did many other countries at this time. Socialist eastern European governments opened up substantially more room for western popular culture and grassroots initiative.[144] Western European and North American youth cultures increasingly attained a prominent place in society.[145] Similar phenomena occurred around the globe during the 1960s.[146] Such parallels between socialist and nonsocialist countries justify the recent attention given to the "Soviet sixties"; as an important chronological period, it offers a useful basis for analysis that draws comparisons between Soviet and non-Soviet contexts.[147] My evidence suggests that we should date the start of this era, at least in regard to cultural policy, to the party Central Committee revoking of the decree against western-style music in May 1958. The Soviet sixties, although a part of the Thaw that lasted from 1953 to the end of the 1960s, stand out as tangibly different from the early Thaw. In the Soviet sixties, the authorities acknowledged the legitimacy of explicitly building upon western cultural forms in forging an attractive socialist alternative to a western modernity, with youth cafés the clearest example of this practice.

THE HARD-LINE TURN OF THE LATE KHRUSHCHEV YEARS, 1963–1964

In late 1962, the Khrushchev administration faced a series of domestic and foreign challenges. The party leader's signature domestic agricultural programs, the drive to develop the Tselina (Virgin lands), to plant corn across the Soviet Union, and to increase the use of fertilizer, suffered serious problems. A combination of shortages and price reforms inspired discontent among the population, most notably expressing itself in the Novocherkassk uprising of June 1962.[148] Abroad, the Soviet retreat during the Cuban Missile Crisis in October 1962 caused a major loss of face for the Soviet Union. The growing rift with China proved even more critical. The Chinese leadership condemned the Soviets for adopting an intolerably soft-line approach toward building communism.[149] Such developments inspired worries over whether the post-Stalin top officials had chosen the correct path. In particular, such missteps gave conservatives ammunition to criticize de-Stalinizing reforms, placing the Khrushchev administration on the defensive.

As a result, the Kremlin stepped away from some elements of cultural liberalization after mid-1962. In December 1962, Khrushchev famously condemned an exhibit of abstract art at Moscow's Manege as "degenerate." Over the next several months, he gave major speeches decrying cultural liberalism and tolerance toward western cultural influence in front of audiences filled with members of the intelligentsia. Some soft-line officials lost their positions, and hard-liners gained ground.[150] Literary and film production grew more constrained. Bold films produced in the more pluralistic environment of the early 1960s gave way to either heavily edited films or to complete suppression, an example being M. M. Khutsiev's *Mne dvadtsat' let* (I am twenty), which dealt with generational tensions.[151] The Khrushchev administration also adopted a more authoritarian approach in many other areas of governance, for instance, taking an increasingly intolerant stance toward petty offenders.[152]

This policy change had a direct impact on popular culture. At a meeting with cultural figures in March 1963, Khrushchev spoke out against American-style jazz, though clearly leaving room for sovietized jazz.[153] Following Khrushchev's lead, in the Komsomol CC plenum in July 1963, Pavlov criticized dance halls that featured "a boisterous orgy of delirious bodily movements to the wail of jazz music."[154] A Komsomol propaganda department memo accused foreign radio stations of "using young people's interest in [western] dances to spread skeptical and philistine attitudes among Soviet youth."[155] Komsomol newspapers disparaged jazz once more.[156]

Some of the most prominent and innovative jazz-oriented institutions suffered as a consequence. The authorities shut down jazz interest-based clubs in Moscow and in Leningrad.[157] Touring big bands had to limit the number of jazz pieces in their repertoires.[158]

Youth cafés also experienced difficulties. In an internal report, the Komsomol propaganda department disparaged problems in a number of cafés, especially in Moscow. For example, the department censured a November 1963 evening at Molodezhnoe, where the orchestra "played only jazz music and Jewish songs and dances." Events at other cafés during the same month also spurred pointed criticism. A council member of the Aelita club distributed poetry that defended Yevgenii Yevtushenko from official criticism and made accusations of official anti-Semitism in the Soviet Union. The cafés Eksprompt (Impromptu) and Molodezhnoe held exhibits of abstract art.[159] Soon thereafter, in February 1964, a speaker at the Moscow city Komsomol conference associated Aelita and Molodezhnoe with immorality, drunkenness, hooliganism, and religion.[160] Such attacks led to the ouster of some café council heads, including the manager of Aelita, and the toning down of jazz and other café activities associated with western cultural influence.

The swing toward a hard-line approach brought into the open previously submerged tensions between pioneering café activists and their goals and those of the Soviet hierarchy. For the café enthusiasts, providing a fitting setting for unrestrained sociability was the main goal. Their ideal included playing jazz and hosting activities on controversial topics. The Soviet leadership saw the pluralistic atmosphere of cafés as a way to get young people into state-managed spaces and thus socialist time. The tolerant atmosphere of the most daring cafés proved unacceptable to the party as it steered a new course in culture.

However, this shift in policy did not have nearly as much of a grassroots impact as the one in late 1956, because the Khrushchev leadership did not swing as far toward the hard line and because the conditions for jazz and western dancing had changed. Cultural organizations such as the Moscow city cultural department did impose stricter controls over the repertoire of amateur jazz bands and the music played in dance halls.[161] Clubs expressed more hesitancy about hosting the newest western music and dancing. Still, the explosion of amateur and professional jazz bands after the 1958 party CC decree, along with the grassroots demands among the young, hampered top-level efforts to limit western popular culture. Cultural institutions with soft-line officials, as well as ones seeking to achieve ambitious financial goals, continued to play the newest western dances. Consequently, many young people retained access to modern western music and dancing in state-organized cultural recreation, although these genres faced somewhat greater limitations than previously.

Likewise, many youth cafés continued to play American-style jazz and provide an atmosphere of intimate sociability. The growth in the number of cafés did not match the grand intentions of 1962, yet more did open, if not with the frequency originally planned. The most famous youth café in Leningrad, Saigon, opened its doors in September 1964.[162] Likely inspired by the television program *Sinii Plamia* (Blue flame), many clubs organized events termed "K plameni" (To the flame) that were designed to resemble youth cafés. The Moscow Trekhgornaia Manufaktura offered one such event.[163]

Crucially, the Komsomol continued to place a strong emphasis on soliciting initiative from below, though to a lesser degree than it had before. In his speech in July 1963, Pavlov highlighted "a central problem" in Komsomol work: "the suppression of youth initiative." Pavlov went on to say that Komsomol committees must "develop cadres of enthusiasts" through various interest-based leisure activities and "through them enact the influence of the Komsomol" on young people.[164] His words powerfully endorsed grassroots activism and initiative from below, while making clear that the long-term goal was inculcating the party's influence among youth, a goal shared by local Komsomol organizations.[165]

Such a solicitous attitude toward youth initiative blunted the impact of hard-line criticism. Many young grassroots activists engaging in organized cultural recreation enjoyed western popular culture and expressed their initiative by planning activities with contemporary jazz and western dancing. Despite the conservative turn, policy makers' high regard for youth community management—and its vital role in building communism—outweighed their suspicions of western cultural subversion. This prioritization helped safeguard most initiative-based youth amateur collectives that had elements of western popular culture, with only some of the most well-known and controversial ones experiencing suppression. It is thus no wonder that in my interviews with jazz enthusiasts, the vast majority did not speak of any sharp break associated with the end of 1962. In fact, they tended to agree with Garanian's statement that, from the early 1960s onward, the atmosphere became better for jazz.[166]

Consequently, my findings suggest that the hard-line turn in 1963 had much more impact on the small minority of cultural elites than on the broader cultural field. This analysis adds nuance to historical narratives of Soviet cultural policy that tend to focus on the state's interactions with the cultural intelligentsia. Such works, reflecting the concerns and conceptions of their elite historical subjects, generally depict December 1962 as a fundamental turning point away from Thaw-era liberalism.[167] However, the experience of the multitude of non-elite cultural producers in the amateur arts underscores that the Manege events did not constitute a sharp and momentous break in the vast majority of youth lives and cultural practices.

By mid-1958, policy makers were gradually realizing that the didactic aesthetic upbringing campaign had alienated a significant proportion of youth from collective recreation spaces and socialist time. The hard-line policies of late 1956 and 1957 undermined the Khrushchev administration's social contract and efforts to strengthen youth activism. Furthermore, high officials began to recognize that censorship did not compete successfully on the Cold War cultural front's new battleground of leisure, pleasure, consumption, and fun.

These factors informed the Khrushchev leadership's change in strategy toward building a socialist version of modernity through state-sponsored popular culture that included a much greater tolerance for western popular culture and more support for youth initiative. The authorities revised their approach to gardening cultural consumption desires and aesthetic preferences. From late 1956 to mid-1958, the party line proclaimed the superiority of the orthodox cultural canon and treated all deviations as indicative of improper cultural tastes; now, official discourse considerably extended the boundaries of the tolerable. While continuing to uphold the normative cultural canon as the best option, policy makers allowed Soviet youth to indulge in a substantial degree of western popular culture and still consider themselves cultured and worthy New Soviet People. Such policy shifts dovetailed with a series of parallel developments in the ways that societies approached youth cultural practices in eastern Europe, in western states, and around the globe, underscoring convergences between and the mutual influences of the Soviet Union and the rest of the world.

Soviet policy makers achieved some marked successes. The reforms proved highly popular, particularly among the large subgroup that enjoyed western popular culture, which the Kremlin had failed to reach via the aesthetic upbringing campaign. Consequently, the authorities managed to reinvigorate the social contract and decrease the gap that had grown between youth and the state from the end of 1956, while getting the young to spend more of their leisure in socialist time.

The changes in the official line denoted a turn toward a looser emotional regime, with a greatly broadened range of appropriate emotional expression. The overarching Soviet emotional community now encompassed within its borders many young people marginalized from late 1956 to mid-1958, especially those enamored of jazz and western dancing. The joy, pleasure, and enthusiasm expressed in the interviews by young people regarding party-state support for western popular culture and youth initiative symbolized the strengthened emotional connections between the bureaucracy and youth, owing to the increasingly shared conception between official policy and young people of what constituted socialist fun. The Soviet system's new line helped ensure that the formation of social relationships, emotional catharsis, community bonds, and individual and collective identities took place within officially managed contexts. The reforms in state-sponsored popular culture, especially the youth cafés, also contributed to forging shestidesiatniki.

In pursuing the new course in mid-1958, the Kremlin reacted to the systemic problems associated with a hard-line course toward organized cultural recreation. Simultaneously, policy makers went against the objections of many conservative bureaucrats. The top rulers sided with pluralistic officials and the large majority of young urbanites in the strident conflicts about popular initiative and western popular culture. This shift underscores how the actual desires and tastes of young people influenced state policy. It also emphasizes that the shape of state-sponsored popular culture resulted from a combination of broader processes and contests among those holding diverse perspectives on how to interpret these developments.

The new initiatives underscore the importance of the Cold War's domestic cultural front. On the one hand, these reforms responded to western propaganda, highlighting the impact of western public diplomacy on Soviet internal cultural policy and everyday life for Soviet youth. On the other hand, the reforms also benefited Soviet domestic cultural diplomacy. Jazz groups and youth cafés helped the party-state showcase the Soviet Union as an appealing socialist alternative to a western modernity, one that had a modern version of popular culture and offered specifically socialist fun untainted by market relations or racist discrimination, against, for example, jazz musicians. Such domestic cultural diplomacy may have had the most impact on visitors from former colonial states, but it also impressed western guests. The changes helped Soviet leaders realize that the Cold War struggle for hearts and minds, whether of domestic or foreign audiences, was moving toward the sphere of pleasure, leisure, and cultural consumption, making the cafés the new, Thaw-era sites for displaying socialism. The new party line in state-sponsored popular culture thus influenced Soviet foreign policy.

Furthermore, the reforms in the sphere of state-sponsored popular culture provided greater opportunities for daily interactions between Soviet and foreign youth. These grassroots interactions arguably made both sets of youngsters more likely to have a sympathetic attitude toward the foreign "Other" and less willing to support hostile and jingoistic foreign policies. The rising exposure of Soviet youth to western popular culture likely had a particularly powerful role in pushing them to adopt a more peaceful stance as they grew up and took power, most clearly illustrated by the peace-oriented course of the Gorbachev years.[168] Further research on the long-term impact of exposure to Soviet domestic cultural diplomacy will help reveal to what extent the altered outlook of foreign visitors to the Soviet Union influenced western public opinion and government policy.[169] More than likely, the information about Soviet state-sponsored popular culture brought back by visitors and published in newspapers within western countries contributed to an erosion of the western postwar consensus about the Soviet Union as an evil monolith. Helping spread a more complex and multifaceted view of socialist societies, Soviet domestic cultural diplomacy arguably enabled formulation of a more nuanced US foreign policy, thus helping institute détente.[170] Overall, my findings point to the importance of going beyond traditional diplomacy channels to investigate multilevel and multipolar interactions and thus reveal their powerful role in shaping the daily experience and overarching course of the Cold War.

By establishing youth cafés and, more broadly, permitting western popular culture such as the most recent American-style jazz and western dancing, the authorities aimed to domesticate western popular culture within socialist settings. To lessen the forbidden appeal of what Alexei Yurchak termed the "Imaginary West," the Khrushchev leadership sought to co-opt what it deemed to be acceptable elements of western cultural influence and make them part of the official Soviet model.[171] Sending Soviet tourists abroad and inviting foreign visitors to the Soviet Union served a similar function. My findings complicate triumphalist accounts that ascribe the fall of the Soviet Union to western cultural penetration and propaganda, and they show the role played by the agency of the Soviet state in managing the stream of external influences.[172] The Soviet system in the Thaw proved quite flexible and adaptable in its endeavor to build an alternative, socialist version of modernity.

Reacting to a series of blunders in domestic and foreign policy, in 1963 and 1964 the authorities pursued a more ideologically militant policy toward literature and art, which bred resentment among cultural elites. However, despite some criticism of and limitations on jazz and western dancing, the impact on club activities proved slight, to a large degree owing to the continuing endorsement of youth initiative from below by the Khrushchev administration. The hard-line policies of 1963 and 1964 had a much stronger influence on the cultural intelligentsia than on the cultural activities of the millions of non-elite amateur artists. For them, December 1962 did not mark the ending of the cultural liberalism of the Thaw.

CHAPTER 8
AMBIGUITY AND BACKLASH
State-Sponsored Popular Culture, 1965–1970

In early May 1967, numerous jazz musicians, promoters, and fans gathered in Tallinn, Estonia, for a remarkable event—a massive jazz festival, Tallinn-67. Organized by local Komsomol organs, trade unions, cultural institutions, and city authorities, this festival had concerts with attendance reaching three thousand. The largest Soviet jazz festival up to that point, Tallinn-67 received domestic and foreign press coverage and featured jazz bands from across the Soviet Union, eastern Europe, and beyond the Iron Curtain. A Komsomol propaganda department report praised the "vast majority of ensembles for showing a quite high mastery" of jazz.[1]

Historical accounts generally associate the Brezhnev period, from late 1964 to 1982, with a hard-line, militant cultural policy and depict this period as a time of "stagnation" when the new leadership reversed many of Khrushchev's de-Stalinizing reforms.[2] Going against this trend, several recent works have challenged this paradigm, in the cultural as well as the political sphere.[3] The story of the jazz festival movement contributes to and extends this more nuanced view, especially in the context of the increasing cultural restrictiveness in the last Khrushchev years. The post-Khrushchev era began with a time of ambiguity. The new collective leadership offered a renewed social contract and sought to get young people enthused over the Soviet way of life by appealing to people's desires for western popular culture. However, there emerged a growing militancy against youth autonomy and self-management. Political officials and cultural professionals acquired greater authority over state-sponsored popular culture, and young cultural activists lost out. The end of the decade, when Leonid Brezhnev took full charge, witnessed further suppression of youth agency and a brief turn against western influence following the invasion of Czechoslovakia. This gradual transformation in cultural policy served as a constituent element in the demise of the Thaw-era endeavor to build an appealing socialist modernity with mass grassroots participation, a development that seriously undermined the Soviet project, helping lead to its eventual demise.

NONCONTROVERSIAL CLUB ACTIVITIES IN THE EARLY POST-KHRUSHCHEV YEARS

Ambiguity pervaded the Soviet Union from late 1964 to August 1968. Top officials launched a coup against Khrushchev in October 1964, accusing him of economic mismanagement, international adventurism, excessive and poorly considered reforms, and rudeness. During the mid-1960s, a collective leadership shared the reins of power, with a contest for supremacy taking place behind the scenes. The dynamics of this struggle fed into the complex and shifting official policy at this time as the party-state searched for a post-Khrushchev path. Brezhnev gradually emerged as the dominant leader. His faction defeated an alternative clique led by the former Komsomol head Aleksander Shelepin in mid-1967. The invasion of Czechoslovakia in August 1968 consolidated Brezhnev's authority.[4]

The population had high expectations for the new leaders. Khrushchev's ouster met with little public opposition, as he had lost support among many key social groups by the mid-1960s. Economic setbacks beginning in the early 1960s resulted in widespread shortages of basic goods. A substantial portion of the populace disagreed with Khrushchev's denunciations of Stalin and the nature and extent of many de-Stalinizing reforms.[5] Among the cultural intelligentsia, many felt dismayed by Khrushchev's militant rhetoric and policies after December 1962 and hoped for a return to the soft-line policies of 1958 to 1962.[6] Although an intensification of militancy occurred in the literary arena, other cultural fields faced a more ambiguous policy environment.[7] The new leadership tamped down hard-line criticism in most areas, scaling back the late Khrushchev-era campaign against abstract art, as well as restrictions on film and art music.[8]

In regard to state-sponsored popular culture, there was considerable continuity in policy. The Soviet government kept reducing length of the work week.[9] Komsomol discourse underscored the importance of providing organized activities to fill this increase in youth free time.[10] The increasing availability of individual apartments meant a concomitant increase in competition between private recreation and state-sponsored collective activities.[11]

Yet, some differences appeared soon after the coup. Within the broad field of organized recreation activities for youth, the Khrushchev administration had given club activities equal or slightly more focus than the sphere of sports and military preparation, but the new leadership reversed this prioritization, partly because post-Khrushchev officials used World War II as a new basis of legitimacy.[12] The party Central Committee and the Council of Ministers passed a joint resolution on improving athletics and another on military preparation in 1966. The Komsomol Central Committee (CC), the Fifteenth Komsomol Congress (1966), and branch Komsomol committees also highlighted sports and military preparation.[13]

Nevertheless, state-sponsored popular culture remained an important aspect of Komsomol work. In orthodox club activities, aesthetic upbringing remained a priority, as conveyed by Sergei Pavlov's keynote at the Komsomol congress in 1966.[14] The Komsomol continued to promote work where youth lived, with a Komsomol CC resolution in 1966 calling for improved cultural activities in apartment complexes.[15] There were more than 700,000 amateur circles in the Soviet Union by 1970, though their growth had slowed considerably since the early 1960s—there were 600,000 circles in 1962, up from 350,000 eight years before—partly because of inadequate Komsomol attention.[16]

WESTERN POPULAR CULTURE IN THE MASS CULTURAL NETWORK, 1964-1967

The mid-1960s marked a shift toward more tolerance for jazz. National newspapers carried articles that expressed support for jazz, and Soviet radio established a weekly half-hour segment on this music. The state's chief recording enterprise, Melodiia, produced records by contemporary Soviet jazz bands. Jazz enthusiasts gained the opportunity to have their commentary on jazz published in the Soviet press and even foreign periodicals, including the famous Polish magazine *Jazz*.[17]

Youth clubs reflected this liberal attitude. The Leningrad interest-based club for jazz enthusiasts, Kvadrat (Square), appeared in December 1964.[18] The Komsomol CC expressed a renewed commitment to youth cafés in a 1966 resolution.[19] In Voronezh, the youth café Rossiianka (Russian woman) opened, and new cafés opened in Moscow and Saratov.[20]

The post-Khrushchev authorities also sought to accommodate rock and roll. Rock and roll's popularity exploded in 1963, when the songs of the Beatles entered the Soviet Union and eastern Europe.[21] During the last years of the Khrushchev regime, the Komsomol leadership expressed nothing but antipathy for rock and roll, as did Pavlov (in July 1963) and the Komsomol newspapers.[22]

Soon after Khrushchev's fall from power, this attitude began to change, as officials strove to co-opt rock and roll by inserting some of its elements into the Soviet mainstream. The party-state established a new rock-style professional genre known as the *vokal'no-instrumental'nyi ansambl'* (VIA, or vocal-instrumental ensemble). Professional VIAs had rock music equipment, including electric guitars, electric organs, amplifiers,

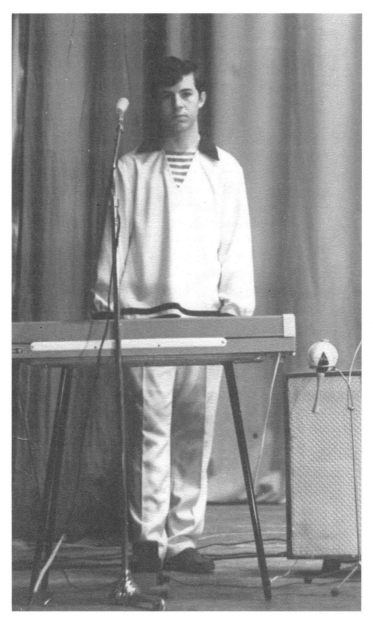

Fig. 8.1. Boris Vishnevkin performing in the amateur group Chaika (Seagull). Note the keyboard, microphone, and amplifiers, evocative of the sound equipment available to a *vokal'no-instrumental'nyi ansambl'* (vocal-instrumental ensemble), better known as a VIA. Vishnevkin's costume reflects the club's ownership by the sailors' trade union. Courtesy of the private archive of Boris Vishnevkin.

FIG. 8.2. Musicians take a bow after the conclusion of a performance by their group Chaika (Seagull). Note the saxophone, evocative of jazz, and the electric guitars, generally associated with rock, illustrating the blending of rock and jazz music in early VIAs. Later, rock would predominate. Courtesy of the private archive of Boris Vishnevkin.

and microphones. However, the authorities directed VIAs to include some brass and folk instruments and to play mostly folk, jazz, and Soviet-written pieces in their repertoires, with only one or two covers of English-language rock songs permitted at each performance. The most well-known professional VIAs performed in large concert halls, had their songs broadcast on radio, appeared on television, and released official records.[23] At the same time, some young people, unhappy with any restrictions on repertoire and equipment and enamored of the rebellious spirit of western rock and roll, formed underground bands that played only at unofficial concerts.[24]

Between these extremes lay a host of amateur VIA groups. These rock-style ensembles had looser limitations on their repertoire and equipment but had much less government financing and played to small audiences in club spaces. A typical example of one such VIA-style amateur ensemble, Chaika (Seagull) was formed at the sailors' trade union club in Baku, a port city and the capital of the Azerbaijan republic. A talented adolescent named Boris Vishnevkin was fourteen when he joined the collective in 1966 (fig. 8.1).

Chaika played a mix of genres: Azeri and Russian folk songs; Soviet variety, revolutionary, and war pieces; melodies from other Soviet republics and from socialist countries; and socialist-themed tunes from nonsocialist states. The last category also included foreign rock-style numbers by explicitly socialist-friendly western musicians, such as Dean Reed, an

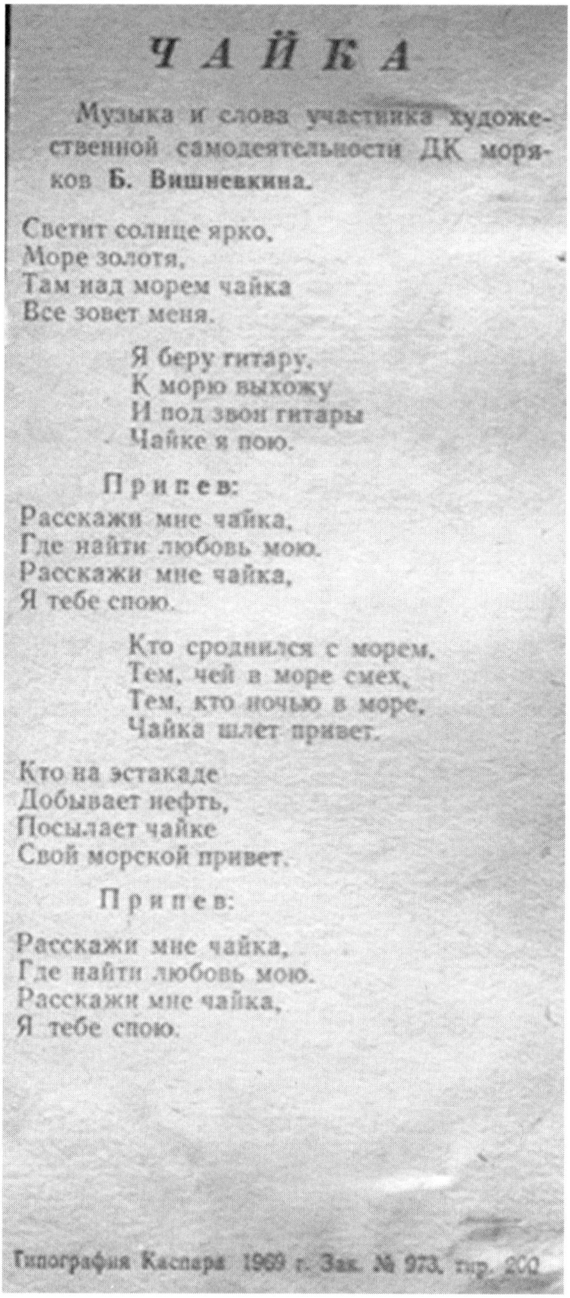

ЧАЙКА

Музыка и слова участника художе-
ственной самодеятельности ДК моря-
ков Б. Вишневкина.

Светит солнце ярко,
Море золотя,
Там над морем чайка
Все зовет меня.

Я беру гитару,
К морю выхожу
И под звон гитары
Чайке я пою.

Припев:
Расскажи мне чайка,
Где найти любовь мою.
Расскажи мне чайка,
Я тебе спою.

Кто сроднился с морем,
Тем, чей в море смех,
Тем, кто ночью в море,
Чайка шлет привет.

Кто на эстакаде
Добывает нефть,
Посылает чайке
Свой морской привет.

Припев:

Расскажи мне чайка,
Где найти любовь мою.
Расскажи мне чайка,
Я тебе спою.

Типография Каспара 1969 г. Зак. № 973, тир. 200

FIG. 8.3. The lyrics to the song "Seagull." Courtesy of the private archive of Boris Vishnevkin.

American. Members of Chaika enjoyed performing jazz as well, considering it the essence of improvisation (fig. 8.2).

Vishnevkin, the musical director of Chaika, refashioned some traditional Azeri folk songs into rock- and jazz-style pieces. He also wrote some numbers for the group, for example, their signature piece "Chaika," named after the band. This song spoke of love, music, seagulls, and working on oil platforms, something particularly meaningful for members of the sailors' trade union in Baku (fig. 8.3).

Vishnevkin expressed regret that the censorship apparatus limited their repertoire, banning the Beatles, for instance. He and the other musicians felt stifled by and resented these restrictions, unable to express their full musical creativity. Nonetheless, Chaika members worked within the limitations to find numbers that pleased their sailors' trade union audiences. They felt true joy over such success; "we loved it," Vishnevkin told me. Still, this amateur collective gave Vishnevkin access to resources, venues, instruments, audiences, professional development, and a network of other performers and music officials. Furthermore, Chaika represented for him and the other musicians a circle of friends that revolved, to a great extent, around music. They gathered at private parties, playing whatever they wanted. They also borrowed the trade union club's instruments to perform at paid events, using Chaika as a springboard to subsequent professional careers as popular musicians. Vishnevkin recalled performing in Chaika as a vital moment in his life and those of other participants, a center of meaning-making, emotional connections, economic activity, and social life—in other words, their identity and socioeconomic position.[25]

Although rock gained in popularity, jazz had more young adherents across the Soviet Union until at least the early 1970s, making the large-scale jazz festivals from the mid-1960s onward especially significant. Postwar festivals originated in the jazz sanctuary of the Baltics, which hosted the first officially sponsored jazz event in 1956.[26] Moscow held the first non-Baltic jazz festival in 1962, a small event held at the club Molodezhnoe and that attracted several local bands.[27] Jazz enthusiasts planned larger events, but the official turn against jazz in 1963 undermined their plans.[28]

Consequently, the first massive jazz festivals in the Soviet center occurred only in the mid-1960s. Jazz musicians gathered from around the Soviet Union to perform for large audiences at official concerts, jamming and socializing with each other before and after the performances. Moscow hosted the first such event, in 1965, with substantial official sponsorship from the Moscow Komsomol committee, the city's cultural authorities, and the Soiuz kompozitorov (Composers' union), with Vano Muradeli serving as jury head. This festival received official support from the press.[29] The jazz festival in 1966 received even more official recognition, with Melodiia releasing festival records and a youth-oriented radio station broadcasting the performances.[30] Large-scale, officially supported festivals took place in Leningrad as well.[31] The Baltic festivals grew, culminating in Tallinn-67. Georgii Garanian recalled the mid-1960s jazz festivals as "huge events" with packed halls.[32] In the late 1960s, jazz festivals began appearing in other cities, including Donetsk, Voronezh, Kuibyshev, Saratov, and others.[33] Reportedly, certain prominent Soviet officials, such as Aleksei Kosygin, the head of government, and Aleksei Adzhubei, Khrushchev's son-in-law and a high-ranking journalist, liked and patronized jazz, using their personal authority to promote these festivals.[34] Nikolai Butov, who rose through the Komsomol hierarchy in the 1960s to become deputy head of the Komsomol propaganda department in the 1970s and 1980s, recalled the organization of jazz festivals as a means of propagandizing jazz.[35]

The endorsement from the higher levels of the Komsomol and the Soiuz kompozitorov necessitated that jazz musicians fit their repertoire to official requirements, which generally meant balancing American and western European jazz pieces with sovietized jazz.[36] However, the definition of sovietized jazz expanded to include pieces written by jazz musicians, the vast majority of whom did not belong to the Soiuz kompozitorov. Thus, Mikhail Kull' recollected that, according to the rules for Dzhazz-67, the jazz festival held in Moscow in 1967, no less than half of each ensemble's program had to have Soviet origins. His band played "Moskovskie prospekty" (Moscow boulevards), a piece written by Kull', which he based on the style of Argentine-American jazz musician Lalo Schifrin. The group also played "Doodlin'," by the American jazz musician Horace Silver, and an arrangement by Kull' of the English jazz saxophonist Johnny Dankworth's "Magenta Midget," along with two other pieces written and arranged by another band member.[37] Jazz musicians frequently chose works by members of the Soiuz kompozitorov that closely resembled American-style jazz, such as those by Isaak Dunaevskii.[38] At Saratov jazz festivals, Lev Figlin's band took famous Soviet songs and "played them in a jazz style."[39]

This focus on works with native origins, even ones performed in the latest American style, underscores a broadening of standards for sovietized jazz. The cultural authorities undertook a new effort to create a truly viable and popular Soviet jazz, one that satisfied jazz musicians and fans while also distinguishing itself from western variants. Officials intended the homegrown character of the new compositions to divest jazz as a genre of its western and capitalist character and instead instill it with a native and socialist spirit.

The mass jazz festivals from the mid-1960s onward attracted jazz musicians from across the Soviet Union. Oleg Cherniaev's Voronezh ensemble played at Kuibyshev and Donetsk events.[40] Aleksei Kuznetsov, the Muscovite jazz guitarist, performed in many regional festivals.[41] In part, such travel proved possible because Komsomol organizations, patrons of jazz festivals, or trade unions generally covered travel and lodging costs.[42] Festival performers occasionally received a small honorarium.[43]

Simultaneously, the issue of finances contributed to the Komsomol's internal corrosion. The Komsomol hierarchy used the large audiences at festival concerts to fill its coffers. Plenty among the Komsomol officialdom saw jazz as somewhat ideologically questionable and would have refused to risk sanctioning jazz festivals based only on the need to satisfy youth desires. For these cadres, financial considerations provided an additional, and often convincing, argument, according to Dubiler, who organized a jazz club and several jazz festivals in Donetsk. He explained to me that such Komsomol officials saw jazz festivals "as a means of making money" for the Komsomol organization, from the tickets sold at the festival concerts. For each festival, Dubiler had to present a budget, and Donetsk authorities refused to grant approval for the event unless sufficient profit, generally several thousand rubles, remained for the Komsomol.[44] In this sense, the festivals served as the antecedent to the corruption of organized cultural activities that grew increasingly widespread in the 1970s.[45] Such practices formed one aspect of a broader expansion of underground economic activities during that time.[46]

The ideological perspectives of local administrators often determined the fate of jazz festivals. Both Dubiler and Cherniaev made the point that many cadres, regardless of top-level endorsement or financial incentives, refused to support jazz festivals because they perceived that music style to be subversive. Dubiler described how, in 1970, a newly appointed head of the Donetsk party committee forbade a jazz festival in Donetsk that year, despite the fact that the city had hosted a successful one the previous year. When Cherniaev tried to organize jazz festivals in Voronezh, some bureaucrats told him that jazz "is not our own, this is American music," and suggested that he instead hold folk music festivals.[47] Fortunately for jazz enthusiasts, the combination of top-level sanction, the policy of appealing to youth desires, and the financial motive enabled some regions with more permissive officials to hold jazz festivals.

These events helped give birth to union-wide jazz networks; in the 1950s, jazz networks had been only local affairs. The jazz clubs and youth cafés of the early 1960s offered the first stepping stone to extending links between musicians and promoters, making it possible to coordinate joint events with similar establishments in other cities. The clubs and cafés also offered visiting jazz enthusiasts a place to meet local performers.[48] Jazz festivals gave jazz musicians from around the country the opportunity for officially sponsored travel to meet one another, evaluate the quality of each other's performance, and form personal contacts at private jam sessions and parties.

Such ties led to later jazz exchanges and the continued strengthening of union-wide linkages. For instance, as the founder of a Donetsk jazz club, Dubiler received an invitation to Tallinn-67, where he established contacts with other musicians. He invited them to his Donetsk jazz festivals and received invitations in return. Dubiler kept up contacts both by visiting festivals elsewhere and by exchanging letters with jazz musicians and promoters.[49] Cherniaev described the emergence of "a group of [jazz] enthusiasts," living in a number of Soviet cities, who "kept up contacts with each other[,] and due to these, [jazz] exchanges took place," generally "via jazz festivals."[50]

In another crucial development, a wave of foreign jazz musicians and promoters came to Soviet jazz festivals and on individual tours. The Khrushchev authorities did not invite any western jazz musicians to perform during 1963 and 1964. However, in May 1966, an American jazz ensemble led by Earl "Fatha" Hines toured the Soviet Union. When in Moscow, many of the sidemen came to Molodezhnoe and jammed with Soviet jazz musicians.[51] The first performance at a Soviet jazz festival by an American group, Charles Lloyd's quartet, occurred at Tallinn-67. The group finished its tour in Moscow's Molodezhnoe.[52] Moscow's Dzhazz-67 featured the visit of Willis Conover, the host of *Jazz Hour* on Voice of America.[53] Duke Ellington arrived in 1971.[54]

Jazz players from other socialist states also came. They played at major events in Moscow, Leningrad, and the Baltics; for instance, Polish jazz musicians played at Tallinn-67.[55] They also toured Soviet provincial cities. Dubiler invited musicians from Czechoslovakia, Poland, and Romania to perform at Donetsk. Dubiler first made contacts with eastern European jazz enthusiasts in the mid-1960s by perusing Polish jazz journals and finding the names and addresses of potential contacts in a section entitled "We want to write to each other." Dubiler eventually started to write to nonsocialist foreigners, and they sent him jazz materials in return for Soviet souvenirs.[56] A Voronezh jazz enthusiast similarly established cross-border contacts by exchanging letters.[57]

Thus, from the mid-1960s on, Soviet jazz networks were becoming integrated into broad jazz networks across the eastern bloc, a process advanced by Soviet jazz musicians participating in eastern European jazz festivals. The most famous such event, the Jazz Jamboree, took place in Warsaw and featured jazz bands from around the world. The first Soviet attendees arrived in 1962, a number of them being jazz musicians, including Kozlov, who had had a good showing at the Moscow jazz festival in 1962. At the Jazz Jamboree, the Soviet jazz musicians played Thelonious Monk's "Straight, No Chaser," as well as three pieces written by the musicians themselves. They received enthusiastic applause, which Kozlov attributed not to the quality of their performance, which did not equal that of the best Polish jazz musicians, but to the fact that "the appearance at the festival of people from the USSR playing in an American style was so unexpected that it produced a sensation." Kozlov and the other Soviet jazz musicians established friendly relations with Polish and other socialist jazz musicians and even jammed with the visiting American jazz trumpeter Don Ellis. The Soviet musicians returned home full of euphoria and hoped for more such visits in the near future.[58]

However, the militant cultural policy of 1963 and 1964 closed the door to international jazz events. Only after the new leadership took power did such visits become a regular occasion. In 1965, Garanian's ensemble went to a Prague jazz festival. Soviet jazz musicians performed and jammed with socialist jazz musicians, as well as prominent western stars, including the Americans Theodore "Ted" Curson and Don Cherry.[59] Similar cross-border jazz exchanges within the Soviet bloc took place in the late 1960s and 1970s.[60] Still, such visits constituted a privilege available only to a select group of jazz musicians. Cherniaev, for example, remembered his resentment over a refusal for a visit to East Germany.[61]

The international jazz contacts between the superpowers served the interests of American cultural diplomacy. The appearance of American jazz musicians in front of large Soviet audiences made Americans seem less threatening, thus reducing Cold War tensions. Jazz tours helped raise the United States' prestige among the citizens of its superpower competitor.[62]

The Soviet Union benefited as well and also sought to defuse tensions through jazz exchanges. Lacking direct contact with Soviet jazz, American citizens read press reports about American jazz activities in the Soviet Union. The *Village Voice* published an article about the 1966 tour by Hines's group, including mention of the jam with Soviet musicians in Molodezhnoe.[63] The visit by Lloyd's quartet received coverage in *Down Beat*.[64] Very positive comments by Don Ellis about the quality of Soviet jazz musicians appeared in the American press, too.[65] *Newsweek* carried an article about the 1965 jazz festival in Moscow and ran a photograph of Kleinot with it.[66] Such foreign press coverage helped the Soviet Union's domestic cultural diplomacy by convincing outsiders that it welcomed contemporary jazz. Doing so countered western propaganda about the suppression of jazz behind the Iron Curtain. Moreover, depictions of Soviet jazz events contributed to the Soviet Union's aim of presenting itself as having a homegrown, socialist version of jazz, offering socialist fun as part of an alternative modernity.

For the Soviet party-state, jazz exchanges within the Soviet bloc served cultural diplomacy purposes as well. The liberal Komsomol cultural officials who sponsored the visits of Soviet jazz musicians abroad claimed that such trips helped strengthen a progressive socialist version of jazz, while the wide acknowledgment of Soviet jazz in eastern Europe supposedly meant a victory for Soviet culture.[67] By promoting such cultural contacts, the authorities aimed to strengthen a sense of cohesion and community within the Soviet bloc and to create a common socialist popular culture in opposition to a capitalist one.

The growth of international jazz exchanges brought problems unique to those forums, especially in relation to American visitors. The invitation for the Lloyd quartet to play at Tallinn-67 came on the initiative of the festival organizing committee, rather than through typical diplomatic channels. The American musicians obtained tourist visas but received conflicting messages over whether they would have permission to play; not having in hand the official sanction to play, they missed their scheduled performance, only to receive approval two days later, just in time to play an unscheduled session on the last day of the festival.[68] These problems arose despite the fact that, according to the US State Department's official list of cultural exchanges, the quartet had received confirmation that it would be part of the program.[69] Kleinot, who attended the festival, described the outrage felt by the festival-goers over such treatment of the visiting musicians. Rumors circulated that Kosygin had intervened to permit Lloyd's quartet to perform.[70] The Komsomol propaganda department report on the festival censured the festival organizers for having violated "government discipline" in circumventing the proper diplomatic channels and provoking difficulties with regard to the performance of American artists. Such problems, in turn, "enabled some dishonest foreign journalists to twist the essence of the issue into political speculation" and present the local authorities as "preventing the performance of black jazz musicians before an Estonian audience," while "heating up separatist tendencies" among Estonians and undermining party authority.[71] Indeed, *Down Beat* spent about half its article about the tour describing the difficulties experienced by Lloyd's quartet in trying to perform, also hinting that racial discrimination may have played a role.[72] The implications of racism may have been especially problematic given propaganda claims that juxtaposed the Soviet Union's supposed racial unity and a racist western model.[73]

Another incident at Moscow's Dzhazz-67 highlighted continuing tensions over American jazz in the Soviet Union. Conover invited many jazz musicians and promoters to visit the American embassy for a postfestival reception in his honor, prompting much excitement among jazz musicians, according to Kozlov. However, the liberal Komsomol officials who had organized the festival sought to prevent Soviet jazz musicians from attending the reception, which they believed could constitute a "serious threat to the future of Soviet jazz," if, for instance, the US press discovered that Moscow's jazz festival had ended with a reception at the American embassy. Having apparently received an order from above, Kozlov's Komsomol contacts warned the people who received an invitation, such as Kozlov, that those who attended would never again receive permission for international travel. With a heavy heart, Kozlov and most other jazz musicians and promoters decided that this occasion, however unique, was not worth ruining relations with their Komsomol allies or risking the negative impact of articles appearing in American newspapers.[74] The main problem was not Soviet jazz musicians visiting foreign embassies. Vadif Sadykhov and Kleinot had played at the American and other embassies, where they were well paid and given gifts such as foreign cigarettes and beer.[75] The crux of the issue lay in the potentially harmful impact of western public attention on Soviet jazz.

The actions of US representatives underscore how they pursued American cultural diplomacy goals in regard to Soviet youth. A US embassy report on this topic reveals that the American officials stationed at the heart of the Soviet Union tried "by 'all feasible means' to increase [their] contacts with Soviet youth."[76] The United States Information Agency (USIA) paid specific attention to the young. For instance, a 1966 research memorandum labeled "The Soviet Youth Problem" stated that the claims made by Soviet authorities that "alien influences are responsible for the existence of youth problems [were] not without foundation. Interest in Western music and art [was] continually being reinforced by listening to foreign radios, viewing foreign films, [and] contacts with Western tourists."[77] The USIA later produced similar documentation that highlighted western influence on Soviet young people through direct channels, which the report defined as western radio, cultural and commercial exchanges, and international travel.[78] Such records indicate the attention from American government officials devoted to using cultural diplomacy to subvert Soviet youth.

Consequently, Soviet authorities walked a narrow path in their approach toward international jazz exchanges. They tried to make sure that such activities provided more benefit than harm to the Soviet Union's domestic and foreign interests. Nonetheless, the actions of foreign agents at the ground level occasionally undermined the Soviet Union's own cultural diplomacy efforts, underscoring the complexities involved in cross-border jazz exchanges.

International jazz contacts had detrimental consequences for Soviet jazz enthusiasts in addition to beneficial ones. Such disadvantages included the incidents at Tallinn-67 and Dzhazz-67 and increasing scrutiny from the security agency (KGB). Youth cafés, which hosted foreign dignitaries, musicians, and tourists, proved especially vulnerable to KGB attention. When practicing at youth cafés before business hours, Sadykhov occasionally saw "how [KGB operatives] attached microphones in a niche above the stage," and he attributed such surveillance to the "socializing with foreigners" that went on in the café. He recalled one incident in the late 1960s when a KGB colonel met with him and some other jazz musicians, discouraging them from interacting with Americans. The secret police also used informers to monitor youth cafés. Moreover, Sadykhov related that the KGB successfully co-opted some jazz musicians to work on its behalf.[79] The KGB investigated Garanian extensively due to the defection of two jazz musicians performing in a professional Soviet variety troupe visiting Japan; these musicians had played with Garanian's band, Zolotoi vosem' (Golden eight).[80] The KGB imprisoned Andrei Tovmasian, a prominent Soviet jazz trumpeter, after discovering that he had engaged in illegal trade in foreign goods.[81] Dubiler experienced more KGB monitoring than most, due to his foreign contacts. The KGB, which undoubtedly read his letters, called in Dubiler on several occasions, pressing him for information about his contacts. He strove to play dumb, replying to the agents that "certainly, if we find spies, I will let you know," and thus avoiding cooperating with them beyond the minimum.[82] The desire of jazz musicians and promoters, especially those involved in organizing jazz events, to retain the significant profiles they had gained during the 1960s likely made them more willing to share basic information with the KGB.

The international jazz contacts underscore the importance of adopting a multipolar and multilevel paradigm on Cold War interactions and also indicate the need to expand this framework. Sari Autio-Sarasmo and Katalin Miklossy's model highlights the crucial yet informal diplomatic role of interactions across the Iron Curtain. Specifically, these authors focus on how mid- and lower-level agents engaged with each other in mutually beneficial arrangements, ones that did not necessarily fit the overarching goals of the two superpowers.[83] Indeed, the interactions of Soviet jazz musicians with foreign ones occasionally departed from the Cold

War aims of the Soviet Union. Likewise, Soviet jazz performers gained substantial dividends from their contacts with those outside the country, though they also suffered the consequences of interactions with foreigners, as did other Soviet citizens.[84]

My analysis also indicates that we should apply a multipolar and multilevel paradigm to intrabloc interactions as well. Soviet jazz musicians and audiences interacted on multiple levels with performers and spectators from eastern Europe. Similar patterns characterized other musical spheres. For instance, winning the bloc-wide international song festivals in Sopot, Poland, helped launch or strengthen the careers of Soviet variety stars such as Alla Pugacheva and Irina Ponarovskaia.[85] Classical music exchanges within the eastern bloc proved important for both Soviet and eastern European performers.[86] These musical interchanges shaped the course of the Cold War's cultural competition in complex ways. On the one hand, they strengthened Soviet bloc unity by creating a more cohesive socialist musical sphere, with the various countries reinforcing each other's cultural production. On the other hand, such cross-border interplay made possible the rapid spread of western cultural influence from the most westernized socialist countries to the Soviet Union.

Unsurprisingly, Soviet jazz musicians expressed pleasure and enthusiasm over the pluralistic turn toward jazz in the mid-1960s. Garanian told me that at jazz festivals, both jazz musicians and audiences felt "very good," and he was pleasantly surprised with the active support of certain Komsomol cadres.[87] Kuznetsov remarked that jazz festivals denoted the official acceptance of jazz into the Soviet mainstream.[88] The jazz festivals, along with the positive commentary about jazz in Soviet newspapers, the opportunity to attain information about jazz in the burgeoning jazz clubs, the broadcasts of jazz on Soviet radio, the first official releases of jazz records, and the chance to listen to foreign jazz musicians, undoubtedly pleased many and thereby reinforced the regime's popularity. This conclusion nuances previous scholarship that stressed how interactions among Soviet bloc and foreign youth bred discontent among the former, weakening the socialist system as a whole.[89]

The mid-1960s developments irrevocably transformed the Soviet jazz scene. While still seen as excessively western by some of the most hard-line officials, jazz moved into the Soviet mainstream. Many formerly amateur jazz musicians joined professional ensembles in state agencies. They played popular jazz-style variety music commercially, while performing more esoteric jazz music, such as bebop and cool jazz, for minimal payment in youth cafés and at jazz festivals in front of appreciative audiences. Some even formed their own professional groups playing only jazz, although most of these bands did not prove financially viable owing to the growing popularity of rock and roll. Several experimented with blending jazz and rock. In a further sign that jazz was no longer countercultural, those who decided to play jazz professionally experienced no challenges to the authenticity of their music from other performers, promoters, or fans, in contrast to what rock-and-roll musicians encountered.[90] Other amateur jazz musicians chose not to make jazz their full-time career, although many pursued jazz-related activities during their free time as promoters, critics, amateur musicians, or simply avid fans, having gained the opportunity to enjoy jazz through officially sanctioned sources.[91]

Party-state support for jazz removed the reasons for the existence of the jazz enthusiast counterculture and alternative emotional community. The former counterculture transitioned into a professional milieu of jazz musicians and promoters, along with a jazz fan community of their supporters and amateur performers—just one among many Soviet artistic communities. Furthermore, by the Brezhnev years, the jazz fan community of the 1950s and early 1960s was older and better educated, while young people, especially those from working-class backgrounds, searched for a countercultural space in the rock-and-roll scene. Still, the jazz scene retained a slightly unorthodox ambiance due to its history of suppression and its taint of western cultural influence.

Scholarship on Soviet cultural life from the end of 1964 to early 1968 tends to depict this period as "stagnation," a time of conservative ideologues gradually taking control over Soviet official culture and instituting hard-line policies. A recent typical account by Vladislav Zubok, who, like most historians, relies on sources produced largely by cultural elites, terms the mid-1960s the years of "creeping Stalinization," a gradual reversal of de-Stalinization and cultural liberalism associated with Khrushchev's Thaw harking back to the ideological militancy of the late Stalinist cultural model.[92]

However, juxtaposing the last Khrushchev years and the mid-1960s reveals a significant improvement in the day-to-day experience of the many millions of young people enthusiastic about western popular culture. This finding suggests that terming the mid-1960s a time of "creeping Stalinization" in culture does not sufficiently acknowledge the complexities and contingencies in central policy. Moreover, that label overvalues the point of view of the cultural elites—always a small minority—and undercounts that of the myriad non-elite cultural producers and consumers.

Arguably, the pluralistic policy toward western popular culture served to satisfy popular youth desires, representing one clause of a new social contract extended to the young by the post-Khrushchev collective leadership and similar to the agreement offered to youth in the early Thaw. The visits by western musicians were highlighted as demonstrating to domestic and foreign audiences that the Soviet Union enabled its citizens to participate in global cultural trends, while those by foreign socialist ones strengthened the unity of socialist popular culture across the eastern bloc. Other aspects of the new leadership's approach to state-sponsored popular culture similarly departed from late Stalinist precedents, for instance, the emphasis on organized cultural leisure as a means of dealing with youth crime. Likewise, the drive for aesthetic upbringing and cultural work taking place where youth lived originated during the late 1950s and early 1960s, not under Stalin. Admittedly, the stress on sports and military preparation did reflect late Stalinist preferences, as did the increasingly cautious attitude toward youth initiative. On balance, the period of the mid-1960s deserves to be labeled one of ambiguity, conflict, and uncertainty in cultural policy, when some pluralistic tendencies gained ground and others lost out.

YOUTH INITIATIVE AND STATE-SPONSORED POPULAR CULTURE, 1964–1967

The growing emphasis on sports, military preparation, and patriotic upbringing in youth policy hints at the changes in values desired by the post-Khrushchev Kremlin in youth-oriented recreation activities. Indeed, top-level statements and policies foregrounded discipline, obedience, and consciousness, while initiative, autonomy, and spontaneity slowly retreated into the background. This shift took place gradually, and its impact took a while to percolate throughout state-sponsored popular culture, especially since Khrushchev-era policies ramped up institutions and notions associated with youth leadership from below.

The policy began to shift soon after the coup that ousted Khrushchev. At the Fifteenth Komsomol Congress, in 1966, Brezhnev delivered a speech in which he did not mention the development of youth initiative as one of the overarching goals for the Komsomol, instead stressing the need for discipline. Brezhnev also did not praise activism in organized recreation.[93] Brezhnev's deemphasis of youth initiative marked a sharp departure from Khrushchev's statements at the 1958 and 1962 Komsomol congresses. Similarly, Pavlov did not list eliciting initiative from below as one of the Komsomol's main aims, instead calling for strengthening "the discipline and cohesion of [Komsomol] ranks." Pavlov, unlike Brezhnev, did advocate for young people to show activism in organizing interest-based clubs, and he commended Ukraine for helping develop the initiative of school-age Komsomol members.[94] Such signals reached Komsomol cadres, who carefully observed top-level statements for signs of the post-Khrushchev direction. Following the coup, Saratov city Komsomol conferences stopped calling for the development of grassroots activism.[95]

Still, many club activities associated with youth initiative, particularly interest-based clubs, continued to grow. In tune with Pavlov's statements at the congress, branch Komsomol conferences and the Komsomol press expressed support for interest-based associations.[96] Paralleling top-level pronouncements, most of these statements emphasized greater efforts on interest-based clubs for adolescents, as opposed to those for older youth.[97] With such support, the numbers of youth clubs and interest-based associations increased quickly. Most notably, interest-based clubs for adolescents grew by more than 450 percent from the 1962 Komsomol congress to the 1966 one, reaching approximately twelve thousand by 1967.[98]

The encouragement from above to promote interest-based clubs for adolescents arose from several factors. First, the number of adolescents as a proportion of the population grew substantially owing to the demographic imbalances following the war.[99] Second, the authorities perceived adolescents as easier to influence than older youth and more liable to engage in criminal behavior.[100] Interest-based associations also focused on a single issue or social group rather than on the broad range that youth initiative clubs encompassed and were therefore considered less likely to express inappropriately channeled initiative or to escape the control of the hierarchy. All of these factors help explain why Komsomol speeches and conference resolutions in the mid-1960s downplayed youth initiative clubs and rarely mentioned interest-based clubs targeted at older youth.

Youth cafés represent one exception to the trend of a shift away from support for organized cultural recreation for those of college age. However, the expansion of youth cafés came with a price: a decrease in grassroots management. Youth cafés began to shift from being experimental and daring entities to a normal component of Komsomol work, one not only sanctioned but also demanded by the Komsomol leadership. Furthermore, the increasing use of cafés for cultural diplomacy resulted in closer monitoring by party-state organs. As a result, much of the spirit of enthusiasm and freedom permeating the first wave of youth cafés declined, disenchanting some visitors. The Saratovite Mikhail Ryskin stopped going to youth cafés after his initial excitement, as the "air of freedom" he had enjoyed so much began to dissipate.[101]

Also appealing to older youth and rapidly burgeoning during this period were the *kluby samodeiatel'nykh pesen* (clubs of amateur songs). These institutions served as officially sanctioned platforms in which to write and perform guitar poetry.[102] Aleksander Vygnanov, who served in the Komsomol committee of a Moscow technical institute in the mid- and late 1960s, told me that many in the Komsomol bureaucracy had a "skeptical" view of these clubs, believing they harbored "unhealthy" and even "slightly anti-Soviet tendencies."[103] In light of these official attitudes and the wider tendencies militating against youth initiative, the spread of these clubs during the mid-1960s deserves note. To a significant extent, this development resulted from the desire of the authorities to prevent young people from following bard celebrities and engaging in nonconformist musical activities in private settings. Clubs of amateur songs, in other words, represent the further institutionalization of guitar poetry, as officialdom strove to co-opt this genre to serve party-state goals. The clubs, at the same time, constitute a case study of how unofficial culture influenced the mass cultural network, causing it to grant youths more of what they desired.

Even mainstream interest-based associations faced opposition from some strongly militant cadres. A Komsomol propaganda department report from 1967 noted that some regions had plenty of interest-based clubs, yet others had few or none, in large part because Komsomol cadres had "widely varying" attitudes toward interest-based clubs. For instance, one high Komsomol official in Chitinsk Province considered clubs a "harmful invention" and declared that "Chitinsk Province has no and will not have any youth clubs, and if one shows up, then we will try to make sure that it dies quietly." The report's authors claimed that "plenty of similar instances can be cited." The report criticized such views and claimed that interest-based clubs needed to expand. Moreover, the report praised the shift in the focus of these associations. In the late 1950s, they emphasized "satisfying youth needs for interesting and enjoyable leisure." By the mid-1960s, interest-based clubs stressed community activism and politically oriented activities, such as expressing one's opinions on and discussing pressing issues of the day, as well as "influencing the political, cultural, and economic life of one's city, neighborhood, and village."[104] By the mid-1960s, the civic spirit that had emerged in youth initiative-based institutions in the 1950s had grown substantially. Soft-line cadres, such those who authored the Komsomol propaganda department's report, celebrated this development, while hard-liners intent on managing community affairs from above undoubtedly opposed it.

Such tensions also emerge in a proposal, advanced in 1966 by several high-level Komsomol officials, to establish the Vsesoiuznoe podrostkovoe ob"edinenie (Union-wide adolescent association), which would unite interest-based institutions for adolescents. The proposal's authors noted that among those Komsomol cadres consulted, a minority expressed concern that the new entity might "decrease the interest of adolescents toward the Komsomol." Proponents rejected this view, arguing that the association would actually "significantly improve communist upbringing."[105] However, in the environment of the top-level turn against grassroots initiative, hard-line skepticism proved more potent, preventing the association's establishment.[106]

Young amateur artists confronted rising censorship. Ryskin, who took part in a Saratov amateur satirical theater troupe in the 1950s and 1960s, recounted that the Khrushchev years witnessed several zigzags of tolerance and limitations for satire but that after Khrushchev censorship grew ever stronger.[107] The Saratovite Nelli Popkova stated that she began to feel the pressure of the party line on amateur arts only after 1964.[108] More independent-minded literary associations began to close down, as recalled by Volodia Gertsik, an Arkhimed (Archimedes) member and unofficial Soviet poet still active today.[109] Owing to such developments, many young poets formed alternative groups in nonofficial settings, turned toward underground publishing (*samizdat*), and published in other countries (*tamizdat*), with some even participating in political dissent.[110] Gertsik and his friends did all three.

Arkhimed faced mounting difficulties. Iurii Gaponov, the longtime director of the Arkhimed collective, emphasized that student autonomy and initiative began to deteriorate in the mid-1960s, which he explicitly associated with the coup against Khrushchev. Thus, in 1965, militants in the Saratovskii gosudarstvennyi universitet (SGU) physics department's party committee managed to break the departmental Komsomol cell into smaller and weaker units. Likewise, hard-liners successfully prevented the celebration of Den' fizikov (Physicists' day) and the attendant staging of the *Arkhimed* opera that year. However, many physics students and Arkhimed alumni refused to accept this outcome and formed the Arkhimed studio, which meant a more permanent and autonomous status.[111] Moreover, at the physics department Komsomol conference in 1966, those committed to Arkhimed and to student self-rule schemed together to replace the Komsomol committee that accommodated the conservatives with one oriented toward student initiative. The conference voted to reinstate the Den' fizikov celebration.[112] As one *Arkhimed* performer highlighted when commenting about these conflicts, "Naturally we all held to the [official] ideology, but this does not mean that there were no disputes within it."[113]

With a global view of the sixties, it is apparent that changes in the Soviet Union paralleled developments within western societies. The apogee of youth-oriented movements for pluralistic social transformation in capitalist democracies occurred in 1968, with conservative forces gradually rising in strength and limiting the options for reforms originating from below thereafter.[114] Jeremi Suri has noted that, beginning in the late 1960s, both capitalist and socialist systems offered their citizens better consumption options and stability in order to gain popular support and legitimacy while preventing substantial political and social changes, even adopting détente in pursuit of these goals.[115]

The evidence from state-sponsored popular culture indicates that, in the Soviet Union, the roots of this approach to foreign and domestic policy stem from mid-1960s internal politics. Soviet authorities increasingly stressed discipline and hierarchy. Hampering cultural innovation, this governing style increased stability and continuity, while also inspiring some youth discontent. To compensate, the party-state not only provided more orthodox club activities but also instituted greater openness toward western culture, appeasing young people's desires to some extent. Satisfied with the results it achieved in the mid-1960s, the authorities carried this domestic practice into foreign policy at the end of the 1960s, which assisted the emergence of détente. This conclusion reinforces the literature arguing that domestic interests, priorities, and perspectives defined Thaw-era Soviet foreign policy.[116]

STATE-SPONSORED POPULAR CULTURE, 1968–1970s

Historical accounts generally consider the Soviet-led invasion of Czechoslovakia in August 1968 as a sharp and defining hard-line turning point that marked the bitter end of Thaw-era liberalism.[117] However, my evidence indicates that policies toward organized youth leisure from 1968 to 1970 and beyond continued, with slight modifications, and that the trends were already visible in the mid-1960s. Ted Hopf's framework implies that the decision to use armed force in Prague largely resulted from Soviet domestic priorities, an issue not receiving much attention in geopolitics-focused scholarship on Soviet foreign policy. The Czechoslovak Communist Party proclaimed a vision of "socialism with a human face" in January 1968, launching a period of liberalization known as the Prague Spring. This policy represented, from the perspective of the post-Khrushchev leaders, an unpardonable expression of initiative. Moreover, the pluralistic trends of the Prague Spring, which encouraged the Czechoslovak population to exhibit unconstrained grassroots activism while staying within the socialist framework, departed from the increasingly hard-line domestic stance taken by Soviet top officials. Newly empowered after triumphing over Shelepin, Brezhnev chose to invade Czechoslovakia, thus acting in accord with Soviet domestic policies calling for obedience from below and closing down institutions that refused to oblige. These internal trends shaped the Brezhnev Kremlin's perceptions of the Soviet Union's geopolitical and ideological priorities and help explain the use of military force. Other considerations also were in play, such as a desire to maintain superpower status and to deny the western powers a propaganda victory.[118]

While powerfully influenced by Soviet domestic priorities, the invasion had consequences that also affected internal policies. The Komsomol hierarchy placed even greater emphasis on sports, military preparation, and patriotic education. At the Komsomol congress in 1970, E. M. Tiazhel'nikov, who took over leadership of the Komsomol from Pavlov in June 1968, spent little time speaking of clubs and amateur arts, instead focusing on sports and military preparation.[119] Regional Komsomol organizations did so as well.[120]

Western popular culture suffered only slightly after the attack and quickly rebounded. Some short-term restraints cast a brief pall on the jazz scene, and the authorities canceled a Leningrad jazz festival.[121] No jazz festivals took place in 1968 or afterward in Leningrad, Moscow, or Tallinn, the major sites of the mid-1960s jazz festivals. However, the authorities began to sanction regional jazz festivals, probably because the sort problems with foreigners that had marred the Dzhazz-67 and Tallinn-67 festivals were less likely to occur in regional cities, which were much more difficult for foreigners to access.[122] Yet, jazz musicians and fans from across the eastern bloc could attend, and Soviet propaganda could successfully claim that the Soviet Union sponsored jazz.

The post-Khrushchev party-state's promotion of discipline and devaluing of grassroots voluntarism helped bring about the Prague Spring, and the crushing of that uprising intensified the party-state's resolve to uproot grassroots initiative. In contrast to Pavlov's speech at the Komsomol congress in 1966, Tiazhel'nikov's keynote at the congress in 1970 did not discuss the need to develop youth initiative or strengthen individual community activism, though it devoted considerable attention to the Komsomol's role in youth upbringing.[123] Thus, the situation for youth community leadership, which began to deteriorate after the coup, had grown substantially worse by 1970. From then on, the Brezhnev leadership encouraged young people to express initiative from below only in economic production. The key Komsomol construction project of that era, the Baikal-Amur mainline railroad, shows the failure of such policies.[124]

The clampdown on youth community leadership expressed itself in state-sponsored popular culture. The separate archival folders devoted to initiative-oriented cultural institutions such as youth clubs and cafés had disappeared by 1968, underscoring the diminished importance of these entities.[125] The Komsomol leadership feared that associations based on grassroots enthusiasm would slip out of its control.[126] Having gained more power after the invasion, conservatives in the administration banned Den' fizikov in 1969 and forced the Arkhimed studio out of the university in 1970.[127] Hard-liners also closed the Leninskie gory (Lenin hills) theater studio, where Anatolii Krichevich, a member of Arkhimed, had performed. This establishment had used dramatic performance as a tool of political satire that mocked systemic problems in the Soviet Union, a strategy that was acceptable under Khrushchev but unwelcome in the late 1960s.[128] In 1968, Novosibirsk authorities closed down the Pod integralom (Under the integral) youth café for its controversial program.[129]

The Brezhnev Kremlin's approach to managing the bureaucracy also minimized youth initiative. In place of the Khrushchev administration's orientation toward encouraging citizens to participate in local governance, the Brezhnev regime instituted the "stability of cadres."[130] This policy gave officials much greater authority over their individual administrative fiefdoms and minimized the space in which ordinary people could undertake community leadership and oppose the bureaucracy. Since many cadres at the grassroots level disliked initiative-oriented cultural collectives, which disrupted traditional patterns and challenged bureaucratic complacency, the new Kremlin policy enabled local administrators to undermine such institutions.

A further factor hampered grassroots activism: systematization. This term refers to the escalating combined efforts by the Komsomol, the Ministry of Culture, trade unions, educational organs, and other central organs to create a unified structure of organized cultural recreation for young people. Liubov Baliasnaia related that such systematization had roots in the late 1950s in the collaborative interagency efforts to organize leisure activities where youth lived. However, the crucial moment, in her words, occurred in 1966, when a party Central Committee resolution demanded the active coordination of agencies working on organized recreation for school-age youngsters.[131] This resolution applied to older youth as well, with Komsomol cadres calling for a system of youth aesthetic upbringing in the mid-1960s.[132] Nikolai Butov told me that at the local level, this systematization "meant a cohesive program, with the district party committee, Komsomol committee, police, and cultural organs creating a unified plan, and everything tied with it controlled very closely." This approach "applied equally to all the territories of the Soviet Union."[133] This systematization fit within a broader post-Khrushchev Komsomol policy that called for "the establishment of a unified, cohesive program for the communist upbringing of the young," beginning in 1966.[134] Other sectors of public life likewise witnessed increasing bureaucratic control.[135] Such systematization left little room for grassroots activism.

Some limited spaces existed for initiative-oriented cultural collectives. After finishing his studies, Gaponov secured a position at Moscow's Kurchatovskii Institut (Kurchatov institute), and, with his assistance, the Arkhimed studio managed to move to the institute's club in 1970. Having become a cult hit, *Arkhimed* the opera continued its existence, with the studio continuing to stage this work on a regular basis, up to the present.[136] The studio videotaped the opera's fiftieth anniversary performance in 2000 and made it available for viewing over the Internet.[137] In 1965, Georgii Frid and several other musical experts created the Moskovskii molodezhnii muzykal'nii klub (Moscow youth musical club), an institution with a democratic and open atmosphere.[138] Certain amateur theaters in Moscow emphasized grassroots involvement by audiences.[139]

Owing to the stronger regulatory mechanisms in the center, the Soviet regions frequently offered more room for initiative from below during this time of increasingly hard-line approaches promulgated from above. The Saratovite Vladimir Rozhkov recalled the Thaw lasting longer in Saratov than in Moscow.[140] The historian Nina Deviataikina, who studied and then worked as a professor in SGU's history department from 1961 onward, told me that the department's tradition of pluralistic amateur cultural activities, developed under Khrushchev, kept going in the early Brezhnev years.[141] Vladimir Veshnev led a grassroots effort to establish a youth café in the physics department of SGU during the late 1960s.[142] This tendency reflected a pattern of decreased controls and greater room for the expression of popular desires similar to those this study has revealed for the anticosmopolitan years.

This overview of state-sponsored popular culture from 1965 to 1970 clarifies the Brezhnev approach to governance. In the mid-1960s, the post-Khrushchev collective leadership was already undermining the early Thaw social contract by increasingly moving against cultural activities imbued with a spirit of grassroots activism despite knowing that the youth greatly enjoyed these highly popular club forms. To offset this loss to the youth, policy makers gave young people substantially greater access to western music and dancing, aiming to retain the legitimacy of the party-state among youth by satisfying at least some popular desires. Apparently, the new top officials decided that channeling cultural consumption desires toward western culture represented a safer and wiser course than permitting homegrown youth initiative and civic spirit. Upon consolidating power, the Brezhnev administration intensified this approach and continued it into the 1970s and early 1980s, tamping down youth self-management while gradually allowing more western cultural influence.[143] This policy constituted part of a broader social contract, Brezhnev's "Little Deal," that put aside any substantive reforms and strove to keep the population satisfied by appeasing consumerist desires.[144] A technocracy staffed by political managers and professional experts with minimal citizen involvement came to define the Soviet system.[145]

In tune with the Soviet hegemon, other socialist eastern European states followed suit. Their party-states increasingly rejected grassroots self-management and instead focused on supplying consumer products and services to their populations.[146] Thus, a new style of rule acquired dominance throughout the bloc. This approach to governance closely paralleled what Zygmunt Bauman has termed the "patronage state," which is one that promises "personal provision and security" but "demands surrender of the right to choose and to self-determine."[147]

In interviews, Komsomol officials and cultural activists underscored the negative long-term consequences of the new focus on discipline. Butov recollected that, prior to the 1970s, the party-state strongly endorsed cultural activities arising from below, and he expressed regret that after 1970 the authorities came to direct such a great proportion of club activities from above. He personally fought to promote innovative and daring cultural activities during the Brezhnev years, thus facing threats to his career from conservatives. Yet, Butov lamented, the general tendency "was the complete opposite" of what he wished to occur, "resulting in the growth of underground culture," with young people expressing their cultural creativity in nonofficial settings.[148] Popkova told me that, in the Khrushchev years, the authorities had "welcomed and praised" youth initiative, listening to what young people themselves wanted, allowing them to organize their own cultural activities, and providing them with club spaces and equipment. As a result of this attitude from above, Popkova recalled that neither she nor her friends developed feelings of cynicism. After 1964, the situation gradually changed, with rule by directives from above and few opportunities to argue with authority figures, leading, in Popkova's view, to cynicism among a majority of young people.[149] Ol'ga Lebedikhina underscored how directives for cultural activities from above ruined initiative from below, with young performers losing the feeling of enthusiasm and excitement.[150] Liudmila Gerasimova related that amateur arts had grown more professionalized and controlled by the 1970s, which tamped down the spark of enthusiasm that had fueled arts activities. According to her, in the early 1960s she and many other young Komsomol cadres believed that "we [could] make [the system] better," in order to ensure that "everything [was] honest, wise, just." During the 1970s, this sentiment changed, with Komsomol officials increasingly "placing the organization first" and "everything growing more formalized." As a consequence of all these developments, "official life and inner life increasingly grew farther apart"; Gerasimova and her friends found themselves more "focus[ed] on individual concerns during the 1970s."[151]

Gerasimova's words speak to a prominent phenomenon of the 1970s and 1980s: the shift away from social activism, official collectives, and Marxist-Leninist ideology and the movement toward personal life, individual self-satisfaction, friends, family, and the home.[152] As official ideology grew less significant and authentic for many Soviet citizens, they found meaning in consumerism, careerism, nationalism, religion, sport, countercultures, and even dissent.[153] Of course, plenty remained engaged with the endeavor to build communism and worked for reforms from within the system, as exemplified by Gorbachev and others.[154] However, everincreasing numbers turned away from areas of life associated with officialdom and the state. This development makes the traditional archetype of the private and public divide more relevant for the late 1960s to the mid-1980s than for earlier decades, although the dividing lines between these categories still remained much more diffuse and porous than the classical model suggests.

The Brezhnev era transformations undermined the legitimacy of the Soviet project, making the populace less willing to undertake the selfsacrifice Gorbachev called for during perestroika and more ready to accept the demise of the Soviet system.[155] Young people were particularly likely to harbor such attitudes. In the middle of the Stalin years, the young expressed substantially more support for the Soviet system than did other age groups.[156] By the late Brezhnev era, however, these ratios had reversed themselves, with youth offering significantly less support.[157] The Brezhnev Kremlin's dismissal of grassroots community management in exchange for significant increases in consumer products represented only one among several elements leading to this outcome. However, this factor played a key part in causing the population and especially youth to experience disillusionment and to disengage from the system, and it deserves much more attention than it has heretofore received from scholars.[158]

From the mid-1960s forward, the rest of the Soviet bloc also experienced a growing distance between the population and officialdom. This development proved especially acute among the young. In socialist eastern Europe, young people grew apathetic and disenchanted. They turned away from social engagement and official ideology and invested their energies in individual pleasures, family and friends, and consumerism.[159] Adults displayed similar attitudes, if to a lesser extent.[160] Further research will likely reveal that such tendencies resulted, to a significant extent, from the official shift away from endorsing grassroots self-management in favor of increased consumerist offerings as a means of ensuring social legitimacy.

The new collective leadership pursued an ambiguous leisure policy. It placed more emphasis on filling youth free time with sports, patriotic education, and military preparation. Still, the party-state continued to expand some aspects of organized cultural recreation, especially those associated with aesthetic upbringing and work where people were living. In contrast to 1963 and 1964, the mid-1960s witnessed a growing tolerance toward, along with efforts to co-opt, controversial music. The post-Khrushchev administration permitted performances of professional and amateur bands that incorporated elements of rock. Clubs devoted to guitar poetry expanded rapidly. Much more room opened up for jazz, including American-style pieces, with the burgeoning growth of jazz clubs and youth cafés. The definition of appropriately Soviet jazz expanded to include any pieces composed by Soviet jazz musicians. Such liberalism resulted from the official effort to create a homegrown socialist jazz as an alternative to the western version in the context of the Cold War cultural contest.

The massive jazz festivals that appeared in the mid-1960s drew musicians and promoters from around the Soviet Union, the eastern bloc, and the globe. Soviet jazz musicians also began to perform regularly at international socialist jazz festivals. Despite opposition from hard-line bureaucrats, these reforms brought jazz into the Soviet mainstream. This development inexorably led to the gradual demise of the jazz enthusiast alternative youth culture, which underwent transformation into a professional milieu and fan community.

For the Soviet and western governments alike, jazz-based diplomacy aimed to reduce Cold War tensions. Soviet authorities benefited by presenting their country as having a viable, socialist version of fun and by countering western propaganda about the suppression of jazz behind the Iron Curtain, thus advancing domestic cultural diplomacy efforts. Jazz exchanges within the Soviet bloc contributed to the strengthening of bonds between the Soviet Union and eastern Europe and to the forging of a more unified, bloc-wide socialist popular culture. Still, some problems, such as those that occurred at Tallinn-67, marred the party-state's efforts, underscoring how grassroots agents may hamper domestic cultural diplomacy. Soviet jazz enthusiasts expressed joy over the chance to socialize with foreigners, with the formerly "Imaginary West" growing less imaginary and more real to jazz musicians, promoters, and fans. This finding complicates earlier scholarship that suggested Soviet citizens formed their conception of western culture and style without tangible contacts with the outside world.[161] Such jazz activities led to the formation of union-wide jazz networks, with some nodes extending to the Soviet bloc nations. However, jazz musicians and promoters suffered as well, especially from greater KGB monitoring. The evidence attests to the need to expand the multipolar and multilevel paradigm to acknowledge possible negative consequences of exchanges for participants and also to analyze intrabloc interactions via the multipolar and multilevel lens.

The post-Khrushchev collective leadership adopted an increasingly hard-line policy on youth agency during the mid-1960s. The authorities began to discourage initiative from below and promoted discipline as a cardinal value. This new approach undercut club activities and collectives associated with grassroots activism and civic spirit. Still, due to the ambiguities of the mid-1960s and the lack of clarity over the future course at the top, liberal officials and cultural activists hoped and struggled to reverse this trend.

The historiography on Soviet culture during the mid-1960s generally depicts this time as a slide into Brezhnevian "stagnation," characterized by creeping Stalinization that slowly dismantled the cultural liberalism of the post-Stalin Thaw. The data presented above nuance this standard narrative, suggesting that scholars have relied too much on the accounts of cultural elites in evaluating the Soviet cultural field. The mid-1960s proved a significant improvement for the multitude of fans of western popular culture. As for the large numbers in initiative-oriented cultural collectives, most of these institutions had not yet suffered, with only several of the most daring ones being suppressed.

The invasion of Czechoslovakia, undoubtedly an important event, arguably represented the carryover into foreign policy of mid-1960s domestic policies that favored discipline at the expense of self-management. The crushing of the Prague Spring hardly served as a crucial break. Instead, this event reinforced existing tendencies that had originated in the mid-1960s. After a brief chill, western popular culture bounced back quickly. The authorities further strengthened the emphasis on obedience. Considering that these patterns continued throughout the Brezhnev years, the Brezhnev faction's victory likely had much more weight in determining the course of state-sponsored popular culture than the invasion did. From the perspective of youth cultural policy, the Thaw, understood as post-Stalinist liberalizing reforms, did not end with a harsh rupture in August 1968 but petered out in a gradual decline, confirmed fully at the

Komsomol congress of 1970, a fitting date for the ending of the Thaw and the Soviet equivalent of the sixties.

The policy toward organized cultural recreation highlights the Brezhnevian social contract. In part to compensate for disappointing young people who enjoyed initiative-based club activities, top officials offered greater access to western music and dancing to appease popular desires. This policy marked the Soviet Union's transition to a patronage-state ruling style, one that guaranteed personal consumption and security for the individual while dismissing citizen self-management and reform efforts from below. Placing power in the hands of a technocracy dominated by political managers and professional experts, the new leadership relied much less on letting ordinary citizens voice their opinions and shape their local communities, moving away from the infrastructural power-informed governance style under Khrushchev. The Soviet Union's willingness to adopt détente emerged from the need, based on the post-Khrushchev social contract, to ensure stability and rising consumption levels. Other Soviet bloc states followed the Soviet Union's lead in shifting to the patronage-state method of rule. By the late 1960s, western societies had likewise offered their young people greater consumption options and stability and had limited opportunities for social reforms to arise from below. This parallel highlights how Cold War needs combined with conservative backlash to define the shape of the systems in both blocs.[162]

The post-Khrushchev dismissal of youth initiative from below left young people with minimal opportunities to express themselves and their cultural creativity in official settings. As a consequence, young people increasingly articulated their artistic energies in nonofficial settings, as Butov noted, and the gap between official life and inner life grew wide, as Gerasimova related. The young shifted their energies, efforts, and time away from the club network and, more generally, from the party-state, social activism, and Marxist-Leninist ideology, focusing instead on family, friends, the home, daily life, and consumption.

Analogous developments took place in youth emotional communities. During the Thaw, the official emotional regime strongly promoted enthusiasm, optimism, and idealism among youth. In response, many young amateur artists articulated and, to a large extent, experienced such officially endorsed sentiments, which became central to the overarching emotional community of the Thaw. From the mid-1960s on, the authorities slowly reoriented official policy to favor patriotism, pragmatism, and obedience, leading to a new, Brezhnev-era emotional regime. Due to the disparity between the emerging post-1964 emotional regime and the desires and values of many among the young, my interviewees associated the mid-1960s shift with a changing emotional experience—the loss of optimism and enthusiasm, the growth of cynicism and apathy—that increasingly came to define youth emotional communities under Brezhnev. State-sponsored popular culture served as a key arena for bringing about this transition. My finding corresponds to the central role of consumption and leisure in other historical cases of changing emotional regimes and emotional communities.[163]

The new method of governance spotlights a transformation in the Soviet model of socialist modernity into a new, Brezhnev-era framework. During the Thaw, the authorities aimed to provide an alluring alternative to western modernity by appealing to popular desires and interests in two ways: by satisfying consumerist wants and by encouraging citizens to express their agency and voice through grassroots self-management. The latter had particular importance in ensuring that citizens engaged with the Soviet project's ideological goals, by making people feel that, by making a meaningful difference in the life of their communities, they advanced the cause of communist construction. Furthermore, communal activism assisted in controlling and channeling the growth of consumerism. Encouraging self-management served to appease popular desires to some degree and made the Soviet system better fit grassroots needs, which permitted the party-state to provide fewer consumer goods and services in order to achieve the same level of public acclaim. Initiative from below also resulted in the Soviet citizenry concentrating more of their time, energy, emotions, and efforts on communal voluntarism and collective benefits rather than on consumerism and individual desires. The Brezhnevian model of socialist modernity discarded citizen participation in local communal governance, consequently relying to a much greater extent on consumption to ensure legitimacy.

These findings offer a glimpse into the emergent contours of a Brezhnev-era version of a socialist consumer society. The Khrushchev leadership had attempted to use the satisfaction of cultural and material consumer wants both to legitimate the party-state and to get people involved actively in the renewal of the ideological drive. By the Brezhnev years, the authorities had increasingly abandoned the latter component, while the young consumers of state-sponsored popular culture felt entitled to demand and act to ensure that the party-state provided them with what they desired. This growing sense of consumption rights reflected what occurred in consumer societies in other contexts.[164] Certainly, had it retained the Khrushchev-era approach, the Brezhnev leadership would still have had to offer ever-increasing amounts of and better quality consumer products to satisfy the population. Nonetheless, the rate of increase would not have needed to be substantially greater.

Moreover, an ideological imperative essential to the Soviet project from the start, of involving citizens in the struggle to move the Soviet Union toward a communist utopia, proved at odds with the Brezhnev version of socialist modernity. Enacting a patronage-state method of governance effectively rejected the notion of individuals taking active part in restructuring the country and helping achieve the communist future. Instead, this strategy gave authority over the Soviet project to an elite technocratic vanguard. In the long term, this aspect of the Brezhnev-era socialist modernity served to undermine the founding basis of the Soviet Union and dealt a serious blow to its survival, and to socialist eastern Europe as well. By contrast, the more flexible governing policies adopted in China enabled that country and its Communist Party to survive and thrive.[165] Other socialist states, such as socialist Tanzania, also adopted more flexible consumerist policies.[166]

By minimizing initiative from below, the Brezhnev-era version of socialist modernity weakened the Soviet Union vis-à-vis the United States. Drawing distinctions between the two systems played a key role in Soviet, as well as American, public diplomacy on display to domestic and foreign audiences alike. Through the Brezhnev Kremlin's emphasis on discipline as opposed to grassroots activism, the Soviet propaganda machine lost an attractive element that it had used to distinguish the Thaw-era version of socialist modernity from the western model. No longer could the Soviet Union's promoters make nearly as strong an argument that the socialist alternative provided an opportunity for meaningful citizen activism.

Perhaps most important in terms of the Cold War contest, giving up such grassroots engagement from below forced the Brezhnev authorities to fight in an arena defined by and comfortable for the United States: consumption. The western model of modernity had much broader capacity to target, inflame, and satisfy consumption desires, domestically and globally.[167] The Brezhnev administration's policy choices resulted in its version of an alternative socialist modernity competing on an uneven playing field, one that benefited the market economy. Bauman has identified a weakness of the patronage-state ruling style: the government, having taken upon itself the responsibility to guarantee material security and stability for all individuals, receives the blame for any problems in these areas.[168] By rejecting the idea of grassroots responsibility for local community affairs, the Brezhnevian model of socialist modernity helped lead to governments across the Soviet bloc bearing the brunt of popular anger over economic or social problems. In contrast, western capitalist governing structures, which did not make such vast claims or take on such burdens, had the opportunity to shift blame to the supposedly impartial market or to purportedly self-determining citizens who fully controlled their own fate. The patronage-state ruling style, combined with the ratcheting of consumerist expectations, made the Soviet bloc's long-term prospects questionable and the gradual weakening of Soviet Cold War positions predictable.[169] In other words, the Soviet Union was not necessarily doomed to fail in its cultural consumption competition with capitalist states, contrary to what other scholars suggest.[170] It was the Brezhnev leadership's choices that seriously undermined the Soviet Union's long-term success.

CONCLUSION

Socialist fun was serious business. For Soviet citizens, especially young people, state-sponsored popular culture provided a central venue in which to fulfill their cultural consumption desires, to express themselves through cultural production, to socialize with others in their free time, to form friendship and romantic bonds, and to enjoy themselves. For the authorities, club activities offered the opportunity to instill officially prescribed cultural values and tastes, to ensure social control and appropriate leisure, and to satisfy popular desires and thereby gain legitimacy. More broadly, the party-state intended state-sponsored popular culture to help build a socialist, alternative version of modernity.

Even under Stalin, Soviet citizens had fun in state-sponsored popular culture. At the height of the militant anticosmopolitan campaign, plenty among the young genuinely enjoyed the limited range of heavily politicized cultural activities promoted in top-level cultural policy. Expressing conformist agency and without internal reservations, many ideologically committed youths sang songs praising Stalin. Other youngsters conformed outwardly but disagreed, to a greater or lesser extent, with some of the ideologically loaded cultural programming. They performed pieces whose content they did not believe in because doing so afforded them the opportunity to partake in the other benefits of organized cultural recreation. Nonetheless, such mixed motivations led to at least partial alienation from the party-state structure and lack of enthusiasm for the Soviet project. Exploring these diverse perspectives complicates our view of the anticosmopolitan campaign, which currently relies overwhelmingly on sources from the cultural intelligentsia that almost invariably disparage the campaign's cultural impact.

Some youth sought to engage in activities within state-managed settings that departed from top-level cultural policies. They danced in the banned western styles they liked and performed forbidden jazz tunes, often with the approval and sponsorship of local club workers and Komsomol officials. This surprising collaboration between ordinary citizens and lower-level cadres resulted from the structure of the Soviet cultural system, which provided incentives to officials who found ways of satisfying the population. Consequently, mass grassroots desires for prohibited cultural forms, especially western ones, functioned like consumer demand in market economies, undermining the late Stalinist Kremlin's ideologically militant stance. Moreover, the powerful cultural control organs made it harder for youngsters in the capital cities to enjoy forbidden activities during periods of cultural militancy than for youth in some provincial settings, where cultural controls were weaker. This finding challenges the idea that those in capital cities enjoyed greater access to consumption opportunities than those in the regions. More broadly, these insights underscore the importance of distinguishing between different agencies within the official cultural structure, as their varying missions were often at cross purposes. Overall, the evidence nuances our understanding of the Soviet cultural industry, which, at least from the perspective of ordinary citizens, was significantly less top-down and more responsive to popular demands than previously thought, even during an era of Soviet history that many scholars see as the most authoritarian.

The post-Stalin leadership substantially revised Soviet cultural policies. Top officials invested more material resources into the club network; they also pushed club workers to place less emphasis on political propaganda and more on entertaining cultural offerings that genuinely appealed to popular desires. Cultural workers' efforts to achieve that goal included co-opting some elements of western popular culture. Furthermore, policy makers encouraged widespread youth initiative and autonomy in organizing and managing cultural activities in official institutions. The post-Stalin leadership thus offered a new, Thaw-era model of socialist fun, one not only collectivist, egalitarian, and altruistic but also characterized by an orientation toward popular desires and broad grassroots engagement. Soviet discourse juxtaposed the socialist model against the mainstream western capitalist model, portrayed as one instilling passiveness, consumerism, individualism, and class divisions and as serving the interests of the capitalist bourgeoisie instead of ordinary citizens. The post-Stalin reforms reflect the broader goal of the new leadership: to build a Thaw-era version of socialist modernity with wide appeal among domestic and foreign audiences. Creating such an image was crucial in the context of the Cold War struggle for cultural hegemony at home and abroad.

Young people responded with great enthusiasm for the Thaw-era model of socialist fun, which gave them much more room to express their agency and enjoy the kind of cultural activities they actually wanted. The post-Stalin reforms succeeded in making many more among the young feel like their own interests and preferences fit the Thaw-era official cultural system. This sense of satisfaction contributed to youth optimism regarding the Thaw-era version of socialist modernity and helped close the gap between the young and policy makers that loomed large in the late Stalin years.

The post-Stalin departures in state-sponsored popular culture did not occur without numerous conflicts and policy zigzags. Such tensions date back to prerevolutionary and early Soviet struggles over whether to rely on spontaneity versus consciousness, indicating the importance of these disagreements for the course of Soviet history. In the Thaw, cultural bureaucrats of a conservative orientation decried most or all of the reforms, struggling to return to the late Stalinist model. More liberal officials, aided by many ordinary young cultural activists, opposed the ideological militants, and, for most of the Khrushchev years, they did so successfully. At times, cultural policy did grow more conservative, generally because of major Cold War reverses that gave ammunition to cultural hard-liners. At those times, the cultural hierarchy narrowed the range of the permissible and privileged didactic cultural activities meant to inculcate prescribed cultural norms and direct youth aesthetic tastes. This emphasis, however, undermined important aims of the Khrushchev leadership, namely, satisfying cultural consumption desires and soliciting initiative from below. These latter goals, along with the growing realization that censorship alienated Soviet youth in the Cold War cultural struggle, led to an overall soft-line inclination under Khrushchev.

Once Brezhnev consolidated power after the ambiguities of the first post-Khrushchev years, the new administration decided to retreat from some key elements of the Thaw-era model of socialist fun. Top-level policy increasingly limited room for youth initiative in state-sponsored popular culture, giving much more control to cultural bureaucrats, club workers, and cultural professionals, with the goal of minimizing the possibility for youth misbehavior and disobedience. While this change harked back to the late Stalin years, the Brezhnev administration retained the Khrushchev-era orientation toward satisfying popular desires for consumption of cultural entertainment in clubs, permitting even more western popular culture than in the Khrushchev years, all meant to ensure social legitimacy for the leadership. The Brezhnev reforms shifted the ideal of model Soviet citizenship from the Thaw-era vision of individuals as active subjects to passive objects receiving and practicing whatever the cultural authorities offered. This step undermined a uniquely appealing element of socialist fun in the Cold War struggle: now, both western and socialist popular culture positioned people primarily in a passive role as consumers of cultural entertainment. The resulting playing field was decidedly not a level one during the cultural Cold War, due to the powerful orientation of American popular culture toward entertainment and its resultant competitive advantage.

Socialist fun and the socialist version of modernity grew less appealing to domestic and foreign audiences alike. The Brezhnev policies made youth feel that their interests and preferences did not align with the official cultural structure, thus alienating youngsters from the official cultural system and the Soviet project as a whole. This development, I argue, seriously undermined the Soviet Union's long-term social stability and cohesion.

While primarily concerned with Soviet history after 1945, my narrative likewise illuminates topics of interdisciplinary humanistic and social scientific relevance. Consumerism constitutes one key theme. Although rooted in the Stalin years, a Soviet socialist consumer society emerged only in the Thaw-era Soviet Union, when the authorities emphasized satisfying the cultural and material consumption desires of the citizenry as a whole, not just socially mobile elites. Organized cultural recreation proved crucial to the Khrushchev version of a socialist consumer society, which differed from a western capitalist consumer society by encouraging consumers to also function as active producers of cultural content and by prioritizing collective, not individual, consumption. Although retaining and in some respects intensifying the orientation toward fulfilling popular desires, the Brezhnev version of socialist consumerism shifted away from encouraging grassroots cultural production and collective cultural recreation. This shift moved the Brezhnev-era socialist consumer society closer to the western version and undermined the idea, vital during the Cold War, that the Soviet Union offered an alternative way of life.

A further distinction between Soviet and western consumer societies lay in the Soviet Union's efforts to shape the population's cultural tastes. The party-state's efforts to ensure cultural hegemony by cultivating normative aesthetic tastes resulted primarily from ideological and Cold War concerns rather than the goal of reinforcing class distinctions. The endeavor to define popular cultural preferences, which began during the early Soviet years, took on a mass character in 1957 with the aesthetic upbringing campaign. Based on the perceived need to oppose western cultural propaganda and the globalization of American popular culture, the Soviet drive waxed and waned depending on whether the leadership pursued hard- or soft-line policies. Aesthetic upbringing represented an important area of continuity between the Brezhnev and Khrushchev socialist consumer societies. It achieved significant success among those already predisposed toward prescribed tastes and also among socially mobile urban youngsters yearning for cultural uplift, but it failed to reach many others who lacked this urge, particularly fans of western popular culture. Overall, youth tastes shifted significantly over time, and while the party-state's efforts to guide cultural preferences had some impact, young people also formed their tastes based on a wide variety of other factors, from peer influence to changing global youth tastes. My exploration suggests the benefits to scholarship of exploring the understudied topic of the struggles over and the social role and impact of aesthetic preferences within socialist and nonsocialist contexts alike, in relation to domestic processes and to transnational ones such as the Cold War and globalization.

Western popular culture acquired a worldwide reach after 1945, drawing strength from its entertaining, consumer-driven cultural content, the market power of multinational media corporations, and extensive assistance from the US and other western governments eager to secure Cold War cultural victories and economic gain. The western cultural industry proved especially well suited to co-opting and commercializing youth countercultures, turning them into appealing products that western government officials and business leaders believed would spread western precepts and values. Yet, at least under Khrushchev, the party-state was surprisingly effective at mediating the impact of western cultural influence. Soviet cultural officials combined some elements of western popular culture with mainstream Soviet culture while providing youngsters with uniquely socialist elements such as opportunities to establish and manage their own cultural spaces within official settings. Likewise, Soviet youths did not absorb all of the messages propounded by western cultural diplomacy; instead, they refashioned western cultural products to suit their own needs and preferences. Indeed, large numbers of Soviet youngsters who greatly admired western popular culture, such as jazz enthusiasts, actually preferred the Thaw-era socialist modernity and way of life to the western model. Overall, the international exchanges of cultural products, ideas, and people across the Soviet Union's borders had a powerful but complex impact on Soviet society, one that deserves far greater attention in the scholarly literature.

The framework of globalization and attempts to mediate its impact does not suffice to explain the scope of Soviet responses to foreign cultural influence. To get the other side of the story requires paying attention to sub-state interactions and actors as part of a multipolar and multilevel approach to Cold War transnational history. Both capitalist democratic and socialist authoritarian governments consciously deployed cultural diplomacy to target citizens of the other blocs and of nonaligned states. Substantial research has proved that the US government strongly, and frequently covertly, influenced the cultural scene in its own bloc. In turn, my findings help illuminate Soviet efforts to use cultural diplomacy in eastern Europe in order to create a unified socialist popular culture across the Soviet bloc. Government officials practiced foreign and domestic cultural diplomacy, cooperating extensively with their citizenry to create a positive impression on outsiders. Many Soviet citizens conformed fully to official dictates, while some cultural activists took more risks and pushed the boundaries, often gaining what they wanted but in some cases facing punishments, such as disruption of their continued ability to interact with foreigners, career roadblocks, and even imprisonment. Soviet cultural diplomacy, foreign and domestic, strongly influenced Soviet and non-Soviet youth in a wide variety of ways. One consistent pattern apparent across my sources was that cultural diplomacy in the 1950s and 1960s reduced hostility and made youngsters more tolerant and curious of about each other, leading to more peacefulness and understanding in international relations as this cohort grew up and took greater authority, a pattern well illustrated by the Gorbachev leadership.

Such evidence indicates that the clash between the superpowers had a powerful impact on Soviet cultural life from 1945 to 1970, underscoring that the Soviet Union represented one among many Cold War cultures. Wary of engaging in Cold War determinism, I have in this account disentangled and opened the curtain on those aspects of Soviet daily cultural practices within club activities attributable to the struggle between the socialist and capitalist blocs. The post-1945 Soviet Union experienced a wave of foreign cultural influence stemming from a combination of internal dynamics, namely, the population's cultural consumption desires and the systemic incentives of the official cultural network, and external drivers, such as globalization and western public diplomacy. Such diplomacy had more influence than globalization in the Soviet Union in comparison to nonsocialist states, owing both to the lack of market opportunities for large multinationals in the Soviet Union and the fact that, after the early 1950s, American public diplomacy became more extensive, subtle, and entertaining, thus increasing its effectiveness. Soviet top officials formulated cultural policies that reacted to foreign cultural influence, and their approach evolved over time, depending on external and internal historical developments and their personal interpretations of the significance of such cultural influence, with both achievements and notable failures in their effort to mediate the impact of foreign popular culture on the Soviet population. In this sense, Cold War cultural struggles had a substantial impact on the organized cultural recreation offered to youngsters. Additionally, party-state efforts at foreign and domestic cultural diplomacy frequently relied on citizen involvement in state-sponsored popular culture, yet another effect of the Cold War on Soviet club-goers. The foreign cultural diplomacy of the west also deserves acknowledgment, as it provided not only entertaining programming and information on western popular culture but also opportunities for direct personal interactions via cultural exchanges such as youth groups traveling to the Soviet Union. Likewise, the domestic cultural diplomacy of the west had an influence on the small numbers of Soviet citizens who traveled abroad, which translated into some, if minor, impacts on club activities.

While we derive analytical benefit from looking at the Soviet Union as a Cold War culture and considering how its citizens, like those of many other states, experienced the superpower struggle within their day-to-day cultural activities, it bears repeating that this polity was also distinct; the Soviet Union led the eastern bloc, was relatively centralized, and encompassed great geographical diversity. One important consequence of the Soviet position of power in the socialist bloc meant that its cultural policy had a strong impact on other socialist states, especially those in Soviet-dominated eastern Europe.

As a Cold War story, my account also illuminates emotional expression and experience in daily cultural life. The anticosmopolitan campaign brought about a rapid shift to a strict emotional regime within state-sponsored popular culture. Comfortable for many true believers, the newly narrowed affective guidelines and hard discipline caused distress, apathy, and alienation for the many others who did not have the prescribed sentiments. This situation contributed to the growing gap between the party-state and many young people, moving the overarching youth emotional community further from the government. The emotional regime loosened significantly in the Thaw, although with occasional reverses. This relaxation paved the way for a closer alignment of the mainstream youth emotional community and the party-state, with many young people engaged in club activities expressing much enthusiasm for and optimism over socialist fun and socialist modernity and finding meaning, purpose, and a sense of community and belonging in state-sponsored popular culture. However, a more severe emotional regime took hold under Brezhnev. A large proportion of youngsters experienced deep disappointment and emotional alienation in the Brezhnev years, turning away from official cultural activities. My narrative enriches our understanding of the central role of emotions both in political mobilization and in ensuring social stability and cohesion, especially regarding youth—those at the most crucial stage in their integration into society and the formation of their public identity.

The special case of jazz enthusiasts underscores the importance of teasing out the diversity of emotional experience and its societal implications. Harsh late Stalinist cultural policies ended up creating deviance by narrowing the boundaries of acceptable behavior. Avid fans of jazz coalesced into an alternative youth culture of jazz enthusiasts, which func-

tioned simultaneously as a subordinate emotional community. Jazz enthusiasts represented one among several groupings that deviated openly from
official cultural and emotional norms. The looser post-Stalin emotional
regime transformed the relationship between policy makers and jazz enthusiasts, making many among the latter group excited over the Soviet
system. Jazz enthusiasts increasingly joined official cultural amateur activities, blurring the boundaries between them and the mainstream. The
more severe emotional regime under Brezhnev had a complex impact on
jazz enthusiasts. While disliking the tamping down of autonomous grassroots activism, many jazz enthusiasts appreciated the Brezhnev authorities
for expressing more tolerance toward their favored cultural form than had
the Khrushchev administration. They now could make a professional career out of playing jazz, and avid fans had many more opportunities to
listen to and purchase recordings from domestic and foreign jazz artists;
international jazz networks sprang up. Consequently, the jazz enthusiast
alternative youth culture and emotional community gradually became a
fan community, one among many others, although with a hint of mar-
ginality. Tracing the history of the birth, life path, and end of the jazz
enthusiasts as a coherent grouping permits a deeper comprehension of the
nature of alternative youth cultures and emotional communities in relation
to their broader social setting.

The powerful emotions experienced by many youths who participated in organized cultural recreation, the strong social bonds they formed
within amateur collectives in clubs, and the extensive civic activism exhibited by cultural activists after Stalin all challenge the traditional notions
of public and private in the Soviet setting. Reproducing the narrow vision
of critical Soviet intelligentsia from the Khrushchev and Brezhnev years,
the binary perspective on public and private does not represent the experience and viewpoints of many members of the Soviet population. It hardly
speaks to the everyday life of tens of millions of youngsters who performed
enthusiastically as amateurs in state-sponsored popular culture, investing
substantial time, resources, and emotional energy, and finding meaning,
friendships, pleasure, fun, and a sense of personal meaning and purpose
within official cultural activities. Moreover, during the Thaw, plenty of cultural activists at the grassroots actively organized together and even fought
to promote what they wanted in clubs, and they achieved notable successes
at some risk to their own life path within the Soviet system. Their civic
engagement illustrates a commitment to improving official cultural life and
their own cultural opportunities. The public and private spheres, from the
perspective of organized cultural recreation, had no hard and fast boundaries. Frequently, young people easily transitioned between official and unof-

ficial settings to find ways of satisfying their cultural consumption desires and expressing themselves culturally. Those I interviewed frequently shared that they experienced no substantial distinction between the cultural activities they practiced in their apartments versus those in state-managed cultural institutions. They often formed friendship bonds with members of their cultural collectives, socializing and enjoying themselves together at home and in club spaces alike. This conclusion is most applicable to the Thaw period and less to the Brezhnev years, during which cultural censorship and suppression of grassroots initiative led to more distinctions between cultural activity in private apartments versus clubs, although not nearly the strict boundaries envisioned by the traditional public-private paradigm. Post-Khrushchev developments encouraged many youngsters to turn their cultural production and consumption toward unofficial cultural activities, weakening the state's ability to reach and mobilize its youth.

Young people had particular importance for the Soviet authorities, both for their prominent ideological role within Marxism-Leninism and their demographic significance within the Soviet Union. Consequently, the party-state from its early years implemented a very active youth policy designed to mold its young people into model citizens of the communist tomorrow. Still, the officially promoted notion of young New Soviet People shifted over time. In the anticosmopolitan years, the Stalinist Kremlin pronounced the ideal to be disciplined, militant, and politicized citizens rejecting any western influence. Under Khrushchev, this vision changed to New Soviet Women and Men as collective-oriented young enthusiasts ready to take charge of the project of building communism and managing society at the grassroots. The authorities expanded the space in which model citizens could partake in entertaining cultural activities with western elements in official settings, but they also called on Thaw-era New Soviet Individuals to acquire a broad cultural education. Policy makers stressed varying elements of this model during different times depending on the political situation, with soft-line policies prevailing for most of the Khrushchev era. In the post-Khrushchev years, the new top officials gradually changed their approach to present the ideal as passive, obedient, and patriotic New Soviet Individuals who enjoyed a steadily increasing level of cultural consumption, including consumption of western popular culture. An examination of organized cultural recreation enabled me to trace party-state efforts to construct and reconstruct the category of young people under three administrations, as well as the transitions between their distinct models of the ideal young individual.

This now apparent forging of young people into the type of citizen the party-state desired advances our overall understanding of Soviet policies designed to garden the population to fit the leadership's needs. The late Stalin administration took a highly coercive approach to such social engineering. In the mid-1950s, the new leadership adopted softer social control policies, shifting from relying on coercive, authoritarian power to favoring infrastructural power that involved negotiation with the population and engaging the citizenry in social management. Under Brezhnev, the gardening aspects of state-sponsored popular culture became more ambiguous. On the one hand, escalating cultural censorship and the suppression of grassroots initiative indicate increasing use of coercive power. On the other hand, the authorities provided greater opportunities to consume culture, including western popular culture—an infrastructural–power tactic. Along with some significant successes, such gardening through state-sponsored popular culture resulted in notable failures, especially during the more authoritarian periods in cultural policy. These failures resulted from the mismatch during those times between the Kremlin's intentions and young people's desires, along with the challenges the center faced in observing and controlling the implementation of its desired policy at the grassroots.

Indeed, young people were not simply obedient objects gardened by officialdom but active subjects showing agency in shaping their everyday environments, including those within state-managed cultural structures. Some exhibited conformist agency, upholding and strengthening top-level initiatives that fit their needs. However, especially during times of cultural militancy, the center's cultural policies did not match the desires and interests of many club-goers. Less compliant young people responded in different ways. Some chose to withdraw, to a lesser or greater extent, from state-sponsored popular culture. Others pursued a different path, maneuvering and negotiating within official structures to attain those cultural opportunities that they wanted. They achieved a surprising degree of success, winning many small victories, as a result of the systemic incentives that allowed lower-level club and Komsomol officials to appeal to popular preferences. This multitude of minute expressions of grassroots agency combine to produce a major impact on the shape of Soviet state-sponsored popular culture. Likewise, Kremlin officials, in formulating their policies, ended up responding to the pressures of young people and their desires, at least after Stalin, when the Khrushchev administration sought to elicit grassroots activism among the young and also pursued a social contract that obliged the state to appease popular wants. Additionally, the changes in youth preferences over time also brought about corresponding shifts in the offerings of the Soviet cultural industry. In other words, young people and their voices, agency, tastes, and interests genuinely mattered, helping define broader historical developments. The story of Soviet organized cultural recreation is thus as much a story of young amateur participants and audience members as government bureaucrats and official structures.

In an example of this complexity, the Khrushchev Kremlin's support for youth initiative greatly expanded the space for youth agency within the Soviet system, helping bring about the active post-Stalin generation. The last Stalin generation lacked a generational consciousness: although sharing some common traits, those who grew up in the late Stalin years generally did not identify and organize together with other members of their age cohort to push for social change. To a significant degree, the passive nature of the last Stalin generation stemmed from the late Stalin leadership's approach to young people, which discouraged youth from banding together, did not assign the young great social prominence, and suppressed autonomous youth initiative. The Khrushchev administration pursued diametrically opposite policies in these three areas; its discourse also explicitly positioned the young cohort in the mid- and late 1950s as a generation distinct from previous ones. This differing approach, along with societal dynamics relating to postwar recovery, greater affluence, mass enrollments in higher education, and more free time, led to the emergence of an active post-Stalin generation. Its members shared a generational consciousness and exhibited a civic spirit in collaborating together with others within their age cohort to pursue social reforms of interest to young people and in daring to stand up to older authority figures in doing so. The post-Stalin generation's activism paid off, substantially affecting state-sponsored popular culture. Exploring the last Stalin generation and the post-Stalin generation through organized cultural recreation illuminates how government youth policy interacted with other domestic and external historical developments to influence generational formation and cohesiveness in complex and unexpected ways.

These diverse topics combine to advance our understanding of modernity. The Soviet version of socialist modernity represented one among a number of socialist modernities, one that was also affected by other socialist modernities in complex ways, through intrabloc cultural networks, for instance. More broadly, Soviet socialist modernity constituted one among multiple modernities, although made distinct by the post-Stalin leadership's endeavor to forge the most influential alternative to the capitalist democratic model. Placing the Soviet Union within the multiple modernities framework and thus in a global context provides a substantial analytical benefit, paving the way for international comparisons of the Soviet case study with a range of countries.

Informed by this approach, my account draws attention to the similarities and differences between Soviet and non-Soviet society. In terms of popular culture, the Soviet state-sponsored version has the most overlap with those of other socialist states, particularly the ones in the Soviet bloc but also those outside it. The parallels resulted from a combination of the influence of the Soviet model, as well as these states' similar goal of trying to move toward communism; distinctions emerged from their varying histories, internal dynamics, and international geopolitical factors. Moreover, Soviet organized cultural recreation activities resembled in many ways those in nonsocialist authoritarian twentieth-century European states. Direct Soviet influence played little role here, although the example of the Soviet model provided a reference point, positive or negative. Most important for explaining commonalities between the Soviet Union and these polities was the shared pattern of state structures striving to garden their populations in order to reach a utopian future, in this instance via government-managed cultural activities designed to reforge cultural norms and ideals while also satisfying cultural consumption desires. Differences from the Soviet case stemmed from both the unique history of each society and its domestic and geopolitical situation, as well as varying ideological perspectives on the utopian future, which caused countries such as Italy and especially Germany to rely, at least somewhat, on market mechanisms. In socialist and nonsocialist authoritarian countries alike, gardening through state-sponsored popular culture faced challenges. Tensions arose between popular desires and top-level prescriptions meant to reshape the citizenry's cultural norms. Policy makers experienced difficulties implementing central policy at the grassroots, owing to the conflicting priorities and incentives within differing government structures, as well as the diverse perspectives among officials about the best methods for forging the idealized future.

Most distant from the Soviet case, in western capitalist democracies the market rather than the government functioned as the primary venue for providing cultural activities, with a minor role for nonprofit organizations. My account spotlights the need to expand current scholarly paradigms, based overwhelmingly on evidence from western capitalist democracies, to take much greater account of government structures, non-market methods, and settings outside of the North Atlantic region when considering issues of humanistic and social scientific concern. This book in particular helps nuance our views on consumerism, tastes, emotions, popular culture, globalization, cultural diplomacy, Cold War cultures, public and private spheres, social engineering, agency, mainstream youth, alternative youth cultures, community, generations, and, not least, modernity. Still, certain commonalities also emerged from comparing the Soviet case to western capitalist democracies, owing to parallel experiences of the impact of postwar recovery and the escalating Cold War, the growing social prominence of young people and their cultural practices, and similarities in technological developments and consequent social changes.

A study of Soviet state-sponsored popular culture offers pragmatic lessons for contemporary life. While the Soviet Union lost the Cold War, its dissolution should not discredit all aspects of Soviet society; many former citizens speak with longing of organized cultural recreation as one of the best aspects of the Soviet Union. No wonder: after all, those of all social backgrounds could use the club network to gain access to state-funded opportunities for widely diverse cultural production, cultural knowledge, and cultural consumption, with the clubs serving as spaces for socialization, leisure, friendship, and romance. State-sponsored popular culture engaged youth in the system, provided entertaining fun, filled their free time, and encouraged cultural expression. Capitalist democracies may well draw some useful lessons from considering these elements of the Soviet model, perceived by those who grew up in the Soviet Union as generally positive, while making sure to avoid its many negative aspects.

Another topic of direct relevance to current-day society relates to transnational cultural influences. An exploration of western cultural diplomacy's impact on the Soviet Union and efforts by the Soviet leadership to mediate this influence provides insights on how current-day authoritarian countries may react to such targeted cultural influence. A broader understanding of this issue would enable western governments to improve their cultural diplomacy, foreign and domestic alike. Such knowledge has particular importance relative to the Cold War context, since future large-scale conflicts between capitalist democracies and major nondemocratic states will likely resemble the Cold War pattern of cultural, social, economic, and political competition rather than direct military action, with extensive deployment of cultural diplomacy on both sides. Better appreciation of how western cultural diplomacy played out in the Soviet Union would also be particularly applicable to the multiple contemporary conflicts between western democracies and countries whose leadership explicitly rejects the capitalist democratic model and pursues its own path to the future. Such knowledge may lead to a recalibration of the balance between hard-power tactics, such as sanctions and interventions, and potentially more effective soft-power ones, for instance, cultural diplomacy.

A final broad lesson, perhaps the most important one, relates to contemporary perceptions of societies that take a hostile stance toward western capitalist democratic modernity. When discussing such countries, public discourse overwhelmingly emphasizes authoritarian governance, coercion, and repression. The combination of media discourse and public opinion also sways the actions of government officials. In reality, any society that has long-term social stability and cohesion must gratify the needs and wants of many of its members and therefore possesses many positive and creative elements. Systems hang together internally when they make people feel like they lead meaningful lives through engagement with and contributing to the system's own goals, whether by giving citizens what they want or by shaping their desires to conform to what the system actually offers or, as is usually the case, a combination of both. Acknowledging this truth in media discourse, public opinion, and policy making would go a long way toward advancing cultural understanding and improving international relations.

State-sponsored popular culture represented one important element that brought positive and joyful feelings to the Soviet population, letting citizens express themselves culturally and satisfy their cultural consumption desires and making people think and feel that their desires and tastes functioned to serve the system. Socialist fun helps explain why the Soviet Union, despite its numerous problems, maintained its stability and cohesion for so long. Socialist fun also casts light on some of the reasons for the eventual failure of the Soviet system, as the Brezhnev reforms in organized cultural recreation helped undermine perceptions that individual interests and wants were in line with the system's goals. Socialist fun was serious business indeed.

NOTES

ABBREVIATIONS USED IN THE NOTES

d.	*delo*
f.	*fond*
FO	Foreign Office
GANISO	Gosudarstvennyi arkhiv noveishei istorii Saratovskoi oblasti (State Archive of Contemporary History of Saratov Oblast)
GARF	Gosudarstvennyi arkhiv Rossiiskoi Federatsii (State Archive of the Russian Federation)
GASO	Gosudarstvennyi arkhiv Saratovskoi oblasti (State Archive of Saratov Oblast)
l.	*list*
ll.	*listy*
NACP	National Archives at College Park, MD
op.	*opis'*
PRO	Public Record Office
RG	Record Group
RGALI	Rossiiskii gosudarstvennyi arkhiv literatury i iskusstva (Russian State Archive of Literature and Art)
RGANI	Rossiiskii gosudarstvennyi arkhiv noveishei istorii (Russian State Archive of Contemporary History)
RGASPI	Rossiiskii gosudarstvennyi arkhiv sotsial'no-politicheskoi istorii (Russian State Archive of Socio-Political History)
TNA	The National Archives of the United Kingdom
TsAGM	Tsentral'nyi arkhiv goroda Moskvy (Central Archive of the City of Moscow)
TsAOPIM	Tsentral'nyi arkhiv obshchestvenno-politicheskoi istorii Moskvy (Central Archive of Social-Political History of Moscow)

INTRODUCTION

1. On the film *Karnaval'naia noch'* and the controversies surrounding it, see Josephine Woll, *Real Images: Soviet Cinema and the Thaw* (New York: I. B. Tauris, 2000), 51–56.

2. In this book I do not capitalize "western," "west," or "western Europe" to avoid giving the impression of homogenizing a widely varied set of historical experiences and dividing a supposedly cohesive "West" from "East." See Martin W. Lewis and Karen E. Wigen, *The Myth of Continents: A Critique of Metageography* (Berkeley: University of California Press, 1997), 1–19; and Edward Said, *Orientalism* (New York: Vintage Books, 1979), 1–30.

3. For a broader take on Russian popular culture that considers cultural activities produced both by and for the masses, see Louise McReynolds, "Russia's Popular Culture in History and Theory," in *A Companion to Russian History*, ed. Abbott Gleason (London: Wiley-Blackwell, 2009), 295–310. For more on post-1945 amateur arts, see Susan Costanzo, "Amateur Theaters and Amateur Publics in the Russian Republic, 1958–71," *Slavonic and East European Review* 86, no. 2 (April 2008): 372–94; Bella Ostromoukhova, "Le Dégel et les troupes amateur: Changements politiques et activités artistiques des étudiants, 1953–1970," *Cahiers du Monde russe* 47, no. 1–2 (January–June 2006): 303–25; and A. G. Borzenkov, *Molodezh' i politika: Vozmozhnosti i predely studencheskoi samodeiatel'nosti na vostoke Rossii (1961–1991 gg.), Chast' 2* (Novosibirsk: Novosibirskii gosudarstvennyi universitet, 2002), 2–4. For an analysis of the debates about elite-oriented versus mass-oriented cultural production, see Herbert J. Gans, *Popular Culture and High Culture: An Analysis and Evaluation of Taste* (New York: Basic Books, 1999).

4. For 1953, see RGASPI, f. M-1, op. 32, d. 741, l. 3. For 1962, see S. P. Pavlov, *Otchet Tsentral'nogo Komiteta VLKSM i zadachi komsomola, vytekaiushchie iz reshenii XXII s'ezda KPSS* (Moscow: Molodaia gvardiia, 1962), 51. Like all Soviet statistics, these were probably manipulated by lower-level officials eager to inflate their accomplishments. Still, this evidence reflects the reality of widespread participation in amateur arts. Moreover, as local bureaucrats were just as likely to massage numbers in 1953 and 1962, we can validly speak about the growth of participation in amateur arts over this period.

5. O. K. Makarova, *Kul'turnoe stroitel'stvo SSSR: Statisticheskii sbornik* (Moscow: Gosudarstvennoe statisticheskoe izdatel'stvo, 1956), 273.

6. I define "identity" as a concept encompassing an individual's personal worldview and beliefs—their selfhood or subjectivity. I will thus use these terms interchangeably. For criticism of the undefined use of "identity," see Rogers Brubaker and Frederick Cooper, "Beyond 'Identity,'" *Theory and Society* 29, no. 1 (February 2000): 1–47.

7. Anthony Giddens, *The Consequences of Modernity* (Stanford: Stanford University Press, 1990), 1; Zygmunt Bauman, *Modernity and Ambivalence* (Ithaca: Cornell University Press, 1991), 263. For a variety of historically informed perspectives on modernity, see "*AHR* Roundtable: Historians and the Question of 'Modernity,'" *American Historical Review* 116, no. 3 (June 2011): 631–751.

8. On the Stalinist leadership's shift, see David L. Hoffmann, "Was There a 'Great Retreat' from Soviet Socialism? Stalinist Culture Reconsidered," *Kritika* 5, no. 4 (Fall 2004): 651–74. On the term "Thaw," see Stephen V. Bittner, *The Many Lives of Khrushchev's Thaw: Experience and Memory in Moscow's Arbat* (Ithaca: Cornell University

Press, 2008), 1–13; and Nancy Condee, "The Cultural Codes of Khrushchev's Thaw," in *Nikita Khrushchev*, ed. William Taubman, Sergei Khrushchev, and Abbott Gleason (New Haven: Yale University Press, 2000), 160–76.

9. On the global appeal of socialist modernity after 1945, see Vladislav M. Zubok, *A Failed Empire: The Soviet Union in the Cold War from Stalin to Gorbachev* (Chapel Hill: University of North Carolina Press, 2007), 131; Odd A. Westad, *The Global Cold War: Third World Interventions and the Making of Our Times* (New York: Cambridge University Press, 2005), 79–109; and Kate A. Baldwin, *Beyond the Color Line and the Iron Curtain: Reading Encounters between Black and Red, 1922–1963* (Durham: Duke University Press, 2002), 202–52. On interwar efforts to impress visiting cultural intellectuals with Soviet culture, see Michael David-Fox, *Showcasing the Great Experiment: Cultural Diplomacy and Western Visitors to the Soviet Union, 1921–1941* (New York: Oxford University Press, 2011), 1–27; Katerina Clark, *Moscow, the Fourth Rome: Stalinism, Cosmopolitanism, and the Evolution of Soviet Culture, 1931–1941* (Cambridge: Harvard University Press, 2011), 1–41; and Liudmila Stern, *Western Intellectuals and the Soviet Union, 1920–1940: From Red Square to the Left Bank* (New York: Routledge, 2007), 1–11.

10. On cultural hegemony, see Antonio Gramsci, *Selections from the Prison Notebooks of Antonio Gramsci*, ed. and trans. Quintin Hoare and Geoffrey Nowell Smith (New York: International Publishers, 1971), 57–58, 263–76.

11. David L. Hoffmann, *Stalinist Values: The Cultural Norms of Soviet Modernity, 1917–1941* (Ithaca: Cornell University Press, 2003), 1–14; Stephen Kotkin, *Magnetic Mountain: Stalinism as a Civilization* (Berkeley: University of California Press, 1995), 355–66.

12. Martin Malia, *The Soviet Tragedy: A History of Socialism in Russia, 1917–1991* (New York: Free Press, 1994), 1–20; György Péteri, "Introduction: The Oblique Coordinate Systems of Modern Identity," in *Imagining the West in Eastern Europe and the Soviet Union*, ed. György Péteri (Pittsburgh: University of Pittsburgh Press, 2010), 1–12. On multiple modernities, see the essays in Dominic Sachsenmaier, Shmuel N. Eisenstadt, and Jens Riedel, eds., *Reflections on Multiple Modernities: European, Chinese, and Other Interpretations* (Boston: Brill, 2001); Shmuel N. Eisenstadt, ed., *Multiple Modernities* (New Brunswick: Transaction Publishers, 2002); and Eliezer Ben-Rafael with Yitzhak Sternberg, eds., *Identity, Culture, and Globalization* (Boston: Brill, 2001). For an application of this idea to the Soviet Union, see David L. Hoffmann, *Cultivating the Masses: Modern State Practices and Soviet Socialism, 1914–1939* (Ithaca: Cornell University Press, 2011), 3. On modernization theory, see David C. Engerman, Nils Gilman, Mark H. Haefele, and Michael E. Latham, eds., *Staging Growth: Modernization, Development, and the Global Cold War* (Amherst: University of Massachusetts Press, 2003), 1–24. On moving beyond Eurocentrism, see Dipesh Chakrabarty, *Provincializing Europe: Postcolonial Thought and Historical Difference* (Princeton: Princeton University Press, 2000), 3–26.

13. On debates over modernization projects in other contexts, see James C. Scott, *Seeing Like a State: How Certain Schemes to Improve the Human Condition Have Failed* (New Haven: Yale University Press, 1998), 1–8; Susan Buck-Morss, *Dreamworld and Catastrophe: The Passing of Mass Utopia in East and West* (Cambridge: MIT Press, 2000), 2–39; Mike Featherstone, *Consumer Culture and Postmodernism*, 2nd ed. (Los Angeles: SAGE, 2007), 1–12; and Raymond Williams, *The Politics of Modernism: Against the New Conformists*, ed. and intro. Tony Pinkney (New York: Verso, 1989), 1–30.

14. For two different scholarly takes on early Soviet debates over spontaneity versus consciousness, see Anna Krylova, "Beyond the Spontaneity-Consciousness Paradigm: 'Class Instinct' as a Promising Category of Historical Analysis," *Slavic Review* 62, no. 1 (Spring 2003): 1–23; and Leopold H. Haimson, "Lenin's Revolutionary Career Revisited: Some Observations on Recent Discussions," *Kritika* 5, no. 1 (Winter 2004): 55–80.

15. Such accounts include Victoria de Grazia, *Irresistible Empire: America's Advance through Twentieth-Century Europe* (Cambridge: Belknap Press of Harvard University Press, 2005), 3–6; and Reinhold Wagnleitner, "The Empire of Fun, or Talkin' Soviet Union Blues: The Sound of Freedom and U.S. Cultural Hegemony in Europe," *Diplomatic History* 23, no. 3 (Summer 1999): 499–524.

16. For New Soviet People, see Igal Halfin, *From Darkness to Light: Class, Consciousness, and Salvation in Revolutionary Russia* (Pittsburgh: University of Pittsburgh Press, 2000), 205–82; and Peter Fritzsche and Jochen Hellbeck, "The New Man in Stalinist Russia and Nazi Germany," in *Beyond Totalitarianism: Stalinism and Nazism Compared*, ed. Michael Geyer and Sheila Fitzpatrick (New York: Cambridge University Press, 2009), 302–44. On young cultural elites, see Vladislav Zubok, *Zhivago's Children: The Last Russian Intelligentsia* (Cambridge: Belknap Press of Harvard University Press, 2009), 1–22; and L. B. Brusilovskaia, *Kul'tura povsednevnosti v epokhu "ottepeli": Metamorfozy stilia* (Moscow: Izdatel'stvo URAO, 2001), 169–74. On countercultural youth, see William J. Risch, *The Ukrainian West: Culture and the Fate of Empire in Soviet Lviv* (Cambridge: Harvard University Press, 2011), 179–250; and Sergei Zhuk, *Rock and Roll in the Rocket City: The West, Identity, and Ideology in Soviet Dniepropetrovsk, 1960–1985* (Baltimore: Johns Hopkins University Press, 2010), 65–106. On western countercultural youth, see the essays in Andy Bennett and Keith Kahn-Harris, eds., *After Subculture: Critical Studies in Contemporary Youth Culture* (New York: Palgrave Macmillan, 2004); and Stuart Hall and Tony Jefferson, eds., *Resistance through Rituals: Youth Subcultures in Post-War Britain*, 2nd ed. (New York: Routledge, 2006).

17. David Caute, *The Dancer Defects: The Struggle for Cultural Supremacy during the Cold War* (New York: Oxford University Press, 2003), 2; Zhuk, *Rock and Roll in the Rocket City*, 3, 6; Wagnleitner, "Empire of Fun"; Alexei Yurchak, *Everything Was Forever, Until It Was No More: The Last Soviet Generation* (Princeton: Princeton University Press, 2006), 219; and Kristin Roth-Ey, *Moscow Prime Time: How the Soviet Union Built the Media Empire That Lost the Cultural Cold War* (Ithaca: Cornell University Press, 2011), 1–5.

18. My definition of agency draws on Arjun Appadurai, *Modernity at Large: Cultural Dimensions of Globalization* (Minneapolis: University of Minnesota Press, 1996), 5–11; Gyan Prakash, "Subaltern Studies as Postcolonial Criticism," *American Historical Review* 99, no. 5 (December 1994): 1475–90; Ken Roberts, *Youth in Transition: Eastern Europe and the West* (New York: Palgrave Macmillan, 2009), 14; and Birgitte Søland, *Becoming Modern: Young Women and the Reconstruction of Womanhood in the 1920s* (Princeton: Princeton University Press, 2000), 3–18. For more on conformist agency, see Gleb Tsipursky, "Conformism and Agency: Model Young Communists and the Komsomol Press in the Later Khrushchev Years, 1961–1964," *Europe-Asia Studies* 65, no. 7 (September 2013): 1396–1416. For more on Soviet youth agency, see Anna Krylova, *Soviet Women in Combat: A History of Violence on the Eastern Front* (New York: Cambridge University Press, 2010), 20–26; and Matthias Neumann, *The*

Communist Youth League and the Transformation of the Soviet Union, 1917–1932 (New York: Routledge, 2011), 1–14.

19. Juliane Fürst, *Stalin's Last Generation: Soviet Youth and the Emergence of Mature Socialism* (New York: Oxford University Press, 2010), 17–18; Benedict Anderson, *Imagined Communities: Reflections on the Origin and Spread of Nationalism* (New York: Verso, 1991), 6–7; Lawrence Grossberg, *We Gotta Get Out of This Place: Popular Conservatism and Postmodern Culture* (New York: Routledge, 1992), 113–27.

20. On cultural consumption in Soviet Ukraine, including in clubs, see Zhuk, *Rock and Roll in the Rocket City*, 7–9. For cultural consumption in the center, see Roth-Ey, *Moscow Prime Time*, 176–222. On socialist Cold War consumption, see the essays in David Crowley and Susan E. Reid, eds., *Pleasures in Socialism: Leisure and Luxury in the Eastern Bloc* (Evanston: Northwestern University Press, 2010); and Péteri, *Imagining the West in Eastern Europe and the Soviet Union*. On how people refashion mainstream products, see Michel de Certeau, *The Practice of Everyday Life*, trans. Steven F. Rendall (Berkeley: University of California Press, 1984), 29–42.

21. For organized cultural recreation in socialist eastern Europe, see Uta G. Poiger, *Jazz, Rock, and Rebels: Cold War Politics and American Culture in a Divided Germany* (Berkeley: University of California Press, 2000), 1–30; Paulina Bren, *The Greengrocer and His TV: The Culture of Communism after the 1968 Prague Spring* (Ithaca: Cornell University Press, 2010), 1–10; and Esther von Richthofen, *Bringing Culture to the Masses: Control, Compromise and Participation in the GDR* (New York: Berghahn Books, 2009), 1–27. For fascist Italy, see Ruth Ben-Ghiat, *Fascist Modernities: Italy, 1922–1945* (Berkeley: University of California Press, 2001), 3–7. For Nazi Germany, see Shelley Baranowski, *Strength through Joy: Consumerism and Mass Tourism in the Third Reich* (New York: Cambridge University Press, 2004), 40–74. On "gardening states," see Bauman, *Modernity and Ambivalence*, 20. For a standard account of consumption that relies only on evidence from the United States and western Europe, see Daniel Miller, *Material Culture and Mass Consumption* (Oxford: Basil Blackwell, 1987), 147–217. On leisure, see Thorstein Veblen, *The Theory of the Leisure Class: An Economic Study of Institutions* (1899; repr., New York: Modern Library, 1934), 68–101. On popular culture, see Richard B. Gruneau, ed., *Popular Cultures and Political Practices* (Toronto: Garamond Press, 1988). On taste, see Pierre Bourdieu, *Distinction: A Social Critique of the Judgment of Taste*, trans. and ed. Richard Nice (Cambridge: Harvard University Press, 1984), 466–85.

22. On reception of popular culture, see Stuart Hall, "Encoding/Decoding," in *Culture, Media, Language: Working Papers in Cultural Studies, 1972–79*, ed. Stuart Hall, Dorothy Hobson, Andrew Lowe, and Paul Willis (1980; repr., London: Routledge, 2005), 107–16; Toby Miller and Alec McHoul, *Popular Culture and Everyday Life* (Thousand Oaks: SAGE, 1998), 1–5. For more on fan communities, see Simon Frith, "The Cultural Study of Popular Music," in *Cultural Studies*, ed. Lawrence Grossberg, Cary Nelson, and Paula A. Treichler (New York: Routledge, 1992), 174–86; and John Storey, *Cultural Theory and Popular Culture: An Introduction* (Essex: Pearson Education, 2009), 223–25. For a typical narrative that considers jazz behind the Iron Curtain as inherently oppositional, see Gertrud Pickhan and Rüdiger Ritter, eds., *Jazz behind the Iron Curtain* (Frankfurt: Peter Lang, 2010), 7–10.

23. Elaine Hatfield, John T. Cacioppo, and Richard L. Rapson, *Emotional Contagion* (New York: Cambridge University Press, 1994), 78–127; William M. Reddy, *The Navigation of Feeling: A Framework for the History of Emotions* (Cambridge: Cambridge

University Press, 2001), 128–29; Barbara H. Rosenwein, *Emotional Communities in the Middle Ages* (Ithaca: Cornell University Press, 2006), 2. Other scholarship on the importance of feelings in history includes Peter N. Stearns and Jan Lewis, eds., *An Emotional History of the United States* (New York: New York University Press, 1998), 1–14; Peter N. Stearns, *American Cool: Constructing a Twentieth-Century Emotional Style* (New York: New York University Press, 1994), 1–15; Randolph Roth, "Measuring Feelings and Beliefs That May Facilitate (or Deter) Homicide: A Research Note on the Causes of Historic Fluctuations in Homicide Rates in the United States," *Homicide Studies* 16, no. 2 (May 2012): 197–216; and Patricia Ticineto Clough, introduction to *The Affective Turn: Theorizing the Social*, ed. Patricia Ticineto Clough with Jean Halley (Durham: Duke University Press, 2007), 1–33. For insights on Soviet emotions, see the essays in Mark D. Steinberg and Valeria Sobol, eds., *Interpreting Emotions in Russia and Eastern Europe* (DeKalb: Northern Illinois University Press, 2011); and Jan Plamper, Schamma Schahadat, and Marc Elie, eds., *Rossiiskaia imperiia chuvstv: Podkhody k kul'turnoi istorii emotsii* (Moscow: Novoe literaturnoe obozrenie, 2010).

24. For the traditional approach to public and private in the Soviet Union, see Vladimir Shlapentokh, *Public and Private Life of the Soviet People: Changing Values in Post-Stalin Russia* (New York: Oxford University Press, 1989), 3–18; Oleg Kharkhordin, *The Collective and the Individual in Russia: A Study of Practices* (Berkeley: University of California Press, 1999), 279–302. For an analysis depicting Soviet state and society as "us" and "them," see Sarah Davies, *Popular Opinion in Stalin's Russia: Terror, Propaganda and Dissent, 1934–1941* (New York: Cambridge University Press, 1997), 124–46. For recent challenges to the traditional private-public paradigm, see Lewis H. Siegelbaum, "Introduction: Mapping Private Spheres in the Soviet Context," in *Borders of Socialism: Private Spheres of Soviet Russia*, ed. Lewis H. Siegelbaum (New York: Palgrave Macmillan, 2006), 1–21; Deborah A. Field, *Private Life and Communist Morality in Khrushchev's Russia* (New York: Peter Lang, 2007); and Benjamin K. Tromly, "Re-Imagining the Soviet Intelligentsia: Student Politics and University Life, 1948–1964" (PhD diss., Harvard University, 2007), 94–150. For a theoretical take on public and private spheres, see Peter U. Hohendahl and Marc Silberman, "Critical Theory, Public Sphere and Culture: Jürgen Habermas and His Critics," *New German Critique* 16 (Winter 1979): 89–119.

25. My definition of the term "soft power" draws on Joseph S. Nye Jr., *Soft Power: The Means to Success in World Politics* (New York: Public Affairs, 2004), x. For cultural diplomacy, see Nicholas J. Cull, *The Cold War and the United States Information Agency: American Propaganda and Public Diplomacy, 1945–1989* (New York: Cambridge University Press, 2008), xv. On cultural relations in international exchanges, see Akira Iriye, *Cultural Internationalism and World Order* (Baltimore: Johns Hopkins University Press, 1997), 1–12. For western cultural diplomacy, see Penny M. Von Eschen, *Satchmo Blows Up the World: Jazz Ambassadors Play the Cold War* (Cambridge: Harvard University Press, 2004), 1–30; and Yale Richmond, *Cultural Exchange and the Cold War: Raising the Iron Curtain* (University Park: Pennsylvania State University Press, 2003), xii–xiv. For literature on the impact of western cultural diplomacy in the Soviet Union, see Donald J. Raleigh, *Soviet Baby Boomers: An Oral History of Russia's Cold War Generation* (New York: Oxford University Press, 2011), 66–267; and Susan E. Reid, "Who Will Beat Whom? Soviet Popular Reception of the American National Exhibition in Moscow, 1959," *Kritika* 9, no. 4 (Fall 2008): 855–904. For an overview

of recent historiography on cultural diplomacy, see Thomas W. Zeiler, "The Diplomatic History Bandwagon: A State of the Field," *Journal of American History* 95, no. 4 (March 2009): 1053–73.

26. Works dealing with western Cold War cultural diplomacy occasionally mention efforts to influence visiting foreigners via cultural activities, but they do not explore this topic in a systematic manner; see, for example, Kenneth Osgood, *Total Cold War: Eisenhower's Secret Propaganda Battle at Home and Abroad* (Lawrence: University Press of Kansas, 2006), 243. On young foreign visitors in particular, see Karen M. Paget, "From Cooperation to Covert Action: The United States Government and Students, 1940–52," in *The US Government, Citizen Groups and the Cold War: The State-Private Network*, ed. Helen Laville and Hugh Wilford (New York: Routledge, 2006), 66–82; Hugh Wilford, *The Mighty Wurlitzer: How the CIA Played America* (Cambridge: Harvard University Press, 2008), 122–28; and Joël Kotek, *Students and the Cold War*, trans. Ralph Blumenau (New York: St. Martin's Press, 1996), 210–24. On the importance of sub-state interactions in the Cold War, see Sari Autio-Sarasmo and Katalin Miklossy, eds., *Reassessing Cold War Europe* (New York: Routledge, 2011). On transnational history as it applies to the Soviet context, see Michael David-Fox, "Introduction: Entangled Histories in the Age of Extremes," in *Fascination and Enmity: Russia and Germany as Entangled Histories, 1914–1945*, ed. Michael David-Fox, Peter Holquist, and Alexander M. Martin (Pittsburgh: University of Pittsburgh Press, 2012), 1–12; and György Péteri, ed., *Nylon Curtain: Transnational and Transsystemic Tendencies in the Cultural Life of State-Socialist Russia and East-Central Europe* (Trondheim: Trondheim Studies on East European Cultures & Societies, 2006), 1–14.

27. On the need for micro-level case studies of the Cold War, see Jeffrey A. Engel, ed., *Local Consequences of the Global Cold War* (Washington: Woodrow Wilson Center Press / Stanford: Stanford University Press, 2007). For Cold War cultures, see Annette Vowinckel, Marcus M. Payk, and Thomas Lindenberger, eds., *Cold War Cultures: Perspectives on Eastern and Western European Societies* (New York: Berghahn Books, 2012); and Rana Mitter and Patrick Major, eds., *Across the Blocs: Cold War Cultural and Social History* (Portland: Frank Cass, 2004). For a nuanced take on the impact of the Cold War on US culture and Cold War determinism, see Peter J. Kuznick and James Gilbert, "US Culture and the Cold War," in *Rethinking Cold War Culture*, ed. Peter J. Kuznick and James Gilbert (Washington: Smithsonian Institution Press, 2001), 1–13. For a different view, see Lary May, ed., *Recasting America: Culture and Politics in the Age of Cold War* (Chicago: University of Chicago Press, 1989), 1–18. For how domestic concerns and priorities, including those about western popular culture, influenced post-Stalin Soviet foreign and internal policy, see Jeremi Suri, *Power and Protest: Global Revolution and the Rise of Détente* (Cambridge: Harvard University Press, 2003), 1–5; Ted Hopf, *Social Construction of International Politics: Identities & Foreign Policies, Moscow, 1955 and 1999* (Ithaca: Cornell University Press, 2002), 39–82; and Ted Hopf, *Reconstructing the Cold War: The Early Years, 1945–1958* (New York: Oxford University Press, 2012).

28. On the divergence of local practice from central directives, and for more on Saratov, see Donald J. Raleigh, ed., *Provincial Landscapes: Local Dimensions of Soviet Power, 1917–1953* (Pittsburgh: University of Pittsburgh Press, 2001), 1–14.

29. Donald J. Raleigh, *Russia's Sputnik Generation: Soviet Baby Boomers Talk about Their Lives* (Bloomington: Indiana University Press, 2006), 10–12; Raleigh, *Soviet Baby Boomers*, 3–15; and Irina Paperno, *Stories of the Soviet Experience: Memoirs, Di-*

aries, Dreams (Ithaca: Cornell University Press, 2009), 209–10. On analyzing autobiographical sources, especially oral ones, in non-Soviet settings, see Harold Rosen, *Speaking from Memory: A Guide to Autobiographical Acts and Practices* (Stoke-on-Trent: Trentham, 1998), 1–15; and Alessandro Portelli, *The Death of Luigi Trastulli, and Other Stories: Form and Meaning in Oral History* (Albany: State University of New York Press, 1991), 45–58.

CHAPTER 1. IDEOLOGY, ENLIGHTENMENT, AND ENTERTAINMENT

1. RGASPI, f. M-1, op. 32, d. 321, l. 57.

2. "Za poleznyi i razumnyi otdykh," *Komsomol'skaia pravda*, July 4, 1946. For the difference between internal and external official discourse, see Donald J. Raleigh, "Languages of Power: How the Saratov Bolsheviks Imagined Their Enemies," *Slavic Review* 57, no. 2 (Summer 1998): 320–49.

3. Louise McReynolds, *Russia at Play: Leisure Activities at the End of the Tsarist Era* (Ithaca: Cornell University Press, 2003), 14–75; E. Anthony Swift, *Popular Theater and Society in Tsarist Russia* (Berkeley: University of California Press, 2002); Gary Thurston, *The Popular Theatre Movement in Russia, 1862–1919* (Evanston: Northwestern University Press, 1998); Kh. A. Khrenov, *Chelovek igraiushchii v russkoi kul'ture* (Saint Petersburg: Aleteia, 2005), 574–76; Kate Transchel, *Under the Influence: Working-Class Drinking, Temperance, and Cultural Revolution in Russia, 1895–1932* (Pittsburgh: University of Pittsburgh Press, 2006), 1–11; Lynn M. Sargeant, "High Anxiety: New Venues, New Audiences, and the Fear of the Popular in Late Imperial Russian Musical Life," *19th-Century Music* 35, no. 2 (Fall 2011): 93–114.

4. V. A. Berezina, ed. *Dopolnitel'noe (vneshkol'noe) obrazovanie detei Rossii* (Moscow: Dialog kul'tur, 2008), 10–11; Joan Neuberger, *Hooliganism: Crime, Culture, Power in St. Petersburg, 1900–1914* (Berkeley: University of California Press, 1993), 205–9.

5. G. G. Karpov and N. D. Sintsov, *Klubnoe delo: Uchebnoe posobie* (Moscow: Sovetskaia Rossiia, 1959), 14; I. S. Rozental', *"I vot obshchestvennoe mnen'e!" Kluby v istorii rossiiskoi obshchestvennoisti; Konets XVIII–nachalo XX v.* (Moscow: Novyi khronograf, 2007), 239–82; Adele Lindenmeyr, "Building Civil Society One Brick at a Time: People's Houses and Worker Enlightenment in Late Imperial Russia," *Journal of Modern History* 84, no. 1 (March 2012): 1–39; Lynn M. Sargeant, "Civil Society as a Do-It-Yourself Project: The People's House in Late Imperial Russia" (unpublished manuscript); Victoria E. Bonnell, *Roots of Rebellion: Workers' Politics and Organizations in St. Petersburg and Moscow, 1900–1914* (Berkeley: University of California Press, 1983), 328–34.

6. While the influence flowed from western Europe in this case, Russia shaped the rest of the world in other ways. See Steven G. Marks, *How Russia Shaped the Modern World: From Art to Anti-Semitism, Ballet to Bolshevism* (Princeton: Princeton University Press, 2003), 1–6.

7. E. P. Thompson, *The Making of the English Working Class* (New York: Pantheon Books, 1964), 401–8.

8. Peter Bailey, *Leisure and Class in Victorian England: Rational Recreation and the Contest for Control, 1830–1885* (Buffalo: University of Toronto Press, 1978), 169–82; Peter Borsay, *A History of Leisure: The British Experience since 1500* (New York: Palgrave Macmillan, 2006).

9. W. Fitzhugh Brundage, "Working in the 'Kingdom of Culture': African Americans and American Popular Culture, 1890–1930," in *Beyond Blackface: African Americans and the Creation of American Popular Culture, 1890–1930*, ed. W. Fitzhugh Brundage (Chapel Hill: University of North Carolina Press, 2011), 1–42.

10. Steven Mintz, *Huck's Raft: A History of American Childhood* (Cambridge: Harvard University Press, 2004), 185–94; John R. Gillis, *Youth and History: Tradition and Change in European Age Relations, 1770–Present* (New York: Academic Press, 1981), 37–131.

11. For western Europe, see Michel Foucault, *Discipline and Punish: The Birth of the Prison* (New York: Vintage Books, 1979), 104–35; Michel Foucault, *The History of Sexuality*, vol. 1, *An Introduction*, trans. Robert Hurley (New York: Pantheon, 1978), 53–73. For social interventionism in late imperial Russia, see Laura Engelstein, *The Keys to Happiness: Sex and the Search for Modernity in Fin-de-Siècle Russia* (Ithaca: Cornell University Press, 1992), 17–56.

12. Joseph Bradley, *Voluntary Associations in Tsarist Russia: Science, Patriotism, and Civil Society* (Cambridge: Harvard University Press, 2009), 254–66; A. S. Tumanova, *Obshchestvennye organizatsii i russkaia publika v nachale XX veka* (Moscow: Novyi khronograf, 2008), 289–94.

13. Daniel Beer, *Renovating Russia: The Human Sciences and the Fate of Liberal Modernity, 1880–1930* (Ithaca: Cornell University Press, 2008), 165–204; Lynn M. Sargeant, *Harmony and Discord: Music and the Transformation of Russian Cultural Life* (New York: Oxford University Press, 2011), 271.

14. Lindenmeyr, "Building Civil Society One Brick at a Time."

15. James Von Geldern, *Bolshevik Festivals, 1917–1920* (Berkeley: University of California Press, 1993); Richard Stites, "Festival and Revolution: The Role of Public Spectacle in Russia, 1917–1918," in *Essays on Revolutionary Culture and Stalinism*, ed. John W. Strong (Columbus: Slavica Publishers, 1990), 9–28.

16. O. Tumim, *Zhenskii klub v derevne* (Petrograd: Nachatki znanii, 1919), 19–31; Gabriele Gorzka, "Proletarian Culture in Practice: Workers' Clubs, 1917–1921," in Strong, *Essays on Revolutionary Culture and Stalinism*, 29–55; Isabel A. Tirado, *Young Guard! The Communist Youth League, Petrograd 1917–1920* (New York: Greenwood Press, 1988), 117–43.

17. Lynn Mally, *Culture of the Future: The Proletkult Movement in Revolutionary Russia* (Berkeley: University of California Press, 1990), 253–59; Sheila Fitzpatrick, *The Commissariat of Enlightenment: Soviet Organization of Education and the Arts under Lunacharsky, October 1917–1921* (New York: Cambridge University Press, 1970), 89–109; Donald J. Raleigh, *Experiencing Russia's Civil War: Politics, Society, and Revolutionary Culture in Saratov, 1917–1922* (Princeton: Princeton University Press, 2002), 208–15.

18. Lewis H. Siegelbaum, *Soviet State and Society between the Revolutions, 1918–1929* (New York: Cambridge University Press, 1992), 135–223; Michael David-Fox, *Revolution of the Mind: Higher Learning among the Bolsheviks, 1918–1929* (Ithaca: Cornell University Press, 1997), 83–132; Igal Halfin, *From Darkness to Light: Class, Consciousness, and Salvation in Revolutionary Russia* (Pittsburgh: University of Pittsburgh Press, 2000), 205–82; Stuart Finkel, *On the Ideological Front: The Russian Intelligentsia and the Making of the Soviet Public Sphere* (New Haven: Yale University Press, 2007), 1–12; Sharon Kowalsky, *Deviant Women: Female Crime and Criminology in Revolu-*

tionary Russia, 1880–1930 (DeKalb: Northern Illinois University Press, 2009), 187–95; Eric Naiman, *Sex in Public: The Incarnation of Early Soviet Ideology* (Princeton: Princeton University Press, 1997), 27–78.

19. David L. Hoffmann, *Cultivating the Masses: Modern State Practices and Soviet Socialism, 1914–1939* (Ithaca: Cornell University Press, 2011), 1–16.

20. Elizabeth A. Wood, *Performing Justice: Agitation Trials in Early Soviet Russia* (Ithaca: Cornell University Press, 2005), 150–73; John B. Hatch, "Hangouts and Hangovers: State, Class and Culture in Moscow's Workers' Club Movement, 1925–1928," *Russian Review* 53, no. 1 (January 1994): 97–117.

21. Anne E. Gorsuch, *Youth in Revolutionary Russia: Enthusiasts, Bohemians, Delinquents* (Bloomington: Indiana University Press, 2000), 41–95, 139–66; Anne E. Gorsuch, *Flappers and Foxtrotters: Soviet Youth in the "Roaring Twenties,"* Carl Beck Papers in Russian and East European Studies, No. 1102 (Pittsburgh: Center for Russian and East European Studies, University Center for International Studies, University of Pittsburgh, 1994), 1–33; S. Frederick Starr, *Red and Hot: The Fate of Jazz in the Soviet Union, 1917–1980* (New York: Oxford University Press, 1983), 37–78; Tricia Starks, *The Body Soviet: Propaganda, Hygiene, and the Revolutionary State* (Madison: University of Wisconsin Press, 2008), 81; Katerina Clark, *Petersburg: Crucible of Cultural Revolution* (Cambridge: Harvard University Press, 1995), 162–65.

22. Sheila Fitzpatrick, *The Cultural Front: Power and Culture in Revolutionary Russia* (Ithaca: Cornell University Press, 1992), 16–36; K. G. Bogemskaia, "Vvedenie," in *Samodeiatel'noe khudozhestvennoe tvorchestvo v SSSR: Ocherki istorii, 1917–1932 gg.*, ed. K. G. Bogemskaia and L. P. Solntseva (Saint Petersburg: Dmitrii Bulanin, 1999), 10–23.

23. S. Dolinskii, *Klub molodezhi v den' 1 maia* (Moscow: Novaia Moskva, 1925); S. Dmitrovskii, *Mezhdunarodnyi iunosheskii den' v klube* (Kiev: Proletarii, 1925); *Molodezh' v rabochem klube* (Moscow: Molodaia gvardiia, 1927); M. A. Rastopchina, *Kak privlech' v klub massu* (Moscow: Izdanie G. F. Mirimanova, 1925). Also see Matthias Neumann, *The Communist Youth League and the Transformation of the Soviet Union, 1917–1932* (New York: Routledge, 2011), 131–32.

24. Michael David-Fox, "What Is Cultural Revolution?," *Russian Review* 58, no. 2 (April 1999): 181–201.

25. V. Kirov, *Klub i byt: Doklad na vsesoiuznom klubnom soveshchanii i rezoliutsii po dokladu* (Moscow, 1930), 4–20; Lynn Mally, *Revolutionary Acts: Amateur Theater and the Soviet State, 1917–1938* (Ithaca: Cornell University Press, 2000), 215–16; S. Iu. Rumiantsev and A. P. Shul'pin, "Samodeiatel'noe tvorchestvo i 'gosudarstvennaia' kul'tura," in *Samodeiatel'noe khudozhestvennoe tvorchestvo v SSSR: Ocherki istorii, 1930–1950 gg.*, ed. K. G. Bogemskaia (Moscow: Gosudarstvennyi institut iskusstvoznaniia, 1995), 7–52; Amy Nelson, *Music for the Revolution: Musicians and Power in Early Soviet Russia* (University Park: Pennsylvania State University Press, 2004), 207–40; Benjamin Harshav, *The Moscow Yiddish Theater: Art on Stage in the Time of Revolution* (New Haven: Yale University Press, 2008), 3–35.

26. Amy E. Randall, *The Soviet Dream World of Retail Trade and Consumption in the 1930s* (New York: Palgrave Macmillan, 2008), 134–57; Jukka Gronow, *Caviar with Champagne: Common Luxury and the Ideals of the Good Life in Stalin's Russia* (New York: Berg, 2003), 1–13; Julie Hessler, *A Social History of Soviet Trade: Trade Policy, Retail Practices, and Consumption, 1917–1953* (Princeton: Princeton University Press, 2004), 197–250; Karen Petrone, *Life Has Become More Joyous, Comrades: Celebrations*

in the *Time of Stalin* (Bloomington: Indiana University Press, 2000), 203–10; Elena Osokina, *Za fasadom "Stalinskogo izobilia": Raspredelenie i rynok v snabzhenii naselenia v gody industrializatsii, 1927–1941* (Moscow: ROSSPEN, 1998).

27. O. K. Makarova, *Kul'turnoe stroitel'stvo SSSR: Statisticheskii sbornik* (Moscow: Gosudarstvennoe statisticheskoe izdatel'stvo, 1956), 273.

28. Lewis H. Siegelbaum, "The Shaping of Soviet Workers' Leisure: Workers' Clubs and Palaces of Culture in the 1930s," *International Labor and Working-Class History* 56 (October 1999): 78–92; Lynne Attwood, "Women Workers at Play: The Portrayal of Leisure in the Magazine *Rabotnitsa* in the First Two Decades of Soviet Power," in *Women in the Stalin Era*, ed. Melanie Ilič (New York: Palgrave, 2001), 29–48; Anne Gorsuch, "'Smashing Chairs at the Local Club': Discipline, Disorder, and Soviet Youth," in *Sowjetjugend 1917–1941: Generation Zwischen Revolution und Resignation*, ed. Corinna Kuhr-Korolev (Essen: Klartext, 2001), 247–61.

29. David MacFadyen, *Songs for Fat People: Affect, Emotion, and Celebrity in the Russian Popular Song, 1900–1955* (Ithaca: McGill-Queen's University Press, 2002), 114–40; Starr, *Red and Hot*, 107–56.

30. Malte Rolf, *Sovetskie massovye prazdniki* (Moscow: ROSSPEN, 2009), 96–97; Alaina Lemon, *Between Two Fires: Gypsy Performance and Romani Memory from Pushkin to Postsocialism* (Durham: Duke University Press, 2000), 124–65; Ali Iğmen, *Speaking Soviet with an Accent: Culture and Power in Kyrgyzstan* (Pittsburgh: University of Pittsburgh Press, 2012), 26; Susannah L. Smith, "From Peasants to Professionals: The Socialist-Realist Transformation of a Russian Folk Choir," *Kritika* 3, no. 3 (Summer 2002): 393–425.

31. Michael David-Fox, *Showcasing the Great Experiment: Cultural Diplomacy and Western Visitors to the Soviet Union, 1921–1941* (New York: Oxford University Press, 2011), 285; Katerina Clark, *Moscow, the Fourth Rome: Stalinism, Cosmopolitanism, and the Evolution of Soviet Culture, 1931–1941* (Cambridge: Harvard University Press, 2011), 307–44.

32. Starr, *Red and Hot*, 157–80; Martin Lücke, "The Postwar Campaign against Jazz in the USSR (1945–1953)," in *Jazz behind the Iron Curtain*, ed. Gertrud Pickhan and Rüdiger Ritter (Frankfurt: Peter Lang, 2010), 83–98. For more on jazz as a musical genre, see Mark C. Gridley with David Cutler, *Jazz Styles: History & Analysis* (Upper Saddle River: Prentice Hall, 2003); and David Meltzer, ed., *Reading Jazz* (San Francisco: Mercury House, 1993).

33. Tara Zahra, *The Lost Children: Reconstructing Europe's Families after World War II* (Cambridge: Harvard University Press, 2011), 1–24.

34. Karpov and Sintsov, *Klubnoe delo*, 20; Starr, *Red and Hot*, 181–203.

35. Mark Slobin, ed., *Retuning Culture: Musical Changes in Central and Eastern Europe* (Durham: Duke University Press, 1996), 1–13.

36. TsAGM, f. 44, op. 1, d. 4, ll. 24–25.

37. For the similar role of incentives in industry, see Joseph S. Berliner, *Factory and Manager in the USSR* (Cambridge: Harvard University Press, 1957).

38. A. A. Alekseeva, *Stroka v biografii* (Moscow: Molodaia gvardiia, 2003), 17–18.

39. E. M. Andreev, L. E. Darskii, and T. L. Khar'kova, *Naselenie Sovetskogo Soiuza, 1922–1991* (Moscow: Nauka, 1993), 63.

40. For more on the Komsomol's structure, see Peter Konecny, *Builders and Deserters: Students, State, and Community in Leningrad, 1917–1941* (Montreal: McGill-Queen's University Press, 1999), 38–100; Neumann, *Communist Youth League*, 126–

45; Ralph Talcott Fisher Jr., *Pattern for Soviet Youth: A Study of the Congresses of the Komsomol, 1918–1954* (New York: Columbia University Press, 1959), 279–91; and Allen Kassof, *The Soviet Youth Program: Regimentation and Rebellion* (Cambridge: Harvard University Press, 1965), 1–8.

41. Elena Zubkova, *Russia after the War: Hopes, Illusions, and Disappointments, 1945–1957*, trans. and ed. Hugh Ragsdale (Armonk: M. E. Sharpe, 1998), 31–39.

42. Jeffrey W. Jones, *Everyday Life and the "Reconstruction" of Soviet Russia during and after the Great Patriotic War, 1943–1948* (Bloomington: Slavica Publishers, 2008); Nicholas Ganson, *The Soviet Famine of 1946–47 in Global and Historical Perspective* (New York: Palgrave Macmillan, 2009); Karl D. Qualls, *From Ruins to Reconstruction: Urban Identity in Soviet Sevastopol after World War II* (Ithaca: Cornell University Press, 2010).

43. Juliane Fürst, *Stalin's Last Generation: Soviet Youth and the Emergence of Mature Socialism, 1945–56* (New York: Oxford University Press, 2010), 32–63.

44. On the need for youth to prepare for war, see Anna Krylova, *Soviet Women in Combat: A History of Violence on the Eastern Front* (New York: Cambridge University Press, 2010), 35–59. On children, see Olga Kurchenko, *Little Soldiers: How Soviet Children Went to War, 1941–1945* (New York: Oxford University Press, 2011), 249–53.

45. Makarova, *Kul'turnoe stroitel'stvo SSSR*, 273.

46. GARF, f. R-5451, op. 24, d. 278, ll. 7–17; RGASPI, f. M-1, op. 32, d. 269, ll. 35–36.

47. RGASPI, f. M-1, op. 32, d. 269, ll. 1–9.

48. On these discussions, see A. V. Pyzhikov, *Khrushchevskaia "ottepel'"* (Moscow: OLMA-PRESS, 2002), 15–40; Alexander Titov, "The 1961 Party Program and the Fate of Khrushchev's Reforms," in *Soviet State and Society under Nikita Khrushchev*, ed. Melanie Ilič and Jeremy Smith (New York: Routledge, 2009), 8–25.

49. RGASPI, f. M-1, op. 3, d. 382, l. 125; RGASPI, f. M-1, op. 3, d. 429, ll. 2–4.

50. "Priblizit' klub k zavodskoi molodezhi!," *Komsomol'skaia pravda*, January 6, 1945.

51. For other such articles, see "Komsomol'tsy sela Tatishchevo," *Komsomol'skaia pravda*, January 6, 1945; "Za poleznyi i razumnyi otdykh," *Komsomol'skaia pravda*, July 4, 1946; and "Khudozhestvennuiu samodeiatel'nost'—na sluzhbu vospitaniia molodezhi," *Komsomol'skaia pravda*, January 7, 1945.

52. On socialist realism, see Jeffrey Brooks, *Thank You, Comrade Stalin! Soviet Public Culture from Revolution to Cold War* (Princeton: Princeton University Press, 2000), 54–105; Katerina Clark, *The Soviet Novel: History as Ritual* (Chicago: University of Chicago Press, 1981), 3–24; and Matthew E. Lenoe, *Closer to the Masses: Stalinist Culture, Social Revolution, and Soviet Newspapers* (Cambridge: Harvard University Press, 2004), 245–54.

53. RGASPI, f. M-1, op. 3, d. 403, ll. 17–22.

54. On Saratov, see RGASPI, f. M-1, op. 32, d. 323, l. 8. On Moscow, see TsAOPIM, f. 635, op. 3, d. 120, ll. 9–10.

55. "Khudozhestvennuiu samodeiatel'nost'—na sluzhbu vospitaniia molodezhi," *Komsomol'skaia pravda*, January 7, 1945.

56. RGASPI, f. M-1, op. 3, d. 433, ll. 17–19.

57. RGASPI, f. M-1, op. 32, d. 321, l. 57.

58. RGASPI, f. M-1, op. 32, d. 378, l. 2.

59. RGASPI, f. M-1, op. 3, d. 403, ll. 17–22.

60. German Krichevskii, born 1934, interview by author, February 6, 2009. Also see his unpublished memoir, "Samoanaliz, ili razveiat' mify," which he graciously provided.

61. RGASPI, f. M-1, op. 3, d. 403, ll. 17–22.

62. RGASPI, f. M-1, op. 3, d. 403, ll. 27–31.

63. On the 1930s, see David L. Hoffmann, *Peasant Metropolis: Social Identities in Moscow, 1929–1941* (Ithaca: Cornell University Press, 1994), 161–64.

64. RGASPI, f. M-1, op. 3, d. 403, ll. 17–22.

65. "Dobro pozhalovat'!," *Komsomol'skaia pravda*, July 13, 1946.

66. RGASPI, f. M-1, op. 32, d. 321, l. 57.

67. "Za poleznyi i razumnyi otdykh," *Komsomol'skaia pravda*, July 4, 1946.

68. RGASPI, f. M-1, op. 32, d. 269, ll. 1–9.

69. Irina Sirotkina, "Pliaska i ekstaz v Rossii ot Serebriannogo veka do kontsa 1920-kh godov," in *Rossiiskaia imperiia chuvstv: Podkhody k kul'turnoi istorii emotsii*, ed. Jan Plamper, Schamma Schahadat, and Marc Elie (Moscow: Novoe literaturnoe obozrenie, 2010), 282–305.

70. Richard Stites, *Russian Popular Culture: Entertainment and Society since 1900* (New York: Cambridge University Press, 1992), 125–26; Josephine Woll, *Real Images: Soviet Cinema and the Thaw* (New York: I. B. Tauris, 2000), 3–4; Sergei Kapterev, "Illusionary Spoils: Soviet Attitudes toward American Cinema during the Early Cold War," *Kritika* 10, no. 4 (Fall 2009): 779–807; Sarah Davies, "Soviet Cinema in the Early Cold War: Pudovkin's *Admiral Nakhimov* in Context," in *Across the Blocs: Cold War Cultural and Social History*, ed. Rana Mitter and Patrick Major (Portland: Frank Cass, 2004), 49–70.

71. TsAGM, f. 44, op. 1, d. 4, l. 19.

72. TsAGM, f. 44, op. 1, d. 4, l. 19.

73. Starr, *Red and Hot*, 205–6; Fürst, *Stalin's Last Generation*, 201–5; Mark Edele, "Strange Young Men in Stalin's Moscow: The Birth and Life of the Stiliagi, 1945–1953," *Jahrbücher für Geschichte Osteuropas* 50, no. 1 (March 2002): 37–61; Gleb Tsipursky, "Living 'America' in the Soviet Union: The Cultural Practices of 'Westernized' Soviet Youth, 1945–1964," in *The Soviet Union and the United States: Rivals of the Twentieth Century; Coexistence and Competition*, ed. Eva-Maria Stolberg (New York: Peter Lang, 2013), 139–64.

74. TsAGM, f. 2011, op. 1, d. 37, l. 86.

75. RGASPI, f. M-1, op. 32, d. 710, ll. 7–9.

76. A conclusion in accord with other findings for a brief postwar relaxation is in Zubkova, *Russia after the War*, 31–39. However, this finding contradicts Sheila Fitzpatrick's view of the postwar Stalin period as exclusively a time of tightening controls; see Fitzpatrick, "Postwar Soviet Society: The 'Return to Normalcy,' 1945–1953," in *The Impact of World War II on the Soviet Union*, ed. Susan J. Linz (Totowa: Rowman & Allanheld, 1985), 129–56.

77. For more on how the war served as a major break, see Juliane Fürst, "Introduction: Late Stalinist Society; History, Policies, People," in *Late Stalinist Russia: Society between Reconstruction and Reinvention*, ed. Juliane Fürst (New York: Routledge, 2006), 1–20.

78. Uta G. Poiger, *Jazz, Rock, and Rebels: Cold War Politics and American Culture in a Divided Germany* (Berkeley: University of California Press, 2000), 31–70.

79. Claire Wallace and Sijka Kovatcheva, *Youth in Society: The Construction and Deconstruction of Youth in East and West Europe* (New York: St. Martin's Press, 1998), 153–84.

80. See the contributions to Sabrina P. Ramet and Gordana P. Crnković, eds., *Kazaaam! Splat! Ploof! The American Impact on European Popular Culture since 1945* (New York: Rowman & Littlefield, 2003); Alexander Stephan, ed., *The Americanization of Europe: Culture, Diplomacy, and Anti-Americanism after 1945* (New York: Berghahn Books, 2006); and Axel Schildt and Detlef Siegfried, eds., *European Cities, Youth, and the Public Sphere in the Twentieth Century* (Burlington: Ashgate Publishing, 2005).

81. James Gilbert, *A Cycle of Outrage: America's Reaction to the Juvenile Delinquent in the 1950s* (New York: Oxford University Press, 1986), 11–61.

CHAPTER 2. IDEOLOGICAL RECONSTRUCTION IN THE CULTURAL RECREATION NETWORK, 1947-1953

1. "Skuchno molodezhi v Kirovograde," *Komsomol'skaia pravda*, June 19, 1948; "Bol'she vnimaniia studencheskim obshchezhitiiam," *Stalinets*, March 25, 1952. The latter newspaper, the organ of the state university at Saratov, changed its name to *Leninskii put'* in January 1957.

2. N. A. Mikhailov, *Otchetnyi doklad na XI s''ezde komsomola o rabote TsK VLKSM* (Moscow: Molodaia gvardiia, 1949), 33–35.

3. Mark B. Smith, *Property of Communists: The Urban Housing Program from Stalin to Khrushchev* (DeKalb: Northern Illinois University Press, 2010), 25–58; Sheila Fitzpatrick, "Postwar Soviet Society: The 'Return to Normalcy,' 1945–1953," in *The Impact of World War II on the Soviet Union*, ed. Susan J. Linz (Totowa: Rowman & Allanheld, 1985), 129–56; A. Z. Vakser, *Leningrad poslevoennyi, 1945–1982 gody* (Saint Petersburg: Izdatel'stvo Ostrov, 2005).

4. Elena Zubkova, *Russia after the War: Hopes, Illusions, and Disappointments, 1945–1957*, trans. and ed. Hugh Ragsdale (Armonk: M. E. Sharpe, 1998): 27–30, 40–56, 101–8, 139–48; Amir Weiner, *Making Sense of War: The Second World War and the Fate of the Bolshevik Revolution* (Princeton: Princeton University Press, 2001), 7–40.

5. Vladislav Zubok, *A Failed Empire: The Soviet Union in the Cold War from Stalin to Gorbachev* (Chapel Hill: University of North Carolina Press, 2007), 1–93; Yoram Gorlizki and Oleg Khlevniuk, *Cold Peace: Stalin and the Soviet Ruling Circle, 1945–1953* (New York: Oxford University Press, 2004), 17–70; A. V. Fateev, *Obraz vraga v sovetskoi propagande, 1945–1954 gg.* (Moscow: Institut rossiiskoi istorii RAN, 1999).

6. Melvyn P. Leffler, "The Cold War: What Do 'We Now Know'?," *American Historical Review* 104, no. 2 (April 1999): 501–24; Geraint Hughes and Saki R. Dockrill, "Introduction: The Cold War as History," in *Palgrave Advances in Cold War History*, ed. Saki R. Dockrill and Geraint Hughes (New York: Palgrave Macmillan, 2006), 1–18.

7. O. K. Makarova, *Kul'turnoe stroitel'stvo SSSR: Statisticheskii sbornik* (Moscow: Gosudarstvennoe statisticheskoe izdatel'stvo, 1956), 273.

8. GARF, f. R-5451, op. 24, d. 900, l. 11.

9. RGASPI, f. M-1, op. 32, d. 630, l. 185; RGASPI, f. M-1, op. 32, d. 741, ll. 1–6.

10. For more on the role of culture in the conflict between the superpowers during the postwar Stalin period, see Tony Shaw and Denise J. Youngblood, *Cinematic Cold War: The American and Soviet Struggle for Hearts and Minds* (Lawrence: University Press of Kansas, 2010), 65–96; Nicholas J. Cull, *The Cold War and the United States Information Agency: American Propaganda and Public Diplomacy, 1945–1989* (New York: Cam-

bridge University Press, 2008), 22–80; David Caute, *The Dancer Defects: The Struggle for Cultural Supremacy during the Cold War* (New York: Oxford University Press, 2003), 441–67; Peter Romijn, Giles Scott-Smith, and Joes Segal, eds., *Divided Dreamworlds? The Cultural Cold War in East and West* (Amsterdam: Amsterdam University Press, 2012); Scott Lucas, *Freedom's War: The American Crusade against the Soviet Union* (New York: New York University Press, 1999), 93–106; Walter L. Hixson, *Parting the Curtain: Propaganda, Culture, and the Cold War* (New York: St. Martin's Press, 1997), 1–56; Michael Nelson, *War of the Black Heavens: The Battles of Western Broadcasting in the Cold War* (Syracuse: Syracuse University Press, 1997), 10–66; Jenny Anderson, "The Great Future Debate and the Struggle for the World," *American Historical Review* 117, no. 5 (December 2012): 1411–30; and Frances Stonor Saunders, *The Cultural Cold War: The CIA and the World of Arts and Letters* (New York: New Press, 1999), 7–84.

11. Jan Plamper, *The Stalin Cult: A Study in the Alchemy of Power* (New Haven: Yale University Press, 2012), 60–85; Jeffrey Brooks, *Thank You, Comrade Stalin! Soviet Public Culture from Revolution to Cold War* (Princeton: Princeton University Press, 2000), 195–232.

12. David Brandenberger, *National Bolshevism: Stalinist Mass Culture and the Formation of Modern Russian Identity, 1931–1956* (Cambridge: Harvard University Press, 2002), 183–96; Robert Edelman, *Spartak Moscow: A History of the People's Team in the Workers' State* (Ithaca: Cornell University Press, 2009), 165–66; Terry Martin, "Modernization or Neo-Traditionalism? Ascribed Nationality and Soviet Primordialism," in *Russian Modernity: Politics, Knowledge, Practices*, ed. David L. Hoffman and Yanni Kotsonis (New York: St. Martin's Press, 2000), 161–84.

13. Sheila Fitzpatrick, *The Cultural Front: Power and Culture in Revolutionary Russia* (Ithaca: Cornell University Press, 1992), 238–57; Ethan Pollock, *Stalin and the Soviet Science Wars* (Princeton: Princeton University Press, 2006), 41–71; V. D. Esakov and E. S. Levina, *Stalinskie "sudy chesti": Delo "KR"* (Moscow: Nauka, 2005).

14. Rósa Magnúsdóttir, "Keeping Up Appearances: How the Soviet State Failed to Control Popular Attitudes toward the United States of America, 1945–1959" (PhD diss., University of North Carolina at Chapel Hill, 2006); Konstantin V. Avramov, "Soviet America: Popular Responses to the United States in Post–World War II Soviet Union" (PhD diss., University of Kansas, 2012); N. I. Nikolaeva, "Nekotorye itogi antiamerikanskoi kampanii v SSSR v kontse 40kh–nachale 50kh godov," in *Novaia i noveishaia istoriia*, ed. A. V. Gladyshev and V. S. Mirzekhanov (Saratov: Izdatel'stvo Saratovskogo universiteta, 2004), 100–112; Eric Shiraev and Vladislav Zubok, *Anti-Americanism in Russia: From Stalin to Putin* (New York: Palgrave, 2000), 7–25.

15. Jonathan Brent and Vladimir P. Naumov, *Stalin's Last Crime: The Plot against the Jewish Doctors, 1948–1953* (New York: HarperCollins, 2003), 1–11, 249–83; Sheila Fitzpatrick, *Tear Off the Masks! Identity and Imposture in Twentieth-Century Russia* (Princeton: Princeton University Press, 2005), 282–300; Yuri Slezkine, *The Jewish Century* (Princeton: Princeton University Press, 2004), 204–371.

16. Richard Stites, *Russian Popular Culture: Entertainment and Society since 1900* (New York: Cambridge University Press, 1992), 116.

17. Reprinted in A. N. Iakovlev, ed., *Vlast' i khudozhestvennaia intelligentsiia: Dokumenty TsK RKP(b)—VKP(b)—OGPU—NKVD o kul'turnoi politike; 1917–1953* (Moscow: Mezhdunarodnyi fond Demokratiia, 1999), 591–96. For the resolution's impact on the circus, see Miriam Neirick, *When Pigs Could Fly and Bears Could Dance: A History of the Soviet Circus* (Madison: University of Wisconsin Press, 2012).

18. RGASPI, f. 17, op. 3, d. 1069, ll. 42–48.

19. Kiril Tomoff, *Creative Union: The Professional Organization of Soviet Composers, 1939–1953* (Ithaca: Cornell University Press, 2006), 97–151; S. Frederick Starr, *Red and Hot: The Fate of Jazz in the Soviet Union, 1917–1980* (New York: Oxford University Press, 1983), 204–33; Martin Lücke, "The Postwar Campaign against Jazz in the USSR (1945–1953)," in *Jazz behind the Iron Curtain*, ed. Gertrud Pickhan and Rüdiger Ritter (Frankfurt: Peter Lang, 2010), 83–98. Contemporary western music arts constituted another target; see Peter J. Schmelz, *Such Freedom, If Only Musical: Unofficial Soviet Music during the Thaw* (New York: Oxford University Press, 2009), 26–27; and Marina Frolova-Walker, *Russian Music and Nationalism: From Glinka to Stalin* (New Haven: Yale University Press, 2007).

20. GARF, f. R-5451, op. 24, d. 900, l. 12; TsAOPIM, f. 667, op. 2, d. 41, l. 10; "Udovletvoriat' kul'turnye zaprosy molodezhi," *Komsomol'skaia pravda*, December 12, 1951.

21. RGASPI, f. M-1, op. 32, d. 630, l. 120.

22. RGASPI, f. M-1, op. 32, d. 475, l. 140.

23. RGASPI, f. M-1, op. 32, d. 630, ll. 149–50.

24. Juliane Fürst, *Stalin's Last Generation: Soviet Youth and the Emergence of Mature Socialism, 1945–56* (New York: Oxford University Press, 2010), 23.

25. On such reinforcement, see Svetlana Boym, *Common Places: Mythologies of Everyday Life in Russia* (Cambridge: Harvard University Press, 1994), 29–120; and Jeffrey W. Jones, *Everyday Life and the "Reconstruction" of Soviet Russia during and after the Great Patriotic War, 1943–1948* (Bloomington: Slavica Publishers, 2008), 8.

26. *V pomoshch' krasnym ugolkam* (Moscow, 1951), 33; GANISO, f. 3234, op. 11, d. 85, l. 15.

27. RGASPI, f. M-1, op. 32, d. 710, ll. 17–18.

28. *Vechera molodezhi* (Odessa, 1952), 6.

29. M. P. Materikova was a senior female shock worker in the factory. See *Kogda konchaetsia smena: Ocherki o kul'turno-massovoi rabote molodezhi na predpriiatii* (Moscow: Molodaia gvardiia, 1952), 41–42.

30. *Postanovleniia chetvertogo plenuma TsK VLKSM (23 avgusta–25 avgusta, 1950 goda)* (Moscow: Molodaia gvardiia, 1950), 7, 12–13.

31. Viktor Stepanchuk, born 1929, interview by author, May 19, 2009.

32. *Vechera molodezhi*, 6; "Na stsene–remeslenniki," *Moskovskii komsomolets*, June 13, 1951. *Moskovskii komsomolets* was the official organ of the Moscow city Komsomol.

33. Untitled article, *Stalinets*, May 6, 1952.

34. *V pomoshch' krasnym ugolkam*, 35–37.

35. "Kontserty dlia izbiratelei," *Moskovskii komsomolets*, January 28, 1951; "Vo dvortse kul'tury avtozavoda," *Moskovskii komsomolets*, October 2, 1951.

36. *Khudozhestvennaia samodeiatel'nost'*, 59–81.

37. "Molodye talanty," *Moskovskii komsomolets*, June 6, 1950.

38. RGASPI, f. M-1, op. 32, d. 630, l. 90.

39. TsAGM, f. 44, op. 1, d. 19, ll. 3–4.

40. "Vecher druzhby," *Moskovskii komsomolets*, February 7, 1953.

41. *Kogda konchaetsia smena*, 13–14.

42. *Vechera molodezhi*, 3, 5.

43. Valentina Miagkova, born 1923, interview by author, April 29, 2009.

44. *V pomoshch' krasnym ugolkam*, 12.

45. *O rabote komsomol'skikh organizatsii vysshikh uchebnykh zavedenii* (Moscow: Molodaia gvardiia, 1952), 5–6.

46. "Razvivat' initsiativu molodezhi," *Komsomol'skaia pravda*, December 9, 1951.

47. GANISO, f. 4529, op. 9, d. 3, l. 289.

48. On this campaign and its limits, see Fürst, *Stalin's Last Generation*, 103–12.

49. On Stalin as source of authority, see Alexei Yurchak, *Everything Was Forever, Until It Was No More: The Last Soviet Generation* (Princeton: Princeton University Press, 2006), 36–76.

50. A. A. Beliaev, "Provintsial'nye komsomol'skie organizatsii v poslevoennykh usloviakh: Osobennosti deiatel'nosti v dukhovnoi sfere (na materialakh Tombovskoi bolasti 1945–1954 gg.)" (Candidate diss., Tambov State University, 2010).

51. Such tightly restricted activism paralleled the 1930s Stalinist prescriptions of appropriate enthusiasm. Malte Rolf, "Expression of Enthusiasm and Emotional Coding in Dictatorship—The Stalinist Soviet Union," *Working Papers*, UCLA Center for European and Eurasian Studies, University of California Los Angeles (December 2004), http://www.escholarship.org/uc/item/6qh736hj#.

52. Ruth Ben-Ghiat, *Fascist Modernities: Italy, 1922–1945* (Berkeley: University of California Press, 2001), 10–11; Victoria de Grazia, *The Culture of Consent: Mass Organization of Leisure in Fascist Italy* (New York: Cambridge University Press, 1981), 1–23, 151–86.

53. Shelley Baranowski, *Strength through Joy: Consumerism and Mass Tourism in the Third Reich* (New York: Cambridge University Press, 2004), 40–74; Detlev J. K. Peukert, *Inside Nazi Germany: Conformity, Opposition, and Racism in Everyday Life* (New Haven: Yale University Press, 1987), 143–69.

54. For an analysis of Soviet state violence that uses the gardening metaphor, see Paul Hagenloh, *Stalin's Police: Public Order and Mass Repression in the USSR, 1926–1941* (Washington: Woodrow Wilson Center Press / Baltimore: Johns Hopkins University Press, 2009), 1–17. For use of the gardening imagery to compare Soviet and Nazi violence, see Jorg Baberowski and Anselm Doering-Manteuffel, "The Quest for Order and the Pursuit of Terror: National Socialist Germany and the Stalinist Soviet Union as Multiethnic Empires," in *Beyond Totalitarianism: Stalinism and Nazism Compared*, ed. Michael Geyer and Sheila Fitzpatrick (New York: Cambridge University Press, 2009), 180–230. For the metaphor of gardening as a means of analyzing fascist Italian efforts against social "deviants," see Ben-Ghiat, *Fascist Modernities*, 3–5.

55. RGASPI, f. M-1, op. 32, d. 630, ll. 108–9.

56. TsAGM, f. 2987, op. 1, d. 1, l. 1.

57. TsAGM, f. 2987, op. 1, d. 13, ll. 1–2.

58. TsAGM, f. 44, op. 1, d. 12, ll. 29–31.

59. "V svobodnye chasy," *Komsomol'skaia pravda*, June 29, 1948; "Nachalsia smotr khudozhestvennoi samodeiatel'nosti," *Stalinets*, December 12, 1952.

60. "150 sel'skikh khorov," *Moskovskii komsomolets*, October 3, 1950; "Molodye talanty," *Moskovskii komsomolets*, June 6, 1950.

61. "Smotr sel'skoi khudozhestvennoi samodeiatel'nost'," *Moskovskii komsomolets*, December 7, 1950; RGASPI, f. M-1, op. 3, d. 523, ll. 3–6.

62. On industrial competitions, see Stephen Kotkin, *Magnetic Mountain: Stalinism as a Civilization* (Berkeley: University of California Press, 1995), 72–105.

63. TsAOPIM, f. 635, op. 6, d. 32, ll. 1–2.

64. "Smotr sel'skoi khudozhestvennoi samodeiatel'nosti," *Moskovskii komsomolets*, December 7, 1950.

65. RGASPI, f. M-1, op. 32, d. 630, l. 110.

66. TsAOPIM, f. 667, op. 2, d. 39, l. 14.

67. Katherine Lebow, "*Kontra Kultura*: Leisure and Youthful Rebellion in Stalinist Poland," in *Pleasures in Socialism: Leisure and Luxury in the Eastern Bloc*, ed. David Crowley and Susan E. Reid (Evanston: Northwestern University Press, 2010), 71–94.

68. Timothy Johnston, *Being Soviet: Identity, Rumour, and Everyday Life under Stalin, 1939–1953* (New York: Oxford University Press, 2011), 149–52.

69. David L. Hoffmann, "Was There a 'Great Retreat' from Soviet Socialism? Stalinist Culture Reconsidered," *Kritika* 5, no. 4 (Fall 2004): 651–74.

70. On Bulgaria, see Karin Taylor, *Let's Twist Again: Youth and Leisure in Socialist Bulgaria* (Vienna: Lit, 2006), 101–2, 122. On East Germany, see Uta G. Poiger, *Jazz, Rock, and Rebels: Cold War Politics and American Culture in a Divided Germany* (Berkeley: University of California Press, 2000), 31–70. On Hungary, see Karl Brown, "Dance Hall Days: Jazz and Hooliganism in Communist Hungary, 1948–1956," in Pickhan and Ritter, *Jazz behind the Iron Curtain*, 267–94.

71. On how this spread of late Stalinist socialism occurred in higher education, see John Connelly, *Captive University: The Sovietization of East German, Czech, and Polish Higher Education* (Chapel Hill: University of North Carolina Press, 2000), 1–18.

72. Dmitrii Gal'tsov, born 1942, interview by author, February 20, 2009.

73. Oleg Cherniaev, born 1946, interview by author, February 22, 2009.

74. Valerii Miliaev, born 1937, interview by author, February 28, 2009; Sergei Semenov, born 1948, interview by author, March 18, 2009.

75. M. S. Gorbachev, *Memoirs*, trans. Georges Peronansky and Tatjana Varsavsky (New York: Doubleday, 1996), 35.

76. For other research on emotions in Russia, see the contributions to Mark D. Steinberg and Valeria Sobol, eds., *Interpreting Emotions in Russia and Eastern Europe* (DeKalb: Northern Illinois University Press, 2011); Jan Plamper, Schamma Schahadat, and Marc Elie, eds., *Rossiiskaia imperiia chuvstv: Podkhody k kul'turnoi istorii emotsii* (Moscow: Novoe literaturnoe obozrenie, 2010); Mark D. Steinberg, *Proletarian Imagination: Self, Modernity, and the Sacred in Russia* (Ithaca: Cornell University Press, 2002); Mary W. Cavender, *Nests of the Gentry: Family, Estate, and Local Loyalties in Provincial Russia* (Newark: University of Delaware Press, 2007); Jan Plamper, "Introduction: Emotional Turn? Feelings in Russian History and Culture," *Slavic Review* 68, no. 2 (Summer 2009): 229–37; Ronald G. Suny, "The Contradictions of Identity: Being Soviet and National in the USSR and After," in *Soviet and Post-Soviet Identities*, ed. Mark Bassin and Catriona Kelly (New York: Cambridge University Press, 2012), 17–36; and Sheila Fitzpatrick, "Happiness and Toska: A Study of Emotions in 1930s Russia," *Australian Journal of Politics and History* 50, no. 3 (2004): 357–71.

77. Nina Petrova, born in the late 1930s, interview by author, May 5, 2009.

78. Valentina Iarskaia, born in the mid-1930s, interview by author, May 30, 2009.

79. Nikolai Troitskii, born 1931, interview by author, May 22, 2009.

80. Francheska Kurilova, born 1936, interview by author May 15, 2009.

81. Svetlana Shchegol'kova, born 1937, interview by author, February 19, 2009.

82. For more on how the Soviet authorities wanted young people to feel pleasure from prescribed cultural activities, see I. V. Narskii, "'Zariad veselosti': S(t)imuliat-

siia radosti v diskurse o sovetskoi tantseval'noi samodeiatel'nosti" (paper presented at Smekhovaia kul'tura v Rossii XVIII–XX vv., Cheliabinsk, Russia, October 2011). On broader research indicative of the powerful relationship between emotions and the arts, see Martha C. Nussbaum, *Upheavals of Thought: The Intelligence of Emotions* (New York: Cambridge University Press, 2001), 238–78; Sianne Ngai, *Ugly Feelings* (Cambridge: Harvard University Press, 2005), 1–7; and Lila Abu-Lughod, "Shifting Politics in Bedouin Love Poetry," in *Language and the Politics of Emotion*, ed. Catherine A. Lutz and Lila Abu-Lughod (New York: Cambridge University Press, 1990), 24–45.

83. RGASPI, f. M-1, op. 32, d. 673, ll. 7–8; RGASPI, f. M-1, op. 32, d. 630, l. 102; RGASPI, f. M-1, op. 32, d. 741, l. 3.

84. David MacFadyen, *Songs for Fat People: Affect, Emotion, and Celebrity in the Russian Popular Song, 1900–1955* (Ithaca: McGill-Queen's University Press, 2002), 3–6.

85. For more on the link between emotions and authenticity in the Russian context, see Catriona Kelly, "Pravo na emotsii, pravil'nye emotsii: Upravlenie chuvstvami v Rossii posle epokhi prosveshcheniia," in Plamper, Schahadat, and Elie, *Rossiiskaia imperiia chuvstv*, 52–77.

86. TsAOPIM, f. 667, op. 2, d. 14, l. 159.

87. RGASPI, f. M-1, op. 32, d. 630, l. 151.

88. "Parki i sady—dlia molodezhi," *Komsomol'skaia pravda*, June 3, 1949.

89. RGASPI, f. M-1, op. 32, d. 710, ll. 19–25.

90. Liubov Baliasnaia, born 1927, interview by author, April 5, 2009. For more on Baliasnaia, see A. A. Alekseeva, *Stroka v biografii* (Moscow: Molodaia gvardiia, 2003), 72.

91. For more on veterans, see Fürst, *Stalin's Last Generation*, 32–63; Mark Edele, *Soviet Veterans of the Second World War: A Popular Movement in an Authoritarian Society, 1941–1991* (New York: Oxford University Press, 2008), 39–101.

92. Anatolii Avrus, born 1930, interview by author, May 28, 2009.

93. Troitskii interview.

94. On such conflicts, see Ludmilla Alexeyeva and Paul Goldberg, *The Thaw Generation: Coming of Age in the Post-Stalin Era* (Boston: Little, Brown, 1990), 29–56; and Fürst, *Stalin's Last Generation*, 32–63.

95. Nikolai Troitskii, *Kniga o liubvi* (Saratov: Privolzhskoe knizhnoe izdatel'stvo, 2006), 43.

96. Troitskii interview.

97. Iarskaia interview.

98. TsAOPIM, f. 635, op. 13, d. 133, l. 49.

99. E. Semenov, *Dom kul'tury na Kubani* (Moscow, 1950), 9–10.

100. For more on celebrations of Victory Day by veterans, see Nina Tumarkin, *The Living and the Dead: The Rise and Fall of the Cult of World War II in Russia* (New York: Basic Books, 1994), 95–124; and Edele, *Soviet Veterans of the Second World War*, 129–58.

101. Avrus interview.

102. Igal Halfin, *From Darkness to Light: Class, Consciousness, and Salvation in Revolutionary Russia* (Pittsburgh: University of Pittsburgh Press, 2000), 205–82; Jochen Hellbeck, *Revolution on My Mind: Writing a Diary under Stalin* (Cambridge: Harvard University Press, 2006), 165–222.

103. On organized cultural recreation, see Esther von Richthofen, *Bringing Culture to the Masses: Control, Compromise and Participation in the GDR* (New York: Berghahn Books, 2009), 13–14. On sports, see Molly W. Johnson, *Training Socialist Citizens: Sports and the State in East Germany* (Boston: Brill, 2008), 3–5. On Soviet–East German relations more broadly, see Hope M. Harrison, *Driving the Soviets up the Wall: Soviet-East German Relations, 1953–1961* (Princeton: Princeton University Press, 2003).

104. On how specific emotions can be deliberately attached to certain behaviors and experiences, see Sara Ahmed, *The Cultural Politics of Emotion* (New York: Routledge, 2004), 1–19.

105. William M. Reddy, *The Navigation of Feeling: A Framework for the History of Emotions* (Cambridge: Cambridge University Press, 2001), 124–29; William M. Reddy, "Comment: Emotional Turn? Feelings in Russian History and Culture," *Slavic Review* 68, no. 2 (Summer 2009): 329–34.

106. Vladimir Shlapentokh, *Public and Private Life of the Soviet People: Changing Values in Post-Stalin Russia* (New York: Oxford University Press, 1989), 153–202; Oleg Kharkhordin, *The Collective and the Individual in Russia: A Study of Practices* (Berkeley: University of California Press, 1999), 1–34, 75–122; Oleg Kharkhordin, "Druzhba: Klassicheskaia teoriia i sovremennye zaboty," in *Druzhba: Ocherki policy teorii praktik*, ed. Oleg Kharkhordin (Saint Petersburg: Izdatel'stvo Evropeiskogo universiteta v Sankt-Peterburge, 2009), 11–47.

107. Lewis H. Siegelbaum, "Introduction: Mapping Private Spheres in the Soviet Context," in *Borders of Socialism: Private Spheres of Soviet Russia*, ed. Lewis H. Siegelbaum (New York: Palgrave Macmillan, 2006), 1–21; Deborah A. Field, *Private Life and Communist Morality in Khrushchev's Russia* (New York: Peter Lang, 2007); Benjamin K. Tromly, "Re-Imagining the Soviet Intelligentsia: Student Politics and University Life, 1948–1964" (PhD diss., Harvard University, 2007), 94–150.

108. Kotkin, *Magnetic Mountain*, 220.

109. For a critical take on "speaking Bolshevik" from a different perspective, see Anna Krylova, "Soviet Modernity: Stephen Kotkin and the Bolshevik Predicament," *Contemporary European History* 23, no. 2 (2014): 167–92.

110. Judith Butler, *Bodies That Matter: On the Discursive Limits of "Sex"* (New York: Routledge, 1993), 2.

111. This point on the key role of the interpreter of texts is informed by Jacques Derrida, *Margins of Philosophy*, trans. and ed. Alan Bass (Chicago: University of Chicago Press, 1982), 307–30; M. M. Bakhtin, *The Dialogic Imagination: Four Essays by M. M. Bakhtin*, ed. Michael Holquist, trans. Cary Emerson and Michael Holquist (Austin: University of Texas Press, 1981), 259–94; and Judith Butler, Ernesto Laclau, and Slavoj Žižek, *Contingency, Hegemony, Universality: Contemporary Dialogues on the Left* (New York: Verso, 2000), 11–43.

112. Michel de Certeau, *The Practice of Everyday Life*, trans. Steven F. Rendall (Berkeley: University of California Press, 1984), 29–42.

CHAPTER 3. IDEOLOGY AND CONSUMPTION

1. RGASPI, f. M-1, op. 32, d. 710, ll. 6–8.

2. Juliane Fürst makes such a claim in her book *Stalin's Last Generation: Soviet Youth and the Emergence of Mature Socialism, 1945–56* (New York: Oxford University Press, 2010), 92–93.

3. "V klube tol'ko tantsuiut . . . ," *Komsomol'skaia pravda*, December 8, 1951.

4. "Klub ili . . . tansploshchadka?," *Moskovskii komsomolets*, January 19, 1950.

5. S. Frederick Starr, *Red and Hot: The Fate of Jazz in the Soviet Union, 1917–1980* (New York: Oxford University Press, 1983), 216–17.

6. RGASPI, op. 32, d. 630, l. 79; RGASPI, op. 32, d. 710, l. 16.

7. TsAGM, f. 2987, op. 1, d. 13, ll. 16, 20.

8. TsAGM, f. 2987, op. 1, d. 20, ll. 2–3, 24–25.

9. TsAGM, f. 44, op. 1, d. 6, ll. 14–16.

10. RGASPI, f. M-1, op. 32, d. 673, ll. 7–8; RGASPI, f. M-1, op. 32, d. 741, l. 3.

11. TsAGM, f. 2987, op. 1, d. 20, ll. 3, 24–25.

12. RGASPI, f. M-1, op. 32, d. 710, ll. 6–8.

13. RGASPI, f. M-1, op. 32, d. 710, ll. 7–8.

14. RGASPI, f. M-1, op. 32, d. 710, ll. 7–8.

15. "Stiliaga," *Krokodil*, March 10, 1949.

16. "Stiliaga," *Krokodil*, March 10, 1949.

17. Fashion had importance for official styles as well. See Cristina Vatulescu, *Police Aesthetics: Literature, Film, and the Secret Police in Soviet Times* (Stanford: Stanford University Press, 2010), 196.

18. Juliane Fürst, "The Importance of Being Stylish: Youth, Culture and Identity in Late Stalinism," in *Late Stalinist Russia: Society between Reconstruction and Reinvention*, ed. Juliane Fürst (New York: Routledge, 2006), 209–30; Mark Edele, "Strange Young Men in Stalin's Moscow: The Birth and Life of the Stiliagi, 1945–1953," *Jahrbücher für Geschichte Osteuropas* 50, no. 1 (2002): 37–61; Timothy Johnston, *Being Soviet: Identity, Rumour, and Everyday Life under Stalin, 1939–1953* (New York: Oxford University Press, 2011), 198–206; Marina Dmitrieva, "Jazz and Dress: *Stiliagi* in Soviet Russia and Beyond," in *Jazz behind the Iron Curtain*, ed. Gertrud Pickhan and Rüdiger Ritter (Frankfurt: Peter Lang, 2010), 239–56.

19. Aleksei Kozlov is one such exception, a prominent jazz musician who did consider himself a *stiliaga*. See his memoir, *"Kozel na sakse": I tak vsiu zhizn'* (Moscow: Vagrius, 1998), 68–100.

20. Aleksei Kuznetsov, born 1941, interview by author, February 21, 2009.

21. Valentina Iarskaia, born in the mid-1930s, interview by author, May 30, 2009.

22. Georgii Garanian, born 1934, interview by author, February 4, 2009.

23. For instance, Feliks Arons, born 1940, interview by author, May 18, 2009.

24. See, for instance, S. G. Kara-Murza, *"Sovok" vspominaet* (Moscow: Algoritm, 2002), 65–79.

25. For the United States, see Howard S. Becker, *Outsiders: Studies in the Sociology of Deviance* (New York: Free Press, 1973), 79–119.

26. For other sources of alternative masculinities in the postwar Stalin years, see Ethan Pollock, "'Real Men Go to the Bania': Postwar Soviet Masculinities and the Bathhouse," *Kritika* 11, no. 1 (Winter 2010): 47–76; Edele, "Strange Young Men."

27. Garanian interview.

28. Iurii Zhimskii, born 1936, interview by author, May 27, 2009.

29. Lev Figlin, born 1938, interview by author, May 25, 2009.

30. Iarskaia interview.

31. Vitalii Kleinot, born 1941, interview by author, February 14, 2009.

32. Zhimskii interview.

33. See another memoir account by this jazz musician: A. S. Kozlov, *Dzhazz, rock, i mednye tuby* (Moscow: Eksmo, 2005), 73.

34. Boris Taigin, interview in "Rastsvet i krakh 'Zolotoi sobaki,'" *Pchela* 20 (May–June 1998), http://www.pchela.ru/podshiv/20/goldendog.htm.

35. RGASPI, f. M-1, op. 32, d. 710, ll. 7–8.

36. Figlin interview.

37. On *fartsa*, see E. R. Iarskaia-Smirnova and P. V. Romanov, "Fartsa: Podpol'e sovetskogo obshchestva potrebleniia," *Neprikosnovennyi zapas: Debaty o politike i kul'ture* 5, no. 43 (2005), http://magazines.russ.ru/nz/2005/43/r012-pr.html; Sergei Zhuk, *Rock and Roll in the Rocket City: The West, Identity, and Ideology in Soviet Dniepropetrovsk* (Baltimore: Johns Hopkins University Press, 2010), 95–105. For the gray economy, see Alena V. Ledeneva, *Russia's Economy of Favours: Blat, Networking, and Informal Exchange* (New York: Cambridge University Press, 1998), 104–38.

38. For such broadcasting and Soviet government efforts against it, see Kristin Roth-Ey, *Moscow Prime Time: How the Soviet Union Built the Media Empire That Lost the Cultural Cold War* (Ithaca: Cornell University Press, 2011), 131–75; Simo Mikkonen, "Stealing the Monopoly of Knowledge? Soviet Reactions to U.S. Cold War Broadcasting," *Kritika* 11, no. 4 (Fall 2010): 771–805; Stephen Lovell, "Broadcasting Bolshevik: The Radio Voice of Soviet Culture, 1920s–1950s," *Journal of Contemporary History* 48, no. 1 (January 2013): 78–97. For the structure of Soviet radio, see T. M. Goriaeva, *Radio Rossii: Politicheskii kontrol' sovetskogo radioveshchaniia v 1920–1930-kh godakh; Dokumental'naia istoriia* (Moscow: ROSSPEN, 2000), 33–171.

39. "Music Is Combatting Communism: Voice of America Shows Bring Universal Harmony," *Down Beat*, October 8, 1952; Starr, *Red and Hot*, 210, 228.

40. Iarskaia interview.

41. Konstantin Marvin, born 1934, interview by author, May 13, 2009.

42. Arons interview. Also see M. I. Kull', *Stupeni voskhozhdeniia*, accessed October 22, 2012, http://www.jazz.ru/books/kull/default.htm; and Kozlov, *"Kozel na sakse,"* 9–16, 90.

43. Eckhardt Derschmidt, "The Disappearance of the Jazu-Kissa: Some Considerations about Japanese 'Jazz-Cafés' and Jazz-Listeners," in *The Culture of Japan as Seen through Its Leisure*, ed. Sepp Linhart and Savine Frühstück (Albany: State University of New York Press, 1998), 285–302.

44. Nicholas J. Cull, *The Cold War and the United States Information Agency: American Propaganda and Public Diplomacy, 1945–1989* (New York: Cambridge University Press, 2008), 51–81; Michael Nelson, *War of the Black Heavens: The Battles of Western Broadcasting in the Cold War* (Syracuse: Syracuse University Press, 1997), 20–45; Philip M. Taylor, *British Propaganda in the Twentieth Century: Selling Democracy* (Edinburgh: Edinburgh University Press, 1999), 225–57; Walter L. Hixson, *Parting the Curtain: Propaganda, Culture, and the Cold War* (New York: St. Martin's Press, 1997), 29–57.

45. File S-18–57, Soviet Listening to Western Radio, 1957, Special Reports (S): 1953–97 (P-160), Office of Research, RG 306, NACP.

46. File R-42–62, Soviet Views of American Radio Broadcasting, Research Reports, 1960–99 (P-142), Office of Research, RG 306, NACP.

47. File R-3–62, Soviet Attitudes toward the Voice of America, Research Reports, 1960–99 (P-142), Office of Research, RG 306, NACP.

48. Kleinot interview; Kuznetsov interview; Garanian interview; Zhimskii interview; Figlin interview.

49. See the following memoirs: V. P. Aksenov, *V poiskakh grustnogo bebi: Kniga ob Amerike* (New York: Liberty Publishing House, 1987), 14–22; V. I. Slavkin, *Pamiatnik neizvestnomu stiliage* (Moscow: Artist. Rezhiser. Teatr, 1996), 5; and Kozlov, *"Kozel na sakse,"* 82–98.

50. Figlin interview.

51. Oleg Cherniaev, born 1946, interview by author, February 22, 2009; Viktor Dubiler, born 1941, interview by author, February 22, 2009.

52. Kozlov, *Dzhazz, rock, i mednye tuby*, 97.

53. B. P. Pustyntsev, interview in "Soprotivlenie na nevskom prospekte," *Pchela* 11 (October–November 1997), http://www.pchela.ru/podshiv/11/pustyncev.htm.

54. For how western broadcasting helped inspire political opposition in the Soviet borderlands, see Vladimir Tolz with Julie Corwin, "Soviet Reactions to Foreign Broadcasting in the 1950s," in *Cold War Broadcasting: Impact on the Soviet Union and Eastern Europe*, ed. Ross A. Johnson and R. Eugene Parta (New York: Central European University Press, 2010), 277–99.

55. Garanian interview; Marvin interview; Kozlov, *"Kozel na sakse,"* 134–35.

56. Garanian interview.

57. Amir Weiner, *Making Sense of War: The Second World War and the Fate of the Bolshevik Revolution* (Princeton: Princeton University Press, 2001), 82–190.

58. V. B. Feiertag, *Istoriia dzhazovogo ispolnitel'stva v Rossii* (Saint Petersburg: Skifiia, 2010), 140.

59. Zhimskii interview.

60. Figlin interview.

61. Figlin interview.

62. Michael May, "Swingin' under Stalin: Russian Jazz during the Cold War and Beyond," in *"Here, There and Everywhere": The Foreign Politics of American Popular Culture*, ed. Reinhold Wagnleitner and Elaine T. May (Hanover: University Press of New England, 2000), 179–91; Tiit Lauk, "Estonian Jazz before and behind the 'Iron Curtain,'" in Pickhan and Ritter, *Jazz behind the Iron Curtain*, 153–64.

63. As Juliane Fürst notes, for stiliagi, "differentiation, not pure entertainment, was their driving force." See Fürst, *Stalin's Last Generation*, 220–22.

64. On western youth countercultures in the postwar decade, see the contributions to Stuart Hall and Tony Jefferson eds., *Resistance through Rituals: Youth Subcultures in Post-war Britain*, 2nd ed. (New York: Routledge, 2006); Reinhold Wagnleitner, *Coca-Colonization and the Cold War: The Cultural Mission of the United States in Austria after the Second World War*, trans. Diana M. Wolf (Chapel Hill: University of North Carolina Press, 1994), 275–96; Uta G. Poiger, *Jazz, Rock, and Rebels: Cold War Politics and American Culture in a Divided Germany* (Berkeley: University of California Press, 2000), 31–70; Josie McLellan, *Love in the Time of Communism: Intimacy and Sexuality in the GDR* (New York: Cambridge University Press, 2011), 51; and Lewis A. Erenberg, "Things to Come: Swing Bands, Bebop, and the Rise of a Postwar Jazz Scene," in *Recasting America: Culture and Politics in the Age of Cold War*, ed. Lary May (Chicago: University of Chicago Press, 1989), 221–46. On 1930s zoot suiters, see James Gilbert, *A Cycle of Outrage: America's Reaction to the Juvenile Delinquent in the 1950s* (New York: Oxford University Press, 1986), 11–41. On German swing youth,

see Detlev J. K. Peukert, *Inside Nazi Germany: Conformity, Opposition, and Racism in Everyday Life* (New Haven: Yale University Press, 1987), 143–69.

65. For the powerful effect of labeling a group as deviant, see the historiography on labeling theory, which posits that "deviants" become "deviant" when those with power successfully attach this label to them: Emile Durkheim, *The Rules of the Sociological Method*, ed. George E. G. Catlin, trans. Sarah A. Solovay and John H. Mueller (New York: Free Press, 1965), 47–75; Stephen Pfohl, *Images of Deviance and Social Control: A Sociological History* (New York: McGraw-Hill, 1994), 345–98; and Stuart H. Traub and Craig B. Little, eds., *Theories of Deviance* (Itasca: F. E. Peacock, 1985), 277–332. For a work that utilizes labeling theory in the Soviet context, see Brian LaPierre, *Hooligans in Khrushchev's Russia: Defining, Policing, and Producing Deviance during the Thaw* (Madison: University of Wisconsin Press, 2012), 8.

66. Golfo Alexopoulos, "Amnesty 1945: The Revolving Door of Stalin's Gulag," *Slavic Review* 64, no. 2 (Summer 2005): 274–306.

67. My view of resistance is informed by Lynne Viola, "Popular Resistance in the Stalinist 1930s: Soliloquy of a Devil's Advocate," *Kritika* 1, no. 1 (Winter 2000): 45–70; Anna Krylova, "The Tenacious Liberal Subject in Soviet Studies," *Kritika* 1, no. 1 (Winter 2000): 119–46; and Jochen Hellbeck, "Speaking Out: Languages of Affirmation and Dissent in Stalinist Russia," *Kritika* 1, no. 1 (Winter 2000): 71–96.

68. Elena Zubkova, *Russia after the War: Hopes, Illusions, and Disappointments, 1945–1957*, trans. and ed. Hugh Ragsdale (Armonk: M. E. Sharpe, 1998), 109–16; N. A. Mitrokhin, *Russkaia partiia: Dvizhenie russkikh natsionalistov v SSSR, 1953–1985 gody* (Moscow: Novoe literaturnoe obozrenie, 2003), 187–91; Fürst, *Stalin's Last Generation*, 327–35.

69. Garanian interview.

70. Kuznetsov interview.

71. N. Sh. Leites, interview in "Klub 'Kvadrat': Dzhaz-shmaz i normal'nye liudi," *Pchela* 11 (October–November 1997), http://www.pchela.ru/podshiv/11/jazzshmaz.htm.

72. Pickhan and Ritter, *Jazz behind the Iron Curtain*, 7–10 (quote, 8).

73. Rüdiger Ritter, "The Radio—A Jazz Instrument of Its Own," in Pickhan and Ritter, *Jazz behind the Iron Curtain*, 35–55 (quote, 37; original emphasis). Also see Ruth Leiserowitz, "Jazz in Soviet Lithuania—a Nonconformist Niche," in Pickhan and Ritter, *Jazz behind the Iron Curtain*, 183–90; and Irina Novikova, "Black Music, White Freedom: Times and Space of Jazz Countercultures in the USSR," in *Blackening Europe: The African American Presence*, ed. Heike Raphael-Hernandez (New York: Routledge, 2004), 73–84.

74. Katherine Verdery, *What Was Socialism, and What Comes Next?* (Princeton: Princeton University Press, 1996), 29.

75. Anatolii Avrus, born 1930, interview by author, May 28, 2009.

76. Nina Petrova, born in the late 1930s, interview by author, May 5, 2009.

77. Liubov Baliasnaia, born 1927, interview by author, April 5, 2009.

78. For more on the hard postwar living conditions, see Donald Filtzer, *The Hazards of Urban Life in Late Stalinist Russia: Health, Hygiene, and Living Standards, 1943–1953* (New York: Cambridge University Press, 2010), 1–22.

79. Zhimskii interview.

80. Nelli Popkova, born 1936, interview by author, May 20, 2009.

81. On separate schooling, see E. Thomas Ewing, *Separate Schools: Gender, Policy, and Practice in Postwar Soviet Education* (DeKalb: Northern Illinois University Press, 2010), 90–129.

82. Francheska Kurilova, born 1936, interview by author, May 15, 2009.

83. Zhimskii interview.

84. Figlin interview.

85. Alexei Yurchak, *Everything Was Forever, Until It Was No More: The Last Soviet Generation* (Princeton: Princeton University Press, 2006), 36–125.

86. TsAGM, f. 2011, op. 1, d. 164, ll. 17–18.

87. RGASPI, f. M-1, op. 32, d. 710, ll. 7–9.

88. This issue received no attention in the keynotes of the last postwar Stalinist Moscow and Saratov city Komsomol conferences. TsAOPIM, f. 635, op. 13, d. 133; GANISO, f. 4529, op. 9, d. 3.

89. RGASPI, op. 32, d. 742, l. 95.

90. Stephen Lovell, *The Russian Reading Revolution: Print Culture in the Soviet and Post-Soviet Eras* (New York: St. Martin's Press, 2000), 18.

91. For the post-Stalin decades, see Sergei I. Zhuk, *Popular Culture, Identity, and Soviet Youth in Dniepropetrovsk, 1959–1984*, Carl Beck Papers in Russian and East European Studies, No. 1906 (Pittsburgh: Center for Russian and East European Studies, University Center for International Studies, University of Pittsburgh, 2008), 1–67; Sudha Rajagopalan, *Indian Films in Soviet Cinema: The Culture of Movie-going after Stalin* (Bloomington: Indiana University Press, 2008), 1–28.

92. Richard Taruskin, *The Danger of Music and Other Anti-Utopian Essays* (Berkeley: University of California Press, 2009), 447–65.

93. For more on the differing missions of central cultural organs, see Kiril Tomoff, *Creative Union: The Professional Organization of Soviet Composers, 1939–1953* (Ithaca: Cornell University Press, 2006), 1–10.

94. For the concept of totalitarianism in western scholarship on the Soviet Union, see David C. Engerman, *Know Your Enemy: The Rise and Fall of America's Soviet Experts* (New York: Oxford University Press, 2009), 153–234. One influential work that treats the Soviet Union as totalitarian is Martin Malia, *The Soviet Tragedy: A History of Socialism in Russia 1917–1991* (New York: Free Press, 1994), with pages 291–314 describing the postwar years.

95. Theodor W. Adorno, *The Culture Industry: Selected Essays on Mass Culture*, ed. J. M. Bernstein (London: Routledge, 1991), 53–84.

96. Daniel Miller, "Consumption as the Vanguard of History: A Polemic by Way of an Introduction," in *Acknowledging Consumption: A Review of New Studies*, ed. Daniel Miller (New York: Routledge, 1995), 1–57; Kate Soper and Frank Trentmann, eds., *Citizenship and Consumption* (New York: Palgrave Macmillan, 2008); Emma Casey and Lydia Martens, eds., *Gender and Consumption: Domestic Cultures and the Commercialisation of Everyday Life* (Burlington: Ashgate, 2007), 1–11; Joseph Heath and Andrew Potter, *The Rebel Sell: Why the Culture Can't Be Jammed* (Toronto: HarperCollins, 2004), 1–9.

97. Rósa Magnúsdóttir, "Keeping Up Appearances: How the Soviet State Failed to Control Popular Attitudes toward the United States of America, 1945–1959" (PhD diss., University of North Carolina at Chapel Hill, 2006), 1–17.

98. On such crackdowns, see John Springhall, *Youth Popular Culture and Moral*

Panics: Penny Gaffs to Gangsta-Rap, 1830–1996 (New York: St. Martin's Press, 1998), 121–46; Stanley Cohen, Folk Devils and Moral Panics: The Creation of the Mods and Rockers, 2nd ed. (New York: Basil Blackwell, 1987), 71–91.

99. Fürst, Stalin's Last Generation, 1–21 (quote, 3–4). For more on generations in Russia, see Stephen Lovell, ed., Generations in Twentieth-Century Europe (New York: Palgrave Macmillan, 2007), 1–18; and Rex A. Wade, "Generations in Russian and Soviet History," Soviet and Post-Soviet Review 32, no. 1 (2005): 125–41. On generational consciousness, see Karl Mannheim, Essays on the Sociology of Knowledge, trans. and ed. Paul Kecskemeti (New York: Oxford University Press, 1952), 276–80.

100. For another example of where officially prescribed affective expression in popular culture fit well with the emotions that Soviet citizens themselves wanted to express, if not for all the same reasons, see Neringa Klumbyte, "Political Intimacy: Power, Laughter, and Coexistence in Late Soviet Lithuania," East European Politics and Societies 25, no. 4 (November 2011): 658–77.

101. For parallels to youth in other contexts, see Peter Wicke, "Music, Dissidence, Revolution, and Commerce: Youth Culture between Mainstream and Subculture," in Between Marx and Coca-Cola: Youth Cultures in Changing European Societies, 1960–1980, ed. Axel Schildt and Detlef Siegfried (New York: Berghahn Books, 2006), 109–26; and Jeremy Gilbert and Ewan Pearson, Discographies: Dance Music, Culture, and the Politics of Sound (New York: Routledge, 1999), 158–86.

CHAPTER 4. STATE-SPONSORED POPULAR CULTURE IN THE EARLY THAW, 1953–1956

1. "Druzheskie sharzhi," Leninskii put', April 5, 1958.

2. Jeremy Smith, introduction to Khrushchev in the Kremlin: Policy and Government in the Soviet Union, 1953–1964, ed. Jeremy Smith and Melanie Ilič (New York: Routledge, 2011), 1–8; William Taubman, Khrushchev: The Man and His Era (New York: Norton, 2003), 236–99.

3. Polly Jones, "The Dilemmas of De-Stalinization," in The Dilemmas of De-Stalinization: Negotiating Cultural and Social Change in the Khrushchev Era, ed. Polly Jones (New York: Routledge, 2006), 1–18; Deborah A. Field, Private Life and Communist Morality in Khrushchev's Russia (New York: Peter Lang, 2007), 1–9.

4. Miriam Dobson, Khrushchev's Cold Summer: Gulag Returnees, Crime, and the Fate of Reform after Stalin (Ithaca: Cornell University Press, 2009), 21–49.

5. Iu. V. Aksiutin and O.V. Volobuev, XX s"ezd KPSS: Novatsii i dogmy (Moscow: Politizdat, 1991).

6. P. L. Vail and A. A. Genis, 60-e: Mir sovetskogo cheloveka (Ann Arbor: Ardis, 1988), 160–75.

7. Ted Hopf, Social Construction of International Politics: Identities & Foreign Policies, Moscow, 1955 and 1999 (Ithaca: Cornell University Press, 2002), 39–82; Aleksandr Fursenko and Timothy Naftali, Khrushchev's Cold War: The Insider Story of an American Adversary (New York: Norton, 2006), 5–32; Vladislav Zubok, A Failed Empire: The Soviet Union in the Cold War from Stalin to Gorbachev (Chapel Hill: University of North Carolina Press, 2007), 62–94.

8. Research on Soviet young people in the Thaw has focused on college students. See Benjamin K. Tromly, "Re-Imagining the Soviet Intelligentsia: Student Politics and University Life, 1948–1964" (PhD diss., Harvard University, 2007); L. V. Silina, Nastroeniia sovetskogo studenchestva, 1945–1964 (Moscow: Russkii mir, 2004);

and S. L. Merzliakov, "Saratovskii gosudarstvennyi universitet v gody voiny i mira (1941–1964 gg.)" (Candidate diss., Saratov State University, 2008).

9. L. B. Brusilovskaia, *Kul'tura povsednevnosti v epokhu "ottepeli": Metamorfozy stilia* (Moscow: Izdatel'stvo URAO, 2001), 169–74; Alexander Prokhorov, "The Myth of the 'Great Family' in Marlen Khutsiev's *Lenin's Guard* and Mark Osep'ian's *Three Days of Victor Shernyshev*," in *Cinepaternity: Fathers and Sons in Soviet and Post-Soviet Film*, ed. Helena Goscilo and Yana Hashamova (Bloomington: Indiana University Press, 2010), 29–51.

10. Mark B. Smith, *Property of Communists: The Urban Housing Program from Stalin to Khrushchev* (DeKalb: Northern Illinois University Press, 2010), 59–99; Christine Varga-Harris, "Forging Citizenship on the Home Front: Reviving the Socialist Contract and Constructing Soviet Identity during the Thaw," in Jones, *Dilemmas of De-Stalinization*, 101–16; Lynne Attwood, "Housing in the Khrushchev Era," in *Women in the Khrushchev Era*, ed. Melanie Ilič, Susan E. Reid, and Lynne Attwood (New York: Palgrave Macmillan, 2004), 177–202.

11. See the contributions to David Crowley and Susan E. Reid, eds., *Pleasures in Socialism: Leisure and Luxury in the Eastern Bloc* (Evanston: Northwestern University Press, 2010); and E. R. Iarskaia-Smirnova and P. V. Romanov, eds., *Sovetskaia sotsial'naia politika: Stseny i deistvuiushchie litsa, 1940–1985* (Moscow: Variant, 2008). Also see N. B. Lebina and A. N. Chistikov, *Obyvatel' i reformy: Kartiny povsednevnoi zhizni gorozhan v gody nepa i khrushchevskogo desiatiletiia* (Saint Petersburg: Dmitrii Bulanin, 2003).

12. There are superficial accounts of organized cultural recreation in the Soviet Union in Anne White, *De-Stalinization and the House of Culture: Declining State Control over Leisure in the USSR, Poland, and Hungary, 1953–89* (New York: Routledge, 1990); and K. G. Bogemskaia, ed., *Samodeiatel'noe khudozhestvennoe tvorchestvo v SSSR: Ocherki istorii, konets 1950-kh–nachalo 1990-kh godov* (Saint Petersburg: Dmitrii Bulanin, 1999).

13. RGASPI, f. M-1, op. 32, d. 741, ll. 8–10.

14. A. N. Shelepin, *Otchetnyi doklad TsK VLKSM XII s"ezdu komsomola* (Moscow: Molodaia gvardiia, 1954), 44–45.

15. Liubov Baliasnaia, born 1927, interview by author, April 5, 2009; "Otkroite eti zaly dlia molodezhi," *Komsomol'skaia pravda*, May 25, 1956; "Khudozhestvennoi samodeiatel'nosti—postoiannoe vnimanie," *Stalinets*, October 22, 1955; "Uchis' otdykhat'!," *Zaria molodezhi* (Saratov), December 14, 1956.

16. John Bushnell, "Urban Leisure Culture in Post-Stalin Russia: Stability as a Social Problem?," in *Soviet Society and Culture: Essays in Honor of Vera S. Dunham*, ed. Terry L. Thompson and Richard Sheldon (Boulder: Westview Press, 1988), 58–86; Jiri Zuzanek, *Work and Leisure in the Soviet Union: A Time-Budget Analysis* (New York: Praeger, 1980), 39–49.

17. See the contributions to Ilič, Reid, and Attwood, *Women in the Khrushchev Era*.

18. RGASPI, f. M-1, op. 3, d. 877, ll. 3–4.

19. TsAOPIM, f. 635, op. 13, d. 484, l. 30.

20. Stephen E. Hanson, *Time and Revolution: Marxism and the Design of Soviet Institutions* (Chapel Hill: University of North Carolina Press, 1997), 171–75.

21. RGASPI, f. M-1, op. 32, d. 741, ll. 23–25.

22. RGANI, f. 5, op. 30, d. 179, ll. 45–46.

23. E. Iu. Zubkova, L. P. Koshelova, G. A. Kuznetsova, A. I. Miniuk, and L. A.

Rogovaia eds., *Sovetskaia zhizn', 1945–1953* (Moscow: ROSSPEN, 2003), 194–210. One instance of violent crime was the murder in December 1952 of a fourth grader by a school Komsomol secretary. RGASPI, f. M-1, op. 32, d. 742, ll. 25–26.

24. RGANI, f. 5, op. 30, d. 80, l. 18.

25. TsAOPIM, f. 635, op. 14, d. 546, l. 47.

26. Baliasnaia interview.

27. M. S. Gorbachev, *Memoirs*, trans. Georges Peronansky and Tatjana Varsavsky (New York: Doubleday, 1996), 64–65.

28. Juliane Fürst, *Stalin's Last Generation: Soviet Youth and the Emergence of Mature Socialism, 1945–56* (New York: Oxford University Press, 2010), 20–29; Julie Hessler, *A Social History of Soviet Trade: Trade Policy, Retail Practices, and Consumption, 1917–1953* (Princeton: Princeton University Press, 2004), 296–336.

29. David R. Shearer, *Policing Stalin's Socialism: Repression and Social Order in the Soviet Union* (New Haven: Yale University Press, 2009), 404–36; A. V. Pyzhikov, *Khrushchevskaia "ottepel'"* (Moscow: OLMA-PRESS, 2002), 15–40; Manon van de Water, *Moscow Theaters for Young People: A Cultural History of Ideological Coercion and Artistic Innovation, 1917–2000* (New York: Palgrave Macmillan, 2006), 67; and Smith, *Property of Communists*, 25–58. In this way, Soviet officials echoed the "enlightened bureaucrats" of the nineteenth century. See W. Bruce Lincoln, *The Great Reforms: Autocracy, Bureaucracy, and the Politics of Change in Imperial Russia* (DeKalb: Northern Illinois University Press, 1990), chaps. 1 and 3.

30. Kristin Roth-Ey, *Moscow Prime Time: How the Soviet Union Built the Media Empire That Lost the Cultural Cold War* (Ithaca: Cornell University Press, 2011), 176–222.

31. Vera Dunham, *In Stalin's Time: Middleclass Values in Soviet Fiction* (New York: Cambridge University Press, 1976).

32. For Soviet social welfare, see David L. Hoffmann, *Cultivating the Masses: Modern State Practices and Soviet Socialism, 1914–1939* (Ithaca: Cornell University Press, 2011), 17–69; and Alec Nove, "Social Welfare in the USSR," in *Russia under Khrushchev: An Anthology from "Problems of Communism,"* ed. Abraham Brumberg (New York: Praeger, 1962), 571–90.

33. For the dashing of popular expectations, see Elena Zubkova, *Russia after the War: Hopes, Illusions, and Disappointments, 1945–1957*, trans. and ed. Hugh Ragsdale (Armonk: M. E. Sharpe, 1998), 31–39.

34. On material consumer goods, see Susan E. Reid, "Cold War in the Kitchen: Gender and the De-Stalinization of Consumer Taste in the Soviet Union," *Slavic Review* 61, no. 2 (Summer 2002): 211–52; Christine Varga-Harris, "Constructing the Soviet Hearth: Home, Citizenship, and Socialism in Russia, 1956–1964" (PhD diss., University of Illinois at Urbana-Champaign, 2005), 1–24.

35. The Stalinist leadership, demanding exemplary leisure conduct from the new managerial and communist elite in the 1930s, paid much less attention to managing the free-time activities of the masses. See David L. Hoffmann, *Stalinist Values: The Cultural Norms of Soviet Modernity, 1917–1941* (Ithaca: Cornell University Press, 2003), 57–88. For the expansion of surveillance during the Thaw, see the contributions to Karl Schlögel, ed., *Mastering Russian Spaces: Raum und Raumbewältigung als Problem der russischen Geschichte* (Berlin: Oldenbourg-Verlag, 2011), esp. Susan E. Reid's chapter; and Edward D. Cohn, "Sex and the Married Communist: Family

Troubles, Marital Infidelity, and Party Discipline in the Postwar USSR, 1945–64," *Russian Review* 68, no. 3 (July 2009): 429–50.

36. On "rational" leisure, see RGASPI, f. M-1, op. 32, d. 770, l. 20; and Z. A. Petrova and M. P. Rymkevich, eds., *Novoe v rabote klubov* (Moscow: Sovetskaia Rossiia, 1962), 85.

37. For the classical analysis of how surveillance is meant to manage behavior, see Michel Foucault, *Discipline and Punish: The Birth of the Prison* (New York: Vintage Books, 1979), 178–79. For insights on Soviet surveillance, see Paul Hagenloh, *Stalin's Police: Public Order and Mass Repression in the USSR, 1926–1941* (Washington: Woodrow Wilson Center Press / Baltimore: Johns Hopkins University Press, 2009), 324–33; Peter Holquist, *Making War, Forging Revolution: Russia's Continuum of Crisis, 1914–1921* (Cambridge: Harvard University Press, 2002), 237–39; and Amir Weiner and Aigi Rahi-Tamm, "Getting to Know You: The Soviet Surveillance System, 1939–57," *Kritika* 13, no. 1 (Winter 2012): 5–45.

38. Michael Mann, "The Autonomous Power of the State: Its Origins, Mechanisms and Results," in *States in History*, ed. John H. Hall (New York: Basil Blackwell, 1986), 109–36.

39. On this shift in rhetoric in 1957, see Donald J. Raleigh, *Soviet Baby Boomers: An Oral History of Russia's Cold War Generation* (New York: Oxford University Press, 2011), 67. For more on how the Soviet authorities compared the Soviet Union to the United States, see Alan M. Ball, *Imagining America: Influence and Images in Twentieth-Century Russia* (Lanham: Rowman & Littlefield, 2003), xi. On comparing social welfare benefits from different systems, see Brij Mohan, ed., *Toward Comparative Social Welfare* (Cambridge: Schenkman Books, 1985), vii–viii.

40. Anne E. Gorsuch, *All This Is Your World: Soviet Tourism at Home and Abroad after Stalin* (New York: Oxford University Press, 2011), 106–29; Eleonory Gilburd, "Books and Borders: Sergei Obraztsov and Soviet Travels to London in the 1950s," in *Turizm: The Russian and East European Tourist under Capitalism and Socialism*, ed. Anne E. Gorsuch and Diane P. Koenker (Ithaca: Cornell University Press, 2006), 227–47; Radina Vučetić, "Soviet Cosmonauts and American Astronauts in Yugoslavia: Who Did the Yugoslavs Love More?," in *Soviet Space Culture: Cosmic Enthusiasm in Socialist Societies*, ed. Eva Maurer, Julia Richers, Monica Rüthers, and Carmen Scheide (New York: Palgrave Macmillan, 2011), 188–205; and Zubok, *Failed Empire*, 103.

41. *XX s"ezd KPSS: Stenograficheskii otchet; Ch. 1* (Moscow: Gospolitizdat, 1956), 606–7. The festival itself is described in chapter 6.

42. "Navstrechu festivaliu iunosti," *Komsomol'skaia pravda*, February 5, 1956; *Dokumenty piatogo plenuma TsK VLKSM* (Moscow: Molodaia gvardiia, 1956), 19–21.

43. TsAGM, f. 429, op. 1, d. 538, ll. 218–33.

44. "The College Student in the Soviet Union," *USSR*, no. 7–13 (1956): 1–7.

45. "The Sixth World Youth Festival," *USSR*, no. 7–13 (1956): 60–61.

46. "A Quintet of Talents," *USSR*, no. 7–13 (1956): 41–43.

47. TNA: PRO FO 371/129156 BW 2/563, p. 10.

48. TNA: PRO BW 2/575 GB/460/48FAC, pp. 34–35.

49. Lynn Mally, "Hallie Flanagan and the Soviet Union: New Heaven, New Earth, New Theater," in *Americans Experience Russia: Encountering the Enigma, 1917 to the Present*, ed. Choi Chatterjee and Beth Holmgren (New York: Routledge, 2013), 31–49.

50. Steven Fielding, Peter Thompson, and Nick Tiratsoo, *"England Arise!" The Labour Party and Popular Politics in 1940s Britain* (New York: Manchester University Press, 1995), 135–68.

51. David B. Wolcott, *Cops and Kids: Policing Juvenile Delinquency in Urban America, 1890–1940* (Columbus: Ohio State University Press, 2005), 193–98; Suzanne Wasserman, "Cafes, Clubs, Corners and Candy Stores: Youth Leisure-Culture in New York City's Lower East Side during the 1930s," *Journal of American Culture* 14, no. 4 (Winter 1991): 43–48. Some corporations did still continue to provide organized recreation for their workforce. See David L. Stebenne, "IBM's 'New Deal': Employment Policies of the International Business Machines Corporation, 1933–1956," *Journal of the Historical Society* 5, no. 1 (2005): 47–77; Sanford S. Jacoby, *Modern Manors: Welfare Capitalism since the New Deal* (Princeton: Princeton University Press, 1997), 35–94.

52. Hopf, *Social Construction of International Politics*, 39–82, 183–51.

53. GARF, f. R-5451, op. 24, d. 900, l. 11.

54. GARF, f. R-5451, op. 24, d. 1543, l. 19.

55. O. K. Makarova, *Kul'turnoe stroitel'stvo SSSR: Statisticheskii sbornik* (Moscow: Gosudarstvennoe statisticheskoe izdatel'stvo, 1956), 46–49, 276.

56. A. Bratenkov, *Klubom rukovodit sovet: Iz opyta raboty kluba Krasnoiarskogo lespromkhoza* (Tomsk, 1955), 4–5.

57. GANISO, f. 4158, op. 20, d. 472, l. 10.

58. TsAGM, f. 44, op. 1, d. 19, ll. 1–4.

59. TsAGM, f. 44, op. 1, d. 50, ll. 5–6.

60. TsAGM, f. 1988, op. 1, d. 49, ll. 2–3.

61. RGASPI, f. M-1, op. 32, d. 630, l. 102.

62. Shelepin, *Otchetnyi doklad TsK VLKSM XII s"ezdu komsomola*, 46.

63. S. P. Pavlov, *Otchet Tsentral'nogo Komiteta VLKSM i zadachi komsomola, vytekaiushchie iz reshenii XXII s"ezda KPSS* (Moscow: Molodaia gvardiia, 1962), 51.

64. GANISO, f. 654, op. 1, d. 16, l. 166; GANISO, f. 654, op. 1, d. 12, l. 37.

65. TsAOPIM, f. 635, op. 13, d. 484, l. 51; TsAOPIM, f. 635, op. 12, d. 1, l. 31.

66. Anatolii Avrus, born 1930, interview by author, May 28, 2009.

67. TsAGM, f. 1988, op. 1, d. 49, ll. 2–3.

68. TsAOPIM, f. 6803, op. 1, d. 1, l. 138.

69. RGANI, f. 5, op. 34, d. 17, l. 43.

70. V. K. Khromov, interview in "My vsegda zanimalis' tol'ko iskusstvom: Interv'iu s Valentinom Khromovym," accessed October 22, 2012, http://aptechka.agava.ru/statyi/knigi/inter6.html.

71. S. Frederick Starr, *Red and Hot: The Fate of Jazz in the Soviet Union, 1917–1980* (New York: Oxford University Press, 1983), 261–88.

72. GARF, f. R-5451, op. 24, d. 1543, ll. 13–25; Shelepin, *Otchetnyi doklad TsK VLKSM XII s"ezdu komsomola*, 44.

73. RGALI, f. 2329, op. 10, d. 16, l. 4 (original emphasis).

74. TsAGM, f. 2987, op. 1, d. 39, l. 39.

75. RGALI, f. 2329, op. 10, d. 324, ll. 4–6.

76. Irina Sirotkina, "Pliaska i ekstaz v Rossii Serebriannogo veka do kontsa 1920-kh godov," in *Rossiiskaia imperiia chuvstv: Podkhody k kul'turnoi istorii emotsii*, ed. Jan Plamper, Schamma Schahadat, and Marc Elie (Moscow: Novoe literaturnoe obozrenie, 2010), 282–305.

77. TsAGM, f. 2987, op. 1, d. 58, l. 37.

78. E. Makhlin, *Opyt raboty kul'turno-prosvititel'nykh uchrezhdenii na zhelezno-dorozhnom transporte* (Moscow: Gudok, 1957), 102.

79. Feliks Arons, born 1940, interview by author, May 18, 2009.

80. Avrus interview.

81. "Na ostrie pera . . . ," *Molodoi stalinets*, August 21, 1955.

82. Baliasnaia interview.

83. TsAGM, f. 2987, op. 1, d. 39, ll. 29–30.

84. TsAGM, f. 2987, op. 1, d. 45, ll. 25–26.

85. TsAGM, f. 1988, op. 1, d. 29, ll. 9–11.

86. Georgii Garanian, born 1934, interview by author, February 4, 2009. For more on the Zolotoi vosem', see Starr, *Red and Hot*, 245–47.

87. A. S. Kozlov, *"Kozel na sakse": I tak vsiu zhizn'* (Moscow: Vagrius, 1998), 134–35.

88. Valentina Iarskaia, born in the mid-1930s, interview by author, May 30, 2009.

89. Iurii Zhimskii, born 1936, interview by author, May 27, 2009.

90. RGASPI, f. M-1, op. 32, d. 873, ll. 105–26.

91. On conflicts over films, see Josephine Woll, *Real Images: Soviet Cinema and the Thaw* (New York: I. B. Tauris, 2000), 3–14, 59–66. On art music, see Peter J. Schmelz, *Such Freedom, If Only Musical: Unofficial Soviet Music during the Thaw* (New York: Oxford University Press, 2009), 26–66. On literature, see Emily Lygo, *Leningrad Poetry, 1953–1975: The Thaw Generation* (Bern: Peter Lang, 2010), 13–82. For a broad depiction of conflicts within the cultural intelligentsia, see M. R. Zezina, *Sovetskaia khudozhestvennaia intelligentsia i vlast' v 1950-e–60-e gody* (Moscow: Dialog-MGU, 1999), 104–53.

92. For this recent scholarship, see Stephen V. Bittner, *The Many Lives of Khrushchev's Thaw: Experience and Memory in Moscow's Arbat* (Ithaca: Cornell University Press, 2008), 1–13; and Dobson, *Khrushchev's Cold Summer*, 156–85. For the opposing position, the classic piece is Stephen F. Cohen, "The Friends and Foes of Change: Reformism and Conservatism in the Soviet Union," in *The Soviet Union since Stalin*, ed. Stephen F. Cohen, Alexander Rabinowitch, and Robert Sharlet (Bloomington: Indiana University Press, 1980), 11–31.

93. Baliasnaia interview.

94. For the role of anxieties in shaping Thaw-era developments, see Dobson, *Khrushchev's Cold Summer*, 156–85; Jones, "Dilemmas of De-Stalinization"; Iu. V. Aksiutin, *Khrushchevskaia "Ottepel'" i obshchestvennye nastroeniia v SSSR v 1953–1964 gg.* (Moscow: ROSSPEN, 2004).

95. Melanie Ilič, introduction to *Soviet State and Society under Nikita Khrushchev*, ed. Melanie Ilič and Jeremy Smith (New York: Routledge, 2009), 1–8; Bittner, *Many Lives of Khrushchev's Thaw*, 75–104, 211–19; Taubman, *Khrushchev*, 236–99.

96. Aleksei Kuznetsov, born 1941, interview by author, February 21, 2009; "Aleksei Kuznetsov: Polveka v dzhaze," *Jazz.ru* 15 (August 2008): 1–3; A. S. Kozlov, *Dzhazz, rock, i mednye tuby* (Moscow: Eksmo, 2005), 116–17.

97. Garanian interview.

98. Kuznetsov interview; Vitalli E. Kleinot, born 1941, interview by author, February 14, 2009; M. I. Kull', *Stupeni voskhozhdeniia*, accessed October 22, 2012, http://www.jazz.ru/books/kull/default.htm.

99. Garanian interview.

100. Zhimskii interview.

101. Lev Figlin, born 1938, interview by author, May 25, 2009.

102. Garanian interview.

103. Arons interview.

104. Figlin interview. For more on marginal homosocial spheres in the Soviet Union, see Dan Healey, *Homosexual Desire in Revolutionary Russia: The Regulation of Sexual and Gender Dissent* (Chicago: University of Chicago Press, 2001), 259–50.

105. Iarskaia interview.

106. Sarah Thornton, *Club Cultures: Music, Media and Subcultural Capital* (Hanover: Wesleyan University Press, 1996), 163–68; Pierre Bourdieu, *Distinction: A Social Critique of the Judgment of Taste*, trans. and ed. Richard Nice (Cambridge: Harvard University Press, 1984), 1–7.

107. Kozlov, *"Kozel na sakse,"* 72.

108. "Nam stydno za nashu podrugu," *Komsomol'skaia pravda*, June 21, 1955.

109. On stiliagi in the early and late Thaw, see Gleb Tsipursky, "Living 'America' in the Soviet Union: The Cultural Practices of 'Westernized' Soviet Youth, 1945–1964," in *The Soviet Union and the United States: Rivals of the Twentieth-Century; Coexistence and Competition*, ed. Eva-Maria Stolberg (Frankfurt: Peter Lang, 2013), 139–64.

110. On this antidelinquency campaign, see Juliane Fürst, "The Arrival of Spring? Changes and Continuities in Soviet Youth Culture and Policy between Stalin and Khrushchev," in Jones, *Dilemmas of De-Stalinization*, 135–53; Brian LaPierre, "Defining, Policing, and Punishing Hooliganism in Khrushchev's Russia" (PhD diss., University of Chicago, 2006), 164–233; V. A. Kozlov, *Mass Uprisings in the USSR: Protest and Rebellion in the Post-Stalin Years*, trans. and ed. Elaine M. MacKinnon (Armonk: M. E. Sharpe, 2002), 136–62; Louise I. Shelley, *Policing Soviet Society: The Evolution of State Control* (New York: Routledge, 1996), 44–45; Sheila Fitzpatrick, "Social Parasites: How Tramps, Idle Youth, and Busy Entrepreneurs Impeded the Soviet March to Communism," *Cahiers du Monde russe* 47, no. 1–2 (2006): 377–408; and Gleb Tsipursky, "Citizenship, Deviance, and Identity: Soviet Youth Newspapers as Agents of Social Control in the Thaw-Era Leisure Campaign," *Cahiers du Monde russe* 49, no. 4 (September–October 2008): 1–22.

111. Lisa E. Davenport, *Jazz Diplomacy: Promoting America in the Cold War Era* (Jackson: University Press of Mississippi, 2009), 33; Penny M. Von Eschen, *Satchmo Blows Up the World: Jazz Ambassadors Play the Cold War* (Cambridge: Harvard University Press, 2004), 13–17; Naima Prevots, *Dance for Export: Cultural Diplomacy and the Cold War* (Hanover: Wesleyan University Press, 1998), 1–7.

112. Figlin interview.

113. Viktor Dubiler, born 1941, interview by author, February 22, 2009.

114. Margo S. Rosen, "The Independent Turn in Soviet-Era Russian Poetry: How Dmitry Bobyshev, Joseph Brodsky, Anatoly Naiman and Evgeny Rein Became the 'Avvakumites' of Leningrad" (PhD diss., Columbia University, 2011), 184–87.

115. Figlin interview.

116. Kleinot interview.

117. Ann Komaromi, "Samizdat and Soviet Dissident Publics," *Slavic Review* 71, no. 1 (Spring 2012): 70–90.

118. Dubiler interview.

119. On bringing back jazz records from international travel, see Kleinot interview. On the broader context of Soviet travel abroad after 1953, see Gorsuch, *All This Is Your World*, 79–167; and Gilburd, "Books and Borders," 227–47.

120. Boris Taigin, interview in "Rastsvet i krakh 'Zolotoi sobaki,'" *Pchela* 20 (May–June 1998), http://www.pchela.ru/podshiv/20/goldendog.htm.

121. Figlin interview.

122. Dubiler interview.

123. Katerina Clark, *Petersburg: Crucible of Cultural Revolution* (Cambridge: Harvard University Press, 1995), 162.

124. Garanian interview.

125. Figlin interview.

126. "Stiliagi," *Zaria molodezhi*, February 17, 1957.

127. Tsipursky, "Citizenship, Deviance, and Identity."

128. For a similar dynamic in rock and roll in the 1970s and 1980s, see Alexei Yurchak, *Everything Was Forever, Until It Was No More: The Last Soviet Generation* (Princeton: Princeton University Press, 2006), 164–65.

129. Kleinot interview; Kuznetsov interview; Garanian interview; Iarskaia interview.

130. Vadif Sadykhov, born 1946, interview by author, February 24, 2009.

131. Kleinot interview.

132. Sadykhov interview.

133. On East Germany and Hungary, Uta G. Poiger, *Jazz, Rock, and Rebels: Cold War Politics and American Culture in a Divided Germany* (Berkeley: University of California Press, 2000), 106–36; Karl Brown, "Dance Hall Days: Jazz and Hooliganism in Communist Hungary, 1948–1956," in *Jazz behind the Iron Curtain*, ed. Gertrud Pickhan and Rüdiger Ritter (Frankfurt: Peter Lang, 2010), 267–94. On Bulgaria, Karin Taylor, *Let's Twist Again: Youth and Leisure in Socialist Bulgaria* (Vienna: Lit, 2006), 122.

134. See William J. Risch, *The Ukrainian West: Culture and the Fate of Empire in Soviet Lviv* (Cambridge: Harvard University Press, 2011), 226–32; Susan E. Reid, "The Exhibition *Art of Socialist Countries*, Moscow 1958–9, and the Contemporary Style of Painting," in *Style and Socialism: Modernity and Material Culture in Post-War Eastern Europe*, ed. Susan E. Reid and David Crowley (Oxford: Berg, 2000), 101–32.

135. Another of those areas was sexuality. See Josie McLellan, *Love in the Time of Communism: Intimacy and Sexuality in the GDR* (New York: Cambridge University Press, 2011), 13. On eastern Europe and leisure more broadly, see Cathleen M. Giustino, Catherine J. Plum, and Alexander Vari, eds., *Socialist Escapes: Breaking Away from Ideology and Everyday Routine in Eastern Europe, 1945–1989* (New York: Berghahn Books, 2013).

136. On conflicts over hegemony in capitalist popular culture, see the contributions to Tony Bennett, Colin Mercer, and Janet Woollcott, eds., *Popular Culture and Social Relations* (Philadelphia: Open University Press, 1986); and Richard B. Gruneau, ed., *Popular Cultures and Political Practices* (Toronto: Garamond Press, 1988).

137. For other scholarship on emotional transformation during the Thaw, see Polly Jones, "Breaking the Silence: Iurii Bondarev's Quietness between the 'Sincerity' and 'Civic Emotions' of the Thaw," in *Interpreting Emotions in Russia and Eastern Europe*, ed. Mark D. Steinberg and Valeria Sobol (DeKalb: Northern Illinois University Press, 2011), 152–76; Catriona Kelly, "Pravo na emotsii, pravil'nye emotsii: Upravlenie chuvstvami v Rossii posle epokhi prosveshcheniia," in Plamper, Schahadat, and Elie, *Rossiiskaia imperiia chuvstv*, 52–77; and Glennys Young, "Emotsii, politika osparivaniia i obshchestvennaia pamiat': Iz istorii novocherkasskoi tragedii," in Plamper, Schahadat, and Elie, *Rossiiskaia imperiia chuvstv*, 457–79.

138. On the benefits of such positive feelings, see the contributions to Felicia A. Huppert, Nick Baylis, and Berry Keverne, eds., *The Science of Well-Being* (New York: Oxford University Press, 2005); and C. R. Snyder and Shane J. Lopez, eds., *Handbook of Positive Psychology* (New York: Oxford University Press, 2002).

139. David Crowley and Susan E. Reid, "Introduction: Pleasures in Socialism," in Crowley and Reid, *Pleasures in Socialism*, 3–52.

140. Marina Balina and Evgeny Dobrenko, eds., *Petrified Utopia: Happiness Soviet Style* (New York: Anthem Press, 2009), xv–xxiv.

141. Darrin M. McMahon, *Happiness: A History* (New York: Atlantic Monthly Press, 2006), 454–80.

142. Greg Castillo, *Cold War on the Home Front: The Soft Power of Midcentury Design* (Minneapolis: University of Minnesota Press, 2010), 139–72; Ruth Oldenziel and Karin Zuchman, "Kitchens as Technology and Politics: An Introduction," in *Cold War Kitchen: Americanization, Technology, and European Users*, ed. Ruth Oldenziel and Karin Zuchman (Cambridge: MIT Press, 2009), 1–32.

CHAPTER 5. YOUTH INITIATIVE AND THE 1956 YOUTH CLUB MOVEMENT

1. Iurii Sokolov, born 1940, interview by author, April 16, 2009.

2. RGANI, f. 5, op. 34, d. 11, ll. 64–67.

3. RGANI, f. 5, op. 30, d. 38, l. 127.

4. RGASPI, f. M-1, op. 32, d. 811, ll. 1–13.

5. *XX s'ezd KPSS: Stenograficheskii otchet; Ch. 1* (Moscow, 1956), 603, 606–8.

6. RGASPI, f. M-1, op. 3, d. 880, l. 36; RGASPI, f. M-1, op. 3, d. 971, ll. 62–63.

7. "Videt' i podderzhivat' komsomol'skuiu initsiativu," *Leninskii put'*, June 1, 1957; A. Disudenko and A. Skrypnik, *Zakon komsomol'skoi zhizni* (Moscow: Molodaia gvardiia, 1966), 96; TsAOPIM, f. 635, op. 14, d. 484, l. 20.

8. Soo-Hoon Park, "Party Reform and 'Volunteer Principle' under Khrushchev in Historical Perspective" (PhD diss., Columbia University, 1993); George Breslauer, "Khrushchev Reconsidered," in *The Soviet Union since Stalin*, ed. Stephen F. Cohen, Alexander Rabinowitch, and Robert Sharlet (Bloomington: Indiana University Press, 1980), 50–70.

9. N. S. Khrushchev, *Vospityvat' aktivnykh i soznatel'nykh stroitelei kommunisticheskogo obshchestva (rech' na XIII s'ezde VLKSM 18 aprelia 1958 goda)* (Moscow: Molodaia gvardiia, 1961), 40.

10. A. N. Shelepin, *Otchetnyi doklad Tsentral'nogo Komiteta Vsesoiuznogo leninskogo kommunisticheskogo soiuza molodezhi XIII s'ezdu komsomola (15 aprelia 1958 g.)* (Moscow: Molodaia gvardiia, 1958), 63–65.

11. RGASPI, f. M-1, op. 3, d. 946, ll. 12–13.

12. Sabina Mihelj, "Negotiating Cold War Culture at the Crossroads of East and West: Uplifting the Working People, Entertaining the Masses, Cultivating the Nation," *Comparative Studies in Society and History* 53, no. 2 (June 2011): 509–39.

13. Esther von Richthofen, *Bringing Culture to the Masses, Control, Compromise and Participation in the GDR* (New York: Berghahn Books, 2009), 153–70; Thomas Lindenberger, "The Fragmented Society: 'Social Activism' and Authority in GDR State Socialism," *Zeitgeschichte* 37, no. 1 (January–February 2010): 3–20.

14. See the contributions to Stuart C. Aitken, Anne Trine Kjorholt, and Ragnhild Lund eds., *Global Childhoods: Globalization, Development, and Young People* (New

York: Routledge, 2008); as well as Claire Wallace and Sijka Kovatcheva, *Youth in Society: The Construction and Deconstruction of Youth in East and West Europe* (New York: St. Martin's Press, 1998), 209–12.

15. For how the authorities called on journalists to inspire enthusiasm in the Thaw, see Thomas C. Wolfe, *Governing Soviet Journalism: The Press and the Soviet Person after Stalin* (Bloomington: Indiana University Press, 2005), 33–70.

16. Gleb Tsipursky, "Coercion and Consumption: The Khrushchev Leadership's Ruling Style in the Campaign against 'Westernized' Youth, 1954–64," in *Youth and Rock in the Soviet Bloc: Youth Cultures, Music, and the State in Russia and Eastern Europe*, ed. William J. Risch (Lanham: Lexington Books, 2015), 55–80.

17. Benjamin K. Tromly, "Re-Imagining the Soviet Intelligentsia: Student Politics and University Life, 1948–1964" (PhD diss., Harvard University, 2007), 370–424.

18. Michaela Pohl, "Women and Girls in Virgin Lands," in *Women in the Khrushchev Era*, ed. Melanie Ilič, Susan E. Reid, and Lynne Attwood (New York: Palgrave Macmillan, 2004), 52–74.

19. RGASPI, f. M-1, op. 32, d. 811, ll. 14–20.

20. Kristin Roth-Ey, "Playing for Cultural Authority: Soviet TV Professionals and the Game Show in the 1950s and 1960s," in *Pleasures in Socialism: Leisure and Luxury in the Eastern Bloc*, ed. David Crowley and Susan E. Reid (Evanston: Northwestern University Press, 2010), 147–76; Bella Ostromoukhova, "KVN—'molodezhnaia kul'tura shestidesiatykh'?," *Neprikosnovennyi zapas: Debaty o politike i kul'ture* 36, no. 4 (September 2004), http://magazines.russ.ru/nz/; Alexander Prokhorov, "Tri Buratino: Evoliutsiia sovetskogo kinogiroiia," in *Veselye chelovechki: Kul'turnye geroi sovetskogo detstva*, ed. Il'ia Kukulin, Mark Lipovetskii, and Mariia Maiofis (Moscow: Novoe literaturnoe obozrenie, 2008), 153–80; Mark Koenig, "Media and Reform: The Case of Youth Programming on Soviet Television (1955–1990)" (PhD diss., Columbia University, 1995), 108–12.

21. RGASPI, f. M-1, op. 32, d. 861, l. 76. For more on such brigades, see M. V. Iunisov, "Agitatsionno-khudozhestvennye brigady," in *Samodeiatel'noe khudozhestvennoe tvorchestvo v SSSR: Ocherki istorii, konets 1950-kh—nachalo 1990-kh godov*, ed. K. G. Bogemskaia (Saint Petersburg: Dmitrii Bulanin, 1999), 309–32.

22. Emily Lygo, *Leningrad Poetry, 1953–1975: The Thaw Generation* (Bern: Peter Lang, 2010), 35–38.

23. For more on the impact of youth initiative-oriented activities in the mass cultural network, see Gleb Tsipursky, *Having Fun in the Thaw: Youth Initiative Clubs in the Post-Stalin Years*, Carl Beck Papers in Russian and East European Studies, No. 2201 (Pittsburgh: Center for Russian and East European Studies, University Center for International Studies, University of Pittsburgh, 2012), 1–69.

24. "Po initsiative komsomol'tsev: Svoimi rukami," *Komsomol'skaia pravda*, January 15, 1955. For similar stories, see "Vse mozhno sdelat' svoimi rukami," *Komsomol'skaia pravda*, August 4, 1955; and "Postroim klub svoimi rukami!," *Leninskii put'*, October 26, 1957.

25. RGASPI, f. M-1, op. 32, d. 838, l. 120.

26. M. E. Nepomniashchii, ed., *Entuziasty: Sbornik o peredovikakh kul'turno-prosvititel'noi raboty* (Moscow: Sovetskaia Rossiia, 1959), 38–39. For another example of promoting initiative, see E. Makhlin, *Opyt raboty kul'turno-prosvititel'nykh uchrezhdenii na zheleznodorozhnom transporte* (Moscow: Gudok, 1957), 3.

27. On trade unions in the Thaw, see Jumbae Jo, "Dismantling Stalin's Fortress: Soviet Trade Unions in the Khrushchev Era," in *Soviet State and Society under Nikita Khrushchev*, ed. Melanie Ilič and Jeremy Smith (New York: Routledge, 2009), 122–41.

28. RGASPI, f. M-1, op. 32, d. 858, l. 8. For similar complaints, see RGASPI, f. M-1, op. 3, d. 912, l. 5; RGASPI, f. M-1, op. 32, d. 811, l. 8; and RGASPI, f. M-1, op. 32, d. 838, l. 119.

29. RGASPI, f. M-1, op. 32, d. 811, l. 14; *XX s'ezd KPSS*, 607–8.

30. On this turn in the mid-1930s, see Lynn Mally, *Revolutionary Acts: Amateur Theater and the Soviet State, 1917–1938* (Ithaca: Cornell University Press, 2000), 146–212; Malte Rolf, *Sovetskie massovye prazdniki* (Moscow: ROSSPEN, 2009), 96–97 (or in Malte Rolf, *Soviet Mass Festivals, 1917–1991*, trans. Cynthia Klohr [Pittsburgh: University of Pittsburgh Press, 2013]); and Susannah Lockwood Smith, "From Peasants to Professionals: The Socialist-Realist Transformation of a Russian Folk Choir," *Kritika* 3, no. 3 (Summer 2002): 393–425.

31. RGASPI, f. M-1, op. 3, d. 901, l. 168; "Klub devushek," *Komsomol'skaia pravda*, September 5, 1956.

32. Anne White, *De-Stalinization and the House of Culture: Declining State Control over Leisure in the USSR, Poland, and Hungary, 1953–89* (New York: Routledge, 1990), 2.

33. RGASPI, f. M-1, op. 32, d. 858, l. 133.

34. "Klub starsheklassnikov," *Zaria molodezhi*, September 13, 1957.

35. RGASPI, f. M-1, op. 32, d. 838, l. 120.

36. RGASPI, f. M-1, op. 32, d. 839, l. 22.

37. Douglas R. Weiner, *A Little Corner of Freedom: Russian Nature Protection from Stalin to Gorbachev* (Berkeley: University of California Press, 2001), 312–39.

38. RGASPI, f. M-1, op. 32, d. 1055, l. 133.

39. Boris Pshenichner, born 1933, interview by author, April 29, 2009. For more on the circle devoted to space, see E. V. Bashlii, *Zvezdnyi dom na Vorob'evykh gorakh: K 40-letiiu otdela astronomii i kosmanavtiki posviashchaetsia* (Moscow: MGDD[Iu] T, 2002), 1–2. On the Dvorets pionerskaia (Pioneer palace), see Susan E. Reid, *Khrushchev in Wonderland: The Pioneer Palace in Moscow's Lenin Hills, 1962*, Carl Beck Papers in Russian and East European Studies, No. 1606 (Pittsburgh: Center for Russian and East European Studies, University Center for International Studies, University of Pittsburgh, 2002), 1–53. On early forms of Soviet aeronautics circles, see Asif A. Siddiqi, *The Red Rockets' Glare: Spaceflight and the Soviet Imagination* (New York: Cambridge University Press, 2010), 114–54. For other space clubs, see Monica Rüthers, "Children and the Cosmos as Projects of the Future and Ambassadors of Soviet Leadership," in *Soviet Space Culture: Cosmic Enthusiasm in Socialist Societies*, ed. Eva Maurer, Julia Richers, Monica Rüthers, and Carmen Scheide (New York: Palgrave Macmillan, 2011), 206–28. For an in-depth study of how an archaeological circle functioned in the late Soviet period, see B. S. Gladarev, "Formirovanie i funktsionirovanie milieu (na primere arkheologicheskogo kruzhka LDPDTIu 1970–2000 gg.)," accessed October 22, 2012, http://www.indepsocres.spb.ru/boriss.htm.

40. For this postwar Stalinist approach, see Juliane Fürst, "The Importance of Being Stylish: Youth, Culture and Identity in Late Stalinism," in *Late Stalinist Russia: Society between Reconstruction and Reinvention*, ed. Juliane Fürst (New York: Routledge, 2006), 209–30.

41. B. A. Grushin, *Chetyre zhizni Rossii v zerkale oprosov obshchestvennogo mneniia: Ocherki massovogo soznaniia rossiian vremen Khrushcheva, Brezhneva, Gorbacheva i Eltsina v 4-kh knigakh; Zhizn' 1-ia, epokha Khrushcheva* (Moscow: Progress-Traditsiia, 2001); Vladimir Shlapentokh, *Public and Private Life of the Soviet People: Changing Values in Post-Stalin Russia* (New York: Oxford University Press, 1989), 14–18.

42. Alexander Prokhorov, "The Unknown New Wave: Soviet Cinema of the Sixties," in *Springtime for Soviet Cinema: Re/Viewing the 1960s*, ed. Alexander Prokhorov (Pittsburgh: Pittsburgh Russian Film Symposium, 2001), 7–28.

43. Stephen Lovell, *The Russian Reading Revolution: Print Culture in the Soviet and Post-Soviet Eras* (New York: St. Martin's Press, 2000), 46–48.

44. Liubov Baliasnaia, born 1927, interview by author, April 5, 2009.

45. For Bulgaria, see Karin Taylor, *Let's Twist Again: Youth and Leisure in Socialist Bulgaria* (Vienna: Lit, 2006), 95.

46. TsAOPIM, f. 635, op. 13, d. 484, l. 94; TsAOPIM, f. 6083, op. 1, d. 1, ll. 164–65; GANISO, f. 652, op. 1, d. 3, ll. 51–52.

47. "Molodezhnyi klub v TsPKiO," *Moskovskii komsomolets*, May 23, 1957; "Fakel," *Zaria molodezhi*, October 3, 1956; "Klub kul'tury," *Leninskii put'*, March 21, 1959.

48. "Boi serosti i skuki," *Komsomol'skaia pravda*, September 6, 1956; RGASPI, f. M-1, op. 32, d. 858, ll. 213–18.

49. RGASPI, f. M-1, op. 32, d. 858, l. 112.

50. One directive, for example, was aimed at Saratov; see "Fakel," *Zaria molodezhi*, October 3, 1956.

51. RGANI, f. 5, op. 34, d. 11, ll. 64–67.

52. RGASPI, f. M-1, op. 32, d. 811, l. 26; RGASPI, f. M-1, op. 3, d. 912, l. 6.

53. RGASPI, f. M-1, op. 32, d. 858, l. 111.

54. RGASPI, f. M-1, op. 32, d. 858, ll. 107–12. Hilary Pilkington touches on the post-Stalin drive to get youth used to supposedly rational leisure in her essay "'The Future Is Ours': Youth Culture in Russia, 1953 to the Present," in *Russian Cultural Studies: An Introduction*, ed. Catriona Kelly and David Shepherd (New York: Oxford University Press, 1998), 368–86.

55. S. P. Pavlov, *Ob itogakh iun'skogo Plenuma TsK KPSS "Ocherednye zadachi ideologicheskoi raboty partii" i roli komsomol'skikh organizatsii v vospitanii sovetskoi molodezhi na sovremennom etape stroitel'stva kommunizma: Doklad pervogo sekretaria TsK VLKSM tov. Pavlova S. P. na III plenume TsK VLKSM 9 iulia 1963 g.* (Moscow: Molodaia gvardiia, 1963). On Pavlov, see A. A. Alekseeva, *Stroka v biografii* (Moscow: Molodaia gvardiia, 2003), 20–21.

56. Sokolov interview.

57. TNA: PRO FO 371/129156 GB/460/48P, pp. 2–4.

58. RGASPI, f. M-1, op. 32, d. 858, ll. 107–12.

59. S. P. Pavlov, *Otchet Tsentral'nogo Komiteta VLKSM i zadachi komsomola, vytekaiushchie iz reshenii XXII s"ezda KPSS* (Moscow: Molodaia gvardiia, 1962), 37; RGASPI, f. M-1, op. 34, d. 141, l. 95.

60. RGASPI, f. M-1, op. 32, d. 858, l. 110.

61. RGASPI, f. M-1, op. 32, d. 858, ll. 110–11; Anna Rotkirch, "'What Kind of Sex Can You Talk About?' Acquiring Sexual Knowledge in Three Soviet Generations," in *On Living through Soviet Russia*, ed. Daniel Bertaux, Paul Thompson, and Anna Rotkirch (New York: Routledge, 2003), 193–219. On youth and sex in the early

Soviet years, see Frances L. Bernstein, *The Dictatorship of Sex: Lifestyle Advice for the Soviet Masses* (DeKalb: Northern Illinois University Press, 2007), 129–58.

62. RGASPI, f. M-1, op. 32, d. 858, l. 109.

63. While the late Stalinist state allowed debates on literary works, cultural institutions very rarely held such events, likely due to the potential for significant repercussions if something went awry, as well as grassroots reluctance to disagree so publicly with official interpretations of literature. I found no records of postwar Stalinist debates on topics other than literary works. For more on the challenges of organizing debates on literary works under Stalin, see TsAOPIM, f. 635, op. 11, d. 31, ll. 15–16.

64. RGASPI, f. M-1, op. 32, d. 858, ll. 216–18.

65. RGASPI, f. M-1, op. 32, d. 858, l. 114.

66. RGASPI, f. M-1, op. 32, d. 811, ll. 25–28.

67. RGASPI, f. M-1, op. 32, d. 814, ll. 17–18. Also see an instruction booklet on youth debates: M. P. Kapustin, *Kak provesti molodezhno-komsomol'skie disputy v klube* (Tashkent, 1959).

68. RGASPI, f. M-1, op. 32, d. 811, l. 28.

69. Nelli Popkova, born 1936, interview by author, May 20, 2009.

70. On unofficial youth debate groups, often repressed by the state, in the late Stalin era, see Elena Zubkova, *Russia after the War: Hopes, Illusions, and Disappointments, 1945–1957*, trans. and ed. Hugh Ragsdale (Armonk: M. E. Sharpe, 1998), 109–38; Juliane Fürst, *Stalin's Last Generation: Soviet Youth and the Emergence of Mature Socialism, 1945–56* (New York: Oxford University Press, 2010), 95–136; and E. V. Markasova, "A vot praktiku my znaem po geroiam Krasnodona," *Neprikosnovennyi zapas* 58, no. 2 (2008), http://magazines.russ.ru/nz/2008/2/ma18.html.

71. Robert Hornsby, *Protest, Reform and Repression in Khrushchev's Soviet Union* (New York: Cambridge University Press, 2013), chap. 3; Benjamin Tromly, "Intelligentsia Self-Fashioning in the Postwar Soviet Union: Revol't Pimenov's Political Struggle, 1949–57," *Kritika* 13, no. 1 (Winter 2012): 151–76; Kathleen E. Smith, "A New Generation of Political Prisoners: 'Anti-Soviet' Students, 1956–1957," *Soviet and Post-Soviet Review* 32, no. 1 (2005): 191–208.

72. GANISO, f. 652, op. 1, d. 3, ll. 51–52.

73. On how 1960s amateur theater troupes functioned to instill a similar orientation toward public engagement, see Susan Costanzo, "Amateur Theatres and Amateur Publics in the Russian Republic, 1958–71," *Slavonic and East European Review* 86, no. 2 (April 2008): 372–94. During the perestroika years, clubs offered a space for meetings of dissenting political groups; see A. G. Borzenkov, *Molodezh' i politika: Vozmozhnosti i predely studencheskoi samodeiatel'nosti na vostoke Rossii (1961–1991 gg.); Chast' 2* (Novosibirsk: Novosibirskii gosudarstvennyi universitet, 2002), 166–67. For post-Soviet youth civic activism, see Julie Hemment, "Nashi, Youth Voluntarism, and Potemkin NGOs: Making Sense of Civil Society in Post-Soviet Russia," *Slavic Review* 71, no. 2 (Summer 2012): 234–60. Other socialist states, such as China, also adopted models that sought to channel and guide civic engagement; see Nara Dillon, "Governing Civil Society: Adapting Revolutionary Methods to Serve Post-Communist Goals," in *Mao's Invisible Hand: The Political Foundations of Adaptive Governance in China*, ed. Sebastian Heilmann and Elizabeth J. Perry (Cambridge: Harvard University Press, 2011), 138–64.

74. RGASPI, f. M-1, op. 32, d. 858, ll. 67–68; Sokolov interview.

75. RGASPI, f. M-1, op. 32, d. 830, l. 14a.

76. D. L. Bykov, *Bulat Okudzhava* (Moscow: Molodaia gvardiia, 2009), 252.

77. Ludmilla Alexeyeva and Paul Goldberg, *The Thaw Generation: Coming of Age in the Post-Stalin Era* (Pittsburgh: University of Pittsburgh Press, 1993).

78. For the importance of poetry in the Thaw, see L. B. Brusilovskaia, *Kul'tura povsednevnosti v epokhu ottepeli: Metamorfozy stilia* (Moscow: Izdatel'stvo URAO, 2001), 169–74.

79. The case study regarding the poets and their compromise effort primarily draws on a published collection of primary sources composed of published interviews with participants, as well as on extensive quotes from newspaper articles and archival documents; see L. V. Polikovskaia, *My predchustviie . . . predtecha . . . ploshchad' Maiakovskogo, 1958–1965* (Moscow: Zvenia, 1997), 143–52. I also rely on a memoir by a former participant, V. K. Bukovskii, *"I vozvrashchaetsia veter . . . "* (New York: Khronika Press, 1978), 129–37.

80. Here, my research complicates the conclusions in Juliane Fürst, "Friends in Private, Friends in Public: The Phenomena of Kompaniia among Soviet Youth in the 1950s and 1960s," in *Borders of Socialism: Private Spheres of Soviet Russia*, ed. Lewis H. Siegelbaum (New York: Palgrave Macmillan, 2006), 229–50. For another critical approach to Fürst's take on kompanii, see Tromly, "Re-Imagining the Soviet Intelligentsia," 155–56.

81. On Soviet physics, see Ethan Pollock, *Stalin and the Soviet Science Wars* (Princeton: Princeton University Press, 2006), 72–103. On MGU in the 1950s and 1960s, see O. G. Gerasimova, *Obshchestvenno-politicheskaia zhizn' studenchestva MGU v 1950-e–seredine 1960-kh gg.* (Moscow: Moskovskii gosudarstvennyi universitet, 2008).

82. This information and the description of *Arkhimed* that follows come from a group memoir of the Arkhimed collective: Svetlana Kovaleva, *Ty pomnish' fizfak? Neformal'nye traditsii fizfaka MGU* (Moscow: Pomatur, 2003), 76–86, 362.

83. On these tropes, see P. L. Vail and A. A. Genis, *60-e: Mir sovetskogo cheloveka* (Ann Arbor: Ardis, 1988), 64–87, 100–111, 160–76.

84. Tatiana Tkacheva, born 1945, interview by author, January 20, 2009.

85. D. V. Gal'tsⓍv, born 1942, interview by author, February 20, 2009.

86. Sergei Semenov, born 1948, interview by author, March 18, 2009.

87. Ol'ga Lebedikhina, born 1947, interview by author, December 25, 2008.

88. Svetlana Shchegol'kova, born 1937, interview by author, February 19, 2009.

89. Svetlana Kovaleva, born in the mid-1930s, interview by author, March 3, 2009.

90. Semenov interview.

91. Iurii Gaponov, born 1934, interview by author, April 28, 2009.

92. Oleg Kharkhordin, "Druzhba: Klassicheskaia teoriia i sovremennye zaboty," in *Druzhba: Ocherki policy teorii praktik*, ed. Oleg Kharkhordin (Saint Petersburg: Izdatel'stvo Evropeiskogo universiteta v Sankt-Peterburge, 2009), 11–47.

93. Daniel Goleman, *Social Intelligence: The New Science of Human Relationships* (New York: Bantam Dell, 2006); Joseph LeDoux, *The Emotional Brain: The Mysterious Underpinnings of Emotional Life* (New York: Touchstone, 1996).

94. Sokolov interview.

95. Irina Sokol'skaia, born 1947, interview by author, November 8, 2008.

96. Nona Kozlova, born 1933, interviewed April 29, 2009; Pshenichner interview.

97. Valentina Miagkova, born 1923, interview by author, April 29, 2009.

98. Tkacheva interview.

99. Valerii Miliaev, born 1937, interview by author, February 28, 2009.

100. Nina Deviataikina, born 1947, interview by author, May 20, 2009.

101. For the center and the Soviet-era Russian provinces, see Donald J. Raleigh, *Soviet Baby Boomers: An Oral History of Russia's Cold War Generation* (New York: Oxford University Press, 2011), 66–119. For Ukraine, see William J. Risch, *The Ukrainian West: Culture and the Fate of Empire in Soviet Lviv* (Cambridge: Harvard University Press, 2011), 1–16.

102. Lebedikhina interview.

103. Gleb Tsipursky, *Find Your Purpose Using Science* (Westerville: Intentional Insights, 2015).

104. Fürst, *Stalin's Last Generation*, 19.

105. RGASPI, f. M-1, op. 32, d. 1096, l. 3.

106. Baliasnaia interview.

107. RGASPI, f. M-1, op. 32, d. 858, l. 113.

108. RGANI, f. 5, op. 34, d. 11, ll. 69–70. For more on complaint letters written during the Thaw, see Gleb Tsipursky, "'As a Citizen, I Cannot Ignore These Facts': Whistleblowing in the Khrushchev Era," *Jahrbücher für Geschichte Osteuropas* 58, no. 1 (March 2010): 52–69.

109. RGANI, f. 5, op. 34, d. 11, l. 71.

110. Sokolov interview; "Kak tushili 'Fakel,'" *Komsomol'skaia pravda*, December 9, 1956.

111. RGALI, f. 2329, op. 10, d. 183, ll. 28–31; RGASPI, f. M-1, op. 32, d. 830, ll. 11–14.

112. G. G. Karpov and N. D. Sintsov, *Klubnoe delo: Uchebnoe posobie* (Moscow: Sovetskaia Rossiia, 1959), 26.

113. RGASPI, f. M-1, op. 32, d. 1096, ll. 3–16.

114. TsAGM, f. 1988, op. 1, d. 114, ll. 38–39.

115. TsAGM, f. 718, op. 1, d. 258, ll. 34–36.

116. See Gerald S. Smith, *Songs to Seven Strings: Russian Guitar Poetry and Soviet "Mass Song"* (Bloomington: Indiana University Press, 1984); S. Iu. Rumiantsev, "Liubitel'skii muzykal'nyi teatr: Avtorskaia pesnia," in Bogemskaia, *Samodeiatel'noe khudozhestvennoe tvorchestvo v SSSR*, 19–76.

117. Timothy W. Ryback, *Rock around the Bloc: A History of Rock Music in Eastern Europe and the Soviet Union* (New York: Oxford University Press, 1990), 35–49.

118. Rossen Djagalov, "Guitar Poetry as the Genre of 1960s Democratic Socialism: A Global History" (paper presented at the "Socialist 1960s: Popular Culture and the City in Global Perspective" conference, University of Illinois, Urbana-Champaign, June 2010).

119. A praiseworthy exception to the usually narrow focus on the most controversial bards is Rachel S. Platonov, *Singing the Self: Guitar Poetry, Community, and Identity in the Post-Stalin Period* (Evanston: Northwestern University Press, 2012).

120. TsAGM, f. 2987, op. 1, d. 70, l. 31.

121. Miliaev interview. For Miliaev's bard activities, see a website dedicated to guitar poetry: "Miliaev Valerii Aleksandrovich," accessed October 22, 2012, http://www.bards.ru/archives/author.php?id=1682.

122. Again, one exception is Platonov's work, yet even this study excessively emphasizes the marginal elements within bard music. See Platonov, *Singing the Self*, 101–53.

123. Sergei Krylov, born 1941, interview by author, March 2, 2009; Miliaev interview.

124. TsAGM, f. 718, op. 1, d. 254, ll. 13–14.

125. Mark Pinkhasik, born in the late 1930s or early 1940s, interview by author, May 13, 2009; Konstantin Il'in, born 1944, interview by author, May 20, 2009; Galina Petrova, born in the late 1930s or early 1940s, interview by author, May 13, 2009; GANISO, f. 652, d. 3, l. 239; "Zasedanie soveta kluba," *Leninskii put'*, November 17, 1962; "Tol'ko nachalo," *Leninskii put'*, December 1, 1962.

126. Kovaleva, *Ty pomnish' fizfak?*, 81–82; Kovaleva interview.

127. Gaponov interview.

128. Quoted in Kovaleva, *Ty pomnish' fizfak?*, 86–87.

129. Kovaleva interview; Gaponov interview; Tkacheva interview; Volodia Gertsik, born 1946, interview by author, November 10, 2008; TsAOPIM, f. 6083, op. 1, d. 52, l. 18; "Arkhimed' v MGU," *Iunost'* 7 (1963): 108; Kovaleva, *Ty pomnish' fizfak?*, 81–97.

130. Gaponov interview.

131. Miliaev interview.

132. On such high-level struggles, see Jeremy Smith's introduction to *Khrushchev in the Kremlin: Policy and Government in the Soviet Union, 1953–1964*, ed. Jeremy Smith and Melanie Ilič (New York: Routledge, 2011), 1–8.

133. Shchegol'kova interview; Kovaleva, *Ty pomnish' fizfak?*, 82.

134. Kovaleva interview.

135. Rebecca Friedman, *Masculinity, Autocracy, and the Russian University, 1804–1863* (New York: Palgrave Macmillan, 2005), 1–13.

136. Miliaev interview.

137. Gaponov interview.

138. Gal'tsov interview.

139. Semenov interview.

140. On multiple meanings in Soviet cultural activities, see Richard Taruskin, *On Russian Music* (Berkeley: University of California Press, 2009), 307. On the challenges of receiving prescribed signals, see Stuart Hall, "Encoding/Decoding," in *Culture, Media, Language: Working Papers in Cultural Studies, 1972–79*, ed. Stuart Hall, Dorothy Hobson, Andrew Lowe, and Paul Willis (New York: Routledge, 2005), 107–16.

141. G. V. Sapgir, interview in "Lianazovo i drugie (gruppy i kruzhki kontsa 50kh)," *Arion* 3 (1997), http://magazines.russ.ru/arion/1997/3/sabgir.html; A. V. Laiko, interview in "Aleksandr Laiko: 'Liubov', i zhizn', i smert'—vse smertnaia vina v Moskovii moei," *Evreiskaia gazeta*, August 8, 2006. For some of Laiko's poetry, see A. V. Laiko, "Krasnye Mal'vy," *Znamia* 12 (2004), http://magazines.russ.ru/znamia/2004/12/la7.html.

142. "Marochki: Interv'iu Aleksandra Levina s Andreem Sergeevym," *Russkii Zhurnal*, August 16, 1998.

143. Risch, *Ukrainian West*, 179–81; Sergei Zhuk, *Rock and Roll in the Rocket City: The West, Identity, and Ideology in Soviet Dniepropetrovsk* (Baltimore: Johns Hopkins University Press, 2010), 31–52; Larisa Honey, "Pluralizing Practices in Late-Socialist Moscow: Russian Alternative Practitioners Reclaim and Redefine Individualism," in *Soviet Society in the Era of Late Socialism, 1964–1985*, ed. Neringa Klumbyte and Gulnaz Sharafutdinova (Lanham: Lexington Books, 2012), 117–42. For more on alternative medical practices in the Thaw-era Soviet Union, see Birgit Menzel, "Occult and

Esoteric Movements in Russia from the 1960s to the 1980s," in *The New Age of Russia: Occult and Esoteric Dimensions*, ed. Birgit Menzel, Michael Hagemeister, and Bernice G. Rosenthal (Berlin: Verlag Otto Sagner, 2012), 151–85.

144. RGASPI, f. M-1, op. 32, d. 1170, ll. 97–100.

145. Polikovskaia, *My predchustviie*, 143–52.

146. V. D. Dudintsev, *Ne khlebom edinym* (Munich: Zope, 1957).

147. Denis Kozlov, "Naming the Social Evil: The Readers of *Novyi mir* and Vladimir Dudintsev's *Not by Bread Alone*, 1956–59 and Beyond," in *The Dilemmas of De-Stalinization: Negotiating Cultural and Social Change in the Khrushchev Era*, ed. Polly Jones (New York: Routledge, 2006), 80–98.

148. Anatolii Avrus, born 1930, interview by author, May 28, 2009; Liudmila Gerasimova, born in the mid-1930s, interview by author, May 27, 2009; Popkova interview.

149. GANISO, f. 652, op. 1, d. 3, ll. 48–49. Also see "Za vysokuiu ideinost' i printsipial'nost'!," *Leninskii put'*, June 8, 1957.

150. TsAOPIM, f. 6083, op. 1, d. 52, ll. 166–67.

151. Susan E. Reid, "In the Name of the People: The Manege Affair Revisited," *Kritika* 6, no. 4 (Fall 2005): 673–716. For more on Soviet abstract art in the Thaw, see Matthew J. Jackson, *The Experimental Group: Ilya Kabakov, Moscow Conceptualism, Soviet Avant-Gardes* (Chicago: University of Chicago Press, 2010), 47–91.

152. Pavlov, *Ob itogakh iun'skogo Plenuma TsK KPSS*, 39.

153. Arjun Appadurai, *Modernity at Large: Cultural Dimensions of Globalization* (Minneapolis: University of Minnesota Press, 1996), 7.

154. On Nazi Germany, see Shelley Baranowski, *Strength through Joy: Consumerism and Mass Tourism in the Third Reich* (New York: Cambridge University Press, 2004), 1–9; Rolf, *Sovetskie massovye prazdniki*, 7–36; and Detlev J. K. Peukert, *Inside Nazi Germany: Conformity, Opposition, and Racism in Everyday Life* (New Haven: Yale University Press, 1987), 143–69. On fascist Italy, see Victoria de Grazia, *The Culture of Consent: Mass Organization of Leisure in Fascist Italy* (New York: Cambridge University Press, 1981), 151–224. However, note that the fascist Italian regime called on young cultural intellectuals to express their initiative in their own voices, giving their own takes on the fascist version of a modern culture. See Ruth Ben-Ghiat, *Fascist Modernities: Italy, 1922–1945* (Berkeley: University of California Press, 2001), 13–14.

155. Nicole Eustace, *Passion Is the Gale: Emotion, Power, and the Coming of the American Revolution* (Chapel Hill: University of North Carolina Press, 2008), 3–16; R. Marie Griffith, "'Joy Unspeakable and Full of Glory': The Vocabulary of Pious Emotion in the Narratives of American Pentecostal Women, 1910–1945," in *An Emotional History of the United States*, ed. Peter N. Stearns and Jan Lewis (New York: New York University Press, 1998), 218–40.

156. On the minimal incidence of spectacular deviationism among Soviet youth in comparison to youth countercultures in western contexts, see Jeremi Suri, *Power and Protest: Global Revolution and the Rise of Détente* (Cambridge: Harvard University Press, 2003), 1–5. For more on western youth countercultures in these years, see James Gilbert, *A Cycle of Outrage: America's Reaction to the Juvenile Delinquent in the 1950s* (New York: Oxford University Press, 1986); John Springhall, *Youth Popular Culture and Moral Panics: Penny Gaffs to Gangsta-Rap, 1830–1996* (New York: St. Martin's Press, 1998), 121–46; Steven Mintz, *Huck's Raft: A History of American Childhood* (Cambridge: Harvard University Press, 2004), 310–33; and Stuart Hall and Tony

Jefferson, eds., *Resistance through Rituals: Youth Subcultures in Post-War Britain*, 2nd ed. (New York: Routledge, 2006).

157. Oleg Kharkhordin, *The Collective and the Individual in Russia: A Study of Practices* (Berkeley: University of California Press, 1999), 279–302. Also see Oleg Kharkhordin, *Oblichat' i litsemerit': Genealogiia rossiiskoi lichnosti* (Saint Petersburg: Evropeiskii universitet v Sankt-Peterburge, 2002), 363–434.

158. Kharkhordin, *Oblichat' i litsemerit'*, 416–17.

159. For scholarship equating Komsomol management to social control, see Allen Kassof, *The Soviet Youth Program: Regimentation and Rebellion* (Cambridge: Harvard University Press, 1965), 171–86; and Ralph Talcott Fisher Jr., *Pattern for Soviet Youth: A Study of the Congresses of the Komsomol, 1918–1954* (New York: Columbia University Press, 1959), 285–86.

160. Alexei Yurchak, *Everything Was Forever, Until It Was No More: The Last Soviet Generation* (Princeton: Princeton University Press, 2006), 36–76.

161. I do not use the term "Thaw generation," as the Thaw covered a long period spanning several generations. For more on the term "Thaw generation," see Alexeyeva and Goldberg, *Thaw Generation*.

162. June Edmunds and Bryan S. Turner, eds., *Generational Consciousness, Narrative, and Politics* (New York: Rowman & Littlefield, 2002), 1–12; June Edmunds and Bryan S. Turner, *Generations, Culture and Society* (Philadelphia: Open University Press, 2002), 16–23. For more on the ties between successive cohorts and social change, see Judith Burnett, *Generations: The Time Machine in Theory and Practice* (Farnham, Surrey: Ashgate, 2010), 1–8; and Norman B. Ryder, "The Cohort as a Concept in the Study of Social Change," *American Sociological Review* 30, no. 6 (1965): 843–61. For criticism of the usefulness of the concept of generation for analysis, however, see Homi K. Bhabha, *The Location of Culture* (New York: Routledge, 1994).

CHAPTER 6. THE 1957 INTERNATIONAL YOUTH FESTIVAL AND THE BACKLASH

1. A. N. Shelepin, *Ob uluchshenii ideino-vospitatel'noi raboty komsomol'skikh organizatsii sredi molodezhi (Doklad na VII plenum TsK VLKSM 1957 g.)* (Moscow: Molodaia gvardiia, 1957), 48–49.

2. On students going beyond the permissible, see RGASPI, f. M-1, op. 32, d. 821, ll. 96–99; A. N. Shelepin, *Otchetnyi doklad Tsentral'nogo Komiteta Vsesoiuznogo leninskogo kommunisticheskogo soiuza molodezhi XIII s'ezdu komsomola (15 aprelia 1958 g.)* (Moscow: Molodaia gvardiia, 1958), 33; and Benjamin K. Tromly, "Intelligentsia Self-Fashioning in the Postwar Soviet Union: Revol't Pimenov's Political Struggle, 1949–57," *Kritika* 13, no. 1 (Winter 2012): 151–76. For more on the consequences of the Secret Speech, see Polly Jones, "From the Secret Speech to the Burial of Stalin: Real and Ideal Responses to De-Stalinization," in *The Dilemmas of De-Stalinization: Negotiating Cultural and Social Change in the Khrushchev Era*, ed. Polly Jones (New York: Routledge, 2006), 41–63; Cynthia Hooper, "What Can and Cannot Be Said: Between the Stalinist Past and New Soviet Future," *Slavonic and East European Review* 86, no. 2 (April 2008): 306–27; and V. A. Kozlov, *Mass Uprisings in the USSR: Protest and Rebellion in the Post-Stalin Years*, trans. Elaine M. MacKinnon (Armonk: M. E. Sharpe, 2002), 112–36.

3. Katya Vladimirov, "The Art of the Arcane: The June Plenum of 1957 and the Clash of Generations," *Soviet and Post-Soviet Review* 32, no. 1 (2005): 175–90.

4. Denis Kozlov, "'I Have Not Read, but I Will Say': Soviet Literary Audiences and Changing Ideas of Social Membership, 1958–66," *Kritika* 7, no. 3 (Summer 2006): 557–97; Deming Brown, *Soviet Russian Literature since Stalin* (New York: Cambridge University Press, 1978), 253–309; Emily Lygo, *Leningrad Poetry, 1953–1975: The Thaw Generation* (Bern: Peter Lang, 2010), 43.

5. Stephen V. Bittner, *The Many Lives of Khrushchev's Thaw: Experience and Memory in Moscow's Arbat* (Ithaca: Cornell University Press, 2008), 40–74.

6. Christina Ezrahi, *Swans of the Kremlin: Ballet and Power in Soviet Russia* (Pittsburgh: University of Pittsburgh Press, 2012).

7. Shelepin, *Ob uluchshenii ideino-vospitatel'noi raboty*, 7–9, 45–48.

8. RGANI, f. 5, op. 34, d. 17, ll. 41–43.

9. RGANI, f. 5, op. 30, d. 179, l. 87; "Moscow's Jet Set Rides High," *New York Times*, November 4, 1956.

10. RGANI, f. 5, op. 36, d. 46, ll. 51–56.

11. For a description of anxiety and optimism as the key drivers of Thaw-era policy, see Miriam Dobson, *Khrushchev's Cold Summer: Gulag Returnees, Crime, and the Fate of Reform after Stalin* (Ithaca: Cornell University Press, 2009), 157–58.

12. RGASPI, f. M-1, op. 3, d. 930, l. 12.

13. TsAOPIM, f. 635, op. 13, d. 484, l. 33.

14. GANISO, f. 4529, op. 12, d. 24, l. 203.

15. Shelepin, *Ob uluchshenii ideino-vospitatel'noi raboty*, 43, 48–49.

16. Liubov Baliasnaia, born 1927, interview by author, April 5, 2009.

17. On Stalin-era culturedness, see David L. Hoffmann, *Cultivating the Masses: Modern State Practices and Soviet Socialism, 1914–1939* (Ithaca: Cornell University Press, 2011), 234; Vadim Volkov, "The Concept of *Kul'turnost'*: Notes on the Stalinist Civilizing Process," in *Stalinism: New Directions*, ed. Sheila Fitzpatrick (New York: Routledge, 2000), 210–30; and Sheila Fitzpatrick, *Everyday Stalinism: Ordinary Life in Extraordinary Times; Soviet Russia in the 1930s* (New York: Oxford University Press, 1999), 75–88.

18. Michael David-Fox, *Showcasing the Great Experiment: Cultural Diplomacy and Western Visitors to the Soviet Union, 1921–1941* (New York: Oxford University Press, 2011), 1–27.

19. Nicholas J. Cull, *The Cold War and the United States Information Agency: American Propaganda and Public Diplomacy, 1945–1989* (New York: Cambridge University Press, 2008), 22–188; Kenneth Osgood, *Total Cold War: Eisenhower's Secret Propaganda Battle at Home and Abroad* (Lawrence: University Press of Kansas, 2006), 214–16; Hugh Wilford, *The Mighty Wurlitzer: How the CIA Played America* (Cambridge: Harvard University Press, 2008), 1–10; Naima Prevots, *Dance for Export: Cultural Diplomacy and the Cold War* (Hanover: Wesleyan University Press, 1998), 1–7, 69–93; Nathan D. Abrams, "Struggling for Freedom: Arthur Miller, the *Commentary* Community, and the Cultural Cold War" (PhD diss., University of Birmingham, 1998); Serge Guilbaut, *How New York Stole the Idea of Modern Art: Abstract Expressionism, Freedom, and the Cold War*, trans. Arthur Goldhammer (Chicago: University of Chicago Press, 1983), 1–15; Frances Stonor Saunders, *The Cultural Cold War: The CIA and the World of Arts and Letters* (New York: New Press, 1999), 1–6.

20. RGASPI, f. M-1, op. 3, d. 930, ll. 4–6.

21. Juliane Fürst, *Stalin's Last Generation: Soviet Youth and the Emergence of Mature Socialism, 1945–56* (New York: Oxford University Press, 2010), 16, 232–33.

22. "Ob uluchshenii ideino-vospitatel'noi raboty komsomol'skikh organizatsii sredi komsomol'tsev i molodezhi," *Zaria molodezhi*, March 1, 1957; TsAOPIM, f. 635, op. 13, d. 546, ll. 6–62; GANISO, f. 4529, op. 14, d. 2, l. 19.

23. Shelepin, *Otchetnyi doklad Tsentral'nogo Komiteta [komsomola]*, 32.

24. Josephine Woll, *Real Images: Soviet Cinema and the Thaw* (New York: I. B. Tauris, 2000); Alexander Prokhorov, "The Myth of the 'Great Family' in Marlen Khutsiev's *Lenin's Guard* and Mark Osep'ian's *Three Days of Victor Shernyshev*," in *Cinepaternity: Fathers and Sons in Soviet and Post-Soviet Film*, ed. Helena Goscilo and Yana Hashamova (Bloomington: Indiana University Press, 2010), 29–51; Aleksander Prokhorov, "The Unknown New Wave: Soviet Cinema of the Sixties," in *Springtime for Soviet Cinema: Re/Viewing the 1960s*, ed. Aleksander Prokhorov (Pittsburgh: Pittsburgh Russian Film Symposium, 2001), 7–28.

25. Margaret Peacock, "Contested Innocence: Images of the Child in the Cold War" (PhD diss., University of Texas at Austin, 2008), 125–26. Also see her book, *Cold War Kids: The Politics of Childhood in the Soviet Union and the United States, 1945–1968* (Chapel Hill: University of North Carolina Press, 2014)

26. On this and previous international youth festivals, see Pia Koivunen, "Overcoming Cold War Boundaries at the World Youth Festivals," in *Reassessing Cold War Europe*, ed. Sari Autio-Sarasmo and Katalin Miklossy (New York: Routledge, 2011), 175–92; Pia Koivunen, "The 1957 Moscow Youth Festival: Propagating a New, Peaceful Image of the Soviet Union," in *Soviet State and Society under Nikita Khrushchev*, ed. Melanie Ilič and Jeremy Smith (New York: Routledge, 2009), 46–65; Margaret Peacock, "The Perils of Building Cold War Consensus at the 1957 Moscow World Festival of Youth and Students," *Cold War History* 12, no. 1 (February 2012): 1–21; and Kristin Roth-Ey, "'Loose Girls' on the Loose: Sex, Propaganda and the 1957 Youth Festival," in *Women in the Khrushchev Era*, ed. Melanie Ilič, Susan E. Reid, and Lynne Attwood (New York: Palgrave Macmillan, 2004), 75–96. On the 1968 youth festival, see Nick Rutter, "Look Left, Drive Right: Internationalisms at the 1968 World Youth Festival," in *The Socialist Sixties: Crossing Borders in the Second World*, ed. Anne E. Gorsuch and Diane P. Koenker (Bloomington: Indiana University Press, 2013), 193–212.

27. Memorandum of Conversation: "American Youth Participation in World Festival of Youth in Moscow," January 22, 1957, File 1431(e)—Sixth World Youth Festival, Moscow, 1957, Bilateral Political Relations Subject Files, 1921–73 (A1-5345), General Records of the Department of State, 1756–1999, RG 59, NACP.

28. On the US government providing the funding for this and other supposedly independent youth associations, see Karen Paget, "From Stockholm to Leiden: The CIA's Role in the Formation of the International Student Conference," in *The Cultural Cold War in Western Europe, 1945–1960*, ed. Giles Scott-Smith and Hans Krabbendam (Portland: Frank Cass, 2003), 134–67; Joël Kotek, "Youth Organizations as a Battlefield in the Cold War," in Scott-Smith and Krabbendam, *Cultural Cold War in Western Europe*, 168–91; and Wilford, *Mighty Wurlitzer*, 123–48. More broadly on US state-private networks, see Inderjeet Parmar, "Conceptualizing the State-Private Network in American Foreign Policy," in *The US Government, Citizen Groups and the Cold War: The State-Private Network*, ed. Helen Laville and Hugh Wilford (New York: Routledge, 2006), 13–28.

29. TNA: PRO FO 371/129156 NS 2042/1, p. 2.

30. TNA: PRO FO 371/129156 NS 2042/1, p. 2. For British government financing of domestic youth organizations, see Richard Aldrich, "Putting Culture into the

Cold War: The Cultural Relations Department (CRD) and British Covert Information Warfare," in Scott-Smith and Krabbendam, *Cultural Cold War in Western Europe*, 109–38.

31. TNA: PRO FO 371/129155 NS 2041/1, pp. 2–8.

32. Memorandum of Conversation: "Proposed US Participation in Sixth International Youth Festival," February 25, 1957, File 1431(e)—Sixth World Youth Festival, Moscow, 1957, Bilateral Political Relations Subject Files, 1921–73 (A1-5345), General Records of the Department of State, 1756–1999, RG 59, NACP.

33. Review of *Komsomol'skaia pravda* article, "Barbara Gets Phone Call from USSR Paper," March 17, 1957, File 1431(e)—Sixth World Youth Festival, Moscow, 1957, Bilateral Political Relations Subject Files, 1921–73 (A1-5345), General Records of the Department of State, 1756–1999, RG 59, NACP.

34. "'Festival' pridet v Moskvu," *Komsomol'skaia pravda*, January 17, 1957. Also see *Moskovskii komsomolets*, March 10, 16, 1957.

35. GANISO, f. 4158, op. 1, op. 20, d. 625, ll. 12–13.

36. TsAGM, f. 44, op. 1, d. 50, ll. 39–40.

37. RGASPI, f. M-1, op. 32, d. 742, l. 78.

38. RGASPI, f. M-1, op. 32, d. 770, l. 24.

39. RGASPI, f. M-1, op. 32, d. 798a, l. 24.

40. "Festivaliu navstrechu," *Moskovskii komsomolets*, May 25, 1957. Also see *Komsomol'skaia pravda*, January 10, 1957; *Zaria molodezhi*, October 28, 1956; and *Moskovskii komsomolets*, May 26, 1957.

41. TsAGM, f. 1988, op. 1, d. 46, l. 14.

42. TsAGM, f. 44, op. 1, d. 55, ll. 40–41; TsAGM, f. 2987, op. 1, ll. 1–2.

43. A. S. Kozlov, *Dzhazz, rock, i mednye tuby* (Moscow: Eksmo, 2005), 113.

44. RGANI, f. 5, op. 36, d. 46, ll. 54–56.

45. TsAGM, f. 429, op. 1, d. 517, ll. 24–25.

46. TsAGM, f. 44, op. 1, d. 55, l. 43; "Ansambl' 'Romashka,'" *Komsomol'skaia pravda*, May 26, 1957; RGASPI, f. M-1, op. 32, d. 830, l. 14a.

47. TsAGM, f. 2987, op. 1, d. 58, l. 23.

48. RGASPI, f. M-1, op. 32, d. 873, ll. 105–26.

49. Lev Figlin, born 1938, interview by author, May 25, 2009.

50. For jazz at the festival, see V. B. Feiertag, *Istoriia dzhazovogo ispolnitel'stva v Rossii* (Saint Petersburg: Skifiia, 2010), 154; and S. Frederick Starr, *Red and Hot: The Fate of Jazz in the Soviet Union, 1917–1980* (New York: Oxford University Press, 1983), 248–51.

51. Kozlov, *Dzhazz, rock, i mednye tuby*, 106–7.

52. Georgii Garanian, born 1934, interview by author, February 4, 2009; Starr, *Red and Hot*, 248–51.

53. RGASPI, f. M-1, op. 32, d. 874, ll. 44–51.

54. Garanian interview; Vitalii E. Kleinot, born 1941, interview by author, February 14, 2009; A. S. Kozlov, *"Kozel na sakse": I tak vsiu zhizn'* (Moscow: Vagrius, 1998), 100–16; Starr, *Red and Hot*, 248–51.

55. William J. Risch, *The Ukrainian West: Culture and the Fate of Empire in Soviet Lviv* (Cambridge: Harvard University Press, 2011), 221–22. For more on how western-style music originating in one socialist state influenced other socialist countries, see Dean Vuletic, "Sounds Like America—Yugoslavia's Soft Power in Eastern Europe," in *Divided Dreamworlds? The Cultural Cold War in East and West*, ed. Pe-

ter Romijn, Giles Scott-Smith, and Joes Segal (Amsterdam: Amsterdam University Press, 2012), 115–32.

56. Aleksei Kuznetsov, born 1941, interview by author, February 21, 2009; Kozlov, *Dzhazz, rock, i mednye tuby*, 109–10.

57. Kleinot interview.

58. Kozlov, *Dzhazz, rock, i mednye tuby*, 109–10.

59. "Voices of America in Moscow," *New York Times*, August 11, 1957.

60. Garanian interview; "Georgii Garanian," accessed October 22, 2012, http://www.garanian.ru/biografic.html.

61. TASS, "Barbara Perry: Youth Rally Aids Peace," August 8, 1957, File 1431(e)—Sixth World Youth Festival, Moscow, 1957, Bilateral Political Relations Subject Files, 1921–73 (A1-5345), General Records of the Department of State, 1756–1999, RG 59, NACP.

62. This quote and subsequent ones come from the exchange of letters between the State Department and Charlotte Saxe, September 1957, File 1431(e)—Sixth World Youth Festival, Moscow, 1957, Bilateral Political Relations Subject Files, 1921–73 (A1-5345), General Records of the Department of State, 1756–1999, RG 59, NACP.

63. Report of a conversation with two members of the British delegation to the festival, File 1431(e)—Sixth World Youth Festival, Moscow, 1957, Bilateral Political Relations Subject Files, 1921–73 (A1-5345), General Records of the Department of State, 1756–1999, RG 59, NACP.

64. British memorandum on the festival, File 1431(e)—Sixth World Youth Festival, Moscow, 1957, Bilateral Political Relations Subject Files, 1921–73 (A1-5345), General Records of the Department of State, 1756–1999, RG 59, NACP. For more on the importance of African and Asian youth to the Soviet Union, see David C. Engerman, "The Second World's Third World," *Kritika* 12, no. 1 (Winter 2011): 183–211.

65. TsAGM, f. 2987, op. 1, d. 58, l. 35.

66. TNA: PRO FO 371/129155 NS 2041/1, pp. 2–8.

67. On the impact of cultural exchanges on Soviet citizens and on inadequate funding by western governments, see Yale Richmond, *Cultural Exchange and the Cold War: Raising the Iron Curtain* (University Park: Pennsylvania State University Press, 2003), 179–83.

68. Baliasnaia interview.

69. RGASPI, f. M-1, op. 32, d. 839, l. 26.

70. Garanian interview; Starr, *Red and Hot*, 250–51.

71. GANISO, f. 3234, op. 13, d. 96, l. 8.

72. TsAOPIM, f. 667, op. 3, d. 26, l. 58.

73. TsAGM, f. 2987, op. 1, d. 58, l. 31.

74. TsAGM, f. 2987, op. 1, d. 64, ll. 9–10.

75. RGASPI, f. M-1, op. 32, d. 1011, l. 11; "Muzykal'nyi patrul'," *Komsomol'skaia pravda*, July 1, 1960; L. Tiutikov and M. Sishigin, eds., *Sila obshchestvennogo pochina* (Moscow: Molodaia gvardiia, 1962), 29–39.

76. RGASPI, f. M-1, op. 32, d. 858, l. 137.

77. Konstantin Marvin, born 1934, interview by author, May 13, 2009.

78. Robert Hornsby, *Protest, Reform and Repression in Khrushchev's Soviet Union* (New York: Cambridge University Press, 2013), chap. 4; Dobson, *Khrushchev's Cold Summer*, 109–32.

79. Garanian interview; Iurii Zhimskii, born 1936, interview by author, May 27, 2009; Kuznetsov interview; Marvin interview; Kozlov, *Dzhazz, rock, i mednye tuby*, 127–29.

80. Shelepin, *Ob uluchshenii ideino-vospitatel'noi raboty*, 52.

81. *XX s"ezd KPSS: Stenograficheskii otchet; Ch. 1* (Moscow, 1956), 603, 606–8.

82. RGASPI, f. M-1, op. 32, d. 838, l. 131.

83. For instance, RGASPI, f. M-1, op. 32, d. 858, l. 144.

84. RGASPI, f. M-1, op. 32, d. 858, ll. 159–63.

85. Ruth Ben-Ghiat, *Fascist Modernities: Italy, 1922–1945* (Berkeley: University of California Press, 2001), 13–14.

86. Nara Dillon, "Governing Civil Society: Adapting Revolutionary Methods to Serve Post-Communist Goals," in *Mao's Invisible Hand: The Political Foundations of Adaptive Governance in China*, ed. Sebastian Heilmann and Elizabeth J. Perry (Cambridge: Harvard University Press, 2011), 138–64; Jeremi Suri, "The Rise and Fall of an International Counterculture, 1960–1975," *American Historical Review* 114, no. 1 (February 2009): 45–68; Hung Chang-tai, "A Political Park: The Working People's Cultural Palace in Beijing," *Journal of Contemporary History* 48, no. 3 (July 2013): 556–77.

87. Shelepin, *Ob uluchshenii ideino-vospitatel'noi raboty*, 48–49; "Zametiki ob esteticheskom vospitanii," *Leninskii put'*, April 13, 1957.

88. M. A. Solov'ev, *Materialy po kul'turno-prosvetitel'noi rabote* (Moscow: Sovetskaia Rossiia, 1959), 78–82.

89. RGASPI, f. M-1, op. 3, d. 967, ll. 113–14.

90. RGASPI, f. M-1, op. 32, d. 858, ll. 138–39.

91. RGASPI, f. M-1, op. 32, d. 858, ll. 139–44.

92. RGASPI, f. M-1, op. 3, d. 967, ll. 113–15; RGASPI, f. M-1, op. 32, d. 839, ll. 22–27.

93. For more on such Soviet rituals, see Christel Lane, *The Rites of Rulers: Ritual in Industrial Society—The Soviet Case* (New York: Cambridge University Press, 1981). More broadly on weddings and other rituals, see the contributions to *Contemporary Consumption Rituals: A Research Anthology*, ed. Cele C. Otnes and Tina M. Lowrey (Mahwah: Lawrence Erlbaum Associates, 2004).

94. RGASPI, f. M-1, op. 32, d. 770, l. 111; RGASPI, f. M-1, op. 32, d. 838, l. 124.

95. "U nas komsomol'skaia svad'ba," *Komsomol'skaia pravda*, July 11, 1957. On the Khrushchev antireligious campaign, see Emily B. Baran, "Faith on the Margins: Jehovah's Witnesses in the Soviet Union and Post-Soviet Russia, Ukraine, and Moldova, 1945–2010" (PhD diss., University of North Carolina at Chapel Hill, 2011), 150–73.

96. TsAOPIM, f. 635, op. 13, d. 546, l. 54.

97. On the role of performance in shaping gender norms, see Judith Butler, *Gender Trouble: Feminism and the Subversion of Identity* (New York: Routledge, 1990), x–xi; and Judith Butler, *Bodies That Matter: On the Discursive Limits of "Sex"* (New York: Routledge, 1993), 1–4.

98. RGASPI, f. M-1, op. 32, d. 943, ll. 39–42.

99. RGASPI, f. M-1, op. 32, d. 902, l. 51; RGASPI, f. M-1, op. 32, d. 946, ll. 164–70; GANISO, f. 4529, op. 14, d. 2, l. 27.

100. R. Kh. Migranov, *V pokhod za kul'turu* (Moscow: Molodaia gvardiia, 1959).

101. RGASPI, f. M-1, op. 32, d. 1011, l. 3.

102. GANISO, f. 4529, op. 14, d. 7, l. 258.

103. RGASPI, f. M-1, op. 32, d. 1011, ll. 8–9; A. Dimentman, *Kul'turu v massy: Iz opyta raboty pervykh universitetov kul'tury* (Moscow: Iskusstvo, 1960), 5; S. P. Pavlov, *Otchet Tsentral'nogo Komiteta VLKSM i zadachi komsomola, vytekaiushchie iz reshenii XXII s"ezda KPSS* (Moscow: Molodaia gvardiia, 1962), 46–47.

104. RGANI, f. 5, op. 36, d. 141, ll. 116–18.

105. N. S. Khrushchev, *Vospityvat' aktivnykh i soznatel'nykh stroitelei kommunisticheskogo obshchestva (rech' na XIII s"ezde VLKSM 18 aprelia 1958 goda)* (Moscow: Molodaia gvardiia, 1961), 35–37.

106. Shelepin, *Otchetnyi doklad Tsentral'nogo Komiteta [komsomola]*, 44–45.

107. Obshchestvo znanii (Knowledge society) was dedicated to advancing official propaganda, largely through providing lecturers and lecture materials on various topics.

108. RGASPI, f. M-1, op. 32, d. 943, ll. 72–73. For other examples of similar rhetoric, see TsAGM, f. 718, op. 1, d. 398, l. 18; and GASO, f. 2520, op. 2, d. 104, l. 58.

109. GASO, f. 2520, op. 2, d. 104, ll. 11–12.

110. *Informatsionnyi biulleten' Ministerstva kul'tury SSSR* (Moscow: Iskusstvo, 1959), 36–49.

111. GASO, f. 2520, op. 2, d. 104, ll. 11–12; Dimentman, *Kul'turu v massy*, 22–23.

112. RGASPI, f. M-1, op. 32, d. 973, l. 2.

113. V. I. Travin, *Deistvennoe sredstvo vospitaniia molodezhi* (Leningrad: LDNTP, 1968), 3–9.

114. Lynn M. Sargeant, "High Anxiety: New Venues, New Audiences, and the Fear of the Popular in Late Imperial Russian Musical Life," *19th-Century Music* 35, no. 2 (Fall 2011): 93–114.

115. Donald J. Raleigh, *Experiencing Russia's Civil War: Politics, Society, and Revolutionary Culture in Saratov, 1917–1922* (Princeton: Princeton University Press, 2002), 208–15, 231–36; Lynn M. Sargeant, *Harmony and Discord: Music and the Transformation of Russian Cultural Life* (New York: Oxford University Press, 2011), 279; *Molodezh' v rabochem klube* (Moscow: Molodaia gvardiia, 1927), 48; *Saratovskii voskresnyi universitet* (Saratov, 1928), 1–15. For a rare exception to the Stalin-era tendency to eschew entertainment in public lectures, see V. M. Abramkin, *Universitet literatury i iskusstva: Programmy, plany lektsii, bibliografiia; 1948–49 uchebnyi god* (Leningrad, 1948), 3.

116. RGASPI, f. M-1, op. 32, d. 858, l. 143; RGASPI, f. M-1, op. 3, d. 967, ll. 114–15.

117. Shelepin, *Otchetnyi doklad Tsentral'nogo Komiteta [komsomola]*, 43–44.

118. Baliasnaia interview.

119. *Informatsionnyi biulleten' Ministerstva kul'tury SSSR*, 30–50; RGALI, f. 2329, op. 10, d. 652, l. 4.

120. Dimentman, *Kul'turu v massy*, 6.

121. RGASPI, f. M-1, op. 32, d. 1011, ll. 125–26; RGALI, f. 2329, op. 10, d. 652, l. 1; RGALI, f. 2329, op. 10, d. 652, l. 37.

122. GASO, f. 2520, op. 2, d. 104, l. 24; RGALI, f. 2329, op. 10, d. 652, l. 34; RGASPI, f. M-1, op. 32, d. 943, l. 73; RGASPI, f. M-1, op. 32, d. 973, l. 2.

123. Katerina Clark, *Petersburg: Crucible of Cultural Revolution* (Cambridge: Harvard University Press, 1995), 21; Benjamin K. Tromly, "Re-Imagining the Soviet In-

telligentsia: Student Politics and University Life, 1948–1964" (PhD diss., Harvard University, 2007), 40–93.

124. TsAGM, f. 718, op. 1, d. 398, l. 64; *Klub—stroiteliam kommunizma* (Moscow: Profizdat, 1961), 184.

125. GASO, f. 2520, op. 2, d. 104, l. 25; G. G. Karpov and N. D. Sintsov, *Klubnoe delo: Uchebnoe posobie* (Moscow: Sovetskaia Rossiia, 1959), 282; Dimentman, *Kul'turu v massy*, 12.

126. RGASPI, f. M-1, op. 32, d. 973, l. 3; Karpov and Sintsov, *Klubnoe delo*, 282; *Informatsionnyi biulleten' Ministerstva kul'tury SSSR*, 34; *Klub—stroiteliam kommunizma*, 184.

127. Aleksander Vygnanov, born 1942, interview by author, February 13, 2009.

128. For more on these reforms, see Tromly, "Re-Imagining the Soviet Intelligentsia," 310–48; Laurent Coumel, "The Scientist, the Pedagogue, and the Party Official: Interest Groups, Public Opinion and Decision-Making in the 1958 Education Reform," in Ilič and Smith, *Soviet State and Society under Nikita Khrushchev*, 66–85.

129. Brian LaPierre, *Hooligans in Khrushchev's Russia: Defining, Policing, and Producing Deviance during the Thaw* (Madison: University of Wisconsin Press, 2012), 107.

130. RGASPI, f. M-1, op. 32, d. 973, l. 5.

131. RGALI, f. 2329, op. 10, d. 652, l. 38.

132. LaPierre, *Hooligans in Khrushchev's Russia*, 163.

133. Sargeant, "High Anxiety."

134. GASO, f. 2520, op. 2, d. 104, l. 13.

135. RGASPI, f. M-1, op. 32, d. 1011, l. 130.

136. RGALI, f. 2329, op. 10, d. 652, l. 38.

137. RGASPI, f. M-1, op. 32, d. 1011, ll. 11–12.

138. GASO, f. 2520, op. 2, d. 104, ll. 11–12.

139. RGASPI, f. M-1, op. 32, d. 1011, ll. 129–31.

140. TsAGM, f. 718, op. 1, d. 398, ll. 64–66.

141. TsAGM, f. 718, op. 1, d. 257, l. 55.

142. On the corn campaign, see Anatolii Strelianyi, "Khrushchev and the Countryside," in *Nikita Khrushchev*, ed. William Taubman, Sergei Khrushchev, and Abbott Gleason (New Haven: Yale University Press, 2000), 113–37.

143. RGASPI, f. M-1, op. 32, d. 973, l. 4.

144. GASO, f. 2520, op. 2, d. 104, l. 29.

145. RGASPI, f. M-1, op. 32, d. 1055, l. 9.

146. RGASPI, f. M-1, op. 32, d. 943, l. 75.

147. Dimentman, *Kul'turu v massy*, 6–7.

148. Nelli Popkova, born 1936, interview by author, May 20, 2009.

149. Iurii Sokolov, born 1940, interview by author, April 16, 2009.

150. Vygnanov interview.

151. Viktor Sobolev, born 1953, interview by author, April 29, 2009.

152. Nikolai Troitskii, born 1931, interview by author, May 22, 2009.

153. Baliasnaia interview.

154. Sari Autio-Sarasmo and Katalin Miklossy, "The Cold War from a New Perspective," in Autio-Sarasmo and Miklossy, *Reassessing Cold War Europe*, 1–15; Sari Autio-Sarasmo and Brendan Humphreys, "Cold War Interactions Reconsidered," in *Winter Kept Us Warm: Cold War Interactions Reconsidered*, ed. Sari Autio-Sarasmo and Brendan Humphreys (Helsinki: Aleksanteri Institute, 2010), 16–22.

155. This work thus helps answer the call for micro-level studies of the local impact

of the Cold War made in Jeffrey A. Engel and Katherine C. Engel, "Introduction: On Writing the Local within Diplomatic History—Trends, Historiography, Purposes," in *Local Consequences of the Global Cold War*, ed. Jeffrey A. Engel (Washington: Woodrow Wilson Center Press / Stanford: Stanford University Press, 2007), 1–32.

156. Annette Vowinckel, Marcus M. Payk, and Thomas Lindenberger, eds., *Cold War Cultures: Perspectives on Eastern and Western European Societies* (New York: Berghahn Books, 2012); Peter J. Kuznick and James Gilbert, eds., *Rethinking Cold War Culture* (Washington: Smithsonian Institution Press, 2001); Lary May, ed., *Recasting America: Culture and Politics in the Age of Cold War* (Chicago: University of Chicago Press, 1989). For how this Cold War culture played out in Hungary, see Danielle Fosler-Lussier, *Music Divided: Bartók's Legacy in Cold War Culture* (Berkeley: University of California Press, 2007).

157. On the emphasis on World War II, see Amir Weiner, *Making Sense of War: The Second World War and the Fate of the Bolshevik Revolution* (Princeton: Princeton University Press, 2001), 7–40.

158. Bruce Horner, "Discourse," in *Key Terms in Popular Music and Culture*, ed. Bruce Horner and Thomas Swiss (Malden: Blackwell, 1999), 18–34; Herbert J. Gans, *Popular Culture and High Culture: An Analysis and Evaluation of Taste* (New York: Basic Books, 1999); Frank Mort, *Cultures of Consumption: Masculinities and Social Space in Late Twentieth-Century Britain* (New York: Routledge, 1996), 1–15.

159. Ben-Ghiat, *Fascist Modernities*, 3–6.

160. Paulina Bren, *The Greengrocer and His TV: The Culture of Communism after the 1968 Prague Spring* (Ithaca: Cornell University Press, 2010), 1–10.

161. Polly Jones, "Introduction: The Dilemmas of De-Stalinization," in Jones, *Dilemmas of De-Stalinization*, 1–18.

162. For how the Khrushchev authorities pursued Cold War aims by showcasing for global audiences the Soviet population as being creative and well educated, see Vladislav Zubok, *A Failed Empire: The Soviet Union in the Cold War from Stalin to Gorbachev* (Chapel Hill: University of North Carolina Press, 2007), 164.

163. Risch, *Ukrainian West*, 181–84; Sergei Zhuk, *Rock and Roll in the Rocket City: The West, Identity, and Ideology in Soviet Dniepropetrovsk* (Baltimore: Johns Hopkins University Press, 2010), 1–17.

164. James C. Scott, *Seeing Like a State: How Certain Schemes to Improve the Human Condition Have Failed* (New Haven: Yale University Press, 1998), 1–8; Zygmunt Bauman, *Modernity and Ambivalence* (Ithaca: Cornell University Press, 1991), 11–17.

165. On global youth movements, see John Springhall, *Youth Popular Culture and Moral Panics: Penny Gaffs to Gangsta-Rap, 1830–1996* (New York: St. Martin's Press, 1998); Claire Wallace and Sijka Kovatcheva, *Youth in Society: The Construction and Deconstruction of Youth in East and West Europe* (New York: St. Martin's Press, 1998); Steven Mintz, *Huck's Raft: A History of American Childhood* (Cambridge: Harvard University Press, 2004), 310–33; Stuart Hall and Tony Jefferson, eds., *Resistance through Rituals: Youth Subcultures in Post-War Britain*, 2nd ed. (New York: Routledge, 2006); and Jeremy Varon, Michael S. Foley, and John McMillian, "Time Is an Ocean: The Past and Future of the Sixties," *Sixties* 1, no. 1 (June 2008): 1–7.

CHAPTER 7. A REFORMIST REVIVAL

1. RGASPI, f. M-1, op. 32, d. 1096, ll. 29–32.

2. TsAGM, f. 718, op. 1, d. 257, ll. 48–49.

3. Z. A. Petrova and M. P. Rymkevich, eds., *Novoe v rabote klubov* (Moscow: Sovetskaia Rossiia, 1962), 84–85.

4. Jiri Zuzanek, *Work and Leisure in the Soviet Union: A Time-Budget Analysis* (New York: Praeger, 1980), 41.

5. "Arifmetika dvukh sistem," *Komsomol'skaia pravda*, July 29, 1960.

6. TsAOPIM, f. 635, op. 14, d. 313, ll. 149–50.

7. RGASPI, f. M-1, op. 32, d. 1024, l. 79. Karpinskii served as the head of the propaganda department from July 1959 to May 1962. See A. A. Alekseeva, *Stroka v biografii* (Moscow: Molodaia gvardiia, 2003), 78.

8. TsAGM, f. 718, op. 1, d. 257, l. 26.

9. RGASPI, f. M-1, op. 32, d. 1011, ll. 4, 22.

10. "Tvoi dosug—tvoe bogatstvo," *Komsomol'skaia pravda*, August 7, 1960; "Chasy tvoego dosuga," *Komsomol'skaia pravda*, July 29, 1960; A. Komissarova, *10 vecherov molodezhi* (Moscow: Molodaia gvardiia, 1963), 5–7.

11. S. P. Pavlov, *Otchet Tsentral'nogo Komiteta VLKSM i zadachi komsomola, vytekaiushchie iz reshenii XXII s'ezda KPSS* (Moscow: Molodaia gvardiia, 1962), 47.

12. On instilling the new moral code via club activities, see Z. A. Petrova, *Resheniia XXII s'ezda KPSS pretvoriaiutsia v zhizn'* (Moscow: Sovetskaia Rossiia, 1963), 128. For more on this code and its implementation, see Deborah A. Field, *Private Life and Communist Morality in Khrushchev's Russia* (New York: Peter Lang, 2007), 9–27.

13. RGASPI, f. M-1, op. 32, d. 1011, l. 16.

14. V. E. Bondarenko, *Propaganda iskusstva v klube* (Moscow: Minkul't RSFSR, 1963), 1–6, 40–65; G. S. Frid, *Muzyka, obshchenie, sud'by: O Moskovskom molodezhnom muzykal'nom klube; Stat'i i ocherki* (Moscow: Sovremennyi Kompozitorov, 1987); TsAGM, f. 718, op. 1, d. 536, ll. 26–27; L. Tiutikov and M. Sishigin, eds., *Sila obshchestvennogo pochina* (Moscow: Molodaia gvardiia, 1962), 39–43.

15. Christine Varga-Harris, "Constructing the Soviet Hearth: Home, Citizenship and Socialism in Russia, 1956–1964" (PhD diss., University of Illinois at Urbana-Champaign, 2005), 132–86; Elena Zhidkova, "Praktiki razresheniia semeinykh konfliktov: Obrashcheniia grazhdan v obshchestvennye organizatsii i partiinye iacheiki," in *Sovetskaia sotsial'naia politika: Stseny i deistvuiushchie litsa, 1940–1985*, ed. E. R. Iarskaia-Smirnova and P. V. Romanov (Moscow: Variant, 2008), 266–89.

16. Susan E. Reid, "Happy Housewarming! Moving into Khrushchev-Era Apartments," in *Petrified Utopia: Happiness Soviet Style*, ed. Marina Balina and Evgeny Dobrenko (New York: Anthem Press, 2009), 133–60.

17. RGASPI, f. M-1, op. 32, d. 1024, l. 62; "Komsomol'skim organizatsiam po mestu zhitel'stva—byt'!," *Moskovskii komsomolets*, September 2, 1962; E. Murav'ev, *Ot vse dushi—liudiam* (Smolensk: Smolenskoe knizhnoe izdatel'stvo, 1963), 3–29.

18. RGASPI, f. M-1, op. 32, d. 1018, l. 32; TsAOPIM, f. 635, op. 13, d. 370, ll. 44–48.

19. RGASPI, f. M-1, op. 32, d. 1011, l. 22.

20. RGASPI, f. M-1, op. 67, d. 41, ll. 40–41, 44–47.

21. A. N. Shelepin, *Otchetnyi doklad Tsentral'nogo Komiteta Vsesoiuznogo leninskogo kommunisticheskogo soiuza molodezhi XIII s'ezdu komsomola (15 aprelia 1958 g.)* (Moscow: Molodaia gvardiia, 1958), 63.

22. RGASPI, f. M-1, op. 32, d. 1096, l. 7.

23. RGASPI, f. M-1, op. 32, d. 1024, l. 86.

24. Pavlov, *Otchet Tsentral'nogo Komiteta VLKSM*, 39–40.

25. Pavlov, *Otchet Tsentral'nogo Komiteta VLKSM*, 40.

26. RGASPI, f. M-1, op. 32, d. 1024, l. 87.

27. Liubov Baliasnaia, born 1927, interview by author, April 5, 2009.

28. M. A. Solov'ev, *Materialy po kul'turno-prosvetitel'noi rabote* (Moscow: Sovetskaia Rossiia, 1959), 43–45.

29. Similarly, the decree legitimated western music styles. See Peter J. Schmelz, *Such Freedom, If Only Musical: Unofficial Soviet Music during the Thaw* (New York: Oxford University Press, 2009), 26–66.

30. [Vasilii Aksenov], "Dobro pozhalovat', tovarishch Dzhaz," *Moskovskii komsomolets*, September 9, 1962. For more on youth writers, see Deming Brown, *Soviet Russian Literature since Stalin* (New York: Cambridge University Press, 1978), 180–217; Laura J. Olsen, *Performing Russia: Folk Revival and Russian Identity* (New York: RoutledgeCurzon, 2004), 35–67.

31. "Tem, kto liubit muzyku," *Leninskii put'*, March 2, 1963.

32. V. P. Aksenov, *V poiskakh grustnogo bebi: Kniga ob Amerike* (New York: Liberty Publishing House, 1987), 14.

33. V. P. Aksenov, *Sobranie sochinenii* (Moscow: Iunost', 1994), 1:195–96, 353. For a scholarly analysis of *Zvezdnyi bilet*, see Alexander Prokhorov, *Unasledovannyi diskurs: Paradigmy stalinskoi kul'tury v literature i kinematografii "ottepeli"* (Saint Petersburg: Akademecheskii proekt, 2007).

34. Liudmila Gerasimova, born in the late 1930s, interview by author, May 27, 2009.

35. A. N. Strugatskii and B. N. Strugatskii, *Ponedel'nik nachinaetsia v subbotu* (1965; repr., Moscow: Tekst, 1992), 100–101.

36. Penny M. Von Eschen, *Satchmo Blows Up the World: Jazz Ambassadors Play the Cold War* (Cambridge: Harvard University Press, 2004), 92–120; Lisa E. Davenport, *Jazz Diplomacy: Promoting America in the Cold War Era* (Jackson: University of Mississippi Press, 2009), 114–29; S. Frederick Starr, *Red and Hot: The Fate of Jazz in the Soviet Union, 1917–1980* (New York: Oxford University Press, 1983), 270–72.

37. Nicholas J. Cull, *The Cold War and the United States Information Agency: American Propaganda and Public Diplomacy, 1945–1989* (New York: Cambridge University Press, 2008), 149–70; Marsha Siefert, "From Cold War to Wary Peace: American Culture in the USSR and Russia," in *The Americanization of Europe: Culture, Diplomacy, and Anti-Americanism after 1945*, ed. Alexander Stephan (New York: Berghahn Books, 2006), 185–217; Philip M. Taylor, *British Propaganda in the Twentieth Century: Selling Democracy* (Edinburgh: Edinburgh University Press, 1999), 225–57; Susan E. Reid, "In the Name of the People: The Manege Affair Revisited," *Kritika* 6, no. 4 (Fall 2005): 673–716; Sudha Rajagopalan, *Indian Films in Soviet Cinemas: The Culture of Movie-going after Stalin* (Bloomington: Indiana University Press, 2008), 66–97.

38. Vladislav Zubok, *A Failed Empire: The Soviet Union in the Cold War from Stalin to Gorbachev* (Chapel Hill: University of North Carolina Press, 2007), 103.

39. Naima Prevots, *Dance for Export: Cultural Diplomacy and the Cold War* (Hanover: Wesleyan University Press, 1998), 69–93; Victoria Hallinan, "Cold War Cultural Exchange and the Moiseyev Dance Company: American Perception of Soviet Peoples" (PhD diss., Northeastern University, 2013).

40. "Moscow 1962," last accessed December 11, 2012, http://www.youtube.com/watch?feature=player_embedded&v=w0kb3ErhI5w.

41. David Caute, *The Dancer Defects: The Struggle for Cultural Supremacy during the Cold War* (New York: Oxford University Press, 2003), 1–17.

42. Paula A. Michaels, "Comrades in the Labor Room: The Lamaze Method of Childbirth Preparation and France's Cold War Home Front," *American Historical Review* 115, no. 4 (October 2010): 1031–60.

43. Anne E. Gorsuch, *All This Is Your World: Soviet Tourism at Home and Abroad after Stalin* (New York: Oxford University Press, 2011), 106–29. On citizen diplomacy in the United States, see the essays in Helen Laville and Hugh Wilford, eds., *The US Government, Citizen Groups and the Cold War: The State-Private Network* (New York: Routledge, 2006); and Scott Lucas, *Freedom's War: The American Crusade against the Soviet Union* (New York: New York University Press, 1999), 109–27.

44. Shawn Salmon, "Marketing Socialism: Intourist in the Late 1950s and Early 1960s," in *Turizm: The Russian and East European Tourist under Capitalism and Socialism*, ed. Anne E. Gorsuch and Diane P. Koenker (Ithaca: Cornell University Press, 2006), 187–204; Jeffrey S. Hardy, "Gulag Tourism: Khrushchev's 'Show' Prisons in the Cold War Context, 1954–59," *Russian Review* 71, no. 1 (January 2012): 49–78.

45. RGASPI, f. M-1, op. 67, d. 41; Andrei Kozovoi, "Eye to Eye with the Main Enemy: Soviet Youth Travel to the United States," *Ab Imperio* 2 (June 2011): 221–37.

46. Constantin Katsakioris, "Afrikanskie studenty v SSSR: Ucheba i politika vo vremia dekolonizatsii—shestidesiatye gody," in *Sotsial'naia istoriia: Ezhegodnik*, ed. N. L. Pushkareva (Saint Petersburg: Aleteiia, 2009), 209–30; Katsakioris, "Soviet Lessons for Arab Modernization: Soviet Educational Aid towards Arab Countries after 1956," *Journal of Modern European History* 8, no. 1 (March 2010): 85–105.

47. File R-44–60, Foreign Students in Western European, Soviet Bloc, and American Universities, 1950–59: A Statistical Analysis, Research Reports, 1960–99 (P-142), Office of Research, RG 306, NACP.

48. TNA: PRO FO 371/129155 NS 2041/1, pp. 2–3; TNA: PRO FO 371/129156 GB/460/48P, pp. 2–4.

49. TNA: PRO FO 371/129156 ER 78/613, p. 2.

50. TNA: PRO FO 371/129156 NS 2042/3, p. 3.

51. TNA: PRO FO 371/129156 Whitehall 7191/2, p. 1.

52. Giles Scott-Smith, "Building a Community around the Pax Americana: The US Government and Exchange Programs during the 1950s," in Laville and Wilford, *US Government, Citizen Groups and the Cold War*, 83–99.

53. On the Soviet leadership's desire to be acknowledged and respected as a major global power, see Zubok, *Failed Empire*, 94–122; Michael David-Fox, *Showcasing the Great Experiment: Cultural Diplomacy and Western Visitors to the Soviet Union, 1921–1941* (New York: Oxford University Press, 2011), 312–24.

54. Dean MacCannell, *The Tourist: A New Theory of the Leisure Class* (1976; repr., Berkeley: University of California Press, 1999), 1–16.

55. Michael Abeßer, "Between Cultural Opening, Nostalgia and Isolation—Soviet Debates on Jazz between 1953 and 1964," in *Jazz behind the Iron Curtain*, ed. Gertrud Pickhan and Rüdiger Ritter (Frankfurt: Peter Lang, 2010), 99–116, esp. 115.

56. Kristin Roth-Ey, *Moscow Prime Time: How the Soviet Union Built the Media Empire That Lost the Cultural Cold War* (Ithaca: Cornell University Press, 2011), 131–75; Miriam Dobson, *Khrushchev's Cold Summer: Gulag Returnees, Crime, and the Fate of Reform after Stalin* (Ithaca: Cornell University Press, 2009), 133–55.

57. TsAGM, f. 2987, op. 1, d. 81, l. 1; Susan Costanzo, "Amateur Theatres and Amateur Publics in the Russian Republic, 1958–71," *Slavonic and East European Review* 86, no. 2 (April 2008): 372–94; Susan Costanzo, "Reclaiming the Stage:

Amateur Theater-Studio Audiences in the Late Soviet Era," *Slavic Review* 57, no. 2 (Summer 1998): 398–424; A. P. Shul'pin, *Molodezhnye teatry Rossii* (Saint Petersburg: Dmitrii Bulanin, 2004).

58. Petrova and Rymkevich, *Novoe v rabote klubov*, 8.

59. TsAGM, f. 718, op. 1, d. 269, ll. 2–12.

60. TsAGM, f. 718, op. 1, d. 258, l. 20.

61. TsAGM, f. 718, op. 1, d. 262, l. 52.

62. TsAGM, f. 718, op. 1, d. 262, ll. 58–60.

63. TsAGM, f. 2987, op. 1, d. 70, l. 32.

64. TsAGM, f. 718, op. 1, d. 257, l. 26. For more on the impact of western cultural propaganda in the German Democratic Republic (East Germany), see Uta G. Poiger, *Jazz, Rock, and Rebels: Cold War Politics and American Culture in a Divided Germany* (Berkeley: University of California Press, 2000), 33–47; and Mark Fenemore, *Sex, Thugs and Rock 'n' Roll: Teenage Rebels in Cold-War East Germany* (New York: Berghahn Books, 2007), 132–83.

65. See two interviews with interest-based club activists for jazz: for E. S. Barban, "Dzhaz v epokhu Khrushcheva: 'Na kostiakh' i tol'ko na tantsakh," accessed October 22, 2012, http://news.bbc.co.uk/hi/russian/in_depth/newsid_4753000/4753692.stm; and for N. Sh. Leites, "Klub 'Kvadrat': Dzhaz-shmaz i normal'nye liudi,'" *Pchela* 11 (October–November 1997), http://www.pchela.ru/podshiv/11/jazzshmaz.htm.

66. M. I. Kull', *Stupeni Voskhozhdeniia*, accessed October 22, 2012, http://www.jazz.ru/books/kull/default.htm; Starr, *Red and Hot*, 263; A. S. Kozlov, *"Kozel na sakse": I tak vsiu zhizn'* (Moscow: Vagrius, 1998), 112–13.

67. Abram Derzhavets, born 1935, interview by author, April 28, 2009; Irina Sokol'skaia, born 1947, interview by author, November 8, 2008.

68. Iurii Sokolov, born 1940, interview by author, April 16, 2009; Viktor Sobolev, born 1953, interview by author, April 29, 2009; D. V. Gal'tsov, born 1942, interview by author, February 20, 2009.

69. Sokol'skaia interview.

70. Sarah Thornton, *Club Cultures: Music, Media and Subcultural Capital* (Hanover: Wesleyan University Press, 1996), 163–68.

71. Francheska Kurilova, born 1936, interview by author, May 15, 2009.

72. Svetlana Kovaleva, born in the mid-1930s, interview by author, March 3, 2009.

73. TsAGM, f. 718, op. 1, d. 257, ll. 56–57.

74. TsAGM, f. 718, op. 1, d. 258, l. 13.

75. RGASPI, f. M-1, op. 32, d. 1096, ll. 55–56.

76. RGASPI, f. M-1, op. 32, d. 1102, ll. 150–51.

77. William J. Risch, "Soviet 'Flower Children': Hippies and the Youth Counterculture in 1970s L'viv," *Journal of Contemporary History* 40, no. 3 (July 2005): 565–84; T. B. Shchepanskaia, "Trassa: Pipl i telegi 80kh," *Neprikosnovennyi zapas* 36, no. 4 (2004), http://magazines.russ.ru/nz/2004/4/sh7.html; B. S. Gladarev, "Zhiznennye miry 'osoboi' leningradskoi molodezhi," *Neprikosnovennyi zapas* 36, no. 4 (2004), http://magazines.russ.ru/nz/2004/4/glad6.html.

78. TsAGM, f. 718, op. 1, d. 257, ll. 30–39, 45–53; RGASPI, f. M-1, op. 34, d. 69, ll. 15–30; G. Dubrova and N. Proshchunin, *Sputnik komsomol'skogo aktivista: Spravochnaia knizhka* (Moscow: Molodaia gvardiia, 1962), 234–36.

79. For more on the Thaw-era style, see Susan E. Reid, "Cold War in the Kitchen: Gender and the De-Stalinization of Consumer Taste in the Soviet Union," *Slavic Review* 61, no. 2 (Summer 2002): 211–52.

80. TsAGM, f. 718, op. 1, d. 257, l. 32.

81. Dubrova and Proshchunin, *Sputnik komsomol'skogo aktivista*, 234.

82. "Kofe na hodu," *Moskovskii komsomolets*, May 24, 1959; Viktor Krivulin, "Nevskii do i posle velikoi kofeinoi revoliutsii," *Pchela* 6 (October 1996), http://www.pchela.ru/podshiv/6/coffee.htm; Gorsuch, *All This Is Your World*, 63.

83. RGASPI, f. M-1, op. 32, d. 1096, l. 22.

84. Dubrova and Proshchunin, *Sputnik komsomol'skogo aktivista*, 234–36; RGASPI, f. M-1, op. 34, d. 69, ll. 15. Also, see an interview with a former Voronezh café council member in "Istoriia s geografiei: Molodezhnye kafe 60-kh," accessed October 22, 2012, http://www.nestor.minsk.by/jz/articles/2000/ad/av1201.html.

85. RGASPI, f. M-1, op. 32, d. 1096, ll. 35–39.

86. Vadif Sadykhov, born 1946, interview by author, February 24, 2009.

87. Starr, *Red and Hot*, 269; RGASPI, f. M-1, op. 32, d. 1011, l. 20.

88. TsAOPIM, f. 635, op. 14, d. 329, l. 3; "Do vstrechi za stolikom," *Komsomol'skaia pravda*, May 20, 1961; Vitalii Kleinot, born 1941, interview by author, February 14, 2009; TsAGM, f. 718, op. 1, d. 257, ll. 30–39; Aleksei A. Kuznetsov, born 1941, interview by author, February 21, 2009; Starr, *Red and Hot*, 269; Krivulin, "Nevskii do i posle velikoi kofeinoi revoliutsii."

89. V. M. Ponomarev, *Na obratnoi storone zvuka* (Moscow: Agraf, 2003), 35.

90. Kozlov, *"Kozel na sakse,"* 157–58.

91. TsAGM, f. 718, op. 1, d. 257, l. 36; Kleinot interview.

92. RGASPI, f. M-1, op. 32, d. 1096, l. 39.

93. Emily Lygo, *Leningrad Poetry, 1953–1975: The Thaw Generation* (Bern: Peter Lang, 2010), 62–63. Also see Margo S. Rosen, "The Independent Turn in Soviet-Era Russian Poetry: How Dmitry Bobyshev, Joseph Brodsky, Anatoly Naiman and Evgeny Rein Became the 'Avvakumites' of Leningrad" (PhD diss., Columbia University, 2011), 116–61.

94. RGASPI, f. M-1, op. 32, d. 1096, ll. 100–101.

95. "My vypivali kazhdyi den'," *Pchela* 6 (October 1996), http://www.pchela.ru/podshiv/6/drink.htm; Krivulin, "Nevskii do i posle velikoi kofeinoi revoliutsii."

96. "Uiut, a ne roskosh'," *Komsomol'skaia pravda*, May 20, 1961.

97. For Estonia, see Gorsuch, *All This Is Your World*, 63–64. For Lithuania, see Ruth Leiserowitz, "Jazz in Soviet Lithuania—a Nonconformist Niche," in Pickhan and Ritter, *Jazz behind the Iron Curtain*, 183–90.

98. Liubov Baliasnaia interview; Konstantin Il'in, born 1944, interview by author, May 20, 2009.

99. Eckhardt Derschmidt, "The Disappearance of the Jazu-Kissa: Some Considerations about Japanese 'Jazz-Cafés' and Jazz-Listeners," in *The Culture of Japan as Seen through Its Leisure*, ed. Sepp Linhart and Savine Frühstück (Albany: State University of New York Press, 1998), 285–302; Karin Taylor, *Let's Twist Again: Youth and Leisure in Socialist Bulgaria* (Vienna: Lit, 2006), 99.

100. RGASPI, f. M-1, op. 34, d. 69, ll. 16–18.

101. RGASPI, f. M-1, op. 34, d. 69, ll. 2–16; Tiutikov and Sishigin, *Sila obshchestvennogo pochina*, 121.

102. A. S. Kozlov, *Dzhazz, rock, i mednye tuby* (Moscow: Eksmo, 2005), 155.

103. TNA: PRO FO 1110/1482 PR 171/287, pp. 12–15.

104. Kleinot interview.

105. Kozlov, *Dzhazz, rock, i mednye tuby*, 155, 159.

106. Ponomarev, *Na obratnoi storone zvuka*, 47, 35.

107. Kleinot interview.

108. Harding Ganz, born 1938, interview by author, May 10, 2012.

109. David-Fox, *Showcasing the Great Experiment*, 98–141, 175–206.

110. Dubrova and Proshchunin, *Sputnik komsomol'skogo aktivista*, 234; TsAGM, f. 718, op. 1, d. 257, ll. 46–47; Ganz interview.

111. Valerii Miliaev, born 1937, interview by author, February 28, 2009; Kleinot interview; Il'in interview.

112. Kozlov, *"Kozel na sakse,"* 157–58.

113. Sadykhov interview.

114. Mikhail Ryskin, born 1938, interview by author, June 1, 2009.

115. Georgii Garanian, born 1934, interview by author, February 4, 2009; Kleinot interview; Krivulin, "Nevskii do i posle velikoi kofeinoi revoliutsii."

116. TsAGM, f. 718, op. 1, d. 257, l. 32.

117. TsAGM, f. 718, op. 1, d. 257, ll. 47–52 (Likhodeev quote); P. L. Vail and A. A. Genis, *60-e: Mir sovetskogo cheloveka* (Ann Arbor: Ardis, 1988).

118. RGASPI, f. M-1, op. 32, d. 1096, l. 33.

119. Sadykhov interview.

120. Sadykhov interview.

121. Kozlov, *"Kozel na sakse,"* 124–25; Garanian interview.

122. Kozlov, *Dzhazz, rock, i mednye tuby*, 166–67; Kleinot interview.

123. Oleg Cherniaev, born 1946, interview by author, February 22, 2009; Lev Figlin, born 1938, interview by author, May 25, 2009.

124. TsAGM, f. 718, op. 1, d. 257, ll. 47–52. For this slogan in top-level discourse, see Pavlov, *Otchet Tsentral'nogo Komiteta VLKSM*, 40.

125. Kleinot interview.

126. Sadykhov interview.

127. RGASPI, f. M-1, op. 32, d. 1024, l. 78.

128. RGASPI, f. M-1, op. 34, d. 69, l. 22.

129. Victoria de Grazia, *Irresistible Empire: America's Advance through Twentieth-Century Europe* (Cambridge: Belknap Press of Harvard University Press, 2005), 336–75; Reinhold Wagnleitner and Elaine T. May, eds., *"Here, There and Everywhere": The Foreign Politics of American Popular Culture* (Hanover: University Press of New England, 2000); Alexander Stephan, "Cold War Alliances and the Emergence of Transatlantic Cooperation: An Introduction," in *The Americanization of Europe: Culture, Diplomacy, and Anti-Americanism after 1945*, ed. Alexander Stephan (New York: Berghahn Books, 2006), 1–20; Sabrina P. Ramet and Gordana P. Crnković, eds., *Kazaaam! Splat! Ploof! The American Impact on European Popular Culture since 1945* (New York: Rowman & Littlefield, 2003); Danielle Fosler-Lussier, "Cultural Diplomacy as Cultural Globalization: The University of Michigan Jazz Band in Latin America," *Journal of the Society for American Music* 4, no. 1 (February 2010): 59–93. For Russia in particular, see Hilary Pilkington, "Youth Strategies for Glocal Living: Space, Power and Communication in Everyday Cultural Practice," in *After Subculture: Critical Studies in Contemporary Youth Culture*, ed. Andy Bennett and Keith Kahn-Harris (New York: Palgrave Macmillan, 2004), 119–34; Catherine Evtuhov, introduction

to *The Cultural Gradient: The Transmission of Ideas in Europe, 1789–1991*, ed. Catherine Evtuhov and Stephen Kotkin (New York: Rowman & Littlefield, 2003), 1–10; Richard Kuisel, "Americanization for Historians," *Diplomatic History* 24, no. 3 (Summer 2000): 509–16; Axel Schildt and Detlef Siegfried, eds., *Between Marx and Coca-Cola: Youth Cultures in Changing European Societies, 1960–1980* (New York: Berghahn Books, 2006), 82–105; Jennifer Cole and Deborah Durham, "Introduction: Globalization and the Temporalities of Children and Youth," in *Figuring the Future: Globalization and the Temporalities of Children and Youth*, ed. Jennifer Cole and Deborah Durham (Sante Fe: School for Advanced Research Press, 2008), 3–25; Deana Campbell Robinson, Elizabeth B. Buck, Marlene Cuthbert, and the ICYI, *Music at the Margins: Popular Music and Global Cultural Diversity* (Newbury Park: SAGE Publications, 1991), 3–4; and Yves Cohen and Stephanie Lin, "Circulatory Localities: The Example of Stalinism in the 1930s," *Kritika* 11, no. 1 (Winter 2010): 11–45.

130. A rare exception is an examination of how the French state sponsored American hip-hop; see Felicia McCaren, "Monsieur Hip-Hop," in *Blackening Europe: The African American Presence*, ed. Heike Raphael-Hernandez (New York: Routledge, 2004), 157–70.

131. Vladislav M. Zubok, *Zhivago's Children: The Last Russian Intelligentsia* (Cambridge: Belknap Press of Harvard University Press, 2009), 162; L. Lur'e and I. Maliarova, *1956 god: Seredina veka* (Saint Petersburg: Neva, 2007), 3–4; L. B. Brusilovskaia, *Kul'tura povsednevnosti v epokhu "ottepeli": Metamorfozy stilia* (Moscow: Izdatel'stvo URAO, 2001), 169–74; M. R. Zezina, *Sovetskaia khudozhestvennaia intelligentsiia i vlast' v 1950-e–60-e gody* (Moscow: Dialog-MGU, 1999), 179–278; Roger D. Markwick, *Rewriting History in Soviet Russia: The Politics of Revisionist Historiography, 1956–1974* (New York: Palgrave Macmillan, 2001), 181–82; Schmelz, *Such Freedom, If Only Musical*, 179–215.

132. Zubok, *Failed Empire*, 163–91; Brusilovskaia, *Kul'tura povsednevnosti v epokhu "ottepeli*," 169–74.

133. Karl Mannheim, *Essays on the Sociology of Knowledge*, trans. and ed. Paul Kecskemeti (New York: Oxford University Press, 1952), 305–7.

134. For Russian nationalism, see N. A. Mitrokhin, *Russkaia partiia: Dvizhenie russkikh natsionalistov v SSSR, 1953–1985 gody* (Moscow: Novoe literaturnoe obozrenie, 2003), 141–79; and Yitzhak M. Brudny, *Russian Nationalism and the Soviet State, 1953–1991* (Cambridge: Harvard University Press, 1998), 8–13. On Ukrainian nationalism, see William J. Risch, *The Ukrainian West: Culture and the Fate of Empire in Soviet Lviv* (Cambridge: Harvard University Press, 2011), 170–219.

135. TsAGM, f. 718, op. 1, d. 257, ll. 78–79.

136. TsAGM, f. 718, op. 1, d. 257, ll. 62–63.

137. TsAGM, f. 718, op. 1, d. 257, l. 37.

138. "Rozy i shipy," *Moskovskii komsomolets*, March 28, 1962; TsAGM, f. 718, op. 1, d. 257, ll. 54–56.

139. TsAGM, f. 718, op. 1, d. 262, l. 7.

140. TsAGM, f. 718, op. 1, d. 258, ll. 14–15; TsAGM, f. 718, op. 1, d. 257, l. 56; TsAGM, f. 718, op. 1, d. 257, l. 35; RGASPI, f. M-1, op. 32, d. 1096, ll. 30–34.

141. "Rozy i shipy," *Moskovskii komsomolets*, May 30, 1962.

142. Valentina Shatrova, "Tot samyi 'Goluboi Ogonek,'" *Zhurnalist* 5 (May 2008): 49.

143. "Rozy i shipy," *Moskovskii komsomolets*, March 28, 1962; RGASPI, f. M-1, op. 32, d. 1096, l. 35; Il'in interview; GANISO, f. 652, op. 1, d. 4, l. 253.

144. Ana Hoffman, *Staging Socialist Femininity: Gender Politics and Folklore Performances in Serbia* (Boston: Brill, 2010), 35–65; Marta Domurat, "The Jazz Press in the People's Republic of Poland: The Role of *Jazz* and *Jazz Forum* in the Past and Today," in Pickhan and Ritter, *Jazz behind the Iron Curtain*, 117–28; Raymond Patton, "The Communist Culture Industry: The Music Business in 1980s Poland," *Journal of Contemporary History* 47, no. 2 (April 2012): 427–49.

145. Reinhold Wagnleitner, *Coca-Colonization and the Cold War: The Cultural Mission of the United States in Austria after the Second World War*, trans. Diana M. Wolf (Chapel Hill: University of North Carolina Press, 1994), 166–221; Angela Lopez, "Youth in the 1990s and Youth in the 1960s in Spain: Intergenerational Dialogue and Struggle," in *Generational Consciousness, Narrative, and Politics*, ed. June Edmunds and Bryan S. Turner (New York: Rowman & Littlefield, 2002), 111–31; Michael Brake, *Comparative Youth Culture: The Sociology of Youth Cultures and Youth Subcultures in America, Britain, and Canada* (New York: Routledge, 1985), 83–115.

146. Jeremy Varon, Michael S. Foley, and John McMillian, "Time Is an Ocean: The Past and Future of the 1960s," *The 1960s* 1, no. 1 (June 2008): 1–7.

147. For scholarship on the Soviet sixties, see Anne E. Gorsuch and Diane P. Koenker, eds., *The Socialist Sixties: Crossing Borders in the Second World* (Bloomington: Indiana University Press, 2013), esp. 1–24. For an earlier work that treats the Soviet sixties as a distinct period, see Vail and Genis, *60-e*.

148. Samuel H. Baron, *Bloody Saturday in the Soviet Union: Novocherkassk, 1962* (Stanford: Stanford University Press, 2002).

149. Aleksandr Fursenko and Timothy Naftali, *Khrushchev's Cold War: The Inside Story of an American Adversary* (New York: Norton, 2006), 469–528; Aleksandr Fursenko and Timothy J. Naftali, *One Hell of a Gamble: Khrushchev, Castro, and Kennedy, 1958–1964* (New York: Norton, 1997), 240–89; Zubok, *Failed Empire*, 123–91; Odd A. Westad, *The Global Cold War: Third World Interventions and the Making of Our Times* (New York: Cambridge University Press, 2005), 160–70.

150. Zubok, *Zhivago's Children*, 193–225; Stephen V. Bittner, *The Many Lives of Khrushchev's Thaw: Experience and Memory in Moscow's Arbat* (Ithaca: Cornell University Press, 2008), 44; Reid, "In the Name of the People"; Zezina, *Sovetskaia khudozhestvennaia intelligentsiia i vlast'*, 294–321.

151. Lygo, *Leningrad Poetry*, 74–81; Brown, *Soviet Russian Literature since Stalin*, 253–309; Josephine Woll, *Real Images: Soviet Cinema and the Thaw* (New York: I. B. Tauris, 2000), 101–60.

152. Sheila Fitzpatrick, "Social Parasites: How Tramps, Idle Youth, and Busy Entrepreneurs Impeded the Soviet March to Communism," *Cahiers du Monde russe* 47, no. 1–2 (2006): 377–408; Dobson, *Khrushchev's Cold Summer*, 189–214; Leon Lipson, "Hosts and Pests: The Fight against Parasites," in *The Soviet Political System: A Book of Readings*, ed. Richard Cornell (Englewood Cliffs: Prentice Hall, 1970), 323–33.

153. Starr, *Red and Hot*, 273–75.

154. S. P. Pavlov, *Ob itogakh iun'skogo Plenuma TsK KPSS "Ocherednye zadachi ideologicheskoi raboty partii" i roli komsomol'skikh organizatsii v vospitanii sovetskoi molodezhi na sovremennom etape stroitel'stva kommunizma: Doklad pervogo sekretaria TsK VLKSM tov. Pavlova S. P. na III plenume TsK VLKSM 9 iulia 1963 g.* (Moscow: Molodaia gvardiia, 1963), 43–44.

155. RGASPI, f. M-1, op. 32, d. 1055, l. 13.

156. "Dzhaz i molitvennyi ekstaz," *Moskovskii komsomolets*, October 1, 1963.

157. "Klub 'Kvadrat': Dzhaz-shmaz i normal'nye liudi,'" *Pchela* 11 (October–November 1997), http://www.pchela.ru/podshiv/11/jazzshmaz.htm; Kull', *Stupeni Voskhozhdeniia*.

158. Starr, *Red and Hot*, 275.

159. RGASPI, f. M-1, op. 32, d. 1055, ll. 135–37.

160. TsAOPIM, f. 635, op. 15, d. 188, l. 50.

161. TsAGM, f. 429, op. 1, d. 803a, ll. 6–17, 44.

162. Viktor Toporov, "My vypivali kazhdyi den'," *Pchela* 6 (October 1996), http://www.pchela.ru/podshiv/6/drink.htm.

163. TsAGM, f. 718, op. 1, d. 406, l. 44; TsAGM, f. 718, op. 1, d. 398, l. 20.

164. Pavlov, *Ob itogakh iun'skogo Plenuma TsK KPSS*, 33–41.

165. TsAOPIM, f. 635, op. 15, d. 188, l. 56; TsAOPIM, f. 667, op. 4, d. 1, l. 31; *Zapiska otdelov komsomol'skikh organov TsK VLKSM ob itogakh otchetov i vyborov v komsomole* (Moscow: Molodaia gvardiia, 1964), 7–8.

166. Garanian interview. Also see Sadykhov interview; Kuznetsov interview; and Kleinot interview.

167. Zubok, *Zhivago's Children*, 193–225; Zezina, *Sovetskaia khudozhestvennaia intelligentsiia i vlast'*, 294–321.

168. For more on how the tolerant atmosphere of the Thaw played a key role in the emergence of Gorbachev's reforms, see Zubok, *Failed Empire*, 163–91; and Robert D. English, *Russia and the Idea of the West: Gorbachev, Intellectuals, and the End of the Cold War* (New York: Columbia University Press, 2000), 49–81, 193–228.

169. Also deserving research is the question of how various groups in western countries sought to undermine Soviet external and domestic cultural diplomacy. For instance, some members of Soviet diaspora communities tried to subvert the Soviet Union's cultural diplomacy by boycotting performances by the Bol'shogo teatra ballet company. William J. Risch, personal communication, December 21, 2012.

170. On the undermining of this consensus, see Geraint Hughes and Saki R. Dockrill, "Introduction: The Cold War as History," in *Palgrave Advances in Cold War History*, ed. Saki R. Dockrill and Geraint Hughes (New York: Palgrave Macmillan, 2006), 1–18. Regarding youth in particular, see Jeremi Suri, "The Rise and Fall of an International Counterculture, 1960–1975," *American Historical Review* 114, no. 1 (February 2009): 45–68.

171. Alexei Yurchak, *Everything Was Forever, Until It Was No More: The Last Soviet Generation* (Princeton: Princeton University Press, 2006), 158–206.

172. For example, see Walter L. Hixson, *Parting the Curtain: Propaganda, Culture, and the Cold War* (New York: St. Martin's Press, 1997), 215–28; and Reinhold Wagnleitner, "The Empire of Fun, or Talkin' Soviet Union Blues: The Sound of Freedom and U.S. Cultural Hegemony in Europe," *Diplomatic History* 23, no. 3 (Summer 1999): 499–524. For more criticism of such accounts, see Gorsuch, *All This Is Your World*, 169.

CHAPTER 8. AMBIGUITY AND BACKLASH

1. RGASPI, f. M-1, op. 34, d. 146, ll. 1–5.

2. For examples of historians relying on the concept of "stagnation," see Thomas C. Wolfe, *Governing Soviet Journalism: The Press and the Socialist Person after Stalin* (Bloomington: Indiana University Press, 2005), 71–142; Roger D. Markwick, *Rewriting History in Soviet Russia: The Politics of Revisionist Historiography, 1956–1974* (New

York: Palgrave Macmillan, 2001), 199–247; V. A. Kozlov, *Mass Uprisings in the USSR: Protest and Rebellion in the Post-Stalin Years*, trans. and ed. Elaine M. MacKinnon (Armonk: M. E. Sharpe, 2002), 303; and Mark Slobin, ed., *Retuning Culture: Musical Changes in Central and Eastern Europe* (Durham: Duke University Press, 1996), 1–13.

3. For recent criticisms of this paradigm, see Neringa Klumbyte and Gulnaz Sharafutdinova, "Introduction: What Was Late Socialism?," in *Soviet Society in the Era of Late Socialism, 1964–1985*, ed. Neringa Klumbyte and Gulnaz Sharafutdinova (Lanham: Lexington Books, 2012), 1–14; and Edwin Bacon, "Reconsidering Brezhnev," in *Brezhnev Reconsidered*, ed. Edwin Bacon and Mark Sandle (New York: Palgrave Macmillan, 2002), 1–21. On the cultural sphere more specifically, see Tony Shaw and Denise J. Youngblood, *Cinematic Cold War: The American and Soviet Struggle for Hearts and Minds* (Lawrence: University Press of Kansas, 2010), 159–214; and Kristin Roth-Ey, *Moscow Prime Time: How the Soviet Union Built the Media Empire That Lost the Cultural Cold War* (Ithaca: Cornell University Press, 2011), 176–280.

4. William Taubman, *Khrushchev: The Man and His Era* (New York: Norton, 2003), 3–17, 620–46; Ian D. Thatcher, "Brezhnev as Leader," in Bacon and Sandle, *Brezhnev Reconsidered*, 22–37; N. A. Mitrokhin, *Russkaia partiia: Dvizhenie russkikh natsionalistov v SSSR, 1953–1985 gody* (Moscow: Novoe literaturnoe obozrenie, 2003), 338–56.

5. Iu. V. Aksiutin, *Khrushchevskaia "Ottepel'" i obshchestvennye nastroeniia v SSSR v 1953–1964 gg.* (Moscow: ROSSPEN, 2004), chap. 4.

6. Vladislav Zubok, *Zhivago's Children: The Last Russian Intelligentsia* (Cambridge: Belknap Press of Harvard University Press, 2009), 259–96; P. L. Vail and A. A. Genis, *60-e: Mir sovetskogo cheloveka* (Ann Arbor: Ardis, 1988), 190–207.

7. On the literary field, see Emily Lygo, *Leningrad Poetry, 1953–1975: The Thaw Generation* (Bern: Peter Lang, 2010), 83–89, 94–95; Deming Brown, *Soviet Russian Literature since Stalin* (New York: Cambridge University Press, 1978), 331–52; and Denis Kozlov, "'I Have Not Read, but I Will Say': Soviet Literary Audiences and Changing Ideas of Social Membership, 1958–66," *Kritika* 7, no. 3 (Summer 2006): 557–97.

8. Zubok, *Zhivago's Children*, 259–96; Josephine Woll, *Real Images: Soviet Cinema and the Thaw* (New York: I. B. Tauris, 2000), 161–98; Peter J. Schmelz, *Such Freedom, If Only Musical: Unofficial Soviet Music during the Thaw* (New York: Oxford University Press, 2009), 199–214; Richard Taruskin, *On Russian Music* (Berkeley: University of California Press, 2009), 299–321.

9. *XV s'ezd vsesoiuznogo leninskogo kommunisticheskogo soiuza molodezhi (17–21 maia 1966 goda): Stenograficheskii otchet* (Moscow: Molodaia gvardiia, 1966), 29.

10. TsAOPIM, f. 635, op. 17, d. 50, l. 51.

11. For more on individual apartments and leisure activities in the early post-Khrushchev years, see Steven E. Harris, "'I Know All the Secrets of My Neighbors': The Quest for Privacy in the Era of the Separate Apartment," in *Borders of Socialism: Private Spheres of Soviet Russia*, ed. Lewis H. Siegelbaum (New York: Palgrave Macmillan, 2006), 171–90.

12. Nina Tumarkin, *The Living and the Dead: The Rise and Fall of the Cult of World War II in Russia* (New York: Basic Books, 1994), 95–157; Mark Edele, *Soviet Veterans of the Second World War: A Popular Movement in an Authoritarian Society, 1941–1991* (New York: Oxford University Press, 2008), 129–52; Scott W. Palmer, "How Memory Was Made: The Construction of the Memorial to the Heroes of the Battle of Stalingrad," *Russian Review* 68, no. 3 (July 2009): 373–407; Elena Prokhorova, "Mend-

ing the Rupture: The War Trope and the Return of the Imperial Father in 1970s Cinema," in *Cinepaternity: Fathers and Sons in Soviet and Post-Soviet Film*, ed. Helena Goscilo and Yana Hashamova (Bloomington: Indiana University Press, 2010), 51–69.

13. RGASPI, f. M-1, op. 67, d. 146, ll. 16–25; RGASPI, f. M-1, op. 3, d. 137, ll. 16–17; *XV s'ezd vsesoiuznogo leninskogo kommunisticheskogo soiuza molodezhi*, 28, 53–55; V. K. Krivoruchenko, *XIV–XVI s'ezdy VLKSM* (Moscow: Molodaia gvardiia, 1989), 121–27; GANISO, f. 4529, op. 15, d. 7, ll. 59–60; TsAOPIM, f. 635, op. 17, d. 50, ll. 49–51.

14. S. P. Pavlov, *Ob itogakh iun'skogo Plenuma TsK KPSS "Ocherednye zadachi ideo-logicheskoi raboty partii" i roli komsomol'skikh organizatsii v vospitanii sovetskoi molodezhi na sovremennom etape stroitel'stva kommunizma: Doklad pervogo sekretaria TsK VLKSM tov. Pavlova S. P. na III plenume TsK VLKSM 9 iulia 1963 g.* (Moscow: Molodaia gvardiia, 1963), 52.

15. RGASPI, f. M-1, op. 34, d. 121, ll. 2–7.

16. *XVI s'ezd Vsesoiuznogo Leninskogo Kommunisticheskogo Soiuza Molodezhi: Stenograficheskii otchet* (Moscow: Molodaia gvardiia, 1971), 56; Krivoruchenko, *XIV–XVI s'ezdy VLKSM*, 134–35; S. P. Pavlov, *Otchet Tsentral'nogo Komiteta VLKSM i zadachi komsomola, vytekaiushchie iz reshenii XXII s'ezda KPSS* (Moscow: Molodaia gvardiia, 1962), 51; A. N. Shelepin, *Otchetnyi doklad TsK VLKSM XII s'ezdu komso-mola* (Moscow: Molodaia gvardiia, 1954), 46.

17. Frederick Starr, *Red and Hot: The Fate of Jazz in the Soviet Union, 1917–1980* (New York: Oxford University Press, 1983), 275–77.

18. N. Sh. Leites, interview in "Klub 'Kvadrat': Dzhaz-shmaz i normal'nye liudi,'" *Pchela* 11 (October–November 1997), http://www.pchela.ru/podshiv/11/jazzshmaz .htm.

19. RGASPI, f. M-1, op. 34, d. 69, l. 2.

20. Oleg Cherniaev, born 1946, interview by author, February 22, 2009; TsAOP-IM, f. 6083, op. 1, d. 109, l. 231; GANISO, f. 652, op. 1, d. 31, ll. 27–28.

21. William J. Risch, *The Ukrainian West: Culture and the Fate of Empire in So-viet Lviv* (Cambridge: Harvard University Press, 2011), 226–32; Sergei Zhuk, *Rock and Roll in the Rocket City: The West, Identity, and Ideology in Soviet Dniepropetrovsk, 1960–1985* (Baltimore: Johns Hopkins University Press, 2010), 65–106; Artemy Troitskii, *Back in the USSR: The True Story of Rock in Russia* (Winchester: Faber and Faber, 1988), 21–28. For more on Soviet rock and roll, see Yngvar B. Steinholt, *Rock in the Reservation: Songs from the Leningrad Rock Club, 1981–86* (New York: MMMSP, 2005); Timothy W. Ryback, *Rock around the Bloc: A History of Rock Music in Eastern Europe and the Soviet Union* (New York: Oxford University Press, 1990), 50–65; and Thomas Cushman, *Notes from Underground: Rock Music Counterculture in Russia* (Albany: State University of New York Press, 1995), 17–88; Mark Fenemore, *Sex, Thugs and Rock 'n' Roll: Teenage Rebels in Cold-War East Germany* (New York: Berghahn Books, 2007); Uta G. Poiger, *Jazz, Rock, and Rebels: Cold War Politics and Ameri-can Culture in a Divided Germany* (Berkeley: University of California Press, 2000), 168–205; Sabrina P. Ramet, "Shake, Rattle, and Self-Management: Rock Music and Politics in Socialist Yugoslavia, and After," in *Kazaaam! Splat! Ploof! The American Impact on European Popular Culture since 1945*, ed. Sabrina P. Ramet and Gordana P. Crnković (New York: Rowman & Littlefield, 2003), 173–97; Vladimir Trendafilov, "The Formation of Bulgarian Countercultures: Rock Music, Socialism, and After," *East Central Europe* 2–3, no. 38 (2011): 238–54; and Caius Dobrescu, "The Phoenix

That Could Not Rise: Politics and Rock Culture in Romania, 1960–1989," *East Central Europe* 2–3, no. 38 (2011): 255–90.

22. Pavlov, *Ob itogakh iun'skogo Plenuma TsK KPSS*, 43–44; "Tem, kto liubit muzyku," *Leninskii put'*, March 2, 1963.

23. L. K. Bubennikova, "VIA i rok-gruppy," in *Samodeiatel'noe khudozhestvennoe tvorchestvo v SSSR: Ocherki istorii, konets 1950-kh–nachalo 1990-kh godov*, ed. K. G. Bogemskaia (Saint Petersburg: Dmitrii Bulanin, 1999), 79–104; David MacFadyen, *Red Stars: Personality and the Soviet Popular Song, 1955–1991* (Ithaca: McGill-Queen's University Press, 2001), 147–48.

24. Zhuk, *Rock and Roll in the Rocket City*, 79–94; Risch, *Ukrainian West*, 223–32.

25. B. D. Vishnevkin, born 1952, interview by author, July 30, 2012.

26. Tiit Lauk, "Estonian Jazz before and behind the 'Iron Curtain,'" in *Jazz behind the Iron Curtain*, ed. Gertrud Pickhan and Rüdiger Ritter (Frankfurt: Peter Lang, 2010), 153–64; V. B. Feiertag, *Istoriia dzhazovogo ispolnitel'stva v Rossii* (Saint Petersburg: Skifiia, 2010), 164.

27. A. S. Kozlov, *Dzhazz, rock, i mednye tuby* (Moscow: Eksmo, 2005), 171–72.

28. Feiertag, *Istoriia dzhazovogo ispolnitel'stva v Rossii*, 158–63; Starr, *Red and Hot*, 261–88.

29. Vitalii Kleinot, born 1941, interview by author, February 14, 2009; Kozlov, *Dzhazz, rock, i mednye tuby*, 186.

30. Kleinot interview; Viktor Dubiler, born 1941, interview by author, February 22, 2009.

31. Leites interview in "Klub 'Kvadrat.'"

32. Georgii Garanian, born 1934, interview by author, February 4, 2009.

33. Cherniaev interview; Dubiler interview.

34. Kleinot interview; Cherniaev interview; Dubiler interview.

35. Nikolai Butov, born 1944, interview by author, February 16, 2009.

36. Aleksei Kuznetsov, born 1941, interview by author, February 21, 2009.

37. M. I. Kull', *Stupeni voskhozhdeniia*, accessed October 22, 2012, http://www.jazz.ru/books/kull/default.htm.

38. Kleinot interview.

39. Lev Figlin, born 1938, interview by author, May 25, 2009.

40. Cherniaev interview.

41. Kuznetsov interview.

42. Dubiler interview; Cherniaev interview.

43. Vadif Sadykhov, born 1946, interview by author, February 24, 2009.

44. Dubiler interview.

45. For the increasing corruption in cultural activities of the 1970s and 1980s, see Zhuk, *Rock and Roll in the Rocket City*, 215–38; and Christopher J. Ward, *Brezhnev's Folly: The Building of BAM and Late Soviet Socialism* (Pittsburgh: University of Pittsburgh Press, 2009), 42–68.

46. Steven L. Solnick, *Stealing the State: Control and Collapse in Soviet Institutions* (Cambridge: Harvard University Press, 1998), 42–124; Alena V. Ledeneva, *Russia's Economy of Favours: Blat, Networking, and Informal Exchange* (New York: Cambridge University Press, 1998), 139–74; William A. Clark, *Crime and Punishment in Soviet Officialdom: Combating Corruption in the Political Elite, 1965–1990* (Armonk: M. E. Sharpe, 1993), 71–99.

47. Dubiler interview; Cherniaev interview.

48. Dubiler interview; Sadykhov interview; V. M. Ponomarev, *Na obratnoi storone zvuka* (Moscow: Agraf, 2003), 49.

49. Dubiler interview.

50. Cherniaev interview.

51. Ponomarev, *Na obratnoi storone zvuka*, 51–53.

52. "Charles Lloyd in Russia: Ovations and Frustrations," *Down Beat*, July 13, 1967; Ponomarev, *Na obratnoi storone zvuka*, 53–56.

53. Kozlov, *Dzhazz, rock, i mednye tuby*, 201–4.

54. Kozlov, *Dzhazz, rock, i mednye tuby*, 220–23; Harvey G. Cohen, "Visions of Freedom: Duke Ellington in the Soviet Union," *Popular Music* 30, no. 3 (October 2011): 297–318.

55. Feiertag, *Istoriia dzhazovogo ispolnitel'stva v Rossii*, 164.

56. Dubiler interview. For more on Polish jazz journals, see Marta Domurat, "The Jazz Press in the People's Republic of Poland: The Role of *Jazz* and *Jazz Forum* in the Past and Today," in Pickhan and Ritter, *Jazz behind the Iron Curtain*, 117–28.

57. Cherniaev interview.

58. Kozlov, *Dzhazz, rock, i mednye tuby*, 173–85 (quote, 178); Kleinot interview.

59. Kozlov, *Dzhazz, rock, i mednye tuby*, 193–95; Garanian interview.

60. Kuznetsov interview.

61. Cherniaev interview.

62. Penny M. Von Eschen, *Satchmo Blows Up the World: Jazz Ambassadors Play the Cold War* (Cambridge: Harvard University Press, 2004), 92–120; Lisa E. Davenport, *Jazz Diplomacy: Promoting America in the Cold War Era* (Jackson: University Press of Mississippi, 2009), 114–29; Danielle Fosler-Lussier, "Cultural Diplomacy as Cultural Globalization: The University of Michigan Jazz Band in Latin America," *Journal of the Society for American Music* 4, no. 1 (February 2010): 59–93.

63. Ponomarev, *Na obratnoi storone zvuka*, 51–53.

64. "Charles Lloyd in Russia: Ovations and Frustrations," *Down Beat*, July 13, 1967.

65. Kozlov, *Dzhazz, rock, i mednye tuby*, 181.

66. Kleinot interview.

67. Kozlov, *Dzhazz, rock, i mednye tuby*, 184.

68. "Charles Lloyd in Russia: Ovations and Frustrations," *Down Beat*, July 13, 1967.

69. Department of State Report on Exchanges with the Soviet Union and Eastern Europe, No. 29, 1967, p. 12, Reports on Exchanges with the Soviet Union and Eastern Europe, 1960–70 (P-183), Office of Research and Assessment/Office of the Historian, RG 306, NACP.

70. Kleinot interview.

71. RGASPI, f. M-1, op. 34, d. 146, ll. 4–5.

72. "Charles Lloyd in Russia: Ovations and Frustrations," *Down Beat*, July 13, 1967.

73. Julie Hessler, "Death of an African Student in Moscow: Race, Politics, and the Cold War," *Cahiers du Monde russe* 47, no. 1–2 (January–June 2006): 33–64.

74. Kozlov, *Dzhazz, rock, i mednye tuby*, 204–7.

75. Sadykhov interview; Kleinot interview.

76. File SOC 16, Youth, Youth Problems, Bilateral Political Relations Subject Files, 1921–73 (A1-5345), General Records of the Department of State, 1756–1999,

RG 59, NACP.

77. File M-240-66, The Soviet Youth Problem, Research Memoranda, 1963–99 (P-64), Office of Research and Media Reaction, RG 306, NACP.

78. File M-7-24-85, Western Popular Culture and Soviet Youth: A Case Study of the "Muslim" Regions, Research Memoranda, 1963–99 (P-64), Office of Research and Media Reaction, RG 306, NACP.

79. Sadykhov interview.

80. Garanian interview.

81. See the memoirs of Andrei Tovmasian, "Vospominaniia," *Jazz.ru*, no. 161–62 (May 2002), http://www.jazz.ru/mag/162/tovmasian.htm.

82. Dubiler interview.

83. Sari Autio-Sarasmo and Katalin Miklossy, "The Cold War from a New Perspective," in *Reassessing Cold War Europe*, ed. Sari Autio-Sarasmo and Katalin Miklossy (New York: Routledge, 2011), 1–15.

84. Barbara Walker, "The Moscow Correspondents, Soviet Human Rights Activists, and the Problem of the Western Gift," in *Americans Experience Russia: Encountering the Enigma, 1917 to the Present*, ed. Choi Chatterjee and Beth Holmgren (New York: Routledge, 2013), 139–60.

85. MacFadyen, *Red Stars*, 148, 217.

86. Kiril Tomoff, "A Pivotal Turn: Prague Spring 1948 and the Soviet Construction of a Cultural Sphere," in *Nylon Curtain: Transnational and Transsystemic Tendencies in the Cultural Life of State-Socialist Russia and East-Central Europe*, ed. György Péteri (Trondheim: Trondheim Studies on East European Cultures & Societies, 2006), 54–80; Danielle Fosler-Lussier, "'Multiplication by Negative One': Musical Values in East-West Engagement," in Péteri, *Nylon Curtain*, 14–32.

87. Garanian interview.

88. Kuznetsov interview.

89. Pia Koivunen, "Overcoming Cold War Boundaries at the World Youth Festivals," in Autio-Sarasmo and Miklossy, *Reassessing Cold War Europe*, 175–92.

90. Polly McMichael, "The Boundaries of Soviet Rock Culture: Mashina vremeni and Roskontsert," paper presented at the Association for Slavic, East European, and Eurasian Studies national convention, Washington, DC, November 2011; Trendafilov, "Formation of Bulgarian Countercultures."

91. Iurii Zhimskii, born 1936, interview by author, May 27, 200; Figlin interview.

92. Even the fact that Zubok focuses on the experience of the intelligentsia does not explain the term "creeping Stalinization," since jazz musicians deserve to be counted among the ranks of the intelligentsia. See Zubok, *Zhivago's Children*, 259–96. For a perspective similar to Zubok's, see M. R. Zezina, *Sovetskaia khudozhestvennaia intelligentsiia i vlast' v 1950-e–60-e gody* (Moscow: Dialog-MGU, 1999), 329–51.

93. *XV s'ezd vsesoiuznogo leninskogo kommunisticheskogo soiuza molodezhi*, 23; Krivoruchenko, *XIV–XVI s'ezdy VLKSM*, 16.

94. *XV s'ezd vsesoiuznogo leninskogo kommunisticheskogo soiuza molodezhi*, 52, 79–80, 89–90.

95. GANISO, f. 4529, op. 15, d. 7, ll. 52–71; GANISO, f. 4529, op. 17, d. 1, ll. 192–200.

96. TsAOPIM, f. 667, d. 75, l. 38; "Grazhdaninom byt' obiazan . . . ," *Leninskii put'*, June 12, 1965.

97. GANISO, f. 4529, op. 17, d. 1, l. 197.

98. RGASPI, f. M-1, op. 34, d. 141, l. 95; Krivoruchenko, *XIV–XVI s'ezdy VLKSM*, 139.

99. *XV s'ezd vsesoiuznogo leninskogo kommunisticheskogo soiuza molodezhi*, 43–44.

100. Pavlov, *Ob itogakh iun'skogo Plenuma TsK KPSS*, 32; RGASPI, f. M-1, op. 67, d. 62, l. 133.

101. Mikhail Ryskin, born 1938, interview by author, June 1, 2009.

102. TsAOPIM, f. 6083, op. 1, d. 109, l. 201. Also see Rachel S. Platonov, *Singing the Self: Guitar Poetry, Community, and Identity in the Post-Stalin Period* (Evanston: Northwestern University Press, 2012), 77–78.

103. Aleksander Vygnanov, born 1942, interview by author, February 13, 2009.

104. RGASPI, f. M-1, op. 34, d. 141, ll. 95–101.

105. RGASPI, f. M-1, op. 3, d. 127, ll. 139–42.

106. Krivoruchenko, *XIV–XVI s'ezdy VLKSM*, 139.

107. Ryskin interview.

108. Nelli Popkova, born 1936, interview by author, May 20, 2009.

109. Volodia Gertsik, born 1946, interview by author, November 10, 2008. For a sample of his poetry, see Volodia Gertsik, at Russkaia virtual'naia biblioteka, accessed October 22, 2012, http://www.rvb.ru/np/publication/01text/35/06gertsyk.htm.

110. Ann Komaromi, "Samizdat and Soviet Dissident Publics," *Slavic Review* 71, no. 1 (Spring 2012): 70–90; Lygo, *Leningrad Poetry*, 86–95, 120–21.

111. Iurii Gaponov, born 1934, interview by author, April 28, 2009.

112. Gertsik interview; Gaponov interview; S. K. Kovaleva, *Ty pomnish' fizfak? Neformal'nye traditsii fizfaka MGU* (Moscow: Pomatur, 2003), 98.

113. Sergei Semenov, born 1948, interview by author, March 18, 2009.

114. Steven Mintz, *Huck's Raft: A History of American Childhood* (Cambridge: Harvard University Press, 2004), 310–34; John R. Gillis, *Youth and History: Tradition and Change in European Age Relations, 1770–Present* (New York: Academic Press, 1981), 185–210; Jeremy Varon, Michael S. Foley, and John McMillian, "Time Is an Ocean: The Past and Future of the Sixties" *Sixties* 1, no. 1 (June 2008): 1–7; Axel Schildt and Detlef Siegfried, "Youth, Consumption, and Politics in the Age of Radical Change," in *Between Marx and Coca-Cola: Youth Cultures in Changing European Societies, 1960–1980*, ed. Axel Schildt and Detlef Siegfried (New York: Berghahn Books, 2006), 1–38; William Marotti, "Japan 1968: The Performance of Violence and the Theater of Protest," *American Historical Review* 114, no. 1 (February 2009): 97–135; Timothy Brown, "'1968' East and West: Divided Germany as a Case Study in Transnational History," *American Historical Review* 114, no. 1 (February 2009): 69–96; Gerd-Rainer Horn, *The Spirit of '68: Rebellion in Western Europe and North America, 1956–1976* (New York: Oxford University Press, 2007).

115. Jeremi Suri, *Power and Protest: Global Revolution and the Rise of Détente* (Cambridge: Harvard University Press, 2003), 1–5, 216–59.

116. Ted Hopf, *Social Construction of International Politics: Identities & Foreign Policies, Moscow, 1955 and 1999* (Ithaca: Cornell University Press, 2002), 39–82, 183–51.

117. Zubok, *Zhivago's Children*, 259–96; Vail and Genis, *60-e*, 310–23.

118. For more on the invasion, see Vladislav Zubok, *A Failed Empire: The Soviet Union in the Cold War from Stalin to Gorbachev* (Chapel Hill: University of North Carolina Press, 2007), 192–226; Mike Bowker, "Brezhnev and Superpower Relations," in Bacon and Sandle, *Brezhnev Reconsidered*, 90–109; and Mitchell Lerner, "'Trying to

Find the Guy Who Invited Them': Lyndon Johnson, Bridge Building, and the End of the Prague Spring," *Diplomatic History* 32, no. 1 (January 2008): 77–103.

119. *XVI s'ezd vsesoiuznogo leninskogo kommunisticheskogo soiuza molodezhi*, 39, 56–61. On Tiazhel'nikov, see A. A. Alekseeva, *Stroka v biografii* (Moscow: Molodaia gvardiia, 2003), 22.

120. GANISO, f. 4529, op. 17, d. 14, ll. 197–201.

121. Starr, *Red and Hot*, 289–315; Leites interview in "Klub 'Kvadrat.'"

122. On closed cities, see Sergei I. Zhuk, "Closing and Opening Soviet Society (Introduction to the Forum)," *Ab Imperio* 2 (June 2011): 123–58.

123. *XV s'ezd vsesoiuznogo leninskogo kommunisticheskogo soiuza molodezhi*, 33, 74.

124. Ward, *Brezhnev's Folly*, 151–57.

125. These files included RGASPI, f. M-1, op. 34, d. 68; and RGASPI, f. M-1, op. 34, d. 141.

126. Krivoruchenko, *XIV–XVI s'ezdy VLKSM*, 139–40.

127. Gaponov interview; Semenov interview; Kovaleva, *Ty pomnish' fizfak?*, 98.

128. Anatolii Krichevich, born 1950, interview by author, December 12, 2008.

129. RGASPI, f. M-1, op. 34, d. 69, ll. 24–31. For more on Pod integralom, see Paul R. Josephson, *New Atlantis Revisited: Akademgorodok, the Siberian City of Science* (Princeton: Princeton University Press, 1997); and A. G. Borzenkov, *Molodezh' i politika: Vozmozhnosti i predely studencheskoi samodeiatel'nosti na vostoke Rossii (1961–1991 gg.); Chast' 2* (Novosibirsk: Novosibirskii gosudarstvennyi universitet, 2002), 170.

130. Mark Sandle, "Brezhnev and Developed Socialism: The Ideology of *Zastoi?*," in Bacon and Sandle, *Brezhnev Reconsidered*, 165–87.

131. Liubov Baliasnaia, born 1927, interview by author, April 5, 2009.

132. GANISO, f. 652, op. 1, d. 4, l. 167.

133. Butov interview.

134. Krivoruchenko, *XIV–XVI s'ezdy VLKSM*, 133.

135. Mark Sandle, "A Triumph of Ideological Hairdressing? Intellectual Life in the Brezhnev Era Reconsidered," in Bacon and Sandle, *Brezhnev Reconsidered*, 135–64.

136. Semenov interview; Kovaleva, *Ty pomnish' fizfak?*, 98–101; Gaponov interview; Iurii Gaponov, "Traditsii 'fizicheskogo iskusstva' v rossiskom fizicheskom soobshchestve 50–90-kh godov," accessed October 22, 2012, http://www.abitura.com/happy_physics/traditions.html; Iurii Gaponov, "Rozhdenie traditsii," accessed October 22, 2012, http://kvant.info/arch/kikoin_gaponov.htm; Igor Oleinik, "O studii 'Arkhimed': Kogda my byli molodymi molodymi i chush' prekrasnuiu nesli," accessed October 22, 2012, http://www.respectme.ru/blog/273; "Chto takoe Den' Fizika?," accessed October 22, 2012, http://www.dubinushka.ru/subtopics.php?sid=50.

137. "Miuzikl (opera) Arkhimed—Chast' 1," accessed October 22, 2012, http://www.youtube.com/watch?v=LOYc_VmQaCU.

138. G. S. Frid, *Muzyka, obshchenie, sud'by: O Moskovskom molodezhnom muzykal'nom klube; Stat'i i ocherki* (Moscow: Sovremennyi Kompozitorov, 1987), 15–16, 35; A. Tsuker and A. Selitskii, *Grigorii Frid: Put' khudozhnika* (Moscow: Sovremennyi kompozitor, 1990), 93.

139. Susan Costanzo, "Reclaiming the Stage: Amateur Theater-Studio Audiences in the Late Soviet Era," *Slavic Review* 57, no. 2 (Summer 1998): 398–424.

140. Vladimir Rozhkov, born 1947, interview by author, May 26, 2009.

141. Nina Deviataikina, born 1947, interview by author, May 20, 2009.

142. Vladimir Veshnev, born in the early 1940s, interview by author, May 18, 2009; GANISO, f. 652, op. 1, d. 31, l. 47.

143. On growing western influence in music, see Zhuk, *Rock and Roll in the Rocket City*, 215–38; Steinholt, *Rock in the Reservation*; Ryback, *Rock around the Bloc*, 102–14; and Cushman, *Notes from Underground*, 77–80. On Soviet television, see Roth-Ey, *Moscow Prime Time*, 176–222; Christine Evans, "*Song of the Year* and Soviet Mass Culture in the 1970s," *Kritika* 12, no. 3 (Summer 2011): 615–45; and Joshua First, "From Spectator to 'Differentiated' Consumer: Film Audience Research in the Era of Developed Socialism (1965–80)," *Kritika* 9, no. 2 (Spring 2008): 317–44. On the variety stage, see MacFadyen, *Red Stars*, 210–67; and Olga Partan, "Alla, the Jester-Queen of Russian Pop Culture," *Russian Review* 66, no. 3 (July 2007): 483–500. More broadly on organized cultural recreation under Brezhnev, see Mari Ristolainen, *Preferred Realities: Soviet and Post-Soviet Amateur Art in Novorzhev* (Jyväskylä: Gummerus Printing, 2008), 109–68; Brian Donahoe and Joachim Otto Habeck, eds., *Reconstructing the House of Culture: Community, Self, and the Makings of Culture in Russia and Beyond* (New York: Berghahn Books, 2011), 4–7.

144. James R. Millar, "The Little Deal: Brezhnev's Contribution to Acquisitive Socialism," *Slavic Review* 44, no. 4 (Winter 1985): 694–706. For a more recent take on consumer goods in the Brezhnev years, see Lewis H. Siegelbaum, *Cars for Comrades: The Life of the Soviet Automobile* (Ithaca: Cornell University Press, 2008), 173–252. On social services, see E. R. Iarskaia-Smirnova, P. V. Romanov, and N. B. Lebina, "Sovetskaia sotsial'naia politika i povsednevnost', 1940–85," in *Sovetskaia sotsial'naia politika: Stseny i deistvuiushchie litsa, 1940–1985*, ed. E. R. Iarskaia-Smirnova and P. V. Romanov (Moscow: Variant, 2008), 7–33.

145. Sandle, "Triumph of Ideological Hairdressing?"

146. Paulina Bren, *The Greengrocer and His TV: The Culture of Communism after the 1968 Prague Spring* (Ithaca: Cornell University Press, 2010), 177–200; Judd Stitziel, *Fashioning Socialism: Clothing, Politics and Consumer Culture in East Germany* (New York: Berg, 2005), 1–11; Katherine Verdery, *What Was Socialism, and What Comes Next?* (Princeton: Princeton University Press, 1996), 26–29; Sabina Mihelj, "The Politics of Privatization: Television Entertainment and the Yugoslav Sixties," in *The Socialist Sixties: Crossing Borders in the Second World*, ed. Anne E. Gorsuch and Diane P. Koenker (Bloomington: Indiana University Press, 2013), 251–67; Mary Neuberger, "Inhaling Luxury: Smoking and Anti-Smoking in Socialist Bulgaria, 1947–1989," in *Pleasures in Socialism: Leisure and Luxury in the Eastern Bloc*, ed. David Crowley and Susan E. Reid (Evanston: Northwestern University Press, 2010), 239–58.

147. Zygmunt Bauman, *Modernity and Ambivalence* (Ithaca: Cornell University Press, 1991), 278.

148. Butov interview.

149. Popkova interview.

150. Ol'ga Lebedikhina, born 1947, interview by author, December 25, 2008.

151. Liudmila Gerasimova, born in the late 1930s, interview by author, May 27, 2009.

152. Donald J. Raleigh, *Soviet Baby Boomers: An Oral History of Russia's Cold War Generation* (New York: Oxford University Press, 2011), 168–266; Oleg Kharkhordin, *The Collective and the Individual in Russia: A Study of Practices* (Berkeley: University of California Press, 1999), 329–62; Vladimir Shlapentokh, *Public and Private Life of*

the Soviet People: Changing Values in Post-Stalin Russia (New York: Oxford University Press, 1989), 153–63; Alexander Prokhorov, *Unasledovannyi diskurs: Paradigmy stalinskoi kul'tury v literature i kinematografii 'ottepeli'* (Saint Petersburg: Akademecheskii proekt, 2007), 7–9; Basile Kerblay, *Modern Soviet Society* (New York: Routledge, 1983), chap. 11.

153. On consumerism, see Jukka Gronow and Sergei Zhuravlev, "Soviet Luxuries from Champagne to Private Cars," in Crowley and Reid, *Pleasures in Socialism*, 121–46. On nationalism in Russia, see Mitrokhin, *Russkaia partiia*, 338–526. On non-Russian nationalism, see Elena Zubkova, "Vlast' i razvitie etnokonfliktnoi situatsii v SSSR, 1953–1985 gody," *Otechestvennaia istoriia* 4 (2004): 3–32. On religion, see Sergei Zhuk, "Religion, 'Westernization,' and Youth in the 'Closed City' of Soviet Ukraine, 1964–84," *Russian Review* 67, no. 4 (October 2008): 661–79. On sports, see the contributions to Nikolaus Katzer, Sandra Budy, Alexandra Kohring, and Manfred Zeller, eds., *Euphoria and Exhaustion: Modern Sport in Soviet Culture and History* (Frankfurt: Campus Verlag, 2010). On countercultures, see John Bushnell, *Moscow Graffiti: Language and Subculture* (Boston: Unwin Hyman, 1990). On dissent, see Barbara Walker, "Pollution and Purification in the Moscow Human Rights Networks of the 1960s and 1970s," *Slavic Review* 68, no. 2 (Summer 2009): 376–95; and B. M. Firsov, *Raznomyslie v SSSR, 1940–1960-e gody: Istoriia, teoriia i praktiki* (Saint Petersburg: Evropeiskii Dom, 2008), 1–16.

154. See the following memoirs of reformist cadres: M. S. Gorbachev, *Memoirs*, trans. Georges Peronansky and Tatjana Varsavsky (New York: Doubleday, 1996), 84–107; G. A. Arbatov, *The System: An Insider's Life in Soviet Politics* (New York: Times Books, 1992); A. S. Cherniaev, *Moia zhizn' i moe vremia* (Moscow: Mezhdunarodnye otnosheniia, 1995); F. M. Burlatskii, *Khrushchev and the First Russian Spring: The Era of Khrushchev through the Eyes of His Advisor* (New York: Scribner's, 1991). Also see Robert D. English, *Russia and the Idea of the West: Gorbachev, Intellectuals, and the End of the Cold War* (New York: Columbia University Press, 2000), 117–92; and David L. Ruffley, *Children of Victory: Young Specialists and the Evolution of Soviet Society* (Westport: Praeger, 2003), 47–84.

155. Raleigh, *Soviet Baby Boomers*, 268–310; Alexei Yurchak, *Everything Was Forever, Until It Was No More: The Last Soviet Generation* (Princeton: Princeton University Press, 2006), 282–98; Stephen Kotkin, *Armageddon Averted* (New York: Oxford University Press, 2001), 10–30.

156. Alex Inkeles and Raymond A. Bauer, *The Soviet Citizen: Daily Life in a Totalitarian Society* (Cambridge: Harvard University Press, 1959), chap. 11.

157. Donna Bahry, "Politics, Generations, and Change in the USSR," in *Politics, Work, and Daily Life in the USSR: A Survey of Former Soviet Citizens*, ed. James R. Millar (New York: Cambridge University Press, 1987), 61–99.

158. On the implications for clubs and political engagement during the Gorbachev years, see Carole Sigman, *Clubs politiques et perestroïka en Russie: Subversion sans dissidence* (Paris: Editions Karthala, 2009). For how these dynamics played out in post-Soviet Russian political activism by youth, see D. V. Gromov, *Ulichnye aktsii (molodezhnyi politicheskii aktivizm v Rossii)* (Moscow: IEARAN, 2012). For its implication for post-Soviet popular culture, see Eliot Borenstein, *Overkill: Sex and Violence in Contemporary Russian Popular Culture* (Ithaca: Cornell University Press, 2008).

159. Sabrina P. Ramet, *Social Currents in Eastern Europe: The Sources and Consequences of the Great Transformation*, 2nd ed. (Durham: Duke University Press, 1995),

262–76; Gabor Klaniczay and Balazs Trencsenyi, "Introduction: Mapping the Merry Ghetto: Musical Countercultures in East Central Europe, 1960–1989," *East Central Europe* 2–3, no. 38 (2011): 169–79; Karin Taylor, *Let's Twist Again: Youth and Leisure in Socialist Bulgaria* (Vienna: Lit, 2006), 122–29; Sabina Mihelj, "The Politics of Privatization: Television Entertainment and the Yugoslav Sixties," in Gorsuch and Koenker, *Socialist Sixties*, 251–67; Fenemore, *Sex, Thugs and Rock 'n' Roll*, 156–242.

160. Esther von Richthofen, *Bringing Culture to the Masses: Control, Compromise and Participation in the GDR* (New York: Berghahn Books, 2009), 190–207; Scott Moranda, "Camping in East Germany: Making 'Rough' Nature More Comfortable," in Crowley and Reid, *Pleasures in Socialism*, 197–219; Mike Dennis, "Kicking the Ball Over the Wall: Football and Agency in Communist East Germany," in *Winter Kept Us Warm: Cold War Interactions Reconsidered*, ed. Sari Autio-Sarasmo and Brendan Humphreys (Helsinki: Aleksanteri Institute, 2010), 192–207; Josie McLellan, "'Even under Socialism, We Don't Want to Do without Love': East German Erotica," in Crowley and Reid, *Pleasures in Socialism*, 219–38; Bren, *Greengrocer and His TV*, 201–8.

161. Yurchak, *Everything Was Forever, Until It Was No More*, 158–206.

162. For more on parallels between authoritarianism and consumerism in the United States and the Soviet Union, see Kate Brown, *Plutopia: Nuclear Families, Atomic Cities, and the Great Soviet and American Plutonium Disasters* (New York: Oxford University Press, 2013).

163. On the key role of consumption and leisure in the changes of emotional expression and experience, see Peter N. Stearns and Jan Lewis, eds., *An Emotional History of the United States* (New York: New York University Press, 1998), 1–14; Peter N. Stearns, "Consumerism and Childhood: New Targets for American Emotions," in Stearns and Lewis, *Emotional History of the United States*, 396–416; and Peter N. Stearns, *American Cool: Constructing a Twentieth-Century Emotional Style* (New York: New York University Press, 1994), 1–15, 264–84.

164. Paul Glennie, "Consumption within Historical Studies," in *Acknowledging Consumption: A Review of New Studies*, ed. Daniel Miller (New York: Routledge, 1995), 164–203; Gary Cross, *Time and Money: The Making of Consumer Culture* (New York: Routledge, 1993); Ian R. Jones, Paul Higgs, and David J. Ekerdt, eds., *Consumption and Generational Change: The Rise of Consumer Lifestyles* (New Brunswick: Transaction Publishers, 2009); Michael Kammen, *American Culture, American Tastes: Social Change and the 20th Century* (New York: Knopf, 1999), 162–89; Neil McKendrick, John Brewer, and J. H. Plumb, *The Birth of a Consumer Society: The Commercialization of Eighteenth-Century England* (Bloomington: Indiana University Press, 1982), 265–85.

165. Sebastian Heilmann and Elizabeth J. Perry, "Embracing Uncertainty: Guerrilla Policy Style and Adaptive Governance in China," in *Mao's Invisible Hand: The Political Foundations of Adaptive Governance in China*, ed. Sebastian Heilmann and Elizabeth J. Perry (Cambridge: Harvard University Press, 2011), 1–29.

166. Laura Fair, "Drive-In Socialism: Debating Modernities and Development in Dar es Salaam, Tanzania," *American Historical Review* 118, no. 4 (October 2013): 1077–104.

167. On the domestic scene, see Tibor Scitovsky, *The Joyless Economy: The Psychology of Human Satisfaction and Consumer Dissatisfaction* (New York: Oxford University Press, 1976), 133–39; John K. Galbraith, *The Affluent Society* (Cambridge: Riverside

Press, 1958), 152–60; and the contributions to Neva R. Goodwin, Frank Ackerman, and David Kiron, eds., *The Consumer Society* (Washington: Island Press, 1997).

168. Bauman, *Modernity and Ambivalence*, 278.

169. On the weakening of the Soviet Union's Cold War positions under Brezhnev, see David S. Foglesong, *The American Mission and the Evil Empire: The Crusade for a "Free Russia" since 1881* (New York: Cambridge University Press, 2007), 174–95; and Zubok, *Failed Empire*, 265–335.

170. For instance, David Caute proclaims that "the cultural defeat of the Soviet system was set in motion as soon as the cold war began." Caute, *The Dancer Defects: The Struggle for Cultural Supremacy during the Cold War* (New York: Oxford University Press, 2003), 2. Also see Reinhold Wagnleitner, "The Empire of the Fun, or Talkin' Soviet Union Blues: The Sound of Freedom and U.S. Cultural Hegemony in Europe," *Diplomatic History* 23, no. 3 (Summer 1999): 499–524.

BIBLIOGRAPHY

PRIMARY SOURCES

Archival Sources

Russia

Gosudarstvennyi arkhiv noveishei istorii Saratovskoi oblasti (GANISO, State Archive of Contemporary History of Saratov Oblast), Saratov
f. 652   Saratov State University Komsomol Committee
f. 654   Saratov Third State Ball-Bearing Plant Komsomol Committee
f. 3234   Kirov Neighborhood Komsomol Committee
f. 4158   Saratov Oblast Komsomol Committee
f. 4529   Saratov City Komsomol Committee
Gosudarstvennyi arkhiv Rossiiskoi Federatsii (GARF, State Archive of the Russian Federation), Moscow
f. R-5451   All-Union Central Council of Trade Unions
op. 24, General Department
op. 28, Department of Cultural Mass Work
f. R-8131   Procuracy
Gosudarstvennyi arkhiv Saratovskoi oblasti (GASO, State Archive of Saratov Oblast), Saratov
f. 2520   Cultural Department of the Saratov City Executive Committee
Rossiiskii gosudarstvennyi arkhiv literatury i iskusstva (RGALI, Russian State Archive of Literature and Art), Moscow
f. 2329   USSR Ministry of Culture
op. 10, 27, Department of Cultural Enlightenment Institutions
Rossiiskii gosudarstvennyi arkhiv noveishei istorii (RGANI, Russian State Archive of Contemporary History), Moscow
f. 5   Communist Party Central Committee, 1953–1991
op. 30, General Department
op. 34, Department of Propaganda and Agitation
op. 36, Department of Culture
Rossiiskii gosudarstvennyi arkhiv sotsial'no-politicheskoi istorii (RGASPI, Russian State Archive of Socio-Political History), Moscow
f. M-1   Komsomol

op. 3, 67, Bureau of the Komsomol Central Committee

op. 32, 34, Department of Propaganda and Agitation

f. 17   Communist Party Central Committee, 1917–1953

op. 3, Documents in Preparation for Politburo Meetings

op. 125, 132, Department of Propaganda and Agitation

Tsentral'nyi arkhiv goroda Moskvy (TsAGM, Central Archive of the City of Moscow), Moscow

f. 44   Moscow Gor'kii House of Culture

f. 2011   Division of Cultural Enlightenment Institutions of the Moscow Executive Committee, 1917–1953

f. 429   Division of Cultural Enlightenment Institutions of the Moscow Executive Committee, 1953–1991

f. 718   Moscow City Trade Union Council

f. 1988   Department of Cultural Enlightenment Work of the Krasnopresnenskii Neighborhood Executive Committee

f. 2987   Moscow House of Folk Creativity

f. R-523   Department of Culture of the Kuibyshev Neighborhood Executive Committee

Tsentral'nyi arkhiv obshchestvenno-politicheskoi istorii Moskvy (TsAOP-IM, Central Archive of Social-Political History of Moscow), Moscow

f. 635   Moscow City Komsomol Committee

f. 667   Krasnopresnenskii Neighborhood Komsomol Committee

f. 6083   Moscow State University Komsomol Committee

United Kingdom

The National Archives of the United Kingdom (TNA): Public Record Office (PRO), London

FO   Foreign Office

United States

National Archives at College Park (NACP), College Park, MD

RG 59   General Records of the Department of State

RG 306   Records of the US Information Agency

Document Collections

Iakovlev, A. N., ed. *Vlast' i khudozhestvennaia intelligentsiia: Dokumenty TsK RKP(b)–VKP(b)–OGPU–NKVD o kul'turnoi politike; 1917–1953.* Moscow: Mezhdunarodnyi fond Demokratiia, 1999.

Newspapers and Journals

Down Beat
Izvestiia
Jazz.ru
Komsomol'skaia pravda
Krokodil
Literaturnaia Gazeta
Molodoi stalinets/Zaria molodezhi
Moskovskii komsomolets
Moskovskii universitet
New York Times
Pchela
Stalinets/Leninskii put'
USSR/Soviet Life

Films

Karnaval'naia noch'. Directed by E. A. Riazanov. Moscow: Mosfil'm, 1956.
Mne dvadtsat' let. Directed by M. M. Khutsiev. Moscow: Gorky Film Studio, 1965.

Literature

Aksenov, V. P. *Sobranie sochinenii*. Volume 1. Moscow: Iunost', 1994.
Dudintsev, V. D. *Ne khlebom edinym*. Munich: Zope, 1957.
Strugatskii, A. N., and B. N. Strugatskii. *Ponedel'nik nachinaetsia v subbotu*. 1965. Reprint, Moscow: Tekst, 1992.

Interviews by the Author

Anno, Evgenii Iosifovich. Born 1946, interviewed January 21, 2009.
Arons, Feliks Matveevich. Born 1940, interviewed May 18, 2009.
Avrus, Anatolii Il'ich. Born 1930, interviewed May 28, 2009.
Baliasnaia, Liubov Kuz'michova. Born 1927, interviewed April 5, 2009.
Butov, Nikolai Ivanovich. Born 1944, interviewed February 16, 2009.
Cherniaev, Oleg Vital'evich. Born 1946, interviewed February 22, 2009.
Derzhavets, Abram Semenovich. Born 1935, interviewed April 28, 2009.
Derzhavets, Larissa Ivanovna. Born 1939, interviewed April 28, 2009.
Deviataikina, Nina Ivanovna. Born 1947, interviewed May 20, 2009.
Dobrushina, Irina. Born 1928, interviewed November 10, 2008.
Dubiler, Viktor Abramovich. Born 1941, interviewed February 22, 2009.
Figlin, Lev Aronovich. Born 1938, interviewed May 25, 2009.
Gal'tsov, Dmitrii Vladimirovich. Born 1942, interviewed February 20, 2009.

Ganz, Harding. Born 1938, interviewed May 10, 2012.

Gaponov, Iurii Vladimirovich. Born 1934, interviewed April 28, 2009.

Garanian, Georgii Aramovich. Born 1934, interviewed February 4, 2009.

Gerasimova, Liudmila. Born in the late 1930s, interviewed May 27, 2009.

Gertsik, Volodia. Born 1946, interviewed November 10, 2008.

Gomonkov, Fedor Stepanovich. Born in mid-1930s, interviewed February 11, 2009.

Guseva, Lidiia Viktorovna. Born 1935, interviewed June 1, 2009.

Iarskaia, Valentina Nikolaevna. Born in the mid-1930s, interviewed May 30, 2009.

Il'in, Konstantin. Born 1944, interviewed May 20, 2009.

Kleinot, Vitalii E. Born 1941, interviewed February 14, 2009.

Kovaleva, Svetlana. Born in mid-1930s, interviewed March 3, 2009.

Kozlova, Nona Vladimirovna. Born 1933, interviewed April 29, 2009.

Krichevich, Anatolii Nikolaevich. Born 1950, interviewed December 12, 2008.

Krichevskii, German. Born 1934, interviewed February 6, 2009.

Krylov, Sergei Anatolevich. Born 1941, interviewed March 2, 2009.

Kurilova, Francheska Aleksandrovna. Born 1936, interviewed May 15, 2009.

Kuznetsov, Aleksei A. Born 1941, interviewed February 21, 2009.

Lebedikhina, Ol'ga Matveevna. Born 1947, interviewed December 25, 2008.

Marvin, Konstantin Alekseevich. Born 1934, interviewed May 13, 2009.

Miagkova, Valentina Stepanovna. Born 1923, interviewed April 29, 2009.

Miliaev, Valerii A. Born 1937, interviewed February 28, 2009.

Parfenov, Aleksander Vladimirovich. Born 1941, interviewed February 8, 2009.

Parfenova, Zinaida Adreevna. Born 1942, interviewed February 8, 2009.

Petrova, Galina Nikolaevna. Born in the mid-1930s, interviewed May 13, 2009.

Petrova, Nina Konstantinovna. Born in the late 1930s, interviewed May 5, 2009.

Pinkhasik, Mark Abramovich. Born in the mid-1930s, interviewed May 13, 2009.

Platonovna, Ekaterina Pavlova. Born 1949, interviewed February 8, 2009.

Platonovna, Svetlana Andreevna. Born 1949, interviewed February 8, 2009.

Popkova, Nelli. Born 1936, interviewed May 20, 2009.

Pshenichner, Boris Grigorevich. Born 1933, interviewed April 29, 2009.

Raikova, Nina Petrovna. Born 1938, interviewed April 28, 2009.

Rozhkov, Vladimir Petrovich. Born 1947, interviewed May 26, 2009.

Ryskin, Mikhail Il'ich. Born 1938, interviewed June 1, 2009.

Sadykhov, Vadif E. Born 1946, interviewed February 24, 2009.

Semenov, Sergei Viktorevich. Born 1948, interviewed March 18, 2009.

Shchegol'kova, Svetlana Nikolaevna. Born 1937, interviewed February 19, 2009.

Sobolev, Viktor E. Born 1953, interviewed April 29, 2009.

Sokolov, Iurii Vladimirovich. Born 1940, interviewed April 16, 2009.

Sokolova, Irina Nikolaevna. Born 1945, interviewed April 16, 2009.

Sokol'skaia, Irina Borisovna. Born 1947, interviewed November 8, 2008.

Stepanchuk, Viktor Petrovich. Born 1929, interviewed May 19, 2009.

Tkacheva, Tatiana Mikhailovna. Born 1945, interviewed January 20, 2009.

Troitskii, Nikolai Alekseevich. Born 1931, interviewed May 22, 2009.

Veshnev, Vladimir Petrovich. Born early 1940s, interviewed May 18, 2009.

Vishnevkin, Boris D. Born 1952, interviewed July 30, 2012.

Vygnanov, Aleksander A. Born 1942, interviewed February 13, 2009.

Zhimskii, Iurii P. Born 1936, interviewed May 27, 2009.

Other Personal Accounts

Aksenov, V. P. *V poiskakh grustnogo bebi: Kniga ob Amerike*. New York: Liberty Publishing House, 1987.

Arbatov, G. A. *The System: An Insider's Life in Soviet Politics*. New York: Times Books, 1992.

Bukovskii, V. K. *"I vozvrashchaetsia veter. . . ."* New York: Khronika Press, 1978.

Burlatskii, F. M. *Khrushchev and the First Russian Spring: The Era of Khrushchev through the Eyes of His Advisor*. New York: Scribner's, 1991.

Cherniaev, A. S. *Moia zhizn' i moe vremia*. Moscow: Mezhdunarodnye otnosheniia, 1995.

Frid, G. S. *Muzyka, obshchenie, sud'by: O Moskovskom molodezhnom muzykal'nom klube; Stat'i i ocherki*. Moscow: Sovremennyi kompozitorov, 1987.

Gorbachev, M. S. *Memoirs*. Translated by Georges Peronansky and Tatjana Varsavsky. New York: Doubleday, 1996.

Kovaleva, S. K. *Ty pomnish' fizfak? Neformal'nye traditsii fizfaka MGU*. Moscow: Pomatur, 2003.

Kozlov, A. S. *Dzhazz, rock, i mednye tuby*. Moscow: Eksmo, 2005.

Kozlov, A. S. *"Kozel na sakse": I tak vsiu zhizn'*. Moscow: Vagrius, 1998.

Krichevskii, German. "Samoanaliz, ili razveiat' mify." Unpublished memoir.

Kull', M. I. *Stupeni voskhozhdeniia*. Accessed October 22, 2012. http://www.jazz.ru/books/kull/default.htm.

Miagkova, V. S. *O dome kotoryi stroili vmeste: Vospominaniia rezhisera-pedagoga Evgenii Vasil'evny Galkinoi*. Moscow: MGDD(Iu)T, 2007.

Miliaev, V. A. *Laskaiushchiisia ezh*. Moscow: Dobrosovet, 2007.

Polikovskaia, L. V. *My predchustviie . . . predtecha . . . ploshchad' Maiakovskogo, 1958–1965.* Moscow: Zvenia, 1997.

Ponomarev, V. M. *Na obratnoi storone zvuka.* Moscow: Agraf, 2003.

Slavkin, V. I. *Pamiatnik neizvestnomu stiliage.* Moscow: Artist. Rezhiser. Teatr, 1996.

Other Published Primary Sources

XV s'ezd Vsesoiuznogo leninskogo kommunisticheskogo soiuza molodezhi (17–21 maia 1966 goda): Stenograficheskii otchet. Moscow: Molodaia gvardiia, 1966.

XVI s'ezd Vsesoiuznogo Leninskogo Kommunisticheskogo Soiuza Molodezhi: Stenograficheskii otchet. Moscow: Molodaia gvardiia, 1971.

XX s'ezd KPSS: Stenograficheskii otchet; Ch. 1. Moscow, 1956.

Abramkin, V. M. *Universitet literatury i iskusstva: Programmy, plany lektsii, bibliografiia; 1948–49 uchebnyi god.* Leningrad, 1948.

Amosova, T., and E. Ivanova. *Tematicheskie molodezhnye vechera k 40-letiu Leninskogo komsomola.* Alma-Ata, 1958.

Andreev, E. M., L. E. Darskii, and T. L. Khar'kova. *Naselenie Sovetskogo Soiuza, 1922–1992.* Moscow: Nauka, 1993.

Bashlii, E. V. *Zvezdnyi dom na Vorob'evykh gorakh: K 40-letiiu otdela astronomii i kosmanavtiki posviashchaetsia.* Moscow: MGDD(Iu)T, 2002.

Bondarenko, V. E. *Propaganda iskusstva v klube.* Moscow: Minkul't RSFSR, 1963.

Bratenkov, A. *Klubom rukovodit sovet: Iz opyta raboty kluba Krasnoiarskogo lespromkhoza.* Tomsk, 1955.

Brudnyi, V. I. *V klube gde vsem interesno: Iz opyta raboty kluba na obshchestvennykh nachalakh.* Moscow: Profizdat, 1962.

Dimentman, A. *Kul'turu v massy: Iz opyta raboty pervykh universitetov kul'tury.* Moscow: Iskusstvo, 1960.

Disudenko, A., and A. Skrypnik. *Zakon komsomol'skoi zhizni.* Moscow: Molodaiia gvardiia, 1966.

Dmitrovskii, S. *Mezhdunarodnyi iunosheskii den' v klube.* Kiev: Proletarii, 1925.

Dokumenty piatogo plenuma TsK VLKSM. Moscow: Molodaia gvardiia, 1956.

Dolinskii, S. *Klub molodezhi v den' 1 maia.* Moscow: Novaia Moskva, 1925.

Dubrova, G., and N. Proshchunin. *Sputnik komsomol'skogo aktivista: Spravochnaia knizhka.* Moscow: Molodaia gvardiia, 1962.

Iakovlev, A. N. *Vlast' i khudozhestvennaia intelligentsiia: Dokumenty TsK RKP(b)–VKP(b)–OGPU–NKVD o kul'turnoi politike, 1917–1953.* Moscow: Mezhdunarodnyi fond Demokratiia, 1999.

Informatsionnyi biulleten' Ministerstva kul'tury SSSR. Moscow: Iskusstvo, 1959.

Kapustin, M. P. *Kak provesti molodezhno-komsomol'skie disputy v klube.* Tashkent, 1959.

Karpov, G. G., and N. D. Sintsov. *Klubnoe delo: Uchebnoe posobie.* Moscow: Sovetskaia Rossiia, 1959.

Khrushchev, N. S. *Sluzhit' delu kommunizma (rechi na XIII i XIV s"ezdakh VLKSM).* Moscow: Molodaia gvardiia, 1963.

Khrushchev, N. S. *Vospityvat' aktivnykh i soznatel'nykh stroitelei kommunisticheskogo obshchestva (rech' na XIII s"ezde VLKSM 18 aprelia 1958 goda).* Moscow: Molodaia gvardiia, 1961.

Kirov, V. *Klub i byt: Doklad na vsesoiuznom klubnom soveshchanii i rezoliutsii po dokladu.* Moscow, 1930.

Klub—stroiteliam kommunizma. Moscow: Profizdat, 1961.

Kogda konchaetsia smena: Ocherki o kul'turno-massovoi rabote molodezhi na predpriiatii. Moscow: Molodaia gvardiia, 1952.

Komissarova, A. *10 vecherov molodezhi.* Moscow: Molodaia gvardiia, 1963.

Kozudlin, B. *Kul'turno-prosvetitel'naia rabota sredi molodezhi.* Sverdlovsk: Sverdlovskoe knizhnoe izdanie, 1954.

Krivoruchenko, V. K. *XIV–XVI s"ezdy VLKSM.* Moscow: Molodaia gvardiia, 1989.

Kutasova, T. *Samodeiatel'nyi tantseval'nyi kollektiv.* Moscow: Profizdat, 1954.

Lenin, V. I. *Uchitsia kommunizmu, kniga 1: V. I. Lenin, KPSS; O partiinom rukovodstve komsomola.* Moscow: Izdatel'stvo politicheskoi literatury, 1982.

Makarova, O. K. *Kul'turnoe stroitel'stvo SSSR: Statisticheskii sbornik.* Moscow: Gosudarstvennoe statisticheskoe izdatel'stvo, 1956.

Makhlin, E. *Opyt raboty kul'turno-prosvititel'nykh uchrezhdenii na zheleznodorozhnom transporte.* Moscow: Gudok, 1957.

Migranov, R. Kh. *V pokhod za kul'turu.* Moscow: Molodaia gvardiia, 1959.

Mikhailov, N. A. *Otchetnyi doklad na XI s"ezde komsomola o rabote TsK VLKSM.* Moscow: Molodaia gvardiia, 1949.

Molodezh' v rabochem klube. Moscow: Molodaia gvardiia, 1927.

Murav'ev, E. *Ot vsei dushi—liudiam.* Smolensk: Smolenskoe knizhnoe izdatel'stvo, 1963.

Nepomniashchii, M. E., ed. *Entuziasty: Sbornik o peredovikakh kul'turno-prosvititel'noi raboty.* Moscow: Sovetskaia Rossiia, 1959.

Nikolaeva, I. N. *Rabota kluba s molodezh'iu.* Moscow: Sovetskaia Rossiia, 1957.

O rabote komsomol'skikh organizatsii vysshikh uchebnykh zavedenii. Moscow: Molodaia gvardiia, 1952.

Orlov, V. N. *Klub interesnykh vstrech.* Moscow: Moskovskii rabochii, 1964.

Pavlov, S. P. *Ob itogakh iun'skogo Plenuma TsK KPSS "Ocherednye zadachi ideologicheskoi raboty partii" i roli komsomol'skikh organizatsii v vospitanii sovetskoi molodezhi na sovremennom etape stroitel'stva kommunizma: Doklad pervogo sekretaria TsK VLKSM tov. Pavlova S. P. na III plenume TsK VLKSM 9 iulia 1963 g.* Moscow: Molodaia gvardiia, 1963.

Pavlov, S. P. *Otchet Tsentral'nogo Komiteta VLKSM i zadachi komsomola, vy-tekaiushchie iz reshenii XXII s'ezda KPSS.* Moscow: Molodaia gvardiia, 1962.

Petrova, Z. A. *Resheniia XXII s'ezda KPSS pretvoriaiutsia v zhizn'.* Moscow: Sovetskaia Rossiia, 1963.

Petrova, Z. A., and M. P. Rymkevich, eds. *Novoe v rabote klubov.* Moscow: Sovetskaia Rossiia, 1962.

Poliakov, L. I. *Sbornik rukovodiashchikh materialov po kul'turno-massovoi rabo-te.* Moscow: Profizdat, 1957.

Postanovleniia chetvertogo plenuma TsK VLKSM. (23 avgusta–25 avgusta, 1950 goda). Moscow: Molodaia gvardiia, 1950.

Postanovleniia vos'mogo plenuma TsK VLKSM. Moscow: Molodaia gvardiia, 1952.

Programma Kommunisticheskoi partii Sovetskogo Soiuza. Moscow: Politizdat, 1974.

Rastopchina, M. A. *Kak privlech' v klub massu.* Moscow: Izdanie G. F. Miri-manova, 1925.

Roshchin, M. M. *Chto ty delaesh' vecherom?* Moscow: Molodaia gvardiia, 1961.

Saratovskii voskresnyi universitet. Saratov, 1928.

Semenov, E. *Dom kul'tury na Kubani.* Moscow, 1950.

Shelepin, A. N. *Ob uluchshenii ideino-vospitatel'noi raboty komsomol'skikh or-ganizatsii sredi molodezhi (Doklad na VII plenum TsK VLKSM 1957 g.).* Moscow: Molodaia gvardiia, 1957.

Shelepin, A. N. *Otchetnyi doklad Tsentral'nogo Komiteta Vsesoiuznogo leninskogo kommunisticheskogo soiuza molodezhi XIII s'ezdu komsomola (15 aprelia 1958 g.).* Moscow: Molodaia gvardiia, 1958.

Shelepin, A. N. *Otchetnyi doklad TsK VLKSM XII s'ezdu komsomola.* Moscow: Molodaia gvardiia, 1954.

Sizov, N. *V klubakh i dvortsakh kul'tury.* Moscow: Profizdat, 1954.

Solov'ev, M. A. *Materialy po kul'turno-prosvititel'noi rabote.* Moscow: Sovets-kaia Rossiia, 1959.

Tiutikov, L., and M. Sishigin, eds. *Sila obshchestvennogo pochina.* Moscow: Molodaia gvardiia, 1962.

Travin, V. I. *Deistvennoe sredstvo vospitaniia molodezhi.* Leningrad: LDNTP, 1968.

Tsentral'noe Statisticheskoe Upravlenie: Itogi vsesoiuznoi perepisi naseleniia 1959 goda. Moscow, 1963.

Tsuker, A., and A. Selitskii. *Grigorii Frid: Put' khudozhnika.* Moscow: Sovre-mennyi kompozitor, 1990.

Tumim, O. *Zhenskii klub v derevne.* Petrograd: Nachatki znanii, 1919.

V pomoshch' klubnomu rabotniku goroda i derevni. Tula: Izdanie tulgubpolitpro-
sveta, 1924.

V pomoshch' krasnym ugolkam. Moscow, 1951.

Vechera molodezhi. Odessa, 1952.

Volkova, O. I. *Narodnye universitety.* Saratov: Saratovskoe knizhnoe izdatel'stvo, 1962.

*Zapiska otdelov komsomol'skikh organov TsK VLKSM ob itogakh otchetov i vybo-
rov v komsomole.* Moscow: Molodaia gvardiia, 1964.

Zubkova, E. Iu., L. P. Koshelova, G. A. Kuznetsova, A. I. Miniuk, and L. A.
Rogovaia, eds. *Sovetskaia zhizn', 1945–1953.* Moscow: ROSSPEN, 2003.

SECONDARY SOURCES

Dissertations, Theses, and Unpublished Manuscripts

Abrams, Nathan D. "Struggling for Freedom: Arthur Miller, the *Commentary* Community, and the Cultural Cold War." PhD diss., University of
Birmingham, 1998.

Avramov, Konstantin V. "Soviet America: Popular Responses to the United
States in Post–World War II Soviet Union." PhD diss., University of Kansas, 2012.

Baran, Emily B. "Faith on the Margins: Jehovah's Witnesses in the Soviet
Union and Post-Soviet Russia, Ukraine, Moldova, 1945–2010." PhD diss.,
University of North Carolina at Chapel Hill, 2011.

Beliaev, A. A. "Provintsial'nye komsomol'skie organizatsii v poslevoennykh
usloviakh: Osobennosti deiatel'nosti v dukhovnoi sfere (na materialakh
Tombovskoi bolasti 1945–1954 gg.)." Candidate diss., Tambov State University, 2010.

Hallinan, Victoria. "Cold War Cultural Exchange and the Moiseyev Dance
Company: American Perception of Soviet Peoples." PhD diss., Northeastern University, 2013.

Koenig, Mark. "Media and Reform: The Case of Youth Programming on Soviet Television (1955–1990)." PhD diss., Columbia University, 1995.

LaPierre, Brian. "Defining, Policing, and Punishing Hooliganism in Khrushchev's Russia." PhD diss., University of Chicago, 2006.

Magnúsdóttir, Rósa. "Keeping Up Appearances: How the Soviet State Failed
to Control Popular Attitudes toward the United States of America, 1945–
1959." PhD diss., University of North Carolina at Chapel Hill, 2006.

Merzliakov, S. L. "Saratovskii gosudarstvennyi universitet v gody voiny i mira
(1941–1964 gg.)." Candidate diss., Saratov State University, 2008.

Park, Soo-Hoon. "Party Reform and 'Volunteer Principle' under Khrushchev
in Historical Perspective." PhD diss., Columbia University, 1993.

Peacock, Margaret. "Contested Innocence: Images of the Child in the Cold War." PhD diss., University of Texas at Austin, 2008.

Rosen, Margo S. "The Independent Turn in Soviet-Era Russian Poetry: How Dmitry Bobyshev, Joseph Brodsky, Anatoly Naiman and Evgeny Rein Became the 'Avvakumites' of Leningrad." PhD diss., Columbia University, 2011.

Roth-Ey, Kristin. "Mass Media and the Remaking of Soviet Culture, 1950s–1960s." PhD diss., Princeton University, 2003.

Sargeant, Lynn M. "Civil Society as a Do-It-Yourself Project: The People's House in Late Imperial Russia." Unpublished manuscript.

Tromly, Benjamin K. "Re-Imagining the Soviet Intelligentsia: Student Politics and University Life, 1948–1964." PhD diss., Harvard University, 2007.

Varga-Harris, Christine. "Constructing the Soviet Hearth: Home, Citizenship, and Socialism in Russia, 1956–1964." PhD diss., University of Illinois at Urbana-Champaign, 2005.

Books and Articles

Adorno, Theodor W. *The Culture Industry: Selected Essays on Mass Culture.* Edited by J. M. Bernstein. New York: Routledge, 1991.

Ahmed, Sara. *The Cultural Politics of Emotion.* New York: Routledge, 2004.

"*AHR* Roundtable: Historians and the Question of 'Modernity.'" *American Historical Review* 116, no. 3 (June 2011): 631–751.

Aitken, Stuart C., Anne Trine Kjorholt, and Ragnhild Lund, eds. *Global Childhoods: Globalization, Development, and Young People.* New York: Routledge, 2008.

Aksiutin, Iu. V. *Khrushchevskaia "Ottepel'" i obshchestvennye nastroeniia v SSSR v 1953–1964 gg.* Moscow: ROSSPEN, 2004.

Aksiutin, Iu. V., and O. V. Volobuev. *XX s"ezd KPSS: Novatsii i dogmy.* Moscow: Politizdat, 1991.

Alekseeva, A. A. *Stroka v biografii.* Moscow: Molodaia gvardiia, 2003.

Alexeyeva, Ludmilla, and Paul Goldberg. *The Thaw Generation: Coming of Age in the Post-Stalin Era.* Boston: Little, Brown, 1990.

Alexopoulos, Golfo. "Amnesty 1945: The Revolving Door of Stalin's Gulag." *Slavic Review* 64, no. 2 (Summer 2005): 274–306.

Anderson, Benedict. *Imagined Communities: Reflections on the Origin and Spread of Nationalism.* New York: Verso, 1991.

Anderson, Jenny. "The Great Future Debate and the Struggle for the World." *American Historical Review* 117, no. 5 (December 2012): 1411–30.

Appadurai, Arjun. *Modernity at Large: Cultural Dimensions of Globalization.* Minneapolis: University of Minnesota Press, 1996.

Applebaum, Anne. *Gulag: A History*. New York: Doubleday, 2003.

Arnett, Jeffrey J. *Adolescence and Emerging Adulthood: A Cultural Approach*. Upper Saddle River: Prentice Hall, 2001.

Autio-Sarasmo, Sari, and Brendan Humphreys, eds. *Winter Kept Us Warm: Cold War Interactions Reconsidered*. Helsinki: Aleksanteri Institute, 2010.

Autio-Sarasmo, Sari, and Katalin Miklossy, eds. *Reassessing Cold War Europe*. New York: Routledge, 2011.

Bacon, Edwin, and Mark Sandle, eds. *Brezhnev Reconsidered*. New York: Palgrave Macmillan, 2002.

Bailey, Peter. *Leisure and Class in Victorian England: Rational Recreation and the Contest for Control, 1830–1885*. Buffalo: University of Toronto Press, 1978.

Bakhtin, M. M. *The Dialogic Imagination: Four Essays by M. M. Bakhtin*. Edited by Michael Holquist. Translated by Cary Emerson and Michael Holquist. Austin: University of Texas Press, 1981.

Baldwin, Kate A. *Beyond the Color Line and the Iron Curtain: Reading Encounters between Black and Red, 1922–1963*. Durham: Duke University Press, 2002.

Balina, Marina, and Evgeny Dobrenko, eds. *Petrified Utopia: Happiness Soviet Style*. New York: Anthem Press, 2009.

Ball, Alan M. *Imagining America: Influence and Images in Twentieth-Century Russia*. Lanham: Rowman & Littlefield, 2003.

Baranowski, Shelley. *Strength through Joy: Consumerism and Mass Tourism in the Third Reich*. New York: Cambridge University Press, 2004.

Barker, Adele, and Jehanne M. Gheith, eds. *A History of Women's Writing in Russia*. Cambridge: Cambridge University Press, 2002.

Baron, Samuel H. *Bloody Saturday in the Soviet Union: Novocherkassk, 1962*. Stanford: Stanford University Press, 2002.

Bassin, Mark, and Catriona Kelly, eds. *Soviet and Post-Soviet Identities*. New York: Cambridge University Press, 2012.

Bauman, Zygmunt. *Modernity and Ambivalence*. Ithaca: Cornell University Press, 1991.

Becker, Howard S. *Outsiders: Studies in the Sociology of Deviance*. New York: Free Press, 1973.

Beer, Daniel. *Renovating Russia: The Human Sciences and the Fate of Liberal Modernity, 1880–1930*. Ithaca: Cornell University Press, 2008.

Ben-Ghiat, Ruth. *Fascist Modernities: Italy, 1922–1945*. Berkeley: University of California Press, 2001.

Ben-Rafael, Eliezer, and Yitzhak Sternberg, eds. *Identity, Culture, and Globalization*. Boston: Brill, 2001.

Bennett, Andy, and Keith Kahn-Harris, eds. *After Subculture: Critical Studies in Contemporary Youth Culture*. New York: Palgrave Macmillan, 2004.

Bennett, Tony, Colin Mercer, and Janet Woollcott, eds. *Popular Culture and Social Relations*. Philadelphia: Open University Press, 1986.

Berezina, V. A., ed. *Dopolnitel'noe (vneshkol'noe) obrazovanie detei Rossii*. Moscow: Dialog kul'tur, 2008.

Berliner, Joseph S. *Factory and Manager in the USSR*. Cambridge: Harvard University Press, 1957.

Bernstein, Frances L. *The Dictatorship of Sex: Lifestyle Advice for the Soviet Masses*. DeKalb: Northern Illinois University Press, 2007.

Bertaux, Daniel, Paul Thompson, and Anna Rotkirch. *On Living through Soviet Russia*. New York: Routledge, 2004.

Bhabha, Homi K. *The Location of Culture*. New York: Routledge, 1994

Bittner, Stephen V. *The Many Lives of Khrushchev's Thaw: Experience and Memory in Moscow's Arbat*. Ithaca: Cornell University Press, 2008.

Bogemskaia, K. G., ed. *Samodeiatel'noe khudozhestvennoe tvorchestvo v SSSR: Ocherki istorii, 1930–1950 gg*. Moscow: Gosudarstvennyi institut iskusstvoznaniia, 1995.

Bogemskaia, K. G., ed. *Samodeiatel'noe khudozhestvennoe tvorchestvo v SSSR: Ocherki istorii, konets 1950-kh–nachalo 1990-kh godov*. Saint Petersburg: Dmitrii Bulanin, 1999.

Bogemskaia, K. G., and L. P. Solntseva, eds. *Samodeiatel'noe khudozhestvennoe tvorchestvo v SSSR: Ocherki istorii, 1917–1932 gg*. Saint Petersburg: Dmitrii Bulanin, 2000.

Bonnell, Victoria E. *Roots of Rebellion: Workers' Politics and Organizations in St. Petersburg and Moscow, 1900–1914*. Berkeley: University of California Press, 1983.

Borenstein, Eliot. *Overkill: Sex and Violence in Contemporary Russian Popular Culture*. Ithaca: Cornell University Press, 2008

Borsay, Peter. *A History of Leisure: The British Experience since 1500*. New York: Palgrave Macmillan, 2006.

Borzenkov, A. G. *Molodezh' i politika: Vozmozhnosti i predely studencheskoi samodeiatel'nosti na vostoke Rossii (1961–1991 gg.), Chast' 2*. Novosibirsk: Novosibirskii gosudarstvennyi universitet, 2002.

Bourdieu, Pierre. *Distinction: A Social Critique of the Judgment of Taste*. Translated and edited by Richard Nice. Cambridge: Harvard University Press, 1984.

Boym, Svetlana. *Common Places: Mythologies of Everyday Life in Russia*. Cambridge: Harvard University Press, 1994.

Bradley, Joseph. *Voluntary Associations in Tsarist Russia: Science, Patriotism, and Civil Society*. Cambridge: Harvard University Press, 2009.

Brake, Michael. *Comparative Youth Culture: The Sociology of Youth Cultures and Youth Subcultures in America, Britain, and Canada*. New York: Routledge, 1985.

Brandenberger, David. *National Bolshevism: Stalinist Mass Culture and the Formation of Modern Russian Identity, 1931–1956*. Cambridge: Harvard University Press, 2002.

Bren, Paulina. *The Greengrocer and His TV: The Culture of Communism after the 1968 Prague Spring*. Ithaca: Cornell University Press, 2010.

Bren, Paulina. "Mirror, Mirror, on the Wall . . . Is the West the Fairest of Them All? Czechoslovak Normalization and Its (Dis)Contents." *Kritika* 9, no. 4 (Fall 2008): 831–54.

Brent, Jonathan, and Vladimir P. Naumov. *Stalin's Last Crime: The Plot against the Jewish Doctors, 1948–1953*. New York: HarperCollins, 2003.

Brooks, Jeffrey. "Declassifying a 'Classic.'" *Kritika* 5, no. 4 (Fall 2004): 709–19.

Brooks, Jeffrey. *Thank You, Comrade Stalin! Soviet Public Culture from Revolution to Cold War*. Princeton: Princeton University Press, 2000.

Brown, Deming. *Soviet Russian Literature since Stalin*. New York: Cambridge University Press, 1978.

Brown, Kate. *Plutopia: Nuclear Families, Atomic Cities, and the Great Soviet and American Plutonium Disasters*. New York: Oxford University Press, 2013.

Brown, Timothy. "'1968' East and West: Divided Germany as a Case Study in Transnational History." *American Historical Review* 114, no. 1 (February 2009): 69–96.

Browning, Christopher R., with contributions by Jürgen Matthäu. *The Origins of the Final Solution: The Evolution of Nazi Jewish Policy, September 1939–March 1942*. Lincoln: University of Nebraska Press / Jerusalem: Yad Vashem, 2004.

Brubaker, Rogers, and Frederick Cooper. "Beyond 'Identity.'" *Theory and Society* 29, no. 1 (February 2000): 1–47.

Brudny, Yitzhak M. *Russian Nationalism and the Soviet State, 1953–1991*. Cambridge: Harvard University Press, 1998.

Brumberg, Abraham, ed. *Russia under Khrushchev: An Anthology from "Problems of Communism."* New York: Praeger, 1962.

Brundage, W. Fitzhugh, ed. *Beyond Blackface: African Americans and the Creation of American Popular Culture, 1890–1930*. Chapel Hill: University of North Carolina Press, 2011.

Brusilovskaia, L. B. *Kul'tura povsednevnosti v epokhu "ottepeli": Metamorfozy stilia*. Moscow: Izdatel'stvo URAO, 2001.

Buck-Morss, Susan. *Dreamworld and Catastrophe: The Passing of Mass Utopia in East and West*. Cambridge: MIT Press, 2000.

Burnett, Judith. *Generations: The Time Machine in Theory and Practice*. Farnham, Surrey: Ashgate Publishing, 2010.

Bushnell, John. *Moscow Graffiti: Language and Subculture*. Boston: Unwin Hyman, 1990.

Butler, Judith. *Bodies That Matter: On the Discursive Limits of "Sex."* New York: Routledge, 1993.

Butler, Judith. *Gender Trouble: Feminism and the Subversion of Identity.* New York: Routledge, 1990.

Butler, Judith, Ernesto Laclau, and Slavoj Žižek. *Contingency, Hegemony, Universality: Contemporary Dialogues on the Left.* New York: Verso, 2000.

Bykov, D. L. *Bulat Okudzhava.* Moscow: Molodaia gvardiia, 2009.

Casey, Emma, and Lydia Martens, eds. *Gender and Consumption: Domestic Cultures and the Commercialization of Everyday Life.* Burlington: Ashgate Publishing, 2007.

Castillo, Greg. *Cold War on the Home Front: The Soft Power of Midcentury Design.* Minneapolis: University of Minnesota Press, 2010.

Caute, David. *The Dancer Defects: The Struggle for Cultural Supremacy during the Cold War.* New York: Oxford University Press, 2003.

Cavender, Mary W. *Nests of the Gentry: Family Estate, and Local Loyalties in Provincial Russia.* Newark: University of Delaware Press, 2007.

Certeau, Michel de. *The Practice of Everyday Life.* Translated by Steven F. Rendall. Berkeley: University of California Press, 1984.

Chakrabarty, Dipesh. *Provincializing Europe: Postcolonial Thought and Historical Difference.* Princeton: Princeton University Press, 2000.

Chang-tai, Hung. "A Political Park: The Working People's Cultural Palace in Beijing." *Journal of Contemporary History* 48, no. 3 (July 2013): 556–77.

Chatterjee, Choi. *Celebrating Women: Gender, Festival Culture, and Bolshevik Ideology, 1910–1939.* Pittsburgh: University of Pittsburgh Press, 2002.

Chatterjee, Choi, and Beth Holmgren, eds. *Americans Experience Russia: Encountering the Enigma, 1917 to the Present.* New York: Routledge, 2013.

Chatterjee, Choi, and Karen Petrone. "Models of Selfhood and Subjectivity: The Soviet Case in Historical Perspective." *Slavic Review* 67, no. 4 (Winter 2008): 967–86.

Clark, Katerina. *Moscow, the Fourth Rome: Stalinism, Cosmopolitanism, and the Evolution of Soviet Culture, 1931–1941.* Cambridge: Harvard University Press, 2011.

Clark, Katerina. *Petersburg: Crucible of Cultural Revolution.* Cambridge: Harvard University Press, 1995.

Clark, Katerina. *The Soviet Novel: History as Ritual.* Chicago: University of Chicago Press, 1981.

Clark, William A. *Crime and Punishment in Soviet Officialdom: Combating Corruption in the Political Elite, 1965–1990.* Armonk: M. E. Sharpe, 1993.

Clough, Patricia Ticineto, with Jean Halley, eds. *The Affective Turn: Theorizing the Social.* Durham: Duke University Press, 2007.

Cohen, Harvey G. "Visions of Freedom: Duke Ellington in the Soviet Union." *Popular Music* 30, no. 3 (October 2011): 297–318.

Cohen, Stanley. *Folk Devils and Moral Panics: The Creation of the Mods and Rockers*. 2nd ed. New York: Basil Blackwell, 1987.

Cohen, Stephen F., Alexander Rabinowitch, and Robert Sharlet, eds. *The Soviet Union since Stalin*. Bloomington: Indiana University Press, 1980.

Cohen, Yves, and Stephanie Lin. "Circulatory Localities: The Example of Stalinism in the 1930s." *Kritika* 11, no. 1 (Winter 2010): 11–45.

Cohn, Edward D. "Sex and the Married Communist: Family Troubles, Marital Infidelity, and Party Discipline in the Postwar USSR, 1945–64." *Russian Review* 68, no. 3 (July 2009): 429–50.

Cole, Jennifer, and Deborah Durham, eds. *Figuring the Future: Globalization and the Temporalities of Children and Youth*. Santa Fe: School for Advanced Research Press, 2008.

Connelly, John. *Captive University: The Sovietization of East German, Czech, and Polish Higher Education*. Chapel Hill: University of North Carolina Press, 2000.

Cornell, Richard, ed. *The Soviet Political System: A Book of Readings*. Englewood Cliffs: Prentice Hall, 1970.

Costanzo, Susan. "Amateur Theaters and Amateur Publics in the Russian Republic, 1958–71." *Slavonic and East European Review* 86, no. 2 (April 2008): 372–94.

Costanzo, Susan. "Reclaiming the Stage: Amateur Theater-Studio Audiences in the Late Soviet Era." *Slavic Review* 57, no. 2 (Summer 1998): 398–424.

Costlow, Jane T., Stephanie Sandler, and Judith Vowles, eds. *Sexuality and the Body in Russian Culture*. Stanford: Stanford University Press, 1993.

Cross, Gary. *Time and Money: The Making of Consumer Culture*. New York: Routledge, 1993.

Crowley, David, and Susan E. Reid, eds. *Pleasures in Socialism: Leisure and Luxury in the Eastern Bloc*. Evanston: Northwestern University Press, 2010.

Cull, Nicholas J. *The Cold War and the United States Information Agency: American Propaganda and Public Diplomacy, 1945–1989*. New York: Cambridge University Press, 2008.

Cushman, Thomas. *Notes from Underground: Rock Music Counterculture in Russia*. Albany: State University of New York Press, 1995.

Dallin, Alexander. *German Rule in Russia, 1941–1945: A Study of Occupation Policies*. Boulder: Westview Press, 1981.

Davenport, Lisa E. *Jazz Diplomacy: Promoting America in the Cold War Era*. Jackson: University Press of Mississippi, 2009.

David-Fox, Michael. *Revolution of the Mind: Higher Learning among the Bolsheviks, 1918–1929*. Ithaca: Cornell University Press, 1997.

David-Fox, Michael. *Showcasing the Great Experiment: Cultural Diplomacy and Western Visitors to the Soviet Union, 1921–1941*. New York: Oxford University Press, 2011.

David-Fox, Michael. "What Is Cultural Revolution?" *Russian Review* 58, no. 2 (April 1999): 181–201.

David-Fox, Michael, Peter Holquist, and Alexander M. Martin, eds. *Fascination and Enmity: Russia and Germany as Entangled Histories, 1914–1945.* Pittsburgh: University of Pittsburgh Press, 2012.

Davies, Sarah. *Popular Opinion in Stalin's Russia: Terror, Propaganda and Dissent, 1934–1941.* New York: Cambridge University Press, 1997.

Derrida, Jacques. *Margins of Philosophy.* Translated and edited by Alan Bass. Chicago: University of Chicago Press, 1982.

de Grazia, Victoria. *The Culture of Consent: Mass Organization of Leisure in Fascist Italy.* New York: Cambridge University Press, 1981.

de Grazia, Victoria. *Irresistible Empire: America's Advance through Twentieth-Century Europe.* Cambridge: Belknap Press of Harvard University Press, 2005.

de Grazia, Victoria, and Ellen Furlough, eds. *The Sex of Things: Gender and Consumption in Historical Perspective.* Berkeley: University of California Press, 1996.

Djagalov, Rossen. "Guitar Poetry as the Genre of the 1960s Democratic Socialism: A Global History." Paper presented at "The Socialist 1960s: Popular Culture and the City in Global Perspective" conference, University of Illinois, Urbana-Champaign, June 2010.

Dobrenko, Evgeny. "Socialism as Will and Representation, or What Legacy Are We Rejecting?" *Kritika* 5, no. 4 (Fall 2004): 675–708.

Dobrescu, Caius. "The Phoenix That Could Not Rise: Politics and Rock Culture in Romania, 1960–1989." *East Central Europe* 2–3, no. 38 (2011): 255–90.

Dobson, Miriam. "Contesting the Paradigms of De-Stalinization: Readers' Responses to *One Day in the Life of Ivan Denisovich.*" *Slavic Review* 64, no. 3 (Fall 2005): 580–600.

Dobson, Miriam. *Khrushchev's Cold Summer: Gulag Returnees, Crime, and the Fate of Reform after Stalin.* Ithaca: Cornell University Press, 2009.

Domrin, Alexander N. "Ten Years Later: Society, 'Civil Society,' and the Russian State." *Russian Review* 62, no. 2 (April 2003): 193–211.

Donahoe, Brian, and Joachim Otto Habeck, eds. *Reconstructing the House of Culture: Community, Self, and the Makings of Culture in Russia and Beyond.* New York: Berghahn Books, 2011.

Dunham, Vera S. *In Stalin's Time: Middleclass Values in Soviet Fiction.* New York: Cambridge University Press, 1976.

Durkheim, Emile. *The Rules of the Sociological Method.* Edited by George E. G. Catlin. Translated by Sarah A. Solovay and John H. Mueller. New York: Free Press, 1965.

Edele, Mark. *Soviet Veterans of the Second World War: A Popular Movement in an Authoritarian Society, 1941–1991*. New York: Oxford University Press, 2008.

Edele, Mark. "Strange Young Men in Stalin's Moscow: The Birth and Life of the Stiliagi, 1945–1953." *Jahrbücher für Geschichte Osteuropas* 50, no. 1 (March 2002): 37–61.

Edelman, Robert. *Spartak Moscow: A History of the People's Team in the Workers' State*. Ithaca: Cornell University Press, 2009.

Edmunds, June, and Bryan S. Turner, eds. *Generational Consciousness, Narrative, and Politics*. New York: Rowman & Littlefield, 2002.

Edmunds, June, and Bryan S. Turner. *Generations, Culture and Society*. Philadelphia: Open University Press, 2002.

Eisenstadt, Shmuel N., ed. *Multiple Modernities*. New Brunswick: Transaction Publishers, 2002.

Engel, Jeffrey A., ed. *Local Consequences of the Global Cold War*. Washington: Woodrow Wilson Center Press / Stanford: Stanford University Press, 2007.

Engelstein, Laura. "Combined Underdevelopment: Discipline and the Law in Imperial and Soviet Russia." *American Historical Review* 98, no. 2 (April 1993): 338–53.

Engelstein, Laura. *The Keys to Happiness: Sex and the Search for Modernity in Fin-de-Siècle Russia*. Ithaca: Cornell University Press, 1992.

Engerman, David C. *Know Your Enemy: The Rise and Fall of America's Soviet Experts*. New York: Oxford University Press, 2009.

Engerman, David C. "The Second World's Third World." *Kritika* 12, no. 1 (Winter 2011): 183–211.

Engerman, David C., Nils Gilman, Mark H. Haefele, and Michael E. Latham, eds. *Staging Growth: Modernization, Development, and the Global Cold War*. Amherst: University of Massachusetts Press, 2003.

English, Robert D. *Russia and the Idea of the West: Gorbachev, Intellectuals, and the End of the Cold War*. New York: Columbia University Press, 2000.

Esakov, V. D., and E. S. Levina. *Stalinskie "sudy chesti": Delo "KR."* Moscow: Nauka, 2005.

Etkind, Alexander. "Soviet Subjectivity: Torture for the Sake of Salvation?" *Kritika* 6, no. 1 (Winter 2005): 171–86.

Eugenia, Paulicelli, and Hazel Clark, eds. *The Fabric of Cultures: Fashion, Identity, Globalization*. New York: Berg, 2008.

Eustace, Nicole. *Passion Is the Gale: Emotion, Power, and the Coming of the American Revolution*. Chapel Hill: University of North Carolina Press, 2008.

Evans, Christine. "*Song of the Year* and Soviet Mass Culture in the 1970s." *Kritika* 12, no. 3 (Summer 2011): 615–45.

Evtuhov, Catherine, and Stephen Kotkin, eds. *The Cultural Gradient: The Transmission of Ideas in Europe, 1789–1991*. New York: Rowman & Littlefield, 2003.

Ewing, E. Thomas. *Separate Schools: Gender, Policy, and Practice in Postwar Soviet Education*. DeKalb: Northern Illinois University Press, 2010.

Ezrahi, Christina. *Swans of the Kremlin: Ballet and Power in Soviet Russia*. Pittsburgh: University of Pittsburgh Press, 2012.

Fair, Laura. "Drive-In Socialism: Debating Modernities and Development in Dar es Salaam, Tanzania." *American Historical Review* 118, no. 4 (October 2013): 1077–104.

Fateev, A. V. *Obraz vraga v sovetskoi propagande, 1945–1954 gg.* Moscow: Institut rossiiskoi istorii RAN, 1999.

Featherstone, Mike. *Consumer Culture and Postmodernism*. 2nd ed. Los Angeles: SAGE Publications, 2007.

Feiertag, V. B. *Istoriia dzhazovogo ispolnitel'stva v Rossii*. Saint Petersburg: Skifiia, 2010.

Fenemore, Mark. *Sex, Thugs and Rock 'n' Roll: Teenage Rebels in Cold-War East Germany*. New York: Berghahn Books, 2007.

Field, Deborah A. *Private Life and Communist Morality in Khrushchev's Russia*. New York: Peter Lang, 2007.

Fielding, Steven, Peter Thompson, and Nick Tiratsoo. *"England Arise!" The Labour Party and Popular Politics in 1940s Britain*. New York: Manchester University Press, 1995.

Filtzer, Donald. *The Hazards of Urban Life in Late Stalinist Russia: Health, Hygiene, and Living Standards, 1943–1953*. New York: Cambridge University Press, 2010.

Finkel, Stuart. *On the Ideological Front: The Russian Intelligentsia and the Making of the Soviet Public Sphere*. New Haven: Yale University Press, 2007.

Firsov, B. M. *Raznomyslie v SSSR, 1940–1960-e gody: Istoriia, teoriia i praktiki*. Saint Petersburg: Evropeiskii Dom, 2008.

First, Joshua. "From Spectator to 'Differentiated' Consumer: Film Audience Research in the Era of Developed Socialism (1965–80)." *Kritika* 9, no. 2 (Spring 2008): 317–44.

Fisher, Ralph Talcott, Jr. *Pattern for Soviet Youth: A Study of the Congresses of the Komsomol, 1918–1954*. New York: Columbia University Press, 1959.

Fitzpatrick, Sheila. *The Commissariat of Enlightenment: Soviet Organization of Education and the Arts under Lunacharsky, October 1917–1921*. New York: Cambridge University Press, 1970.

Fitzpatrick, Sheila. *The Cultural Front: Power and Culture in Revolutionary Russia*. Ithaca: Cornell University Press, 1992.

Fitzpatrick, Sheila. *Everyday Stalinism: Ordinary Life in Extraordinary Times; Soviet Russia in the 1930s*. New York: Oxford University Press, 1999.

Fitzpatrick, Sheila. "Happiness and Toska: A Study of Emotions in 1930s Russia." *Australian Journal of Politics and History* 50, no. 3 (2004): 357–71.

Fitzpatrick, Sheila. "Social Parasites: How Tramps, Idle Youth, and Busy Entrepreneurs Impeded the Soviet March to Communism." *Cahiers du Monde russe et soviétique* 47, no. 1–2 (2006): 377–408.

Fitzpatrick, Sheila, ed. *Stalinism: New Directions.* New York: Routledge, 2000.

Fitzpatrick, Sheila. *Tear Off the Masks! Identity and Imposture in Twentieth-Century Russia.* Princeton: Princeton University Press, 2005.

Foglesong, David S. *The American Mission and the Evil Empire: The Crusade for a "Free Russia" since 1881.* New York: Cambridge University Press, 2007.

Fosler-Lussier, Danielle. "Cultural Diplomacy as Cultural Globalization: The University of Michigan Jazz Band in Latin America." *Journal of the Society for American Music* 4, no. 1 (February 2010): 59–93.

Fosler-Lussier, Danielle. *Music Divided: Bartók's Legacy in Cold War Culture.* Berkeley: University of California Press, 2007.

Foucault, Michel. *Discipline and Punish: The Birth of the Prison.* New York: Vintage Books, 1979.

Foucault, Michel. *The History of Sexuality.* Volume 1, *An Introduction.* Translated by Robert Hurley. New York: Pantheon, 1978.

Friedman, Rebecca. *Masculinity, Autocracy, and the Russian University, 1804–1863.* New York: Palgrave Macmillan, 2005.

Frolova-Walker, Marina. *Russian Music and Nationalism: From Glinka to Stalin.* New Haven: Yale University Press, 2007.

Fursenko, Aleksandr, and Timothy Naftali. *Khrushchev's Cold War: The Inside Story of an American Adversary.* New York: Norton, 2006.

Fursenko, Aleksandr, and Timothy Naftali. *One Hell of a Gamble: Khrushchev, Castro, and Kennedy, 1958–1964.* New York: Norton, 1997.

Fürst, Juliane. "Between Salvation and Liquidation: Homeless and Vagrant Children and the Reconstruction of Soviet Society." *Slavonic and East European Review* 86, no. 2 (April 2008): 232–48.

Fürst, Juliane. *Late Stalinist Russia: Society between Reconstruction and Reinvention.* New York: Routledge, 2006.

Fürst, Juliane. *Stalin's Last Generation: Soviet Youth and the Emergence of Mature Socialism, 1945–56.* New York: Oxford University Press, 2010.

Fürst, Juliane, Polly Jones, and Susan Morrissey. "The Relaunch of the Soviet Project, 1945–64: Introduction." *Slavonic and East European Review* 86, no. 2 (April 2008): 201–7.

Galbraith, John Kenneth. *The Affluent Society.* Cambridge: Riverside Press, 1958.

Gans, Herbert J. *Popular Culture and High Culture: An Analysis and Evaluation of Taste.* New York: Basic Books, 1999.

Ganson, Nicholas. *The Soviet Famine of 1946–47 in Global and Historical Perspective.* New York: Palgrave Macmillan, 2009.

Gaponov, Iu. V. "Rozhdenie traditsii." Accessed October 22, 2012. http://kvant.info/arch/kikoin_gaponov.htm.

Gaponov, Iu. V. "Traditsii 'fizicheskogo iskusstva' v rossiiskom fizicheskom soobshchestve 50–90-kh godov." Accessed October 22, 2012. http://www.abitura.com/happy_physics/traditions.html.

Gerasimova, O. G. *Obshchestvenno-politicheskaia zhizn' studenchestva MGU v 1950-e–seredine 1960-kh gg.* Moscow: Moskovskii gosudarstvennyi universitet, 2008.

Geyer, Michael, and Sheila Fitzpatrick, eds. *Beyond Totalitarianism: Stalinism and Nazism Compared.* New York: Cambridge University Press, 2009.

Giddens, Anthony. *The Consequences of Modernity.* Stanford: Stanford University Press, 1990.

Gienow-Hecht, Jessica. "Academics, Cultural Transfer, and the Cold War—A Critical Review." *Diplomatic History* 24, no. 3 (Summer 2000): 465–94.

Gilbert, James. *A Cycle of Outrage: America's Reaction to the Juvenile Delinquent in the 1950s.* New York: Oxford University Press, 1986.

Gilbert, Jeremy, and Ewan Pearson. *Discographies: Dance Music, Culture, and the Politics of Sound.* New York: Routledge, 1999.

Gillis, John R. *Youth and History: Tradition and Change in European Age Relations, 1770–Present.* New York: Academic Press, 1981.

Giustino, Cathleen M., Catherine J. Plum, and Alexander Vari, eds. *Socialist Escapes: Breaking Away from Ideology and Everyday Routine in Eastern Europe, 1945–1989.* New York: Berghahn Books, 2013.

Gladarev, B. S. "Formirovanie i funktsionirovanie milieu (na primere arkheologicheskogo kruzhka LDPDTIu 1970–2000 gg.)." Accessed October 22, 2012. http://www.indepsocres.spb.ru/boriss.htm.

Gladarev, B. S. "Zhiznennye miry 'osoboi' leningradskoi molodezhi." *Neprikosnovennyi zapas* 36, no. 4 (2004). http://magazines.russ.ru/nz/2004/4/glad6.html.

Gladyshev, A. V., and V. S. Mirzekhanov, eds. *Novaia i noveishaia istoriia.* Saratov: Izdatel'stvo Saratovskogo universiteta, 2004.

Gleason, Abbott, ed. *A Companion to Russian History.* London: Wiley-Blackwell, 2009.

Gleason, Abbott, Peter Kenez, and Richard Stites, eds. *Bolshevik Culture: Experiment and Order in the Russian Revolution.* Bloomington: Indiana University Press, 1985.

Goodwin, Neva R., Frank Ackerman, and David Kiron, eds. *The Consumer Society.* Washington: Island Press, 1997.

Goleman, Daniel. *Social Intelligence: The New Science of Human Relationships.* New York: Bantam Dell, 2006.

Goriaeva, T. M. *Radio Rossii: Politicheskii kontrol' sovetskogo radioveshchaniia v 1920–1930-kh godakh; Dokumental'naia istoriia.* Moscow: ROSSPEN, 2000.

Gorlizki, Yoram, and Oleg Khlevniuk. *Cold Peace: Stalin and the Soviet Ruling Circle, 1945–1953.* Oxford: Oxford University Press, 2004.

Gorsuch, Anne E. *All This Is Your World: Soviet Tourism at Home and Abroad after Stalin.* New York: Oxford University Press, 2011.

Gorsuch, Anne E. *Flappers and Foxtrotters: Soviet Youth in the "Roaring Twenties."* Carl Beck Papers in Russian and East European Studies, No. 1102. Pittsburgh: Center for Russian and East European Studies, University Center for International Studies, University of Pittsburgh, 1994.

Gorsuch, Anne E. *Youth in Revolutionary Russia: Enthusiasts, Bohemians, Delinquents.* Bloomington: Indiana University Press, 2000.

Gorsuch, Anne E., and Diane P. Koenker, eds. *The Socialist Sixties: Crossing Borders in the Second World.* Bloomington: Indiana University Press, 2013.

Gorsuch, Anne E., and Diane P. Koenker, eds. *Turizm: The Russian and East European Tourist under Capitalism and Socialism.* Ithaca: Cornell University Press, 2006.

Goscilo, Helena, and Yana Hashamova, eds. *Cinepaternity: Fathers and Sons in Soviet and Post-Soviet Film.* Bloomington: Indiana University Press, 2010.

Goscilo, Helena, and Beth Holmgren, eds. *Russia–Women–Culture.* Bloomington: Indiana University Press, 1996.

Gramsci, Antonio. *Selections from the Prison Notebooks of Antonio Gramsci.* Translated and edited by Quintin Hoare and Geoffrey Nowell Smith. New York: International Publishers, 1971.

Gridley, Mark C., with David Cutler. *Jazz Styles: History & Analysis.* 8th ed. Upper Saddle River: Prentice Hall, 2003.

Griesse, Malte. "Soviet Subjectivities: Discourse, Self-Criticism, Imposture." *Kritika* 9, no. 3 (Summer 2008): 609–24.

Gromov, D. V. *Ulichnye aktsii (molodezhnyi politicheskii aktvizm v Rossii).* Moscow: IEARAN, 2012.

Gronow, Jukka. *Caviar with Champagne: Common Luxury and the Ideals of the Good Life in Stalin's Russia.* New York: Berg, 2003.

Grossberg, Lawrence. *We Gotta Get Out of This Place: Popular Conservatism and Postmodern Culture.* New York: Routledge, 1992.

Grossberg, Lawrence, Cary Nelson, and Paula A. Treichler, eds. *Cultural Studies.* New York: Routledge, 1992.

Gruneau, Richard B., ed. *Popular Cultures and Political Practices.* Toronto: Garamond Press, 1988.

Grushin, B. A. *Chetyre zhizni Rossii v zerkale oprosov obshchestvennogo mneniia: Ocherki massovogo soznaniia rossiian vremen Khrushcheva, Brezhneva, Gorbacheva i Eltsina v 4-kh knigakh; Zhizn' 1-ia, epokha Khrushcheva.* Moscow: Progress-Traditsiia, 2001.

Guilbaut, Serge. *How New York Stole the Idea of Modern Art: Abstract Expressionism, Freedom, and the Cold War.* Translated by Arthur Goldhammer. Chicago: University of Chicago Press, 1983.

Günther, Hans. *The Culture of the Stalin Period.* New York: St. Martin's Press, 1990.

Gurova, Olga. *Sovetskoe nizhnee bel'e: Mezhdu ideologiei i povsednevnost'iu.* Moscow: Novoe literaturnoe obozrenie, 2008.

Hagenloh, Paul. *Stalin's Police: Public Order and Mass Repression in the USSR, 1926–1941.* Washington: Woodrow Wilson Center Press / Baltimore: Johns Hopkins University Press, 2009.

Haimson, Leopold H. "Lenin's Revolutionary Career Revisited: Some Observations on Recent Discussions." *Kritika* 5, no. 1 (Winter 2004): 55–80.

Halfin, Igal. "Between Instinct and Mind: The Bolshevik View of the Proletarian Self." *Slavic Review* 62, no. 1 (Spring 2003): 34–40.

Halfin, Igal. *From Darkness to Light: Class, Consciousness, and Salvation in Revolutionary Russia.* Pittsburgh: University of Pittsburgh Press, 2000.

Hall, John. H, ed. *States in History.* New York: Basil Blackwell, 1986.

Hall, Stuart, Dorothy Hobson, Andrew Lowe, and Paul Willis, eds. *Culture, Media, Language: Working Papers in Cultural Studies, 1972–79.* London: Routledge, 2005.

Hall, Stuart, and Tony Jefferson, eds. *Resistance through Rituals: Youth Subcultures in Post-War Britain.* 2nd ed. New York: Routledge, 2006.

Hanson, Stephen E. *Time and Revolution: Marxism and the Design of Soviet Institutions.* Chapel Hill: University of North Carolina Press, 1997.

Hardy, Jeffrey S. "Gulag Tourism: Khrushchev's 'Show' Prisons in the Cold War Context, 1954–59." *Russian Review* 71, no. 1 (January 2012): 49–78.

Harrison, Hope M. *Driving the Soviets up the Wall: Soviet-East German Relations, 1953–1961.* Princeton: Princeton University Press, 2003.

Harshav, Benjamin. *The Moscow Yiddish Theater: Art on Stage in the Time of Revolution.* New Haven: Yale University Press, 2008.

Hatch, John B. "Hangouts and Hangovers: State, Class and Culture in Moscow's Workers' Club Movement, 1925–1928." *Russian Review* 53, no. 1 (January 1994): 97–117.

Hatfield, Elaine, John T. Cacioppo, and Richard L. Rapson, *Emotional Contagion.* New York: Cambridge University Press, 1994.

Healey, Dan. *Homosexual Desire in Revolutionary Russia: The Regulation of Sexual and Gender Dissent.* Chicago: University of Chicago Press, 2001.

Heath, Joseph, and Andrew Potter. *The Rebel Sell: Why the Culture Can't Be Jammed.* Toronto: HarperCollins, 2004.

Heilmann, Sebastian, and Elizabeth J. Perry, eds. *Mao's Invisible Hand: The Political Foundations of Adaptive Governance in China.* Cambridge: Harvard University Press, 2011.

Hellbeck, Jochen. *Revolution on My Mind: Writing a Diary under Stalin*. Cambridge: Harvard University Press, 2006.

Hellbeck, Jochen. "Speaking Out: Languages of Affirmation and Dissent in Stalinist Russia." *Kritika* 1, no. 1 (Winter 2000): 71–96.

Hellbeck, Jochen, and Klaus Heller, eds. *Autobiographical Practices in Russia / Autobiographische Praktiken in Russland*. Goettingen: Vandenhoek & Ruprecht, 2004.

Hemment, Julie. "Nashi, Youth Voluntarism, and Potemkin NGOs: Making Sense of Civil Society in Post-Soviet Russia." *Slavic Review* 71, no. 2 (Summer 2012): 234–60.

Hendrick, Harry. *Images of Youth: Age, Class, and the Male Youth Problem, 1880–1920*. Oxford: Clarendon Press, 1990.

Hessler, Julie. "Death of an African Student in Moscow: Race, Politics, and the Cold War." *Cahiers du Monde russe* 47, no. 1–2 (January–June 2006): 33–64.

Hessler, Julie. *A Social History of Soviet Trade: Trade Policy, Retail Practices, and Consumption, 1917–1953*. Princeton: Princeton University Press, 2004.

Hessler, Julie. "The Soviet Reception of Exhibits and Performances from the Third World." Paper presented at the Association for Slavic, East European, and Eurasian Studies national convention, Los Angeles, CA, November 18–21, 2010.

Hixson, Walter L. *Parting the Curtain: Propaganda, Culture, and the Cold War*. New York: St. Martin's Press, 1997.

Hoffmann, Ana. *Staging Socialist Femininity: Gender Politics and Folklore Performances in Serbia*. Boston: Brill, 2010.

Hoffmann, David L. *Cultivating the Masses: Modern State Practices and Soviet Socialism, 1914–1939*. Ithaca: Cornell University Press, 2011.

Hoffmann, David L. *Peasant Metropolis: Social Identities in Moscow, 1929–1941*. Ithaca: Cornell University Press, 1994.

Hoffmann, David L. *Stalinist Values: The Cultural Norms of Soviet Modernity, 1917–1941*. Ithaca: Cornell University Press, 2003.

Hoffmann, David L. "Was There a 'Great Retreat' from Soviet Socialism? Stalinist Culture Reconsidered." *Kritika* 5, no. 4 (Fall 2004): 651–74.

Hoffmann, David L., and Yanni Kotsonis, eds. *Russian Modernity: Politics, Knowledge, Practices*. New York: St. Martin's Press, 2000.

Hohendahl, Peter U., and Marc Silberman. "Critical Theory, Public Sphere and Culture: Jürgen Habermas and His Critics." *New German Critique* 16 (Winter 1979): 89–118.

Holquist, Peter. *Making War, Forging Revolution: Russia's Continuum of Crisis, 1914–1921*. Cambridge: Harvard University Press, 2002.

Hooper, Cynthia. "What Can and Cannot Be Said: Between the Stalinist Past and New Soviet Future." *Slavonic and East European Review* 86, no. 2 (April 2008): 306–27.

Hopf, Ted. *Reconstructing the Cold War: The Early Years, 1945–1958.* New York: Oxford University Press, 2012.

Hopf, Ted. *Social Construction of International Politics: Identities & Foreign Policies, Moscow, 1955 and 1999.* Ithaca: Cornell University Press, 2002.

Horn, Gerd-Rainer. *The Spirit of '68: Rebellion in Western Europe and North America, 1956–1976.* New York: Oxford University Press, 2007.

Horner, Bruce, and Thomas Swiss, eds. *Key Terms in Popular Music and Culture.* Malden: Blackwell, 1999.

Hornsby, Robert. *Protest, Reform and Repression in Khrushchev's Soviet Union.* New York: Cambridge University Press, 2013.

Hudson, George E. "Civil Society in Russia: Models and Prospects for Development." *Russian Review* 62, no. 2 (April 2003): 212–22.

Hughes, Geraint, and Saki R. Dockrill, eds. *Palgrave Advances in Cold War History.* New York: Palgrave Macmillan, 2006.

Huppert, Felicia A., Nick Baylis, and Berry Keverne, eds. *The Science of Well-Being.* New York: Oxford University Press, 2005.

Iarskaia-Smirnova, E. R., and P. V. Romanov. "Fartsa: Podpol'e sovetskogo obshchestva potrebleniia." *Neprikosnovennyi zapas: Debaty o politike i kul'ture* 5, no. 43 (2005). http://magazines.russ.ru/nz/2005/43/r012-pr.html.

Iarskaia-Smirnova, E. R., and P. V. Romanov, eds. *Sovetskaia sotsial'naia politika: Stseny i deistvuiushchie litsa, 1940–1985.* Moscow: Variant, 2008.

Iğmen, Ali. *Speaking Soviet with an Accent: Culture and Power in Kyrgyzstan.* Pittsburgh: University of Pittsburgh Press, 2012.

Ilič, Melanie, ed. *Women in the Stalin Era.* New York: Palgrave, 2001.

Ilič, Melanie, Susan E. Reid, and Lynne Attwood, eds. *Women in the Khrushchev Era.* New York: Palgrave Macmillan, 2004.

Ilič, Melanie, and Jeremy Smith, eds. *Soviet State and Society under Nikita Khrushchev.* New York: Routledge, 2009.

Inkeles, Alex, and Raymond A. Bauer. *The Soviet Citizen: Daily Life in a Totalitarian Society.* Cambridge: Harvard University Press, 1959.

Iriye, Akira. *Cultural Internationalism and World Order.* Baltimore: Johns Hopkins University Press, 1997.

Jackson, Matthew J. *The Experimental Group: Ilya Kabakov, Moscow Conceptualism, Soviet Avant-Gardes.* Chicago: University of Chicago Press, 2010.

Jacoby, Sanford S. *Modern Manors: Welfare Capitalism since the New Deal.* Princeton: Princeton University Press, 1997.

Johnson, Molly W. *Training Socialist Citizens: Sports and the State in East Germany.* Boston: Brill, 2008.

Johnson, Ross A., and R. Eugene Parta, eds. *Cold War Broadcasting: Impact on the Soviet Union and Eastern Europe.* New York: Central European University Press, 2010.

Johnston, Timothy. *Being Soviet: Identity, Rumour, and Everyday Life under Stalin, 1939–1953*. New York: Oxford University Press, 2011.

Jones, Ian R., Paul Higgs, and David J. Ekerdt, eds. *Consumption and Generational Change: The Rise of Consumer Lifestyles*. New Brunswick: Transaction Publishers, 2009.

Jones, Jeffrey W. *Everyday Life and the "Reconstruction" of Soviet Russia during and after the Great Patriotic War, 1943–1948*. Bloomington: Slavica Publishers, 2008.

Jones, Polly, ed. *The Dilemmas of De-Stalinization: Negotiating Cultural and Social Change in the Khrushchev Era*. New York: Routledge, 2006.

Josephson, Paul R. *New Atlantis Revisited: Akademgorodok, the Siberian City of Science*. Princeton: Princeton University Press, 1997.

Kammen, Michael. *American Culture, American Tastes: Social Change and the 20th Century*. New York: Knopf, 1999.

Kapterev, Sergei. "Illusionary Spoils: Soviet Attitudes toward American Cinema during the Early Cold War." *Kritika* 10, no. 4 (Fall 2009): 779–807.

Kara-Murza, S. G. *"Sovok" vspominaet*. Moscow: Algoritm, 2002.

Kassof, Allen. *The Soviet Youth Program: Regimentation and Rebellion*. Cambridge: Harvard University Press, 1965.

Kats, R. S. *Istoriia sovetskoi fantastiki*. 3rd ed. Saint Petersburg: Izdatel'stvo St. Petersburgskogo universiteta, 2004.

Katsakioris, Constantin. "Soviet Lessons for Arab Modernization: Soviet Educational Aid towards Arab Countries after 1956." *Journal of Modern European History* 8, no. 1 (March 2010): 85–105.

Katzer, Nikolaus, Sandra Budy, Alexandra Kohring, and Manfred Zeller, eds. *Euphoria and Exhaustion: Modern Sport in Soviet Culture and History*. Frankfurt: Campus Verlag, 2010.

Kelly, Catriona. *Children's World: Growing Up in Russia, 1890–1991*. New Haven: Yale University Press, 2007.

Kelly, Catriona. *Refining Russia: Advice Literature, Polite Culture, and Gender from Catherine to Yeltsin*. New York: Oxford University Press, 2001.

Kelly, Catriona, and David Shepherd, eds. *Russian Cultural Studies: An Introduction*. New York: Oxford University Press, 1998.

Kerblay, Basile. *Modern Soviet Society*. New York: Routledge, 1983.

Kharkhordin, Oleg. *The Collective and the Individual in Russia: A Study of Practices*. Berkeley: University of California Press, 1999.

Kharkhordin, Oleg, ed. *Druzhba: Ocherki policy teorii praktik*. Saint Petersburg: Izdatel'stvo Evropeiskogo universiteta v Sankt-Peterburge, 2009.

Kharkhordin, Oleg. *Oblichat' i litsemerit': Genealogiia rossiiskoi lichnosti*. Saint Petersburg: Evropeiskii universitet v Sankt-Peterburge, 2002.

Khrenov, Kh. A. *Chelovek igraiuschii v russkoi kul'ture*. Saint Petersburg: Aleteia, 2005.

Klaniczay, Gabor, and Balzas Trencsenyi. "Introduction: Mapping the Merry Ghetto; Musical Countercultures in East Central Europe, 1960–1989." *East Central Europe* 2–3, no. 38 (2011): 169–79.

Klumbyte, Neringa. "Political Intimacy: Power, Laughter, and Coexistence in Late Soviet Lithuania." *East European Politics and Societies* 25, no. 4 (November 2011): 658–77.

Klumbyte, Neringa, and Gulnaz Sharafutdinova, eds. *Soviet Society in the Era of Late Socialism, 1964–1985.* Lanham: Lexington Books, 2012.

Koenker, Diane P. "Mad Men in Moscow: Sex and Style in the Soviet 1960s." Paper presented at the Association for Slavic, East European, and Eurasian Studies national convention, Los Angeles, CA, November 18–21, 2010.

Koenker, Diane P., and Anne E. Gorsuch. "The Socialist 1960s: Popular Culture and the City in Global Perspective." Workshop held in Urbana-Champaign, IL, June 24–26, 2010.

Komaromi, Ann. "Samizdat and Soviet Dissident Publics." *Slavic Review* 71, no. 1 (Spring 2012): 70–90.

Konecny, Peter. *Builders and Deserters: Students, State, and Community in Leningrad, 1917–1941.* Montreal: McGill-Queen's University Press, 1999.

Koshar, Rudy, ed. *Histories of Leisure.* New York: Berg, 2002.

Kotek, Joël. *Students and the Cold War.* Translated by Ralph Blumenau. New York: St. Martin's Press, 1996.

Kotkin, Stephen. *Armageddon Averted.* New York: Oxford University Press, 2001.

Kotkin, Stephen. *Magnetic Mountain: Stalinism as a Civilization.* Berkeley: University of California Press, 1995.

Kowalsky, Sharon. *Deviant Women: Female Crime and Criminology in Revolutionary Russia, 1880–1930.* DeKalb: Northern Illinois University Press, 2009.

Kozlov, Denis. "'I Have Not Read, but I Will Say': Soviet Literary Audiences and Changing Ideas of Social Membership, 1958–66." *Kritika* 7, no. 3 (Summer 2006): 557–97.

Kozlov, V. A. *Mass Uprisings in the USSR: Protest and Rebellion in the Post-Stalin Years.* Translated and edited by Elaine M. MacKinnon. Armonk: M. E. Sharpe, 2002.

Kozovoi, Andrei. "Eye to Eye with the Main Enemy: Soviet Youth Travel to the United States." *Ab Imperio* 2 (June 2011): 221–37.

Krylova, Anna. "Beyond the Spontaneity-Consciousness Paradigm: 'Class Instinct' as a Promising Category of Historical Analysis." *Slavic Review* 62, no. 1 (Spring 2003): 1–23.

Krylova, Anna. "Soviet Modernity: Stephen Kotkin and the Bolshevik Predicament." *Contemporary European History* 23, no. 2 (2014): 167–92.

Krylova, Anna. *Soviet Women in Combat: A History of Violence on the Eastern Front*. New York: Cambridge University Press, 2010.

Krylova, Anna. "The Tenacious Liberal Subject in Soviet Studies." *Kritika* 1, no. 1 (Winter 2000): 119–46.

Kuhr-Korolev, Corinna, ed. *Sowjetjugend 1917–1941: Generation Zwischen Revolution und Resignation*. Essen: Klartext, 2001.

Kuisel, Richard. "Americanization for Historians." *Diplomatic History* 24, no. 3 (Summer 2000): 509–16.

Kukulin, Il'ia, Mark Lipovetskii, and Mariia Maiofis, eds. *Veselye chelovechki: Kul'turnye geroi sovetskogo detstva*. Moscow: Novoe literaturnoe obozrenie, 2008.

Kurchenko, Olga. *Little Soldiers: How Soviet Children Went to War, 1941–1945*. New York: Oxford University Press, 2011.

Kuznick, Peter J., and James Gilbert, eds. *Rethinking Cold War Culture*. Washington: Smithsonian Institution Press, 2001.

Lane, Christel. *The Rites of Rulers: Ritual in Industrial Society—The Soviet Case*. New York: Cambridge University Press, 1981.

LaPierre, Brian. *Hooligans in Khrushchev's Russia: Defining, Policing, and Producing Deviance during the Thaw*. Madison: University of Wisconsin Press, 2012.

LaPierre, Brian. "Making Hooliganism on a Mass Scale: The Campaign against Petty Hooliganism in the Soviet Union, 1956–1964." *Cahiers du Monde russe* 47, no. 1–2 (January–February 2006): 349–75.

Laville, Helen, and Hugh Wilford, eds. *The US Government, Citizen Groups and the Cold War: The State-Private Network*. New York: Routledge, 2006.

Lebina, N. B., and A. N. Chistikov. *Obyvatel' i reformy: Kartiny povsednevnoi zhizni gorozhan v gody nepa i khrushchevskogo desiatiletiia*. Saint Petersburg: Dmitrii Bulanin, 2003.

Ledeneva, Alena V. *Russia's Economy of Favours: Blat, Networking, and Informal Exchange*. New York: Cambridge University Press, 1998.

LeDoux, Joseph. *The Emotional Brain: The Mysterious Underpinnings of Emotional Life*. New York: Touchstone, 1996.

Leffler, Melvyn P. "The Cold War: What Do 'We Now Know'?" *American Historical Review* 104, no. 2 (April 1999): 501–24.

Lemon, Alaina. *Between Two Fires: Gypsy Performance and Romani Memory from Pushkin to Postsocialism*. Durham: Duke University Press, 2000.

Lenoe, Matthew E. *Closer to the Masses: Stalinist Culture, Social Revolution, and Soviet Newspapers*. Cambridge: Harvard University Press, 2004.

Lenoe, Matthew E. "In Defense of Timasheff's Great Retreat." *Kritika* 5, no. 4 (Fall 2004): 721–30.

Lerner, Mitchell. "'Trying to Find the Guy Who Invited Them': Lyndon Johnson, Bridge Building, and the End of the Prague Spring." *Diplomatic History* 32, no. 1 (January 2008): 77–103.

Lewis, Martin W., and Karen E. Wigen. *The Myth of Continents: A Critique of Metageography*. Berkeley: University of California Press, 1997.

Lincoln, W. Bruce. *The Great Reforms: Autocracy, Bureaucracy, and the Politics of Change in Imperial Russia*. DeKalb: Northern Illinois University Press, 1990.

Lindenberger, Thomas. "The Fragmented Society: 'Social Activism' and Authority in GDR State Socialism." *Zeitgeschicht* 37, no. 1 (January–February 2010): 3–20.

Lindenmeyr, Adele. "Building Civil Society One Brick at a Time: People's Houses and Worker Enlightenment in Late Imperial Russia." *Journal of Modern History* 84, no. 1 (March 2012): 1–39.

Linhart, Sepp, and Sabine Frühstück, eds. *The Culture of Japan as Seen through Its Leisure*. Albany: State University of New York Press, 1998.

Linz, Susan J., ed. *The Impact of World War II on the Soviet Union*. Totowa: Rowman & Allanheld, 1985.

Lovell, Stephen. "Broadcasting Bolshevik: The Radio Voice of Soviet Culture, 1920s–1950s." *Journal of Contemporary History* 48, no. 1 (January 2013): 78–97.

Lovell, Stephen. "From Genealogy to Generation: The Birth of Cohort Thinking in Russia." *Kritika* 9, no. 3 (Summer 2008): 567–94.

Lovell, Stephen, ed. *Generations in Twentieth-Century Europe*. New York: Palgrave Macmillan, 2007.

Lovell, Stephen. *The Russian Reading Revolution: Print Culture in the Soviet and Post-Soviet Eras*. New York: St. Martin's Press, 2000.

Lovell, Stephen. *Summerfolk: A History of the Dacha, 1710–2000*. Ithaca: Cornell University Press, 2003.

Lucas, Scott. *Freedom's War: The American Crusade against the Soviet Union*. New York: New York University Press, 1999.

Lur'e, L., and I. Maliarova. *1956 god: Seredina veka*. Saint Petersburg: Neva, 2007.

Lutz, Catherine A., and Lila Abu-Lughod, eds. *Language and the Politics of Emotion*. New York: Cambridge University Press, 1990.

Lygo, Emily. *Leningrad Poetry, 1953–1975: The Thaw Generation*. Bern: Peter Lang, 2010.

MacCannell, Dean. *The Tourist: A New Theory of the Leisure Class*. 1976. Reprint, Berkeley: University of California Press, 1999.

MacFadyen, David. *Red Stars: Personality and the Soviet Popular Song, 1955–1991.* Ithaca: McGill-Queen's University Press, 2001.

MacFadyen, David. *Songs for Fat People: Affect, Emotion, and Celebrity in the Russian Popular Song, 1900–1955.* Ithaca: McGill-Queen's University Press, 2002.

Maiorova, A. S., ed. *Neofitsial'naia zhizn' gorozhan: Zapad-Rossiia-Vostok.* Saratov: Nauka, 2007.

Malia, Martin. *The Soviet Tragedy: A History of Socialism in Russia, 1917–1991.* New York: Free Press, 1994.

Mally, Lynn. *Culture of the Future: The Proletkult Movement in Revolutionary Russia.* Berkeley: University of California Press, 1990.

Mally, Lynn. *Revolutionary Acts: Amateur Theater and the Soviet State, 1917–1938.* Ithaca: Cornell University Press, 2000.

Mannheim, Karl. *Essays on the Sociology of Knowledge.* Translated and edited by Paul Kecskemeti. New York: Oxford University Press, 1952.

Markasova, E. V. "A vot praktiku my znaem po geroiam Krasnodona." *Neprikosnovennyi zapas* 58, no. 2 (2008). http://magazines.russ.ru/nz/2008/2/ma18.html.

Marks, Steven G. *How Russia Shaped the Modern World: From Art to Anti-Semitism, Ballet to Bolshevism.* Princeton: Princeton University Press, 2003.

Markwick, Roger D. *Rewriting History in Soviet Russia: The Politics of Revisionist Historiography, 1956–1974.* New York: Palgrave Macmillan, 2001.

Marotti, William. "Japan 1968: The Performance of Violence and the Theater of Protest." *American Historical Review* 114, no. 1 (February 2009): 97–135.

Maurer, Eva, Julia Richers, Monica Rüthers, and Carmen Scheide, eds. *Soviet Space Culture: Cosmic Enthusiasm in Socialist Societies.* New York: Palgrave Macmillan, 2011.

May, Lary, ed. *Recasting America: Culture and Politics in the Age of Cold War.* Chicago: University of Chicago Press, 1989.

McCracken, Grant. "The History of Consumption: A Literature Review and Consumer Guide." *Journal of Consumer Policy* 10 (June 1987): 139–66.

McKendrick, Neil, John Brewer, and J. H. Plumb. *The Birth of a Consumer Society: The Commercialization of Eighteenth-Century England.* Bloomington: Indiana University Press, 1982.

McLellan, Josie. *Love in the Time of Communism: Intimacy and Sexuality in the GDR.* New York: Cambridge University Press, 2011.

McMahon, Darrin M. *Happiness: A History.* New York: Atlantic Monthly Press, 2006.

McMichael, Polly. "The Boundaries of Soviet Rock Culture: Mashina vremeni and Roskontsert." Paper presented at the Association for Slavic, East

European, and Eurasian Studies national convention, Washington DC, November 2011.

McReynolds, Louise. *Russia at Play: Leisure Activities at the End of the Tsarist Era*. Ithaca: Cornell University Press, 2003.

Meltzer, David, ed. *Reading Jazz*. San Francisco: Mercury House, 1993.

Menzel, Birgit, Michael Hagemeister, and Bernice G. Rosenthal, eds. *The New Age of Russia: Occult and Esoteric Dimensions*. Berlin: Verlag Otto Sagner, 2012.

Michaels, Paula A. "Comrades in the Labor Room: The Lamaze Method of Childbirth Preparation in France's Cold War Home Front." *American Historical Review* 115, no. 4 (October 2010): 1031–60.

Mihelj, Sabina. "Negotiating Cold War Culture at the Crossroads of East and West: Uplifting the Working People, Entertaining the Masses, Cultivating the Nation." *Comparative Studies in Society and History* 53, no. 2 (June 2011): 509–39.

Mikkonen, Simo. "Stealing the Monopoly of Knowledge? Soviet Reactions to U.S. Cold War Broadcasting." *Kritika* 11, no. 4 (Fall 2010): 771–805.

Millar, James R. "The Little Deal: Brezhnev's Contribution to Acquisitive Socialism." *Slavic Review* 44, no. 4 (Winter 1985): 694–706.

Millar, James R., ed. *Politics, Work, and Daily Life in the USSR: A Survey of Former Soviet Citizens*. New York: Cambridge University Press, 1987.

Miller, Daniel, ed. *Acknowledging Consumption: A Review of New Studies*. New York: Routledge, 1995.

Miller, Daniel. *Material Culture and Mass Consumption*. Oxford: Basil Blackwell, 1987.

Miller, Toby, and Alec McHoul. *Popular Culture and Everyday Life*. Thousand Oaks: SAGE Publications, 1998.

Mintz, Steven. *Huck's Raft: A History of American Childhood*. Cambridge: Harvard University Press, 2004.

Mitrokhin, N. A. *Russkaia partiia: Dvizhenie russkikh natsionalistov v SSSR, 1953–1985 gody*. Moscow: Novoe literaturnoe obozrenie, 2003.

Mitter, Rana, and Patrick Major, eds. *Across the Blocs: Cold War Cultural and Social History*. Portland: Frank Cass, 2004.

Mohan, Brij, ed. *Toward Comparative Social Welfare*. Cambridge: Schenkman Books, 1985.

Mort, Frank. *Cultures of Consumption: Masculinities and Social Space in Late Twentieth-Century Britain*. New York: Routledge, 1996.

Naiman, Eric. "On Soviet Subjects and the Scholars Who Make Them." *Russian Review* 60, no. 3 (July 2001): 307–15.

Naiman, Eric. *Sex in Public: The Incarnation of Early Soviet Ideology*. Princeton: Princeton University Press, 1997.

Narskii, I. V. "'Zariad veselosti': S(t)imuliatsiia radosti v diskurse o sovetskoi tantseval'noi samodeiatel'nosti." Paper presented at Smekhovaia kul'tura v Rossii XVIII–XX vv., Cheliabinsk, Russia, October 2011.

Neirick, Miriam. *When Pigs Could Fly and Bears Could Dance: A History of the Soviet Circus*. Madison: University of Wisconsin Press, 2012.

Nelson, Amy. *Music for the Revolution: Musicians and Power in Early Soviet Russia*. University Park: Pennsylvania State University Press, 2004.

Nelson, Amy. "The Struggle for Proletarian Music: RAPM and the Cultural Revolution." *Slavic Review* 59, no. 1 (Spring 2000): 101–32.

Nelson, Michael. *War of the Black Heavens: The Battles of Western Broadcasting in the Cold War*. Syracuse: Syracuse University Press, 1997.

Neuberger, Joan. *Hooliganism: Crime, Culture, and Power in St. Petersburg, 1900–1914*. Berkeley: University of California Press, 1993.

Neumann, Matthias. *The Communist Youth League and the Transformation of the Soviet Union, 1917–1932*. New York: Routledge, 2011.

Ngai, Sianne. *Ugly Feelings*. Cambridge: Harvard University Press, 2005.

Nordlander, David. "Khrushchev's Image in the Light of Glasnost and Perestroika." *Russian Review* 52, no. 2 (April 1993): 248–64.

Nurske, Ragnar. *Problems of Capital Formation in Underdeveloped Countries*. New York: Oxford University Press, 1953.

Nussbaum, Martha C. *Upheavals of Thought: The Intelligence of Emotions*. New York: Cambridge University Press, 2001.

Nye, Joseph S., Jr. *Soft Power: The Means to Success in World Politics*. New York: Public Affairs, 2004.

Oldenziel, Ruth, and Karin Zuchman, eds. *Cold War Kitchen: Americanization, Technology, and European Users*. Cambridge: MIT Press, 2009.

Olsen, Laura J. *Performing Russia: Folk Revival and Russian Identity*. New York: RoutledgeCurzon, 2004.

O'Meara, Patrick. "'All the World's a Stage': Aspects of the Historical Interplay of Culture and Society with Myth and Mask in 18th- and Early 19th-Century Russia." *Kritika* 7, no. 3 (Summer 2006): 619–32.

Osgood, Kenneth. *Total Cold War: Eisenhower's Secret Propaganda Battle at Home and Abroad*. Lawrence: University Press of Kansas, 2006.

Osokina, Elena. *Za fasadom "Stalinskogo izobilia": Raspredelenie i rynok v snabzhenii naseleniia v gody industrializatsii, 1927–1941*. Moscow: ROSSPEN, 1998.

Ostromoukhova, Bella. "KVN–'molodezhnaia kul'tura shestidesiatykh'?" *Neprikosnovennyi zapas: Debaty o politike i kul'ture* 36, no. 4 (September 2004). http://magazines.russ.ru/nz.

Ostromoukhova, Bella. "Le Dégel et les troupes amateur: Changements politiques et activités artistiques des étudiants, 1953–1970." *Cahiers du Monde russe* 47, no. 1–2 (January–June 2006): 303–25.

Otnes, Cele C., and Tina M. Lowrey, eds. *Contemporary Consumption Rituals: A Research Anthology*. Mahwah: Lawrence Erlbaum Associates, 2004.

Palmer, Scott W. "How Memory Was Made: The Construction of the Memorial to the Heroes of the Battle of Stalingrad." *Russian Review* 68, no. 3 (July 2009): 373–407.

Paperno, Irina. "Personal Accounts of the Soviet Experience." *Kritika* 3, no. 4 (Fall 2002): 577–610.

Paperno, Irina. *Stories of the Soviet Experience: Memoirs, Diaries, Dreams*. Ithaca: Cornell University Press, 2009.

Partan, Olga. "Alla, the Jester Queen of Russian Pop Culture." *Russian Review* 66, no. 3 (July 2007): 483–500.

Patton, Raymond. "The Communist Culture Industry: The Music Business in 1980s Poland." *Journal of Contemporary History* 47, no. 2 (April 2012): 427–49.

Peacock, Margaret. *Cold War Kids: The Politics of Childhood in the Soviet Union and the United States, 1945–1968*. Chapel Hill: University of North Carolina Press, 2014.

Peacock, Margaret. "The Perils of Building Cold War Consensus at the 1957 Moscow World Festival of Youth and Students." *Cold War History* 12, no. 1 (February 2012): 1–21.

Péteri, György, ed. *Imagining the West in Eastern Europe and the Soviet Union*. Pittsburgh: University of Pittsburgh Press, 2010.

Péteri, György, ed. *Nylon Curtain: Transnational and Transsystemic Tendencies in the Cultural Life of State-Socialist Russia and East-Central Europe*. Trondheim: Trondheim Studies on East European Cultures & Societies, 2006.

Péteri, György. "The Occident Within—or the Drive for Exceptionalism and Modernity." *Kritika* 9, no. 4 (Fall 2008): 929–37.

Petrone, Karen. *Life Has Become More Joyous, Comrades: Celebrations in the Time of Stalin*. Bloomington: Indiana University Press, 2000.

Peukert, Detlev J. K. *Inside Nazi Germany: Conformity, Opposition, and Racism in Everyday Life*. New Haven: Yale University Press, 1987.

Pfohl, Stephen. *Images of Deviance and Social Control: A Sociological History*. New York: McGraw-Hill, 1994.

Pickhan, Gertrud, and Rüdiger Ritter, eds. *Jazz behind the Iron Curtain*. Frankfurt: Peter Lang, 2010.

Pilkington, Hilary. *Russia's Youth and Its Culture: A Nation's Constructors and Constructed*. New York: Routledge, 1994.

Pilkington, Hilary, and Richard Johnson. "Peripheral Youth: Relations of Identity and Power in Global/Local Context." *European Journal of Cultural Studies* 6, no. 3 (August 2003): 259–83.

Plamper, Jan. "Foucault's Gulag." *Kritika* 3, no. 2 (Spring 2002): 255–80.

Plamper, Jan. "Introduction: Emotional Turn? Feelings in Russian History and Culture." *Slavic Review* 68, no. 2 (Summer 2009): 229–37.

Plamper, Jan. *The Stalin Cult: A Study in the Alchemy of Power*. New Haven: Yale University Press, 2012.

Plamper, Jan, Schamma Schahadat, and Marc Elie, eds. *Rossiiskaia imperiia chuvstv: Podkhody k kul'turnoi istorii emotsii*. Moscow: Novoe literaturnoe obozrenie, 2010.

Platonov, Rachel S. *Singing the Self: Guitar Poetry, Community, and Identity in the Post-Stalin Period*. Evanston: Northwestern University Press, 2012.

Platt, Anthony M. *The Child Savers: The Invention of Delinquency*. Chicago: University of Chicago Press, 1969.

Poiger, Uta G. *Jazz, Rock, and Rebels: Cold War Politics and American Culture in a Divided Germany*. Berkeley: University of California Press, 2000.

Pollock, Ethan. "'Real Men Go to the Bania': Postwar Soviet Masculinities and the Bathhouse." *Kritika* 11, no. 1 (Winter 2010): 47–76.

Pollock, Ethan. *Stalin and the Soviet Science Wars*. Princeton: Princeton University Press, 2006.

Portelli, Alessandro. *The Death of Luigi Trastulli, and Other Stories: Form and Meaning in Oral History*. Albany: State University of New York Press, 1991.

Prakash, Gyan. "Subaltern Studies as Postcolonial Criticism." *American Historical Review* 99, no. 5 (December 1994): 1475–90.

Prevots, Naima. *Dance for Export: Cultural Diplomacy and the Cold War*. Hanover: Wesleyan University Press, 1998.

Prokhorov, Alexander, ed. *Springtime for Soviet Cinema: Re/Viewing the 1960s*. Pittsburgh: Pittsburgh Russian Film Symposium, 2001.

Prokhorov, Alexander. *Unasledovannyi diskurs: Paradigmy stalinskoi kul'tury v literature i kinematografii "ottepeli."* Saint Petersburg: Akademecheskii proekt, 2007.

Pushkareva, N. L., ed. *Sotsial'naia istoriia: Ezhegodnik*. Saint Petersburg: Aleteiia, 2009.

Pyzhikov, A. V. *Khrushchevskaia "ottepel'."* Moscow: OLMA-PRESS, 2002.

Qualls, Karl D. *From Ruins to Reconstruction: Urban Identity in Soviet Sevastopol after World War II*. Ithaca: Cornell University Press, 2010.

Rajagopalan, Sudha. *Indian Films in Soviet Cinemas: The Culture of Moviegoing after Stalin*. Bloomington: Indiana University Press, 2008.

Raleigh, Donald J. *Experiencing Russia's Civil War: Politics, Society, and Revolutionary Culture in Saratov, 1917–1922*. Princeton: Princeton University Press, 2002.

Raleigh, Donald J. "Languages of Power: How the Saratov Bolsheviks Imagined Their Enemies." *Slavic Review* 57, no. 2 (Summer 1998): 320–49.

Raleigh, Donald J., ed. *Provincial Landscapes: Local Dimensions of Soviet Power, 1917–1953*. Pittsburgh: University of Pittsburgh Press, 2001.

Raleigh, Donald J. *Russia's Sputnik Generation: Soviet Baby Boomers Talk about Their Lives*. Bloomington: Indiana University Press, 2006.

Raleigh, Donald J. *Soviet Baby Boomers: An Oral History of Russia's Cold War Generation*. New York: Oxford University Press, 2011.

Ramet, Sabrina P., ed. *Rocking the State: Rock Music and Politics in Eastern Europe and Russia*. Boulder: Westview Press, 1994.

Ramet, Sabrina P. *Social Currents in Eastern Europe: The Sources and Consequences of the Great Transformations*. 2nd ed. Durham: Duke University Press, 1995.

Ramet, Sabrina P., and Gordana P. Crnković, eds. *Kazaaam! Splat! Ploof! The American Impact on European Popular Culture since 1945*. New York: Rowman & Littlefield, 2003.

Randall, Amy E. *The Soviet Dream World of Retail Trade and Consumption in the 1930s*. New York: Palgrave Macmillan, 2008.

Raphael-Hernandez, Heike, ed. *Blackening Europe: The African American Presence*. New York: Routledge, 2004.

Reddy, William M. "Comment: Emotional Turn? Feelings in Russian History and Culture." *Slavic Review* 68, no. 2 (Summer 2009): 329–34.

Reddy, William M. *The Navigation of Feeling: A Framework for the History of Emotions*. Cambridge: Cambridge University Press, 2001.

Reid, Susan. "Cold War in the Kitchen: Gender and the De-Stalinization of Consumer Taste in the Soviet Union." *Slavic Review* 61, no. 2 (Summer 2002): 211–52.

Reid, Susan. "In the Name of the People: The Manege Affair Revisited." *Kritika* 6, no. 4 (Fall 2005): 673–716.

Reid, Susan. *Khrushchev in Wonderland: The Pioneer Palace in Moscow's Lenin Hills, 1962*. Pittsburgh: University of Pittsburgh Press, 2002.

Reid, Susan. "Making Oneself at Home in the Soviet Sixties." Paper presented at the Association for Slavic, East European, and Eurasian Studies national convention, Los Angeles, CA, November 18–21, 2010.

Reid, Susan. "Who Will Beat Whom? Soviet Popular Reception of the American National Exhibition in Moscow, 1959." *Kritika* 9, no. 4 (Fall 2008): 855–904.

Reid, Susan E., and Crowley, David, eds. *Style and Socialism: Modernity and Material Culture in Post-War Eastern Europe*. Oxford: Berg, 2000.

Richmond, Yale. *Cultural Exchange and the Cold War: Raising the Iron Curtain*. University Park: Pennsylvania State University Press, 2003.

Richthofen, Esther von. *Bringing Culture to the Masses: Control, Compromise and Participation in the GDR*. New York: Berghahn Books, 2009.

Riordan, James, ed. *Soviet Youth Culture*. Basingstoke: Macmillan, 1989.

Risch, William J. "Soviet 'Flower Children': Hippies and the Youth Counter-culture in 1970s L'viv." *Journal of Contemporary History* 40, no. 3 (July 2005): 565–84.

Risch, William J. *The Ukrainian West: Culture and the Fate of Empire in Soviet Lviv*. Cambridge: Harvard University Press, 2011.

Risch, William J., ed. *Youth and Rock in the Soviet Bloc: Youth Cultures, Music, and the State in Russia and Eastern Europe*. Lanham: Lexington Books, 2015.

Ristolainen, Mari. *Preferred Realities: Soviet and Post-Soviet Amateur Art in Novorzhev*. Jyväskylä: Gummerus Printing, 2008.

Roberts, Ken. *Youth in Transition: Eastern Europe and the West*. New York: Palgrave Macmillan, 2009.

Robinson, Deana Campbell, Elizabeth B. Buck, Marlene Cuthbert, and the ICYI. *Music at the Margins: Popular Music and Global Cultural Diversity*. Newbury Park: SAGE Publications, 1991.

Rolf, Malte. "Constructing a Soviet Time: Bolshevik Festivals and Their Rivals during the First Five-Year Plan; A Study of the Central Black Earth Region." *Kritika* 1, no. 3 (Summer 2000): 447–73.

Rolf, Malte. "Expression of Enthusiasm and Emotional Coding in Dictatorship—The Stalinist Soviet Union." *Working Papers*, UCLA Center for European and Eurasian Studies, UC Los Angeles, December 2004. http://www.escholarship.org/uc/item/6qh736hj#.

Rolf, Malte. "A Hall of Mirrors: Sovietizing Culture under Stalinism." *Slavic Review* 68, no. 3 (Fall 2009): 601–30.

Rolf, Malte. *Soviet Mass Festivals, 1917–1991*. Translated by Cynthia Klohr. Pittsburgh: University of Pittsburgh Press, 2013.

Rolf, Malte. *Sovetskie massovye prazdniki*. Moscow: ROSSPEN, 2009.

Romanov, P. V., and E. R. Iarskaia-Smirnova, eds. *Sovetskaia sotsial'naia politi-ka 1920–1930-kh godov: Ideologiia i povsednevnost'*. Moscow: Variant, 2007.

Romijn, Peter, Giles Scott-Smith, and Joes Segal, eds. *Divided Dreamworlds? The Cultural Cold War in East and West*. Amsterdam: Amsterdam University Press, 2012.

Rosen, Harold. *Speaking from Memory: A Guide to Autobiographical Acts and Practices*. Stoke-on-Trent: Trentham, 1998.

Rosenwein, Barbara H. *Emotional Communities in the Middle Ages*. Ithaca: Cornell University Press, 2006.

Rosenwein, Barbara H. "Worrying about Emotions in History." *American Historical Review* 107, no. 3 (June 2002): 821–45.

Roth, Randolph. "Measuring Feelings and Beliefs That May Facilitate (or Deter) Homicide: A Research Note on the Causes of Historic Fluctuations in Homicide Rates in the United States." *Homicide Studies* 16, no. 2 (May 2012): 197–216.

Roth-Ey, Kristin. *Moscow Prime Time: How the Soviet Union Built the Media Empire That Lost the Cultural Cold War.* Ithaca: Cornell University Press, 2011.

Rozental', I. S. *"I vot obshchestvennoe mnen'e!" Kluby v istorii rossiiskoi obshchestvennoisti; Konets XVIII–nachalo XX v.* Moscow: Novyi khrongraf, 2007.

Ruffley, David L. *Children of Victory: Young Specialists and the Evolution of Soviet Society.* Westport: Praeger, 2003.

Ryback, Timothy W. *Rock around the Bloc: A History of Rock Music in Eastern Europe and the Soviet Union.* New York: Oxford University Press, 1990.

Ryder, Norman B. "The Cohort as a Concept in the Study of Social Change." *American Sociological Review* 30, no. 6 (1965): 843–61.

Sachsenmaier, Dominic, Shmuel N. Eisenstadt, and Jens Riedel, eds. *Reflections on Multiple Modernities: European, Chinese, and Other Interpretations.* Boston: Brill, 2001.

Said, Edward. *Culture and Imperialism.* New York: Vintage Books, 1993.

Said, Edward. *Orientalism.* New York: Vintage Books, 1979.

Sargeant, Lynn M. *Harmony and Discord: Music and the Transformation of Russian Cultural Life.* New York: Oxford University Press, 2011.

Sargeant, Lynn M. "High Anxiety: New Venues, New Audiences, and the Fear of the Popular in Late Imperial Russian Musical Life." *19th-Century Music* 35, no. 2 (Fall 2011): 93–114.

Saunders, Frances Stonor. *The Cultural Cold War: The CIA and the World of Arts and Letters.* New York: New Press, 1999.

Schildt, Axel, and Detlef Siegfried, eds. *Between Marx and Coca-Cola: Youth Cultures in Changing European Societies, 1960–1980.* New York: Berghahn Books, 2006.

Schildt, Axel, and Detlef Siegfried, eds. *European Cities, Youth, and the Public Sphere in the Twentieth Century.* Burlington: Ashgate Publishing, 2005.

Schlögel, Karl, ed. *Mastering Russian Spaces: Raum und Raumbewältigung als Problem der russischen Geschichte.* Berlin: Oldenbourg-Verlag, 2011.

Schmelz, Peter J. *Such Freedom, If Only Musical: Unofficial Soviet Music during the Thaw.* New York: Oxford University Press, 2009.

Scitovsky, Tibor. *The Joyless Economy: The Psychology of Human Satisfaction and Consumer Dissatisfaction.* New York: Oxford University Press, 1976.

Scott, James C. *Seeing Like a State: How Certain Schemes to Improve the Human Condition Have Failed.* New Haven: Yale University Press, 1998.

Scott-Smith, Giles, and Hans Krabbendam, eds. *The Cultural Cold War in Western Europe, 1945–1960.* Portland: Frank Cass, 2003.

Seniavskaia, E.S. *Protivniki Rossii v voinakh XX veka: Evolutsiia "obraza vraga" v soznanii armii i obshchestva.* Moscow: ROSSPEN, 2006.

Shaw, Tony, and Denise J. Youngblood. *Cinematic Cold War: The American and Soviet Struggle for Hearts and Minds.* Lawrence: University Press of Kansas, 2010.

Shchepanskaia, T. B. "Trassa: Pipl i telegi 80 kh." *Neprikosnovennyi zapas* 36, no. 4 (2004). http://magazines.russ.ru/nz/2004/4/sh7.html.

Shearer, David R. *Policing Stalin's Socialism: Repression and Social Order in the Soviet Union.* New Haven: Yale University Press, 2009.

Shelley, Louise I. *Policing Soviet Society: The Evolution of State Control.* New York: Routledge, 1996.

Shiraev, Eric, and Vladislav Zubok. *Anti-Americanism in Russia: From Stalin to Putin.* New York: Palgrave, 2000.

Shlapentokh, Vladimir. *Public and Private Life of the Soviet People: Changing Values in Post-Stalin Russia.* New York: Oxford University Press, 1989.

Shul'pin, A. P. *Molodezhnye teatry Rossii.* Saint Petersburg: Dmitrii Bulanin, 2004.

Siddiqi, Asif A. *The Red Rockets' Glare: Spaceflight and the Soviet Imagination.* New York: Cambridge University Press, 2010.

Siegelbaum, Lewis H., ed. *Borders of Socialism: Private Spheres of Soviet Russia.* New York: Palgrave Macmillan, 2006.

Siegelbaum, Lewis H. *Cars for Comrades: The Life of the Soviet Automobile.* Ithaca: Cornell University Press, 2008.

Siegelbaum, Lewis H. "The Shaping of Soviet Workers' Leisure: Workers' Clubs and Palaces of Culture in the 1930s." *International Labor and Working-Class History* 56 (October 1999): 78–92.

Siegelbaum, Lewis H. *Soviet State and Society between the Revolutions, 1918–1929.* New York: Cambridge University Press, 1992.

Sigman, Carole. *Clubs politiques et perestroïka en Russie: Subversion sans dissidence.* Paris: Editions Karthala, 2009

Silina, L. V. *Nastroeniia sovetskogo studenchestva, 1945–1964.* Moscow: Russkii mir, 2004.

Slezkine, Yuri. *The Jewish Century.* Princeton: Princeton University Press, 2004.

Slobin, Mark, ed. *Retuning Culture: Musical Changes in Central and Eastern Europe.* Durham: Duke University Press, 1996.

Smith, Gerald S. *Songs to Seven Strings: Russian Guitar Poetry and Soviet "Mass Song."* Bloomington: Indiana University Press, 1984.

Smith, Jeremy, and Melanie Ilič, eds. *Khrushchev in the Kremlin: Policy and Government in the Soviet Union, 1953–1964.* New York: Routledge, 2011.

Smith, Kathleen E. "A New Generation of Political Prisoners: 'Anti-Soviet' Students, 1956–1957." *Soviet and Post-Soviet Review* 32, no. 1 (2005): 191–208.

Smith, Mark B. "Individual Forms of Property in the Urban Housing Fund of the Soviet Union, 1944–64." *Slavonic and East European Review* 86, no. 2 (April 2008): 283–305.

Smith, Mark B. *Property of Communists: The Urban Housing Program from Stalin to Khrushchev.* DeKalb: Northern Illinois University Press, 2010.

Smith, Susannah Lockwood. "From Peasants to Professionals: The Socialist-Realist Transformation of a Russian Folk Choir." *Kritika* 3, no. 3 (Summer 2002): 393–425.

Snyder, C. R., and Shane J. Lopez, eds. *Handbook of Positive Psychology.* New York: Oxford University Press, 2005.

Søland, Birgitte. *Becoming Modern: Young Women and the Reconstruction of Womanhood in the 1920s.* Princeton: Princeton University Press, 2000.

Solnick, Steven L. *Stealing the State: Control and Collapse in Soviet Institutions.* Cambridge: Harvard University Press, 1998.

Solomon, Peter H., Jr. *Soviet Criminal Justice under Stalin.* Cambridge: Cambridge University Press, 1996.

Soper, Kate, and Frank Trentmann, eds. *Citizenship and Consumption.* New York: Palgrave Macmillan, 2008.

Springhall, John. *Coming of Age: Adolescence in Britain, 1860–1960.* Dublin: Gill and Macmillan, 1986.

Springhall, John. *Youth Popular Culture and Moral Panics: Penny Gaffs to Gangsta-Rap, 1830–1996.* New York: St. Martin's Press, 1998.

Starks, Tricia. *The Body Soviet: Propaganda, Hygiene, and the Revolutionary State.* Madison: University of Wisconsin Press, 2008.

Starr, S. Frederick. *Red and Hot: The Fate of Jazz in the Soviet Union, 1917–1980.* New York: Oxford University Press, 1983.

Statiev, Alexander. "The Nature of Anti-Soviet Armed Resistance, 1942–44: The North Caucasus, the Kalmyk Autonomous Republic, and Crimea." *Kritika* 6, no. 2 (Spring 2005): 285–318.

Stearns, Peter N. *American Cool: Constructing a Twentieth-Century Emotional Style.* New York: New York University Press, 1994.

Stearns, Peter N., and Jan Lewis, eds. *An Emotional History of the United States.* New York: New York University Press, 1998.

Stebenne, David L. "IBM's 'New Deal': Employment Policies of the International Business Machine Corporation, 1933–1956." *Journal of the Historical Society* 5, no. 1 (2005): 47–77.

Steinberg, Mark D. *Proletarian Imagination: Self, Modernity, and the Sacred in Russia.* Ithaca: Cornell University Press, 2002.

Steinberg, Mark D., and Valeria Sobol, eds. *Interpreting Emotions in Russia and Eastern Europe.* DeKalb: Northern Illinois University Press, 2011.

Steinholt, Yngvar B. *Rock in the Reservation: Songs from the Leningrad Rock Club, 1981–86.* New York: MMMSP, 2005.

Stephan, Alexander, ed. *The Americanization of Europe: Culture, Diplomacy, and Anti-Americanism after 1945*. New York: Berghahn Books, 2006.

Stern, Liudmila. *Western Intellectuals and the Soviet Union, 1920–1940: From Red Square to the Left Bank*. New York: Routledge, 2007.

Stites, Richard. *Russian Popular Culture: Entertainment and Society since 1900*. New York: Cambridge University Press, 1992.

Stitziel, Judd. *Fashioning Socialism: Clothing, Politics and Consumer Culture in East Germany*. New York: Berg, 2005.

Stolberg, Eva-Maria, ed. *The Soviet Union and the United States: Rivals of the Twentieth Century; Coexistence and Competition*. Frankfurt: Peter Lang, 2013.

Storey, John. *Cultural Theory and Popular Culture: An Introduction*. Essex: Pearson Education, 2009.

Stourac, Richard, and Kathleen McCreery. *Theatre as a Weapon: Workers' Theatre in the Soviet Union, Germany and Britain, 1917–1934*. New York: Routledge & Kegan Paul, 1986.

Strong, John W., ed. *Essays on Revolutionary Culture and Stalinism*. Columbus: Slavica Publishers, 1990.

Suri, Jeremi. *Power and Protest: Global Revolution and the Rise of Détente*. Cambridge: Harvard University Press, 2003.

Suri, Jeremi. "The Rise and Fall of an International Counterculture, 1960–1975." *American Historical Review* 114, no. 1 (February 2009): 45–68.

Swift, E. Anthony. *Popular Theater and Society in Tsarist Russia*. Berkeley: University of California Press, 2002.

Taruskin, Richard. *The Danger of Music and Other Anti-Utopian Essays*. Berkeley: University of California Press, 2009.

Taruskin, Richard. *On Russian Music*. Berkeley: University of California Press, 2009.

Taubman, William. *Khrushchev: The Man and His Era*. New York: Norton, 2003.

Taubman, William, Sergei Khrushchev, and Abbott Gleason, eds. *Nikita Khrushchev*. New Haven: Yale University Press, 2000.

Taylor, Karin. *Let's Twist Again: Youth and Leisure in Socialist Bulgaria*. Vienna: Lit, 2006.

Taylor, Philip M. *British Propaganda in the Twentieth Century: Selling Democracy*. Edinburgh: Edinburgh University Press, 1999.

Thompson, E. P. *The Making of the English Working Class*. New York: Pantheon Books, 1964.

Thompson, Terry L., and Richard Sheldon, eds. *Soviet Society and Culture: Essays in Honor of Vera S. Dunham*. Boulder: Westview Press, 1988.

Thornton, Sarah. *Club Cultures: Music, Media and Subcultural Capital*. Hanover: Wesleyan University Press, 1996.

Thurston, Gary. *The Popular Theatre Movement in Russia, 1862–1919.* Evanston: Northwestern University Press, 1998.

Tirado, Isabel A. *Young Guard! The Communist Youth League, Petrograd, 1917–1920.* New York: Greenwood Press, 1988.

Tomoff, Kiril. *Creative Union: The Professional Organization of Soviet Composers, 1939–1953.* Ithaca: Cornell University Press, 2006.

Traub, Stuart H., and Craig B. Little, eds. *Theories of Deviance.* Itasca: F. E. Peacock, 1985.

Transchel, Kate. *Under the Influence: Working-Class Drinking, Temperance, and Cultural Revolution in Russia, 1895–1932.* Pittsburgh: University of Pittsburgh Press, 2006.

Trendafilov, Vladimir. "The Formation of Bulgarian Countercultures: Rock Music, Socialism, and After." *East Central Europe* 2–3, no. 38 (2011): 238–54.

Troitskii, Artemy. *Back in the USSR: The True Story of Rock in Russia.* Winchester: Faber and Faber, 1988.

Troitskii, Nikolai. *Kniga o liubvi.* Saratov: Privolzhskoe knizhnoe izdatel'stvo, 2006.

Tromly, Benjamin. "Intelligentsia Self-Fashioning in the Postwar Soviet Union: Revol't Pimenov's Political Struggle, 1949–57." *Kritika* 13, no. 1 (Winter 2012): 151–76.

Tsipursky, Gleb. "'As a Citizen, I Cannot Ignore These Facts': Whistleblowing in the Khrushchev Era." *Jahrbücher für Geschichte Osteuropas* 58, no. 1 (March 2010): 52–69.

Tsipursky, Gleb. "Citizenship, Deviance, and Identity: Soviet Youth Newspapers as Agents of Social Control in the Thaw-Era Leisure Campaign." *Cahiers du Monde russe* 49, no. 4 (September–October 2008): 1–22.

Tsipursky, Gleb. "Conformism and Agency: Model Young Communists and the Komsomol Press in the Later Khrushchev Years, 1961–1964." *Europe-Asia Studies* 65, no. 7 (September 2013): 1396–1416.

Tsipursky, Gleb. *Find Your Purpose Using Science.* Westerville: Intentional Insights, 2015.

Tsipursky, Gleb. *Having Fun in the Thaw: Youth Initiative Clubs in the Post-Stalin Years.* Carl Beck Papers in Russian and East European Studies, No. 2201. Pittsburgh: Center for Russian and East European Studies, University Center for International Studies, University of Pittsburgh, 2008.

Tumanova, A. A. *Obshchestvennye organizatsii i russkaia publika v nachale XX veka.* Moscow: Novyi khronograf, 2008.

Tumarkin, Nina. *The Living and the Dead: The Rise and Fall of the Cult of World War II in Russia.* New York: Basic Books, 1994.

Vail, P. L., and A. A. Genis. *60-e: Mir sovetskogo cheloveka.* Ann Arbor: Ardis, 1988.

Vakser, A. Z. *Leningrad poslevoennyi, 1945–1982 gody.* Saint Petersburg: Izdatel'stvo Ostrov, 2005.

van de Water, Manon. *Moscow Theaters for Young People: A Cultural History of Ideological Coercion and Artistic Innovation, 1917–2000.* New York: Palgrave Macmillan, 2006.

Varon, Jeremy, Michael S. Foley, and John McMillian. "Time Is an Ocean: The Past and Future of the Sixties." *The Sixties* 1, no. 1 (June 2008): 1–7.

Vatulescu, Cristina. *Police Aesthetics: Literature, Film, and the Secret Police in Soviet Times.* Stanford: Stanford University Press, 2010.

Veblen, Thorstein. *The Theory of the Leisure Class: An Economic Study of Institutions.* 1899. Reprint, New York: Modern Library, 1934.

Verdery, Katherine. *What Was Socialism, and What Comes Next?* Princeton: Princeton University Press, 1996.

Viola, Lynne. *Peasant Rebels under Stalin: Collectivisation and the Culture of Peasant Resistance.* New York: Oxford University Press, 1996.

Viola, Lynne. "Popular Resistance in the Stalinist 1930s: Soliloquy of a Devil's Advocate." *Kritika* 1, no. 1 (Winter 2000): 45–70.

Vladimirov, Katya. "The Art of the Arcane: The June Plenum of 1957 and the Clash of Generations." *Soviet and Post-Soviet Review* 32, no. 1 (2005): 175–90.

Von Eschen, Penny M. *Satchmo Blows Up the World: Jazz Ambassadors Play the Cold War.* Cambridge: Harvard University Press, 2004.

Von Geldern, James. *Bolshevik Festivals, 1917–1920.* Berkeley: University of California Press, 1993.

Vowinckel, Annette, Marcus M. Payk, and Thomas Lindenberger, eds. *Cold War Cultures: Perspectives on Eastern and Western European Societies.* New York: Berghahn Books, 2012.

Wade, Rex A. "Generations in Russian and Soviet History." *Soviet and Post-Soviet Review* 32, no. 1 (2005): 125–41.

Wagnleitner, Reinhold. *Coca-Colonization and the Cold War: The Cultural Mission of the United States in Austria after the Second World War.* Translated by Diana M. Wolf. Chapel Hill: University of North Carolina Press, 1994.

Wagnleitner, Reinhold. "The Empire of Fun, or Talkin' Soviet Union Blues: The Sound of Freedom and U.S. Cultural Hegemony in Europe." *Diplomatic History* 23, no. 3 (Summer 1999): 499–524.

Wagnleitner, Reinhold, and Elaine Tyler May, eds. *"Here, There and Everywhere": The Foreign Politics of American Popular Culture.* Hanover: University Press of New England, 2000.

Walker, Barbara. "Pollution and Purification in the Moscow Human Rights Networks of the 1960s and 1970s." *Slavic Review* 68, no. 2 (Summer 2009): 376–95.

Wallace, Claire, and Sijka Kovatcheva. *Youth in Society: The Construction and Deconstruction of Youth in East and West Europe*. New York: St. Martin's Press, 1998.

Ward, Christopher J. *Brezhnev's Folly: The Building of BAM and Late Soviet Socialism*. Pittsburgh: University of Pittsburgh Press, 2009.

Wasserman, Suzanne. "Cafes, Clubs, Corners and Candy Stores: Youth Leisure-Culture in New York City's Lower East Side during the 1930s." *Journal of American Culture* 14, no. 4 (Winter 1991): 43–48.

Weiner, Amir. *Making Sense of War: The Second World War and the Fate of the Bolshevik Revolution*. Princeton: Princeton University Press, 2001.

Weiner, Amir, and Aigi Rahi-Tamm. "Getting to Know You: The Soviet Surveillance System, 1939–57." *Kritika* 13, no. 1 (Winter 2012): 5–45.

Weiner, Douglas R. *A Little Corner of Freedom: Russian Nature Protection from Stalin to Gorbachev*. Berkeley: University of California Press, 2001.

Westad, Odd A. *The Global Cold War: Third World Interventions and the Making of Our Times*. New York: Cambridge University Press, 2005.

White, Anne. *De-Stalinization and the House of Culture: Declining State Control over Leisure in the USSR, Poland, and Hungary, 1953–89*. New York: Routledge, 1990.

Wilford, Hugh. *The Mighty Wurlitzer: How the CIA Played America*. Cambridge: Harvard University Press, 2008.

Williams, Raymond. *The Politics of Modernism: Against the New Conformists*. Edited and introduced by Tony Pinkney. New York: Verso, 1989.

Wolcott, David B. *Cops and Kids: Policing Juvenile Delinquency in Urban America, 1890–1940*. Columbus: Ohio State University Press, 2005.

Wolfe, Thomas C. *Governing Soviet Journalism: The Press and the Socialist Person after Stalin*. Bloomington: Indiana University Press, 2005.

Woll, Josephine. *Real Images: Soviet Cinema and the Thaw*. New York: I. B. Tauris, 2000.

Wood, Elizabeth A. *Performing Justice: Agitation Trials in Early Soviet Russia*. Ithaca: Cornell University Press, 2005.

Yekelchyk, Serhy. *Stalin's Empire of Memory: Russian-Ukrainian Relations in the Soviet Historical Imagination*. Toronto: University of Toronto Press, 2004.

Youngblood, Denise J. *Movies for the Masses: Popular Cinema and Soviet Society in the 1920s*. New York: Cambridge University Press, 1992.

Yurchak, Alexei. *Everything Was Forever, Until It Was No More: The Last Soviet Generation*. Princeton: Princeton University Press, 2006.

Zahra, Tara. *The Lost Children: Reconstructing Europe's Families after World War II*. Cambridge: Harvard University Press, 2011.

Zakharova, L. V. "'Naibolee raspostranennoi iavliaetsia forma priamogo pal'to s odnoborotnoi zastezhkoi': O sovetstkoi mode epokhi 'ottepeli.'" *Neprikosnovennyi Zapas: Debaty o Politike i Kul'ture* 45, no. 1 (2006). http://magazines.russ.ru/nz/2006/1/za24.html.

Zeiler, Thomas W. "The Diplomatic History Bandwagon: A State of the Field." *Journal of American History* 95, no. 4 (March 2009): 1053–73.

Zelnik, Reginald E. "A Paradigm Lost? Response to Anna Krylova." *Slavic Review* 62, no. 1 (Spring 2003): 24–33.

Zezina, M. R. *Sovetskaia khudozhestvennaia intelligentsiia i vlast' v 1950-e–60-e gody.* Moscow: Dialog-MGU, 1999.

Zhuk, Sergei. "Closing and Opening Soviet Society (Introduction to the Forum)." *Ab Imperio* 2 (June 2011): 123–58.

Zhuk, Sergei. *Popular Culture, Identity, and Soviet Youth in Dniepropetrovsk, 1959–1984.* Carl Beck Papers in Russian and East European Studies, No. 1906. Pittsburgh: Center for Russian and East European Studies, University Center for International Studies, University of Pittsburgh, 2008.

Zhuk, Sergei. "Religion, 'Westernization,' and Youth in the 'Closed City' of Soviet Ukraine, 1964–84." *Russian Review* 67, no. 4 (October 2008): 661–79.

Zhuk, Sergei. *Rock and Roll in the Rocket City: The West, Identity, and Ideology in Soviet Dniepropetrovsk.* Baltimore: Johns Hopkins University Press, 2010.

Zubkova, Elena. *Russia after the War: Hopes, Illusions, and Disappointments, 1945–1957.* Translated and edited by Hugh Ragsdale. Armonk: M. E. Sharpe, 1998.

Zubkova, Elena. "Vlast' i razvitie etnokonfliktnoi situatsii v SSSR, 1953–1985 gody." *Otechestvennaia istoriia* 4 (2004): 3–32.

Zubok, Vladislav. *A Failed Empire: The Soviet Union in the Cold War from Stalin to Gorbachev.* Chapel Hill: University of North Carolina Press, 2007.

Zubok, Vladislav. *Zhivago's Children: The Last Russian Intelligentsia.* Cambridge: Belknap Press of Harvard University Press, 2009.

Zuzanek, Jiri. *Work and Leisure in the Soviet Union: A Time-Budget Analysis.* New York: Praeger, 1980.

INDEX

Astriev, N. A., 85–86
authoritarian states, 78–79, 158; commonalities in popular culture of, 10, 131, 232; liberalization followed by backlash in, 147–48; using grassroots initiatives, 152–53
Autio-Sarasmo, Sari, 202
Avrus, Anatolii, 47, 49, 65, 84, 86, 111, 129
Azarov, A. K., 86

Babushkiny skazki (Old wives' tales), 48
Baletnaia truppa Bol'shogo teatra (Bolshoi ballet), 168
Baliasnaia, Liubov, 46–47, 65, 76–77, 90, 137, 211; on western influence, 86–87, 145, 166; on youth festivals, 145, 166; on youth initiative, 107, 120, 152, 175
Baltic region, jazz festivals in, 195–96
bard movement, 123–24, 207
Bashkiriia Komsomol, 148–49, 152
Bauman, Zygmunt, 4–5, 10, 213, 219
Beatles, popularity of, 4
Bierman, Wolf, 123
Big Deal, 78
black market, jazz recordings on, 59–60
Bogoslavskii, N. V., 178
Bohr, Niels, 124–25, *125*
Bol'shaia druzhba (Great friendhip, Muradeli), 34–35
Bolsheviks, 19, 102, 152
Bourdieu, Pierre, 92–93
Boy Scouts/Girl Scouts, 18
Brassens, Georges, 123
Bren, Paulina, 159
Brezhnev, Leonid, 190, 227, 230; access to western culture under, 212–13, 228; cultural policy under, 189, 216–17, 223; cultural "stagnation" under, 189, 204, 216; effects of regime, 214–15, 219–20; focus on discipline *vs.* initiative, 7, 205, 209–11; governance under, 212, 218–20; "Little Deal" of,

212–13; regime compared to Stalinism, 204–5
Britain, 144; cultural diplomacy of, 60, 168–69; efforts to undermine Moscow youth festival, 139–40, 144; influence of international youth festival on, 143–44; popular culture in, 18, 82
British Broadcasting Corporation, Russian Service of, 60–61
Bulgaria, 96
bureaucracy, Soviet, 115, 211; agencies working at cross-purposes, 9, 132, 136
Butov, Nikolai, 196, 211, 213, 217

Cacioppo, John T., 11
Castro, Raul, 176–77
Caute, David, 8
censorship, 3, 35, 141; of amateur arts, 195, 208; effects of, 186, 223; evasion of, 8, 94, 146–47
Central Intelligence Agency, Radio Free Europe by, 60
Chaika (Seagull) group, *192–93,* 193–95
Cherniaev, Oleg V., 44, 61–62, 179, 197–98
Cherry, Don, 199
China, 147, 183, 219
citizens, 39, 137; distance from officialdom, 214, 217; increasing travel as tourists, 168, 188; interactions with foreigners, 202–3; Soviet, 143–44; Soviet efforts to shape, 10, 75–76, 78–79, 224. *See also* New Soviet (Young) Persons
civil war (1917–1922), 19
class, social, 98, 137, 160; aesthetic upbringing campaign and, 154, 161; musical taste and, 58, 204
clubs, 19, 22, 82; activities in, 35, 38, 41, 74, 124, 190–91, 215; aesthetic upbringing campaign and, 148, 191; amateur arts and, 23–24, 87; annual

plans for, 4, 23, 28; attendance at, 4, 28–29, 67, 87; buildings for, 3, 83, 148–49, 165; conformist agency of youth participating in, 72; control from above *vs.* grassroots, 20, 206, 213; criticisms of, 28, 46, 163, 170; entertainment at, 1, 17, 21, 27–28, 30–31, 222; finances of, 23–24, 29–30, 41; ideology in, 12, 27, 32–34; ideology *vs.* entertainment in, 1–2, 5, 35, 74, 84–85; influence of young people's desires on offerings of, 9, 30–31, 99, 228; international youth festival and, 80, 140–141; jazz in, 62–63, 87, 91–92, 145, 167; Komsomol models for, 37–38; Komsomol's influence on, 20, 26, 32, 83–84, 210; Komsomol weddings in, 149; lectures at, 24, 84–85; managers of, 4, 23, 105, 170; number of, 21, 26, 33; participation in, 4, 47, 87; pressure to meet financial plans, 28, 67–68, 87; priorities of, 23, 28, 69, 76, 222; resources of, 22–23, 27, 33, 83, 96, 148; rural, 22; staff for, 23, 27; Sunday universities at, 152; tolerance for western popular culture in, 54, 56–57, 70–71, 167, 172, 184; universities of culture under, 151, 153, 155; used in cultural diplomacy, 80–82, 97; young people's enthusiastic participation in, 3–4, 32, 227–28; youth cafés and, 181, 185. *See also* interest-based clubs; trade union clubs; volunteer clubs; workers' clubs; youth initiative clubs

Cold War, 13, 109, 134, 172; building communism in context of, 5, 91; cultural competition in, 12, 60–62, 100, 187; cultural diplomacy in, 82, 135–36, 199, 215; détente in, 209, 217; escalation of, 33, 42; as existential threat to Soviet Union, 6; influence on domestic policies, 33, 72,

137, 158, 187, 226; Soviet loss of, 233

Cold Warriors, efforts to shape young people into, 49–50, 71, 73, 138–39

Coltrane, John, 4

communism, 160, 179; competing visions of, 30, 105, 180; cultural activities in path to, 19, 79, 121–22; efforts to generate youth enthusiasm for, 11, 78, 97, 131; efforts to move from socialism to, 5, 34, 42, 74–75, 214; grassroots activism in building, 102, 119, 218–19; paths to, 87, 91, 131, 134, 136–37; youth groomed to construct, 75–76, 103, 109, 137; youth's faith in, 95, 99, 119

Communist Party, 2, 4–5, 130, 164, 167; anticosmopolitan campaign and, 54–55, 58–59; on clubs, 38, 191; conflicts within, 120–22; cultural recreation and, 123–24, 211; demise of Soviet project and, 219; loyalty to, 38–39, 50; obstacles to cultural hegemony, 67–68; universities of culture and, 151, 153; youth and, 38–39, 72, 138, 150. *See also* party-state

competition, 203; for amateur artistic circles, 24, 80; of variety ensembles, 89; at youth festivals, 80, 140–41, 144. *See also* cultural competition

concerts: in clubs, 28, 29; jazz elements snuck into, 62–63; in universities of culture, 152, 156. *See also* music

conformist agency, 8, 45; in aesthetic upbringing campaign, 134, 160; public and private spheres in, 51–52; of youth, 48, 50, 72

Conover, Willis, 198, 201

consumerism/consumption, 60, 65; agency and, 9, 130–31; appeasing population with, 213–15; cultural, 59, 98, 187, 212, 223, 229; effects of increased, 99–100, 224; increased, 209, 214, 217; market forces in, 68–69, 71, 78; socialist, 9, 53, 159, 177;

Soviet Union's weakness in, 219–20; youth's, 78, 166, 218–19

corruption, 115, 129, 197

counterculture, 173, 214, 225; jazz as mainstream *vs.*, 204, 215; jazz enthusiasts as, 45–46, 54, 63–64, 93–94, 99, 227

crime, 33, 77, 93, 183, 205

Cuban Missile Crisis, 183

cultural activities, 126; availability of, 77, 83, 150; content of, 47–50, 55; effectiveness of, 165, 166, 197; roles of, 19, 79. *See also* cultural recreation

cultural agencies, 151, 153, 170; supporting youth clubs, 116

cultural agitation brigades, 104

cultural collectives, 104–5, 132–33. *See also* interest-based clubs; youth initiative clubs

cultural competition, 79, 160; Cold War, 12–13, 60–62, 137, 168; Soviet methods in, 157, 160, 164

cultural diplomacy, 187, 225–26; cultural recreation used in Soviet, 97, 125; effectiveness of, 143, 188, 226–27, 233; exchange of magazines in, 80, *81;* influence on Soviet domestic front, 139–140; jazz in, 176, 199–203, 215; Soviet, 12–13, 79, 82, 168–69; Soviet domestic *vs.* foreign, 12–13, 157; on Soviet youth copying westerners, 135–36; US, 138, 199, 201, 226–27; western, 143–44, 168–69, 225; youth cafés used in, 176–77, 206

cultural education, 229; as goal, 20, 27; by intelligentsia, 18–19, 152–54, 160. *See also* aesthetic upbringing campaign

cultural exchanges, 167; effects of, 144, 225, 227

cultural hegemony, 6, 67–68, 98, 157

cultural policy, 98, 209, 224, 227; under Brezhnev, 189, 190, 204–5, 216–17;

223; continuity in, 164–65; under Khrushchev, 223, 225; post-Stalin, 222; during Thaw, 96–97, 181

cultural recreation, 12, 211; activism in, 205, 217; goals of, 18, 33–34, 39, 52, 77, 205; influences on, 30, 77; Komsomol and, 26, 46–47, 52, 164–65; market forces in, 68–69, 71, 232; official *vs.* unofficial, 228–29; officials of, 69–70; in other authoritarian states, 131, 232; in postwar period, 17, 27; propaganda about, 5, 80, *81,* 125; in western countries, 82, 223–24, 232–33; young peoples' response to, 99, 186, 228; at youth cafés, 173–75; youth desires for, 47–48, 73, 85, 133, 169, 230

cultural reforms, 74, 77, 89–90, 96–97, 99

culture: in cultural education, 160–61; influence of western, 175–76, 180–81; influences on, 18, 158, 226; low *vs.* high, 18, 186; western, 8, 61, 182. *See also* popular culture

Curson, Theodore "Ted," 199

Czechoslovakia, 159; invasion of, 189–90, 209, 216. *See also* eastern Europe

dance: acceptable and improper forms of, 37, *88,* 148; at clubs, 17, 28; expanded scope of activities banned under anticosmopolitanism, 70; to jazz music, 91–92, 93, 178–79, 183

dance, western: access to, 86, 142, 144, 217; anticosmopolitan attacks on, 34–35, 54, 56–57; in *Arkimed,* 126–28, *127;* at clubs, 167, 184; continuing in spite of anticosmopolitanism, 65–67, 70–71; courtly ball styles allowed, 54–55; inconsistent efforts to ban, 85–86; increasing tolerance for, 85–87, 95–96, 163, 171; to jazz music, 55, 59; objections to, 28, 39, 86,

172; popularity of, 4, 29–30, 65, 73, 135, 159–60, 171–72; tolerance for, 21, 69–70, 85, 160

Dankworth, Johnny, 196

David-Fox, Michael, 177

de Certeau, Michel, 53

de Grazia, Victoria, 39

de-Stalinization: ambiguities in, 90; criticisms of, 183; criticized as too far too fast, 135; cultural reforms and, 77; gradual reversal of under Brezhnev, 204; grassroots activism and, 103; hard-liners' opposition to, 89; youth initiative in, 102, 121; youth support for, 119

Den' fizikov (Physicists' day), 113–18, *114*, 124–26; banning of, 211; prevention of celebration of, 208

Derzhavets, Abram, 171

détente, 209, 217

Deviataikina, Nina, 119, 212

discussions/debates, 214; at youth cafés, 175; by youth initiative clubs, 110–11, 129–30

dissent, clampdown on, 146

diversity, acknowledged in Thaw, 107, 130

Doctor Zhivago (Pasternak), 135

Dom khudozhestvennoi. *See* Doma narodnogo tvorchestva (houses of folk creativity)

Doma narodnogo tvorchestva (houses of folk creativity), 22, 108, 120, 123, 181; amateur arts and, 40, 87; complaining about jazz, 141, 145; management of, 69, 170; Moscow's, 55–56, 63, 85–86; on youth festivals, 141, 144

domestic policy, Soviet; effects of Cold War on, 33, 72, 187; invasion of Czechoslovakia and, 209, 216

Donetsk, jazz festivals in, 197–98

drama. *See* theater

Dubiler, Viktor, 61–62, 93–94, 197–98, 202

Dudintsev, V. D., 129

Dulles, John F., 143

Dunaevskii, Isaak, 196

Dunham, Vera, 78

Dvorets pionerskaia, 118–19

Dylan, Bob, 123

Dzhazz-67 (jazz festival), 196, 198, 201, 202, 210

East Germany, 51, 96, 103, 123, 164

eastern Europe, 135, 214, 217, 219; cultural exchanges with, 139, 203; cultural practices in, 123, 142, 182, 186; grassroots initiatives in, 131, 213; jazz exchanges with, 198–99, 215–16; Soviet Union and, 42–43, 95–97, 225–27

Edmunds, June, 133

Eisenhower, Dwight, 138, 143

Eksprompt (Impromtu, youth café), 184

elites, 19; cultural, 137, 188, 204, 216, 228

Ellington, Duke, 198

Ellis, Don, 199

Ellison, Jeff, 142

emotional communities: jazz enthusiasts as, 64, 70, 227–28; of youth, 186, 217–18

emotional regimes, 11, 119, 159; anticosmopolitan campaign shaping, 51, 64, 227; under Brezhnev, 217–18, 227; loosening, 99, 186, 227

Entuziast volunteer club, 122, 124

Europe, 18, 26, 39; youth in, 31, 64, 107

families, efforts to increase stability of, 149

Feather, Leonard, 60

Figlin, Lev, 59–61, 63, 66, 92–94, 142, 179, 196

Figotin, B. S., 87

Five-Year Plan (1946–1950), 26

foreign policy, Soviet, 75, 83, 209, 216
fox-trot. *See* dance, western
freedom, 131, 166; youth cafés and, 177–78, 206
Frid, Georgii, 212
fun: in clubs' goals, 27–28; positive portrayals of socialist, 115, 215; socialist, 131, 159, 186–87, 222, 234; socialist compared to western, 187, 222, 223–24; youth's desire for, 31, 76–77
Fürst, Juliane, 8–9, 72, 112–13

Galich, Aleksandr, 123
Gal'tsov, Dmitrii, 43–44, 117, 128
Ganz, Harding, 177
Gaponov, Iurii, 117–18, 128, 132, 208, 212
Garanian, Georgii, 10, 58, 61–62, 64, 202; on jazz festivals, 196, 199, 203; playing jazz, 87, 91, 94, 145
"gardening" (shaping citizens as), 10, 224, 232; changing styles of, 75–76, 78–79, 137, 186. *See also* aesthetic upbringing campaign
gender norms, 127, 149
generational tensions, 138, 161–62, 183
generations: cohesiveness of, 9, 133; consciousness of, 72, 162, 231; post-Stalin, 133, 162, 231; *Shestidesiatniki* (people of the sixties) as, 180; "Stalin's last generation," 72, 231
Gerasimova, Liudmila, 129, 157, 167, 213–14, 217
Germany, 31; Nazi, 39, 131, 152–53
Gershwin, George, 135
Gertsik, Volodia, 208
Giddens, Anthony, 4
Gnesinykh Muzyka Pedagogika-institut (Gnessin music-pedagogy institute), 135
Goodman, Benny, 60, 167
Gorbachev, M. S., 44, 77, 187–88, 214
Gor'kill dom kul'tury (Moscow), 23, 29, 84

grassroots activism, 19, 67, 103, 169, 209, 211, 217; appeasing population with consumption *vs.*, 213–14, 218–19; Brezhnev curtailing, 7, 211, 218–19; control from above *vs.*, 20–21, 216; encouraged during Thaw, 5, 101–2; Khrushchev supporting, 130, 211; Komsomol and, 102, 185; party-state not promoting, 37–38, 210, 213–14; party-state supporting, 101–2, 121, 163, 166, 228; popularity of, 109, 181–82, 212; squelching of, 37–38, 213–15; universities of culture as, 152. *See also* agency; youth initiative
Grossberg, Lawrence, 9
guitar poetry, clubs for, 215
Gulag, prisoners brought back from, 75
Gvozdiki nuzhny vliublennym (Lovers need carnations), 125

hard-liners, 132, 145, 167; condemnation of jazz by, 141–42, 203; gaining influence under Brezhnev, 189, 204, 211; increasing influence of, 147, 186; influence of, 163–65; interpretations of Marxist-Leninist ideology, 34, 38–39; in late Khrushchev years, 182–85; opposing youth initiatives, 102, 124–26, 147, 208, 216; opposition to youth cafés, 163, 180–81; soft-liners *vs.*, 19–20, 30, 71, 89–90, 120–22, 136, 155–56, 181, 223; values of, 2, 74, 85; on youth activities, 4, 17, 136, 207
Hatfield, Elaine, 11
hedonism, youth, 31, 139
Hines, Earl "Fatha," 198–99
hobby circles, *vs.* interest-based clubs, 105–6
Hoffman, David, 6
hooliganism, 27, 77, 112
Hopf, Ted, 209
houses of folk creativity. *See* Doma narodnogo tvorchestva (houses of folk creativity)

Hundred Flowers campaign (China, 1956–1957), 147
Hungary, 96, 129, 135. *See also* eastern Europe

Iaroslavskii, B. M., 136
Iarskaia, Valentina, 44, 48, 58–59, 72–73, 87, 92
ideology, 35, 97, 155, 208, 214, 218, 229; in amateur arts repertoires, 40, 45–46, 48; in club activities, 72, 76, 84–85, 170; in cultural activities, 51–52, 145, 221; entertainment and, 37, 68–69; of jazz enthusiasts, 64–65; militancy of, 204; not inhibiting pleasure from participation, 44–46, 51–52, 72; in postwar Stalinist era, 34, 42. *See also* propaganda, Soviet
ideology, foreign, 61, 166
Il'in, Konstantin, 175–76
industrialization, 18
intelligentsia, 135, 180; cultural, 185, 188 (*see also* elites, cultural); cultural education by, 18–19, 152–54, 160; cultural recreation of, 28, 113, 178
interest-based clubs, 105–7, 118–20, 132, 148, 206; jazz in, 171, 183, 191, 197–98; Komsomol supporting, 185, 205–6; proposal to unite, 207–8
isolationism, Soviet, 5, 21, 42, 79–80, 167–68
Italy, fascist, 39, 131, 147

James, Harry, 145
jazz, 39, 92, 178, 197; in amateur artistic collectives, 170–171; American-style, 29–30, 55–56, 89, 141, 146, 183, 196; anticosmopolitan attacks on, 34–35, 54, 57–65; in appealing socialist modernity, 187; backlash against after youth festival, 144–47; becoming mainstream, 203, 215; in cultural diplomacy, 176, 200, 215; dancing to, 91–92, 178–79, 183; elements of,

29–30, 35, 62–63, 67–68, 87, 89, 146; on foreign radio, 60, 93–94; increasing tolerance for, 87–89, 94–96, 167, 185, 191, 215; instruments used in, 145–46; interest-based clubs playing, 171, 183; international exchanges in, 198, 201–3, 215–16; limitations *vs.* ban on, 145–46, 210; popularity of, 4, 10, 96, 135, 142–43, 195; socialist, 215; Soviet, 21, 91–96, 196, 199; sovietized, 21, 35, 55–56, 74, 85, 93–94, 183, 196; tolerance for, 21, 96, 228; by variety ensembles, 87, 195; in youth cafés, 163–64, 173–77, 184; at youth festivals, 135–36, 141–42
jazz enthusiasts, 70, 99, 160; accepting Soviet life, 64–65; as counterculture, 10, 54, 58–60, 63–64, 93–94, 227; not necessarily desiring American culture, 61–62, 72, 95; stiliagi *vs.*, 94–95
jazz festivals, 189, 195–97, 200, 202–3, 210, 215
Jazz Jamboree (Warsaw), 199
jazz musicians, 178, 196, 201; amateurs becoming professional, 203–4; appearance of, 87–89; foreign, 167, 200; networking by, 91, 142, 197–99; persecution of, 35, 85, 145
Jews, 34
juvenile delinquency, 77, 93

"K plameni" (To the flame), 185
Kafe poetov (Poets' cafe), 175
Kaluga Fakel (Kaluga torch collective), 101, 108, 111–12, 118, 121
Karnaval'naia noch' (Carnival night, movie), 1–2, 85, 138
Karpinskii, Len, 164, 166, 179
Kemerovo, 105, 147
KGB, scrutiny of jazz scene by, 202, 216
Kharkhordin, Oleg, 51, 132
Khrennikov, Tikhon, 136, 150
Khromov, V. K., 85

Khrushchev, N. S., 97, 129, 149; aesthetic upbringing campaign and, 137, 229; Brezhnev *vs.*, 217–18; coup against, 7, 135, 190, 205, 208; cultural competition under, 79, 225; cultural policies under, 150, 160, 183, 191, 223; denouncing crimes of Stalin, 75, 134–35; encouraging grassroots activism, 103, 130, 153, 211; hard-liners and, 182–86; promoting youth initiative, 101, 188, 205, 231; social contract of, 186, 189, 230; tolerance for satire under, 208, 211; trying to build communism, 5, 11, 74–75, 119, 160; youth and, 119–20

Khutsiev, Marlen M., 138, 183

Kleinot, Vitalii, 59, 61, 91, 94, 142, 177, 179; jazz festivals and, 199–201

Klub kul'tury (Club of culture, Saratov), 124

kluby samodeiatel'nykh pesen (clubs of amateur songs), 206–7

kompanii (bohemian youth cliques), 112–13

Komsomol, 67, 102, 118, 168; aesthetic upbringing campaign of, 134, 136–39, 148–51; amateur artists circles and, 40, 46, 48–49, 84, 191, 207; conflicting priorities for, 68–69; criticisms of, 46, 138, 144–47; cultural recreation activities provided by, 27, 37, 46–47, 52, 83, 164–65, 211; efforts to increase cultural recreation for youth, 26–27, 164–65, 191; finances of, 26, 69, 197; focus of, 26, 35, 164–65, 210; focus on discipline *vs.* youth initiative, 205, 213; focus on ideology *vs.* entertainment, 17, 32; goals for youth, 136, 165–66, 190; goals of, 24, 25, 150; interest-based clubs and, 171, 205–8; jazz and, 144–47, 167, 171, 183, 200; jazz festivals and, 195–97, 201, 203; membership in, 3, 24–25, 68–69, 115–16;

organization of, 24–25; participation in, 68, 87, 115–16; postwar state of, 26, 27, 31; problems in, 68–69, 102, 120–21; tasks for, 2–3, 17, 26, 55, 77, 115, 132; universities of culture and, 151, 155; volunteering and, 68, 124; western dance and, 66, 86, 171, 183; western popular culture and, 30–31, 68–70, 191; western propaganda and, 109, 135; youth autonomy and, 104, 147, 166, 185, 210; youth cafés and, 173–75, 177, 179, 182, 191, 206; youth clubs and, 20, 26, 37–38, 76, 83–84, 105, 120; youth debates, 110–11, 130; youth festivals and, 80, 136, 139, 141, 144–47; youth initiative clubs and, 101, 107–11, 120–21, 128–29; youth subcultures and, 57–58, 112–13

Kosygin, Aleksei, 196, 200

Kotkin, Stephen, 6, 52, 133

Kovaleva, Svetlana, 117, 124, 127, 172

Kozlov, Aleksei, 62, 87, 93, 95, 142, 176; jazz festivals and, 199, 201; on youth cafés, 177–79

Kozlova, Nona, 118

Krichevich, Anatolii, 211

Krichevskii, German, 27

Kriukhin, Valentin, 111–12

Krylov, Sergei, 123

Kuibyshev, 128–29, 197

Kull,' Mikhail I., 91, 196

Kurchatovskii Institut (Kurchatov Institute, Moscow), 212

Kurilova, Francheska, 44–45, 66, 172

Kuznetsov, Aleksei A., 58, 61, 64, 91–92, 142, 203

Laiko, A. V., 128

Lamaze childbirth method, 168

Landau, L. D., 113, *114,* 124

Lebedikhina, Ol'ga, 117, 119, 213

lectures, 39, 96, 179, 180; changing topics of, 84–85; at clubs, 24, 27–30, 41,

67, 87, 170; in universities of culture, 152, 154–55, 156

Left, *vs.* Right, 19–20

leisure: in changing of emotional regimes, 218; Cold War competition over, 187; concern about youth's use of, 165; increased time for, 164, 190, 215; increasing youth's time in nonofficial settings, 169; spent in socialist time, 97; surveillance of, 78

Leites, N. Sh., 64

Leningrad: interest-based jazz clubs in, 171, 183, 191; jazz disseminated from, 94; jazz festivals, cancellation of, 210; jazz festivals in, 196; jazz musicians returning to, 85; youth cafés in, 175, 177, 184–85; youth initiative clubs in, 108

Leninist principles: search for communism based on, 105

Leninski gory (Lenin hills) theater studio, 211

Leninskoi gvardii (Lenin's guard), 138

Lianozovo poetry group, 128

liberalism, 134, 180, 209; turn away from, 183, 185, 204, 216–17

liberals, 1–2, 126

Likhodeev, Leonid, 163, 178–79

literature, 129, 167; militant policies toward, 188, 190, 208; reduced tolerance for liberalism in, 135, 183; in universities of culture, 151, 156

"Little Deal" (Brezhnev's), 212–13

living conditions, 25; efforts to improve, 21, 159; improvements in, 33, 78

Lloyd, Charles, 198–99, 200

Lovell, Stephen, 68, 107

Lundstrom, Oleg, 145–46

Maiakovskii Ploshchad,' poets of, 112

Manege event, 183, 185

Mann, Michael, 78

Mannheim, Karl, 180

march for culture. *See* aesthetic upbringing campaign

market forces, 71, 155, 232

Marvin, Konstantin, 60, 146

Marxism, pre-revolutionary, 101

Marxist-Leninist ideology, 20, 51, 71; hard-line interpretations of, 19, 34, 38–39

mass cultural network, 22, 26, 71, 130, 207; reforms of, 83–85; western popular culture in, 191–205; youth in, 39, 72–73, 96

Mezhdunarodnyi forum molodezhi i studentov (International forum of youth and students), 176

Mezhdunarodnyi molodezhnyi festival' (youth festival), 89, 134, 135

Miagkova, Valentina, 38, 118–19

Mikhailov, Nikolai, 24, 32, 55

Miklossy, Katalin, 202

Miliaev, Valerii, 117, 119, 123, 126–28

military preparation: club activities compared to, 190–91; party-state emphasis on, 205, 210, 215

military, Soviet, 22

Ministry of Culture, 69; on clubs, 23, 38, 83; on universities of culture, 151, 153–56; on youth initiative clubs, 121–22

Mne dvadtsat' let (I am twenty, Khutsiev), 183

modernity: efforts to create nonwestern, 147–48; socialist *vs.* capitalist, 4–6; western, 6

modernity, socialist, 4; accommodating youth's tastes to increase appeal, 172; aesthetic upbringing for, 165; appeal of, 5; balancing individual desires and communist construction, 133; under Brezhnev relying on consumption *vs.* agency, 218–19; building on western cultural forms, 182; building through state-sponsored popular culture, 186; coercion's failure to create, 41–42, 50; cultured people building and living in, 160; efforts to co-opt youth into building, 95; efforts to create appealing, 131; efforts to show as appealing, 168–69; enthusiasm for, 222–23; grassroots activism in, 130; given up on, 189; increased leisure time as advantage of, 164; jazz and youth cafés in image as appealing, 187; less appealing, compared to American, 223–24; need for grassroots leadership in, 101; need for socialist fun in, 6; post-Stalin efforts to create, 74, 83, 97; promoting youth activism for, 103; role of state-sponsored popular culture in, 221; Soviet *vs.* other, 6–7, 231; under Stalin, 83; values of, 5; youth cafés in forging of, 179

Moiseyev tantsa (Moiseyev dance company), 168

Molodezhnoe (Moscow youth café), 173–78, 181, 184, 195, 198–99

molodezhnye kafe. See youth cafés

Moscow: Dvorets pionerskaia in, 118–19; effectiveness of suppression of jazz in, 63; folk arts house in, 40; Gor'kill dom kul'tury in, 23; interest-based jazz club in, 171; international youth festival in, 139–44; jazz concerts in, 30; jazz disseminated from, 94; jazz festivals, lack of, 210, jazz festivals in, 195–96, 199, 201; jazz interest-based clubs in, shut down, 183; jazz musicians returning to, 85; Komsomol activities in apartments in, 165; least safe for jazz enthusiasts under anticosmopolitanism, 70; plan to construct youth palace for interest-based clubs, 105; provincials' cultural inferiority compared to, 156; Saratov compared to, 13; visiting Americans praising, 143; volunteer clubs in, 122, 124; western popular culture more successfully squelched in, 69; youth cafés in, 173–76, 182, 183–84, 191; youth festival in, 80; youth initiative clubs in, 109–10

Moscow Fakel, 108, 120–21, 128

Moskovskii gosudarstvennyi universitet (MGU, Moscow state university), 13–14, 172; amateur arts at, 43–44; Arkimed studio and, 113–18, 211; cultural recreation at, 124–26; youth initiative clubs at, 107–8, 130

Moskovskii molodezhnii muzykal'nii klub (Moscow youth musical club), 212

movies, 148; at clubs, 17, 28–29; content of, 138, 183; popularity of, 1–2, 28–29; in universities of culture, 151–52

Muradeli, Vano, 34–35, 195

museums, 148, 156

music: amateur, 24, 145, 170, 206–7; in anticosmopolitanism campaign, 36, 70; bard movement, 123; choruses promoted over other, 36–37; content of, 36, 122, 145, 196, 215; guitar, 206–7, 215; international exchanges in, 203, 205; as popular entertainment during WWII, 22; public taste in, 18, 158; rock and roll, 4, 191–95, 204, 215; in universities of culture, 151–52; by variety ensembles, 87, 146, 170–71; VIA (vocal-instrumental ensemble), 191–95; for western dancing, 66, 85. *See also* jazz

music, western, 135, 184; anticosmopolitan prohibitions on, 34–35, 55–56; end of attacks on, 85, 217; increasing tolerance for, 95, 163; popularity of, 29–30, 73. *See also* jazz

Music USA program, on Voice of America, 93–94

Mussolini, 147

muzyka'nye patruli (music patrols), 145, 179

narodnye teatry (people's theaters), 170

nationalism, 37, 50, 214; xenophobic, 39, 42, 48

Ne khlebom (Dudintsev), 129

New Economic Policy (NEP), 105; cultural pluralism of, 21, 90–91; popular culture in, 19–20, 30

New Soviet (Young) People, 31, 41, 186; anticosmopolitan campaign and, 38–39, 47–48; changing standards for, 95, 97, 229; efforts to shape, 4, 7, 49–50, 52, 137, 229–30; ideal desires of, 27, 45, 70; images of, 38–39, 103, 165; methods of grooming, 3–4, 78, 151; standards for, 107, 160

1917 October Revolution, 145

Norris, Philip, 168

Novocherkassk uprising (1962), 183

Novosibirsk, 211

Obshchestvo znanii (Knowledge society), 151, 154–55

Odessa, 110

O'Hara, Barratt, 140

Okudzhava, Bulat, 112, 123

Orsk, 172–73

Paperno, Irina, 15

parks of culture and leisure (*parki kul'tury i otdykha*), 22, 30, 69

party-state, 106, 146, 204; absolved of guilt for terror under Stalin, 134–35; ambiguity in leadership, 190, 216; emphasis on discipline and hierarchy, 209, 210, 216; governance by, 78–79, 155; trying to shape cultural tastes, 158, 165; young peoples' relation to, 130, 170, 186, 221, 224, 227; youth cafés and, 176, 184, 206. *See also* Communist Party; Soviet system

Pasternak, B. L., 135

Pateticheskoe (Pathos, youth café), 175

patriotic education, 210, 215

patriotism, 34, 38, 48, 205

patronage state, 213, 217, 219–20

Pavlov, Sergei, 109, 128–29, 165, 185, 205–6, 210

peace, 187–88

perestroika, 214

Perry, Barbara, 140, 143

personal lives, focus shifting toward, 214, 217

Petrova, Nina, 44, 65

Pinkhasik, Mark, 124

pluralism, 30, 85; advocates of, 2, 129; inconsistent acceptance of, 69–70; increasing, 11, 74, 89, 170, 203; of NEP, Stalin ending, 21; postwar, 17, 28–31

Pod integralom (Under the integral) youth café, 211

poetry, 175, 184, 208, 215

Poland, 135, 199. *See also* eastern Europe

Polish Blue Jazz Band, 142

political reform, 64

Ponarovskaia, Irina, 203

Ponedel'nik nachinaetsia v subbotu (Monday begins on Saturday, Strugatskii brothers), 167

Ponomarev, Valerii, 175, 177

Popkova, Nelli, 66, 111, 156, 208, 213

popular culture: of British working-class, 18; functions of, 22; intelligentsia sponsoring for lower-class, 18–19; official *vs.* unofficial, 3; socialist *vs.* western, 2, 12; youth status and, 92–93, 96; youth's desires for, 10, 41

popular culture, socialist, 157, 200, 205, 225–26

popular culture, state-sponsored, 3, 9, 38, 76, 107, 190, 233; access to, 30, 150; conflicts over, 4, 9, 20, 69, 98, 126, 181, 222; control of, 2–3, 40, 98, 189; in cultural diplomacy, 12–13, 140–41, 188; definition of, 2; efforts to increase youth participation in, 87, 163, 165–66; enthusiasm for, 44–46, 99, 119; evolution of, 18–19, 30, 50; goals of, 20, 80–82, 186, 229–30, 232; influences on, 21–22, 99–100,

169, 181; post-Stalin, 83; Soviet *vs.* other, 39, 43, 231–32; western elements in, 56–57, 65–67, 94–95, 136; young people's influence on, 101, 130, 187, 230–31; young people's relation to, 72–73, 79, 124, 131–32, 221; youth initiative and, 104, 205. *See also* aesthetic upbringing campaign; anticosmopolitanism

popular culture, western, 20, 69–70, 172; access to, 172, 185, 204, 212, 216, 217; American focus on entertainment, 223–24; clampdown on, 21, 134, 144–47; concern about influence of, 13, 90, 95, 134, 164; cultural education on, 160–61; demand for, 221–22; global influence of, 224–25; increasing tolerance for, 96, 169, 186, 189, 209; influence of, 163, 184, 201; limitations on, 22, 145, 184; in mass cultural network, 191–205; not necessarily anti-Soviet, 4, 31, 73; popularity of, 4, 30–31, 57–58, 66, 226; Soviet efforts to counteract, 134, 144–47, 188, 224; Soviet image of, 13, 215–16; Soviet response to, 188, 225; suppression of, 21, 161, 189; tolerance for, 5, 17, 21, 68, 183; young people's demand for, 135, 150, 166, 181–82; youth's increased exposure to, 187, 212. *See also* dance, western; jazz; music, western

populist ruling style, in Thaw, 103–4

Prague Spring, 209, 216

Presley, Elvis, 4

Proletkult, 19

propaganda, Soviet, 80, 100, 145; clubs and, 27, 32, 33–34, 170; clubs and popular culture used in, 80–82, *81;* effectiveness of, 41, 72, 219; goals of, 34, 51, 77; international youth festival called, 139, 143; in universities of culture, 155–56; youth resistance to, 52. *See also* ideology

propaganda, western, 134, 138, 166, 200; aesthetic upbringing campaign to counter, 137, 150–51, 153, 157; efforts to counteract, 169, 224; Soviet responses to, 61, 135, 187

provinces. *See* regions

Pshenichner, Boris, 106, 118

public sphere, *vs.* private, 11–12, 51–52, 71, 132, 214; official *vs.* unofficial recreation in, 228–29

Pugacheva, Alla, 203

Pustyntsev, B. P., 62

racism, 200–201

Radio Free Europe (Central Intelligence Agency), 60

radio stations; foreign, 60, 183; Soviet, 85, 191

Raleigh, Donald, 14

Rapson, Richard L., 11

recordings, 123, 135; of jazz, 59–60, 94, 191, 196

"red corners" *(krasnye ugolki),* 22–23, 83

Reddy, William, 11, 51

regions, 149, 156; cultural recreation in, 182, 210; weaker cultural controls in, 70, 212, 222. *See also* specific locations

religion, 149, 214

Riazanov, El'dar, 1

Right, *vs.* Left, 19–20

Rosenwein, Barbara, 11

Rosner, Eddie, 30

Rossiianka (Russian woman youth café), 191

Rostov Province, 105, 149

Roth-Ey, Kristin, 8, 77

Rozhkov, Vladimir, 212

Rusakov dom kul'tury (house of culture), 170

Russia, imperial, 152; culture of, 30, 37; social reformers in, 18–19

Russian Service (British Broadcasting Corporation), 60–61

Ryskin, Mikhail, 178, 206

Sadykhov, Vadif, 95, 174, 178, 201–2

sailors' trade union, Chaika sponsored by, 193–95

Sapgir, G. V., 128

Saratov, 37; cultural recreation in, 86, 105, 191; jazz in, 63, 92, 196; Komsomol in, 149, 165, 206; Moscow compared to, 13, 212

Saratov pedagogicheskii institut (Saratov pedagogical institute), 88–89, *90*

Saratovskii gosudarstvennyi universitet (SGU, Saratov state university), 86, 124, 212; amateur arts at, 37, 49; youth initiatives at, 107–8, 129–30, 208

satire, tolerance for, 208, 211

Saul'skii, Iu. V., 87, 89, 142, 145

Saxe, Charlotte, 143

Schifrin, Lalo, 196

science, 115

Seeger, Pete, 123

Semenov, Sergei, 117, 128

Semichastnyi, V. E., 40

Shchegol'kova, Svetlana, 45, 117, 126–27

Shelepin, Aleksander, 76–77, 79–80, 145, 152; aesthetic upbringing campaign and, 85, 134, 136–39, 148, 150; Brezhnev *vs.*, 190, 209; on grassroots activism, 102–3, 109, 147, 166; on western influence, 135–36

shestidesiatniki (people of the sixties), 180, 187

Shestoi Mezhdunarodnyi molodezhnyi festival' (Sixth international youth festival, 1957), 80. *See also* youth festivals

Shlapentokh, Vladimir, 51

Silver, Horace, 196

sistema (hippie counterculture), 173

Sobolev, Viktor, 157

sociability, as focus of youth cafés, 164, 173, 177–79, 184

social contracts: under Brezhnev, 212–13, 217; under Khrushchev, 169, 186, 212, 230; post-Khrushchev, 186, 189, 204–5; post-Stalin, 78, 83, 97, 150

social reforms, 18–19, 42, 135, 186

socialism, 5, 43; efforts to move to communism from, 5–6

socialist realism, 27

"socialist time"; efforts to increase youth's, 78, 97, 165–66, 169–70; increasing, 106, 109, 120, 131, 184, 186

sociology, during Thaw, 107

Soiuz kompozitorov (Composers' union), 136, 195–96

Soiuz Pisatelei (Writers' union), 135

Sokolov, Iurii, 101, 121, 156

Sokol'skaia, Irina, 118, 171

Solov'ev-Sedoi, Vasilii, 178

Soviet bloc. *See* eastern Europe

Soviet Life, in magazine exchange, 80, *81*

Soviet reality, plays on, 34

Soviet sixties, 182

Soviet system, 135, 181, 209; citizens' acceptance of, 61–62, 64–65, 72, 95, 119; declining legitimacy of, 214–15, 224; influences on feelings toward, 189, 203, 213–15; western popular culture and, 171, 189, 228. *See also* party-state

Soviet Union: Cold War as existential threat to, 6, 233; foreign image of, 79–80, 139, 143, 166; foreigners visiting, 79–80, 79–82, 167, 172; as socialist model, 42, 95–97; weakened *vs.* US, 219–20

"spontaneity" *vs.* "consciousness" paradigm, 7, 19, 102, 121–22, 132, 205, 223

sports: club activities compared to, 190–91; at international youth festivals, 140–41; party-state emphasis on, 205, 210, 214–15

Stalin, Joseph, 50, 135; cult of personality, 34, 42, 77, 91, 103, 121; cultural policies under, 21–22, 36–37, 48, 97;

variety ensembles, 87, 89, 203

Velikaia druzha (Great friendship), 167

Veshnev, Vladimir, 212

Vishnevkin, Boris, *192*, 193, 195

Voice of America (United States Information Agency), 60–61, 93–94

vokal'no-instrumetal'nyi ansambl' (VIA, vocal-instrumental ensemble music), 191–95

volunteer clubs, 122, 124

volunteering, 109; in aesthetic upbringing campaign, 148–49; in Komsomol projects, 68, 83, 104, 165, 210; for universities of culture, 153–54; youth cafés based on, 173–74

Voronezh Province, 149, 152, 191

Vostochnoe (Eastern youth café), 174–75

Vsesoiuznoe podrostkovoe ob"edinenie (Union-wide adolescent association), 207–8

Vsesoiuznyi Leninskii Kommunisticheskii Soiuz Molodezhi. *See* Komsomol

Vygnanov, Aleksander, 153, 157, 206–7

Vysotskii, Vladimir, 123, 175

Wagnleitner, Reinhold, 8

weddings, Komsomol, 149

women, 76, 92

workers, 18, 76

workers' clubs, 18

World War II, 25, 43; effects on state-sponsored popular culture, 21–22, 30; ideology after, 34, 42–43; influence of, 158, 190; Komsomol and, 26, 31, 47; pluralism following, 17, 22, 28–31; reconstruction after, 25–26, 31, 34; veterans of, 47, 49

Yevtushenko, Yevgenii, 184

youth, 3, 18; aesthetic upbringing campaign and, 134, 136, 148–51, 156–57, 160–61, 163, 186; alienated from party-state, 97, 120, 186, 223–24, 227; allowed more nonconformity, 131–33; in amateur arts, 23, 43–44, 46, 56, 67, 84, 145; anticosmopolitanism and, 70, 97; approval of cultural reforms, 74, 95, 119; commitment to Soviet system, 7–8, 35; communism and, 75–76, 99, 103, 119; consumerism of, 166; consumption wishes accommodated, 78, 85; countercultures among, 57–58, 63–64, 225; cultural activities and, 4, 51–52, 87, 163, 165, 170; cultural desires of, 98, 101, 159, 169, 172; cultural recreation desires, 47–48, 71, 73, 76–77, 90, 133; cultural recreation for, 5, 26–27, 39, 46–47, 52, 211, 217, 228; desires in club offerings, 30–31, 41; disillusionment of, 214, 217–18; efforts to dictate feelings of, 38, 51, 99; efforts to generate enthusiasm for building communism among, 11, 78, 97, 131; empowerment of, 78, 130; entertainment aimed at, 17, 37; entertainment desires of, 41, 68–69; enthusiastic participation in club activities by, 3–4, 99, 227; evenings' entertainments for, 37, 84; failing as Cold Warriors, 49–50, 138–39; forming social bonds, 118–20; grassroots activism of, 120, 181–82, 212, 213–15, 228; growing prominence of, 75–76, 233; identifying as distinct social group, 133; importance of, 9, 229; influences on, 32, 57, 72, 99, 166, 168–69, 172, 201, 226; Komsomol and, 24, 26–27, 46–47, 52, 68, 76–77; "last Stalin generation" *vs.* "post-Stalin generation," 8–9; lectures at clubs aimed at, 27, 85; leisure activities of, 76, 165, 172–73, 190; mass cultural network and, 72–73, 96; noncomformist, 7–8; popularity of western culture with, 30–31, 54, 57–58, 142–43, 171–72; relations with party-state, 72, 99,

130, 135, 170, 181, 186, 214, 217, 221, 227; resistance to propaganda/ideological content, 41, 52, 221; sense of entitlement of, 99–100, 218–19; in socialist time, 120, 186; state-sponsored popular culture and, 10, 30, 79, 221, 230–31; state's goals for, 95, 161; status and popular culture among, 92–93, 96; underground groups of, 64, 111; volunteering by, 83, 149; western popular culture and, 135, 150, 166, 181–82, 184, 187, 204, 209. *See also* New Soviet (Young) People

youth, foreign, 31, 109, 141, 172, 186, 187; exchanges with US and Britain, 139–40; Soviet youth copying, 135–36; visiting the Soviet Union, 79–82, 168–69

youth agency, 9, 130, 133, 216, 230–31

youth cafés, 202, 211; atmosphere of, 176–79, 206; in development of shestidesiatniki, 180, 187; jazz in, 163–64, 197–98

Komsomol and, 191, 210; opposition to, 163, 180–81; popularity of, 177–79, 184–85, 215; uses of, 176–77, 187

youth clubs, 105, 109, 128, 191; benefits from, 119–20; of Komsomol, 120, 210. *See also* clubs; interest-based clubs

youth exchanges, 168–69

youth festivals, international, 149; clubs preparing for, 140–41; effects of, 134, 143–47, 166; jazz at, 89, 135, 141–42, 144–47; in Moscow, 80, 139–44; western efforts to undermine, 139–40

youth initiative, 42, 103, 109; Arkimed (Archimedes) studio as example of,

113–18, 208; in China, 147; clampdowns on, 7, 37–38, 134, 147–48, 189, 208, 216, 223; conflicts over, 120–30, 170; continuation of, 185, 206; cultural collectives managed by, 104–5; effects of allowing, 119, 126–28, 132, 181; excesses of, 181, 210; in fascist Italy, 147; fears of increasing, 26, 210; hard-liners on, 20, 102; increased during Thaw, 8, 101; Komsomol on, 102, 104, 185, 210; opposition to, 120–22, 124–26, 134, 189, 208; support for, 147, 170, 186, 188, 205, 222

youth initiative clubs, 101, 107–12, 119, 147; Archimed studio as, 113–18; Komsomol and, 128–29; popularity of, 116–17, 122, 128–29; space and resources for, 120, 122, 128–29; youth cafés compared to, 173–74. *See also* interest-based clubs; volunteer clubs

youth movements, worldwide, 162, 182, 208–9

Yugoslavia, 103. *See also* eastern Europe

Yurchak, Alexei, 8, 67, 132–33, 188

Zhak, Sergei, 8

Zhdanov, Andrei, 34

Zhimskii, Iurii, 58–59, 61, 74, *75, 90;* on dances, 66, 92; on increasing tolerance for jazz, 87–89; on playing jazz, 62–63, 92, 146

Zhuravleva, L. S., 170

Zolotoi vosem' (Golden eight), 87, 91, 202

Zubok, Vladislav, 204

Zuev club (Moscow), 27, 181

Zvezdnyi bilet (Ticket to the stars, Aksenov), 167